Principles of Economics

HOLT, RINEHART AND WINSTON, INC.   New York   Chicago
San Francisco Atlanta Dallas Montreal Toronto London Sydney

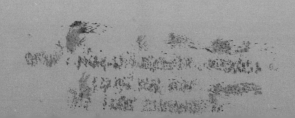

Principles of Economics

DONALD A. NICHOLS
The University of Wisconsin

CLARK W. REYNOLDS
Stanford University

Preface

Purpose

The purpose of this text is to provide an analytical framework that can be used to simplify and guide one's thinking about economic problems. The framework presented here differs from that of other texts in ways that should make it easier for the student to think about the breadth of problems likely to be encountered in the future.

This volume is not built around a particular set of institutions; rather, it presents economics as a cohesive body of thought that is felt to be a useful way of looking at many different problems. Institutions may be expected to evolve rapidly in the coming decades. Any knowledge that can be applied to only one set of conditions is certain to become obsolete. And if one is to understand the economic problems of a number of countries, regions, or groups, this knowledge cannot be restricted to a single pattern of behavior. A presentation of monetary systems, for example, if it focuses on the Federal Reserve System of the United States and its required reserve ratios for member banks, does not offer the student a framework in which to evaluate the international monetary system, the systems of other nations, or the history of money. It leaves him helpless during discussions of the impact of computer money, credit cards, or other such innovations of modern technology.

Instead, a presentation of money that (1) focuses on its economic role — its ability to lower the costs of transactions — and (2) shows the historical development of money from commodities to gold, to coinage, and finally to checks, as a progressive lowering of transaction costs, can easily accommodate further evolution in the financial structure and be used to evaluate alternative systems of liquidity. This is the approach followed in the text. We feel that this approach, while more subtle than the institutional approach, is no more difficult and is much more accurate and interesting.

In this spirit, the text introduces many of the most recent developments in the theory of resource allocation, public goods, money and finance, physical and human capital, growth, income determination, international trade, and development. While no attempt is made to provide the reader with an encyclopedia of doctrine, the most advanced economic thinking is selectively presented in a way that we feel makes it easily understood.

In addition to its unified analytical structure, this book offers the reader a framework that recognizes that economic problems have political dimensions affecting their solutions. The social and political framework in which economic problems arise can be ignored only in times of political consensus and social stability. When the goals of all citizens largely coincide, then it is appropriate for a text in economics to take these goals as given and to focus on the narrower question of how to attain them. But in turbulent times such as these, it is important to sketch in the links between political desires and economic problems, and to show how political and economic equilibria interact. Today's reader can be expected to object if such relationships are not discussed.

We have confronted this problem directly by presenting a framework of political equilibrium in Chapter 1 and by referring to that discussion and expanding upon it whenever it is useful to clarify an economic issue. The framework is based on the principle of the *social compact* of John Locke. Of particular appeal to economists, the social compact permits political equilibrium to be attained through a process of bargaining over the freedoms to be retained by each individual. Do I sacrifice the freedom to murder in exchange for the freedom from being murdered? If all such trades are conducted to improve individual well-being, then a social compact may be said to be established—a political equilibrium. As a further example, do I profit from sacrificing the freedom to pollute in exchange for the freedom from the pollution of others?

Treatment of Current Problems

The purpose of the text, as we have stated, is to aid in analyzing economic problems. To allow it to fulfill this role, there must be a discussion of problems. We have chosen a host of current problems to analyze, and we weave their analysis into our presentation of the relevant principles. In this manner, the problems not only illustrate and simplify the analysis by offering concrete examples, but they also stimulate the student to learn the principles of economics in order to understand the problems and their solutions. We realize that economic problems change rapidly with the passage of time and that it is difficult to select a single set of problems that will remain constant during the life of even a single edition of a basic textbook. Nonetheless, this danger must be confronted, since the alternative is to consider yesterday's problems or even no problems at all and thereby acquire the odious label, *irrelevant*.

Accordingly, we devote a chapter to the economics of public goods with pollution as the example, another chapter to location theory and urban development, two chapters to international poverty and the potential for eliminating it through economic development, a chapter and a half to central planning, a chapter and a half to inflation and the possibility of financial collapse, a chapter to advertising and information theory, a chapter to the political issue of consumer sovereignty, two chapters to the Malthusian problems of population and growth, and a chapter to the economics of natural resources.

Problems that were solved by previous generations are not ignored if they are problems that can arise again in the absence of appropriate policy. Thus the economic and political aspects of the issue of free trade are discussed. Chapters are devoted to unemployment. But old problems that no longer captivate modern audiences receive light treatment. Thus we do not present the Taft-Hartley Act as a burning issue; minimum attention is paid to the problems of American agriculture, or whether it is appropriate to centralize completely the direction of economic activity. The history of debates resolved is touched only briefly to allow room for an adequate presentation of modern issues.

It is our intention that this book present economics in a way that shows its usefulness in dealing with social problems and at the same time establishes a firm foundation for future study. We wish to give the student a feeling for the uncertainty an economist feels when making any professional pronouncement and a respect for the difficulties the economist encounters when trying to improve on the reliability of his statements. Above all, we hope that the student will begin to understand the humility of the scholar, why the scholar feels it is almost impossible to be certain about any proposition, and why anyone who does feel certain about the way in which society functions probably does not know what he is talking about.

Course Scheduling

The text can be used in either one-semester or two-semester courses with either the microeconomic or the macroeconomic sections coming first. In the text, we present the microeconomic material first since it is our feeling that the full understanding of macroeconomics rests on firm microeconomic foundations. However, it should be pointed out that the lectures on which this book is based were delivered in courses that dealt with macroeconomics first. To guarantee the possibility of choice on this matter, we have included a section (III) early in the book entitled *Equilibrium in a Simple Economy*. This section contains elements of both macroeconomics and microeconomics, and serves as a useful departure to the further study of either set of issues.

Thus Chapters 1-7 should be the first taught in any semester that introduces a student to economics regardless of what is to be taught next. In these chapters, the student will get an introduction to social science, scientific method, value theory, supply and demand, and the use of prices as a device for allocating scarce resources.

In a two-semester course with microeconomics taught first, the first twenty-two chapters could be used in the first semester leaving eighteen for the second semester. Or, Chapter 18 on central planning and either Chapter 11 on advertising or Chapter 12 on consumer sovereignty could be switched to the second semester if an equal load of twenty chapters is desired for each semester.

In a two-semester course with macroeconomics taught first, the text assignments for the first semester could consist of Chapter 1-7, 23, and 27-38, leaving twenty chapters for the second semester. Flexibility is possible in this schedule since Chapter 23 on equity and income distributions and Chapters 27 and 28 on economic growth could be left for the second semester and replaced by Chapter

19-21 on factor markets, by Chapters 39-40 on economic development, or by Chapters 24-25 on international trade.

A one-semester course meeting three hours a week that emphasizes analysis and attempts to introduce the student to both microeconomics and macroeconomics has little room for frills. It would contain Chapters 1-9, 13-16, and 29-35, which present the elements of consumer analysis, market organization and aggregative policy. A one-semester course meeting four hours a week might in addition include any other four chapters so long as Chapter 25 is not read without Chapter 24, Chapter 28 without Chapter 27, or Chapter 40 without Chapter 39.

A one-semester course that emphasizes problems could contain Chapters 1-12, 26-32, and 39 and 40.

Biographies, Terms, and Exercises
At the end of each chapter are terms for the student's review, and also questions and problems that provide a solid challenge to his comprehension of the principles and issues introduced in the chapter. Furthermore, biographical sketches of ten famous economists have been prepared by Hans Palmer to show that economics is a continuous, living study that responds to cultural as well as material changes in varied societies. These biographical sketches, listed at the end of the table of contents, are appropriately positioned in the text to demonstrate the historical basis for the development of major principles. At the end of the text, a glossary provides a convenient summation of terms in economics for the student's reference and review. A general index for the text follows the glossary.

Ancillaries
A book of readings, *Issues and Problems in Economics,* has been prepared to complement the analysis of the text with interesting applications, and extends the text analysis to cover many real situations. This book of readings, edited by Charles E. Metcalf and Donald A. Nichols, contains many selections that have not been traditionally considered for the Principles course, but which, with editing, have demonstrated their appropriateness for that purpose.

Charles Metcalf has also prepared a study guide, *Study Guide for Principles of Economics,* to accompany the text. The study guide contains a succinct summary of each chapter plus exercises and questions that are designed to deepen the student's understanding of the important concepts. We feel that the questions and exercises in this guide are interesting, not trivial, and that they will stimulate thinking as well as provide a useful review of the issues presented in the text.

Additionally, an instructor's manual, *Instructor's Manual for Principles of Economics,* prepared by Ernst Berndt, has been developed to accompany this text and is designed to help the instructor organize his own course efficiently. In the manual, each text chapter is summarized, supplementary activities are suggested, a bibliography of background readings is provided, and a variety of test questions are also provided.

Acknowledgments

The ideas presented in this text are those generally accepted by the profession. Except for those conceptual breakthroughs which led to major changes in economic thinking, no reference has been made to their authors. We thank the profession at large for having created the ideas contained in this book. Our contribution is one of organization, not invention. Many useful criticisms of the manuscript were obtained from Ernst Berndt, Robert W. Crandall, Belton Fleisher, Edward Foster, Gerald Gunderson, A. J. Heins, Charles Kennedy, James K. Kindahl, C. Duncan MacRae, Karl Goran Mahler, Charles Metcalf, and Richard Newcomb. Editorial advice was received from Seibert G. Adams and Walter Brownfield of Holt, Rinehart and Winston. Typing at various stages was done cheerfully by Gayle Lee, Linda Anderson, Linda Deutsch, and Lynn Brooks. To all of the above, we owe a great deal of thanks.

In addition to helping us sustain our creative efforts for a period of several years through their encouragement, our wives, Linda Nichols and Dorothy Reynolds, read and commented on long sections of the manuscript for clarity and style. For these services of love and loyalty we dedicate this volume to them. Our students at the University of California (Berkeley), Occidental College, Stockholm School of Economics, Yale University, The University of Wisconsin (Madison), and Stanford University have also rendered many services by providing a forum for the ideas herein expressed, as they were in the process of formation.

Every effort has been made to permit the simplicity and power of economic analysis to speak for itself. Its logical structure may even be said to contain aspects of beauty. Its effectiveness as a tool of social policy makes a knowledge of economic principles indispensible to businessmen, public servants, historians, and social scientists, as well as all informed laymen. Although it is seldom possible for such persons to devote several years to the study of economics, it is often convenient for them to spend all or part of a year on the subject. It is to this group, as well as those who might someday blaze new paths in the discipline, that our book is respectfully submitted.

DONALD A. NICHOLS
Madison, Wisconsin

CLARK W. REYNOLDS
Stanford, California

Contents

Urban Problems and the Location of Population.   A Profile of
Metropolitan Development.   *Questions.   Concepts Discussed.*

Biographical Sketches (prepared by Hans Palmer)

I Introduction

The world is so full of a number of things,
I'm sure we should all be as happy as kings.

ROBERT LOUIS STEVENSON

And you know how happy kings are.

JAMES THURBER

1 Economics and Social Science

What is to be man's relation to man? This basic problem facing every society may be called "the social dilemma." Each society must find some solution to this dilemma in the form of laws or customs that regulate the manner in which men can affect each other's lives. Rarely is a solution maintained for any great length of time as new issues and forces raise new problems and create new opportunities that cause men to desire new forms of behavior.

The study of social science enables us to analyze the nature of this dilemma, to point out alternative resolutions of the dilemma, to prescribe policy that will bring about desired results, and in general, to better understand and predict the social implication of any act. Social science does not judge alternative solutions to the social dilemma as being good or bad, moral or immoral; rather it is concerned with telling us how to attain any particular solution we might desire. If people wish to have a blue society, social science tells us how to get it; social science does not tell us whether blue is the right color. Without a knowledge of social science, it is possible that those who desire a blue society may mistakenly act in such a way as to bring about a green one. The role of social science is to guarantee that we use blue paint when attempting to paint a society blue. It does not tell us whether blue is better than green; that is the role of individual and social conscience.

The Social Compact

One of the earliest frameworks of analysis for the social dilemma was created by a seventeenth-century philosopher, John Locke. It is called the *social compact*. In the framework of the social compact, man is viewed as existing initially in a state of nature with no social laws. He is free to act as an animal with no restrictions on his behavior. He discovers, however, that it is possible to improve upon his precarious existence by sacrificing some of this freedom to a social group. Each man forfeits the right to kill other men—in return he is guaranteed security against his own murder. Additional rights are forfeited until the point is reached where the transfer ceases to increase men's happiness. All rights are willingly sacrificed if the value of protection gained from their exercise by others exceeds the value of the person's own right to exercise them. On the other hand, rights are not relinquished voluntarily if their value to the individual exceeds the value of the protection gained through their uncontrolled use by others. In the development of this theme, Locke explains how a society might determine which laws to create; that is, which freedoms to restrict in order to promote the common good.

The social compact was not designed to explain history. It is merely a way in which to frame a solution to the social dilemma. History, in fact, has left us with societies in which rights are distributed unequally among the members, a possibility ruled out by Locke's manner of choosing laws. These societies may well represent a high degree of social equilibrium even though the bargaining power in future deliberations over the social compact is unequally distributed. One reason that future deliberations are necessary is that certain individuals wish to sacrifice the very rights that others wish to maintain. Tastes differ and because of this no unique optimal social compact exists. Individuals are constantly trying to change the compact in such a way as to improve their own or, in their opinion, society's welfare. Such attempts fill the streets with demonstrators and the newspapers with headlines and editorials. Though not an explanation of history, the social compact is a useful framework within which to view the social dilemma.

The study of social science in general and economics in particular will not allow us to determine one "correct" social compact, although many who pass as social scientists are in reality social evangelists and have such a compact in mind. Social science — hence economics — will permit a student only to assess the implications of different kinds of social compacts. For example, will the means suggested by social evangelists actually bring about the ends they desire? What costs will be incurred in changing the society? Social science does no more than describe how efficient are different actions in achieving stated goals. But this knowledge is absolutely indispensable if our judgements are to be free from confusion and prejudice.

A complete social compact will be a very complex document as it must make some statement about all the possible ways in which men can relate to each other. We can isolate various aspects of such a compact, each of which is associated with a different intellectual discipline. This exercise should illustrate the relation of the various social sciences to each other and serve as a useful background against which to present an outline of the economic problem. No social science studies society as a whole. Rather, each social science selects one dimension of social man to study and pursues that study while ignoring the problems studied by the others. This division of labor has the advantage of carving up the overall complex problem of man's relation to man into smaller, more manageable parts, but it also has the disadvantage of leaving no one able to study efficiently those complex problems that simultaneously involve many topics from several disciplines.

The Social Sciences

A social compact must have some provision for the manner in which social policies can be formed. That is, there must be some form of government. *Political scientists* study government—the distribution of political power, the manner in which social decisions are made, and the relation of the various governing bodies to the citizenry and each other.

Since the collection of individual freedoms that are not sacrificed to the government is yet very complex, the rights of one individual often conflict with those of another. In such a situation, there must be some manner of deciding whose rights are to be upheld and whose must be sacrificed. Such decisions are made within *legal systems*; the study of *law*, or *jurisprudence*, is concerned with the principles under which these decisions are made. Law, of course, is also concerned with the allocation of penalties to those who violate the social compact.

Sociologists and *anthropologists* study how societies differ according to values, attitudes, and group behavior; how authority is distributed within a family structure; how the society indoctrinates the young to accept its values; how the group views nonconformity, creativity, ambition, or generosity; and what groups yield social stimulation, reinforce a common group ethic, or accomplish various other social needs.

Psychologists study some of the same problems that sociologists do but from a different viewpoint. Psychologists are also concerned with why individuals act the way they do, how behavior can be modified or controlled, and how individuals mature and adjust to their environment.

Economics is concerned with the creation and distribution of material satisfaction—who gets what. Economists study this problem but ignore the political and legal system, the family structure, and the problems of attaining psychological maturity. Although it is clear that the social compact contains a solution that is of interest to each of the separate disciplines, no given discipline studies the social compact in its entirety. Each discipline has developed an intellectual framework—a way of looking at problems—that is suited to its own needs but that is not very useful in analyzing other aspects of the social dilemma.

The division of the general social problem into separate little boxes has resulted in some reasonably sophisticated analysis within each box. But increasingly, the pressing social problems of the day—poverty, the environment, urban decay—involve many boxes simultaneously. Since we are only very good at analyzing boxes one at a time, social science has not yet been able to give very profound or confident advice to aid in solving these larger problems. Some way will have to be found to utilize the knowledge of all of the social sciences to allow us to solve these larger problems.

This book is an introduction to principles of economic analysis. As such, we concentrate on problems of material satisfaction. But our concern with broader social questions has led us to construct this book in a manner that we feel most likely to provide bridgeheads to the questions studied by other social scientists. It is our hope that the actual bridges will be constructed by those who use this book as students, if no way is found to construct them sooner.

Much about men remains a mystery; most of their activities are only beginning to be understood. The science of human behavior is very young and is still shaking off its priestly garments. Almost two thousand years have passed since St. Paul remarked to the Corinthians that our perceptions are imperfect – as if seen through a glass, darkly – yet the statement remains true. We are only beginning to understand human behavior, to find ways of studying men that yield fruitful predictions, and to begin to avoid impending social disasters.

On the other hand, recent progress in social science, and in economics in particular, has been dramatic. Many of the actions of men, individually and collectively, are surprisingly orderly and even predictable. Social scientists now understand many of these actions and have constructed simple hypotheses about this behavior that have been found to have great predictive power.

Economics as a Social Science

The material relationships of society, its social "housekeeping," are among the most orderly of human affairs. Because of the inherent order and relative simplicity of its subject matter, the study of *social housekeeping,* or *economics,** has a head start among the social sciences. Many economic variables are easily quantified, or expressed as exact amounts. The simple hypotheses and the quantified variables have allowed economists to bring to bear the power of mathematics on the problems of society. The use of mathematics enables us to state very sharp criteria for economic efficiency at a level of precision that cannot yet be duplicated by the other social sciences. This book will present many of these principles and theorems and indicate why they hold, though it will leave rigorous proofs to more advanced texts.

Because the variables of their discipline are easily quantified, economists have been able to make use of modern mathematical statistics to test their hypotheses and to state precisely the probability or likelihood with which each of their predictions may hold. Modern economics therefore contains many complex, abstract formulations that economists believe represent the manner in which individuals make decisions and that explain how the sum of these decisions in turn affects the individuals. This book will serve as an introduction to the most basic of these economic principles.

The answer to the question "Who gets what?" is a solution to the economic dilemma. To be able to describe such a solution, we must have some means of accounting for all the effects of every economic action. A *general equilibrium system* is the label economists attach to the framework within which they study the interaction of all economic decisions. This book will study the components of such systems as well as explore the interactions of the systems we will construct for simplified economies. Perhaps social scientists will someday be able to construct *social equilibrium systems* of which the economic general equilibrium will be a small part. With such a system social change might actually be predictable, and many costly failures of adjustment such as we observe in contempo-

---

*The word *economics* is derived from the Greek word *oikonomos,* which can be translated as *steward,* or one skilled in the management of a household.

rary society might be avoided. Riots, revolutions, wars, and anarchy may someday be a thing of the past, just as we hope that famine, pestilence, depressions, and poverty will begin to disappear within our own lifetimes. This book will concentrate on the analysis of the latter problems. We hope, however, that the student will view the framework and method of economics as one dimension of social science in general. Our inability to explain, predict, and control war reflects the fact that we have not adequately refined our hypotheses of human behavior. Economics has sufficiently refined hypotheses to explain depression, inflation, and poverty. This is because these latter problems are easier to analyze using current techniques. The proper pursuit of social science should enable us to solve eventually even the more difficult problems. But in order to do so it is necessary to understand the elementary building blocks. Economic principles are among the most important of these.

Positive and Normative Economics

Economics as a social science attempts to identify, analyze, and predict the effects of a given set of social values on men's material relationships. Because it *posits* these values as given and does not call them into question, scientific economics is sometimes called *positive economics*. In an effort to understand better the observed workings of the economy, positive economics maintains an aloofness from many of the deeper philosophical issues that continue to preoccupy mankind. Some economists, unwilling to maintain this pose of objectivity, insert into their analysis considerations not only of what is but what ought to be. Such economics may be called *normative economics,* since it incorporates the subjective elements of the practitioner's own values into its analysis. Since even the most antiseptic attempt at objectivity will be likely to include within its set of initial assumptions or hypotheses to be tested large elements of subjectivity, the dividing line between positive and normative economics is blurred at best.

It is important, however, that we attempt to find that blurry line. The good economist, for example, must be aware of his own values so that he can understand how his manner of asking questions biases the answers he receives. Without such consciousness, he will be unaware of important limitations on his findings and he may be led to erroneous predictions. Professional meetings, journals, textbooks, and courses will become no more than a forum for the expression of prejudice unless we can fully understand our own biases and how they influence our way of looking at problems.

The student beginning economics has already observed the world around him for many years and has formed opinions about how things really are. These often include opinions about the government debt, deficit financing, monopoly profits, unions, income distribution, capitalism, and the efficiency of the free market. In this book, we examine these and many other problems from the vantage of social science. Where a student disagrees with our conclusions, he should examine his own argument to make sure he is thinking as a social scientist, not as a social evangelist. He should examine his and our arguments to see where the bias has crept in to affect the conclusions. We do not pretend to be unbiased individuals. But we do claim to be social scientists, and as such we attempt to be aware of our own prejudices and to make sure that our analysis of what makes the world "tick" is as objective as we can make it. Otherwise, we would reach erroneous conclusions, advocate ineffective policies, and lead frustrated lives. Regardless of our world view, it is essential that we learn how things really work if we are to be effective in pressing toward our goals.

It is likely, of course, that some of the conclusions we present in this book ultimately will be found to be wrong. One need only read some earlier textbooks to be convinced of that. But we were aware of that possibility when we studied each principle. We learned early that *in social science, one can never be sure,* and we wrote this book with this principle in mind. We ask that the student learn this first principle now and be aware of it not only when he scrutinizes our arguments for flaws, but also when he questions his own arguments. If there is a belief about the way society works that the student holds without any doubt at all, then that belief represents an issue that he does not really understand. To truly understand a social hypothesis, one must be aware of the precise conditions under which that hypothesis is false. The difficulty of knowing anything for sure is one reason educated people tend to make humbler statements about the way the world is than do the uneducated. They are much more likely to realize the substantial possibilities of being wrong.

Despite the difficulty of freeing our analysis from bias, we should be able to get together as social scientists and agree upon a great many principles as useful explanations about the way the world operates. As social evangelists, we can argue about the way the world *should* be or *should* operate, but as social scientists, we must strive to find out how it *does* operate. Even if all of us could agree on how the world should turn, we would need to know social science to help us attain that world in the most efficient possible manner.

Questions

1.   The text claims that social science makes no moral statements. Is it possible to create an intellectual structure that makes no moral statements? Does the individual social scientist make a moral statement when choosing to do research on blue societies as opposed to green ones? If each social scientist chooses to study blue societies so that the public receives no information about green ones, has the profession taken a moral stand? Should the individual social scientist worry about who will use his research, and how?

2.   Much of this book will discuss the exchange of commodities. Locke's social compact can be viewed as an exchange of freedoms. One trades the freedom *to* murder for the freedom *from* murder. In this view, the sacrifice of rights could increase rather than decrease freedom. If you were voting on a social compact, would you sacrifice the freedom to speed? To pollute the atmosphere? To disrupt classes? To keep your income? To make war? To use dope?

3.   Is it possible to have a purely positive economics? What is the value of a

positive science? Could a fascist doctor treat pneumonia the same way a socialist doctor would? Could a fascist economist cure inflation the same way a socialist economist would? Unemployment? Poverty?

Concepts Discussed

economics

positive economics

social compact

normative economics

general equilibrium system

2 The Economic Problem

A solution to the economic problem is a distribution of material satisfaction among the society's members. This is an issue about which the members have very strong feelings. This chapter sketches out the essentials of the economic problem, the problem that will concern us for the remainder of the book: How are the members of a society to organize the production and distribution among themselves of those commodities that satisfy human wants?

In the absence of a social compact — and therefore of a government, police force, or legal system — theft might be commonplace. Indeed it is the possibility of theft and other antisocial acts that motivates the establishment of a compact. Theft occurs because a man wishes to increase his own level of material satisfaction; he wishes to satisfy additional human wants by acquiring and using additional commodities. But theft is outlawed by most social compacts partly because it does not increase the total amount of goods available. It merely transfers goods from one person to another. If everyone would stop stealing from each other and, instead, satisfy his desires for additional goods by producing more, there would be a larger total amount of goods available. Society as a whole gets more goods to consume if no effort is devoted to theft. That is one reason why theft is outlawed.

The motivation for theft can serve as an illustration of the two basic forces that give commodities material value. First, man has aspirations, or individual values that include a desire for material consumption. And second, there are restrictions placed on his desires by the generosity of nature. There just are not enough goods to satisfy everyone's aspirations, probably not enough to satisfy anyone's completely. When our *desires* for material satisfaction are frustrated by the *scarcity* of nature, goods acquire value. Their value is precisely their ability to satisfy our desires — to yield satisfaction. Modern economics consists of the study of the conflict of these two forces — desire and scarcity — and therefore of material values.

We are denied the Garden of Eden, a world where we might have all we wish, where theft and even governments would be unnecessary. Instead, we live in a world of scarcity. With only so much to go around, it becomes important that we organize production efficiently so as not to waste happiness. It becomes important that we adjust to frustration as a fact of life. The borders of Eden are patrolled in all dimensions: social, psychological, and economic; and the limitations of material productivity are only one barrier to the boundless aspirations of men.

The Problem of Scarcity in Historical Perspective

Even after two centuries of industrial and agricultural revolution, food, clothing, and shelter remain the principal concerns of most of mankind. The most productive societies in terms of material goods have yet to eliminate pockets of poverty. Even if individuals had limited wants, the increase in the number of mouths to be fed would place increasing demands on available natural resources. Yet the size of the globe remains the same; its natural resources are depleting rather than increasing. New sources of energy and ways to transform them into usable goods must be found if the problem of scarcity is to be alleviated, much less eliminated. The affluence commonly forecast for the future will require great advances in technology and, ultimately, some check on population. We should remember that civilizations have risen and fallen in the past, and that history provides no guarantee that present civilizations will move in only one direction in the future.

Furthermore, the future holds no promise that individual wants will ever be sated regardless of the potential growth of productivity. Our desires go beyond the simple material necessities of life to include better self-understanding, improved relationships with society, expanded knowledge of nature, and the expression of all these faculties in the arts. As long as our span of years is relatively fixed, the resultant limitation of time available to devote to these pursuits will place restrictions on their enjoyment. As long as man's talents are finite, his ability to transform his creative vision into works of literature, sculpture, music, painting, architecture, or economic theory will be limited as well. Happiness will always remain a will-o'-the-wisp, dependent upon our ability to compromise desire and fulfillment. The economic problem of scarcity will never leave us.

Because of scarcity, choice is essential. Intelligent choice implies a decision based upon clear understanding of the alternatives before us. For example, as we know that our days are numbered, we must choose what to do with our time, realizing that this will mean abstaining from some activities in favor of others. Of course, most men would prefer to have more time—time for both study and political activities, time for music lessons, sports, reading, hiking, traveling, painting, and time for ministering to the needs of others. More time would mean more enjoyment, but because our time is limited we must choose carefully to ensure that our lives become a satisfying pattern of activities. Choosing wisely, or efficiently, means maximizing the satisfaction we derive from the use of our time. Choosing inefficiently means satisfaction foregone. As the clock ticks, some choice must be made. This book shows why society, too, must make choices and how happiness can be wasted if these choices are poor ones.

Material Values

We have noted that material *values* arise only when man does not have enough commodities to satisfy all his wants. Modern economists measure the value of a commodity in terms of its ability to satisfy *additional* human wants. *Utility* is the term used to denote satisfaction. It is just one example of the unfortunate jargon economists use in which words have meanings slightly different from those of their everyday usage. Anyone wishing to discuss complex problems in eco-nomics must learn this jargon, however, as it is the language in which the discus-sion is carried out. It is the language of this book.

That the value of a commodity depends on the additional utility it yields follows directly from the fact that commodities take on value only when our wants are not completely satisfied. Thus if we should have on hand a great amount of a particular good — enough to satisfy completely our desires for it — it would have no value because it would not be able to satisfy additional wants. We would give up nothing of value for an additional unit of that commodity because we would already have all we want. Water is of little value to a nonthirsty society even if the reason it is not thirsty is because it has so much water.

If, on the other hand, we have a very small amount of a commodity of which we want a great amount, we would be very happy to acquire additional units of it and would treat these units as objects of great value. We would be willing to trade other commodities in an attempt to acquire more of the desired commodity and thereby satisfy our wants.

Thus the value of an additional unit of a commodity is the amount of addi-tional utility it would yield us. Economists call this *marginal utility*, or the in-crease in satisfaction one derives from having an additional unit of a commodity. It is the marginal utility of a commodity that measures its value in terms of satis-faction. Note that this theory, specified in terms of additional satisfaction — mar-ginal utility — implies that the value of a commodity does not depend solely on its ability to satisfy wants, but that it also depends on the degree to which those wants have already been satisfied. Thus value depends on *desires* and on *scar-city*, for the less we have of a commodity, the more our wants are frustrated and the greater the amount of additional satisfaction we can obtain from an addi-tional unit of that commodity.

Although this theory is simple enough, it is not obvious. That is, it is a prin-ciple understood by few who have not studied economics. In fact, economists searched for the insights embodied in this theory for a century in order to ex-plain the apparent paradoxes they observed. An interesting example of the puz-zles they attempted to explain is presented by the founder of modern economics, Adam Smith, and is called the *diamond-water paradox*.

Adam Smith was a Scottish moral philosopher who attempted to gain insight into men's moral values by studying the material values exhibited in the market-places of eighteenth-century Britain. In 1754 Smith published *The Theory of Moral Sentiments*, an exploration of the relation of moral and material values. His study of markets got him interested in the sources of productive power; in 1776 he published what is considered to be the first work in modern economics, *The Wealth of Nations*.

Smith never did understand the determination of material values. He was troubled by the fact that diamonds were treated as objects of great value whereas water was treated as an object of little value. Clearly water is worth more to society than diamonds. His inability to explain this paradox led him to the belief that goods have a value *in use* that is different from their value *in ex-*

change. Although water ultimately yields more satisfaction than diamonds, men apparently feel it has less value, as they are willing to spend a great amount of money for relatively few diamonds when they could spend the same amount of money on water and thereby acquire a really vast amount of that life-sustaining substance.

Modern economists have replaced the distinction between *use value* and *exchange value* by noting that it is the marginal utility of a commodity that determines its material value, not the total utility derived from consuming all the available units of the commodity. Water has little value in terms of diamonds because men have so much water. They are unwilling to give up additional resources for *more* water. Diamonds, on the other hand, are very scarce. And while they are mere baubles, the fact that there are so few of them and that they do yield satisfaction means that their marginal worth in terms of water is very high. The satisfaction obtained from one *more* diamond is equivalent to that obtained from thousands of gallons of *additional* water. It is the additional or *marginal* usefulness that determines the value of a commodity, then, rather than the total amount of it that is consumed. Men treat each unit of a commodity as if it is the marginal unit (last unit to be consumed). While we realize that water is essential for life, we are quite willing to use it freely since extra water has very little value.

If circumstances were reversed, water might well be worth its weight in diamonds. If, for example, we were wandering lost in the desert parched with thirst, would we not exchange all of our diamonds for a single glass of water? In this case it would be water, rather than diamonds, that is the scarce commodity relative to our needs. If coal could suddenly be converted into diamonds in a simple process of alchemy, what would happen to the worth of the uncut stones in terms of crystal spring water? Would additional diamonds still yield great amounts of satisfaction if our desire for diamonds was already satisfied?

The development of the theory of marginal utility in the late nineteenth century gave economists a foundation on which to erect a theory of material value. Prior to that, most economists, including Marx, had believed in a labor theory of value — that the value of a commodity depends on the amount of labor required for its production. This theory, which ignores men's desires, has trouble explaining many phenomena. It tells us that the value of output will be the same if, for example, doctors build sand castles instead of curing the ill; the doctors' input of labor would be the same. The marginal utility theory of value says that goods have value insofar as they satisfy men's wants; if men prefer being well to owning sand castles, the output of doctors is said to have a higher value curing the ill than it does playing in the sand. The appendix to Chapter 19 is devoted to Marx and the labor theory of value; it discusses further a few of these problems.

Utility is a clumsy foundation, however. First of all, it cannot be measured in absolute terms. No one can say, "Today I am 70 degrees satisfied," and feel confident that others will understand him. Does he think satisfaction is measured from zero to one hundred? Zero to infinity? Minus infinity to infinity? Even if we agreed on a range, we would not know whether 70 means happy or sad. Further-

ADAM SMITH (1732-1790) Although the paternity of modern economics is uncertain, Adam Smith, the Scottish philosopher, can lay good claim to fatherhood. As an eighteenth-century moral philosopher (social scientist), he sought for supposedly "natural" rules of human behavior, the observance of which would yield a maximum of human happiness. Throughout his many careers—professor, tutor to nobility, and civil servant—he continually pursued a quest for these rules, a search that yielded numerous essays and two major books, *Theory of the Moral Sentiments* (1759) and *An Inquiry into the Nature and Causes of the Wealth of Nations* (1776). In the first of these he set forth a set of natural law principles and tensions—selfishness vs. sympathy, convention vs. self-assertion—that explain and determine social behavior. In *Wealth of Nations* Smith sought to formulate rules for action in the economic sphere, partly in a general theoretical framework and partly to provide guides for good economic policy. As the eighteenth century was a period of great economic and social change in England, it is not surprising that much of Smith's attention should have been focused on the process of economic growth, including the relevant social and economic policies. He was, therefore, more concerned with long-run changes in the economy than he was with questions of prices, market structures, and depressions that occupied so much of later economics.

His major axiom was that mankind has a natural urge to "truck and barter" resting largely on different productive advantages. This urge could lead to an intensification of economic activity that leads, in turn, to larger amounts of output and higher incomes for everyone in the society, since wider markets allow greater specialization and division of labor and hence more efficient production. Because the expansion of markets and its accompaniment, technical change, were the result of the conscious activities of the accumulating classes with their urges to save and to invest, it was clearly in the interest of society to see that these classes received an adequate share of society's income. This interest raised the issue of how a society's product was divided among wage earners, landlords, and capitalists (investing entrepreneurs who provided productive facilities and whose wage payments sustained workers until their output could be sold); and this in turn led to consideration of the questions of value and cost.

Although Smith appeared, on occasion, to hold that goods exchanged on the

---

more, we do not even know if different people have the same standards for happiness. There just are no absolute measures of happiness. This poses problems.

Comparing Personal Welfare

One powerful negative conclusion that results from the absence of an absolute measure of satisfaction is that we cannot tell which individual receives a greater amount of satisfaction from consuming a certain group of commodities. We cannot describe the value of a commodity in terms that are the same for all people. It is as if we attempted to use a number to describe heat to people who all owned different kinds of thermometers, Fahrenheit, Centigrade, and so on, and who all associated different numbers with a certain level of heat.

What is the absolute value of an orange to any person? Who can tell? To

basis of the amount of labor they could command, he also held that value, that is, the long-run "natural" price, ultimately would tend to rest on costs of production. Costs were made up of the shares going to each social class; thus over the very long haul, as the stock of capital rose increasing the demand for labor, as population in consequence grew relative to available agricultural land, and as food prices rose, wages and rents (the landlords' share) would go up. Profits would therefore be squeezed, and accumulation would be retarded. Moreover, the rate of profit would tend to fall because of the competition of larger amounts of capital, thus discouraging accumulation further. Technical change and agricultural improvements provided some relief and consequently were to be encouraged if society were to evade this result.

Smith firmly held that the unfettered operation of the market system would maximize the satisfactions from all exchange relationships and would lead to the most desirable distributive arrangements consistent with society's basic capacities to produce. Government interference with the operation of the "invisible hand" would usually reduce the efficiency of the system and probably serve only the interests of a few, hence his strong attack on mercantilism and his rule that government should restrict itself to those activities that private persons could not provide. Stabilization policy was not needed because Smith assumed that there was no problem with long-term unemployment, since production inevitably created its own demand and since the amount of money in the economy affected only the price level. These assumptions were to prove very costly to economics and to Western capitalism throughout much of the nineteenth and twentieth centuries.

Adam Smith placed many key analytical questions in a consistent framework as he sought natural law formulations for economic activity. He set most economic relations of exchange and growth in a structure that undergirded future systematic analysis keyed to the emerging problems of an industrial age. Although he wrote at the outset of the Industrial Revolution, he clearly was the mentor of most economists of the English classical school (including Marx) and set many of the tasks that the dominant schools of economics have chosen to pursue in the intervening period (excluding, of course, short-run fluctuations). His greatest fault lay in not seeing that his analyses were valid mainly in the context of relatively small-scale enterprise.

---

one, an orange may evoke visions of Castille, dreams of green groves with white blossoms, scented air, moonlight, and romance. To another an orange may simply satisfy a craving for a tart, juicy, efficient snack on a busy day. As I cannot describe the degree of utility I obtain from an orange, there is no way to compare my utility with yours. I cannot make this comparison nor can you. The result is that there is no way to know for sure whether total utility is increased or decreased by redistributing income (or oranges) among individuals. *Economists as scientists can say nothing precise about the advantages of one income distribution over another.*

Note that there are two problems that give rise to this result. One is in picking a distribution of satisfaction; the other is in attempting to attain that distribution. Economics tells us nothing about either problem. Even if we could agree on an appropriate distribution of material satisfaction in principle we would not know what distribution of income or goods to advocate since we do not know how to compare the satisfaction different individuals obtain from the same amount of goods. An equal distribution of income may imply an unequal distribution of satisfaction.

Although this is a seemingly negative conclusion, it is a very powerful one. If economics cannot scientifically arbitrate as to which income distribution is best, it is up to each citizen to decide for himself; there will be no objective way to prove anyone wrong. If, as voters, we feel we have the responsibility of determining social policy, it will be up to us to determine the income distribution in whatever manner we feel is right. Though a knowledge of economics is often necessary to determine an efficient social policy, in this case it is useless. We can, of course, argue scientifically over the effects of income distribution on economic variables, and vice versa, but not over the intrinsic merit of alternative distributions.

Relative Measures of Value

Since there is no way to construct an index of satisfaction, it becomes a poor yardstick to use in measuring value. But since the value of a commodity depends on its ability to satisfy, what other measures can be used? Tons, inches, or gallons? Surely not. But we could use any commodity that has value as the measuring rod and compare the value of other commodities to it. That is, we could measure the value of commodities relative to each other or relative to some commodity arbitrarily chosen as an index.

If an individual tells us he has no preference among three apples and two oranges, we know they are of equal value to him, and we also know they increase his satisfaction by the same amount even if we cannot measure the satisfaction. We can say that to this person one apple is worth two-thirds of an orange; that is, its value is two-thirds of an orange. In this case we have used oranges as the index of relative value. On the orange index, apples get a grade of two-thirds.

Once we agree on an index, say, an orange index, then we can add apples and oranges despite the admonitions of our grade-school teachers. If one apple is worth two-thirds of an orange, then six apples plus one orange equals five oranges in value. Alternatively we could use gold as the index of relative value. Or dollars. If one apple is worth four cents and one orange is worth six cents, then six apples plus one orange equal thirty cents in value.

Monetary measures are the traditional ones, of course. One can read in the paper that the nation produced 900 billion dollars' worth of commodities last year, or that an individual left an estate having a total value of $150,000. Both of these aggregates consist of many different kinds of commodities, all of which had to be converted to a common measure of relative value in order to be added together.

What, then, would we lose by measuring value in terms of oranges rather than in terms of satisfaction? Nothing that was not already lost because of the

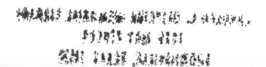

impossibility of measuring value absolutely. We do not know if a 100 percent increase on the orange index represents a doubling of satisfaction or not. We do not know if an income of 5,000 apples satisfies Jones as much as it would Smith. We do not know these things because of the lack of an absolute measure of value, not because we have chosen oranges as our index.

Of what use is the orange index? Admittedly, it is a measuring rod whose units do not correspond exactly to satisfaction. A bundle of goods worth 2,000 oranges does not necessarily yield twice as much satisfaction as a bundle worth 1,000. But the bundle with the larger ranking must yield *more* satisfaction than the smaller one. If we know Smith is always indifferent between 3 apples and 2 oranges, then we know that a bundle of 2,400 apples and 400 oranges is worth more than a bundle containing 300 apples and 800 oranges. The measuring rod works well even if the units are meaningless. We can measure any bundle and tell whether it is larger or smaller than any other bundle.

On this foundation—measurements in terms of relative value—the super-structure of economics is erected.

Diminishing Relative Value

Our discussion of the diamond-water paradox has illustrated how the relative value of commodities depended on the quantities available. The value of diamonds relative to water is large because we have so few diamonds and so much water. If we had a great amount of diamonds and very little water, the reverse would be true. This is one example of what we can call the principle of *diminishing relative value*.* It states that the value to an individual of one commodity in terms of any other commodity declines if he receives more of the first commodity and loses just enough of the second to leave his total utility unchanged. That is, if we take some food from a man, but give him the amount of clothes that makes him just as happy as if he had kept the food, the value this man places on clothes relative to food will fall. This is merely an expression of how relative value depends on relative scarcity. We have already discussed how the *absolute* value of commodities as a whole might depend on the total amount one had, that is, on *absolute scarcity*. The principle just presented is different; it is useful if relative measures of value are to be used.

The principle of diminishing relative value is really a psychological principle, not an economic one. Economists believe it to be valid, however. In fact, it must be a valid principle if we are to be able to explain many of the phenomena we observe. The value of diamonds in terms of water would decline if the quantity of diamonds were to increase. Farmers' incomes are low even though food is necessary for existence. But once we have all the food we need, why pay farmers to grow even more? The prediction about the value of diamonds and the

---

*We are using the term *relative value* to denote what economists usually call the *marginal rate of substitution* (MRS). With value equal to marginal utility, and the MRS equal to the ratio of marginal utilities, the term relative value means precisely the same thing as MRS although it is not usually used that way by economists.

explanation of the value of farmers' output are derived from the principle of diminishing relative value.

Value and Exchange

So far the measures of relative value that we have created are personal. Smith may find three apples as satisfying as two oranges, but Jones may feel that three oranges are worth two apples. We have also noted that the feelings of each person about relative value may change if the relative quantities of apples and oranges held by both change. How can we construct an index of value in terms of oranges, or dollars, if the values of other commodities relative to oranges vary? Which value do we use for apples — Smith's (two-thirds of an orange) or Jones's (three-halves of an orange)?

Since the index is designed to measure value, the rate used to convert apples into oranges must be their relative values to an individual. But if the index is to be used for more than one person, each must assign the same relative values. In our example above, Smith and Jones would need different value indices because they do not agree on the relative value of apples and oranges. This does not pose a problem, however, because most people do assign the same relative values to commodities; the reason they do so becomes clear when we examine the process of exchange.

The exchange of commodities is mutually profitable when individuals disagree about relative values. At its simplest, exchange takes place when each of two people prefers what the other has to what he has himself. After the exchange, both parties are happier than before.

In the example above, Smith likes oranges better than apples while Jones prefers apples. If Smith trades two apples to Jones for two oranges, each should be happier than he would be if he did not trade. As long as Smith and Jones disagree about the relative value of apples and oranges, they should continue to trade in order to increase their happiness. Eventually, they must either agree or run out of things to trade.

Why might they suddenly agree? Why should exchange change their minds about relative value? The answer lies in the principle of diminishing relative value. As Smith gives up more apples and gets back more oranges, the value of apples starts to rise relative to oranges. With oranges all over the house and only a few apples left, he may decide not to exchange the remaining apples for oranges because an apple is now worth as much to him as an orange. Jones's closets are now full of apples and he values his few remaining oranges too dearly to trade them for more apples. Thus exchange can stop before the two parties run out of goods because the relative values will be changing while they trade.

If all individuals who are able to trade with each other exploit all possibilities for mutual gain, they must in the end place the same relative values on all the goods they own. They can disagree about the relative values of goods they have chosen *not* to own, but not about those they have decided to own. Any disagreement about the value of goods owned is a signal that further trade would be desirable.

With everyone having the same relative values, it is possible to construct indices with which everyone will agree. For example, we can agree that a man is better off if he receives a raise in pay for doing a job than if he does not get the raise for doing the same job. The dollar index is one on which everyone can agree because everyone places the same relative value on goods and money. If all do not agree on the relative value of goods and money, one should be traded for the other.

It would be very nice to have absolute measures of value, to be able to compare the happiness of individuals, to have a measure of national satisfaction. Since this is impossible, we must be content with relative measures. The fact that there are so many pages left in this book indicates that quite a few things can be done even with relative value measures.

If commodities have value in proportion to their ability to satisfy men's remaining desires, then the measures of value we have discussed are appropriate for all nations regardless of their politics. We have looked only at the economic aspects of the social dilemma and we have abstracted from political discussions. Despite discussing money and exchange, we have said nothing about the grand organization of the economy, whether capitalist, socialist, or communist. We have spoken of men's desires for material satisfaction, why material values exist, and how to measure them. Everything we have presented applies to men living under all forms of social organization—capitalist suburbs, communist collective farms, communal living groups, monasteries, and autocratic families. In fact, since much of this book is concerned with how satisfaction can be squeezed out of resources, its contents are relevant for all forms of social organization.

Economists are known for their enjoyment of abstract discussion. Above, we discussed the theory of material value without discussing the other relationships between men. We will use the technique of abstraction wherever possible in order to simplify the analysis we present. The use of this technique is not an attempt to slip other issues under the table. Rather, it is an attempt to focus more clearly on issues one at a time in order to understand the fundamental importance of each.

Questions
1. Two ideas of journalistic, if not academic, significance are the following:
    a. That we live or soon will live in an affluent society.
    b. That the population explosion dooms mankind to a future of abject poverty.
Are these views consistent? What are their implications in relation to the importance of allocating resources efficiently?
2. The diamond-water paradox is a good illustration of the two forces that simultaneously determine value in a free market—preference and scarcity. Can the

resolution of this paradox be used to explain the relative incomes of farmers and ball players? Of professors and plumbers? Of artists and salesmen?

3. Why cannot economics help us determine a correct income distribution?

4. Why does the possibility of exchange guarantee that all will place the same relative values on the goods we own?

5. Does the theory of value differentiate between necessities and luxuries?

Concepts Discussed

value	diamond-water paradox
utility	relative value
marginal utility	diminishing relative value

3 Scarcity and Cost

Nature has endowed us with resources that can be used to produce material satisfaction. The endowment is not sufficient to allow us to produce all we wish, however, and therefore choice is essential. We must decide whether a forest is to be allowed to stand in pristine splendor, to be cut into timber for houses, formed into paper for books, or burned off to create land for farming or residential use. We must choose the option that most satisfies us if we are to minimize the inevitable frustration of our material wants.

Productive Resources

The scarce resources that limit economic output are usually broken into three categories. The first and most evident is *natural resources*, including land, mineral reserves, fresh water, and virgin forests, all of which are limited by nature itself. The second category is *labor*. Human productive power is a required input in the production of most economic goods. Given the size of the population, the requirements for rest, and alternative demands on one's time, there is only a limited amount of labor available for the production process. The third category is *capital*. Plant and equipment, inventories, housing, roads, and bridges are all capital goods that are used in one form or another to produce satisfaction. In fact, any good that was produced in the past but not consumed then represents capital today. Since capital is a man-made resource, it is possible for men to expand the resources at their command in the future by accumulating capital in the present. But capital is not free, and if it is to be created, someone in the society must consume less than he would if no capital were created. Note that the economist defines capital to be real, physical, man-made, productive assets rather than financial assets.

We return to the study of resources later when we examine the markets in which they are traded. Our purpose here is to indicate that they are indeed limited.

Production and Cost

Given our limited resources, we can produce only a limited quantity of goods in any period of time. To increase the production of any one commodity requires the use of more resources. This leaves fewer resources for other goods; thus fewer other goods are produced. In this way the limitation of resources imposes a cost on the production of goods, which is an important determinant of the value of those goods. More apples mean fewer oranges. The *cost* of apples in terms of oranges is the amount of oranges given up to get those apples. This is a cost that society must bear regardless of how it is organized. Communist, capitalist, and socialist economies (as well as any other "ists" imaginable) face the common problem of scarcity. Resources are scarce; therefore goods have a cost.

Goods that use scarce resources are called *economic goods*. They bear a cost to society in terms of other goods; they are not free because other goods are not free. This is not circular reasoning, since if we declared all goods to be free and permitted anyone to take anything he wanted, there simply would not be enough to go around. Some people would remain unsatisfied and tensions would arise, requiring that a method be devised to limit consumption once again. For example, take a situation where two roommates pool allowances, each spending as much as he desires under the assumption that the pooled incomes make goods free. Suppose that neither roommate feels compunction to restrain himself simply because the allowances are limited. The reader should be able to predict the outcome of such an experiment. Some new system of self-control or rationing would have to be invented that accounted implicitly for the problem of scarcity and hence the economic value of goods. Otherwise the living situation would break down, and each would be looking for a new roommate. The world may be viewed as a collection of roommates, each having an allowance, or an income. Pooling incomes cannot abolish the fact that the sum is limited — the world is on an allowance.

Since there are simply not enough resources to produce all we need or desire, we must pay for apples with oranges foregone, and therefore apples are not free. What must be given up in order to consume something is called the *opportunity cost* of the object to be consumed. The opportunity cost of air in terms of apples or oranges is zero for most of us, though not for space travelers. The opportunity cost of an apple in terms of oranges is the number of oranges we have to forego in order to have that apple. This holds for society as well; what the society must give up in order to produce something is called the *social opportunity cost* of that commodity. As we will refer to this concept many times throughout the text, it will be abbreviated to *social cost*.

The limitations on production imposed by the scarcity of resources can be illustrated quite plainly by a diagram, Figure 3.1, which shows the maximum amounts of food that can be produced for each attainable amount of manufactures. We call this diagram a production possibility frontier (PPF).

A diagram is a convenient way of condensing a great deal of information. Figure 3.1, for example, illustrates by point Y the maximum amount of food that could be produced if no manufactures were produced. All society's resources are devoted to food production at this point, none to manufacturing; if resources are used efficiently, Y indicates the maximum amount of food that could be produced. There is no way to increase food production beyond Y because there are no additional resources that can be devoted to this purpose. If we wish to increase the production of manufactures, Figure 3.1 indicates that we must give up food. Moving from Y to C involves producing more manufactures and less food.

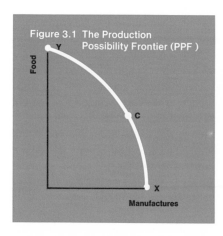

Figure 3.1 The Production Possibility Frontier (PPF)

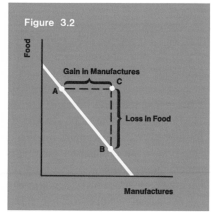

Figure 3.2

Continuing in this fashion, the diagram also tells us *how much* food must be given up in order to get more manufactures as we move along the frontier. In other words, it tells us the *social cost* of manufactures in terms of food, or vice versa. Thus if we know the units in which food and manufactures are expressed in Figure 3.1, the production possibility frontier will help us to determine how many units of manufactures must be given up to produce an additional unit of food at any point, such as C.

We can illustrate this by drawing a simplified production possibility frontier in the form of a straight line. Two such alternative frontiers are presented as examples *A* and *B* in Figures 3.2 and 3.3.

The social cost of a move from *A* to *B* in Figure 3.2 can be analyzed into two steps, the gain in manufactures *AC* and the loss in food *CB*. If we know the amount of food that must be sacrificed in order to gain a unit of manufactured goods, we then know the social cost of manufactured goods. *CB* measures the cost of *AC* units of manufactured goods; therefore *CB/AC* is the social cost of one unit of manufactured goods in terms of food. But this is the definition of the

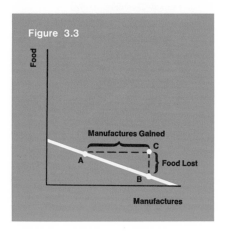

Figure 3.3

slope of line *YX* (a discussion of the concept of *slope* and of *margins* appears in the appendix to this chapter). The slope is a measure of the steepness of the line. If the line is very flat as in Figure 3.3, very little food must be sacrificed in order to get more manufactures whereas in Figure 3.4 the very steep line indicates that much food must be sacrificed to get more manufactured goods. Thus the slope measures the social cost of manufactured goods, while the social cost of food in terms of manufactures is its inverse, AC/CB (one divided by the slope).

In Figure 3.5 the slope changes as we move along the production possibility frontier, more closely approximating conditions faced by real economies. As we have drawn the production possibility frontier, the slope gets steeper as more manufactured goods and less food are produced. That is, as the production of manufactured goods increases, its cost increases in terms of food. Why?

Food and manufactures use different resources. Land is relatively important for food production, whereas factories are required for the production of manufactures. At point *X* all resources including factories are devoted to food production. As we increase the production of manufactures and move to point *A*, we only sacrifice a little food. Many factories are transferred to the production of manufactures, but since they are ill-suited to food production, little food is sacrificed at the outset. Eventually, however, at point *D* virtually all factories will be producing manufactures so that to increase manufacturing output still further we must even transfer land from food production and attempt to utilize it in manufacturing. This will lower food production a great deal though contribute little to manufactures. Because given resources are generally more efficient at producing one commodity than another, the production frontier in the real world bows outward. The cost of food depends on how much food is being produced. The more food we produce, the more expensive it becomes as we must use resources unsuited to food production to gain the additional increments. Thus the cost of food in terms of manufactures is not known until we know at which point on the production frontier we are producing.

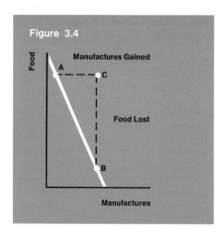

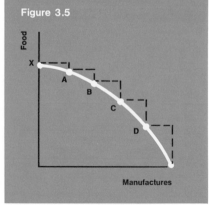

Production Possibilities in *n* Dimensions

The production possibility frontier (PPF) has as many dimensions as there are commodities. In the example above, only two commodities were introduced, food and manufactures, permitting us to illustrate a production possibility frontier and portray its characteristics in a two-dimensional diagram. We have chosen to use two dimensions in order to provide the simplest possible example to describe a more general problem. In practice there are not one or two but a very large number (*n*) of commodities, and therefore the characteristic PPF may be considered *n*-dimensional and might best be expressed algebraically.

Production Efficiency

One obvious requirement of efficiency is that production be at a point on the PPF. The PPF can be thought of as separating attainable from unattainable points. Clearly, producing at point *A* in Figure 3.6 is inferior to producing at point *B*, because more of both commodities are produced at *B* than at *A*. Either or both commodities may be produced in greater quantities at some point on the frontier than at any point within it. Thus production efficiency requires that we be on the frontier, but there are several obstacles that might prevent us from achieving this goal. First, we might not use all of our resources; labor or capital might be unemployed. Second, we might be using inefficient production techniques, techniques that use more of all resources than is absolutely necessary. (As this is a question of engineering rather than economics, we spend little time on this problem.) Third, we might be using resources for the wrong tasks; that is, land might be allocated to the production of manufactures and factories to food production. Under such circumstances, even when technically sound methods of production are used, and even if all of society's resources are fully employed, if the wrong factors are applied to the task at hand it is possible to wind up inside the production frontier. The third reason concerns the economic rather than the

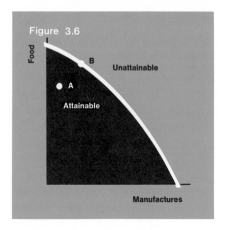

Figure 3.6

VILFREDO PARETO (1848-1923) Vilfredo Pareto, like Léon Walras, gave his name to a concept, Paretian optima, a set of tests for the efficiency of an economic system. Trained as an engineer (as was Walras), Pareto early acquired tools of mathematical analysis and notions of the interrelations within complex systems. From his acquaintance with Walras in Switzerland (where he exiled himself for reasons of disenchantment with Italy's creaky parliamentary government), he increased his understanding of mathematical methods in economics. Coming to his academic post in economics rather late (Lausanne, 1893), he also brought to his theorizing the intellectual benefits of a long career as an industrial and administrative politician. As an aristocrat, he rejected the perfectability of humankind and the natural harmony of men's social arrangements, thus demonstrating attitudes markedly different from the bourgeois radicalism of Walras. He criticized the socialists, especially Marx, for their failure to perceive the need for some form of effective entrepreneurial management and for their naive faith in the communist millennium. Nevertheless, he recognized that the "socialist religion" may well have been the best form of belief for workers in heavy industry and one of the only inspirations for their organizing to defend themselves against entrenched economic power, especially when industrial fluctuations and unemployment were so rampant. His writings reflected these varied influences sprinkled with a contempt for self-annointed bureaucrats and other meddlers (especially socialists and those of *nouveau riche* bourgeois origins). Ironically he was lionized in later life by one of the most authoritarian and self-annointed meddlers of all time, Benito Mussolini, who made him an Italian senator in 1923. Pareto's major works include *Cours d'économie politique* (1896) and *Manuel d'économie politique* (1909), as well as an attack on socialism, *Les systemes socialistes* (1902), and his final sociological treatise *Trattato di sociologia generale* (1916), translated as *Mind and Society* (1935).

Among his many contributions were some path-breaking econometric studies regarding the distribution of income, in which he showed that there is no theoretical way in which to reduce income differences. In the theory of consumer

---

technical efficiency of the production techniques. We discuss economic production efficiency in some detail later. Here we define it as follows:

> *An economy is said to exhibit efficiency in production if there is no way to increase the production of one commodity without decreasing the production of some other commodity.*

Note that this definition tells us that all points on the production possibility frontier exhibit production efficiency whereas all points inside the frontier do not.

Economic Efficiency

Economic efficiency requires more than just production efficiency, however. It requires that individuals get to consume commodities in the proper proportion. Thus although every point on the PPF may represent production efficiency, the society will prefer some points to others. The point at which a great deal of manufactures but no food is produced is probably not a very appealing produc-

choice he attempted to break away from the utility or embodied usefulness notions of many of the marginalists and classicists. Pareto discarded notions of measurable utility and employed his concept of "ophelimity," a neutral form of utility, which had nothing to do with any ethical or hedonistic criteria. Consumers behaved in ways that they thought best, and that was that. By leaving behind such ethical trappings, he was able to define a neutral theory of consumer preference that underlies much modern work.

His most famous contributions, however, came from an attempt to identify conditions of maximal well-being for any given society. These again were emptied of ethical content, save to say that greater well-being is better than less and that well-being is not necessarily a function of the volume of physical, material commodities but rather of any satisfactions that the individual and the society choose. The optimal condition moreover carries no theoretical specification as to the most desirable form of economic organization, socialist or private. Ultimately, the attainment of Pareto optimality or efficiency, given the distribution of income, means that we cannot make one of the maximizers better off without reducing the well-being of another. Briefly stated, his optimality conditions showed that maximal ophelimity for a group could be attained only if certain equalities obtained: prices among consumers, prices among producers, and equal productivity of inputs among all producers.

These optimality conditions set by Pareto have not only given modern economics a touchstone against which to measure the performance of various hypothetical systems (not unexpectedly, pure competition usually comes out best), but they have also provided a rationale for the construction of modern theories in welfare economics (*not* the economics of welfare payments). This powerful tool has also yielded many formulations for the testing and manipulation of planned economic systems. Although theorizing has progressed well beyond Pareto, and indeed often modifies his standards because of the problem of competing goals, we can never escape the implications of the conditions he set if we are to be responsible in our use of economic analysis.

---

tion point regardless of the efficiency of production at that point. Economic efficiency requires that we be at the point on the frontier that yields the most satisfaction to the society. All other points can be considered as wasting satisfaction and therefore inefficient.

But since we know we cannot compare satisfaction among people, it is impossible to determine unambiguously which point yields the most satisfaction. Accordingly, economists define efficiency in a way that allows them to ignore interpersonal comparisons. Therefore efficient allocations of scarce resources do not correspond to allocations that maximize satisfaction, but rather they correspond to points that do not obviously waste satisfaction.

An allocation of resources is said to be efficient if it is impossible to reallocate them in a way that makes at least one person better off and no one else worse off.

If it is possible to make someone better off without making anyone else worse off, satisfaction surely is being wasted. If the only way to increase one man's satisfaction is to decrease another's, then we can never tell whether total satisfaction is being wasted or not. Thus allocations of resources that do not obviously waste satisfaction are defined as efficient allocations. This definition was originated by Vilfredo Pareto (Italian economist, 1848-1923) and is sometimes called a *Pareto optimum* resource allocation.

Every efficient allocation of resources, of course, implies a given distribution of welfare. The question of which welfare distributions are "good" or "bad" must be reserved for politicians, social psychologists, or philosophers. There is little that scientific economics can do to add to this debate, and as a result we carry our analysis little beyond the concept of efficiency defined above. Yet efficiency in such a narrow sense is not to be slighted. Why are some countries rich and others poor? Although a Pareto optimal allocation of resources as defined above may be consistent with extreme income inequality and even starvation, it provides a useful point of departure for an examination of the relative success of alternative economic systems, and often much can be done to improve welfare by following its criteria.

Free Goods

We have defined an economic good as one that uses scarce resources and therefore as one that has a social cost in terms of other goods. A *free good* has no cost. It does not use scarce resources. Increased consumption of a free good does not require us to sacrifice consumption of some other commodity. Examples of free goods are sunshine, air, or the sound of birds. These goods are obtainable to society at zero cost at the margin because their supply is abundant relative to their demand. Their existence does not use up scarce resources, although consumption by some may alter their availability to others. This book is not concerned with *free goods*. It is, however, useful to note how a man values free goods. He will consume as much of these as he wishes as long as there is no cost in the process of consuming them, until the satisfaction he derives from the last unit consumed is zero. An additional unit of consumption after that point will give him no additional satisfaction.

Some free goods, such as mountain vistas, are not distributed evenly over the earth's surface. The cost of consuming them then becomes finite. It becomes necessary for men to sacrifice nonfree or economic goods in order to get to the free goods to consume them. Since such goods are not free for everyone, we may understand why it is the tourists who are always gaping at the scenery rather than the natives. To the natives the scenery is free. They consume so much of it that an extra glance provides less satisfaction than is lost through the effort of raising their heads. But the tourists from the flatlands are willing to spend a month or more of income on vacations that allow them to soak up nature. Scenery provides a very high marginal satisfaction to a tourist who has been deprived of it. He may even go home to New York and write songs about it to sell to others. Similarly, sunshine in the winter, freedom from smog, and cool air in the summer are all goods that are free to some but not to others. The purpose of much traveling is to consume goods that are free to other people.

What about exercise? Is it a free good? Individuals must sacrifice nothing but time in order to consume it. But is time free? Exercise has a cost in terms of reading foregone, or socializing, sleeping, or any other alternative use of time. Thus exercise is not truly free, nor is any good that requires time to consume. Does that leave us with any free goods? Not many. Man is endowed with only one lifetime in which to consume. The consumption of one good requires the sacrifice of some other. The psychological or philosophical problems man faces in adjusting to his finite life span may be similar to those he faces in adjusting to a finite level of material consumption. They are both manifestations of his limited resources. If these adjustments are similar, then the pursuit of the fountain of youth may result from the same motivation as the desire to increase utility.

Concluding Scientific Postscript

The scientific method is a way of inferring truth from facts (data). We observe countless phenomena in our lifetime. To create order out of these phenomena, we must discover the rules (natural, psychological, institutional) that govern them. Learning these principles gives us a shorthand method of understanding the many phenomena. As more principles are discovered, more can be learned from a given year's study. Each generation can thereby acquire a better education than the previous generation and progress can perpetuate itself.

The major social impact of science, however, has been not through man's increased ability to *observe* his environment but through his ability to *control* it. The scientific laws that create order out of data also allow us to *predict* the implications of actions. It is a short step from prediction to the state where we select those actions that bring about the implications we desire. Just as the natural sciences tell us how to transform the earth's natural resources into wondrous products, the human or social sciences tell us how to increase human welfare.

Any discipline that infers truth by using the scientific method is a science. Basically, the method consists of formulating hypotheses and testing them by confrontation with data. The formulation of hypotheses is an art — an act of creation. An hypothesis is a tentative law that man creates to explain the facts he observes. There is, however, no scientific way to manufacture an hypothesis from the facts; someone must have creative insight. Once the hypothesis is intuited, science can proceed. But the hypothesis must be formulated in a manner that allows it to be confronted with the facts. Logic and mathematics are used to derive the implications of the hypothesis and transform it into testable form. Data are then gathered and the evidence either supports the hypothesis, rejects it, or is inconclusive.

Economics has some particular problems that are not shared by all of its sister sciences. First, we cannot create data through experiments under conditions of perfect control. Men will not voluntarily undergo poverty so that we can examine how they would behave if they were poor. They may tell us how they would behave *if* they were poor, but this is not the same thing. We must gather our data by direct observation, as must the other social sciences and astronomy as well. Dependence on direct observation creates particular problems because the world does not generate the data in a manner that makes the laws unambiguously clear. If, for example, we observe that China since turning Communist has remained a very poor country, do we conclude that it remains poor because it is Communist or that it became Communist because it was poor? There is no way to experiment to determine the answer to this question. Sophisticated statistical tools have been created that allow us to answer questions of this kind through comparing the economic performance of many countries, Communist and otherwise, to try to isolate those factors which determine poverty; using statistical methods we can also examine the behavior of individual countries over time. But it is not a simple problem.

Another problem of economics is that our agents are men and men are not all alike. Any hypothesis about human behavior must be an hypothesis about how most men will act. Even chemical agents show slight variations in their behavior and are analyzed subject to statistical probability, but men are not identical to a far greater degree. Therefore, rules formed from observing the behavior of some men do not perfectly predict the behavior of others. Indeed, the same man may change his values and behave differently over time in otherwise almost identical situations. The science of economics is therefore inexact because the agents are not exactly alike. This makes the establishment of scientific principles more difficult in economics than in some other sciences.

Because of these difficulties, economics as a science is very new. The ability to test hypotheses depends upon tools of statistical analysis developed in the twentieth century. Successful attempts to control the economic environment followed this development by a few decades and such attempts are still in their infancy. Indeed, the determination to control the environment has not yet been firmly established in all countries. Because economics is such a new science, it is sometimes mistakenly regarded as no science at all, yet we shall see that directing the power of economic science at social relationships can lead to vast improvements in our environment and way of life. These large potential rewards, translated in terms of human welfare, make economic science a very exciting field in which to work.

Questions

1. What is the opportunity cost to an individual of attending college? Of studying economics? Of being politically active?
2. If two individuals at a picnic both own Coke and hamburgers, why is it inefficient to have one individual think a hamburger is worth four Cokes and the other think a hamburger is worth one Coke?
3. Is air always a free good? Sunshine? Square footage? What is truly a free good?

Concepts Discussed

capital

economic goods

opportunity cost

social cost

production possibility frontier

production efficiency

economic efficiency

Pareto optimum

free goods

APPENDIX: MARGIN AND SLOPE

Margins

A term frequently used in economics is *margin*. We saw that margins, when applied to utility, refer to additional or extra units of a substance. No simpler example is needed. An extra coat is a marginal coat, one more candy bar is a marginal candy bar. Margins refer to increases in the quantity of any item.

When we say *marginal utility*, we refer to additional utility. But when we say the marginal utility *of apples*, we are referring to additional utility and additional apples. Utility is a function of, among other things, apples. A marginal apple (an extra apple) yields some marginal utility. How much? The marginal utility of apples. So the marginal utility of apples refers to the marginal utility of *one* extra apple. The unit of measurement of the marginal utility of apples is: utility per apple.

Similarly, when we say the marginal cost of steak, we refer to the addition to cost brought about by producing *one more* steak. When we refer to the marginal product of labor in producing steak, we mean the amount of *extra* steak produced when *one more* unit of labor is employed. These new terms do not have to be learned here. We define them later when they are needed. They are just examples of the concept we refer to by the word "margin." In fact, this concept is equivalent to one of the basic concepts of calculus — the derivative. However, no prior knowledge of calculus is needed to understand either margins or this book.

Slope

The slope of a line is a measure of the steepness of the line. Its definition between two points is the vertical distance divided by the horizontal distance. In Figure 3A.1, the slope of the line between A and B is the vertical distance (-1) divided by the horizontal distance $(+1)$, or slope $= -1$. The line has a negative slope and can be called *downward sloping*. Note that for straight lines, the slope is constant. That is, the slope of the line between B and C is -1 just as it is between A and C. This gives us a way to measure the slope of a curved line. A curved line does not have the same degree of steepness (slope) at each point, but it clearly does have a slope even though that slope is changing.

In Figure 3A.2, a curved line is drawn *tangent* to straight line BAC. That is, the curved line touches the straight line only at one point, A. To the left of point

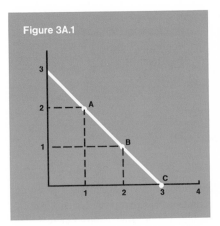

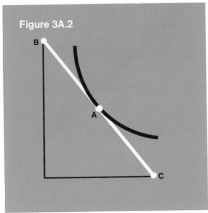

A, the curved line is steeper than the straight line whereas to the right it is flatter. At point A, the curved line and the straight line are equally steep. As slope is a measure of steepness, the two lines must have the same slope at point A. Thus the slope of any curved line can be measured at any point by measuring the slope of the straight line that is tangent to it at that point.

Figure 3A.3 shows a production possibility frontier. The slope of the frontier at A is (300 books) (500 steaks). Since the slope of the line measures the cost of steaks in terms of books, we conclude that the cost is 3/5; that is, the society must give up 3/5 of a book to get another steak.

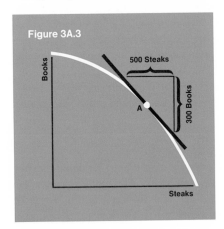

II Elements of Markets

Plus ça change, plus c'est la même chose.

FRENCH SAYING

Having looked at the forces that determine the values of commodities, we now proceed to examine how these forces work in a market system. Preferences and scarce resources, we noted, are attributes of all economies. These forces give rise to material values and make the process of resource allocation important if satisfaction is not to be wasted. The market system, allowing individuals to exchange commodities freely, is one device a society could adopt to allocate resources. It is not the only one. We look at the alternatives in later chapters; in the next two chapters we examine how value is determined in a market.

4 The Elements of the Market

The two sets of forces that determine value — scarcity and utility — exert their influence through markets. A *market* is an arena in which men can trade some commodities for others. The use of markets is therefore one way through which a society can allocate its different commodities, and therefore resources, among its many citizens. It is not, however, the only way. In later chapters we analyze how resources can be allocated through the use of a device called central planning. We will establish criteria to judge which method works better and the effects of both on social welfare. We will find that in different situations and subject to differing social preferences, the market may be preferred for some tasks but not for others. But before we can attack such problems, we must lay foundations. The aims in this chapter are therefore limited to a presentation of the elementary theory of markets.

The marketplace is the setting for the act of exchange. During times of disaster, governments may fall, banks fail, moneys be reduced to worthless paper, but the process of exchange has always survived. The market is inviolate. In civilized societies, the act of exchange is regulated and constrained by laws. The particular social compact that has evolved determines the rules within which the market at that moment must function. In fact, rules against theft, robbery, and physical violence make exchange the appropriate manner in which to acquire objects. With theft and violence illegal, the only legal way to induce someone to part with a desired object is to offer him other desired objects in return. This is called the *act of exchange,* or *trade*. It is through such transactions that society allocates its resources.

Just as there are laws that make exchange the acceptable way to acquire goods, there are laws that limit acquisition by exchange. Obvious examples are the rights to sell oneself into slavery, to buy drugs, or to produce pornography. There are laws to determine who can sell legal or medical services, laws for minimum cleanliness standards for food, and laws against supplying false information about a product. Indeed, the concept of private property that makes acquisition possible is a complex legal phenomenon. Property rights differ greatly from society to society. A given social compact that the members of a society have agreed to observe contains the rules within which exchange may take place. We now examine the act of exchange to see how and why individuals are willing to trade. The only rules we assume at this point are that violence and theft are prohibited. By avoiding all complexities, we can examine exchange in the simplest possible world.

Reciprocal Demand

The basic elements of any act of exchange are complementary desires, or what the economist terms *reciprocal demand*. For an economic transaction to occur, one man must offer what another desires. This must be true for both.parties to the transaction or no exchange will take place. Thus an obvious requirement for trade is that two parties must value two objects differently. The *value* a person places on an object may be expressed in terms of what he is willing to give up for it. The *price* of the object is what he is required to give up for it. If both parties are to agree to trade, each must receive an object of value greater than or equal to its price (the object he sacrifices). The simple purchase of a 10-cent Coke by a student requires that he prefer the Coke to the dime, while the seller must obviously prefer the dime to the Coke. Therefore both parties are made happier by trading.

The principle of diminishing relative value tells us that men desire a variety of goods. Any one commodity loses its value relative to others as more and more of it is consumed. But man does not own a great variety of commodities in his natural state. He must trade if he is to acquire them and thereby satisfy his desires. Thus different men, owning different commodities, find it desirable to trade with each other and widen the variety of experiences they encounter.

A Barter Transaction

To describe a transaction precisely we need list only the quantities of the two commodities that are traded. Economists list this information in the form of a *price* and a *quantity*. *A price is the ratio in which two commodities trade.*

To describe the transaction, "Ten apples were traded for twenty oranges," an economist would say, "Ten apples were sold for two oranges each." The quantity is clearly ten apples while the price is two oranges per apple. Either expression in quotations completely describes the transaction.

As a transaction can be expressed by two measures (dimensions), a point on a diagram can describe it completely. Figure 4.1 measures price on the vertical axis and the number of apples on the horizontal axis. Price is expressed as the ratio in which oranges trade for apples. This price can be called the price of apples *in terms of oranges*. To the consumer, the *price* of an apple and the *cost* of an apple are the same thing.

A Money Transaction

If we wish to describe the transaction, "Ten apples were traded for 25 cents," we plot a point like that in Figure 4.2, which reflects the fact that each apple costs 2½ cents. The price of an apple is 2½ cents per apple.

This latter transaction can no longer be considered barter. *Barter* is the direct exchange of one commodity for another without the use of money. Through the use of money, a barter transaction is broken into two parts. A trade of apples for oranges becomes a trade of apples for money and of money for oranges. The two monetary transactions are easier to conduct than the one barter transaction. This is because of the nature of reciprocal demand.

For example, the seller of apples may wish to buy books whereas the seller of books may wish steak. If the seller of steak wishes apples, then trade can exist. But to arrange such trade by barter is difficult, particularly when we remember that the *quantities* traded must be agreed to by all parties. With money, such transactions become much easier. The seller of apples buys books with the money he receives. But the seller of books can buy anything he wants. In fact, as long as there are some people who are willing to spend money on apples, the apple sellers will have money to spend on whatever else they wish. If an apple seller wishes a book, he need not find a book seller who likes apples. He merely sells his apples for money and uses it to pay for the book.

Thus money is a useful social device because it permits a separation of the acts of selling and acquiring commodities and therefore leads to a generalization of reciprocal demand. As long as the apple seller values some other commodities more highly than his apples, and someone else values those apples more highly than other (perhaps different) commodities, trade can take place. The existence of money frees a man from the necessity of working for General Motors when he wants an automobile or for the bakery when he wants bread. Money allows a man to work where he prefers and still be able to buy the commodities he wishes. We examine money and its effect on the economy in some detail in Chapters 33–38.

Supply and Demand

Some commodities are traded daily in large quantities by large numbers of people. Perishable food is an obvious example of this. Historically, trading of such commodities occurred in a market where the buyers and sellers could meet to bargain and haggle over prices. Originally, such markets were merely open places where anyone who wished to buy or sell could go, being fairly confident that he would meet someone there with reciprocal desires.

Markets are very convenient because they eliminate the need for buyers to visit sellers in spread out locations (the farms, in this case) in order to compare prices and merchandise as well as the need for sellers to visit buyers. Each

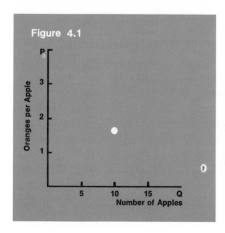

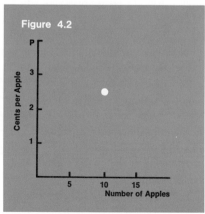

person only need visit the market in order to confront all those who wish to make a trade with him. Thus the existence of a market — a location in time and space where trades can occur — makes the costs of transportation much lower than if such centralization did not exist. In modern economies, it has been found most convenient to use middlemen whose existence allows for the geographical separation of buyers and sellers. Thus the representatives of supermarket chains and cattle growers will meet at markets in the Midwest to trade money for beef. The chains then transport the beef to local retail markets and confront consumers who wish to make the same trade. This arrangement further reduces the traveling buyers and sellers must do to satisfy their desires for trade.

The modern supermarket is a direct descendant of marketplaces where many buyers and sellers met simultaneously to trade. Although the physical appearance may be different, some essential economic aspects are the same and economists have developed special convenient ways to describe them. These descriptions can be grouped under the title of *supply and demand analysis.*

When discussing supply and demand, it is useful to remember the context in which such analyses are applied. First, they are appropriate for markets in which large numbers of people trade large numbers of commodities at a single location. Second, they are most useful in describing markets for homogeneous commodities such as milk, coal, or wheat rather than for unique commodities such as paintings, houses, or real estate. Against this background, it is possible to describe the sum of all the trades for a particular commodity by the same two numbers we used above to describe a single trade. Since the units are identical, we can describe the quantity traded by a single number and we can feel certain that a single price will prevail.

A single price prevails not only because the commodities are identical but also because of the power of *competition.*

In a large retail market, such as that for steak, there is little direct bargaining and haggling over price. The response of a purchaser of steak, if he feels that the price in store A is too high, is to shop in store B. It is much easier to switch stores than it is to haggle over price. Thus if the owner of store A charges very high prices for steak, his sales will be very low. For larger sales, he must lower his price.

This reflects the power of competition. The existence of many sellers of steak gives the buyer a large choice. If he always chooses to buy at the lowest price, then all sellers will have to charge the same low price. The sellers are competing with each other in attempting to gain sales. This competition forces them to charge as low a price as their competitors do if they are to make any sales. Thus one result of the bargaining process that goes on in the buyer's mind is that all sellers must charge the same price if the buyers insist on buying at the lowest possible price. We are therefore able to refer to *the price of steak* as a single number that is the same for all of the transactions occurring over a limited period of time.

We realize, of course, that all steak is not of identical quality, that all stores are not equally pleasant places to shop, that certain locations are more convenient than others, and that for such reasons, the price of steak will vary slightly from store to store. But it is preferable to think of these variations in price as resulting from differences in the commodities rather than in price. A prime steak is preferred to a choice steak. If buyers did not prefer one to the other, we can assume they would buy the cheaper one.

Demand

How do buyers react to different prices? Above, we saw that they would buy steak from B if his price were lower than A's so long as quality remained the same. But if B's quality were a little higher, they might pay a little more for B's steak. What would happen if B attempted to raise his price in order to exploit the situation? As his price increased, he might well discover that his customers were gradually drifting away to A even though A's steaks were of a lower quality. If this is true, we know something very basic about the nature of demand.

The higher the price charged, the less will be the quantity sold. The reason for this is clear; as price increases, individuals *substitute* other goods for the now expensive items. The possibilities for substitution determine the amount that sales will fall as price increases.

We can graph the amount of steak sold by B *as dependent on* the price of steak.* It looks like *DD* in Figure 4.3. Higher prices lead to fewer sales.

Line *DD* is called the *demand curve* for steak or one aspect of the demand function for steak. *The demand curve for steak lists the amount of steak that will be demanded at each price.* By steak demanded, we mean the amount of steak that people will wish to buy. The quantity of steak demanded depends not only on its price but also on consumers' incomes, their preferences for steak, the price of pork and other substitutes, as well as many other factors.

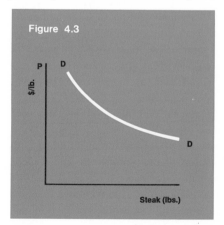

Figure 4.3

P
$/lb.
D

D

Steak (lbs.)

---

*Normally, mathematicians would graph the dependent variable (steak) on the vertical axis and the independent variable (price) on the horizontal axis. But one of the founders of modern economics, Alfred Marshall, reversed the axes in an early exposition of supply and demand curves and most of his successors have continued the tradition.

Thus demand functions are complex functions. We have drawn the demand curve above under the assumption that all other factors are held constant, that tastes have not changed, that the price of pork is constant, etc. In this way, we can isolate the effect of a change in price from all other influences. An economist would say, "*Ceteris paribus* (other things equal), an increase in the price of steak leads to a reduction in the amount of steak demanded." Of course, if other things change, the curve will have to be redrawn.

If a *demand curve* refers to the amount demanded at every price, other things equal, those other things might be called the *conditions of demand*. Changing the conditions of demand will change the position of the demand curve. For example, an increase in the price of pork will lead to an increase in the demand for steak. An increase in consumers' income will also increase the demand for steak. Tastes can change as well. A new belief that steak contains some rare vitamin will increase its demand. In fact, this latter phenomenon explains the huge rise in the price of calves' liver. Before liver was discovered to be a superb source of vitamins, minerals, and protein, it was almost a free good. Butchers would give it away to families with large dogs. Now the price of a pound of calves' liver is equal to that of a pound of steak, yet it still tastes the same.

The technique of assuming that other things remain constant when we examine the workings of a single market results in what economists call a *partial equilibrium*. This technique is most closely associated with Alfred Marshall (see biography on pages 42 and 43).

Demand Equilibrium
Each point on the demand curve represents a potential equilibrium for the buyers. Although we examine consumer equilibrium in detail later, here we note briefly the nature of such an equilibrium. The buyer will try to trade money for steaks if he feels that the steaks will yield more utility than will the other goods on which that money could be spent. Of course, the more steaks he buys, the less utility he receives from each. With enough steak purchases, the utility of steaks will not exceed that of the other goods that the money could buy. The buyer will then be in equilibrium.

For every price, such an equilibrium can be determined. Why does each price imply a different equilibrium quantity of steaks? If the price of steaks is high, the buyer must give up a large amount of money for each steak. This means he is sacrificing a considerable amount of utility, since he could spend that money on other goods. He will make this sacrifice only if steaks yield a great deal of satisfaction relative to the goods foregone. And we know from the principle of diminishing relative value that steaks will yield this satisfaction only if he buys very few of them. On the other hand, a low price for steaks means the consumer will have to trade a smaller amount of money (therefore sacrifice a smaller amount of satisfaction) for each steak. He will trade money for steaks until the satisfaction from the last steak is equal to that of the goods foregone.

Thus diminishing relative value explains the downward slope of the demand curve. An individual will trade money for a steak only if the steak yields more satisfaction than do the other goods that the money could buy. These other goods represent the utility foregone for steak. The consumer acts as if he were actually trading them for steak. If the price of steak is high, he will buy very little of it. Only if he buys very little of it will the marginal utility of steak relative to other goods be high enough to warrant its purchase. If price falls, he can then acquire additional steaks by sacrificing small amounts of money. He increases his steak consumption until the marginal utility of steak is exactly equal to the utility he could get from the other goods that must be sacrificed. Thus a demand curve is a locus of points telling us the value to the demander of the marginal steak.

Our examination of consumers indicates that there are many possible points of equilibrium. Since consumers can adjust to any price they observe, knowledge only of the demand curve is insufficient to tell us how price is finally determined. The demand curve merely tells us the value individuals place on each marginal steak by showing us what price they would be willing to pay for it. We need more information before we can explain why an equilibrium price is indeed an "equilibrium."

Supply

The additional information comes from an examination of the sellers of steak. Just as the buyers are called demanders, the sellers are called *suppliers*. And just as an examination of buyer behavior led to the discovery of a demand curve, an examination of seller behavior reveals the existence of a *supply curve*.

Profits represent the return to a seller in excess of cost. Sellers would like profits to be as large as possible. To make these profits they need to have both high prices and large levels of sales. But it would do them little good to charge very high prices and frighten away all the buyers. So sellers do not charge the highest prices possible. Each is constrained by competition to charge the same price as everyone else. In fact, if all sellers offer an identical product, no one can raise his price above the others' without losing his customers. And if at these prices large profits exist, we can expect further price cuts. Why? If one store charges less than the others, it makes all the sales. Therefore, if there are 20 stores, it will be in the interest of any one store to make half as much profit on each item and sell 20 times as many items. This would raise the store's profits tenfold. Each store realizes this and lowers price until profits have fallen to a point where the store owners are making a level of profits that is low enough to force them to consider moving their capital into other businesses rather than lowering prices further. Traditionally, economists think of these normal profits as a cost of business. They are a payment that must be made to capital regardless of how it is used. Only profits in excess of this are called profits or excess profits by economists.

At each price, there is an equilibrium quantity of goods to be sold that al-

ALFRED MARSHALL (1842–1924)   Founder of the first great modern department of economics, at Cambridge University, Alfred Marshall was also the arche-
type of the modern academic economist with his focus on theory and research,
with his major involvement in advising governments, and with his concern for
social issues. He achieved prominence as economics began to proliferate in
schools in both Europe and America and as it began to emerge as a scientifically
grounded, internally logical discipline having a truly international body of schol-
ars in mutual contact.

For all of his influence on modern economics, Marshall's output was amazingly modest, being found mostly in three books, *Industry and Trade* (1919),
Money, Credit and Commerce (1923), and, above all, *Principles of Economics*
(1890 and seven editions thereafter). He also wrote a number of articles and
served on numerous commissions, but it seems safe to say that his major contributions were in the *Principles* and in his many brilliant students (for example,
Keynes, Pigou, Robertson) at Cambridge. In his and his students' work we find
such key analytical devices as marginalism, a focus on individual decision-
making units (that is, consumers, producers), and the use of precise, mathematical formulations. Although he abhorred analysis widely divorced from reality, his resultant theories were not so much grounded on empirical investigation
as on deductive logic, being developed in a method similar to Ricardo's. Marshall
sought logical propositions about behavior useful in the prediction and explanation of economic phenomena. It must be emphasized, however, that he did
not presume to find mirrors of reality but rather accurate models that were good
predictors of results.

The neoclassical school (which, incidentally, included Walras) did not
pioneer marginal analysis, which had roots in the eighteenth century, but they did
use it as a general rule in economic theory, one that integrated the behavior of all
types of economic decision units. By means of the marginal principle Marshall
was able to derive sets of mutually consistent patterns of economic action for all
private types of economic agents—consumers, firms, factor suppliers—according
to which equilibrium conditions in particular markets could be defined. This
approach led to the specification of the now-familiar supply and demand analysis

---

lows the store owner a normal return on his capital. Lower prices for that quantity of goods would mean that some stores would close, the owners shifting their
capital into other industries. By the same token, a higher price would mean excess profits, causing new firms to enter the market, expand sales, and force the
price back down again, thus eliminating those excess profits. So for each quantity of goods sold, there is some price that leaves all store owners content to continue their operations with no change. All other prices would lead to attempts to
increase or decrease that quantity. The one price that leaves the store owners in
equilibrium can be called the *equilibrium price*.

But profits are only one determinant of the prices stores charge. The remaining determinants are *costs*. The price of a commodity represents cost plus

and its associated curves. The power of the neoclassical method was shown by its applicability to all types of exchange relationships including not only those for the consumer but also those for buyers and sellers of factors of production. Moreover, by shifting attention to the margin in economic decision making, the neoclassicists were able to develop more precise rules for making choices than were the classicists, who could only speak of tendencies based on averages.

In all of this it should be noted that Marshall and the English school relied on what is called partial equilibrium rather than general equilibrium analysis as propounded by Léon Walras. They developed the equilibrium conditions in the markets for individual commodities, and from these partial specifications presumed that they could discern the equilibrium conditions for entire industries, groups of industries, and for the economy. Although their system underlies much modern thinking in microeconomic analysis, it is weak in handling interdependence effects without some rather closely defined supplementary assumptions. Furthermore, although Marshall dealt with monopoly in his analysis, he adhered rather closely to conditions of pure competition for the satisfactory establishment of equilibrium conditions. Indeed, Marshall specified competition as a norm not only for behavior but also for the natural tendency of the economy, an assumption that was to prove costly to later analysis and to policy formulators.

Marshall's analysis shifted the emphasis of economics from long-run developmental questions to shorter-run issues of price determination, concern with distributive shares as returns to productive services, and to questions of efficiency rather than growth. (After all, if one is efficient, growth takes care of itself.) Increasingly, economics in the Marshallian tradition showed that short-run and long-run questions were subject to the same type of analysis, appropriately modified, and thus the distinction between the two as it had been previously perceived was blurred. The long run was for Marshall that period in which certain factors of production could be altered in volume or nature. In the short run they could not. How different that was from Smith or even Mill with their concern for historical development and the conditions for satisfactory economic growth. If we were to fault Marshall, it would be on the grounds that his analysis was too partial, too short-term, and too wedded to pure competition.

---

profit. Cost to the butcher represents the cost of renting his store, of buying steaks from meatpackers, as well as other expenses that can be ignored for the moment. Therefore, for any given quantity of goods sold, the competitive sellers' equilibrium price will equal the cost of those sales per unit including the payment to capital. If the price is below this level, firms leave the industry; if above, new firms enter or existing firms expand.

Different equilibrium sellers' prices will correspond to different quantities of goods sold. This is because unit costs change when the quantity sold changes. As butchers demand more steaks from cattle growers, cattle growers attempt to expand; in order to do this, they have to bid land away from wheat farmers — land that is relatively less productive of cattle than the land already used by cattle growers. Increased costs to cattle growers mean increased costs to butchers. Thus higher levels of output are associated with higher unit costs because resource prices increase when an industry expands. Chapters 13–17 discuss the concept of cost and supply in much greater detail. Here it is sufficient to note the effect of the increased costs on price. Costs per steak increase as sales increase. Consequently, the sellers' equilibrium price must increase as sales increase.

A typical *supply function* or *supply curve, SS,* has been drawn in Figure 4.4. It represents the quantity of steak supplied as a function of the price of steak. The *conditions of supply* are similar to those of demand. The price of steak, for example, depends upon the price of agricultural land, the price of cowboys, the weather, the price of cattle feed, the technical know-how of ranchers, and the amount of "normal profits," or return to capital, required to keep the cattle growers in business. A decline in the price of land, for example, leads to excess profits in the cattle business. As new ranchers enter the industry, the supply of steaks expands and the supply price for a given amount of steak will fall.

Supply and Demand

We now have two functions that relate price to quantity. One tells us all of the alternative points of buyer equilibrium — points at which the value of a commodity equals its price; the other tells us the seller equilibrium points — points at which the cost of a commodity equals its price. If a *market equilibrium* requires that both the buyers and the sellers be in equilibrium, then only a point that lies on both curves can represent a market equilibrium. At that point the value of a commodity equals its cost.

Point *E* in Figure 4.5 is such a point. At *E* both sellers and buyers are in equilibrium. They are content to trade *Q'* steaks at price *P'*. At any other price, there is no equilibrium. In fact, at any other price there exist forces working to change that price. Consider price *P"* in Figure 4.6. If that were the price of steak,

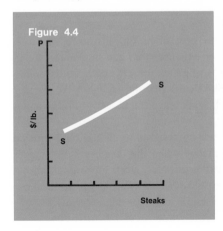

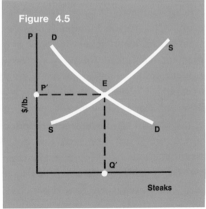

suppliers would wish to supply *B* steaks but buyers would wish to buy only *A* steaks. We say that there is an *excess supply* of steaks. What happens then?

Buyers would buy only *A* steaks and sellers would be disappointed. They would not be achieving the level of sales necessary to keep profits high enough to warrant so many butchers. At the end of each day, there are unsold steaks. One butcher may lower his price in an attempt to increase his own sales. This makes things even worse for the other butchers. They lower price as well. But with lower prices, fewer steaks can be produced at a profit. This example shows that there exist forces that tend to move prices downward from *P''*.

What about price *P** in Figure 4.7? At *P**, a very low price, buyers attempt to buy *F* steaks though sellers wish to sell only *C* at that price. There is an *excess demand* for steaks. The buyers go to the stores and buy *C* steaks, but they wish to buy more. They shop elsewhere and find that all stores have run out of steaks. The buyer may mention to the butcher that he would have bought some more steak if it had been available, or the butcher may notice that he runs out of steak at noon. A buyer then offers to pay extra if the butcher will save some steak for him. Soon the butcher raises the price of steak and increases his profits above the normal level. Thus if a price is set *below* the equilibrium price, forces exist to cause that price to *increase*; a price set *above* the equilibrium price will encounter forces that cause it to *decrease*. The arrows in Figure 4.8 demonstrate that these forces guarantee that an equilibrium price will be attained.

At any price but the equilibrium price, there exist forces of change. As long as supply and demand curves are normally shaped, they guarantee that eventually an equilibrium will be attained. Although the marketplace may appear confused to the observer who watches the hand-waving and head-shaking and listens to the emotional pitch of the crowd, whether at Macy's on the Saturday after Christmas or in Oaxaca, Mexico, on any Sunday, markets are in fact amazingly efficient institutions. That is why they have not changed in principle since the earliest periods of recorded history and today can be analyzed by the anthropologist or market research expert as similar phenomena, whether located in

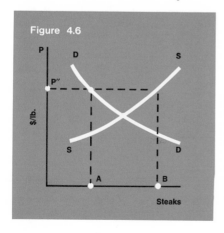

Figure 4.6

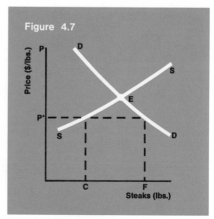

Figure 4.7

Mesoamerica or New York City. In the example above, two groups of people engage in the exhange of two commodities, money and steak. Out of a number of possible points of exchange in the diagram, they will arrive at only one point agreeable to both groups. This is the principle of *equilibrium.*

If excess demand exists initially, the buyers will begin to offer a higher price — though for a smaller number of steaks. The sellers will be willing to supply an increasing number of steaks as the price rises. The position of exchange will move up toward *E* in Figure 4.8.

If excess supply exists initially, the sellers will begin to reduce their price while offering to supply a smaller quantity of steaks. As the price falls, the buyers will be willing to purchase a larger number. The position of exchange will move down toward *E.*

In either case, the process of bargaining itself will bring about a final exchange position at which both buyers and sellers will be satisfied. This is called the position of *equilibrium.* Equilibrium is possible because the supply and demand curves slope in different directions. This is due to the influence of diminishing relative value on the demand curve and increasing product costs on the supply curve.

In Chapter 2 the principles of utility and value were introduced. They have now been shown to underlie the achievement of equilibrium in the market. If people did not know what they wanted, and if a utility maximum were therefore indeterminate, it would not be possible to draw individual demand or supply curves for any commodity. Equilibrium would be meaningless and all would be flux. But since individuals generally do act as though they know their order of preferences for various goods, and because their marginal satisfaction from any one thing relative to other things declines as its ownership increases, demand curves are normally determinate and downward sloping for any commodity relative to any other commodity (whether the unit of exhange is in terms of steak, oranges, or money).

The exact *position* of the demand curve is determined by the *conditions of*

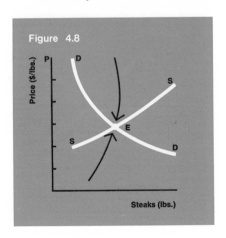

Figure 4.8

demand. These are the following: (1) the prices of other goods and services; (2) the taste patterns of buyers; and (3) the purchasing power (income) of buyers.

When a demand curve is drawn, it is always assumed that except for prices the conditions of demand are held constant. This is an example of the application of the *ceteris paribus* assumption so essential to the use of two-dimensional diagrams. The demand curve *DD* in Figure 4.8 can be drawn only if it is assumed that (1) the price of *other goods* does not change (only the price of steaks in terms of money is allowed to vary), (2) the tastes of the buyer are fixed for the time being, and (3) the purchasing power of the steak buyer is established (by the number of dollars he carries with him). If any of these conditions is permitted to vary, then the curve *DD* will *shift*.

The exact *position* of the supply curve is determined by the *conditions of supply*, which are the following: (1) the prices of other goods and services; (2) the behavior patterns of sellers; and (3) the available technology.

The supply curve *SS* is drawn on the assumption that the following three conditions are unchanging: (1) The price of other goods (including all goods that may be necessary to produce steaks) is fixed; (2) the preference of men for being butchers as opposed to entering other trades is stable; and (3) the supplier's technical capacity to turn beef into steaks remains fixed. If any one of the conditions of supply is permitted to vary, the *SS* curve will shift either to the right or to the left. A simple example illustrates this clearly.

Let us alter condition 1 in the supply of steaks and let the price of inputs (labor time) rise in terms of money. For example, a cowboy engaged in growing steaks may be offered more money for his time to work in the city. This increases the *opportunity cost* of his time spent in growing steaks. In order for the cowboy to continue chasing dogies, he will have to be compensated for this increase in costs with a higher price for every quantity sold. The rancher's costs will increase and he will raise price to the meatpacker who, in turn, will raise price to the butcher. The supply curve will therefore shift to the left, and if the demand curve does not change, the price of steaks will rise.

The student may want to invent changes in conditions 2 and 3 of supply and draw the appropriate shifts in the *SS* curve. The implications of altering the conditions of supply and demand are dealt with in more detail in Chapter 5.

Changes in Supply and Demand

Confusions about supply and demand arise most frequently from a failure to distinguish between a movement *along* a curve and a movement of a curve itself.

Either movement can lead to a change in the *quantity demanded*. The quantity of steaks demanded is a function of the price of steak and of many other variables as well. A change in any of these variables can lead to a change in the quantity of steak demanded. In an analysis of markets, however, we often wish to assess the *cause* of a change in the equilibrium—a change in *both* price and quantity. To make this assessment it is important to distinguish changes in quantity demanded that are brought about by price changes from those brought about by other causes. The former are a result of shifts in the *supply* curve whereas the latter result from shifts in the demand curve.

For example, if the supply curve shifts to the right from S_1S_1 to S_2S_2 in Figure 4.9 (an increase in supply), the price of steak falls and the quantity sold increases. The *quantity* demanded has increased, but it would be erroneous to say that "demand has increased." The increase in the quantity sold results from an increase in *supply*. This causes price to fall and, therefore, the quantity of steaks demanded to increase. So to keep separate the impact of changes in *demand* from changes in *supply*, we reserve the former term for changes in quantity demanded that result from changes in variables *other than price*; that is, we reserve the term for changes that cause the demand curve to shift.

An easy way to remember this distinction is to remember that in equilibrium, the *quantity demanded* always equals the *quantity supplied*. So when the quantity demanded increases, the quantity supplied should increase as well, regardless of the cause of the increase. But we would like to be able to say whether the increase was caused by changes that affected the buyer or by those that affected the seller. So we reserve the term a "change in demand" to refer to a shift in the demand curve and not a movement along the curve caused by a change in price and therefore by a change in supply. Throughout this book the mention of a "change in supply" will always refer to a shift in the supply curve and not a movement along a given curve. And statements that "supply is upward sloping" and that the "quantity supplied will rise as the price rises" will refer to the same thing—a movement along a given supply curve rather than a shift in the curve itself.

The Market and Efficiency

No matter how confused markets may appear to be, they tend to serve as highly efficient instruments of exchange. We shall see in subsequent chapters that the more competitively they operate, the more likely they are to permit an efficient

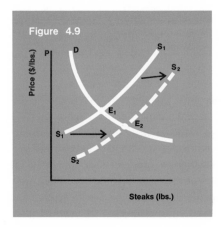

Figure 4.9

allocation of resources. If sellers do not have their own little preserve of buyers but instead must compete freely among themselves in the market, then the price each seller charges for any commodity must eventually be the same and must equal the cost of production. This will help to bring about an efficient allocation of resources. If, for example, there exist two prices for steak, $2 per pound for New York City residents and $1 per pound for residents of Westchester County (assuming no transport costs), resources are not being efficiently allocated. It would be possible to buy one pound in Westchester and sell it to a New York City resident for less than $2. The New York City resident buying the extra steak would be made better off by this process, and no one need be made worse off, provided the social cost of steak were $1. If the cost of a steak is $1 and its value to a consumer $2, that consumer could be made better off by paying $1 for a steak. And since he pays the whole cost of the steak, no one else is made worse off by that transaction.

The beauty of the market as a device for allocating resources efficiently lies in the fact that at an equilibrium the value of a commodity equals its cost. Remember that we can express value and cost in relative terms. Thus if the value of a steak relative to an apple is 40 whereas its social cost is 20, we know we can improve satisfaction by producing 20 less apples and one more steak. The extra steak is worth 40 apples. But if we look at an ordinary supply and demand curve, we can see that whenever the value of a steak exceeds its cost, there will be pressures exerted through the market to increase production. Only when value equals cost are these pressures absent. And when value equals cost, there is nothing to be gained by increasing or decreasing the production of a particular commodity.

Adam Smith called this property of markets the "invisible hand." He felt that the market acts as an invisible hand guiding merchants who attempt to maximize their own profits to do what is best for the society. Today, we know enough about social welfare to label the market equilibrium an *efficient* allocation of resources rather than the *best* allocation of resources. But efficiency is better than nothing. For with an efficient allocation of resources, we know that no utility is being wasted. Later we will study conditions under which free markets are inefficient. But for now, we can say that if the value of the marginal unit of each commodity equals its cost, then the optimal amount is being produced. And value equals cost when sellers and buyers are in equilibrium.

The market allocates commodities to those who are willing to pay the most for them. This leads to efficiency, because steak lovers get a lot of steak, auto lovers get beautiful cars, and oenophiles get vintage wines. But it also means that rich people get more goods than poor people. While we cannot say how this will affect utility, we might feel in our bones that it is unfair, or that it would not be a good thing if carried to an extreme. In Chapters 6 and 7 we examine a simple economy and tell more about the efficiency of competitive markets and the way in which they are related to income distribution.

Attempts to Bypass the Market

Suppose that an economy attempted to circumvent the market by replacing sellers of steaks with a central planning board who would determine the number of steaks to be sold. Individuals are still assumed to decide freely how much to buy. This removes competition on the supply side but preserves it on the demand side. What will happen?

The demand curve will not change. As shown in Figure 4.10, it is still *DD*. The supply curve disappears, however, and becomes just a point. This represents the price and quantity determined by the members of the central planning board. If they are lucky, the point they choose is right on the demand curve (at *A*). If they try *B*, however, unsold steaks will exist and a condition of excess supply will occur. Inventories build up, and the planners will have to either lower the price or decrease the quantity of steaks produced. In the short run, steaks will spoil and be thrown away.

If the planners try point *C*, then people will want more steaks than exist. This results in first-come-first-served, and there is unsatisfied demand. Some people get bargains and others get nothing. Rationing may become necessary in order to preserve a degree of equity; otherwise long queues will result and individuals will "pay" a higher price by spending more time waiting in line. The Soviet Union has tended to substitute lines and waiting for a more flexible competitive price system as a means of allocating resources. In the earlier years in the USSR, position *C* was more frequent than position *B* for more commodities. Long lines and waiting periods were the rule because the value of the commodities exceeded their cost. Recently, pricing policy has been changed to the point where some goods remain unsold at the price that is fixed in the state stores (*B* instead of *C*). Planners do not automatically hit on position *A* and clear the market without lines and waiting or unsold inventories.

Gradually, the authorities are permitting a higher degree of individual autonomy to sellers and plant managers in the Soviet Union, so that a supply curve

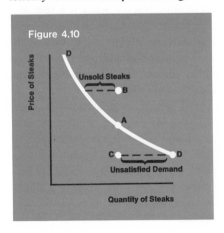

Figure 4.10

is beginning to appear for many commodities. As this continues, Soviet price and output positions will gradually approach those of a purely competitive economy, with attendant welfare gains for both buyers and sellers. Lines will become a thing of the past as will unsold, rotting merchandise. It is important that the student realize that lines and rationing are a result of a method of resource allocation and not of poverty. There are many countries poorer than the Soviet Union where no lines exist for merchandise, though even less is consumed by every citizen. This is because these countries use free markets and in them the value of commodities does not exceed their cost. Soviet authorities simply do not charge high enough prices to eliminate the lines. In very poor countries, incomes are so low that people do not have an effective demand for many commodities. The consumption that they would have to sacrifice to buy these commodities is worth too much to them, so they do without.

The Neutrality of the Market
A perfectly competitive market is a passive instrument that facilitates the process of exchange. Though its transactions mirror the desires of its participants, the prices and quantities determined by a perfect market may be regarded as politically, socially, and ethically neutral, since no single participant has sufficient influence to alter the conditions of supply and demand. Thus the market can be used as an allocating mechanism by any type of social system, regardless of its objectives. It is conceivable that one day the matching of supply and demand (as determined by the underlying conditions of supply and demand) may be achieved by planners with computers, but this is something for the distant future. Meanwhile, the allocation process must rely upon individuals' making thousands of decisions daily, guided by information such as market prices or some substitute for them. For most societies, individual propensities to truck and barter provide a means of achieving essentially the same results more quickly and efficiently than attempts to circumvent the market. But no matter how well the price system serves as a device for rationing, it allocates resources in a manner that depends upon a given distribution of income. Thus the market is of little value as a device for redistributing income. Its very neutrality assures this. But the price system will work in principle for any income distribution or social system.

Questions

1. How does the "invisible hand" work? Why do perfectly free markets lead us to produce the quantity of a commodity for which its value equals its cost? Why is any other quantity of output wasteful?
2. Why do demand curves generally slope downward? Supply curves upward?
3. What forces exist to change a price if it is not at its equilibrium level?
4. How do supply and demand curves portray the interaction of the basic forces of scarcity and utility that determine economic value?

Concepts Discussed

market
reciprocal demand
price
barter
demand curve
supply curve
conditions of demand and supply

demand equilibrium
supply equilibrium
market equilibrium
profit
excess supply or demand
the invisible hand

5 More on Markets

Order and Change

The equilibrium brought about by allowing sellers and buyers to maximize their own utilities in a free market may be one of continual change. As the conditions of supply and demand change, the equilibrium they determine changes as well. Variations in climate, health, tastes, expectations of the future, and population all operate to change the supply or demand curves in one way or another. Therefore price and quantity sold change as well. The more perfectly the market operates, the more quickly changes in the conditions of supply and demand are reflected in the movement of the price and quantity of goods traded. The less perfectly the market operates, the more likely excess supply of some commodities and excess demand for others will arise. The greater the surpluses and deficits, the greater the waste of potential satisfaction. The market permits change to take place in an orderly fashion so that supply and demand continually tend toward a stable equilibrium. Rarely does this orderly behavior break down. This chapter deals with equilibrium in a single market as it is affected by changes in supply and demand. The influence of these changes on the equilibrium will be shown to depend upon the length of the period of adjustment considered.

There are some basic facts about changes in markets that *must* be understood. We must know how price and quantity will respond to shifts in supply or demand. For example, if either supply or demand expands (shifts to the right in Figure 5.1), we should know that the *quantity sold will expand*. To check this, draw in a new supply or demand curve to replace the old one in Figure 5.1. If

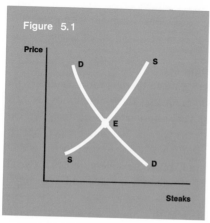

Figure 5.1

Price

D   S

E

S   D

Steaks

the new curve is to the right of the old one, the quantity sold will have to increase. Recognition of this fact should become instinctive to any student of economics. *If buyers try to buy more, or if sellers try to sell more, sales will increase.*

The next basic fact of markets is equally obvious. *If supply increases, price will fall; if demand increases, price will rise.* This, too, should be learned until it is an automatic response on the part of anyone trying to explain a price movement. It can be seen, again, by shifting the curves to the right in Figure 5.1. The reason for this response of price lies in the reasons behind the shape of the supply and demand curves. If supply expands, the new solution will lie to the right on the *same demand curve.* As demand curves with few exceptions slope downward, moving the supply curve to the right requires a new equilibrium with *lower price* and *higher quantity.*

Similarly, an expansion of demand leads to more goods sold at higher prices. An expansion of demand can be represented as a movement *along the supply curve.*

If we remember the forces that come into play when a price other than the equilibrium price exists, we will see why changes in supply or demand have the effects they do. Suppose that a fad of protein dieting sweeps the country and consumer tastes shift toward steak and away from pizza. The effect this will have in the steak market is that butchers will begin to run out of steak; customers will bribe butchers to sell more steak; and the butchers will find that they can increase price and still sell a great deal more steak than before. Thus the increase in demand will be felt in the steak market as a *pressure for an increase in prices.* Alternatively, an expansion in supply due to new methods of growing cattle cheaply will be felt in the market as a *pressure to reduce prices.* For only if prices fall will the sellers be able to induce the buyers to buy more steaks. Buyers, on the other hand, can only cause sellers to increase production by offering them higher prices.

Students *must* understand the effect of changes in supply and demand on price and quantity before proceeding to the remainder of the book. Any future discussion about markets will assume that the student is familiar with the results of a change in supply or demand.

Time Limits on the Adjustment to Change
The shorter the time period studied, the less chance there is for a change in the conditions of supply or demand. The assumption that these conditions are held constant is a realistic assumption only for very short periods of time. We can draw the supply and demand curves for steaks for one day and expect them to approximate the actual market conditions. But when trying to portray the annual market, we are forced to admit that there are likely to be several prices for steak over the year. Unforeseen events are likely to disturb the demand and supply curves many times.

However, *forecasting* is not our problem in this book. We wish to *explain* how prices are determined in markets. This requires that we show how conditions affect price and quantity and how variations in those conditions change the results. It does not require that we forecast the changes. Therefore, we will accept a set of conditions and draw the corresponding supply and demand curves. We will draw annual curves as if the set of conditions would remain constant throughout the year. As long as we know how changes in the conditions affect supply and demand, we know *why* prices and quantities fluctuate. We will be able to explain each new fluctuation by a change in one or more conditions.

The Market for Gasoline: An Example

How much gasoline should the economy produce? This is the planner's question. Even if the market is being permitted to do the "planning" for us, we are still entitled to ask the question. The customary answer is, "Whatever the market will bear." But what will the market bear? "This depends on how much gasoline people consume." And how much gasoline will they consume? "This depends on its cost." What does gasoline cost? "That depends upon how much we produce." The apparent circularity of such questions and answers reflects a basic economic principle. Costs and value are relative concepts and can be defined only in terms of each other. It is necessary to have *both* supply and demand present in order to determine how much gasoline the economy should produce. We must know what each good costs in terms of other goods and what it is worth relative to other goods. We must know how many other goods the society must sacrifice in order to make one more gallon of gasoline. That is the cost of gasoline. And we must know the value of those goods relative to gasoline. If they are worth less than gasoline, that is, they yield less utility than the extra gallon of gasoline, then we should produce that extra gasoline.

The supply curve should show us how much each quantity costs, and the demand curve should show us what each quantity is worth. At equilibrium, the gasoline should be worth exactly what it costs and no more nor less should be produced. But adjustment to an equilibrium takes time. Should a sudden change occur in the supply of gasoline, the immediate effect on price and quantity demanded would be different from the long-run effect. To see why, we will discuss the market for gasoline in some detail.

Let us first consider the short run. What would be the immediate response of consumers to a 10 cent a gallon increase in the price of gasoline? Probably just a lot of grumbling. Fewer trips to the corner might be made in the family car that week. And what would be the response to a 10 cent a gallon decrease in price? A lot of smiling. Father is more willing to let Junior use the car that weekend—of if Junior owns his own car, he may fill it up for the first time in his life.

Therefore, if we draw the demand curve for gasoline for that week, it is likely to be very steep. As drawn in Figure 5.2, a 10 cent per gallon change from an initial price of 30 cents per gallon leads to an increase (or decrease) of about 10 percent in the amount of gasoline sold.

If we were to draw the annual demand for gasoline, we would find a different story. If the price of gasoline went up 10 cents a gallon and stayed there for a year, much larger decreases in gasoline consumption would be observed. Commuters would form carpools to save on gasoline money. Fewer shopping trips would be made. More vacations would be taken by airplane, fewer by car; and shorter distances would be traveled on automobile vacations. Some people would commute by bus or train. Fewer families would buy second or third cars.

All of these responses require more time than one week to exhibit their complete effect. Therefore they do not affect the very short-run demand curve. Habits exist and it takes a while for them to change. Costs of commuting by different systems must be calculated before a switch is made. Therefore, the medium-run (annual) demand curve is flatter than the short-run curve. It is flatter because a year allows people more time to *substitute* other goods for gasoline. Whereas the weekly demand curve in Figure 5.2 shows that a change of 10 cents a gallon leads to a 10 percent change in consumption, the annual curve in Figure 5.3 shows that the 10 cent change in price might lead to a 33 percent change in quantity demanded. This is because there is a greater opportunity to *substitute* other goods for gasoline when there is a longer period in which to adjust. Increases in price lead to *larger* percentage reductions in demand when there are good substitutes for the product than they do when only poor substitutes exist. Carpools are a poor substitute for gasoline in the very short run because they take time to form.

How about the very long run? How might the quantity of gasoline demanded respond to price changes if individuals could complete very long-run adjustments to price changes? If gasoline prices became very high, people would buy cars with smaller engines. In Europe, where gasoline is heavily taxed and costs about 80 cents per gallon, cars have very small engines and very little weight. They will go 30 miles on a gallon of gas—double the American average. With that price, families might decide that one car was better than two. People would live closer to their jobs in order to drive less. In cities more apartments would be built, less suburban real estate developed. Metropolitan areas might

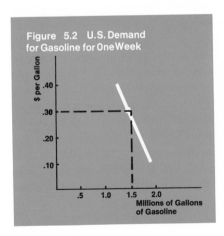

Figure 5.2 U.S. Demand for Gasoline for One Week

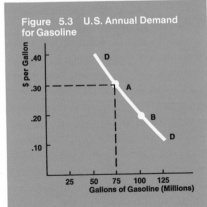

Figure 5.3 U.S. Annual Demand for Gasoline

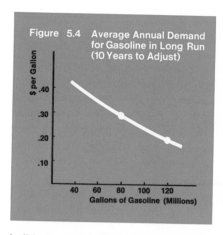

Figure 5.4 Average Annual Demand for Gasoline in Long Run (10 Years to Adjust)

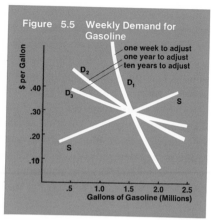

Figure 5.5 Weekly Demand for Gasoline

build new transit lines in response to increased demand for rail service. Bicycles would become more popular, walking more common. In short, people would drive less and they would drive smaller cars.

In Figure 5.4, a very flat demand curve is drawn that allows changes of 50 percent in gasoline demand in response to a 10 cent per gallon change in price. In the very long run, it is possible to do a great deal of substitution for most commodities. Therefore, long-run demand curves will be very much flatter than short-run curves.

In Figure 5.5, we have drawn all three demand curves. Each represents the weekly demand for gasoline—one with one week to adjust to price changes, one with a year for adjustment, and one with ten years to adjust. We now use those three curves to show what would happen to the price and quantity of gasoline in response to a shift in supply. In Figure 5.5, the supply curve is drawn initially so that equilibrium occurs at a price of 30 cents per gallon. This is both a long-run and short-run equilibrium. To understand the difference between these equilibria, we now look at Figure 5.6 in which we assume that the supply curve has

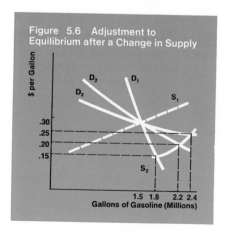

Figure 5.6 Adjustment to Equilibrium after a Change in Supply

shifted outward due to a change in technology. That is, we assume that gasoline has become cheaper to produce and that producers are attempting to sell more by offering lower prices to consumers.

The new supply curve intersects the three demand curves at three different points. This gives us the following information. In the short run, the price of gasoline will fall a great deal (to 15 cents a gallon) and the quantity demanded will only increase to 1.8 million gallons per week. But after a year's adjustment the quantity demanded will have expanded to 2.2 million gallons a week, and this will cause the price to increase to 20 cents a gallon. After 10 years' adjustment to lower prices, demand will increase until 2.4 million gallons are being sold every week at a price of 25 cents per gallon. The longer the adjustment time, the more demand will expand in response to the price decline. Bigger cars will be bought, commuter distances will increase, bus and train transportation will diminish. Thus in this example the discovery of a cheaper way to make gasoline leads initially to a substantial reduction in price and a slight increase in sales. But in the long run, the discovery leads to a substantial increase in sales and a smaller reduction in price. This is because it is easier to substitute gasoline for other commodities in the long run than in the short run. Thus the period for which a supply or demand curve is drawn is a very important thing to know when one is using a demand curve to explain price.

Supply curves are also drawn with particular lengths of time in mind. In the very short run, supply is almost constant. The amount of gasoline, for example, that would be forthcoming in response to a large increase in price depends on how much time the petroleum companies have to adjust to the increase. There is very little they could do to expand supply greatly in one week. Give them a few months and they can open idle refineries and have them all going full blast. Give them a year or two and they can have new refineries, oil tankers, pipelines, dock facilities, and storage areas built. And give them 10 years and they can discover and develop new reserves and create new methods of extracting more gasoline out of every barrel of crude oil.

Thus long-run supply curves are flatter than short-run supply curves. Given this fact, a sudden increase in demand, as shown in Figure 5.7, will lead to a short-run increase in price with a very small quantity increase. In the long run, quantity will increase a great deal and price by only a small amount. The increase in demand moves the economy from the old equilibrium at A to the temporary equilibrium at B and then to the long-run equilibrium at C.

In any market it may take anywhere from a few days to a few decades to adjust to a new invention or idea. There will be an initial short-run adjustment and then a more permanent long-run adjustment. When we observe the world around us, it appears as if all markets are in transition, moving from one equilibrium to another. And as discoveries are made or tastes change rapidly, it is likely that a permanent long-run equilibrium may never be attained. This should not make us despair of the use of supply and demand in explaining prices. Indeed, it is through supply and demand that we understand the whole process of change.

But we should realize that long-run equilibria are not always attained. Change is the order of the day.

Which supply and demand curves should we use, long-run, short-run, or in-between? That depends on our purpose. If we wish to explain why current prices are what they are, we should use the short-run curves. If we wish to explain a series of consecutive prices, we should probably use both curves as was just done above.

Market Instability: Cumulative Expectations, Speculation, and Lagged Response

All of the examples used so far have illustrated the tendency of markets to produce stable equilibria. This means that in Figure 5.1, if the price had moved above point E, forces of excess supply would have arisen to return it to the equilibrium level. If the price had fallen below E, forces of excess demand would have pushed it back up. Sometimes markets do not adjust properly because of unstable expectations or because of lags in the response of supply and demand to price changes. An example of the first disequilibrating mechanism follows.

Suppose that the only way for the suppliers of steak to increase the quantity they supply in the future is by using more cattle for breeding in the present and thus selling less steak in the present. Then if an increase in demand is to *increase* steak output in the long run, it must *decrease* it in the short run. That is, if the long-run supply curve is upward sloping, the short-run supply curve must be downward sloping, as in Figure 5.8.

If the short-run consumer demand curve is very steep—because consumers buy roughly the same amount of steak regardless of price—then the short-run supply and demand curves can be illustrated by Figure 5.9.

As drawn in Figure 5.9, this behavior still determines an equilibrium price and quantity. But what happens if the demand or supply curve shifts slightly, due to some minor force, so that a new equilibrium must be attained? Remember, we rely on the forces of change to guarantee an equilibrium. If, for example, sup-

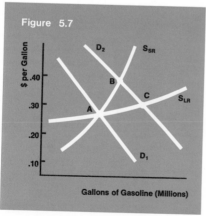

Figure 5.7

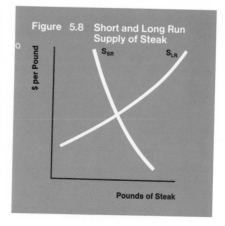

Figure 5.8 Short and Long Run Supply of Steak

ply expands due to some minor deviation, Figure 5.9 tells us that the new equilibrium requires a higher price! But the forces of change are going to lower price. The increased supply means that temporarily there are too many steaks. The only way butchers can unload them is by lowering price. But if price falls, the supply of steak increases by more than the demand! Thus there is an even greater excess supply than before. Prices plummet.

Market forces eliminate excess supply by *lowering* price. But if the supply and demand curves have the peculiar shape of those in Figure 5.9, a decrease in price will cause an even greater excess supply, which in turn will cause an even greater decrease in price. The market forces will be like the arrows in Figure 5.10 that indicate the equilibrium will be unstable.

Note that an important determinant of this instability is the price forecast of the ranchers. Economists call such forecasts *expectations*. If they view price increases as temporary, there is no incentive to hold additional cattle off the market. If they view them as permanent, then they must restrict short-run supply in order to expand long-run output.

What if the increase in price caused the ranchers to forecast further price increases? Their behavior becomes even more troublesome then.

Suppose that the suppliers of steak observe an increase in demand; an increase in price results. This may lead them to anticipate further long-run increases in price. Rather than bring more cattle to market, they bring *less* because they expect the price to go even *higher in the future*. This will be a wise decision if, in fact, prices are going to be higher in the future. The more prices increase, the higher they are expected to go. Therefore, the higher prices go, the fewer cattle the ranchers send to market.

And if the consumers do the same kind of forecasting, their behavior may also be "perverse." If consumers interpret an increase in current prices to signify even higher prices in the future, they may stock up the freezer now. That is, consumers may buy more steaks when prices increase than they do otherwise! Thus an increase in price could cause sellers to restrict the quantity they supply

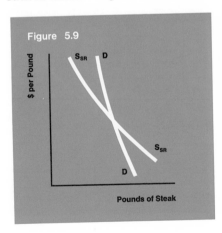

Figure 5.9

S_{SR} D

$ per Pound

S_{SR}

D

Pounds of Steak

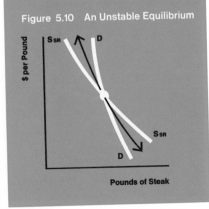

Figure 5.10 An Unstable Equilibrium

S_{SR} D

$ per Pound

S_{SR}

D

Pounds of Steak

and buyers to increase the quantity they demand. This will cause prices to increase still further. This kind of forecasting can make a market unstable. Deviations from the equilibrium price will be reinforced rather than offset by the forces of adjustment.

Is it reasonable to expect this upward spiral of steak prices to go on indefinitely? The answer is, of course, no, anymore than a downward spiral of prices, triggered perhaps by a very good year for cattle production, would be expected to continue indefinitely. In the case discussed above, sharp sellers will soon realize that herds are expanding well beyond normal levels and that eventually this beef will have to be slaughtered. They foresee an end to price increases and therefore attempt to take advantage of current high prices by increasing the supply offered in the present period. As a result, supply will begin to shift to the right again. Buyers, on the other hand, will watch their freezers fill with uneaten steaks and begin to have second thoughts about buying more. Demand will shift to the left. The combined forces will work to reduce prices. Of course, expectations may work in either direction. As prices begin to fall, sellers may anticipate that this new trend will continue and begin dumping beef on the market, reinforcing the downswing in prices. Buyers may decide to wait even longer to purchase steak, also reinforcing the price decline. Again, there will be natural forces at work to prevent cumulative expectations from driving price to zero.

Market forces normally eliminate excess supply by *lowering* price, or excess demand by *raising* price. But if supply and demand curves are strongly influenced by cumulative expectations (assumptions that past trends in price will continue), then a rise in price will cause an even greater excess supply. Even though supply and demand curves are normally shaped, market forces will work *as though* they were perversely shaped.

Are such cases prevalent? No. It is very rare to see prices of anything tending toward zero or infinity. The most common cases of prices going to zero are cases of paper money. We study money later, but it is useful to ask here why it is paper money and not some commodity whose price can go to zero. The answer is that paper money has value because the government says it has value. It is virtually costless to produce. Therefore the value of paper money is not tied to the value of any other commodities by any production link *and people know this*. Because they know that the production of steaks uses up resources, they know that 10 cents a pound is a very low price for steak and that such a bargain is a temporary phenomenon. Most people would be likely to stock up at 10 cents a pound rather than wait for 5 cents a pound. In fact, most people would probably jump at a chance to buy steak at a price that is 20 cents below the price they have previously associated with steak. But when the price of paper money is low, it is not necessarily a bargain.

And on the positive side, even the coolest of cattlemen will be unlikely to hold out for $12 a pound when the price of steaks has risen to $10 a pound. Only the silliest of housewives will increase their steak purchases at this price out of a fear of higher prices. Thus the knowledge on both sides of the market that there exist basic costs of production, and that competition will eventually wipe out excess profits, leads to sanity in most markets. The basic belief that price and cost are closely related prevents prices from deviating too far from cost.

But history does contain some notable examples of price instability. One of the most famous is that of tulip bulbs in eighteenth-century Holland. The price of tulip bulbs rose without any apparent limit. People were paying hundreds of dollars for a single tulip bulb. Many thought the spiral would never end and rushed out to buy more and more tulips. When the long-run conditions of supply and demand eventually restored themselves, the price of tulip bulbs fell back to a level reflecting their actual marginal cost to producers and marginal utility to consumers. When the price of tulips fell to a few cents per bulb, many families were wiped out. They had foolishly transferred all their wealth into tulip bulbs.

Speculation

Another reason that most equilibria are stable is that it only takes a few sharp-witted (and wealthy) speculators to bring order to the markets. When the speculators feel that the price of steaks is below cost, they buy vast quantities as a bet that prices will rise. Their buying causes prices to rise. Similarly, if prices are very high, they sell the steaks they have or sell steaks "short" (sell steaks they do not yet own but promise to deliver in the future, presumably by future purchase). Thus buying and selling by speculators guarantees that prices do not get too far away from the underlying cost conditions. If, in fact, the silly housewives and the cool cattlemen continue to behave in a destabilizing fashion, the speculators will make a lot of money. For the speculators may end up buying steak from the cattlemen at $.25 a pound and selling it to the housewives later at $2.50 a pound. The behavior of housewives and cattlemen makes the market unstable, but the speculator has placed an upper and lower limit on their irrationality. When the price drops to $.25 a pound, the speculator buys so much steak that the cattlemen have no more to sell him and then prices begin to increase. The housewives stampede the stores out of fear of higher prices for steak. This causes a huge increase in steak prices. At $2.50 a pound, the speculator unloads the steaks on the eager housewives until their freezers are full. Then the demand for steak disappears and we begin all over.

Who will be blamed for this irrationality? Why, the speculator, of course. He must be causing this cycle in order to make money. And he *is* making a visible fortune. But really, whose fault is it? It is the fault of the housewives who refuse to buy at $.35 a pound and the cattlemen who refuse to sell at $2.40 a pound. In fact, it is the housewives and cattlemen who are the destabilizing speculators. They buy when prices are increasing and sell when they are decreasing. This magnifies any movement of prices that occurs. The speculator, on the other hand, buys low and sells high to restore the equilibrium; and he makes a handsome profit in the bargain. In the real world, there are many shrewd speculators who make their living stabilizing markets. The competition among them is quite fierce. Competition among speculators increases the price at which they buy steaks and decreases the price at which they sell them. This eliminates any discernible cycle in price and consequently any easy profits.

There has been much discussion through history about whether speculators can create cycles in prices in order to make money. A speculator can only make money by selling something for more than he pays for it, that is, by buying low and selling high. Cycles, on the other hand, can be created or accentuated only by speculators who buy high (in the hopes of selling higher) and sell low (in the hopes of selling lower). But buying high and selling low is not very profitable. Anyone who makes money speculating must have a *stabilizing* influence on the market. He must have bought low (thereby preventing even lower prices) and sold high (thereby preventing even higher prices). Speculators who lose money, usually greedy amateurs, have a destabilizing influence on markets.

The smart speculator fulfills an important social function in a market economy. He is very attentive to shifts in the determinants of supply and demand. His reaction to those shifts causes the price to adjust immediately, reflecting the new underlying conditions of the market. Speculators make money by bringing markets into equilibrium. To do this they must be very sensitive to the real determinants of price — cost and marginal utility. At any one time, speculators may disagree about the future course of prices. Those who feel prices are going to rise are labeled "bullish" while the pessimists are called "bears." If there are more bulls than bears, prices will increase. As prices increase to higher levels, some bulls become bears. This brings about the new equilibrium. Speculators who ignore the fundamentals that determine price are in for some tough sledding when dealing with such professionals. There is a Wall Street adage that says, "The bulls get a little, the bears get a little, but the pigs get nothing." Silly housewives and cool cattlemen take notice. We observe very few unstable markets in the real world. Of course, there is always the possibility that a market may become unstable. But there is a fortune to be made by the man who recognizes the instability and eliminates it. And there is no apparent lack of men in search of fortune.

Another kind of instability is caused by production lags. If farmers observe high prices for corn this winter, they plant a lot of corn. This expands supply so that next winter corn prices are very low. They then plant little corn the following spring and corn prices rise again. If farmers naively act in such a fashion, instability is possible. The cycle of corn prices can get larger and larger without limit.

To see why, we have drawn the long-run demand and supply curves for corn in Figure 5.11. Point E represents a long-run equilibrium. The short-run supply of corn is very different from the long-run supply. Corn takes a whole season to mature. Therefore we have drawn the short-run supply curve in Figure 5.11 as a vertical line. This represents the fact that no changes in price can affect the amount of corn immediately available. In Figure 5.12, the farmers were aiming at E, the equilibrium, but poor weather restricted their output to Q'. This reduction in supply caused price to increase that winter to P'.

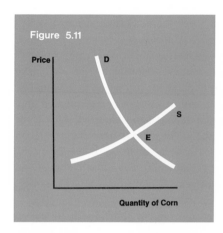

Figure 5.11

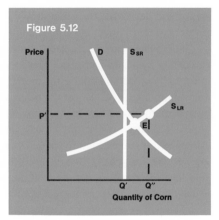

Figure 5.12

In response to this high price, the next season the farmers plant a lot of corn. The farmers have a long-run supply curve that determines the amount of corn they wish to supply at every price. For price P', they intend to supply Q''. But Figure 5.13 shows that when quantity Q'' reaches the market, the price will have to fall to P'' if the corn is to be sold. The demand curve indicates that such a large quantity can be sold only at a very low price.

In response to the low price farmers receive for corn, they plant very little the next year (Q'''). Most of their acreage is transferred to other crops. The student can predict what will happen to price when this corn comes to market.

The dynamic instability just described is called the *cobweb theorem*. The reason for this name can be seen by examining Figure 5.14. The arrow traces out the movements from one equilibrium to the next. Clearly, the successive short-run equilibria are getting further and further from the long-run equilibrium. The market for corn is dynamically unstable. Of course, if corn can be stored (canned or frozen), a shrewd speculator can make a fortune by limiting the extremes of such a cycle. By buying low and selling high, he can restore stability and get rich in the process.

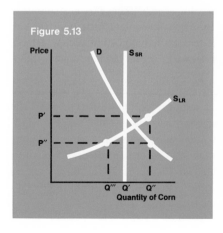

Figure 5.13

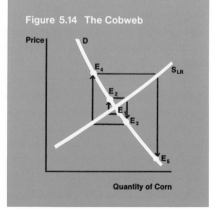

Figure 5.14 The Cobweb

In Figure 5.15, the corn market is dynamically stable even though the same response of farmers is assumed. Thus naive forecasts by farmers (or anyone else) do not necessarily lead to a dynamically unstable market. Certain additional mathematical conditions must be met before instability arises. (This model is unstable if the demand curve is steeper than the supply curve.)

Models with lagged responses form one of the major explanations of business cycles. Above, corn output increases and decreases in a cyclical fashion. It is possible to have such behavior lead to *permanent* cycles if the curves are nonlinear. Figure 5.16 shows a cycle that is stable but does not allow attainment of the long-run equilibrium. No matter what initial conditions are assumed in Figure 5.16, the permanent cycle will be approached. The economy will be at E_1 and E_2 in alternate years.

Measuring the Elasticity of a Curve

Until now we have referred to the shape of supply and demand curves in terms of their steepness or flatness. The reader may have become dissatisfied with such lack of precision. What is a "flat" curve? When does it become "steep"? The terms are ambiguous and do not permit the exact measurement of the relationship between price and quantity that economic analysis requires. A more precise measure of the shape of a curve is required for this. Otherwise it will be impossible to make clear statements about the effect of a shift in supply or demand on the price and quantity of goods sold.

The appendix to Chapter 3 shows how the steepness of a line can be measured by its slope. But slope merely measures the vertical distance divided by the horizontal distance. These distances depend on the units of measurement. For example, Figures 5.17 and 5.18 both represent demand curves for milk, but Figure 5.18 measures quantity in one-half gallons whereas Figure 5.17 measures quantity in gallons. The curve in Figure 5.18 is therefore very much flatter than the curve in 5.17. Each increase in milk consumption represents twice as many horizontal units in Figure 5.18 as it does in Figure 5.17. "Flatness" or "steepness," therefore, tells us little about economic behavior.

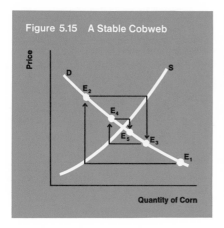

Figure 5.15   A Stable Cobweb

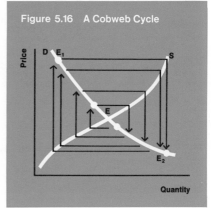

Figure 5.16   A Cobweb Cycle

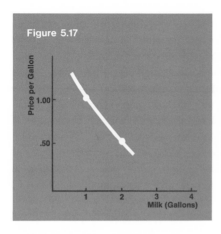

Figure 5.17

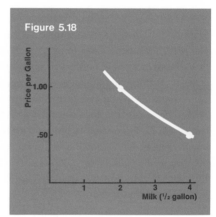

Figure 5.18

But we do need some concept that allows us to judge the relative responsiveness of two commodities to a change in price. To get around the problem of arbitrary units of measure, we speak of the *percentage change* in quantity that results from a 1 percent *change* in price. This is called the own price *elasticity* of the demand curve. Technically, the elasticity of demand is measured as the percentage increase in quantity divided by the percentage increase in price. It is defined at a point on a demand curve.

If a small percentage change in price leads to a large percentage change in demand, the demand curve is said to be very *elastic*. In fact, we use the words *elastic* and *inelastic* to denote those curves with elasticity greater than and less than *one*, respectively.

Figure 5.19 represents an elastic demand curve. When price falls by one-third, quantity demanded doubles. The curve in this figure has an average elasticity of 3.0 between points *A* and *B*. (Negative signs are often dropped from elasticity calculations, because it is common knowledge that demand curves are downward sloping.)

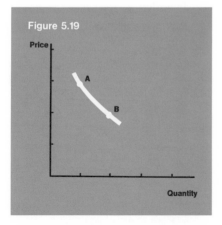

Figure 5.19

Figure 5.20 depicts an inelastic demand curve. Moving from *M* to *N* represents a 50 percent decline in price and a 25 percent increase in quantity demanded. Thus elasticity equals .5 on average between the two points.

Figure 5.21 depicts a curve of unity elasticity. When price falls in half, quantity sold doubles. This curve is neither elastic nor inelastic.

The elasticity of different demand curves will depend on what sort of substitutes exist for the commodity. For example, the demand curve for Sealtest chocolate ice cream will be highly elastic if the potential buyer feels that other ice creams are very similar. A 20 percent increase in the price of Sealtest ice cream might lead to a drop in sales of 70 percent or more, since other ice cream is a good substitute for Sealtest. But if the price of all ice cream were to rise by 20 percent, the quantity of ice cream demanded might fall by only 20 percent or so. Cake is a substitute for ice cream, but it is not a perfect one. Thus elasticity of demand will depend upon the degree to which close substitutes have very elastic demand curves.

The elasticity of demand for a product tells us what happens to expenditures on that product as price changes. Expenditures on a product equal the price of the product times the number sold: $E = P \times Q$. If the quantity bought increases by 1 percent when price falls by 1 percent, expenditures on that product remain constant. If the quantity bought increases by *more than* 1 percent, the *expenditure increases* when price falls. Thus commodities with *elastic* demand curves receive a larger portion of incomes when prices fall—and a smaller portion when prices rise. The opposite is true of commodities with inelastic demand curves. As price rises by 1 percent, the quantity bought falls by less than 1 percent if the demand curve is inelastic. Thus expenditure on that commodity increases as its price increases.

This gives us another view of those commodities that have good substitutes and those that do not. If a good has few good substitutes, we tend to buy it regardless of its price. As its price increases, we buy it anyway and give up some other goods instead, that is, we spend more on this good and have less left to

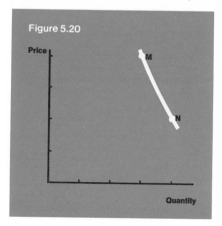

Figure 5.20

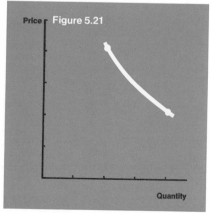

Figure 5.21

spend for other goods. Such goods have been called necessities by noneconomists. As the prices of these goods rise, we give up other goods in order to be able to afford these.

If necessities have inelastic demand curves, luxuries have elastic demand curves. It may be easier to learn this fact in the form just mentioned than in its true form. In fact, the true form is: Necessities are goods with inelastic demand curves and luxuries are goods with elastic demand curves. For there is no way to define a necessity or a luxury except with reference to other goods. Some goods are *more* necessary or *more* luxurious than other goods. If they are more necessary, less money will be spent on *other* goods when the price of necessities rises.

Questions

1.   Why are large financial rewards available to any group that stabilizes an otherwise unstable market?
2.   How might the salaries of computer programmers respond over time to a sudden increase in demand for their services? How might the number of programmers change?
3.   What would happen to the price of tea if the supply of coffee suddenly increased?
4.   If the demand for food is inelastic, what should happen to farmers' incomes when production is abundant? When there is a drought?

Concepts Discussed

long-run supply, demand
short-run supply, demand
stability
expectations
speculation

cobweb theorem
elasticity
necessity
luxury

III Equilibrium in a Simple Economy

Go to the ant, thou sluggard.
Consider his ways and be wise. . . .

And I considered all the work done under the sun,
and lo it was all vanity and vexation of the spirit.

ECCLESIASTES

Supply and demand analysis yields an abstract mathematical view of the nature of equilibrium in a single market. The abstraction is useful in allowing us to explain the value of commodities and how these values are affected by costs and desires.

In Part III we abstract further from the complexities of the real world and apply the model of supply and demand to the economy as a whole. We do this by focusing on the labor market alone. Obviously, we do not believe that the whole economy can be described adequately by such a simple model, but we wish to present a complete economic model as early as possible. Our reason for this is that we want the student to be able to think about the whole system in order to realize how the parts of the economy affect each other. Later in the book, as we learn more about each sector of the economy, we will have a framework in which to place this new knowledge. That theoretical framework will provide a basis for analyzing practical problems of trade and finance, economic growth, employment and the price level, and economic development, as well as questions of product choice, pricing, advertising, decisions to save and invest, and the place of government in the economy.

The model of this section can be thought of as the bare bones of an economy. Later we add the flesh and blood in the form of additional complications. But just as skeletons can give an idea of the nature of the animals they come from, abstract economic models can convey glimpses of how the economy operates. Of course, the more abstract the model, the less it resembles the real world. On the other hand, the more abstract the model, the simpler the analysis becomes. Since we feel it is important to start thinking about the whole economic system as soon as possible, we present a model of it now. And since it must be a very simple model to be understood at this stage, it will not be a complete picture of the economy. If the student views the following two chapters as a cartoon of an economy rather than as a photograph, he will not be disappointed. Good cartoonists can suggest a very complex picture by a few lines.

Chapter 6 analyzes the supply and demand for labor and can be used to deepen one's understanding of market equilibrium. Chapter 7 describes the implications of that equilibrium for income distribution, explores the impact of technology, tastes, and resources on that solution, and provides a glance at the job of a central planner in the same simple world.

Our purpose in these two chapters is to give an idea of how a market economy distributes income, how it decides what to produce, and how the results of this process compare with those obtained under central planning.

6 The Labor Market in a Simple Economy

The Problem

How does a market economy allocate resources among alternative uses? How is the income that is produced distributed among members of the economy? Do you have answers to these questions? If you do, your answers are derived from hypotheses about behavior and their interaction with scarce resources. Do you know whether your hypotheses can withstand scientific empirical tests?

In this chapter, we pose a few hypotheses that most economists believe have been verified by data generated by the real world. We intend to explore the logical implications of these simple hypotheses. This is an exercise in economic theory and it will require a great deal of abstraction. Even common sense involves a considerable amount of mental shorthand. But common sense, or intuition, should not be thought of as a substitute for theory. Both have their roles to play. We use intuition to devise hypotheses about human behavior. We use theory to derive the implications of those hypotheses. We should be particularly careful about using common sense as a substitute for theoretical analysis since common sense can often be wrong. We use common sense to create hypotheses only because we have nothing better. That common sense can be misleading is illustrated by the fact that a scientist's first attempt at a particular hypothesis is rarely correct. That is, rarely does his common sense lead him directly to the truth. But for any set of hypotheses, economic theory should allow us to derive implications without error. Theory is a powerful tool of analysis. Errors are easy to find when theorizing is explicit. The hazy, hand-waving of common sense is of little use for scientific analysis because a better tool exists, namely, theory.

The following assumptions are designed to reduce the analysis to its simplest possible state. They are not thought of as assumptions about the real world. That is, these assumptions are the equivalent of assuming that flesh and blood cannot exist and therefore skeletons can be thought of as people. These assumptions do not imply that we feel that flesh and blood are unimportant. Rather, they imply that we feel it is unnecessary to complicate the analysis with them at this point. Much can be learned from examining skeletons.

Assumptions

We assume that a certain economy exists in which only food (corn) is being produced and only land and labor are used to produce it. There are many farmers;

land is privately owned and cannot be bought or sold (this is simply to reduce the number of markets). Each farmer and laborer attempts to earn as high an income as possible. In fact, only two commodities are bought and sold—corn and labor (manhours).

We want to determine how equilibrium occurs in this simple economy during a given period. How many markets must we look at? If money is kept out of the picture (barter exists), there is only *one market* with one demand and one supply curve reflecting the exchange of corn for labor. We call this the *labor market*. If we can discover at what point this market will achieve equilibrium, we can answer the two questions posed at the beginning of the chapter. To do this, we simply need apply to this market the tools of supply and demand learned earlier (see Chapters 4 and 5). We begin with the demand for labor.

The Analysis of the Demand for Labor

What determines the amount of labor (manhours) that farmers will hire during the period? Let us take the case of a single farmer. His economic problem is *how much corn to produce*, given the following:

1. the price of labor.
2. the price of corn.
3. the amount of land he possesses.
4. the technology at his disposal.

Because he is one farmer among many, we assume his behavior will have little or no independent influence on the prices of labor and corn. He can take these prices as given. He can, of course, sell his corn at a price *below* the market price if he wishes; but we assume he will not do that. And he cannot sell it at any higher price because no one would buy it from him. So we assume that he expects to sell his corn at the price he observes in the market.

The amount of land in his possession is fixed. His technological knowledge is fixed (his son will not return from agricultural college until next year). And there is no machinery in his world. Therefore his output will be related directly to his employment of labor. The amount of labor he employs will be influenced by the relative price of corn and labor. The higher the price of corn relative to labor, the more labor he will hire and the more corn he will produce. The lower the price of corn relative to labor, the less labor he will employ and the less corn he will produce.

Exactly how much labor should he hire? We learned from supply and demand theory that one knows the answer to such a question only when one is given a price. We must know how much it costs the farmer to hire labor. What must he give up to get another manhour of labor? We could have a money price for corn and a money price for labor, such as

$4/manhour
$1/bushel of corn

But we know that a price is the ratio at which quantities trade. So we could also express the price of labor in terms of corn. Let us do that and ignore money.

$$\frac{\$4/\text{manhour}}{\$1/\text{bushel}} = 4 \text{ bushels/manhour}$$

The price of labor in terms of corn is the cost of labor to the farmer. The farmer must know this cost in order to answer the question, "How much labor will I hire?" But this is not enough information. He must also know what labor is "worth" to him before he can decide whether or not he can "afford" to employ another manhour of labor. How does he find out how much labor he can afford? He looks at the *production function*.

The Production Function
The production function tells us the maximum amount of corn that can be produced for each combination of labor and land, given the farmer's technological knowledge. Less than this amount can be produced also, but we assume each producer is as efficient as possible and does not willingly lower his own income. The farmer is assumed to do the best he can with the resources at his disposal. This does not mean that some farmers may not be able to do better than others, but just that each farmer does the best *he* can.

A Hiring Decision Rule
If another manhour can produce 5 more bushels of corn, we know that the farmer should hire more labor if the cost of that labor is 4 bushels per manhour. This will allow him to keep an extra bushel of corn. If another manhour can produce only 3 more bushels, he should not hire any more labor. So the farmer can be assumed to adopt a simple "decision rule": *If a manhour produces more than it costs, hire it; if it produces less than it costs, fire it.*

Profit Maximization
This simple rule seems obvious. Yet it is one of the keys to understanding a market economy. We could call it *the decision rule that arises from the strategy of profit maximization.* Profit maximization is a behavioral assumption that plays an important part in resource allocation theory. It supposes that if it costs the farmer nothing to reallocate resources in order to get more profit (in this case to hire or fire labor), then he will do so. His marginal utility from an additional unit of profit is greater than zero. The farmer is therefore better off with more profits than less from the same amount of land and technology. It is not always true that such adjustments are costless, but such is assumed to be the case for our farmer.

The implications of this decision may not be obvious, nor may its mechanics. But as an aid to understanding, it will be helpful to keep in mind the simplicity of the decision rule. Having established the rule, we ask again, How much labor will the farmer hire? To answer this we now need to look at the production function. The production function for corn is assumed to be as shown in Table 6.1.

Ten units of labor can produce 100 bushels of corn on one acre of land. The production function shows how output responds to various *input combinations*, which we will call "processes." Each process takes a different look at the same production function. The numbers chosen in process 1 below show no advantages (returns) of large- or small-scale production. This example illustrates what is called *constant returns to scale*. Scale, of course, refers to the size of the operation. Constant returns to scale means that when we double *all* of the inputs, output will double. In the real world, there are many examples of *economies of scale*. That is, there are many production functions that yield more than twice as much output when inputs are doubled. Our results are derived from a world where such economies are absent. We see later how these results must be qualified when this complication is added.

Diminishing Returns

We now note a complication in the production function: *diminishing returns*. If output doubles when we double *all* inputs, what happens when we double only *one* input? Output will increase, but it will not double. Thus adding *two* units of labor to one unit of land will not give twice the output obtained by adding *one* unit of labor to that land. This effect is called diminishing returns. It is a technological characteristic of most production functions. It means that the continued addition of extra units of *only one input* (in this case, labor) results in less and less additional output (of corn). In other words, by holding all inputs but one constant, one obtains less and less *extra* output from each *additional* unit of the input that is increased. It is important to remember that diminishing returns refers to cases where only one input is changed, whereas returns to scale refers to proportional changes in all inputs. This is a concept that deals with incremental changes in output relative to input. Hence it is a *marginal* concept. We can call diminishing returns diminishing marginal output, or, as economists choose to say, *diminishing marginal productivity*. The *marginal product* of an input is the

---

Table 6.1   Production Function for Corn

Process 1

Land (Acres)	Labor (Manhours)	Output (Bushels of Corn)
1	10	100
2	20	200
3	30	300
4	40	400

Table 6.2   Production Function for Corn

Process 2

Land (Acres)	Labor (Manhours)	Output (Bushels of Corn)
1	20	150
2	40	300
3	60	450

additional output derived from employing one more unit of that input while holding all other units constant.

To understand diminishing returns we need to know more about the production function. What output, for example, would the farmer get from combining one acre with 20 manhours of labor? For this we need to view the production function in terms of another process, process 2 (see Table 6.2). The farmer is supposed to have the knowledge contained in these tables stored up in his head, in the records he keeps, in technical books at his disposal, or perhaps at a local agricultural extension agency. We simply assume he has the knowledge from one source or another.

One acre and 20 manhours should be able to produce more corn than 1 acre and 10 manhours (100 bushels using process 1), but less than 2 acres and 20 manhours (200 bushels). Output must be more than 100 and less than 200 bushels if both processes are efficient. Let us say that these inputs lead to 150 bushels and that this process also has no large- or small-scale advantages.

We already have enough information to discuss diminishing returns by comparing process 1 with process 2 and noticing what happens to the output from *one acre* of land as more labor is added (Table 6.3).

When 10 manhours are employed on 1 acre of land, they produce 100 bushels; the next 10 manhours added increase output by only 50 bushels. This is not because the new labor is inferior. It is because extra labor is added to work on the same amount of land. Thus each laborer has less land to work with. The original labor now has only one-half acre to use where before they had a whole acre. Thus their output diminishes to 75 bushels. The new labor is given only one-half acre as well, making their output only 75 bushels. Total output in-

Table 6.3   Comparison of Processes 1 and 2

Process	Land	Labor	Output	Marginal Output
1	1	10	100	100
2	1	20	150	50

creases from 100 bushels to 150 bushels as a result of the increase in labor. We say that there are diminishing returns to labor because the last increment of labor added less to output than did the previous increment.

We can envision a third process for producing corn by which 30 manhours and 1 acre could produce 180 bushels of corn. This process can be seen in Table 6.4, where the first two processes have been recorded as well.

Note that the marginal output of the third batch of 10 manhours when added to 1 acre of land is only 30 bushels of corn. Thus the third process allows us to extend the diminishing returns to labor even further. We would have to define additional processes, of course, to fill in the remaining blanks in Table 6.4. As it stands, however, it can be used to illustrate diminishing returns to land by noting the outputs that result from combining 1 and 2 acres of land with 20 manhours of labor.

The farmer does not have to know about diminishing returns; all he has to know is (1) *relative prices*, (2) the *production function*, and (3) the *decision rule*. Suppose he has only one acre of land. Now he attempts to decide how much to produce if he wishes to keep as much corn as possible. If 10 manhours of labor cost him 40 bushels (which we assumed at the beginning of the chapter), how many manhours should he hire?

First, suppose that he hires no labor. Zero manhours means zero profit. If he hires 10 manhours he can produce 100 bushels on the one acre.

> 10 manhours produce 100 bushels of corn
> −10 manhours cost 40 bushels of corn
>   profit = 60 bushels of corn

The farmer's conclusion is clear. *He should hire at least 10 manhours of labor* during the period. But is this enough to maximize his profits? Let us apply the decision rule once again. Suppose that he considers hiring a second 10 manhours. They produce an extra 50 bushels and cost an extra 40. Profits will rise from 60 to 70 bushels of corn. *Hire them.* What about a third 10 manhours? Increasing manhours from 20 to 30 raises output by 30 bushels and raises costs by 40 bushels. Profits will actually decline. *Do not hire them.* The decision rule tells

Table 6.4   Bushels of Corn Produced by Various Combinations of Inputs

Labor Input	10 Manhours	20 Manhours	30 Manhours	40 Manhours
Land Input				
1 Acre	100 (Process 1)	150 (Process 2)	180 (Process 3)	
2 Acres		200 (Process 1)		300 (Process 2)
3 Acres			300 (Process 1)	

the farmer not to hire more than 20 manhours. Process 2 is therefore the best combination of resources for the farmer when the price of 1 manhour of labor is 4 bushels of corn.

A Demand Curve for Labor

This exercise shows us how the cost of labor, the price of corn, the production function for corn, and the farmer's behavior all affect the demand for labor. But this exercise assumed that a unit of labor cost 4 bushels. What would happen if the price were different, say, 6 bushels per manhour. How much labor would then be hired? Answering this question for every possible price will determine the *demand curve for labor*.

Assume the wage is 6 bushels per manhour. At this wage the first 10 manhours would provide 100 bushels of corn and cost 60 bushels. Profits would now be 40 bushels of corn. He should hire at least 10 manhours. But if he attempted to hire an additional 10 manhours, production would increase by 50 bushels and costs by 60 bushels. Therefore, *only 10 manhours should be hired*. This gives us a second point on the demand curve for labor. Both of these points, A and B, are shown in Figure 6.1.

We know that at a price of 60, 10 units are hired whereas at a price of 40, 20 units are hired. Thus the demand curve for labor will be downward sloping. Although in our example the demand curve reflects the assumption that labor increases in units of 10 and therefore descends in steps, in cases where many production processes exist and it is possible to hire fractional amounts of labor, the demand function will be a smooth curve, such as the curve in Figure 6.2. To create a demand curve for the whole economy, we must add up the demands of all the individuals at every price. When we add demand curves, we add them *horizontally*. To find the demand for labor at a wage of 4 bushels per hour, we add the demand of farm 1 to that of farm 2, and so forth. We do *not* find the price at which only one unit of labor is demanded by adding the price farm 1 would pay for one unit to that farm 2 would pay. Such a sum is economically

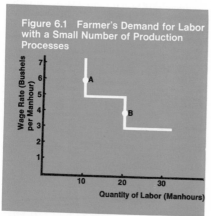

Figure 6.1 Farmer's Demand for Labor with a Small Number of Production Processes

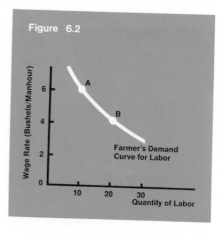

Figure 6.2

meaningless since the labor can be used on one farm only and cannot collect a wage from both. Demand curves are added horizontally simply because we want to know the *total* demand for labor at 4 bushels per hour.

The demand curve for labor of the *whole economy* in our simple example can be determined by summing all of the individual demand curves for each farmer. For simplicity, let us suppose that there are 10,000 farmers in the economy and that each of them has the same production function and the same amount of land (one acre) as the farmer we have just discussed, that it is possible to hire fractional amounts of labor, and that many production processes exist. The demand curve for labor in the whole economy is therefore as shown in Figure 6.3.

This completes the analysis of the behavior of the farmers in our simple economy. We know how much labor farmers would be willing to hire at each wage rate. Now we need to know how labor will behave. We need to know the supply curve of labor.

The Supply of Labor: (1) Fixed Supply

What determines the supply of labor available to farmers? This depends in part on how many workers there are, how much time they have at their disposal during the period, and how they choose to divide it between earning income (work) and leisure. (Nonwork time is called "leisure" by economists even though it may be far more tiring and less satisfying than work time.)

How will one worker divide the 24 hours in a day between work and leisure? Suppose 8 of the 24 hours in a day are the bare minimum required for eating, sleeping, and other necessities of life. We first examine a worker under the assumption that leisure yields *no* utility. We assume that except for his essential 8 hours of rest the worker is so anxious to consume corn that he offers the entire remaining 16 hours to the farmer, regardless of the wage rate. His individual supply curve of labor for a single working day is expressed by the vertical white line in Figure 6.4.

A fixed supply of labor of 16 hours a day involves the strong assumption

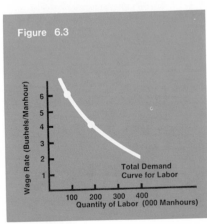

Figure 6.3

Wage Rate (Bushels/Manhour)

Total Demand Curve for Labor

Quantity of Labor (000 Manhours)

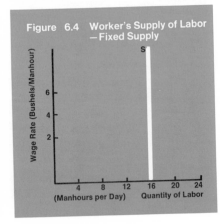

Figure 6.4 Worker's Supply of Labor —Fixed Supply

Wage Rate (Bushels/Manhour)

(Manhours per Day)   Quantity of Labor

that additional leisure yields less utility than additional corn, regardless of the wage. It is always possible for workers to offer their labor services to farmers, receive some wages (corn) in exchange, and be better off. Because corn is the only commodity of value in our economy in this first example, no time will be reserved for leisure. There is no doubt as to the amount of time spent working—*all of the time available.* That is why the supply curve of labor in this model is insensitive to the wage rate (zero price elasticity of supply of labor). The wage rate does not matter in this extreme example since even an hour of additional leisure time yields less marginal utility than the smallest additional amount of corn.

The usefulness of example 1 is that it shows the importance of the fact that leisure yields utility. Nonworking time, just like corn or any other commodity, is subject to the principle of diminishing marginal utility. It is unlikely that workers will offer the same amount of time to farmers regardless of the wages they expect to receive. The more time spent working, the less time available for other activities. The more time spent working, the higher the marginal utility of the time left over. This means that the supply curve of labor need not be perfectly inelastic. Leisure is a substitute for what income can buy.

The Supply of Labor: (2) Variable Supply

If the supply of labor is permitted to vary with the wage rate, the problem becomes somewhat more difficult. Two possible influences on the slope of the supply curve can be imagined. The first is quite typical of all cases of reciprocal demand. If the price of labor rises, more corn can be obtained for each hour of work time. Because of this, workers will tend to exchange time for corn and work longer hours as the wage rises. Another way of looking at this is to recognize that leisure has become more expensive in terms of goods; thus less of it is bought.

Because of this effect, the supply curve for each worker may slope upward and have the traditional shape of supply curves in most markets. An upward-sloping supply curve is produced by the *substitution effect* caused by the increase in wages. Corn is cheaper in terms of labor, making the opportunity cost of leisure in terms of corn higher than before. Workers substitute corn for leisure and work longer hours, as shown in Figure 6.5.

This illustrates the principle of the diminishing relative value of corn in terms of leisure. It tells us that as the consumption of one commodity (corn) rises, its value relative to the other commodity (leisure) falls. More and more corn must be obtained per hour for each additional hour of leisure sacrificed to work. On the other hand, if we work less during a period, so that leisure time rises, then the relative value of leisure in terms of corn will fall. It will take less and less to attract another hour of our time away from leisure toward work.

The Effect of Increasing Income

There is another influence of rising wages on the shape of the labor supply curve that has the opposite effect of that just discussed. It is the fact that rising wages not only make the opportunity cost of leisure greater, but they also make the worker's income higher. Thus he is able to buy both more corn *and more leisure* if he chooses to do so. This is the income effect that works directly against the substitution effect as wages rise. It can be illustrated as follows.

Suppose that a worker begins by working 16 hours a day for 2 bushels an hour. His income is 32 bushels of corn. Now suppose that because of a change in conditions of demand (over which the worker has no control), the wage *doubles* to 4 bushels per hour. The worker's first reaction may be to say, "Now if I take some time off, each hour of leisure will cost me more corn than ever." This is the *substitution effect* in action. But he might then offset this argument by thinking to himself, "Wait a minute. Because wages have doubled, 16 hours of labor brings in twice as much corn as before. Wouldn't it be better to spend a little more time on something else, rather than spending it all earning corn?" This is the *income effect* in action. Taken by itself, the income effect produces a backward-sloping supply curve of labor. Figure 6.6 shows this unusual type of supply curve where only the income effect operates.

Which way will the supply curve slope for a worker in our hypothetical economy? This depends upon the relative strength of the two competing influences as determined by his preferences for corn and leisure. If corn is necessary for survival and leisure is not, we would expect him to offer all his labor at very low wage rates. If very little corn keeps a man alive and extra quantities nauseate him, we would expect him to spend all wage increases on the purchase of leisure. In this case, the income effect will dominate as wages rise. An increasing amount of the income growth will be spent on leisure rather than corn. If, on the other hand, his liking for corn does not diminish rapidly as he increases consumption of it, then the substitution effect may dominate and he may buy more and more corn as his wages rise.

A rise in wages tends to increase the amount of labor offered for corn because corn has become cheaper and leisure more expensive. This is the *substitution effect*. It produces an upward-sloping supply curve of labor.

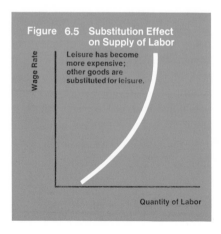

Figure 6.5   Substitution Effect on Supply of Labor

Wage Rate

Leisure has become more expensive; other goods are substituted for leisure.

Quantity of Labor

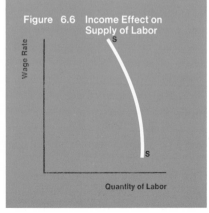

Figure 6.6   Income Effect on Supply of Labor

Wage Rate

S

S

Quantity of Labor

A rise in wages tends to increase the income of workers. This, in turn, tends to increase the demand for leisure as well as corn. This is the *income effect*. It produces a downward-sloping supply curve of labor. When a supply curve slopes downward, economists call it "backward sloping" or "backward bending."

One of the unsolved empirical questions of economics is which influence tends to dominate labor markets, whether in practice there are wages low enough for the income effect to be dominated and wages high enough for the substitution effect to be ignored. Because we cannot tell *a priori* which effect will dominate in our hypothetical economy, the individual worker's supply curve has been drawn to illustrate the influence of both effects at the extremes but is vertical in the midrange where the two effects exactly cancel each other.

In this example of a typical worker's behavior in our economy, the income effect is dominant above a wage of 4 bushels per hour, and the substitution effect is dominant below that wage rate. Therefore the supply curve bends backward above a wage of 4 bushels per manhour.

What will the supply curve of labor look like for the economy as a whole? We mentioned above that this curve is the sum of the individual supply curves and will inherit their shape. For simplicity, we *assume that all workers have identical tastes* for corn and leisure. Thus Figure 6.7 is applicable to each worker. If we know the number of workers and days in the period, the product of the two gives the total number of man-days that potentially can be used for work during the period. In our economy let us say there are 25,000 man-days, or 400,000 manhours, of labor *potentially* available (16 hours per day times 25,000 man-days). This gives us the limit on the horizontal axis of the diagram that shows the market supply curve for labor. We also know from Figure 6.7 how the total number of hours will be divided between work and leisure at each wage for each worker. The total supply of all markets is illustrated in Figure 6.8.

In this figure, the market supply curve for labor is determined from our information about workers' preferences, the number of workers, and the number

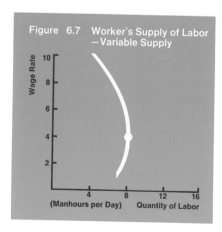

Figure 6.7   Worker's Supply of Labor — Variable Supply

Wage Rate

(Manhours per Day)   Quantity of Labor

Figure 6.8   Market Supply of Labor — Variable Supply

Wage Rate (Bushels/Manhour)

(000 Manhours per Day)   Quantity of Labor

of days during the period. It is a unique curve with supply varying according to the wage rate. We are now ready to show how the actual wage rate in this economy depends on the interaction between forces of supply and demand.

How the "Invisible Hand" Achieves General Equilibrium

Now that both the supply and demand curves for labor have been determined, we can discuss an equilibrium. This occurs at the point of intersection of the two curves, point *E* in Figure 6.9. It does not matter where the curves lie or what shape they have as long as they intersect at one point; this will be an equilibrium. Notice that equilibrium in the market for labor, in this example, means equilibrium for the whole economy. The solutions to a number of variables can be derived from this equilibrium. They are as follows:

1. The *price of labor* in terms of corn is established. It equals the marginal productivity of labor in corn production. The *quantity of labor* actually employed is also established at that point where the demand and supply prices are equal. Both price and quantity of labor are therefore simultaneously determined by the interaction of supply and demand.
2. *National output* (income) in terms of corn now may be determined by applying the production function to the quantity of labor employed. (Note that leisure, although a use of scarce labor, has not been included as output. Economists believe that leisure has value, but it is traditionally omitted from measures of total production.)
3. *Labor income* in terms of corn is determined by multiplying the wage rate times the number of manhours employed.
4. *Rental income* in terms of corn is then the difference between national income and labor income. This is the return to farmers for the use of their land.

These results give us all of the parts of the puzzle necessary to answer the two questions asked at the beginning of the chapter: How will resources be allocated, and how will income be distributed? These answers have been provided by the market mechanism unaided by any intervention.

The Numerical Solution

What are the answers to the two questions? We can calculate actual numbers for each of the economic elements (variables) in the analysis. This should not imply that the reader must be able to reproduce these numerical values to be able to use the analysis of Chapters 6 and 7. On the contrary, the important thing is to understand the principles that are illustrated by the analysis. In practice, it is often impossible to find precise values for the variables. Yet the principles remain powerful tools for explaining how an economy behaves, whether or not actual measurement is possible.

The values are calculated as follows, using Figure 6.9 and the production function data from Table 6.4.

1. The *price of labor* in equilibrium is 4 bushels per manhour.
2. The *quantity of labor* hired during the period is 200,000 manhours in equilibrium.
3. *National output* (national income) in equilibrium is 1,500,000 bushels of corn during the period. We determine this from the production function, Table 6.4, which shows us that when one farmer with one acre of land employs 20 manhours at a wage of 4 bushels/manhour, he will produce 150 bushels of corn. We multiply this output times 10,000, since there are that many identical farmers in our hypothetical economy.
4. *Labor income* is determined by multiplying the wage rate (4 bushels/manhour) times the number of manhours (200,000), giving a result of 800,000 bushels of corn.
5. *Rental income* is obtained by subtracting labor income from national income and is therefore 700,000 bushels of corn.

The numerical answers to our two questions, therefore, are the following:

Question 1: How are scarce resources allocated?

Answer: Since 400,000 manhours were potentially available during the period to use for producing corn or leisure,

   Labor Time: Allocated 50 percent to work
                          50 percent to leisure

   Land Time: Allocated 100 percent to corn production
                          none to leisure

   Production Chosen: 200,000 manhours of leisure
                          1,500,000 bushels of corn

Question 2: How is income distributed?

Answer: 53.3 percent to labor (⁸⁄₁₅)
            46.7 percent to rent (⁷⁄₁₅)

What we just solved was a *theoretical model* of a simple economy. It was necessary in this case merely to determine the supply and demand for a single

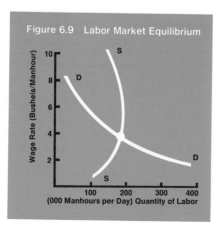

Figure 6.9   Labor Market Equilibrium

market to obtain a solution. This is a solution in one diagram. In the following chapters we do *not* make any more formal models of this kind, but we speak of economies that produce *many commodities* and contain many markets. More commodities than corn could be added to the model above, but each would require another supply and demand relationship that must be solved for a given price and quantity. The calculations could become cumbersome, but the principles would remain as simple as before. Income distribution would be obtained by the same mechanism as in the case above. In fact, once we knew the prices and quantities for all the goods, the operations we would perform to calculate national output, total wage income, and so on, would be much like those we have just performed. Thus our model, while an abstraction from reality, can be used to examine the causes of the distribution of income between wages and profits. This is one of the operations performed in the next chapter where we compare the market solution with an allocation of resources that could result from central planning.

Questions

1. The absurdity of the following questions illustrates well the principle of diminishing returns: Why cannot we grow all of the world's food in a flower pot? Why fear a population explosion? Why not study only courses in one's major field? Why do not athletic teams practice only offense?

2. Why is it impossible to tell whether a man will work more or less when his wage is increased? What effect should an income tax have on labor supply? Can we tell for sure whether leisure will increase in the future as man gets richer through higher wages?

3. Why should certain firms offer employees "time and a half" for hours worked in excess of the normal work week?

Concepts Discussed

production function
constant returns to scale
economies of scale
diminishing returns

marginal product
substitution effect
income effect

7 Market and Planning Solutions Compared

It is now time to isolate the influences of the various determinants of equilibrium in the simple economy presented in Chapter 6 to see how they affect the solution. What would happen to total output and the income distribution if there were more land? If workers changed their taste for leisure? If new production techniques were learned? If a population explosion occurred? Since the equilibrium has been presented by a single supply and demand curve, all we need to do is note how a change in any of these variables would shift the curves and thereby change the solution. The variables mentioned above are all part of the conditions of demand or supply. We know that changes in these conditions can shift the curves. Thus our analysis will be focused on the wage rate—why it is what it is and how it would differ if conditions changed.

Determinants of the Wage

We can see the impact on the wage rate of changes in many of these variables by looking only at the labor supply curve. First, note that an increase in labor supply (a rightward shift of the supply curve) causes the wage rate to fall. This is because the demand curve slopes downward and therefore a rightward shift in supply will cause an increase in the amount of labor sold and a decrease in the wage rate, as shown in Figure 7.1. Remember that this is due to diminishing re-

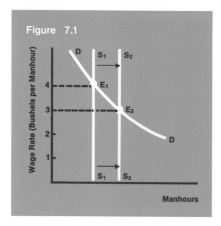

Figure 7.1

turns in production. An increase in the amount of labor used with no increase in the amount of land used lowers the productivity of the marginal worker.

The most obvious way for labor supply to expand is through an increase in the number of laborers. Remember that the aggregate labor supply curve is merely the sum of the individual labor supply curves. More individuals means more curves and a larger sum. Thus an increase in population would lead to a decrease in wage rates, *other things equal.* That is, if all the other conditions of supply and demand remained constant, an increase in the number of workers would lower the wage rate because of diminishing returns. If we were to look at the wage rates of various different nations, we would find that, other things equal, wages in agriculture are lowest where the number of men per acre is highest.

A change in tastes in favor of leisure relative to corn would lead to a decline in labor supply and therefore to an increase in the wage rate, other things equal.

Demand, too, obviously affects the wage. A change in the conditions of demand that caused demand to increase would lead to a higher wage and to more or less labor being sold, depending on whether the labor supply curve sloped upward and backward. The most obvious way for demand to increase is for the amount of land to become larger. This could occur through new discoveries or through irrigation and other devices for creating agricultural land out of desert, tundra, forest, or swamp. This model predicts that, other things equal, the discovery of new land will lead to wage increases. Diminishing returns tells us that with fewer men per acre, the return to the marginal worker will be higher.

An improvement in technology could also shift demand out. At its simplest, we can show an improvement in technology by increasing all of the numbers in Table 6.4, the table that shows how much output can be obtained from various combinations of inputs. If, for example, we doubled all of the numbers in Table 6.4, we would double the marginal product of labor for every possible combination of men and land. Since the demand for labor shows points at which the marginal product of labor equals the wage, the height of the demand curve would be doubled. This illustrates an increase in demand leading to an increase in the wage rate.

The predictions made by this small model are useful when explaining different levels of wage rates around the world. If we note that the role of capital in the real world is similar to that of land in our model—it augments the productive power of labor—we can then predict that those nations that have an abundance of land, buildings, machinery, and roads will have higher wage rates than those that do not. We can furthermore claim that one way to raise wages would be to increase the amount of capital available and to improve the quality of land.

Similarly, those nations using outmoded production techniques will have lower standards of living than those using the latest, most productive techniques. In poor countries, we would expect to see old equipment, inefficient agricultural techniques, and, in general, less technical knowledge than we observe in rich countries.

How about the capitalists? Could we have higher wage rates if the laborers banded together to throw out the capitalists, the owners of the plots of land? Are low wage rates a result of greedy farmers? Throwing over the farmers—nationalizing their land—may redistribute income by sharing the rent among the laborers as well. But that does not change the wage rates in a market economy, nor does it change the share of output that is paid to labor and the share paid to the owners of land. It merely changes the owners of land.

Distributive Shares

In our model the labor share depended upon (1) the tastes of workers, (2) the number of workers, (3) the technology available, and (4) the amount of land (capital). As a result of the interaction of these four elements, the wage level (4 bushels/manhour) provided a labor income share of 53.3 percent of national income. Suppose that technology had improved enough to shift the demand curve in Figure 7.1 to the right. Both real wages and output would rise. If real wages rose more than in proportion to the increase in output as a result of technological improvements in corn farming, then the labor share of national income would rise as well.

In the United States, the share of labor in national income in 1900 was about 70 percent and that of capital plus land about 30 percent. At the present time, the labor share is closer to 80 percent, whereas that of capital is about 20 percent. In the meantime, real wages have risen more than twofold. Most of this improvement in real wages must have been due to increased productivity of labor through education, investment, and technology, rather than through decreases in profits and rents. The decrease in the share of profits can explain an increase in wages of only 14 percent in the last 70 years! That is, if the relative share of labor had gone from 70 to 80 percent but technology remained constant, real wages would have increased by only 14 percent. But the huge increases in output in this century have increased *both* wages and profits substantially. New production techniques have allowed both capitalists and laborers to get rich.

Who gets the rent? The share of rent each person receives in our model depends upon a number of factors.

(1) *Inheritance*: The amount of land inherited determines the rents one enjoys. In fact, in the United States people inherit different quantities of wealth and this partly explains their differences in income.

(2) *Saving*: It is also possible to add to one's wealth by saving. In our model, if we introduce the possibility of trade in land, thrifty farmers might save and buy the land of their less thrifty neighbors, thereby increasing their future share of rents. Laborers might also save out of their wages and buy land from lazy farmers and become farmers themselves.

Total wealth in the United States is less than three times total annual income. If one could accumulate an amount of wealth worth *three times* his annual income, and if he had an average American income, then he would have an average amount of wealth. This may be difficult to achieve through savings alone (without the benefit of gifts or inheritance), but it is certainly possible. One works for 40 years. Saving the income from 3 of these years would do the trick. Thus saving is at least as important as inheritance in determining the distribution of wealth and therefore of rental (profit) income. Indeed, as the national wealth more than doubles every generation, at least half of current wealth represents saving done by this generation.

The split between labor income and profit income need not correspond to different social classes in American society. If the poor save, they will receive profits as a part of future income. There is evidence, however, that some groups have very low incomes and save very little over the course of a lifetime. It is not realistic to expect them to save for future consumption when they have so little in the present. Saving is theoretically possible regardless of one's income, of course, but in fact, we do not observe much saving by the very poor. *The equality of the distribution of wealth then depends ultimately on the equality of income distribution.* Factors such as education and ability that affect income distribution are further analyzed later in the book. Our purpose here is simply to demonstrate how the market does determine national output and distribute income.

The Commissar's Problem

Too many mouths to feed, given the resources available, creates political pressures that make the question of a low wage rate or a low living standard anything but academic. China, with 600 million mouths, is an extreme example of a general problem. In such a case, it is essential that production be organized efficiently in order to prevent disorder or, worse, starvation. Will the market economy or central planning allocate resources in a way that achieves the most output? We have just shown how a simple market economy that produces one good (corn) and employs two factors of production (labor and land) was able to determine output and its composition, distribute output among farmers and workers by determining wage and rental rates (profits), and fix the level of employment. All of these results were accomplished through the unhampered interaction of supply and demand under conditions of perfect competition. Now we examine the possibility of central planning and compare its solution to that of the market. Some conclusions are drawn as to the relative effectiveness of the two systems.

Suppose that the government of our hypothetical economy assigns a commissar the task of maximizing national output (corn production). Farms are abolished, rents are no longer earned by farmers, and workers now await the decision of the commissar-planning as to where they will be employed and on which land. To simplify the problem, we assume that the planner decides to pay the same wages as before and take the rent for the government. To make the problem a bit more interesting, we assume that different plots of land have different levels of productivity. The commissar's problem is to determine how best to allocate the labor he hires to the different plots of land so as to get the most production of corn. Profits are unimportant to him. Output is what he wishes to maximize. Since he knows that the law of diminishing returns is no respecter of political systems, he is aware that it will be easy to make mistakes, particularly at the beginning. There is danger of assigning too much labor to some plots of land and not enough to others. Land and labor are present in the same quantities as before, but the decision as to their use that formerly rested with the 10,000 individual farmers now lies on the shoulders of the planner. When private property was abolished, the decision-making apparatus disappeared along with the farmers. The planner must start from scratch. What is he likely to do?

The Commissar's Decision Rule

Starting from any initial allocation of laborers to the land, the commissar wishes to increase production by transferring laborers from one plot to another until an allocation is obtained that maximizes output. He knows that if a worker is transferred from one plot of land to another, two things will occur: (1) The marginal product of labor on the old plot is lost; (2) the marginal product of labor on the new plot is gained. That is, output changes due to two effects. Output from one plot falls because less labor is employed there. It rises on the other plot because more labor is employed there. The amounts it falls and rises are the respective marginal products of labor.

Since the planner starts from a point of limited experience, the marginal products of labor on the thousands of plots of land almost certainly will be unequal at the outset. How then should labor be moved about to increase productivity? Trial and error offer certain clues to effective planning behavior. If output falls when a worker is moved from one plot to another, the marginal product of labor on the old plot was greater than it is on the new one. On the other hand, if output rises when a worker is moved, then the marginal product of labor on the new plot exceeds that on the initial plot. Thus the following decision rule is formed:

> *Move workers from plots where they have a low marginal product to plots where they have a high marginal product.*

If carefully followed, the planner's decision rule will guide him toward the desired maximization of output. Each move will increase output as the gain exceeds the loss. He should continue to follow that rule until he attains the maximum output possible (given the resources of the economy and its technology). This point represents the most efficient allocation of labor among the various plots of land in the economy.

When is the maximum obtained? Clearly, if the marginal product of labor is ever higher on one plot than on another, the planner can increase output by shifting labor. Thus the maximum must have marginal products equal for all plots of land. But how do the marginal products approach equality if they were initially quite different? The reader will recall that diminishing returns implies that the more labor allocated to a single plot, the lower the *marginal product of* labor on that plot. The less labor allocated to a single plot, the higher the marginal product of labor it will have. So if one plot in the centrally planned economy has a lower marginal product than another plot, the planner shifts a worker from the first to the second. This move *decreases* the marginal product on the second plot and *increases* the marginal product on the first plot, tending to bring the two levels of productivity together. By moving a sufficient amount of labor, the marginal products can be equalized. The maximum level of output can be obtained.

Efficient Allocation through Planning

Maximization of output was accomplished in our example by trial and error. The commissar was able to achieve his result without considering profits or prices, unlike the profit-maximizing farmers in the previous chapters. His actions may have been tedious and time-consuming, requiring long periods of combining and recombining resources before the desired outcome was achieved, but they eventually worked. The larger the economy, the greater the number of workers, the more extensive the land area, the less technological knowledge and organizational skill inherited from the past, the more difficult the planner's problem must be. In our example, we assume that he did finally achieve a solution that maximized output and ideally allocated manpower. We can call this an *efficient allocation* of resources because no recombination would have further increased production. Any alternative combination would have used the same amount of resources but produced less corn.

Since the commissar was able to maximize production, why should not all societies adopt central planning? Why should they rely instead on a system of allocation that depends upon individual farmers' maximizing their profits (rent)?

A Reaffirmation of the Market Economy

An answer to this question can be discovered by re-examining the working of the market economy described in Chapter 6. Farmers in the market economy maximized their profits (rents) by hiring labor whose marginal product was greater than or equal to the wage rate. The last manhour employed by each farmer tended to have a marginal product equal to the wage rate. But here is the surprising result. If the market functions properly, there will be one wage rate faced by all farmers. The labor market achieves equilibrium at *a single price for labor*. No one farmer can influence that price. Therefore each farmer will set the marginal product of labor on his plot of land equal to the same wage rate. *Thus all marginal products will be equal. Thus output is maximized.*

This is an important conclusion. By allowing each farmer to maximize his own profits, the market economy reaches the same allocation of labor as the economy that started out through central planning to maximize output. An important result has just been shown. *Under ideal conditions, both the planning and the price system can maximize output.* How did the price system do it? Those farmers who initially had plots of land on which the marginal product was less than the wage were losing money on the marginal worker. Thus they followed their individual decision rules and fired him. Those with marginal products above the wage rate could make more profits by hiring more labor. Labor, therefore, was automatically shifted from plots with low marginal productivity to plots with high marginal productivity without benefit of central planning or a commissar. That is, workers were shifted from plots where they were producing less than the wage to plots where they could produce more than the wage. No central coordination was necessary to guarantee the efficient reallocation of labor. We recall that Adam Smith called this property of the price system the "invisible hand." The invisible hand guides resources to an efficient allocation if markets work properly and everyone maximizes his profits.

In a free market, the man who is willing to pay the most for a product gets it. In the labor market, this means that the man who can create the most corn by hiring labor is the one who hires it. Thus free labor markets lead to an efficient allocation of labor among the many alternative tasks to which labor could be assigned.

This result is a special case of a more general proposition that we demonstrate later; that is, that the market leads to an efficient allocation of resources only when *private cost equals social cost*. In this case, the farmer had to pay a wage to the laborers that represented the amount they could earn elsewhere, that is, the amount they could produce elsewhere. The cost of a laborer to the farmer was equal to the output lost on other plots by having the laborer work for this farmer. If each farmer hires enough labor to maximize his profits, then the wage rate (the private cost) will equal the marginal product of labor (the social cost) in all plots.

We saw that the way for the planner to maximize output was to make thousands of small decisions about the different plots of land and how much labor to assign to each. In fact, the incentive of profit maximization led the individual farmers to make these identical decisions. When big decisions can be broken into many small ones, it is often possible to decentralize the decision making and allow the little decisions to be made separately. Whether or not this is efficient will depend on other circumstances. For example, each farmer does have a capacity for making decisions. This is a labor resource that should not be wasted. Centralizing decisions wastes the decision-making capacity of the bulk of the populace. On the other hand, there are cases in which decentralized decisions do not work well. We will see these below as examples where markets misallocate resources.

Some noneconomic examples of centralized and decentralized decision making might help us to understand how it is that other circumstances determine the most efficient method. In the army, some decisions are centralized, some not. For example, when a sergeant confronts a squad of men and attempts to line them up in order of height, he says, "If you're taller than the man in front of you, get in front of him." This decentralizes the problem and utilizes the brains of each private. Five men may move at once in response to such an order. If the sergeant made the comparison himself, it would surely take longer to achieve the results. Decentralized decision making appears to be superior in this example.

An alternative example is the decision to invade Normandy on June 6, 1944. This had to be a highly centralized decision because coordinated action of all parties was essential for success. Allowing each private to decide when to invade and at what point would have led to disaster.

Similarly, some social and economic problems are better solved by decentralized decisions, some by centralized decisions. Planning will tend to execute the centralized decisions better whereas the market will better perform the decentralized ones.

In subsequent chapters we analyze problems faced by market systems and planning systems when there are many commodities included in national output, which is to be maximized. Moreover, in this simple example we have allowed the workers in both systems to decide how much leisure and corn to consume. To make sure that the proper amounts of leisure and corn are produced so that the laborers do not get too little of one or the other, it is important that they be made aware of the social cost of leisure. To do this without offering them a market wage rate is difficult, perhaps impossible. Thus our commissar was really allowed to use the market as a crutch. In effect, he allowed this important decision to be made decentrally. And if the wage is used as a basis for decisions in the labor market it is hard to think of it not affecting the distribution of income, particularly in more complex models where there are many different kinds of labor. In this special case, however, there is no such problem. Profits can be divided among the men without adversely affecting their allocation between corn and leisure. Further on it will be discovered that as economies get more complex, there are cases where it is virtually impossible to achieve an efficient solution under central planning and cases where the market itself misfires. And as we have already seen in Chapter 5, even in simple economies equilibria may exist that are unstable or imply severe social costs. In such cases, only *mixed systems* — part market and part planning — may lead to an efficient allocation of resources. That is, in effect, what our planning model was. All of the economies in the world are in reality mixed systems, although some rely more on planning than others.

How does the market allocate resources by itself, how might a central planner modify that solution, and how might a complete planning solution appear? We have seen that for simple problems both methods *can* attain efficiency; under ideal conditions the market system does so in a decentralized fashion while the planning solution is centralized. There are advantages and disadvantages to the two systems; thus the alternative approaches must be painstakingly examined before any decision is reached concerning which to use. Much of the rest of the book analyzes the relative efficiency of these two systems to see the domain in which each is most useful — under which system the most desires are satisfied. With over 600 million people in his country, even Mao Tse-Tung cannot afford not to have an open mind about this question.

Questions

1. How did the market and the planner arrive at the identical allocation of labor to land?

2. If the planner uses wage rates to guide individuals' decisions in the labor market, can he attain any distribution of income he wishes? Alternatively, if he ceases to use wage rates, can he get individuals to work the proper amount of time?

3. Devise examples in which decentralized decision making is more efficient than centralized decision making, and vice versa.

Concepts Discussed

central planning

maximizing national output

planning decision rules

mixed systems

IV The Consumption Decision

There's one born every minute.

P. T. BARNUM

The whole purpose of our complex economic machinery is to satisfy men's material wants. A man is called a consumer when he uses economic goods for his own satisfaction. In the next five chapters, we examine economic issues that affect a person in his role as a consumer.

First, we look more closely at the decision process—how the relative prices and values of commodities affect the quantities of goods that men will buy. Then we look at efficiency once again and show the conditions under which a man's material wants can best be satisfied by allowing him to spend his own income as he chooses. We explain pollution as a problem that arises because these conditions are not met. We show how collective action is necessary to eliminate pollution but that decentralized free markets may lead to efficient allocations of resources for other commodities.

A chapter is devoted to the role of information in allowing the potential consumer to learn which commodities are most likely to satisfy him. Advertising is looked at as a phenomenon that can either provide this information or attempt to fool him. Finally, we look at the question of consumer sovereignty: Who should decide which goods are to be produced? We consider the alternatives and how we might choose among them.

The tools and jargon we present are useful in analyzing most of the problems we deal with in the rest of the book. They should be mastered so that intelligent discussion of these problems is possible.

8 Consumption

The Consumer's Problem

We are continually confronted with the problem of consumer choice. Somehow we must decide which goods to buy, what to do with our time, whether to spend now or save for the future. These decisions get made with or without the aid of conscious choice. The problem of choice has always been with us although the nature of the decisions we confront has changed. In prehistoric days, many of men's decisions were crucial to their survival. As civilizations advanced, the number of decisions increased but the importance of each declined as the pressure of physical survival relaxed. There are still some decisions, however, that must consider the destructive potential of advanced technology, and these decisions bear directly on survival. Technology may also create a need for more decisions. In the future, the demand for self-understanding — mental survival — may well increase as the world becomes more complex. Each action of ours affects other people in new ways, thereby increasing the decisions they must make. Progress, therefore, does not eliminate the problem of choice; it merely changes the decisions that are to be made.

In this chapter we analyze the consumer's problem: how to attain the greatest amount of satisfaction from his limited resources. We effectively ignored this class of decisions when looking at the simple economy in the last few chapters. There the decision of the laborers concerning how much leisure to enjoy and how much corn to buy was mentioned but not analyzed carefully. Such an analysis is the purpose of this chapter.

Once we present the analysis, we discuss the efficiency of the market solution and point out why all nations today allow consumers to decide which goods to buy with their incomes rather than make that decision on a centralized basis. To visualize the problem of the planner in allocating consumption among members of an economy, one might think of him as a socially-appointed god whose eye is on the sparrow and who regulates its consumption from day to day. Is the sparrow better off on the wing, left to its own devices? This depends upon the degree of divine characteristics of omnipotency, omnipresence, and omniscience possessed by the planner. A sparrow in a state of nature has little influence on his environment. Man in a state of nature, alone and unaided, is vulnerable, too. Would sparrows have a better chance of survival if they could band together into societies? How might this influence their consumer behavior? Would smart sparrows hire consumption planners?

The Logic of Consumer Choice

How does the consumer decide what to buy in a market economy? If he confronts himself with the question, What goods will I buy? he needs to know certain facts in order to reply. He must know the price of each commodity that poses itself as a candidate. If there are thousands of choices available, as is true for any society, then he must have all prices in mind before an exact answer can be given. *What do goods cost?* That is the first informational requirement. He also must know how much he has to spend to determine how much of each good he is able to buy. *How large is my income?* That is the second informational requirement. When drawing the demand curves for single goods, we argued that the prices of other goods mattered, even if they were not formally introduced into the analysis. The quantity of steak bought depended on the price of movies, beers, and so on. Now we introduce these prices formally and develop a model that explains their role and that of a consumer's income in determining his demand for specific commodities.

Recall the production possibility frontier presented in Chapter 3. It describes *all of the possible efficient combinations of output* that can be achieved given the limited resources available during a period of time. The production possibility frontier (PPF) drawn below describes the possibilities of producing movies or steak. All points *within* the PPF are attainable. All external points are not possible. By showing what can be consumed, the curve portrays graphically the choice between steaks and movies confronting society. The efficient production possibilities lie along the PPF.

At any point along the frontier the slope of the PPF represents the rate at which society can trade a given quantity of movies for steaks. This is called the *social opportunity cost* of steaks in terms of movies. It is clearly a *price*. It is a price that reflects social cost. The social cost of a steak is the number of movies that must be sacrificed to produce it.

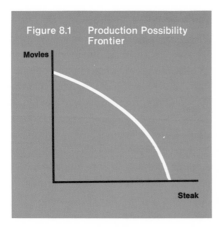

Figure 8.1   Production Possibility Frontier

Movies

Steak

The Consumption Possibility Frontier

Of course no individual "sees" the production possibility curve confronting society as a whole. But individuals, too, have limited resources depending upon their own *incomes* or purchasing power. These resources place a boundary on the quantities of steak or movies that they can consume. Such a boundary can be shown graphically for the individual just as it can for the society. But the boundaries will look different. Not only will the individual's boundary be much smaller than that for the society as a whole, but it will have a different shape as well.

Remember that the reason the PPF is bowed outward is due to the fact that different resources are technologically more useful at producing different products. The more steak we give up to produce movies, the more resources we must transfer that are better at producing steaks than movies. This makes each succeeding movie more expensive in terms of steak. Each individual's income is so small, however, that he can buy as much steak or as many movies as his income permits without his action affecting the prices of those commodities. He can regard the prices facing him as fixed. This means that when he knows his income, the line representing his alternative consumption possibilities between steak and movies will be a straight line. The cost of steak in terms of movies is constant if the prices of steak and movies are constant. This is the *consumption possibility frontier* for the individual (CPF), which has a slope determined by the market prices of steak and movies over which he has no control. The more steak one buys, the less money remains for movies, clothes, and cars. The CPF presents this fact graphically (see Figure 8.2). More steak means fewer movies.

The slope of the individual's consumption possibility frontier (CPF) represents a *price* to the individual just as the slope of society's PPF represents a price to society. Given his income and the prices of steak and movies, he can select any combination within the CPF. The CPF shows us the amounts of steak and movies he can buy if he spends all his resources on these two commodities. We discuss only two commodities because diagrams have only two dimensions.

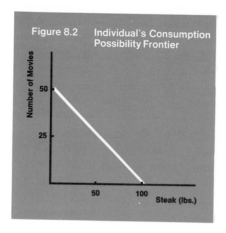

Figure 8.2 Individual's Consumption Possibility Frontier

But the theory of consumer choice can accommodate any number of commodities, each of which would need its own dimension for graphical description of the problem.

In this example movies cost $2 each and steaks $1 per pound. The slope of the CPF is therefore

$$\frac{\text{price steak}}{\text{price movies}} = \frac{\$1}{\$2} = \frac{1}{2}$$

If we assume that the person's income is $100, the various consumption possibilities along the CPF are easy to determine. If he chooses nothing but steak, he ends up with 100 pounds of steak. If he wishes nothing but movies, he can see up to 50 movies ($100/$2 per film = 50 movies). These are the extreme ends of the CPF. Any other combination along the same straight line ends up costing the same amount of money ($100). The more steak bought, the less amount of resources available for movies. We could say that moving from one point to another on the CPF involves a *trade* of steak for movies. Or in *n* dimensions, the purchase of movies requires that other goods be foregone.

The height of the CPF represents income, and its slope represents the ratio of the market prices between movies and steak. A rich person will have large consumption possibilities; therefore his CPF will be to the right of the present curve. A poor person's CPF will be to the left. But the slope of any CPF will be the same as long as market prices remain what they are. If our individual's income rises, the CPF in the diagram will shift to the right, but its slope will not change. That is because the slope of the CPF is determined by market prices, over which the individual has no control.

Budget Constraints

When someone talks about his budget limitations, he is simply discussing the problem illustrated above. That is why the CPF is often called a "budget constraint" by economists. It serves the same purpose for individuals that the PPF serves for society. When we prepare a budget we are attempting to choose from among the points along the CPF. When we shop for bargains we are really deciding which mixture of commodities we will choose from those along the CPF. We wish more steaks and more movies, but we have a limited income. We must choose wisely between steaks and movies in order to become as happy as possible with our limited income. Our mental computers are so accustomed to this selection process that we perform it almost without thinking. We ponder, Is that extra movie worth $2 and an evening? Can I afford to buy this $100 suit? That is, How uncomfortable will I feel without the other commodities that the $100 could buy? The budget constraint forces us to evaluate one commodity in terms of others. We do this so often that we become good at it and do it automatically. Implicitly, we evaluate each commodity relative to what it costs us in terms of other commodities and decide whether or not to buy it.

Tastes and Relative Value

We often say that "there is no accounting for taste." Yet there can be an accounting *of* taste regardless of how it was formed. For example, let us return to the consumption problem just posed. If one knows his income and the relevant prices, he can make a decision between steak and movies and answer the original question, What goods do I want? The prices of the commodities and his income have been translated into a number of alternative consumption possibilities illustrated by a convenient frontier (CPF). Which combination will he select?

This is where psychology enters the picture. For us to predict the consumer's response we need to know his pattern of tastes. Production decisions are made on the basis of resources and technology. They are objective. Consumption decisions are subjective. They rest upon the fundamental values of each individual. How does one value steak relative to movies? Although the choice between steak and movies may seem superficial, it could depend upon profound psychological considerations. If one has been raised strictly in the Puritan tradition, he may feel that movies are sinful and stay away from the theater. If one has been raised strictly as a Hindu, he may feel that eating meat is sinful and never touch a bite. But if one is a typical consumer, he will derive utility from both steak and movies and find himself somewhere between the extreme points on the CPF.

Tastes are a fascinating subject. Their formation depends on education in the broadest sense—the influences of family, neighborhoods, friends, church, school, and work. Tastes are conditioned by books, TV, radio, advertising, and other media. A later chapter, Chapter 11, is devoted to advertising and the formation of tastes. But however they are determined, and whatever they may be, our tastes for almost every commodity are subject to diminishing relative value. This facilitates our analysis of the consumption decision. No matter how one's preferences for steak or movies are formed, they are likely to exhibit diminishing relative value.

Utility Maximization through Consumer Choice

For the present we argue intuitively as to the implications of diminishing relative value. (A more complete mathematical presentation is given in the appendix.) Our intuition is based on the observation of actual behavior. We are simply attempting to formalize that behavior.

Which point on the CPF represents the likely selection? Consider three points, *A*, *B*, and *C*, in Figure 8.3. Which of these points yields the most utility? Point *A* gives one no steaks and therefore leaves one red-eyed and hungry. Point *C* gives one no movies and leaves one stuffed and rather bored. Point *B* gives one some of both and is therefore *likely* to be preferred. One is neither hungry nor bored at *B*.

We can, of course, choose any point on the CPF. We have chosen *B* just as an example. Suppose that one selects *B* as preferable to all other points. If we offer him a combination just near *B*, he will like it better than *A* or *C*, but less than *B* itself. It does not balance his wants properly. In other words, as he moves from *C* towards *B*, or from *A* towards *B*, he gets happier and happier until his utility is finally maximized at *B*. Point *B* represents the maximum level of utility he can attain given his limited resources. A greater income, of course, would allow him to buy more and be happier.

The Consumer's Decision Rule

In a market economy what decision rule might approximate the way in which a consumer goes about miximizing his utility? We can think of him saying to himself:

> *If the last dollar spent on steak yields more utility than the last dollar spent on movies, buy more steak and fewer movies.*

This decision rule will increase total utility, since the marginal utility gained from an additional dollar's worth of steak will more than offset the marginal utility lost from one less dollar's worth of movies. By reallocating spending according to the decision rule, the consumer will approach that allocation of his income that maximizes his utility. Since the rule tells us that resources must be shifted whenever the utility gained from the last dollar spent on steak differs from that gained from the last dollar spent on movies, we know that at an equilibrium these values must be equal. That is, the last dollar spent on movies must yield exactly the same amount of satisfaction as the last dollar spent on steak at the point that maximizes utility. If these values are different, then it is possible to increase utility by spending less on the commodities that yield low levels of satisfaction and more on the ones that yield high levels of satisfaction.

This argument tells us the characteristics of the equilibrium at which the consumer is as happy as he can be with his given level of income. But it does not give us much insight into the reason why such a point is obtained when the decision rule is followed. If a dollar's worth of steak yields more satisfaction than a dollar's worth of movies, why not buy all steak and no movies? The answer lies

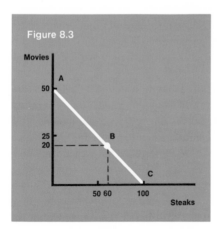

Figure 8.3

in the concept of diminishing relative value. To show the relation between this concept and the decision rule, it is useful to write the decision rule algebraically.

The reciprocal of the price of a commodity gives the number of units that a dollar will purchase. For example, if a magazine costs one-half dollar, then one dollar will buy two magazines. The number of magazines = $1/(price of a magazine) = $1/$½ = 2$. If a movie costs $2, $1 will buy one-half movie or 1/(price of movie). So the number of movies, magazines, or any other commodity that can be bought with one dollar is one dollar divided by the price of the commodity.

Therefore, the words "dollar's worth of steak" can be replaced by "$1/P_{steak}$" units of steak.

But the marginal utility of $(1/P_{steak})$ more units of steak is equal to the marginal utility of one more steak times the number of units of steak* $(1/P_{steak})$. Thus we can rewrite [the marginal utility of $(1/P_{steak})$ units of steak] as [MU_{steak} times $(1/P_{steak})$] which equals [MU_{steak}/P_{steak}]. Our result for consumer equilibrium is then the following:

$$\text{if } \left(\frac{MU_{steak}}{P_{steak}}\right) = \left(\frac{MU_{movies}}{P_{movies}}\right) \text{ then } \begin{pmatrix} \text{the consumer is} \\ \text{in equilibrium} \end{pmatrix}$$

And the decision rule can be expressed as follows:

$$\text{if } \left(\frac{MU_{steak}}{P_{steak}}\right) > \left(\frac{MU_{movies}}{P_{movies}}\right) \text{ then } \begin{pmatrix} \text{buy more steak,} \\ \text{fewer movies.} \end{pmatrix}$$

The relative value of a commodity was defined in Chapter 2 as the value of one commodity relative to another. And since the value of a commodity is its marginal utility, the value of one commodity relative to another is the ratio of marginal utilities of the two commodities. This was discussed in Chapter 2.

The decision rule can be rewritten by multiplying it by P_{steak}/MU_{movies}. Since this number is positive and is multiplied by both sides of the inequality, the operation does not change the inequality. The decision rule now reads

$$\text{if } \left(\frac{MU_{steak}}{MU_{movies}}\right) > \left(\frac{P_{steak}}{P_{movies}}\right) \text{ then } \begin{pmatrix} \text{buy more steak,} \\ \text{fewer movies.} \end{pmatrix}$$

Note that MU_{steak}/MU_{movies} is the value of a steak relative to the value of a movie. It is the number of movies that gives the same satisfaction as one steak. (If an extra steak yields twice as much satisfaction as an extra movie, its value in terms of movies is two.) But note also that P_{steak}/P_{movies} is the price of a steak in terms of movies. Remember that a price is the ratio in which two commodities trade. So if the price of a steak is $1 per steak ($1/1 steak) and the price of a movie is $2 per movie, then the price of a steak in terms of movies is

$$\frac{\$1/\text{steak}}{\$2/\text{movie}} = \frac{1 \text{ movie}}{2 \text{ steaks}}$$

---

*Technically, this statement is not true for large finite quantities of steak. It becomes a better approximation the smaller the quantity of steak, and it is exact only in the limit where infinitesimal quantities of steak are considered.

That is, one-half a movie must be given up if one more steak is to be bought. The ratio in which steaks trade for movies is 2 steaks per movie.

Looking back at the transformed decision rule, we see that it says

If the value of a steak in terms of movies exceeds the cost of a steak in terms of movies, buy more steaks, fewer movies.

And that makes sense too. If the value of a commodity exceeds its cost, we should buy more of it.

Now we can explain the role of diminishing relative value in attaining a maximum level of utility. If the (relative) value of a commodity exceeds its (relative) cost, buy more of it. But as we buy more of it and trade away more of some other commodity, the relative value of the former must fall. As we get more and more steak and fewer and fewer movies, the value of a steak in terms of movies falls. This process is continued until the value of a steak falls to equal its cost. Thus the relation of the decision rule to the equilibrium can be summarized as follows:

$$\text{if} \left(\begin{array}{c}\text{the relative}\\\text{value of steak}\end{array}\right) > \left(\begin{array}{c}\text{the relative}\\\text{cost of steak}\end{array}\right) \text{then (buy more steak)}$$

This will cause the relative value of steak to fall until

$$\left(\begin{array}{c}\text{the relative value}\\\text{of steak}\end{array}\right) = \left(\begin{array}{c}\text{the relative cost}\\\text{of steak}\end{array}\right) \text{thus} \left(\begin{array}{c}\text{utility is}\\\text{maximized}\end{array}\right)$$

We will use this result many times in the future. The student *must* understand that when the consumer follows the decision rule above, he arrives at an equilibrium where the marginal utility divided by the price of any commodity equals that of any other. That is, when the consumer tries to get the most for his money (which is the behavior implied by our decision rule), then the result will be the equilibrium just described.

Private Cost Versus Social Cost

No person who seeks to maximize his welfare will be content until his consumption of steak and movies satisfies this condition of consumer equilibrium. As long as the marginal utility of a pound of steak exceeds one-half the marginal utility of a movie, he will prefer more steak and fewer movies (given that a movie costs twice as much as a steak). If, on the other hand, the marginal utility of a movie exceeds twice the marginal utility of a pound of steak, he will prefer more movies and fewer steaks. Suppose that a consumer attains his utility maximum. How does the rest of society feel about his choice? Does his selfish pursuit of his own happiness make others less happy? More happy? How does the consumer's decision affect others? Let us suppose that everyone else has made a similar consumption decision so that society is consuming at point *F* on its PPF. (See Figure 8.4.)

If society ends up consuming at *F*, we know that the *social opportunity cost* is shown by the slope of the curve at that point (the slope of PPF). This is the cost of steaks *to society* as measured by the munber of movies that society must give up to obtain another pound of steak. If this price is also the price that the individual faces, the society should be indifferent concerning the individual's selection. His choice will affect no other person's utility. Why is this true?

If the prices the individual observes represent the social cost of those commodities, then the consumer's decision to consume more steak and fewer movies allows all other consumers to remain exactly as they were. For when the individual demands one extra steak from the rest of the economy, he sacrifices *enough movies to produce that steak.* Remember that the decision to consume more steak means that less of something else must be consumed. The extra steak one demands requires that the society devote more resources to steak production. Demanding fewer movies means that a lesser amount of resources is devoted to more production. If the value of resources needed to increase the steak production equals the value of resources freed from movie production, then the society can produce the consumer's extra steak with no sacrifice on the part of innocent third parties.

If, however, the social cost of steak *exceeds* the private cost, then the consumption of an extra steak requires that someone else sacrifice some consumption. This is because the resources freed by the decrease in movie production will be insufficient to produce another steak. If individuals face prices that let them give up one-half a movie and buy a steak, but the social cost of steak is a whole movie, then *every extra steak bought by any consumer must lower someone else's welfare.*

This is a very powerful theorem that must be learned. We devote the next chapter entirely to this question. For now, even if the principle is not perfectly understood, the student should get a "feeling" for it.

Only if social cost equals private cost will an individual's consumption decision leave others unaffected.

If the cost to society is more than the individual consumer is asked to pay for any commodity, then his bargain is society's loss.

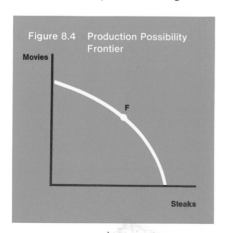

Figure 8.4 Production Possibility Frontier

Movies

F

Steaks

The Implications for Central Planners

The preceding analysis shows that as long as social cost equals private cost, society is indifferent as to where the individual ends up along his CPF. Consider now a collective system (communism) under which the commissar gives bundles of goods to individuals instead of letting them trade in the market. The implications of this can be illustrated using the CPR in Figure 8.5.

How will the commissar know how many movies or how much steak to give to our individual? He must make an arbitrary decision if he does not possess information about that person's pattern of preferences or tastes. It is unlikely that the planner will be able to guess with accuracy the tastes of every individual whose consumption he governs. Therefore, he is likely to pick a point, such as D, that does not reflect the maximum utility for the individual (B is assumed to be the maximum as before). If he gives the person the combination of goods represented by D, what happens to utility? It is lower at D than at B, because B was preferred by the individual to all other points. So $D < B$ as far as utility is concerned, yet it costs society the same amount of scarce resources to produce at D as it does to produce at B. Because all of the points on the CPF represent commodity bundles that use the *same amount* of scarce resources, why not let the individual choose the combination he prefers? He will be happier and no one will be worse off.

We have discovered the basic reason why all countries, even the Soviet Union, tend to allow consumers to determine how to spend their income in terms of the prices they face. People know their own preferences. They are best able to determine which bundle of commodities maximizes their utility within their budget constraint. It would be foolish for the central planner to attempt to determine which point on the CPF (which bundle of commodities) is best for each person. The only way he could be sure he was right would be to ask the individual. But if the individual's feelings are to be considered anyway, why not let him express those feelings in the market rather than in a letter to the commissar? If the individual's feelings are not considered, he might ask, Whose society is this anyway?

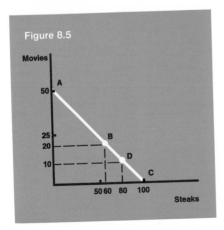

Figure 8.5

As long as other people's consumption choices do not affect us, we can be content to let them make their own decisions. It takes a great deal of arrogance for one person to believe that he should dictate the consumption patterns of another when those patterns affect no one but himself.

What if the planner is democratically elected? The planner who offers the best commodity bundle wins the election. Does that get us around the problem?

No. Tastes differ. Just because the majority prefers a certain proportion of steak to movies does not mean that everyone does. What does the Puritan do with the movies he is given or the Hindu with his steaks? Obviously, they attempt to trade them with each other. Thus a market will spring up anyway. (When such markets are illegal, they are called *black markets*.) But if it costs the society nothing to have a diversity of consumption patterns and if it makes individuals happier, then there is a strong reason to allow consumers to dispose of their incomes as they choose. And for this reason, most countries of the world have largely free consumer's markets. This question is discussed more fully in Chapter 12, which is devoted to the issue of consumer sovereignty.

Of course, if social cost does not equal private cost, then one consumer's decisions will affect others. This case can be called *market failure* because many of the claimed advantages of markets do not exist in these cases. Many following chapters are devoted to market failure where we show why centralized policy is often needed to correct the implications of such failure.

Are we kinder to sparrows by dictating their behavior or by letting them fly when and where they will and eat what they will?

Questions

1. Why do my consumption decisions not affect your welfare if the prices I face are the same as those faced by the society?
2. Why must the relative value of a commodity to a consumer equal its relative cost if the consumer is to be content with his consumption decisions?
3. "If a commodity is worth more than it costs, buy more of it." Why does this decision rule guide a consumer to that bundle of goods that yields the maximum level of utility he can obtain from his income?

Concepts Discussed

consumption possibility frontier
budget constraint
social cost

private cost
market failure
black market

APPENDIX: INDIFFERENCE CURVES

The quantity of a commodity demanded depends on its value and its cost relative to other commodities. In this appendix, we describe these two factors graphically. The role of prices is shown through their effect on the budget constraint just as presented in the body of the chapter. There, however, we did not use any graphical means to describe utility. We remedy that deficiency now.

Consumer Indifference Curves

The basic graphic tool used by economists to describe the role of utility in demand is called an *indifference curve*. Each indifference curve, drawn on a two-dimensional surface, describes the alternative sets of quantities of two different commodities that yield the same utility.

Remember that when we defined value, we said that there must be some quantity of steak (½ ounce, 1 ounce, 1 pound 4 ounces, etc.) that has the *same value* to a person as does a certain book. If a person feels that 1 book is equal in value to 3 pounds of steak, then increasing consumption by 1 book or by 3 pounds of steak will increase utility by exactly the same amount. That person will be *indifferent* between the two situations. Thus different bundles of commodities can yield the same level of utility. An indifference curve shows in two dimensions all of the possible combinations of two commodities that yield the same utility. What shape should an indifference curve take?

Remembering the principle of diminishing relative value, we should be able to realize the nature of the different bundles of commodities that yield the same level of utility. Consider steaks and movies. What alternative combinations of steaks and movies yield the same level of utility? Clearly, more steaks mean more utility and more movies mean more utility. Increasing either commodity leads to an increase in utility; decreasing either decreases utility. Only by increasing one and decreasing the other can we keep the level of utility constant. This leads to proposition 1.

1. *If both goods yield utility, an indifference curve for those two goods must be* downward sloping.

But diminishing relative value tells us even more than that about the shape of an indifference curve. The more steaks one gets, the less each steak is worth relative to movies. Therefore the more steaks one has, the fewer movies one would be willing to sacrifice for another steak. Or, in terms of indifference curves, the more steaks one has, the fewer movies one would sacrifice for a steak *and be as well off after the sacrifice as before.* Therefore, if we measure steak on the horizontal axis, an indifference curve must get flatter and flatter as we acquire more steak; that is, the vertical distance must become smaller relative to the horizontal distance to represent the smaller amount of movies one sacrifices for a given amount of extra steak. This leads to proposition 2.

2. *An indifference curve will be convex to the origin; that is, it will bend "inward" as in Figure 8A.1.*

In Figure 8A.1, we have drawn an indifference curve for a particular individual. It is called U_1U_1 because it represents the same level of utility (U_1) at any point along the curve.

On the indifference curve in Figure 8A.1, for example, the role of diminishing relative value can be described by looking at three points, L, M, and N. At L, the individual consumes 40 movies and 30 pounds of steak per time period—say, one year. This gives him a level of satisfaction we have labeled U_1. This individual would be just as happy with 15 fewer movies if we gave him 10 more pounds of steak. That is, he would be just as happy at point M as he is at point L. Note that between L and M he is willing to trade 15 movies for 10 steaks. We can say that the relative value of steaks in terms of movies is one and one-half. Each steak is worth one and one-half movies.

However, once he has moved from L to M, his increased consumption of steak and decreased consumption of movies decrease the value of steak relative to movies. At M, he will no longer be willing to give up one and one-half movies for each steak. His decreased consumption of movies has made each movie more valuable relative to steak. To illustrate this, we have added point N. A move from M to N involves a sacrifice of 10 movies and a gain of 10 steaks. Between M and N, the value of each steak is only one movie.

Note that the slope of the indifference curve equals the relative value of steak. When the individual is willing to give up one movie to acquire one steak, the slope of the curve must be one. Thus the diminishing relative value of steak is described by the decreasing slope of the indifference curve. Because of diminishing relative value, indifference curves are convex to the origin.

So far, we have spoken of just one indifference curve representing just one level of utility. To represent other utility levels, we need other indifference curves. If we increase the quantity of steak or movies this individual consumes without decreasing his consumption of the other good, he will be better off. Thus points above and to the right of the indifference curve drawn represent higher levels of utility. Each of these points must lie on an indifference curve as well. Higher levels of utility are represented by indifference curves above and to the right of the one drawn.

In Figure 8A.2, some of the many indifference curves are shown. It is impossible to draw all of the indifference curves, because they would lie so close to each other that the whole quadrant would be whitened. That is, every point in the diagram is on some indifference curve. Thus there can be no space between

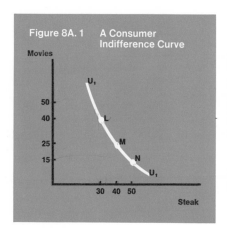

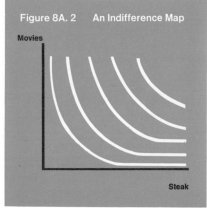

the curves. The whole set of indifference curves, called the *indifference* map, can be thought of as being dense or compact. For purposes of illustration, however, we draw only a few curves so that they can be seen clearly.

It is now possible to illustrate a graphical solution to the problem of utility maximization. Assume that income is $100. The budget line (CPF) shows the extreme limits of consumption possibilities facing our individual if the price of steak is $1 and that of movies $2. It is impossible for him to consume quantities greater than those represented by that straight line, the slope of which depends on the prices of steak and movies that he faces in the market. That line is his budget constraint.

If he maximizes his utility, he will choose the point that just satisfies his budget constraint and that is on as high an indifference curve as possible. Point *B* in Figure 8A.3 is such a point. Note that the highest utility level he can obtain is that represented by the indifference curve that is tangent to his budget constraint. Buying either more steaks (fewer movies) or more movies (fewer steaks) than those represented by point *B* will lower his utility. Such a point will lie on an indifference curve lower than U_2. It will yield an amount of utility equal to some point that has fewer movies and fewer steaks than point *B*. For example, in Figure 8A.3, point *S* and point *R* yield equal utility. They lie on the same indifference curve. But point *S* and point *B* cost the same amount of money. They both lie on the budget constraint. Clearly, point *B* is superior to *R* since *B* contains more steaks and more movies than *R* does. Since *B* yields more utility than *R* and *R* yields the same amount of utility as *S*, *B* yields more utility than *S*.

Figure 8A.4 clearly illustrates the characteristics of the solution we have just mentioned; namely, the point that maximizes utility is one that uses all the consumer's resources, and all points that yield higher levels of utility involve greater expenditures. It should be remembered that we have simplified the problem to two dimensions for purposes of illustration only. One can imagine an *n*-dimensional solution with quantities of *n* commodities being determined. Among these many commodities are goods to be purchased in the future. These

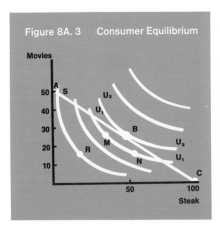

Figure 8A. 3   Consumer Equilibrium

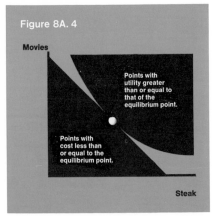

Figure 8A. 4

goods are provided for by present saving. Thus our requirement that a maximizing consumer choose a point from his budget constraint and thereby allocate all his income does not imply that saving is zero. It is merely an assumption that he must utilize all his resources. Some of the points on the *n*-dimensional budget constraint are points that involve saving.

Note that the slope of the budget constraint equals the cost of steak in terms of movies. With the prices of movies and steaks given, it tells us how many movies must be given up to get a steak. Above we noted that the slope of the indifference curve equaled the relative value of steak. That is, it tells us how many movies yield the same utility as a steak. Thus the slope of the indifference curve equals the value of steak, the slope of the budget line equals its cost. At equilibrium, the two curves are tangent and value equals cost. Note that if the consumer buys less steak than the optimal amount (for example, he is at *R* rather than at *B* in Figure 8A.3), the slope of the indifference curve exceeds the slope of the budget line. That is, the value of a steak exceeds its cost. Thus the indifference curves are a way of illustrating why the consumer's decision rule is a good one. If the value of a commodity exceeds cost, buy more; if it is less than cost, buy less; if it equals cost, equilibrium is attained.

The Effect of Increases in Income

In the body of the chapter, we pointed out that increases in income allow the consumer to consume more of both goods if he wishes. Figure 8A.5 illustrates the effect of an increase in income (an increase in the budget constraint) on the demand for steak and movies. The increase in income allows the consumer to obtain an increased level of utility represented by the higher indifference curve he reaches. The arrow shows the locus of equilibrium points for every income level between the two budget constraints drawn.

We mentioned that goods like margarine are called inferior goods because purchases of them actually may decline as income increases. Figure 8A.6 shows what the indifference curves must look like if purchases of margarine are to de-

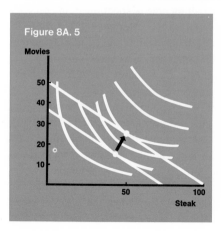

Figure 8A. 5

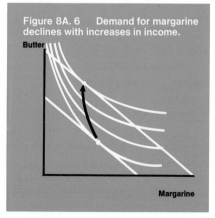

Figure 8A. 6   Demand for margarine declines with increases in income.

cline when income expands. Again, the arrow shows what would happen to the equilibrium for every level of income between the two represented by the budget constraints.

Deriving a Demand Curve

The tools of analysis developed above have many useful properties. For example, it is possible now to show exactly how a consumer demand curve depends upon the pattern of individual tastes underlying the set of consumer indifference curves. Let us derive the demand curve for steak that corresponds to the consumer whose indifference curves we have been studying. He will have one and only one demand curve for steak, which will depend on (1) his *income,* (2) the *prices of the other commodities* (including movies), and (3) his *tastes* (as represented by the set of indifference curves in the diagram). Remember what a demand curve is (see Chapter 4). His demand curve for steak represents the quantity of steak that he will demand at every possible price of steak. We already know from Figure 8A.3 at least *one point* on his demand curve, given that his income is $100 and the price of movies is $2.00 each. That point is the quantity of steak that would be demanded when the price of steak is $1.00 per pound. How can we get other points?

   The other points are derived by varying the assumed price of steak and leaving everything else (income, tastes, and prices of movies) the same as before. How can this be expressed diagrammatically? We know that the slope of the CPF will have to vary to reflect all the possible relative prices of movies and steak. We also know that point A will remain on all budget constraints since his consumption of movies can never exceed 50 regardless of what happens to the price of steak. The price of movies is still $2. Therefore the CPF will rotate from A as the price of steak falls or rises. Each budget constraint can be drawn through point A. The slopes of the budget constraints for each price can be calculated. For example, when the price of steak is $.80 per pound, 125 pounds of steak can be bought if nothing is spent on movies. Thus the new CPF is AC'. Consider a price of $1.25 per pound. When all income is spent on steak, only 80 pounds can be bought. The CPF becomes AC'' in the latter case. For each CPF there will be one optimal consumption point, determined at the point of tangency of the CPF with the highest possible indifference curve, as shown in Fig. 8A.7.

   Notice that these points of equilibrium of our consumer are B, E, and F for the three prices assumed above. The quantity of steak demanded falls as the price rises, from 60 pounds to 50 pounds to 45 pounds as determined by the successive equilibria between the CPFs and the consumer indifference curves U_3, U_2, and U_1. This gives us three points on the consumer's demand curve, one for each of the three prices associated with those points. For any other price, a similar quantity can be derived. The locus of these quantities as a function of the prices is the demand curve for steak. In this case, the demand curve has the normal downward slope since quantity demanded rises when the price of steak

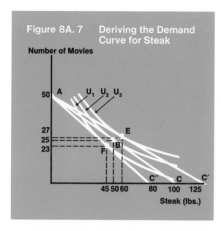

Figure 8A. 7 Deriving the Demand Curve for Steak

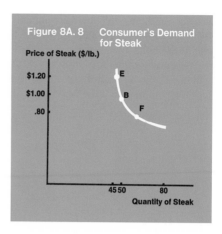

Figure 8A. 8 Consumer's Demand for Steak

falls. The demand curve including points *E, B,* and *F* is drawn in Figure 8A.8. Note that even though money income was kept constant in this example, *what money would buy* changed as the price of steak changed. Thus a rise in the price of steak (when the price of movies was kept constant) actually meant that a dollar could buy fewer real goods than before (movies plus steak). The person's purchasing power in real terms (which we call "real income") therefore declined. When there are very many products in the economy, so that each one constitutes a tiny fraction of a person's total expenditure, the change in that one product's price has a negligible effect on the person's real income. But when a consumer spends a large percentage of his income on one commodity, a change in its price will have a substantial effect on his well-being.

In our example, the amount of money spent on steak declined with the price of steak. That is, the demand curve for steak was inelastic. Had we drawn the demand curve for *movies,* we would have found that it depended on the price of steak. Low prices for steak meant more money left over to spend on movies and thus a higher demand curve for movies than would exist if the price of steak were higher.

The presentation above is very rapid and concentrated. To make certain of learning it, it is useful to do the exercises immediately following as well as those found in the *Study Guide for Principles of Economics* designed to accompany this text. The guide can be obtained through your bookstore.

Exercises
1. Draw a map of indifference curves. Derive the demand curve for steak given income and the price of movies. Now assume that income increases. Derive the new demand curve for steak associated with the new income level.
2. Assume that the price of movies changes. Derive the demand curve for steak again based on the new price for movies.
3. If commodities are good substitutes for each other, the indifference curves

drawn for them will not have much curvature. Why? Derive a demand curve from an indifference map in which the curves are almost straight lines. Is it elastic or inelastic?

4.   If commodities are poor substitutes for each other, the indifference curves will have a great deal of curvature. Why? Derive a demand curve from an indifference map in which the curves are almost right angles. Is it elastic or inelastic?

9 Social and Private Prices

If the prices a consumer faces reflect the true social costs of commodities, his attempts to satisfy his material wants through market transactions will affect no one else's welfare. If he buys more gasoline, less bread, the decrease in bread production will free exactly enough resources to increase gasoline production by the required amount. Everyone else can continue consuming exactly the same commodities he consumed before our consumer changed his mind. This is true, we argued, only when the costs the consumer faces are the same as those faced by the society.

And if the consumer worries only about his own utility when he decides which commodities to buy, the allocation of resources will be efficient only when the prices he faces — private costs — are the same as those faced by the society — social costs. The purpose of this chapter is to demonstrate precisely that. Only when private cost equals social cost for all commodities will an allocation of resources be efficient.

Efficiency was defined in Chapter 3. An allocation of resources is inefficient if it is possible to increase one person's utility without decreasing anyone else's. In Chapter 4 we got a brief look at efficiency of the market system from the standpoint of supply and demand. There we argued that a demand curve is a locus of points at which the *value* of a commodity equals its price, whereas a competitive supply curve is a locus of points at which *cost* equals price. Only at equilibrium is value equal to cost, and only then is utility not wasted.

In Chapter 8 we presented a more sophisticated view of consumer equilibrium. We can use that analysis here to get a better understanding of the relationship between the price system and economic efficiency. Our purpose is to show that the price system yields an efficient allocation of resources only when the prices consumers face equal those faced by the society. First we discuss the relationship between the constraint an individual faces — his budget constraint — and that faced by the society — the production possibility locus. Using that relationship, we then develop the results concerning efficiency.

Budget Constraints and the PPF

Each individual faces a budget constraint like that described in Chapter 8. In competitive markets, all consumers face the same prices, and thus the slope of everyone's budget constraint is the same. The constraints differ from each other only in their distance from the origin, not in their shape. If we add together all these constraints, we get an aggregate budget constraint that shows the alternative amounts of the various commodities that could be bought by the total income of the group at the going prices. This aggregate constraint will have the same shape as each individual's constraint, but it will be much larger. In fact, it will be large enough so that the point selected from it representing the sum of the consumers' demands will lie on the production possibility frontier.

It is not our purpose to examine here the problems of attaining a point on the PPF as opposed to an inefficient point inside it. We devote many following chapters to these problems. For now, we assume that these problems have been solved. This allows us to concentrate our attention on the particular problem of social and private costs. In particular, we assume that production decisions are made efficiently, that equilibrium occurs at a point on the PPF and that consumers' incomes are large enough in the aggregate to buy that production.

We can draw the two curves, the PPF and the aggregate CPF, on the same diagram in several ways. One way is illustrated in Figure 9.1.

In Figure 9.1, point $\overline{B}$ represents the quantities of steak and movies produced and consumed. Note that $\overline{B}$ lies on $\overline{ABC}$, the aggregate consumption possibility frontier faced by consumers given the prices that exist. But note that $\overline{B}$ is the only point on the CPF that is attainable given the resources at the society's disposal. Apparently, people feel they can buy $\overline{A}$ movies when in fact the society can produce only D movies. How is this to be explained?

We assumed that $\overline{B}$ was an equilibrium, that consumers chose it from all the points on line $\overline{ABC}$. Each consumer, of course, selected his own optimum given the prices he faced and not all consumers chose the proportions of steak and movies represented by $\overline{B}$. Point $\overline{B}$ represents the sum of their choices. Each single consumer thought he could change his consumption pattern by spending all his income on steak or all on movies or on any combination that lay on his budget constraint. And in fact he could. That is, any single consumer could choose from any point on his budget constraint. But apparently Figure 9.1 tells us that the same choice is not available to consumers as a whole. Why?

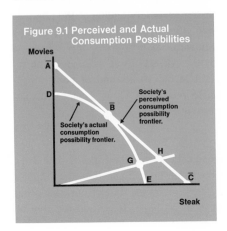

Figure 9.1 Perceived and Actual
Consumption Possibilities

Movies

$\overline{A}$

D

$\overline{B}$

Society's perceived consumption possibility frontier.

Society's actual consumption possibility frontier.

H

G

E

$\overline{C}$

Steak

Any single consumer can change his pattern of consumption without moving the equilibrium appreciably from point $\overline{B}$. Each consumer is such a small part of the total that his decision to switch between steak and movies does not alter appreciably the cost of one commodity in terms of the other. That is, the slope of the PPF does not change over the infinitesimal distance the production point moves when one consumer changes his spending pattern. The resources freed when he decreases steak consumption are sufficient to produce the extra movies he desires given that the social cost (the slope of the PPF) and the private cost (the slope of the CPF) are equal in Figure 9.1. If all consumers attempted to shift in the same direction, however, the change would be appreciable. If everyone tried to consume only steaks, the cost of steak would rise. If large quantities of resources were shifted out of movie production into steak production, their marginal productivities would change. More movies would have to be sacrificed for each additional unit of steak that society wished to consume. Film actresses may look good on the range, but they make poor cattlemen. And not all producers would make good butchers.

Thus each individual faces constant prices because he is an insignificant part of total demand. If he switches from an all-steak-no-movies budget allocation to an all-movies-no-steak position, prices will not change. The producers will not even be aware of his change because they will be busy satisfying the desires of their millions of other customers. Thus prices are constant to an individual only if everyone else continues to act in a constant fashion. If the other millions simultaneously shift their demands, major changes in the resource allocation will have to occur. Prices will change as a result. Any individual can buy as much steak as he wishes at the price posted at the supermarket. If everyone tried to double his purchase of steak, however, the price would rise.

The straight-line CPF represents, therefore, the choices available to an individual *given everyone else's behavior*. If they all try to buy more steak and fewer movies, prices will change and a new CPF will be observed. Thus an individual can buy more steak, fewer movies without changing prices but the society as a whole cannot. An individual CPF is not a fiction. And everyone faces one that is a straight line. But the sum of those CPFs is a fiction. The society is not free to move along such an aggregate consumption line. In the aggregate, prices are not constant. The PPF represents the aggregate consumption possibilities for the society. If the society attempts to move from $\overline{B}$ to H in Figure 9.1, it will find that steak prices increase and it will be able to afford only point G.

We have drawn Figure 9.1 so that social cost and private cost are equal at $\overline{B}$. This will be helpful in illustrating why *resources are only efficiently allocated when social cost equals private cost*. Let us look at $\overline{B}$. We have assumed that at this point the aggregate CPF is tangent to the PPF. Point $\overline{B}$ represents the aggregate consumption of steaks and movies and is the sum of the quantities that maximize individual utilities. It is the point of consumer equilibrium and can be thought of as corresponding to point B in the diagrams for consumer behavior presented in Chapter 8. That means that $\overline{B}$ is preferred to all other points on the fictional aggregate CPF. Individuals were free to select any point on their own CPFs and the net result of these free choices for society is discovered to be $\overline{B}$. For every other point except $\overline{B}$ on the PPF there is a corresponding point on the CPF that is preferable (that is, involves the consumption of more steak *and* more movies). Point H, for example, is better than point G. Thus if $\overline{B}$ is preferred to all points on line $\overline{ABC}$, it is certainly preferable to all other points on the PPF itself. (If $\overline{B}$ is preferred to H and H is preferred to G, $\overline{B}$ must be preferred to G. A similar argument could be established for every other point on the PPF.)

The important thing to note here is that *social cost equals private cost*. The cost to society of producing one more steak is the slope of the PPF. The cost to individuals of one more steak is the slope of the CPF. At point $\overline{B}$, these slopes are equal. As long as these costs are equal, each member of society will be unaffected by the decisions of every other member. One person's decision to buy more steaks and fewer movies neither takes steaks from his neighbor's mouth nor prevents his neighbor from watching movies.

In Figure 9.1, individuals, unaided by any planners, have arrived at a point of total consumption that they prefer to any other that uses resources of the same value. Thus point $\overline{B}$ represents *Pareto efficiency*. It is a point of allocative efficiency because at point $\overline{B}$ it is impossible to improve one person's welfare without harming another's. Each person receives the quantities of steak and movies he prefers to all other quantities available to him given his income and the prevailing prices. Of course, if we allow him to consume quantities in excess of those on his CPF, someone else will have to consume less.

But if social cost does not equal private cost, this result will not hold. It will be possible to improve one person's welfare without lowering that of anyone else. This is now shown.

Allocative Inefficiency

Let us assume that for some reason the social cost now differs from private cost for the two commodities. In Figure 9.2 we have drawn the production possibility frontier $D\overline{B}E$ as before, but now the consumption possibilities facing consumers are shown by line $\overline{LRN}$.

Let point $\overline{R}$ be a point of production equilibrium. How firms might attain such a solution with social costs different from private costs we discuss later. Here we are concerned only with consumers. Point $\overline{R}$ in Figure 9.2 satisfies the same two assumptions as point $\overline{B}$ in Figure 9.1; namely, that it is on the PPF and that consumers' incomes are large enough to buy it—it is on the aggregate CPF. To understand the nature of an equilibrium such as $\overline{R}$, let us look at an individual consumer again and discuss his equilibrium.

In Figure 9.3, we have drawn line $\overline{LRN}$ to represent an individual's CPF. We assume that point R is the point that maximizes his utility. At R, the value of a steak in terms of movies equals the steak's cost (to him) in terms of movies. Note that his ability to attain an equilibrium has nothing to do with social costs.

Private costs, the prices he faces, are all that matter to him in deciding how much of each commodity to buy. His ability to attain an equilibrium is independent of social costs. The importance of social costs lies in their implications for efficiency. Through point R in Figure 9.3 we have drawn dotted line URV whose slope equals the social cost of steak. It is possible for this individual to move from R to any point on URV without affecting anyone else's welfare. But the prices he must pay for commodities restrict him to the points on LRN. In this case, we have portrayed the situation as one in which the private cost of steak exceeds its social cost.

To demonstrate the inefficiency of the solution at R, we need only show that he prefers some other point on URV to point R. If he does in fact prefer some other point on URV to R, he should be allowed to reach that point since his movement toward it will affect no one else's welfare but his own. No one will be made worse off; he will be made better off. Thus if such a point exists, point R — and points like it for all other consumers — will represent an inefficient solution.

Does such a point exist? Very likely one does. Remember that at point R, the *value* of a steak equals its *cost* to the consumer. That is what equilibrium is all about. But we have assumed that at point R, the cost of a steak to the consumer (private cost) exceeds the cost to society. Thus the value of a steak exceeds its social cost. Steaks might be worth two movies each at point R but might cost the society only one movie each to produce. If we let the consumer trade movies for steaks from R at a one-to-one rate, he will do so until the relative value of steaks to movies falls to one. That is, if we let him choose from the points on URV, he will pick the one at which the relative value of steak equals the slope of URV. Since the relative value of each steak is two movies at point R, and the cost is one movie along URV, it is likely that the consumer will buy more steaks and give up movies in order to attain his new equilibrium along URV. Let W signify that point.*

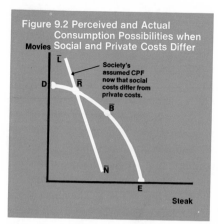

Figure 9.2 Perceived and Actual
Consumption Possibilities when
Social and Private Costs Differ

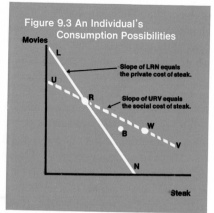

Figure 9.3 An Individual's
Consumption Possibilities

*Those students who read the appendix to Chapter 8 will realize that if an indifference curve is tangent to LRN at point R, there will be some higher indifference curve tangent to URV at some point to the right of R.

Since point W is preferable to R for this consumer, he is better off being allowed to trade at the social cost. No one else is made worse off, because society as a whole is still at point R on the PPF. This means that resources were not at point $\overline{R}$ in Figure 9.2. It is possible to let this consumer improve his welfare without affecting anyone else's satisfaction. Note that by charging him the true social cost he is able to move to points unattainable with his old CPF. Note also that some of his old points are unattainable at the new CPF. This reflects the fact that originally the rest of the society was not indifferent to his decision. Because the price of steak he faced was greater than its social cost, they wished him to consume a large amount of steak. To do this he would have to give up a great many movies. The resources freed from movie production would be more than adequate to produce the new steaks he demanded. In fact, there would be some left over for others to use to build up their own consumption.

We have seen from this behavior that things are not always ideal. When social cost and private cost differ, as at $\overline{R}$ in Figure 9.2, resources are allocated inefficiently; allowing one person to trade from his initial equilibrium at the social prices makes him better off without hurting anyone else. Clearly a solution that denies this possibility wastes satisfaction.

What if the consumer had originally faced a set of prices that reflected social cost? Then he already would have been able to select W, and things could not have been improved upon. The special opportunity to trade at the social price would have made him no better off than before. Thus there is no obvious waste of utility when private prices equal social prices.

When social and private costs are permitted to be the same, the true social choice is faced directly by individuals. Effectively, the price system allows them to choose from the points along the PPF. When social cost does not equal private cost, the individuals feel that they cannot afford some points that are in fact attainable. Prices then mislead them and they choose an inefficient solution. In Figure 9.3, W was attainable by an individual if we charged him the social cost of the commodities. No one was made worse off by permitting him to make this choice. Yet the fact that social and private prices were different had the effect of denying him this possibility. He felt that he could not afford W. Similarly, the whole society feels that it cannot afford its optimum.

Now assume that we let everyone trade from R at the social cost. Let $\overline{URV}$ in Figure 9.4 be the new social CPF, which is the sum of what everyone *thinks* he can consume. Private prices and social prices are equal now, but what is the result? *Everyone* will want more steak and fewer movies than exist at $\overline{R}$ and will want to consume at the collective point $\overline{W}$. And this is not possible!

Demand at the old prices led to an equilibrium at $\overline{R}$. But the quantities demanded at the new price ratio are now at $\overline{W}$. This means excess demand for steak and excess supply of movies. Something will have to give. The likely result will be a rise in the steak price (because of excess demand) and a fall in the movie price (because of excess supply). Production, in responding to the new prices, must move down the PPF from $\overline{R}$ toward $\overline{B}$. Zeroing in on a single consumer shows us why. If prices of steak begin to rise while those for movies fall, the consumer's decision rule tells him to buy less steak and more movies than at W (Figure 9.3). That is because his consumption possibility frontier has shifted back toward B.

We retrace the consumer's steps for the sake of clarity. First, he (and everyone else) faced prices not equal to social cost. He (and they) selected a maximum point (R). This was an inefficient solution. Then we let him (and them) trade at the social cost that existed at R in order to increase his utility. He selected point W, but when everyone else followed suit, the social costs changed. Facing these new social costs, he (and they) no longer preferred W but settled at point B.

The Best for All at Last

What is the result of this new permission (that is, to trade at the social cost) granted to the members of society? Nothing has happened to tastes since Chapter 8, and production possibilities are the same as ever. Therefore the solution will occur at a point of allocative efficiency where both production and consumption are in equilibrium, such as at $\overline{B}$ in Figure 9.5 below. Consumption is in equilibrium at $\overline{B}$ when the slope of the CPF is the same as the slope of the PPF at that point. This was assumed in the last chapter and it is still true. When price ratios are those that are reflected by $\overline{ABC}$ in Figure 9.5, a consumer can buy that combination of goods shown by his CPF (ABC in Figure 8.3). Each will be in equilibrium, maximizing his consumption at a point such as B. From point $\overline{B}$ in Figure 9.5 it will be impossible to improve the welfare of any single individual without lowering that of some other individual. Point $\overline{B}$ represents an efficient allocation of resources, because at that point private prices equal social prices. When private price equals social price it is impossible to make someone better off by allowing him to choose from a set of trades that affect no one else's utility. It is impossible because he already has chosen from those trades since the prices he faces are the social prices at which goods can be traded for each other.

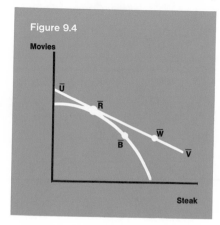

Figure 9.4

Movies

Steak

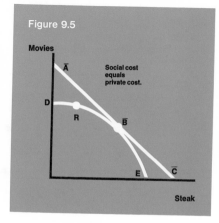

Figure 9.5

Movies

Social cost equals private cost.

Steak

Conclusion

If private prices differ from social prices, an efficient allocation of resources will not be attained. But if the price system is made to function properly, it can signal society's constraints to the individual and thereby allow him to select the best possible consumption point from among all those that are available. We have seen that when social prices equal private prices, individuals operating separately to maximize their utility will lead the society to a point of allocative efficiency. When this condition holds, it will be impossible to make anyone better off without hurting someone else. Whatever a consumer happens to prefer, he ends up paying the society for the resources he consumes. No other allocation system could be more efficient than this.

Questions

1.   Assume that one's before-tax wage rate (say, $4 per hour) accurately reflects the rate at which his labor can be transformed into goods of value through production processes. His after-tax wage rate ($3 per hour) is the rate he uses when deciding how many manhours to work. Does the income tax make the allocation of resources inefficient? Why or why not?
2.   Why is the sum of everyone's budget constraint an illusion?
3.   Why are resources efficiently allocated when private cost equals social cost?

Concepts Discussed

aggregate consumption possibility curve
efficiency

10 Public Goods

There is an exception to the rule that when social cost equals private cost, free consumer choice will lead to an efficient allocation of resources. And that exception will not be an exception if we redefine social and private costs as is done below. This exception is the case of *public goods*.

A public good is a good that can be consumed equally by all regardless of who pays for it. Because of this property, third parties can no longer be indifferent to the manner in which an individual disposes of his income. They clearly prefer him to buy more of the good that yields utility to them. Our rationale for allowing consumers to make their own consumption decisions was that consumers might thereby make themselves better off. If it is possible for consumers to make each other worse off, perhaps they should band together and call a truce. Perhaps they should amend the social compact. Each can give up his right to speed on the highway, for example. Or they can give up the rights to part of their income in order to pay for public goods such as defense, fire protection, or clean air—commodities that when bought by one can be enjoyed by all. If one wishes to have clean air and pays to clean it up, all get to enjoy the benefits.

If the existence of public goods is ignored, a market equilibrium may be reached at which men breathe smog, drink polluted water, and watch their cities decay. This will be true even when society makes an individual pay the cost of production of any commodities he buys. We have to establish new principles to deal with such problems. But first, we exhibit a hypothetical numerical example to indicate why the free market fails to allocate resources properly when public goods exist.

Clean Air—A Fable

Once upon a time the air above human settlements was so clear that smoke signals could be read from horizon to horizon. The smoke that rose in those days created problems other than air pollution. But then the material standard of living changed.

With the increased standard of living came vast increases in the consumption of energy that was freed from raw materials by burning. Each individual found it cheapest to burn his materials in a manner that produced smoke. Slowly, the atmosphere changed. The citizens all hated the dirty air but assumed that it was the price of progress, which was evident all around them.

In Zenith, the primary cause of air pollution was found to be gasoline buggies, the delight of the natives. Each of the one million motorists in Zenith was happy to pay $10 to clean up the air. But no way could be found to clean the air for $10 million.

One day, a bright young inventor discovered a device that would purify the exhaust of automobiles. He set up a business manufacturing the devices at a cost of $1 each, selling them for $5. Each motorist, he reasoned, would happily buy a device since each was willing to pay $10 for clean air. And the inventor would get a handsome reward for his ingenuity.

But no one bought the devices. Puzzled, he lowered the price to $4, $3, $2, and finally to $1. Still no sales. He wept. Why, he wondered, would no one pay $1 for a device that was worth $10.

While the inventor was weeping, his fairy godfather, a wily old economist, appeared. "Of course no one will buy your invention, silly," he said, "because clean air is a public good. You are asking each man to pay for his own device but the benefits will be received by all. Why, you haven't even bought a device for your own car!"

"I know," wept the inventor, "but that is because it would do no good if I alone bought a device. The air would still be dirty and I'd just be out a buck."

"Precisely," said the godfather, "and that is just what everyone else is thinking. Why should anyone buy a device when it is the actions of others that determine the cleanliness of the air? For $1, you are selling them something that improves the cleanliness of the air by only one one-millionth. They will only pay $.00001 for each millionth part of the smog you eliminate."

"But I could never make the device at that cost," the inventor moaned.

"Do not cry," said the godfather, "your invention is excellent. You can clean the air for $1 million, an act for which people will happily pay $10 million. Each device may be worth only $.00001 to each motorist, but that means that each device must be worth $10 to the one million motorists! All you must do is find a way for each man to give each of his neighbors $.00001 in return for buying the device. Then each man who buys a device will receive $9.99999! Your store will be flooded with orders!"

"But why don't they collect from their neighbors already if they can each make a profit doing so?" said the inventor who had studied economics many years ago.

"Because the costs of collection are too great to warrant the transfer of all those thousandths of cents. Why, the postage costs alone would be $59,999.94 for each $9.99999 collected!"

"How can I lower those costs?" asked the inventor.

"You can eliminate them," replied the godfather, "by having a law passed requiring each motorist to install a device on his car. Then all can have clean air for a cost of $1 each."

"You mean $5," grinned the inventor as he called his favorite lobbyist.

This fable portrays the problem of public goods. No one will buy them for himself, yet everyone wants his neighbors to buy them. In the smog case, the action of one individual had such a small influence on the level of smog that he failed to buy the device even though he would have been very happy to pay $1 for clear air. The problem is that his decision to spend the dollar does not give him clean air since the cleanliness of the air depends on the actions of others.

In such cases, the free market fails to allocate resources efficiently. An alternative means must be found if the air is to be kept clean and the nation safe. Laws and political actions are such means. Just as my neighbors and I have surrendered the right to murder each other because this surrender makes us all better off, so we can choose to surrender our rights to pollute the air. And just as we can make it illegal to burn one's house in a crowded city, we can also make it illegal to pay no taxes to support the national military forces. In these cases, laws have been used to replace the market because the market does not perform its allocative function efficiently. Our theorem that proved it was efficient to allow a consumer to maximize his own utility made the crucial assumption that *his behavior affected no one else.* If this assumption does not hold, then the theorem is invalid.

Charity—Individual Purchases with Interdependent Wants

Another way around the problem is to preach to the balking motorist. He could be taught a social ethic that stresses his responsibility to the needs of others. His wants could be shaped to include consideration of the wants of others. Jesus taught his followers to love their enemies, to give their food to the hungry and their cloaks to the shivering. He was in effect urging that wants be made interdependent. Mao teaches his followers to "be kind to our own" (but, alas, "ruthless to our enemies"). This is social awareness on a less inclusive basis. Suppose that preaching caused our motorist to increase his desire for pure air (for the sake of others as well as himself) from $10 to $100 per year. This would still be insufficient for him to act alone in purchasing an antismog device. Why? Because he would reason that a one-millionth reduction in air pollution, though worth more than before, is still only worth $.0001 to him—much less than the cost of the device.

Some powerful preaching would be required to transform the psychological basis of his pattern of demand from individual to interdependent wants to such a degree that he would buy a device on his own. He would have to be willing to pay one million dollars for pure air in order to pay one dollar (the cost of the device) for a mere one-millionth reduction in air pollution. Because the approach of charity continues to rely, as did the market itself, on individual acts of consumption, it is a relatively inefficient way of achieving allocative efficiency in the case of public goods. Though the principle of charity and the selflessness it espouses may do much to elevate the human spirit and preserve peace (itself a public good), it cannot be relied upon as a sole instrument of economic policy.

Planned Consumption—Interdependent Purchases Based on Individual Wants

A more efficient solution to the problem of air pollution in our example would be to let it become a political issue. Here the demand for clean air enters the "political marketplace." Suppose that a candidate for public office arises pledging to eliminate smog at a cost of $1 per motorist. All would consider this a bargain and elect him. As a political entrepreneur he would then be able to tax each motorist $1 and freely distribute antismog devices for all cars. Or he could require that each motorist purchase his own antismog device (for $1). Either way the solution is swifter and cheaper than relying upon each driver to collect $.00001 from every other motorist. It is surer than relying upon ethical teaching to raise every man's evaluation of pure air 100,000 times above its initial level. Yet it provides identical results.

It is easy to see why the demand for public goods moves from the private to the political marketplace. In the example we have chosen, the planned consumption of antismog devices raised the welfare of consumers without decreasing the welfare of anyone. In other cases, however, some might experience a loss of welfare. Those who love to watch orange sunsets through the smog, for example, might be inconvenienced by clear air. The political marketplace can attempt to provide a means of compensation in these cases. These considerations are dealt with later in this book. It is important to note that whereas charity relied upon the formation of collective wants, planned consumption in our example is based solely on individual wants. There is no coercion of consumer demand under such an allocation mechanism, merely an alternative way of expressing the existing demands. Neither is there the need for government intervention in the production or distribution of public goods, only in establishing a mechanism to guarantee their consumption.

The reason for market failure in the case of air pollution is made crystal clear by a device called a *payoff matrix*. Table 10.1 shows four different "payoffs" (outcomes) from alternative sets of conditions. The important thing to notice about this matrix is that one's behavior as an individual motorist has no substantial effect on the outcome. No matter what one does as a consumer, the result will be the same as if he had done the opposite. If one is a typical motorist, he will do the cheapest thing under the circumstances and refrain from buying an antismog device. If everyone behaves in the same manner, the smog will continue and we will all be worse off than if we all buy devices.

This payoff matrix clearly summarizes the alternatives the consumer faces. He can either buy a device or not. If he buys the device, outcomes 1 or 3 will result; that is, the air will be clean or dirty depending on what others do. And similarly,

Table 10.1 Payoff Matrix for Antismog Purchase		
	I Buy a Device	I Do Not Buy a Device
Everyone Else Buys a Device	(1) Air is clean	(2) Air is clean
No One Else Buys a Device	(3) Air is dirty	(4) Air is dirty

if he does not buy the device, the air will be clean or dirty depending on the behavior of others as shown by outcomes 2 and 4. Thus his purchase no longer affects his consumption. His utility rests in the hands of others. He can plead with them to take account of this or, in a democracy, he can enter the political arena and force them to recognize it. But he cannot buy in the open market the goods he wishes to consume.

This establishes one principle by which government intervention in a market economy can be justified: *market failure due to the existence of public goods.* Of course, the political arena itself may be a very inefficient way to make one's wishes felt. Due to this fact, we may sometimes choose to have private consumption decisions determine even the amount of public goods to be produced. But, in principle, if a society wishes to obtain the advantages of efficient resource allocation that the market provides, it should use the market for all consumption activities except the consumption of public goods. For these activities, provision must be made for society to vote for or against the central direction (planning) of consumption. Otherwise, as in the air pollution example, a private market solution is impossible unless some inexpensive way can be found for an individual to collect the payments from everyone else who benefits from his purchase.

The public goods problem results from the fact that these goods yield benefits to others beside the potential purchaser yet these benefits are not considered in his decision to buy. Since this is so, public goods are rarely subject to private ownership. We do not often see private armies, police forces, roads, and the like. The reason for this should now be clear.

We have seen that the problem of collection of payments is closely connected to that of public goods. But even if *collection* costs were zero, there would be additional *bargaining* costs or *coercion* costs associated with pure public goods. Think of the smog example. Even if it were possible to collect the $.00001 from everyone, it would be difficult to induce payments. Each individual may feel that the air will be cleaned up whether he pays or not and therefore he may refuse to pay his share. In any event, his small payment will have no significant effect on the cleanliness of the air that results. It is unlikely we could collect unless a law is passed that forces him to pay for the air he consumes.

Pure Public Goods

It is useful to distinguish between pure public goods, such as clean air, and other public goods. *A pure public good is consumed equally by all.* There are few examples of this, clean air and defense being among them. These goods may be *worth* different amounts to different individuals, but all consume the total *quantity* available. The fact that this quantity is worth different amounts to different people means that some people will be unhappy over the outcome. Those who place a low value on clean air will be angry over the taxes they pay for it. Those who value it highly will be angry that so little is provided. Both sides will furnish the observer with a great deal of political color and amusement. In extreme cases one side will accuse the other of being communists merely because they attempt to use the democratic machinery the way it was designed to be used. The other side will accuse the first of being a selfish inbred power structure that views any political action as a threat to their pocketbooks and privileges. Drama replaces fact on the front page of newspapers while fairy tales replace analysis on the editorial page. The intelligent observer may be both amused and frightened over such developments. Even he himself cannot tell how much of the public good *should be* produced. To do that requires the impossible — a comparison of different people's utility. Whose anger do we value most?

Efficient production of a pure public good requires political action. And political action often leads to a redistribution of utility even while attempting to increase the utility of all. There are two sides to any redistribution of utility. Therefore, public goods form one of the primary issues of political controversy in all countries.

Time Costs

There are various reasons why a public good will not be a pure public good. Some goods, radio and TV broadcasts, for example, would be pure public goods except for the time costs involved in enjoying them. Watching TV takes time and therefore has an opportunity cost. For this reason, individuals ration their own use of these goods and different individuals will consume different amounts. Air and defense, on the other hand, can be enjoyed while doing any other thing. The fact that individuals will choose to enjoy different amounts of TV may eliminate the political bargaining costs. We need simply attach a meter to each person's television set and charge him for the hours he watches. He can refuse to pay by turning off the set. There will be no anger in this case because we measure the value placed on TV by the number of hours it is watched.

But collection costs will still be very high, as backers of "Pay TV" have found. That is why the indirect finance of TV through advertisement or government subsidy is popular. Another reason for indirect finance is that the social cost of having one more person tune in a station is zero. Efficient resource allocation requires that we charge him that price. A way to get around this problem might be to charge a license fee for TV. Each set owner would pay an annual charge and then be free to watch as much as he wished. But here there would be bargaining over the nature of the programs to be offered, the size of the license fee, and so on.

Externalities in Consumption

Some goods have a large private as well as public element. The individual purchaser derives great utility from their consumption although the rest of society is also brought into the act in one way or another. The public element is then called an "externality" because it yields some utility (or disutility) to third persons who did not participate in the initial consumption decision. Wild parties in crowded neighborhoods are a case in point. Whether they wish to or not, sleepy neighbors late at night are required to participate in the music, stamping of feet, hilarity, and revelry of the party. In this case the externalities are negative for the neighbors. If the party giver does not find some way of tempering the enthusiasm or compensating the neighbors for the disutility (by inviting them in or promising to let them have an uninterrupted fling some evening), the neighbors are likely to call the police, who are hired by the community to tame down the kind of behavior that causes negative externalities for others.

Social rules reflect attempts to minimize the negative externalities of unbridled individualism. Take, for example, the case of rules to provide for orderly evacuation of buildings in case of fire. The following table, Table 10.2, is a payoff matrix associated with evacuation of a theater during a fire. If everyone walks, the building will be emptied efficiently. If one person runs, he may be the first out, saving his neck for sure. If everyone else runs, a violent and dangerous stampede occurs. Women and children still suffer and he, too, may be injured. If he stands back from the stampede, he will be the last one out and may be in great danger from the fire.

Thus there is a strong private incentive to run, but the public good requires that everyone walk. The negative externalities from one person's running are great. What may well happen is that society will make outcomes 2, 3, and 4 illegal by outlawing running. This may bother the individual person, because he clearly prefers 2 to 1 and 4 to 3. Indeed, he had planned to run in case of fire, and had spent the entire movie memorizing a plan for escape from the theater in the event of disaster. Unfortunately, everyone else may have had a similar plan. Therefore outcomes 2 and 3 would never have been observed. He would observe either 1 or 4. If it were made illegal to run, only 1 would be possible. At this point society is as well off as it can be, and he must temper his zeal to escape not only for the good of all, but for his own good as well. Otherwise the freedom to run, which he cherishes, may, in the possession of others, mean his own destruction.

In order to be certain of the concept of externalities in consumption, it would be helpful for the reader to construct matrices for other aspects of ev-

TABLE 10.2 Payoff Matrix for Running in Case of Fire		
	Person Walks	**Person Runs**
Everybody Else Walks	(1) The building is quietly and efficiently evacuated with the person among the crowd.	(2) The building is quietly and efficiently evacuated; the person is the first one out.
Everybody Else Runs	(3) A stampede occurs in which many are injured. The person is the last one out.	(4) A stampede occurs in which many are injured. The person leaves with the crowd (or is injured).

eryday behavior, such as litterbugging, speeding, standing up in a stadium, waiting for the stoplight, contributing to charity, or bombing public buildings. Each activity illustrates a positive or negative externality to society from individual behavior. Even apes regulate their behavior to take into consideration the externalities of others in their group. For example, they care for their infants and aged, follow a communal pattern of life, and discipline those who act in pure self-interest. It is not surprising that similar qualities in human behavior are called "good citizenship."

A recognition of the importance of interdependence in consumption takes us from pure economics into the area of moral philosophy. We have retraced the footsteps of Adam Smith to his starting point at the foundation of social ethics. As did he, we recognize that the price system affords no opportunity for us to obtain credit for consideration of the welfare of others in our own consumption decision. Charity is a simple expression of giving without expectation of reward. That is why for many it begins and ends at home. Buying a public good in the marketplace is like giving to charity, as we have seen. But when charity is insufficient to achieve efficient allocation of resources, government intervention in the consumption decision can be tried in an attempt to maximize private as well as social welfare.

Education—A Combined Public and Private Good
Education is an important case of a combined public and private good. One person's education or lack of it can influence the welfare of others. Though one is the prime beneficiary of his own education, what he has learned about economic productivity, social responsibility, and artistic creativity may profoundly affect the lives of others.

Education in the broadest sense is a continuous process. Those whose education is obtained in a subculture of poverty will know something different from those educated in a pampered middle-class environment. Education is partly a private good. As a consumption good, it permits one to improve his welfare directly by expanding his knowledge of men and nature and by sharpening the senses. Education can be the most direct and lasting source of expended consciousness. As an investment good, education also permits the individual to increase his productivity and hence his earning capacity. Individuals may be expected to set aside both time and income to be devoted to their own education, for both investment and consumption purposes.

But education is also a public good. It provides externalities to all of society from the training of each individual. A properly educated society will be likely to possess greater political, ethical, and social responsibility than a poorly educated one. Popular education is regarded as the basis of successful democracy. The externalities of uncensored popular education are often feared by oligarchs whose rule depends upon control of the masses. Those living in democracies, on the other hand, may be expected to derive disutility from mass ignorance or from censorship. If many members of society are unable because of poverty to provide themselves with sufficient formal training to overcome the socially detrimental influence of their environment, this lack of training will work against the welfare of the society as a whole.

How much will individuals pay for private education as a private good? This depends upon the extent to which it provides utility to the person who pays for it. Private demand for education depends upon income, taste, and the price of other goods and services.

But what will an individual pay for education as a public good, one vital to a stable and prosperous democracy? It is almost certain that the market alone will not provide society with sufficient popular education to maximize welfare given the resources at hand. The concept introduced in this chapter illustrates that even for such an important commodity as education, the market is not a reliable allocative mechanism. For this reason most countries have adopted a system of public education, planned by local and state boards of education (central planners responsive to the voters) and funded by tax revenues levied on society as a whole.

We shall see later on why education provides externalities to society not only in terms of its present contribution to welfare, but also in terms of future increases in future knowledge and productivity that it makes possible. Public education is an investment in the future of a country, just as private education is an investment in the future of an individual. Its content as well as its quantity may be regarded as public goods. The lack of education — as in the Russia of the tsars or Mexico at the turn of the century — can be socially disruptive. Of course, education in the hands of misguided leaders can produce negative as well as positive externalities.

Private education, by responding freely to individual demands, provides a safeguard from coercion by the state. Public education permits society to enjoy a greater amount of knowledge than the market would provide in view of its nature as a public good. A mixture of public and private education may therefore provide the highest possible level of social welfare.

The Public Sector
The public sector of the economy refers to those industries that are administered by the government. We have given many examples, such as police, fire protection, and highways. In principle, we want the public sector to consist of public goods and goods whose collection costs are more easily handled in a central fashion.

Consider highways. Highways are a public good in no greater sense than are railroads. Yet most countries produce highways publicly. This is because the collection costs would be very great if highways were privately owned. Toll booths at all intersections and junctions between roads of one company and those of another would require a great cost and inconvenience. So governments provide roads free and pay for them by taxing gasoline. This is a much cheaper device for collecting revenue than are tolls.

Thus the public sector includes many goods that do not satisfy the definition of public goods given above. It is not true that everyone can drive on the same road at the same time without affecting the ability of others to do the same. Thus a highway is not a pure public good. But for reasons of collection costs, it has been found cheaper to produce it publicly.

What about the post office? Is there any reason for mail delivery to be a part of the public sector? Historically, mail service was established by governments to handle their own internal correspondence. The royal couriers who carried this mail were made available to the public in an attempt to defray costs. Governments still do not pay postage on the mail they send. Collection costs are no lower just because mail delivery is publicly owned; there is nothing that makes mail service a public good in principle. It might just as well be a privately owned utility, as is the telephone or the telegraph. In fact, if there are political or organizational problems that make a publicly administered corporation such as the post office inefficient, we might prefer it to be privately owned.

Many public goods have their externalities felt at the local level only. Many people define a good neighbor as one who "keeps up" his property. Certain communities explicitly recognize that one man's behavior affects the value of his neighbor's property as well as the utility he can derive from that property. They do this by restricting the behavior of their citizens in many ways that concern property. Such "zoning" laws modify the social contract so that it recognizes externalities associated with property ownership. It is interesting to note that it is often those people who espouse "free-market" principles in their fight against modifications of the social compact on the national level who live in such "zoned" communities. Perhaps we should conclude that political opinions are more often founded on practical grounds than on those of abstract principles.

Questions
1. Why does the free market not provide an appropriate avenue for the expression of consumer wants in the case of public goods?
2. Construct a payout matrix for the decision to use violence for political ends. To stand up at football games. To steal (if theft were legal).
3. What are the risks associated with relying on charity to provide public goods? On the market? On the political system?

Concepts Discussed
public goods   consumption externalities
payoff matrix

11 Advertising and the Consumption Decision

The Janus Faces of Advertising

Advertising is one of the most glamorous participants in the marketplace. It teases us for attention. It makes us feel wanted. It invites us to a charade in which every taste is awakened and every desire seems capable of fulfillment. Is advertising a hero, a villain, or a character with a tragic flaw in the drama of consumer decision? What would the world be like without it? With no billboards, newspaper, radio, or television ads, no street hawkers, subway posters, or sky-writing, the countryside would be greener, the air clearer, and the city drabber. But along with the razzle-dazzle, something substantial would be missing—consumer information. Housewives would miss the news about sales, theatergoers the details about the latest plays, travelers the facts about food and lodging. Other things besides information would also be affected—those commodities that are supplied by advertising. There would be no more free maps of cities in motel rooms, fewer TV shows, fewer and more expensive newspapers, magazines, and almanacs. This is one side of the question: the fact that advertising provides services to the consumer that he otherwise would have to purchase directly in the marketplace.

But what if all sellers went to extremes and put up posters, billboards, banners, and loudspeakers hawking their wares? What if airplanes flew overhead spilling handbills like snow upon the housetops, announcing a thousand different products? Advertising would then become a nuisance, blighting the landscape and littering the city. Its information would become impossible to assimilate, and the additional services more than the public could ever digest. Furthermore, all of those billboards, airplanes, public address systems, and the people employed to provide them use up scarce resources in the economy. Fewer resources would remain to produce the products that are being advertised. Obviously, we must settle somewhere between the extremes of no advertising and a surfeit of it.

Will the market do a proper job in allocating resources toward advertising? What is the optimal amount of advertising? We know no answers to these questions. We can look at the principles that should be used to determine the answers, but it is difficult to use these principles because they involve concepts that are impossible to measure. Accordingly, even at the end of this chapter we will have given the reader no effective way to measure the various impacts of

133

advertising. We will have discussed the issues, but the answers to our questions will remain matters of judgment rather than of precise scientific measurement.

Uncertainty and Information

Is there an ideal amount of information to supply a consumer to aid him in decision making? How much information would he choose to receive if the choice were his?

In principle, the decision to buy information can be handled in the same manner as the purchase of other commodities, as discussed in Chapter 8. But it does have aspects that differentiate it from the rest of the consumer's decisions. Most important of these aspects is uncertainty. In Chapter 8, we assumed that the consumer knew everything about all the products available. In fact, consumers are very uncertain about the true characteristics of most products they purchase. In the absence of information, they could attain a utility maximum only by chance. Thus the more information they receive, the more likely they are to buy a bundle of commodities that they prefer to all others.

More information is preferred to less information since the utility that is obtained from a given income is likely to increase when the amount of information available increases. Note that this statement differs from the kind of statements we have made previously. It differs by the words "is likely to." We cannot say for sure that more information will lead to a consumer's changing his mind and buying a bundle of goods he prefers to the one he would have bought without the information. It is possible, after all, that he stumbles on the optimal bundle with no information at all. But it is unlikely.

The use of the word "likely" results from the nature of uncertainty. Economists analyze decision making under uncertainty by using a tool of mathematical statistics, *probability theory*. We can do little in this book with probability theory except to give an idea of how it affects decision making. We do this with an example below. But first we must complete our presentation of the framework in which information can be analyzed. Because the information is not guaranteed to improve utility, we can only speak of what is *likely* to happen. We can say that a consumer will *probably* buy a superior bundle of goods once he acquires information, but we cannot be sure.

If information is likely to increase utility, why do we not use all the information we can get? The answer lies in the cost of information. Acquiring information takes valuable time. It may also take minimal amounts of money, but the major cost lies in the time it takes to examine the alternative commodities, to consult friends and experts, or to read the product's specifications in a library. To illustrate the interaction of information costs and consumer decision making, we present an example.

Purchasing an Auto

A young executive has decided to purchase a new car and he intends to buy the quality of car that usually costs about $3,000. From knowledge acquired elsewhere—random magazine reading, discussion with friends, and the like—he knows of five brands that appear to satisfy his needs. He must decide which of these to buy, and to do so he needs further information. How much information should he acquire?

Let us assume that, as readers, we know the true facts although the buyer does not. The facts are that all five cars cost exactly $3,000 but that they will satisfy his needs differently. In fact, we can rank the five cars according to the money value of the satisfaction they will yield him. Car Alpha is really best for him. It would yield him $3,500 worth of satisfaction. Car Beta is next. It will yield $3,400 in satisfaction. Gamma and Delta follow with $3,300 and $3,000, respectively, while Zeta is a poor last and is worth only $1,800 to him. We assume that he knows these numbers, but that he does not know which car is which. That is, he knows that there is a $1,800 lemon on the market, but he cannot remember which it is. In the absence of any information, his choice will be made randomly; he will pick a car by going "eenie, meanie, miney, moe." Since each car is equally likely to be picked, each car has one-fifth of a chance of being selected. How happy is he likely to be if he follows this process?

He may, of course, pick Alpha. But he is only likely to do that one-fifth of the time. Probability theory tells us that to find out how happy he is likely to be, we must find out how happy he will be on average. If he has an equal probability of selecting each car, we need only find the average of their values to find the money value he can be expected to receive from this choice. That is, if he made this same choice many, many times, how satisfied would he be on average? Since he would select each of the five cars one-fifth of the time, their average value will denote the value he can expect to receive from making the choice in this manner. The average value of the above cars is $3,000.

To decide whether or not to acquire information, he must know its cost and the amount it will increase the satisfaction he can expect to receive from the cars he buys. The first step in acquiring information that he considers is to go to the library and read *Consumer Reports*. This will take him two hours and since his wage is $10 an hour, he calculates that this information will cost him $20 worth of time. He also figures that this step alone will help him isolate Zeta from the pack.

He goes to the library and reads about the cars. He finds that Zeta, despite its exotic appearance, has many problems: It is uncomfortable, needs frequent tuning, tips over on fast corners, and its bumpers fall off during rapid braking. He crosses Zeta off his list. The rest of the information he acquires about comfort, styling, and performance does not allow him to distinguish between the other four, however, since some cars are better at one aspect while others excel elsewhere. Now he must choose between Alpha, Beta, Gamma, and Delta. The average value he can expect to receive from these cars is $3,300. Note that by spending $20 on information, he has eliminated the possibility of buying Zeta and this has improved the average value of the cars from which he will choose by $300. Such information is a bargain. Remember that there is no guarantee that this makes him better off. Perhaps initially he would have picked the Alpha by chance, but now he may select the Delta. But if many people do this, on average they will be made better off. Sales of Zeta will fall to zero.

The next step the buyer considers in acquiring information is to visit the showrooms, drive the remaining four cars, and talk to the salesmen. This will take five hours and therefore costs the buyer $50. But the buyer feels that this will be worth the trip because there are various quirks to cars that can be discovered only by sitting in them. He visits the showrooms. He finds that when he enters the Delta, he skins his knee. Knowing his propensity for injury, this information is enough to allow him to eliminate the Delta and many skinned knees from his future. On this visit, he is particularly annoyed by the tasteless interior of the Gamma and decides to restrict his choice to the Alpha and Beta. This we know gives him an expected value of $3,450. Thus the decision to spend five hours ($50) looking at the cars has raised the expected value of the car he will buy by an additional $50.

The next step involves ten hours of study of some data on resale value and engineering specifications that will enable him to select the best car from the remaining two. But since ten hours is worth $100 and will only increase the value of the car he buys by $50, he decides to seek out no further information. He flips a coin to decide between Alpha and Beta.

This illustration gives us an idea of the role of information in reducing uncertainty and therefore allowing consumers to derive greater amounts of utility from their given expenditures. It shows that information, like any other commodity, is something that is purchased when its value exceeds its cost. It also shows information as a special kind of commodity, a commodity that increases the utility one can expect to derive from his income by affecting his choice. In our example, there was an optimal amount of information to be used when buying a car. By allowing the consumer to decide whether or not to buy it, the optimum was obtained.

The sellers of cars, as well as other products, provide information to consumers in the form of advertising. In our example above, one of the reasons the prospective buyer could limit his choice to five cars at the outset was that the advertising he had observed gave him a good idea of the size and nature of the cars available. If we were to judge the value of this advertising from a social viewpoint, we would have to ask: Is it worth the cost? How much higher are car prices because of advertising? Are consumers happier paying the higher prices with the information or would they be happier paying lower prices without it? Answers to such questions are difficult to obtain but, in principle, answers exist.

For other issues concerning advertising, even the principles are not so clear.

Influences of Advertising on Demand

Consumer demand was shown in earlier chapters to depend upon the income, tastes, and relative prices faced by individuals. Tastes were assumed to be given. In considering the influence of advertising on demand, we must analyze this assumption. One of the debates surrounding the value of advertising concerns its influence on tastes. Does advertising passively serve the tastes of consumers and provide information that allows them to satisfy their desires? Or does it actively work to alter tastes? Advertising is traditionally analyzed in terms of two kinds of influences: *information* and *inducement*. We consider these two effects separately, remembering that advertising has a dual personality as both the servant and master of tastes. Indeed, it is difficult to make a psychological distinction between the two influences. In fact, we argue later that advertising really should be broken into categories of information and misinformation. But if information and inducement could be separated, the separated effects would appear as follows in our framework of consumer demand.

Figure 11.1 demonstrates the dilemma of Mr. Horatio A. Economicus. It will be recalled that at our last meeting, Mr. E. had made a decision to consume that combination of steak and movies represented by point *B* on his consumption possibility frontier. He was happiest at that point where

$$\frac{MU_{movies}}{P_{movies}} = \frac{MU_{steak}}{P_{steak}}$$

Advertising as Information

How might advertising increase his welfare by doing nothing more than providing information? Suppose that Mr. E. knew nothing about the availability of movies. Steak he knew about, but movies were something else again. He could begin by consuming at *C* through insufficient knowledge. We might think of his desire for movies as latent—something that can be activated only when he becomes aware that the local music hall has movie shows. One day a poster is plastered up on the side of his neighbor's barn. It says, "Movies are in town." His consumption position, initially at point *C* (since he knew nothing about the availability of movies), now moves toward *B*. The ratio of the marginal utility of movies to their price at *C* is greater than that of steak. Advertising makes him

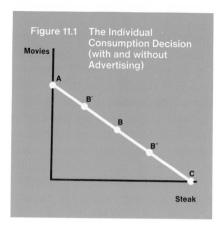

Figure 11.1   The Individual Consumption Decision (with and without Advertising)

aware of consumption possibilities that actually existed before but that he did not know about. Clearly advertising increases Mr. E.'s utility by permitting him to exercise his given taste for movies in moving from *C* to *B*. With the cost of this advertising negligible, we have not shifted his budget constraint, since the price of movies is assumed to have remained constant.

Advertising as Inducement

But advertising can also induce him to *change his tastes*. This can be shown on the same diagram. Suppose that Mr. E. is no longer ignorant of the local action and knows all about the availability of steak and movies. With his initial tastes unchanged, he remains at *B*. This point gives him the greatest possible satisfaction, since

$$\frac{MU_{movies}}{P_{movies}} = \frac{MU_{steak}}{P_{steak}}$$

The sellers of movies wish to fill the theater, however, and they go on advertising. They wish to alter his marginal utility from movies. They put up a new poster on the neighbor's barn that says, "Movies are better than ever." This information actually may be true. If so, movies become a better product than they were before, and Mr. E. may go more often even with his same tastes. But if the same old movies are being shown, he will eventually realize this and give them the same old response, regardless of the new advertising—unless the advertising is successful in *changing his tastes*.

Suppose that the advertisement begins to work on his values. Mulling over its message while plowing the Back Forty, Mr. E. begins to think more and more about movies. The strictures of his grandmother grow less compelling as he passes the picture of Mae West each time he cuts a furrow. His marginal utility of movies will begin to rise (while the marginal utility of steak stays put). If the prices of steak and movies remain the same, he will now find point *B* to be a combination of the two that no longer offers the highest possible satisfaction along *AC*. He will shift from *B* toward *B'* because of the influence of advertising on his tastes.

Since advertising does nothing about Mr. E.'s income, his consumption possibilities remain unchanged. He must give up some steak in order to satisfy his increased taste for movies. Suppose that meat producers now band together to promote the consumption of beef. A new poster is slapped up on the barn wall: "Eat beef." It features the picture of a steer with a compelling smile. Mr. E. is now torn between alternating pressures to shift his tastes in the direction of movies or steak. If the steer wins out over Mae West, Mr. E. may end up consuming at a point such as *B"*. The marginal utility of steak may have risen relative to its price even more than that of movies. He will no longer be in equilibrium at *B* or *B'*. The new ratios will be equal at *B"* and his welfare will be maximized at this new combination of steak and movies as a result of the influence of advertising on his tastes. Note that advertising as an information service in this example did nothing to change his consumption possibilities except make their existence known to him. But as an inducer, it worked on him psychologically to change his preferences among existing consumption possibilities.

Did advertising by inducement make our friend "better off"? The answer to this lies in the realm of psychology rather than economics. When tastes change, our standard for measuring value changes and we can reach no conclusion. Remember that it is utility that we are trying to measure. But utility, we have argued, can never be measured in an absolute sense. Because of this, economists have invented measures of relative value. Steaks are measured in terms of how many movies they are worth. But if the absolute satisfaction yielded by all goods changes, our relative measures will not be able to tell us this. We will still only be able to talk about how many movies a steak is worth and not about how much utility steaks and movies yield. Thus we can say nothing about the effect of a change in tastes on satisfaction. Perhaps we are happier than before, perhaps not. In these areas, we must make judgments about happiness independent of the measures of relative value that are so useful elsewhere.

Advertising as a Public Good

Whether or not the information and inducement effects of advertising made Mr. E. "better off," the posters were not costless. Mr. E. contributed nothing originally to their cost. He received the services that they provided gratis. Since the consumption of the services of advertising was shared by him and other onlookers while someone else paid for the posters, advertising services appeared to have the properties of a public good and should be provided to all at a zero cost since the cost of an extra viewer is zero. But the poster has some cost. Who pays for it? Indirectly, the consumer of steak and movies does, through a somewhat higher price for the commodity (though the producer may also share in the cost through a reduction in profits). The cost of advertising when passed on in the price of a commodity is akin to a tax on the consumer for the service of both information and inducement. But because advertising also provides free externalities to others, the consumer is paying for others' utility as well. Advertising is, in part, a public good. If others enjoy the benefits of advertising, the consumer who pays for it is doing them a service. If they are inconvenienced by the externalities of advertising, he is contributing to their disadvantage. For these and other reasons, advertising is frequently made subject to public control through legislation. To understand why in more detail we examine its dual properties of information and inducement in a few practical examples.

Cases Where Information and Inducement Are Combined

When does information become inducement? Can tastes really be changed? Who is to say that what one man calls a change in tastes may not be called the awakening or refinement of latent tastes by another? If consumers are indeed sovereign, cannot they be permitted to pay to have their tastes refined? After all, this is what finishing schools are all about.

Those who say that advertising can shape the tastes of individuals like putty have a low opinion of the skill of the consumer relative to the craft of advertising men. And those who say that advertising can never bend tastes are arguing for the futility of information. Social history suggests that the answer lies somewhere in between, so that preference patterns and advertising campaigns are engaged in a complex struggle to maximize the interests of both buyers and sellers. If advertising is a game that produces externalities, it must be played according to social rules. These have to do with the kind of information and inducement that are purveyed relative to the values that society has expressed in the political process.

First there is the possibility of altering preferences by providing *misinformation* about a product. "Steak will prevent cancer." This is clearly an abuse of the market and should be prevented. But should this be labeled inducement merely because it is evil? Misinformation appears to be a more appropriate label. The Pure Food and Drugs Act in the United States was a pioneer statute protecting the consumer from such devices and requiring ingredients to be published on the wrappers of all medicines and brand foods sold in interstate commerce. For many commodities the "truth" is still sufficiently ambiguous that misinformation can be passed on to consumers. Ultimately, consumers can be expected to band together and alter the social compact in such a way as to make misinformation illegal.

Abstracting from the clear evil of misinformation, are there other forms of inducement? Can true information be used to compel someone to buy a product that he does not want? This is hard to imagine. How can the truth induce one voluntarily to lower his utility? The real problem is therefore whether undesired wants can be induced or created. Two possibilities exist in this respect: (1) Latent real wants can be uncovered through advertising; and (2) wants can be changed by advertising so that consumers will buy goods they really do not want.

Packaging Wants

No one should object to the first possibility. It refers to the increasing sophistication of consumers. It is the second possibility that the critics of advertising speak of. This last possibility represents brainwashing. Take, for example, the technique that we will call "packaging wants." This is a tack that is used frequently to induce a person to purchase something that otherwise he would not select. The wants for one commodity are linked to those of another in order to sell the latter. One can be induced to want a commodity more if an advertiser can attribute characteristics to the product that satisfy other wants the individual may have. Teenagers, for example, could be induced to buy cigarettes if tobacco companies could successfully link cigarettes with sophistication. Advertisements for clothes, motorcycles, beer, or almost anything else that college students might buy are really advertisements for popularity. The merchants are selling clothes, but the consumer is trying to buy popularity. Attempts such as these to "package" wants may or may not be successful in marketing clothes or motor-bikes. Whether or not they succeed, they receive a great deal of fire from critics. Is packaging of wants "good" or "bad"?

Since this is an objective textbook rather than a polemical treatise on social behavior, we will have to set a rule that conforms to our initial insistence on true versus false information in advertising. We will judge such advertisements as misleading only when they fail to deliver the goods that they purport to sell. If they link wants and all the wants are actually satisfied, then the consumer gets what he pays for and is satisfied. He buys clothes to satisfy the need for both warmth and popularity. If his clothes make him warm and popular, he is satis-fied. (The externalities of such advertising on third persons are neglected here. Some who seek popularity but are unable to buy the new clothes might feel worse off. Others who scorn the advertisements might feel better off now that society's norms are clearly specified and they have a model to feel superior to and to reject by wearing nonconventional clothes. In one case the externalities are negative and in the other positive.)

Let us take a different example. Psychologists commonly hypothesize that males get psychological satisfaction from automobiles; that is, not physical plea-sure but satisfaction of basic emotional needs. Car advertisements play on this factor. Pretty women appear in the advertisements to associate the machine in the buyer's mind with other pleasures. Animals are used as the names of cars or in advertisements to show the buyer how he will feel when driving. One adver-tisement used to show a man in an oil field who has just discovered oil; he dashes to his car and speeds off recklessly. A nice clear shot of the uncapped oil well is then shown. The advertisement was apparently playing on a psycholog-ical want. Is this bad? We answer that by asking whether or not the car satisfies that want as well as providing transportation. In other words, does it deliver the goods?

An individual enjoys fast driving. A psychologist explains to him that the reason he enjoys it is because it satisfies certain inner urges. What does he re-spond? Does he say, "O.K. Now that I understand the situation I will go and buy a Volkswagen"? Or does he say, "Who cares why it's fun. It is"? To tell him that the reason he likes strong, fast cars is because men are biologically prowling hunters, and that he can feel like a man only if he periodically covers lots of territory, is to tell him why he should buy a prowling car. It will satisfy his instinctive needs. It does not say that advertisers are misleading when they sell cars as prowling machines rather than as transportation. For many persons, prowling cars deliver the goods. Clever advertisers are able to use the fact that automobiles satisfy not only transportation needs but other needs as well. They can package the wants without providing any misinformation or deluding the consumer. We would maintain that this is not bad.

How about a counterexample? Remember a certain well-known detergent advertisement that won a *Mad Comics* award? A knight on a white horse comes pounding down the road holding a huge long lance. A background of rhythm is heard and a masculine chorus sings, "Stronger than dirt!" The knight gallops up to the camera pointing his lance, the rhythm gets louder, sun glints from his armor in flashes on the screen, and cymbals crash as he hurtles past the camera. Any lady who bought this detergent expecting that fellow to jump out of the box was disappointed. In her case, the goods were not delivered.

Yet while this advertisement was being run on TV, other soaps had to counter its effect. One detergent made your washing machine ten feet tall; in the advertisement, a lady watches in astonishment as her machine shoots toward the ceiling. Another detergent's advertisement showed a fist popping out of the machine after the soap had been poured in. These advertisements did not deliver the goods that their Freudian images promised — or else there is something about wash-day miracles that we do not understand. Such advertising cannot be said to convey true information about the product. That it plays successfully on housewives' drives is clear. A product that does not counterattack when one of its competitors offers a knight on a white horse rarely lasts long in the soap market. Many soaps and detergents are identical in quality. What distinguishes them is the images created in their advertising campaigns, including their success in playing on the desires of bored housewives stuck at home with the washing.

Another example of packaging wants without delivering comes from cigarette advertising. A manufacturer of a brand of filter cigarettes has apparently decided that the most underdeveloped segment of its market is masculine, possibly due to the feminine image filters initially acquired. Thus the manufacturer attempts to link its filter brand to masculinity (men may be afraid of feminine images but women have no fear of masculine articles). The campaign apparently has been a success although women may still comprise a major segment of this cigarette's market. On the surface, this brand of cigarettes does not appear to deliver masculinity. No paste-on tattoo is included in every carton in an attempt to deliver the goods. Of course, if a buyer really feels more masculine as a result of the purchase of this particular brand of cigarettes, then the goods have been delivered for him. Masculinity, after all, may be a mental state. The cigarette brand delivers the confidence, and the individual the sex appeal, but who cares about that?

The Question of Information

So even in the case of packaged wants, we can distinguish informative from misinformative advertising. We should be against misinformation, not inducement. One clearly leads to lower utility levels whereas we are unsure about the other. Does advertising deliver the goods? Some persuasive advertising clearly does so and can be regarded as information. Some does not and is misinformation. When lies enter the market they are harmful, since they mislead the consumer into decisions that prevent him from maximizing his utility in consumption. Income is scarce, consumption possibilities are limited, and false information that induces the consumer to buy one good reduces the amount of other goods that he can purchase. Lies about the physical characteristics of products, such as were legislated against in the Pure Food and Drugs Act, are no better or worse than lies about products' emotional characteristics. Physical lies are easier to prevent, however.

If we agree that information is good and misinformation is bad, how might we rank advertising in terms of its informational content? Many advertisements are informational and contain a minimum of packaging or emotional content. Attempts to sell machinery and equipment in business magazines offer little chance to use emotional appeals.

Advertisements for consumer goods, on the other hand, often tell the consumer little more than the name of a particular brand. We have heard very often that a brand "tastes good, like a cigarette should." Does this statement provide any real information about the cigarette, other than its name? Who is fooled by it? Why then does the manufacturer buy the advertisement? The company must feel that it conveys information that will increase the sale of its product or it would not purchase the jingle. The advertisement may in fact be conveying information, though it is nothing more than the fixing of a brand name in the mind of the listener.

And this brings us to the last important criticism of advertising. Apparently, many consumers are indifferent between particular brand names of certain products. Their decision to buy is often determined not by qualities of the product but by familiarity, package attractiveness, and so on. For these people advertising up to the brink of nausea may be the telling blow. Rather than flip a coin, a consumer in line at a counter may ask for a particular brand of cigarette because the transistor in line behind him is blaring out the jingle, or it may have been the last thing he heard before leaving his house. As he is really indifferent between the two or more brands available, we might say that it does not matter which brand he chooses, and therefore the advertising is inoffensive. But the advertising is not free. The cigarettes would be cheaper if there were no advertising. If he really is indifferent, would he not prefer cheaper cigarettes?

Information such as the conveying of a brand name uses up scarce resources simply to create an image. Can "image advertisements" really be useful? The American Telephone and Telegraph Company advertises, yet it is a monopoly in most areas of the United States. Why should a company with no competition advertise? American Telephone and Telegraph feels that a better image will help it to recruit bright young scientists and to ward off public criticism when phone service fails to satisfy consumers or when profits seem excessive.

Though much is done by advertising to create images in a market economy, far less is done to convey factual information about the actual cost of consumer goods. We know a great deal about the qualities of products but very little about their costs. Public and private agencies, such as *Consumer's Union*, exist to provide the American consumer with information, some of which is associated with brand names. But few advertisements tell one how much extra expense will be incurred by putting a larger engine in a given automobile model. What will it do to gasoline costs, insurance costs, characteristics of handling, acceleration; air pollution, and so on? In this specific case, some of the information is obtainable not from advertising but from hot-rod magazines. But since most products do not satisfy mass urges the way powerful engines in fast cars do, there are no magazines that provide such information about their costs. What are the costs of renting an apartment as opposed to buying a house? This is the largest budget decision most people face, yet the facts have never been appropriately established.

Recent proposals for consumer legislation focus not on the suppression of advertising so much as on making information about products more readily available to the public and at lower cost. For example, it might be required that a price be stamped on an article in terms of the cents per ounce. That would make comparisons between "Regular" and "Large Economy Size" packages easier to accomplish in the grocery store without a sliderule. Recently the "truth-in-lending" bill passed Congress. It forces lenders to calculate the interest rate on all loans and disclose it to the borrower. Some agencies that had advertised the "consolidation of debts," which often meant paying a higher overall rate of interest than borrowers had previously been paying on their separate accounts, will be less able to induce young couples into overborrowing, which is one of the single most important causes of bankruptcy in the United States today.

Advertising Costs and Benefits

Much has been said about the high cost of advertising in countries with highly developed market economies. The actual costs, however, must be measured not in terms of total cash outlays for advertising but in terms of the number of scarce resources that are used up in the process. The *resource cost* of advertising is only a fraction of its cost to buyers, because of what economists term *value added*. Value added in an industry is the cost of the labor, capital, and land employed in that industry alone. In the case of an advertising agency, most of its sales' proceeds go toward the purchase of services that accompany the advertising, such as space in magazines and newspapers, TV and radio time, and the like. These purchases permit other services to be provided for the public at a lower price than if they were required to buy them in the market. We are provided with free TV and cheap newspapers whose costs are covered by advertising. This is not a giveaway, however, since the consumers of the product are bearing the costs of these services in the form of higher prices (through the "tax" of advertising). But we should not consider these services as part of the social cost of advertising. Rather, we should subtract their value to us from the cost of advertising paid by firms to get a measure of the true social cost of advertising. Of course, the services that advertisers provide are demanded only indirectly by the public. The advertiser himself decides directly what externalities he will provide in the way of TV entertainment or in the choice of the newspaper where he places his advertisements (perhaps because its editorial position agrees with his own). Individuals, we have seen, would prefer to have this money to allocate for themselves rather than receiving it in the form of cheap magazines or newspapers.

Whether or not advertising is worth its cost, we cannot say. Economics is just beginning to assimilate problems that concern the costs of decision making; and the acquisition of valid information is clearly a decision-making cost. It may be that we would be happier if more or fewer resources were devoted to advertising. *We do not yet know how to measure whether this is true or not.* What seems to be a simple problem is really at the frontier of economic science.

We might be able to dream up better ways to dispense information. We could think of much additional information that consumers would like to have before making decisions, information that is unavailable today. In this sense, the advertising industry is probably fairly inefficient from a social viewpoint. More information could be conveyed by using fewer resources. This does not say that advertising today is a bad bargain, but only that it could be a better one.

We have argued that the resource cost (value added) of advertising is much less than the value of the total amount of money spent on advertising. Yet this resource cost is not insignificant in a market economy. And it represents an allocation of resources that need not guarantee efficiency to the consumer, since much advertising is a public good and provides *both* negative and positive externalities to third persons. Individuals are not given the chance to buy more or less advertising without buying more or less of some other commodity, such as newspapers or TV. As this opportunity is missing, we cannot determine whether people, if given the chance, would buy more or less advertising. And how would they know when they needed to buy information? Who would inform them?

Public goods such as TV programs (which all can now view freely regardless of who pays) present a social problem. The alternatives to the present system of commercial TV are subscription or state-supported programming. In either case there is no guarantee of consumer sovereignty. Those who would decide on programming may or may not be better judges of public taste than advertisers who now make the decisions. If there is no easy way to reconcile these problems, it is because in advertising, as in education, the market alone cannot guarantee allocative efficiency. And economists have not yet agreed on how to determine whether more or less advertising is needed. We can only agree that more informative advertising is a good thing.

Questions

1. How could you distinguish informative from persuasive advertising? Can you think of any borderline examples?
2. If teenagers value the alternative uses of their time at a low rate, why might we expect them to acquire a great deal more information than adults do when buying a product?
3. Should advertising be regulated? What regulations would you create? Are you sure that they increase utility?

Concepts Discussed

information costs
information versus inducement

12 Consumer Sovereignty

Sovereignty is a complex political concept. Basically, sovereignty means supreme power. Supreme power entails the right to control every facet of the lives of society's members, to pass laws to regulate behavior or to rule by caprice.

Power can be distributed in many ways among the different members of a society. The purest examples of power distributions are pure dictatorship, in which one man wields all power, or pure democracy, in which power is equally distributed among all the people and majority rule is observed. These are limiting cases that are never observed in fact. In fact, it is impossible for one man to oversee a society of any complexity. A dictator must either delegate some power to subordinates or abdicate the right to control certain aspects of the lives of the people.

On the other hand, the right to vote is rarely accorded to all; the young, the mentally infirm, women, or members of particular races are the groups most often denied this right. But even the right to vote is not a guarantee of an egalitarian distribution of political power. The existence of political parties, machines, pressure groups, and lobbyists all affect the ability of an individual to express his desires in political action. Thus voting is not the only way to exercise one's political powers.

In fact, the political power, and therefore sovereignty, of an individual is a complex function of his right to vote and express himself publicly, his wealth, his profession, how articulate he is, and the political party to which he belongs. If that party is sensitive to ideas from below, he will have more power than in a party controlled by a machine. Indeed, the ability of the political machinery to enact the will of the sovereign people is often in question. In economics, we would call this the question of the efficiency of the political apparatus. Political sovereignty need be no more equally distributed than income, but given any distribution, the ability of the sovereign to have his will carried out depends on the efficiency of the political system.

This is not a text in political science. Therefore, we will spend little time on problems of political efficiency. But it is important that we be aware of the concept's existence. The willingness of a consumer to abdicate his power of market choice to a government planner should depend on his ability to affect the outcome of that plan.

As economists, we take the distribution of political power, or sovereignty, as given. (We do analyze economic power, however.) Modern societies tend to be ruled by laws; individuals make decisions within a legal framework. It is the function of the political sovereign to specify the social compact, the rules that limit free individual action. As the sovereign body has all the political power, it can set any rules it wishes to govern the behavior of men. In fact, one of the major questions we face in this book is what laws should be established to lead to efficient allocations of resources. When should markets be used, when should we plan? In other words, how should the sovereign act so that utility is not wasted? We have already seen how the existence of externalities or public goods will make the market solution inefficient. Thus one principle the sovereign might follow is to use markets except where externalities exist. We will learn more principles later.

Consumer Sovereignty

What is meant by consumer sovereignty? As everyone is a consumer, is consumer sovereignty another term for democracy?

One of the most important decisions to be made by the sovereign concerns the goods to be produced. How many television sets should be produced? What color, size, and quality should they be? If the sovereign has supreme power, he has the power to make such decisions.

Consumer sovereignty denotes a system in which consumers decide which goods are to be produced.

The consumers make their decisions independently of each other by deciding how to spend their incomes. Individually, each consumer may not feel much like a sovereign since his own limited income allows him to buy but a few of the many delights that he sees available in the marketplace. But if he is sovereign, that is, if he has supreme power, why does he not just take those commodities that appeal to him? The answer is twofold. First, consumers are not really sovereign. There exists a political sovereign somewhere who establishes the rules within which consumers may exercise their limited power. Since these rules generally preclude theft, an individual consumer does not have the power to take any commodity that appeals to him without giving some mutually agreed upon payment. And second, a consumer is but one of many, each of whom is sovereign over his own little domain—the spending of his earnings. Thus consumer sovereignty is a term that denotes the freedom of consumers to take certain carefully constrained actions. It does not imply absolute power of consumers to take any action they wish.

How do consumers decide what will be produced? In a market economy, consumers need buy only those goods they wish. Then the consumers will have a say over how many goods can be sold. The only way a seller can induce a consumer to buy more of his good is to lower the price. Thus the consumers are sovereign but within certain limits. They cannot force the sellers to sell at a zero price. They have discretion to buy or not to buy, but they do not have the power to impose their will on the sellers. But the sellers cannot determine production without the consent of consumers. If consumers refuse to buy buggywhips, the seller must cease production (or buy all of his output for himself). To the extent that consumers have an effect on the output produced, we can say they are sovereign.

But how limited is the market power of consumers? Surely they are not ever sovereign. For markets to exist, there must be certain rules agreed upon by the buyers and the sellers. For example, theft may be illegal. It may be illegal to buy narcotics, to consume fireworks in crowds, to smoke in wooden buildings, or to violate the property rights of others. If consumers were really sovereign, they would not have such restrictions on their actions.

Absence of such rules does not denote consumer sovereignty. Absence of all such rules returns us to the jungle where even elementary property rights do not exist. Property, remember, is a social institution. One has the power to own something and the freedom from arbitrary confiscation only when the sovereign guarantees that power. The laws that make up property rights are the first basic rules necessary for markets to have any relevance. There must be rules if there is to be consumer sovereignty. But there is no way to decide how many rules. There is no agreed upon set of rules that can be pointed to as pure consumer sovereignty. Even the concept of property varies from society to society around the world. Indeed, even within Western society the right of trespass varies enormously. In most states of the United States, trespassing can be prohibited at the whim of the owner. It is a right given to the owner by the sovereign body. Other countries have different rules. Access to the beaches of Mexico is made a public right by law, and no private property owner can exclude the right of passage along the coastline of that country. All the forest and farmland of Sweden is endowed with the right of trespass as a public right. Campers and nature lovers willing to respect and preserve the beauty of the Swedish countryside are allowed to roam at will across its length and breadth. Thus in some cases the sovereign body decides that a certain right is an integral part of the institution of ownership while in other cases that right is considered to be separate from ownership.

If the very concept of property is not absolute but depends on the desires of the sovereign body, then obviously consumer sovereignty cannot be an absolute concept. Consumer sovereignty means, more or less, that individual consumers decide how to spend their incomes while obeying certain rules.

In democracies, a consumer will also be a member of the truly sovereign body. As such, he will have a part in all rule making as well as in decisions about public goods. This is because it is the sovereign who decides how much defense to buy, how much to spend to combat pollution, and how much to spend on visiting the moon. Thus the typical consumer will have a say through his political power about what the rules will be that govern the actions of consumers.

Consumer sovereignty and political sovereignty will be distributed differently, of course. Political sovereignty is often theoretically distributed in an egalitarian fashion — one man, one vote — although the existence of political parties, lobby groups, and less-than-honest representatives can magnify the power of some at the expense of others. Consumer sovereignty is distributed among people in proportion to their incomes. A rich man spends more than a poor man and therefore has more to say about the final composition of goods. But regardless of the different manners in which political and consumer sovereignty are distributed, most men have some of both; they have a say in deciding which goods should be produced publicly and they have a great deal of discretion in spending their own incomes on those goods that are produced privately.

Alternatives to Consumer Sovereignty

What are the alternatives to consumer sovereignty? If consumer sovereignty implies that consumers maximize their own utilities, then obvious alternatives would be to have someone else maximize the consumer's utility or to ignore entirely the utility of consumers. Before examining the motives for such systems, we ask what criteria might be used to choose from among these systems.

How do we select which system is best? That depends on our values. Such a decision is called a *value judgement*. We have already warned that in this book we are much more concerned with economic analysis than with value judgements. It is not that we do not find value judgements important; it is that our science says little about them. Nevertheless, it is instructive to view the alternatives to consumer sovereignty even though the choice among those alternatives is one of personal values — a normative choice.

Holy wars have been fought over alternative choices of absolute rules for social behavior. Today it is apparent that scientific analysis will not permit us to say that one value is *instrinsically* superior to another as a standard by which to judge resource allocation. Economic science simply permits us to determine the *implications* of alternative approaches to the allocation problem. Hence we shall never be able to rank values from good to evil independent of our personal opinions or feelings. Therefore questions such as "*should* the market maximize consumers' utility?" must themselves be subjected to the arbitration of each individual.

When P. T. Barnum claimed "There's one born every minute," he was referring to suckers who could be lured into a circus sideshow. But the oddities that he presented attracted the interest of every class and ideology, every educational level, professor, priest, and farm boy. Who is to say that these people were really "suckers" rather than consumers deriving utility from the willful suspension of disbelief? There is no absolute standard of economic value that we can apply to commodities or to the relative importance of the utilities of different people. There is no way to judge these people suckers rather than rational consumers. Similarly, there is no way to judge the correct limits of consumer sovereignty.

We list the alternatives to consumer sovereignty here because it is important that students be aware of their existence. The world yields many examples of these alternatives. Obvious alternatives are to allow an elite to be sovereign or to choose through the political process which goods are to be produced. The elite might decide on one of the following criteria:

1. The economy should maximize the utility of the elite or of a small portion of the society (at the expense of the rest). This is a frequent outcome under autocracy or aristocracy.
2. The economy should maximize the utility of individuals as perceived by an elite. We might call this a paternalistic system. Paternalism may be chosen in order
    a. to save individuals from the cost of maximizing their own utility (professional decision makers are believed *by the elite* to be more efficient at maximizing utility than individuals); or
    b. to force alien values on individuals (people do not know their own best interest).

To get a closer look at such systems and to gain a more subtle understanding of them, we analyze an argument concerning a local symphony orchestra. Should the city government subsidize the orchestra or allow it to exist as best it can on the receipts from ticket sales? Although the context of this discussion is political sovereignty—individuals are attempting to use their political power to maximize their own utilities—it is obviously a question concerning consumers. The question really is, How do we know what a symphony is worth to a city? Who should decide and how? The nature of the arguments used by the participants in the discussion allows us to observe desires for systems other than consumer sovereignty.

Subsidizing a Local Symphony—a Use or Abuse of Consumer Sovereignty?

Should we subsidize culture? To answer this question, we must ask whether a reliance on the market results in too few cultural offerings. What is meant by *too few*? It means that by someone's standards there is not enough in the way of cultural commodities. *Too few for whom*? To answer this, let us look at a number of reasons for subsidizing a local symphony orchestra that might be put forward to the voters. Once the reasons are understood, the motivation may be analyzed.

(1) Music is one of the finer things in life. We should guarantee that people in our town can consume music inexpensively.

Finer sounds like paternalism. Is an elite trying to impose its will on the community? If music is so "fine," then why do folks not pay for it? They pay a great deal for fine whiskey. Is it that they do not appreciate "fine" things? Are they incapable of maximizing their own utilities and therefore must be bribed to listen to music, bribed by setting its price below its social cost?

Why should music be inexpensive? Because it is fine? If it is really highly valued, then people will pay a good price for it. Alternatively, why not subsidize all fine things including fine whiskey?

The elite, in this case, may be relying on their own "superior" values to prevent the masses from foolishly making bad choices. The elite feels that music obviously yields much utility and so the masses will benefit from hearing it. If one trusted consumer sovereignty, he would advocate giving the masses money rather than symphonies and allowing them to decide whether to spend the money on symphonies or something of even greater value.

Perhaps the answer is that symphony music is an acquired taste. The problem may be a dynamic one. If we lure listeners in through low (subsidized) prices, they will eventually appreciate the music enough to pay higher prices. The subsidy is a payment for education in music appreciation. Nevertheless, this does not express the opinion of the masses or else they would undertake the education themselves. It is the opinion of an elite who already appreciates music. Many private firms give away free samples for this reason. If this is the true motivation for the subsidy, a few free concerts a year might do the trick instead.

Perhaps an aristocracy is requesting the symphony. It will be consumed by a small elite. If the whole town pays, it subsidizes the consumption of a few. The aristocracy wishes the goods it consumes to have low prices. If the local government will subsidize music, the elite will receive a bargain at the expense of those who watch TV in undershirts. Thus the elite may be using the political process to make the income distribution even more uneven. If the tax laws will subsidize their yachts, why not see if the city treasury will subsidize their music?

(2) Another argument is that music is a public good. It should be subsidized as such because it provides positive externalities to the whole community.

(a) This may make some sense. As a symphony-goer, citizen A might be willing to pay twice as much if it would ensure a splendid orchestra rather than a mediocre one. But unless all who attend double their contributions, his increased payment will do little to raise the quality of the group. If citizen B, on the other hand, along with everyone else, pays double, A does not have to pay any more to enjoy the benefits of a beautiful new sound. Thus there is an externality involved because each listener benefits from the contribution of others. Yet when buying a ticket, no one takes into account the pleasure he will give other people. He is concerned only with the value of the music to himself.

Because of its public good aspect, no one would pay increased ticket prices unless he immediately received more quality. But improving an orchestra takes time. It requires prior investment in musicians, instruments, and a conductor. Subsidization is an investment in the future welfare of individuals. The symphony does not possess the resources to make these improvements on its own and would find it very difficult to borrow the money.

Firms in the provinces often find it fruitful to take this externality into account. If they subsidize the symphony, they find it easier to attract highly educated personnel, personnel who would otherwise remain in an environment they found to be culturally satisfying. Even sharp-penciled treasurers will open the purse strings once they are aware of the nature of the externalities provided to them by improving their city's cultural environment.

(b) The town may need a great symphony if it is to become a great city. This is an additional aspect of music as a public good: The satisfaction of demand for urban greatness is packaged with the demand for better music. Voters who would never set foot in symphony halls might pay for urban greatness, but would only do so knowing that all others contributed as well. Civic and national pride are used in appeals to gain political support for public goods such as cultural subsidies in France and Germany or the moon race in Russia and the United States. People are induced to pay through taxes for goods that they do not find satisfying enough to pay for at the door. That a city's reputation should depend on music even though most people do not like music enough to pay for it tips us off as to who determines reputation.

Note that we have separated the arguments above into two classes, public goods and others. The public goods represent examples of a broader view of consumer sovereignty. The taxpayers are banding together to accomplish something they want but that would not be provided by the market. The other arguments represent attempts by a small group to have its way against the best interests of others. In such a situation, the others should speak up and use their political sovereignty to defend their interests. An efficient political apparatus will give them an opportunity to express their will.

In our example it is *up to the voters* to determine what they wish in the way of public goods, such as tax support for a local symphony. But sometimes the principle of consumer sovereignty can be abused by an elite that misleads the public through misrepresenting a public good or packaging public wants (those of society) with private wants (those of the elite). This helps to explain the control of dictators such as Stalin, Hitler, and many current national leaders who employ real and artificial threats to national security as devices to gain control over resource allocation. The individuals in society are led to make decisions that abolish their future sovereignty. They are scared into buying national security

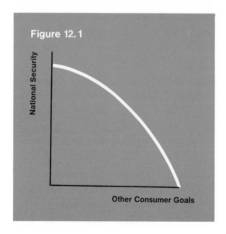

Figure 12.1

National Security

Other Consumer Goals

and undergoing great sacrifices of leisure and other goods in order to pay for it. In fact, the scare is a device to accomplish some end wanted only by the elite, but which the public would never tolerate if it knew the true facts. Propaganda can accomplish many goals, whether the political system is democratic or autocratic.

The further society moves in the direction of national security, the more resources are allocated to programs of national defense and the less other consumer goals can be satisfied. This is illustrated by the production frontier in Figure 12.1. If the threat of security is manufactured, individual welfare will be wasted by this process but the decision-making elite will satisfy its desires for personal importance. The abuse by some politicians of the legitimate demand of the public for national security threatens many societies today with a breakdown of consumer sovereignty in the broadest sense. These politicians form an elite that explicitly or implicitly would impose its standard of values above that of consumer sovereignty. Indeed, the goals of the elite are often no more than the maintenance of power. It is up to the public to choose which standard it will support. For revolutions can always redistribute political power.

Questions

1.   Should local government subsidize symphonies? Theatres? Athletic teams? Conventions? In each case, who pays and who receives the benefits?
2.   Can you justify the actions of a nationalist elite that attempts to make their country great by scaring the peasants into working harder than they would otherwise? Is your answer affected by the effectiveness of the action; that is, whether the action truly makes the nation greater when it would not have been so otherwise?
3.   How sovereign are consumers? How might sovereign consumers buy national security? Cancer research? Wilderness? Pure water?

Concepts Discussed

sovereignty	political efficiency
consumer sovereignty	value judgment

V The Production Decision

What's good for the country
is good for General Motors — and vice versa.

CHARLES E. WILSON

Production is a process in which certain economic goods are created from others. When an economy engages in production, it must give us certain goods and resources in order to receive back the produced commodities. Iron ore, coal, and labor must be sacrificed if we are to create steel. Thus the production process is very much like the act of exchange. Although there is no obvious trading partner who accepts the coal and gives us steel, it is sometimes convenient to view production as a trade with nature. Nature absorbs labor and railroads and gives us back transportation.

Since production can be viewed as exchange, it should not be surprising to find that in some of the most abstract formulations of economic theory, production plays a very minor role. That is, once the conditions for efficiency have been established in a world in which individuals are viewed as endowed with commodities to trade, it requires only a minor extension to view them as endowed with productive factors that can be sold or turned into (traded for) commodities to be sold. A few footnotes must be added about the nature of the available production processes and then all of the results that were generated in the simpler world continue to be valid.

Thus if we were to look only at the mathematics of production processes, we might consider production a trivial qualification to a model of exchange. Yet when we look at the world around us, questions involving production receive a great deal of political attention. Apparently, the way a society organizes its production affects the lives of its citizens in many ways. From very broad issues, such as the degree of capitalism versus socialism, to very specific issues, such as the amount of air pollution to be tolerated, the manner in which goods are to be produced generates food for controversy.

In the following six chapters, we will discuss production from both vantages. First, we look at the possibilities for production from the viewpoint of cost and efficiency. Then we discuss some of the broader social and political problems that arise directly from the mathematics of production. We outline the nature of the choices available to a society and discuss the effect that each could have on the material well-being of the society. We conclude little about the desirability of one production system as opposed to another; we claim that the answers to such questions revolve around empirical issues that have not yet been resolved. Rightness and wrongness we leave to the social evangelists. As scientists, we remain agnostic and claim "it all depends."

13 Profit Maximization and Costs

Production processes use up certain goods and services — inputs — and generate others — outputs. The purpose of production is to allow us to create outputs that are preferred to the inputs that must be sacrificed. Thus the decision whether or not to produce is very much like the decision whether or not to trade. If the value of the outputs exceeds that of the inputs, production can increase satisfaction and it should be carried out.

If we view production as a process similar to trade, we can see that it would be possible to extend the analysis of consumer equilibrium presented in Chapters 8 and 9 by allowing consumers to buy the inputs for a particular production process when they desire to consume more of that output. This extension is so simple that it changes none of the results presented in those chapters.

We might further extend that analysis by allowing the consumer to sell the outputs of the production process. Once this extension is made, however, it becomes convenient to analyze production by itself with no reference to the individual consumer who oversees it. There are two reasons for this convenience. First, if an individual is to sell the output, we need not worry about how much satisfaction the commodity yields him. That is, the issue of the consumer's diminishing relative value for a particular commodity ceases to be important when the output can be sold in a large market at an established price. The question of whether to produce or not turns on the issue of profitability — whether the act of production expands the consumer's budget constraint — and not on whether the consumer can derive pleasure from the output. Since profitability can be examined by itself, the simplest procedure is to ignore issues concerning utility when dealing with the production decision.

The second reason we might like to study production independently of the theory of consumer equilibrium concerns precisely the issue of the budget constraint just raised. If I can buy the inputs to a particular process for $1 and sell the outputs for $2, how much should I buy and sell? Why not buy $1,000 worth or even a million? The point to be noted is that for production decisions, there is no relevant budget constraint like the one that restricts consumers' spending. Since the output is to be sold, the revenue received will pay for the inputs. There is no relevant limit to the amount of inputs that can be bought if they are to be used to produce output that is to be sold.

For these reasons, it is convenient to study production independently of consumer equilibrium even though we might think of it as an extension of consumer theory. Individuals engage in productive activities out of a desire to increase their level of satisfaction. But we can ignore the issue of satisfaction when studying production because the manner in which the process generates satisfaction is by expanding the budget constraint. And since large expansions are always preferred to small expansions, the question of production can be treated as one of maximizing profits.

The Organization of Production

The intellectual leap we have just made, the decision to study production as profit maximization rather than utility maximization, is not just of academic interest. For precisely the reasons that allow us to make this intellectual distinction, it becomes possible for real-world institutions of production to exist and to operate completely independently of any concern for utility. Once we grant that individuals can separate their production decisions from their consumption decisions, we have opened the door to the existence of corporations, planning bureaus, and similar institutions. Once we view an individual as producing wherever he can make the most money, and then spending the returns in a manner that maximizes utility, we have separated his decisions into two groups. And a separate analysis of his production decisions will look suspiciously like an analysis of a firm.

The two groups of decisions that are to be made are the following: (1) An individual owns certain goods and resources that he can trade for other goods and resources yielding more satisfaction. This group of decisions has been studied in Chapters 8 and 9 under the label of consumer theory. (2) An individual can buy goods and resources and combine them via a production process into other goods and services that can be sold. This is the group of decisions we call production theory and we analyze it in this chapter and those that immediately follow. The analyses of production theory will be relevant not only to individuals but to corporations and centrally planned economies as well because those institutions can replace individuals in performing productive activities.

In the rest of this chapter, we study the problem of choosing the best process of production from the many that are available. This problem is one shared by corporations, planning bureaus, and individual producers, the last of whom are called *entrepreneurs*. Accordingly we ignore questions that are concerned with the manner in which production is organized. The reader can assume that individuals are to make these production decisions and that all individuals face the same problems. Later, in Chapters 16 and 18, we discuss some of the social implications of the manner in which production is organized.

Minimizing Costs

To produce a given level of output, the best production technique is the one that costs least, that is, the one that requires the smallest sacrifice of valuable goods and services. The choice of technique can be thought of as representing a host of complex decisions actually made by firms — what kinds of labor, machinery, and resources to use, what services to buy from other firms, what services to produce, whether to spend money on warehouses or airfreight, whether to automate. These and many other problems must be solved if costs are to be minimized.

As always, we discuss a characterization of those problems. We assume a very simple production function that shows the alternatives available to management. The problem is kept simple enough to be represented in two dimensions. But as in the case of our reduction of the problem of consumer choice to two dimensions, we will really be speaking of a much more complex world. Although our consumer diagrams had only two dimensions, the results we obtained were relevant for many more than two commodities. Although our diagrams allow us to represent the choice as one between two factors of production, we should think of that choice as one based on a great number of factors.

The production function, as described in Chapter 6, is a list of all the technologically efficient production processes. Suppose two techniques exist for producing 1 ton of steel, one of which takes 3 tons of iron ore and 15 tons of coal while the other takes 4 tons of ore and 20 tons of coal. Compared with the first process, the second process is technologically inefficient; it should never be used. And it is not one of the techniques that constitute the production function. A production process is *technologically inefficient* if it uses more of at least one productive factor and no less of any other factors than does some other process.

A producer is faced with the problem of choosing the best production process he can from all those available. But clearly he will not choose a technologically inefficient production process. Yet there may be many processes that are technologically efficient. For example, one process may produce 1 ton of steel from 3 tons of ore and 15 tons of coal whereas another uses 4 tons of ore but only 12 tons of coal. Both represent the latest in the engineer's knowledge of how to squeeze steel from coal and ore. Which technique should be used? That depends on the prices of coal and ore. If coal and ore both cost $10 per ton, the second process is clearly the cheaper way to produce steel, but if coal costs $5 per ton and ore costs $20 per ton, the first process is cheaper. When a production decision is made, it is the value of the inputs that must be compared to the value of the outputs. And in a market economy, the value of a resource is its price.

In the appendix to this chapter, we graphically illustrate the problem of minimizing costs in a world where many techniques are available. The graphics are similar to those shown in Chapter 8 for the consumer's problem of maximizing utility. The similarity can also be seen in the graphics illustrating the producer's demand for productive factors.

The producer's decision rule for hiring factors is very similar to the consumer's decision rule for buying commodities. It concerns the relative contribution of alternative factors of production to output, given their price. In Chapter 8, the consumer decided that if the last dollar spent on steak added more to his utility than the last dollar spent on movies, he should buy more steak and fewer movies. In the present case our steel producer decides that

"If the last dollar spent on coal adds more to output than the last dollar spent on ore, hire more coal and less ore."

This simple decision rule leads to the least-cost method of producing any level of output. To make this decision, the producer must know (1) the production function for his firm and (2) the relative price of coal and ore. Execution of this decision rule leads to a general principle quite similar to that associated with consumer utility maximization:

If costs are to be minimized the ratio of marginal productivity to price must be equal for every factor of production.

Let us see why this principle makes sense. The last dollar spent on coal buys (1/price of coal) units of coal. For example, if coal costs $5 per ton, the last dollar spent on coal buys $\frac{1}{5}$ ton of coal. Each unit of coal adds to output the marginal productivity of coal. It should be remembered that the "marginal productivity" of a factor is the contribution that one unit of that factor makes to output while all other factor inputs are held constant. This means that the *amount added to output* by the last dollar spent on coal must be exactly equal to the *marginal product of one unit of coal times the number of units that $1 can purchase*. For example, if the marginal product of a ton of coal happens to be 100 pounds of steel and the price of coal is $5 per ton, the last dollar spent on coal adds 20 pounds of steel to output.

Therefore the amount added to output by $1 worth of a factor can be expressed in the following way. Let X be the factor, P_X the price of X, and MP_X the marginal product of X. Then

$$\frac{MP_X}{P_X} = \frac{\text{the extra output resulting from an additional}}{\text{dollar spent on factor } X}$$

It is the extra output resulting from one extra unit of X multiplied by the number of units of X that one dollar will buy. To execute the decision rule, we obey the following maxim:

$$\text{If } \frac{MP_X}{P_X} > \frac{MP_Y}{P_Y}, \text{ then buy more } X, \text{ less } Y.$$

In other words,

$$\text{If } \begin{pmatrix} \text{the extra output} \\ \text{from another dollar} \\ \text{spent on } X \end{pmatrix} \text{ is greater than } \begin{pmatrix} \text{the extra output} \\ \text{from another dollar} \\ \text{spent on } Y \end{pmatrix}$$

then buy more X, less Y.

If this is done, costs can be lowered for the same level of output, or output can be increased without the expenditure of additional money. Simply by the purchase of fewer Y factors and more X factors, output can be increased while costs are held constant. Why is an equilibrium eventually attained? The answer, the reader will guess from recalling earlier chapters, is due to diminishing returns. If diminishing returns exist for coal (factor X in the case of the steel producer), then shifting dollars from ore to coal in the production of steel will cause the marginal product of coal to fall. But if diminishing returns also exist for ore, then buying less and less ore will cause its marginal productivity to rise. The large ratio declines, the small ratio rises. Thus the ratios will eventually be equal; when they do become equal, the producer will get the most output for his money. The mathematics of this problem is identical to the mathematics of consumer utility maximization. It boils down to a question of where one gets the most for his money. If a dollar spent on coal produces more steel than a dollar spent on ore, then buy coal not ore.

The Graphics of Cost

In Figure 13.1, we have graphed five different technologically efficient production processes (points A–E) and one technologically inefficient one (point F). These points correspond to the production processes described in Table 13.1.
Note that point F is technologically inefficient because there exist other processes that can give the same output using less of at least one input and no more of any other. Regardless of the prices of coal and ore, process F should never be used because processes C and D will always be cheaper.

Diagrams can be used to illustrate the costs of the various processes. Remember that the consumer's budget constraint represents a locus of points of constant money outlay. Similar lines can be drawn for producers to represent loci of constant costs. In Figure 13.2, such a line has been drawn under the assumption that the price of ore is $20 per ton while that of coal is $5 per ton. Every point on the straight line in Figure 13.2 represents a cost of $135.

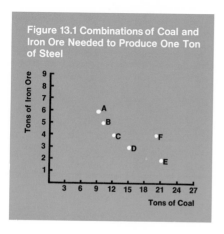

Figure 13.1 Combinations of Coal and Iron Ore Needed to Produce One Ton of Steel

Table 13.1	Alternative Levels of Inputs That Can Produce One Ton of Steel	
Process	Tons of Ore	Tons of Coal
A	6	9
B	5	10
C	4	12
D	3	15
E	2	21
F	4	20

Note that process D is one of the points on that line. If process D is used, a ton of steel can be produced for $135. Note, also, that all the other processes require greater outlays, given the prices of coal and ore. These higher levels of outlays could be shown by additional straight lines further from the origin. Process D is therefore the cheapest process for the given set of prices.

If it is possible to produce a ton of steel using resources worth $135, it would be inefficient to do so by using resources that cost $150 (process B) or $165 (process A). Thus the economically efficient production process is the one that has the lowest cost. Those processes that cost more are economically inefficient. Note that processes A and B are technologically efficient—one cannot switch from them to a process that uses less coal, for example, without increasing the amount of iron ore to be used. But processes A and B are economically inefficient given the prices assumed in Figure 13.2. Whether it is efficient to reduce the use of coal and increase that of ore is a question of cost, not of technology. Process B happens to be inefficient because of cost, not because there exists a process that is technologically superior.

To illustrate this point, let us see what happens when the price of ore drops

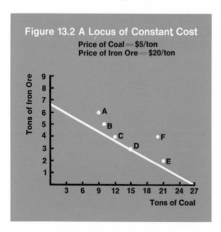

Figure 13.2 A Locus of Constant Cost
Price of Coal = $5/ton
Price of Iron Ore = $20/ton

to $9 per ton while that of coal stays constant. Steel obviously becomes cheaper to produce. Using process D as before, the cost of a ton of steel falls from $135 to $102. But since process B uses relatively more iron than D, the cost of producing steel by this process declines by even more — from $150 per ton to $95 per ton. Thus process B becomes the cheapest way to produce steel. Producers should switch from D to B when the price of iron ore falls from $20 to $9 a ton. Because process B uses relatively more iron ore than D, it becomes economically efficient only at relatively low prices for iron ore.

Graphically the effect of the new prices is shown in Figure 13.3, where the old cost line has been left for purposes of comparison. With the steeper cost line, B is the cheapest production process. Note that one could draw in cost lines of varying slopes to make any of the processes from A to E efficient. That is, there exists some price for coal and ore that would make producers select process A and another price that would make them select process C.

What must be learned from this is that it is the price of the inputs that determine which process is to be used, that is, which process is economically efficient. Processes A through E are all technologically efficient. There is a set of prices for each that makes it the most efficient production process to use. Process F, on the other hand, should never be used. There is no set of positive prices for coal and iron ore that makes F cheaper than C or D.

Costs and Outputs

Firms, of course, do not face budget constraints the way households do. That is because they produce and sell. If we double output and still use process D, costs would double as well. Diagrams like Figures 13.2 and 13.3 are useful in showing us which process to choose. But because the cost lines shown there are not budget constraints, they are of no use in helping us to determine the level of output or the quantity of each factor that will be demanded. These diagrams show the determination of the ratio in which the factors should be used, not the level of use. Here we have been concerned only with minimizing costs for a

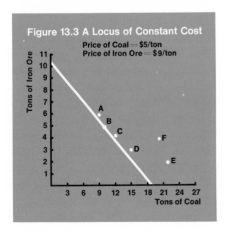

Figure 13.3 A Locus of Constant Cost

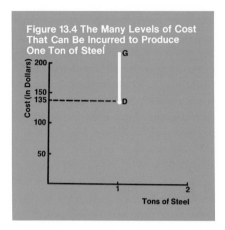

Figure 13.4 The Many Levels of Cost That Can Be Incurred to Produce One Ton of Steel

given level of output. In the next chapter, we will be concerned with choosing the level of output that maximizes profits. There we assume that every possible level of output would be produced by the cheapest method possible.

To make the transition from the problem of selecting a production process to that of selecting a level of output, we construct a relation between cost and the level of output. In Figure 13.2, we saw how for given prices of coal and ore, one ton of steel could be produced either for $135, or for more, possibly very much more, if we use processes that are technologically inefficient. Thus for one ton of output, many different costs are possible. This is shown in Figure 13.4, where the white line has been drawn as if there were an infinite number of economically inefficient production processes. Point D represents the cheapest possible way to produce the ton of steel, and the other points on the white line represent less efficient processes.

There are a great number of processes that can be used to produce any quantity of steel. Thus for each quantity produced, there is some line as line GD in Figure 13.4, which represents all of the possible costs that could be incurred in production. Figure 13.5 shows such a locus for two tons of steel as well as that for one ton.

Figure 13.6 shows by the shaded area all of the loci for all the possible outputs represented on the horizontal axis. That area has been labeled the area of economic inefficiency because points in it will be encountered only if an economically inefficient production process is used. The lower bound of this area is a line that is called the *total cost curve* of the firm. The total cost curve is the locus of the cost of each level of output when the economically efficient production process is being used. In the next few chapters, we will use this concept repeatedly, but we will not redraw the shaded area above the curve. That is, we will assume that the producer has minimized costs properly and that points in this area will never be observed. The only points that will be relevant for further analysis will be the efficient points; they all lie on the total cost curve.

Remember that when factor prices change, the cost curve will change. Dif-

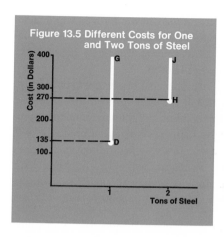

Figure 13.5 Different Costs for One and Two Tons of Steel

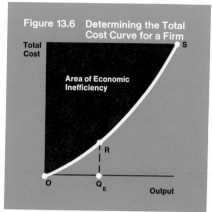

Figure 13.6   Determining the Total Cost Curve for a Firm

ferent production processes may be used for different factor prices, of course, but the total cost curve will always represent the cheapest processes for the particular set of factor prices that exists.

Efficiency and the Production Frontier

In our example, we have expressed the costs of the factors in terms of dollars. Think of expressing those costs in terms of corn instead. Corn is an alternative output to steel, and we could express all prices in terms of corn. If we do this, the problem of minimizing cost can be shown on a production frontier. Figure 13.7 illustrates the role of cost minimization from the viewpoint of conserving society's scarce resources. If the process that uses up the least corn is selected, we can produce OR tons of steel and OT bushels of corn. That is, we can be on the production frontier at point D. If an inefficient process is used, more corn will have to be sacrificed than is necessary and production might be reduced to the quantities shown by point A or even point R. Thus minimizing costs economizes on the use of scarce resources and leaves as many of them as possible to

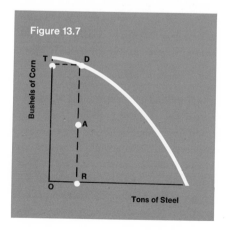

Figure 13.7

be used in producing other commodities. Regardless of the form in which a society organizes its production processes, whether by corporations, planning bureaus, or cooperatives, there will be the greatest amount of goods available if the
economically efficient production processes are chosen.

The price system is a helpful device to use to signal producers to economize
on a particular resource. We have seen that if the price of iron ore increases,
producers will use less of it. If land in Manhattan, uranium, or computer programmers become scarce, the price of those factors will rise and producers will
attempt to get by with fewer of them. They do this by substituting other factors
and using a different process of production. Producers will always hire the factor
that gives the greatest amount of output for the money spent. If iron ore becomes expensive, producers will find it economical to spend less on ore and
more on coal.

It is this fact that led Adam Smith to his "invisible hand" theory, in which
the efforts of every merchant to maximize his own profits lead to the greatest
good for all. If every firm minimizes its costs and all firms compete in the factor
markets for scarce resources, the factors will be employed where their value to
society is greatest, where the value of the goods they produce is greatest. In this
sense, it is true that General Motors and the country as a whole have common
interests. Cost minimization by firms leads to socially efficient production, to a
point on the production possibility frontier. Waste by a firm in any industry can
never be made up by society in some other industry. The wasted resources are
lost forever. Though we would be a little more skeptical today than was Adam
Smith in deciding what is the greatest good for all, it is true that the largest quantity of output occurs when efficient production techniques are used. Who gets
the output is another question, of course.

The firm in an underdeveloped country that responds to the prices it faces
by using very little capital and a lot of labor has economized properly. It has
saved its country's precious capital for other uses. Similarly, the American firm
that automates has saved its country's precious labor resources for other uses.
Labor is very scarce in America; the firm is made aware of this fact by its high
wage rate. The price system can be thought of as a signaling device that tells
firms when to use more of one resource and less of another in order to spread
around society's resources properly. The price system can allocate the precious
resources among competing uses only if producers make each factor pay its own
way.

Our simple sketch of how costs are minimized represents the decisions
made in the production division of a firm. Business school graduates who specialized in operations research and production management determine how best
to produce output given the technical data presented to them by engineers and
the cost data obtained from factor markets. The solution we derived for two factors, coal and ore, can be extended to any number of other factors as well. The
production division of the firm is engaged in a continual search for the most efficient production process given the prices of the factors. Finding this process

becomes increasingly difficult as the number of factors employed and products produced increases. In the next chapter, we see how the production division and the sales division interact to determine the level of output and profits within the constraints imposed by the market.

Questions

1. What is the difference between economic efficiency and technological efficiency?
2. Can you find prices at which each of the processes (A–E) in the example in Table 13.1 are efficient? Can you define a process that dominates A–E, that is, one that makes A–E technologically inefficient?
3. Why do economists study production theory independently of utility maximization?

Concepts Discussed

technologically efficient techniques   total cost curve
economically efficient techniques

APPENDIX: EXHIBITING COST MINIMIZATION BY ISOQUANTS

In the body of the chapter we illustrated how a producer could use the prices of the inputs to choose the cheapest of the available techniques. We assumed that there were a small number of techniques available. For some purposes, it is convenient to think of the number of technologically efficient techniques as being infinite. That is, it is efficient to think of there being a technologically efficient production process for every possible ratio of iron ore to coal. In Figure 13A.1, we have drawn a locus of the inputs required by such processes to produce one ton of steel. Such a locus is called an *isoquant*. The word derives from the Greek *iso* (same) and *quant* (quantity), and its derivation tells us one of its properties.

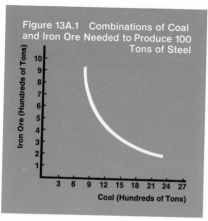

Figure 13A.1 Combinations of Coal and Iron Ore Needed to Produce 100 Tons of Steel

That is, along an isoquant the quantity of output is a constant. An isoquant tells us the various quantities of inputs that can be used to produce a given quantity of output. An isoquant looks very much like a consumer indifference curve. And since the geometry is so similar, we will be quite concise in this appendix, under the assumption that the reader has read the appendix to Chapter 8.

Isoquants differ from indifference curves in the interpretation we place on them if not in their shape. First of all, an indifference curve is a locus of points that signify bundles of goods all yielding the same level of utility. But since we cannot measure utility, the label we place on an indifference curve is arbitrary. There is no reason to prefer the label one to the label ten. With isoquants, however, we are speaking of a measurable quantity of output such as one ton of steel. We can speak of the isoquant for two tons of steel being "twice as large" as that for one ton. No such statement is possible about indifference curves.

The geometry of cost minimization using isoquants is similar to that of utility maximization using indifference curves but not exactly the same. As noted in the body of the chapter, this is due to the fact that the firm has no budget constraint. It can choose to produce two tons of steel or twenty. Thus the firm does not attempt to reach the highest isoquant available, the way a consumer attempts to reach the highest indifference curve available; rather, the firm attempts to maximize profit. One aspect of profit maximization does happen to be cost minimization, and it is this aspect that we illustrate using isoquants. But when illustrating this, we should not lose sight of the larger picture. That is, we should not lose sight of the fact that the other aspect of maximizing profits lies in selecting the proper level of output, or in choosing the appropriate isoquant.

In Figure 13A.2, we show the geometry of cost minimization for a given level of output. In this example, the level of output is 100 tons of steel per week. The same minimizing procedure will have to be done for each possible level of output in order to supply the firm with enough information to allow it to select the proper level of output. For now, however, we will worry about minimizing costs if 100 tons of steel are to be produced. The diagonal lines in Figure 13A.2

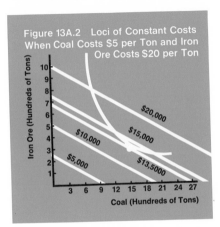

Figure 13A.2 Loci of Constant Costs When Coal Costs $5 per Ton and Iron Ore Costs $20 per Ton

Iron Ore (Hundreds of Tons)

$20,000

$15,000

$10,000

$5,000

$13,500

Coal (Hundreds of Tons)

represent various levels of cost. Each line is drawn using the existing prices of coal and iron ore; along each line, cost remains constant. In Figure 13A.2, we have assumed that the price of ore is $20 per ton whereas that of coal is $5 per ton. Note that $13,500 is the lowest cost at which 100 tons of steel can be produced. All costs below this are unattainable, whereas any level of costs above it can be reached if the firm chooses the wrong production process. At the solution the isoquant is tangent to a constant cost line.

The use of smooth isoquants makes it easier for us to derive the relationship between the marginal products and the prices of factors at the profit maximum. This is because the slope of an isoquant equals the ratio of the marginal products of the factors. To see this, remember that the slope of a curve is defined as the vertical distance divided by the horizontal distance that a point on the curve would travel. But since output is held constant along any isoquant, the extra output produced by traveling from point A to B in Figure 13A.3 must be exactly equal to the decrease in output experienced by moving from B to C. Thus points A and C must represent the same level of output. The amount of extra output produced when moving from A to B is equal by definition to the marginal product of coal times the number of extra tons of coal used. That is, if 1,000 tons of coal are used at A and 1,200 at B, and if 100 tons of steel are produced at A while 110 tons are produced at B, we know that it took 200 extra tons of coal to produce the 10 extra tons of steel. Thus each extra ton of coal can be thought of as contributing an extra $1/20$ of a ton of steel. In other words, the marginal product of coal is $1/20$ between points A and B. And $1/20$ multiplied by 200 gives us the 10 extra tons of steel gained by moving from A to B.

Point C must also represent 100 tons of steel because it lies on the same isoquant as A. Thus the move from B to C involves a decrease in steel production of 10 tons and a decrease in usage of iron ore of 100 tons—from 500 to 400. Thus the marginal product of iron ore must be $1/10$ between points B and C.

Now the slope of the isoquant by definition must be the vertical distance— 100 tons of iron ore—divided by the horizontal distance—200 tons of coal. The

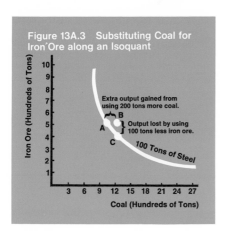

Figure 13A.3 Substituting Coal for Iron Ore along an Isoquant

slope equals ½ multiplied by some dimension that transforms iron ore into coal. Now it so happens that the ratio of marginal products equals ½ as well, and this is no accident. The fact that it is not can be seen by expanding the following simple equation that results from the definition of an isoquant.

(output gained moving from A to B) = (output lost moving from B to C)

We have seen that the gain in output when moving from A to B equals the marginal product of coal times the number of extra tons of coal employed. Thus the equation can be rewritten as

$$
\begin{pmatrix} \text{marginal product of coal times} \\ \text{extra coal employed to move} \\ \text{from } A \text{ to } B \end{pmatrix} = \begin{pmatrix} \text{marginal product of iron ore} \\ \text{times extra iron ore employed} \\ \text{moving from } B \text{ to } C \end{pmatrix}
$$

Now the slope of the line equals the extra ore divided by the extra coal. Thus by cross-multiplying our equation, both sides become equal to the slope of the isoquant.

$$
\frac{\text{marginal product of coal}}{\text{marginal product of iron ore}} = \frac{\text{extra iron ore employed}}{\text{extra coal employed}} = \begin{matrix} \text{slope of} \\ \text{isoquant} \end{matrix}
$$

Thus the slope equals the ratio of the marginal products. And since the slopes of the lines representing constant costs are equal to the ratio of the prices of the inputs, we know that at equilibrium the tangency will guarantee us that the ratio of the marginal products equals the ratio of the costs.

Changing Input Prices

When input prices change, the technique that minimizes costs can change as well. In Figure 13A.4, the same isoquant for 100 tons of steel is drawn, but now we assume that the price of ore has fallen to $9 a ton. Note that the change in

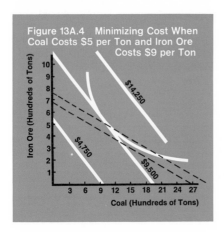

Figure 13A.4   Minimizing Cost When Coal Costs $5 per Ton and Iron Ore Costs $9 per Ton

Iron Ore (Hundreds of Tons)

$14,250

$4,750

$9,500

Coal (Hundreds of Tons)

slope of the cost lines implies the use of factors in different proportions. In this case, the decline in the price of iron ore means that more of it will be used in every ton of steel. When iron ore becomes cheaper, more of it is used but less coal is used.

For further practice in using isoquants, the reader should consult the *Study Guide for Principles of Economics* by Charles Metcalf, which has been designed to accompany this text. An exact reference appears in the preface.

14 Profit Maximization and Sales

We have broken the problem of profit maximization into two parts: (1) the problem of minimizing costs for each level of output; and (2) the problem of choosing the correct level of output. The first of these problems we discussed in Chapter 13, the second we take up here. We continue the discussion in the context of firms but alert the reader that the analysis is relevant for planning bureaus, cooperatives, or any other institution that makes production decisions. The analysis we present here must be understood before we can enter into an intelligent discussion of the importance of the different ways in which a society can organize its production.

The Demand Function for the Firm

The sales division of a firm is faced with a dilemma. The boss keeps hounding them to sell more but he also wants to keep his prices high. The sales division has discovered that the easiest way to increase sales is to lower price. They know that the quantity of their product demanded by consumers depends on price; the lower the price, the more goods consumers will buy. But the boss knows this too. He did not hire his sales division to explain to him the theory of downward-sloping demand. He hired them to shift the demand curve out, thus increasing both price and quantity. Therefore the sales division must use the techniques of marketing that they learned in business school in order to guarantee that all the possibilities for sales are exploited to the extent that it is efficient to do so. In addition, they advertise, use gimmicks, campaigns, and so on, in order to attempt to bend consumer preferences.

Even if they have done all that efficiently, there still exists an undeniable demand function, pushed out though it may be. Just as the engineers were implored to lower costs but ran into a technological limit that we called a production function, the salesmen encounter a behavioral limit that we call a *demand function*. And just as the last dollar spent on labor had to contribute as much to output as the last dollar spent on land if the firm were to be efficient, so the last dollar spent on advertising must contribute as much to sales as the last dollar spent on salesmen. By assuming an efficient cost minimization scheme, we were able to convert the production function into a cost function, a function that told the lowest possible level of costs for each level of output. Similarly, by assuming an efficient sales division in the firm, we can obtain a *revenue function*, a function that tells the highest possible level of revenue for each level of output.

In Figure 14.1, for example, output Q_E can result in any level of revenue from zero (if no sales effort is expended) to R if sales dollars are used efficiently. The boundary of efficient points is called the *total revenue curve*. From here on, we assume that the sales division can manage its job efficiently and that the company operates at some point on its revenue curve rather than at an inefficient point beneath the curve.

This gives us the second important constraint on the firm's actions. (1) They cannot receive more than a limited amount of revenue for each level of sales. Consumers will refuse to buy at higher prices. (2) They cannot reduce costs below some minimum level for each quantity of output. The technology is not sufficiently developed to allow more output from the given inputs. Given these two constraints, the firm chooses that level of output that maximizes profits.

How to Choose the Best Level of Production

The boss is a typical profit maximizer. He loves his wife and children, is a scoutmaster and servant of the community. His motto is, "What's good for the firm is good for society." He has worked hard to find the most efficient combination of productive factors to be used at each level of output so as to minimize costs. He has worked hard to maximize the revenue he can receive for every level of sales. Now he must decide what level of output will maximize profits. To do this he follows a simple decision rule.

If the production of an additional unit of output raises profits, produce it. If it lowers profits, try producing one unit less.

Under normal circumstances this will lead him to the level of output at which profits will be maximized. We shall see how this happens.

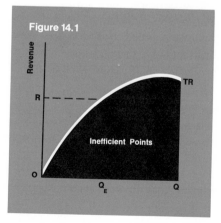

Figure 14.1

The Definition of Profits

Profits are defined as *total dollar receipts from sales* (total revenue) *minus total costs*.

profits = total revenue − total costs

Total costs at different levels of output are illustrated by the firm's cost curve as shown in Figure 13.6. The total cost curve was derived from the production function and the prices of factors of production. Total revenue, as illustrated in Figure 14.1, is derived from the demand function. The boss may decide on the profit-maximizing level of output through trial and error by applying his decision rule, but we can show what that level will be once we know the revenue and cost functions.

Does it seem strange that according to the decision rule the firm may want to *lower* production so as to *raise* profits? Since the boss is usually encouraging the sales manager to *increase* sales, this sounds inconsistent. But remember that sales efforts may be directed at increasing demand through variables other than price. What the boss means is, "Sell as much as you can, given the price." This chapter asks, What price will ensure profit maximization? Or alternatively, What level of output will maximize profits? With the demand function given, the two questions produce the same answer. If the sales division has done its job, the only remaining way for the boss to increase output is to lower the price he charges. It is possible that he will prefer a high price and low output to a low price and high output.

In other words, the boss is not prepared to maximize sales whatever the price might be. If he were, he would end by charging a zero price and giving away his product. This obviously would be the maximum level of sales. Instead, he wishes to maximize *profits*. Profit maximization and sales maximization are mutually inconsistent for most firms. This does not prevent the sales manager from attempting to increase sales *at a given price*. Such attempts represent an effort on his part to shift the demand curve outward. They involve a more complicated sales function than the simple price-quantity relationship. In this chapter we set aside such complications by assuming that the firm is able to attain any point on the demand curve, but that that curve cannot be exceeded. All the firm can do to maximize profits is to find the best price. How will it do this?

Profit Maximization (When the Firm Has No Costs)

The simplest case that will illustrate how a firm arrives at a profit-maximizing price and output is one in which there are no costs. Assume that the firm sells mineral water that costs nothing to raise out of the ground and that is taken home by purchasers in their own containers. Is there a profit-maximizing price and quantity under these unusual circumstances? The answer is made obvious if we look again at Figure 14.1.

It is useful at this point to remember the relationship between the demand curve and the revenue curve that was indicated in Chapter 5. The demand curve tells us how much output will be sold at every price. But total revenue is simply price times quantity. Because the demand curve tells us the price that will be associated with each quantity, we can derive from it the level of revenue that will be received from selling each quantity. Thus we see that these two functions are very closely related. In fact, the demand function is often called *the average revenue function*. This is because it tells us the average revenue, or revenue per unit, that can be obtained for each quantity of sales. Average revenue is simply total revenue divided by the number of units sold. If total revenue is PQ, then average revenue must be $PQ/Q = P$. Average revenue and price are the same thing. And since it is the demand function that relates price to the level of output, the demand function must be the average revenue function.

In Figure 14.2, we have drawn the demand curve for the firm's mineral water. As drawn, Q_1 represents the level of output that leads to maximum revenue. That is because PQ is total revenue and every increase in Q beyond Q_1 leads to a larger percentage decrease in price than the percent by which Q increases; Q increases but P falls. If P falls by a greater percentage than Q increases, the product of the two variables, PQ, falls.*

Clearly, a very high price will lead to no sales; revenue will be zero. Similarly, a zero price will lead to very large quantity of output, but their value will be zero. Some price between these extremes must be chosen if the product is to satisfy the goal of profit maximization. *Even if a firm had no costs of production, so that revenue equaled profits, it would choose to limit its sales.* We will see that this point has important implications for the efficiency of resource allocation.

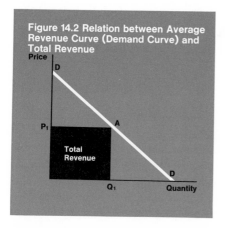

Figure 14.2 Relation between Average Revenue Curve (Demand Curve) and Total Revenue

*Readers will recall that the effect on total revenue of moving up or down the demand curve from A depends on the *elasticity* of the demand curve DD at point A. For example, if the elasticity of DD at A is greater than one, total revenue will fall as price rises above P_1 and rise as price falls below P_1. If the elasticity of DD at A is less than one, total revenue will rise as price rises above P_1. On the other hand, if the elasticity of DD at A is equal to one (unity), total revenue will be maximized at A. See Chapter 5 for the explanation of elasticity.

Marginal Revenue

Marginal revenue is the increase in total revenue that results from the sale of an additional unit. Since marginal revenue is another term for the *change* in total revenue, it gives a clue to the effect of increased sales on profits. If marginal revenue is negative, increasing sales decreases total revenue. The reverse is true if it is positive. A firm should never choose to increase sales if marginal revenue is negative, whatever the costs, since this implies that total revenue (the value of sales) will decrease.

Marginal revenue is most easily understood when divided in two parts. When an additional unit of output is sold, revenue changes in two ways: (1) Revenue increases because one more unit is sold; (2) revenue decreases because price falls. The increase in revenue is equal to the price of output; the decrease is equal to the decline in price times the number of units previously sold. Suppose that the demand curve for the mineral water producer shows that at a price of $10 a gallon, he will sell 10 gallons a day. But at a price of $9 a gallon, he will sell 11 gallons. The marginal revenue from the additional sale of one more gallon is equal to (1) the value of that unit ($9) minus (2) the fall in price on all the other gallons sold: ($1 × 10 gallons = $10) or $9 − $10 = −$1. The firm gains $9 by selling the 11th gallon but loses $10 by charging $1 less for the previous 10 gallons. The marginal revenue at this point is negative, so the profit-maximizing firm is ill-advised to lower price and increase volume. Remember that the definition of marginal revenue is *the change in total revenue that results from an additional unit sold.* Remembering this permits us to arrive at the above result by calculating total revenue both after and before the change in price and taking the difference. The marginal revenue of the 11th gallon of mineral water must be the total revenue that could be received for 11 gallons minus the total revenue that could be received for 10 gallons.

$$\text{marginal revenue} = \$9/\text{gallon} \times 11 \text{ gallons} = \quad \$99$$
$$\text{minus}$$
$$\$10/\text{gallon} \times 10 \text{ gallons} = \underline{\$100}$$
$$-\$1$$

In the example above marginal revenue happened to be negative. A counterexample with marginal revenue positive would occur if the firm had begun by selling mineral water at $20 per gallon and sold 1 gallon. By lowering the price to $19 per gallon, sales might increase to 2 gallons. Marginal revenue from the increased sale is again equal to (1) the revenue from the additional gallon ($19) minus (2) the loss in revenue from the fall in price of all other units sold ($1 × 1 gallon = $1) or $19 − $1 = $18. This must be equal to the change in total revenue, which is $38 − $20 = 18.

In summary, at zero output, total revenue is zero. As output is allowed to expand, revenue expands up to a point. After this point further increases in output will cause revenue to contract. Marginal revenue is positive for small quantities of output but becomes negative as output is increased. Maximum total revenue occurs at that level of output where marginal revenue turns from positive to negative. Maximum total revenue occurs where marginal revenue equals zero. But the firm is interested in profits, not revenue, and profits equal revenue minus cost.

Profit Maximization (When the Firm Has Costs)

Things get a bit more complicated if the well runs dry and our firm has to start manufacturing mineral water by adding minerals to tap water. At this point it begins to cost something to produce the product. If a firm has costs, revenues are no longer equal to profits. The firm now must consider how to maximize profits rather than just revenue. Remembering the original decision rule we established for profits, and noting that profits equal revenue minus cost, we can restate the decision rule as follows:

> *If the production of an additional unit of output adds more to revenue than to cost, produce it; if it adds less to revenue than to cost, reduce output.*

Marginal Cost

How much does one more unit of output add to revenue? Marginal revenue. How much does one more unit of output add to cost? *Marginal cost.* The reader should be able to define marginal cost without hesitation as *the increase in costs caused by producing one more unit of output.* In Chapter 13 we determined the lowest cost for each level of output and connected these efficient points. We called that boundary the *total cost curve. Marginal cost* is simply the increase in total cost brought about by increasing output by one unit. And *average cost* must be total cost divided by the number of units of output. Before we look at cost curves in more detail, let us show how the concepts of marginal cost and marginal revenue permit a restatement of the profit-maximizing decision rule. We can now say that

> *If marginal revenue is greater than marginal cost, increase output; if marginal revenue is less than marginal cost, decrease output.*

This decision rule is very helpful—it is a guide to profit maximization that does not require any knowledge of the absolute level of profits at a given point. If a firm considers entering a new venture, it is interested in how that new venture will affect its *existing level of costs and revenues.* If marginal revenue exceeds marginal cost, it should enter the venture regardless of the absolute profit that such a venture might yield by itself.

For example, a small firm selling batteries through gasoline stations might be losing money although its production is as efficient as possible. A large oil concern might enter the same business and *increase* its profits by doing so. This is because the oil concern already has salesmen who visit all the gasoline stations in order to sell the company's other products. The small firm is losing money because total cost is greater than total revenue, but the large firm is able to raise its profits by entering the business because the marginal cost of entering is less than the marginal revenue. If the larger firm had no oil sales and therefore no reason to have a sales force visit the gasoline stations, it, too, would lose money on the venture. The battery business apparently cannot pay by itself and even in the large firm it does not pay its share of the salesmen's salaries. But the relevant cost to the company is the *additional* cost of selling batteries, not the total cost. Now one can see why some firms are happy to pay a good price to buy out other firms that are losing money.

The curves we have been drawing refer to a single product, of course. But the above example indicates that the decision rule is general enough to apply to the question of new product lines as well.

Before proceeding further, it is useful to understand the relationship between average cost and marginal cost.

Average and Marginal Costs

Costs are related directly to production functions (as the previous chapter showed in some detail). If factor prices are constant and the production function of the firm offers no advantages to either large- or small-scale production — it exhibits constant returns to scale — a firm's total cost function will be a straight line. Costs will rise in proportion to output. Average cost (unit cost) will be constant. As long as average cost does not change, the addition to total cost from each new unit of output will be the same; marginal cost will be constant. It will also be equal to average cost. Figure 14.3 is drawn showing average cost constant and therefore equal to marginal cost.

What happens if the firm has advantages of large-scale production (economies of scale)? The more mineral water the firm produces, the lower the cost of each gallon becomes. If the production function has *economies of scale*, cost per unit will decrease when output is expanded, as shown in Figure 14.4. Where average costs are everywhere decreasing, marginal cost must be less than average cost at every level of output. This is important to understand because it is the key to the relation of marginal to average cost.

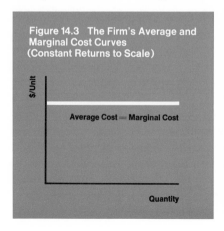

Figure 14.3   The Firm's Average and Marginal Cost Curves (Constant Returns to Scale)

$/Unit

Average Cost = Marginal Cost

Quantity

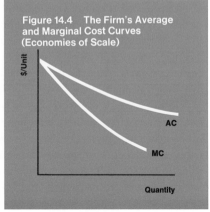

Figure 14.4   The Firm's Average and Marginal Cost Curves (Economies of Scale)

$/Unit

AC

MC

Quantity

Consider the relation between a marginal unit and an average unit of any-thing, such as the height of persons in a room. You enter an empty room. Each new person entering the room represents a new *marginal* height. If the second person is shorter than you are, the average height (your height plus his divided by two) falls, but still it will be greater than the new marginal height (his height alone). Another way of saying the same thing is that if the marginal height is less than the average height, the average must decrease. If a third person enters whose height is above the average, the average will then increase. If the margin exceeds the average, the average is increasing. So it is with costs.

The analogy about height suggests what happens if the production process provides *diseconomies of scale* at all levels of output. Average costs are steadily rising. Figure 14.5 shows that marginal cost in this case must be everywhere above average cost.

A cost function often considered by economists exhibits a more complex pattern of behavior. It assumes the existence of economies of scale for very low levels of production and diseconomies of scale for greater levels of production. The firm's cost curves in this case will be a combination of those in Figures 14.4 and 14.5. We have illustrated it in Figure 14.6.

If a production process first has economies and then diseconomies of scale, its average and marginal cost curves will be U-shaped, as in Figure 14.6. Marginal cost initially would be less than average cost, pulling it down. But when marginal cost exceeds average cost, average cost must increase. This means that at the *minimum point of the average cost curve*

$$MC \text{ (marginal cost)} = AC \text{ (average cost)}$$

Note that at the minimum point on the average cost curve the firm is experiencing neither economies nor diseconomies of scale. The marginal unit neither lowers average cost nor increases it, because it is equal to it.

We shall see later on that U-shaped cost curves are one explanation of why firms are the size they are. Disadvantages of small-scale production enable larger firms to lower price and force smaller producers out of business. Disadvantages

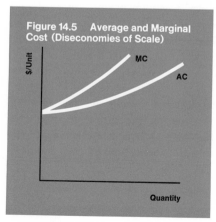

Figure 14.5   Average and Marginal Cost (Diseconomies of Scale)

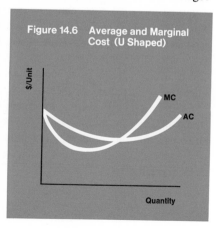

Figure 14.6   Average and Marginal Cost (U Shaped)

of very large-scale production prevent firms from becoming enormous, since smaller producers will be able to sell at lower prices.

What are the technological reasons behind the U-shape of the cost curve?

One of the main reasons for the existence of increasing returns to scale (we will call it decreasing costs from now on) is the division of labor. Adam Smith was the first to notice this in his famous chapter about the pin factory. Smith noticed that when each man performed a special task (making the head of the pin, for example) pin output was much higher than when each man performed all tasks. Ten men could make more pins when each performed a single task than they could if each tried to make the whole pin. The man in charge of pinheads became very efficient at making them, much more so than the man in charge of drawing out the wire into a stem. When the men had to perform all tasks, they never became sufficiently adept at any of them to have a very high productivity. It was the old story of jack-of-all-trades, master-of-none.

In addition to labor skills, there are certain production techniques that are more efficient when used on large-scale operations than otherwise. Simple things such as a boiler being more efficient the larger it gets† can give an indication of the fact that nature need not exhibit constant returns to scale.

Increasing costs, on the other hand, usually arise because of the difficulty of communication. The more people there are that must be aware of the implications of a certain decision, the more difficult it is to make that decision. Bureaucracy and red tape are often the result when large enterprises attempt to eliminate the need to communicate by systematizing operations. It is only since the age of computers that large-scale construction firms have been able to know the whereabouts and condition of all their equipment. Small firms always know this.

In some industries the decreasing costs brought about by the technological efficiency of large-scale production are great enough to offset the costs of communication. Very large firms are likely to exist in such industries.

The Decision Rule Shown Diagrammatically

The decision rule for profit maximization, expressed in terms of marginal revenue and marginal cost, can now be shown diagrammatically. Let us draw a *marginal revenue curve* and an *average revenue curve* for our mineral water producer. The marginal revenue curve simply shows the change in total revenue at each level of output and is drawn everywhere below *DD* (because we know that if an average curve is steadily falling, the marginal curve must lie everywhere below it, pulling it down).

With curves for average and marginal cost and revenue, we can show diagrammatically the maximizing decision based on the firm's decision rule. Drawing both sets of curves (Figures 14.6 and 14.7) in one diagram (Figure 14.8), we see that at one point the marginal cost and marginal revenue curves intersect (at point *E*).

†This is because heat loss is proportional to the size of the surface of the boiler and the size of the surface does not double when the volume is doubled.

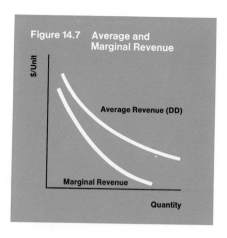

Figure 14.7 Average and Marginal Revenue

At lower output levels than Q_E, marginal revenue (*MR*) is still above marginal cost (*MC*). By the decision rule, the firm should continue to increase output (lower price). This will add more to revenue than to cost, and thus profits will increase. Beyond point *E*, however, things are different. Marginal revenue is below marginal cost for each additional unit of output. The decision rule tells us not to increase output beyond *E* and to reduce output if it is ever greater than *E*. Given these curves, there is one and only one point at which the firm's profits are maximized (where it is impossible to raise profits a cent by changing either price or output). This point is determined by the intersection of *MC* and *MR* at point *E*. Here the quantity produced will be Q_E and the price will be P_E. The firm will make a profit at this point equal to the difference between average cost (*AC*) and average revenue (*AR*) times the number of units sold. This corresponds to the shaded area in the diagram. Note that at no other price and quantity would the shaded area between *AR* and *AC* be as large. Our decision rule has guaranteed this.

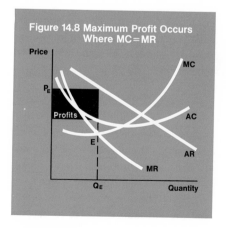

Figure 14.8 Maximum Profit Occurs Where MC=MR

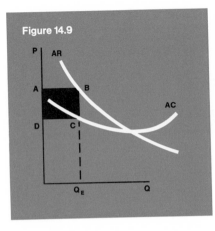

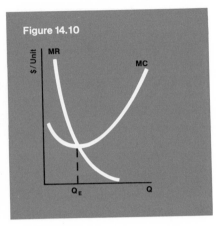

Three Different Ways to View the Profit Maximum

Given that all the cost curves and all the revenue curves are related, we can use any pair of them to depict the point of maximum profits. In Figure 14.9, rectangle $ABCD$ represents profits. Its height is profit per unit; its base is the number of units; therefore its area must be total profits. The largest rectangle, whose height is the difference between AR and AC and whose base is output, shows us the output level that maximizes profit.

In Figure 14.10 maximum profits occur where $MR = MC$. This has been adequately discussed above.

Figure 14.11 shows total revenue and total cost. Total profit is obviously the vertical distance between them. Parallel lines are drawn tangent to the curves at output Q_E. Note that the vertical distance between the curves is greatest at the point of tangency to those parallel lines. All other vertical distances are less than the constant distance between the parallel lines. The reason for this becomes clear once we note that the slope of the total cost function is the change in cost divided by the change in output. But for a change in output of one unit, *this slope must be marginal cost*. Similarly, the slope of the total revenue function is marginal revenue. At that output level where the two slopes are equal, marginal revenue equals marginal cost; profits are at a maximum. To the left of that point in Figure 14.11, MR exceeds MC, as can be seen from the fact that the slope of TR exteeds TC. The decision rule tells us to increase output whenever MR exceeds MC.

Epilogue

The boss's son has returned from college, eager to demonstrate the fruits of his knowledge. He takes up pencil and paper and draws the diagrams we have just drawn to show his father *why* the firm has been choosing P_E and Q_E all along. The old man hates to believe that the profits from all that mineral water have been spent to buy so little education and seemingly have gone down the drain. The diagram shows nothing more than what the old man was able to accom-

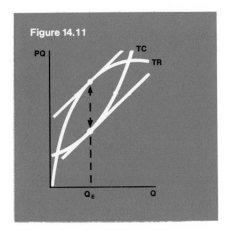

Figure 14.11

plish by a lifetime of trial and error in his efforts to maximize profits. Of what value is this?

What the old man does not know is that as long as firms are maximizing profit (and therefore implicitly if not explicitly setting marginal costs equal to marginal revenue), it is possible to draw some conclusions about allocative efficiency from firm behavior. This is where the diagram comes in handy. The externalities produced by the boy's knowledge about profit maximization and sales must await a less familiar audience. His diagram is used in the next chapter to show the implications for the welfare of society as a whole of the profit-maximizing behavior of a single firm.

Economics is to operations research as physics is to engineering. One must know more than physics in order to build a bridge and one must know more than economics in order to maximize profits. But it is a poor engineer who is devoid of knowledge of physics. The problem is not that the boy learned economics, but that he failed to learn how to use it.

Questions
1. Why does the decision rule described in this chapter eventually lead to a profit maximum? Do we know that profits are maximized whenever $MR = MC$? How do we handle the possibility of shutting the firm down?
2. What technological reasons make cost curves U-shaped? Why does $MC = AC$ at the minimum point of the AC curve?
3. How does the elasticity of the demand curve tell whether MR is positive or negative?

Concepts Discussed
total revenue	marginal cost
profits	average cost
average revenue	decreasing costs
marginal revenue	increasing costs

15 Profit Maximization under Monopoly and Pure Competition

It is time to turn to the question of industrial organization. In this chapter, we look at the narrow question of economic efficiency and how it is affected by the decisions of firms to produce more or less of a particular commodity. We will examine industries with two extreme forms of organization: (1) an industry with one firm, and (2) an industry with many competitive firms. In the next chapter, we look at organizational possibilities in between these extremes, while in the succeeding chapters we look at problems that arise from broadening the analysis. Here we show that the industry that contains many competitive firms is likely to produce the efficient quantity of output whereas the industry that contains one firm only is not likely to do so because that one firm will exploit its market power and raise its prices above the competitive level. We continue to assume that the sole goal of the firms is to maximize profits.

CASE 1: MONOPOLY

Barriers to Entry

A monopoly is an industry with only one firm. As a result, the demand curve for output of the whole industry is the demand curve for the firm. Thus the demand curve a monopolist faces is downward sloping just as in the analysis in Chapter 14. Indeed, the diagram for the mineral water producer in that chapter can now be used to illustrate the behavior of a firm that is the *only seller* of mineral water in the economy. Monopolies can survive provided there is some obstacle to other firms' entering the industry. It may be that the only available mineral water spring is owned by a single firm. Or it may be that the method of extracting and processing mineral water is patented and under exclusive control of one firm. It may even be that the firm threatens to drive any potential competitor out of the industry by legal or illegal means and successfully intimidates all other firms. In any event, we assume there is some barrier to entry into the industry that permits the long-run existence of the mineral water monopoly.

Monopoly Profits

The existence of profits in the case of a monopoly can be seen in the diagram from Chapter 14, reproduced here (Fig. 15.1). The downward-sloping demand curve for the single firm means that marginal revenue is at every point below average revenue. At the point where $MR = MC$ we know that the firm is best off. Profits are earned to the extent of the shaded area between the average revenue and average cost curves. Of what do these profits consist?

profits = total revenue − total cost

Total cost includes payments for the services of *all resources* used by the firm in the process of production: land, labor, capital, and management. Every factor of production is paid at least its "opportunity cost" (what it might earn in the next best alternative employment).

The cost of land to the firm is the rent that land could command from the best possible alternative use. The cost of labor is the amount workers must be paid to prevent them from taking alternative employment. Capital invested in the firm is paid the current rate of interest in the market and the interest payment is part of total cost. The same is true for management. The economic concept of *total cost* therefore measures the services of all scarce resources involved in the production of, for example, mineral water. *Profits*, the remaining revenue after all costs have been covered, do not correspond to the *opportunity cost* of any input. Profits exist whenever total revenue exceeds total cost whether or not the firm is actually a single seller in the market.

The reader should not confuse our definition of profits with the normal accounting use of the term "profits." If a firm owns its own building, it does not make an actual rent payment to itself. An accountant would list the profits of the firm as higher if it owned the building than if it did not. But the use of the building is part of the economic cost of conducting the business and should be so counted when computing economic profits. The building should be thought of as having an opportunity cost. The firm might have chosen to rent that building to someone else. Therefore the income on the building should not be confused with the profit from the business. Firms will often include elements of opportunity cost to land, capital, and management under the heading profits. But these profits

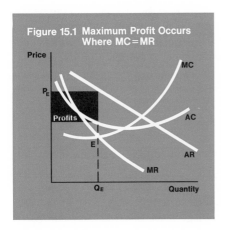

Figure 15.1 Maximum Profit Occurs Where MC = MR

are in reality costs of the production process and must be covered in order for the process to be profitable. Thus the excess of revenue over cost, "economic profits," must be distinguished from "normal profits." It is profits in excess of opportunity cost that interest us. Ownership of the building can be changed without affecting opportunity costs.

Entrepreneurship

If every scarce resource has already been paid its opportunity cost, what is the role of monopoly profits in allocating scarce resources? They play the role of a signal to other producers to enter the market in which the returns above costs are highest, and they therefore serve as an allocative device. In this respect, profits cause those who are thinking about introducing new products or satisfying existing demand to go into action. Take, for example, the initiator of a new product. The person who combines the knowledge of a new invention with the skill to market it successfully is called an *entrepreneur*. His is an exciting and challenging role. Lured by the expectation of economic profits, he goes into business, whether it be producing aluminum (before World War II), ballpoint pens (after the war), hula hoops (in the 1960s), or mineral water. The first producer in any market is a monopolist. The demand curve facing the industry is his own demand curve. How long does this situation last?

Competition and the Survival of Monopoly

As soon as others observe our entrepreneur enjoying economic profits (a return in excess of costs), they will try to enter the market, producing the same product. If successful, they now compete with him for a part of the market and cause his demand curve to shrink. This will have an effect on his profits. When his *AR* and *MR* curves shift to the left, the shaded area of profits will diminish. The monopolist, because he wishes to maximize both present and future profits, will tend to do all he can to prevent others from entering the market. He will use patents, trade secrets, legal charters, copyrights, and intimidation to keep competitors out of his market. Some industries, such as electric power production and distribution, have such economies of scale that they constitute *natural monopolies*. They can survive as single-firm industries by the very nature of their technology. These natural monopolies are immune to the force of competition and are able to sustain economic profits without resorting to legal or illegal barriers to entry. We give them a more careful look later.

CASE 2: PURE COMPETITION

No Barriers to Entry

An industry in pure competition has many firms producing an identical product; there are no barriers to entry and each firm attempts to maximize its own profits independently of the actions of the other firms. Pure competition, like monopoly, is an extreme case among the many market structures that exist in the real world. If we assume that no natural or artificial barriers exist to prevent entry into the market, what will happen to profits? Producers are still profit maximizers. As long as some amount of monopoly profits exists, new firms will enter the market to attempt to capture the return above costs. Since the products of all these firms are identical, consumers will buy from the firm that charges the lowest price. This means that all sellers must charge the same price.

Assume that an equilibrium price is attained in such an industry. Let us see how the demand curve for an individual firm looks in this situation. Someone invents a cheap process that anyone can adopt for making mineral water from tap water. Thousands of firms enter the market, lured by the high profits of the initial firm in the industry. A new price is established in the industry — 10 cents a gallon. How do these market conditions affect an individual seller of mineral water? If he charges more than 10 cents, no one will buy a drop of his water. If he charges less than 10 cents, the world will beat a path to his door. His demand curve will look like *dd* in Figure 15.2. At the market price he can sell as much as he can produce. If he is only one of thousands of firms, his piece of the industry demand curve is so tiny that when stretched out to correspond to the volume he can produce it looks flat.

Economic Profits
Can a producer make an economic profit with a demand curve that is flat? This depends on where his cost curves lie. Let us take the cost curves from the preceding chapter and apply them to this firm. Since profits are the residual between revenue (demand) and cost, we can determine profits under pure competition as in Figure 15.3.

Since the firm is still a profit maximizer, it will produce the level of output at which $MR = MC$. But now that the demand curve (average revenue) is horizontal, the average revenue curve coincides with the marginal revenue curve. Price is determined by the market and is virtually independent of the firm's output. The firm has no incentive to raise price, since that would cut its sales to zero. It has no incentive to lower price, since it can already sell all it is able to produce

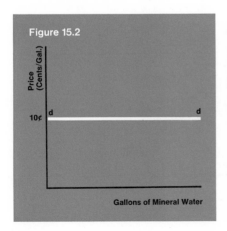

Figure 15.2

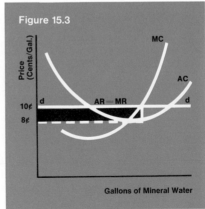

Figure 15.3

at the going market price. These were the conditions we assumed for the corn farmer in Chapter 6. The farmer's output had no influence on the price of corn because he also was only one among many producers of an identical product. The results derived in Chapter 6 are therefore results that will hold true in a world characterized by pure competition.

Note that even in pure competition in the short run, the firm in Figure 15.3 is still making some economic profit by producing at Q_E and selling at 10 cents a gallon. Can such a situation continue? Not if anyone who wishes can still enter the market and experience the same cost conditions (have the same cost curves) as this firm. The short-run equilibrium in Figure 15.3 is not the same as the long-run equilibrium because there is still an inducement for new firms to enter the market and share in the profits.

Competition and the Survival of Economic Profits

As long as economic profits exist, and there are no barriers to entry and if each firm has access to the same technology, more and more firms will enter the market. The long-run solution will be as shown in Figure 15.4.

Remember that the demand curve faced by the competitive firm is a horizontal line at the going price. As other firms enter the industry and attempt to sell their output, they drive the price down. By the individual firm, this is seen as a decrease in the height of its demand curve. Once the demand curve has fallen to the level at which there are no economic profits, there is no more incentive for additional firms to enter the industry. Thus the equilibrium price is the price at which economic profits are zero.

Figure 15.5 illustrates the relationship between the conditions faced by the firm and those within the industry. To understand Figure 15.5, we must note the manner in which an industry supply curve is created from the behavior of the firms we have been studying. The *firm's* supply curve is the locus of points that shows how much output the firm would produce at each price. Now profit maximization tells us that the quantity of output produced will always be the level at which $MR = MC$. But to the competitive firm, we have seen that $MR = AR = P$.

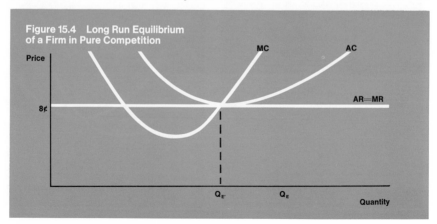

Figure 15.4   Long Run Equilibrium of a Firm in Pure Competition

Thus $P = MC$ is a condition for a profit maximum to exist. And since MC as a function of output is the marginal cost curve, and P as a function of output is the firm's supply curve, the supply curve must coincide with the marginal cost curve if profits are to be maximized.

The industry's supply curve for the given number of firms in the industry is the horizontal sum of the supply curves of the firms, or the sum of the marginal cost curves. As more firms enter the industry, there are more MC curves to sum. Thus the expansion of the industry supply from SS to $S'S'$ in Figure 15.5 results from the entry of new firms.

When enough firms have entered the industry to shift the supply curve out to $S'S'$ so that price falls to P^*, a long-run equilibrium will have been attained. There will be no further incentive for firms to enter since there will be no economic profits in this industry. Firms will be able to earn a return on their own capital, of course, but it will be no more than if they invested it in any other competitive industry.

Can the firm survive? Certainly. Economic profits are a residual after all of the resources used by the firm have already been paid their opportunity cost. Land, labor, capital, and management are fully compensated under total costs. The firm will show accounting profits in its annual report just as any other firm does. It will still earn the market-determined rate of return on the capital it owns and the accountants will label this return "profits." All that is required is that the firm not operate at a loss. If average cost is *above* price, then some of the factors of production cannot be paid their opportunity cost and are likely to find alternative employment. It is, of course, quite possible that the entrepreneur who first set up the mineral water company will be unsatisfied with a salary equal to his "opportunity cost" in the next best employment. The excitement of discovering new sources of windfall profits (and the income it brings) is his meat and drink. Now that the firm has settled into a purely competitive routine, earning only enough revenue to cover costs, the entrepreneur may turn his job over to a manager and strike out in new directions.

What if the price for mineral water fell *below* 8 cents? Then price would not

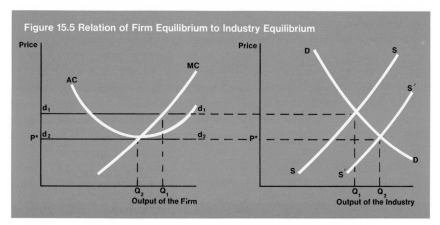

Figure 15.5 Relation of Firm Equilibrium to Industry Equilibrium

cover the firm's average costs and it could not survive over the long run from its own sales. Still, as long as it remained in operation with $P < AC$, its decision to set $MR = MC$ would minimize its losses, just as that decision would maximize profits when $P > AC$.

In the long run, purely competitive firms, by following the same decision rule as monopolies, tend to achieve equilibrium at a point where price equals marginal cost. Such a result eventually *eliminates economic profits* where there are no barriers to entry into the industry. What is the effect of this solution on efficiency? How do competitive industries differ from monopolistic ones in the efficiency of the prices they charge?

Allocative Efficiency under Pure Competition and Monopoly

We now have two quite different results from profit maximization owing to the two different market structures we have analyzed. Both competitors and monopolists set $MR = MC$. But for the competitors, since marginal revenue and average revenue are equal, profit maximization results in price equaling marginal cost. Moreover, the competitor who earns profits faces a situation in which there are no barriers to entry into the industry. Other firms will enter in the long run, serving to increase total production and drive down the market price until it reaches the level of average costs. Thus long-run equilibrium occurs in pure competition at the point of minimum average cost. Competition destroys the economic profits. Competitive firms earn no more than the market rate of return on the capital they own. The monopolist, however, is protected from such an outcome by barriers to entry into his industry. This allows price to remain above both marginal cost and average cost, so that economic profits can be earned even over the long run. How can we compare the efficiency of resource allocation that results from these alternative market structures?

Value and Cost

Resource allocations, we have seen, are efficient whenever the value of commodities equals their cost. We have also seen that prices can be useful signals for the concepts of value and cost. Allowing consumers to maximize utility by buying whatever commodities they wish, given their budget constraint, results in an equilibrium at which the value of a commodity equals its price. If the equilibrium attained by producers is one in which cost is equal to price, then the allocation of resources will be efficient. With cost equal to price and price equal to value, value will be equal to cost and efficiency will characterize the solution.

To analyze the competitive and monopolistic solutions from the viewpoint of efficiency, we only need find which form of organization sets cost equal to price. To do this we must make clear what is meant by cost and see how to derive it from the cost concepts we have been dealing with in this chapter.

If an allocation of resources is to be efficient, it is the social opportunity cost—the slope of the PPF—that must equal the value of a commodity. If the value of a commodity exceeds its social cost, it is possible to produce another unit of it by sacrificing some commodities of lesser value. Some people can be made better off by this trade while no one else need be made worse off. This was shown in Chapter 9 and should be reviewed. Intuitively, this principle can be summarized by the statement, "If the value of a commodity exceeds its cost, more of it should be produced."

Which of the firm's cost concepts corresponds to social opportunity cost? The social cost of a commodity is the other goods that must be sacrificed if one more unit of the commodity is to be produced. The cost to a firm of producing one more unit of a commodity is the marginal cost of that commodity. If prices and costs are expressed in terms of goods instead of money, the marginal cost faced by the firm will be the social cost faced by the society, assuming no external effects of production. Externalities are considered below. Thus it will be the firm's marginal cost that must be set equal to price if resources are to be allocated efficiently—if the value of a commodity is to equal its cost.* Consumers make sure that price is equal to value. Perfectly competitive producers, by maximizing profits, make sure that price equals marginal cost. Thus, at a perfectly competitive equilibrium, value equals cost and resources are allocated efficiently.

Things are different when a monopoly exists. The monopolist sets $MR = MC$, of course, but because the monopolist faces a downward-sloping demand curve, marginal revenue is less than price. Thus marginal cost must be less than price. By the reasoning outlined above, we know that resources are inefficiently allocated when prices differ from marginal cost. To consumers the commodity has a value equal to its price. They are willing to sacrifice other goods of that value for one more unit of the commodity. The producer could produce one more unit for an amount less than the price; he can produce one more at marginal cost. Thus it is possible to make someone better off and no one else worse off by reallocating resources. This is done by having the monopolist produce one more unit of output, paying him his marginal cost so that his profits remain constant, and then selling the commodity at cost to an individual who values it at the market price. The individual is made better off by acquiring a commodity that is worth more to him than it cost him. No one else, including the monopolist, is made worse off.

Figure 15.6 compares the two solutions. Profits are maximized at the point where $MR = MC$. Resources are efficiently allocated where price equals marginal cost. Thus a monopolist misallocates resources by restricting the level of output. If there is less output, people are willing to pay higher prices and economic profits are made possible. Figure 15.6 shows a short-run solution for pure competition in which profits are earned. This output is labeled Q_{CSR}. The long-run output for the competitive firm will be at minimum average cost when enough firms enter to reduce demand to that level. Output for the competitive

*In the appendix to this chapter, we use the PPF to indicate the efficiency of the allocation of resources under perfect competition or monopoly. There we spell out explicitly the conditions that must be satisfied in other markets in order to make the leap from prices expressed in terms of money to those expressed in terms of goods.

industry in the long run will be the amount demanded when price equals min-imum average cost. Thus we see that the free market can misfire on the produc-tion side of the economy if monopolies are tolerated just as it can misfire on the consumption side in the case of public goods.

Regulating Monopolies

What corrective legislation might be imposed on monopolists to prevent them from raising price above marginal cost and restricting production?

(1) Price Regulation. The voters might force monopolists to set price equal to marginal cost. Since a regulatory agency could find it difficult to assess the marginal costs of a monopoly, it might attempt to accomplish this by control-ling the rate of return on capital received by the monopolist. This is the method used by public utility rate commissions. They allow public utilities, such as light and power companies, railroads, airlines, natural gas transmission lines, and tele-phone and telegraph companies, to charge prices that will permit a rate of return on capital equal to the competitive market rate of return, but no more. In effect they are declaring long-run monopoly profits illegal for these enterprises. There are, of course, many technical problems associated with determining the compet-itive rate of return and even with defining the profits of these "natural monopo-lies." Below we will discuss the discretion accountants may use in determining stated profits. But regulatory agencies have been successful in preventing these monopolists from earning economic profits. Returns on capital are allowed and these returns are as close to those earned in the competitive market as the regu-latory agency can make them.

(2) Antitrust. Another regulatory device is antitrust legislation designed to prevent large firms from becoming monopolies by forbidding them to force small firms out of business. This is the intent of the antitrust division of the Jus-tice Department. It attempts to prevent the formation of monopolies. Occasion-ally it has even forced monopolies to divide into several smaller (supposedly competing) firms. An example of this is the tobacco industry. James Duke orga-

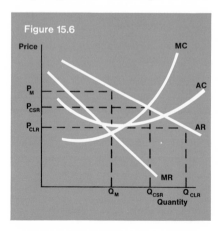

Figure 15.6

nized, around the turn of the century, a huge tobacco firm, the American To-bacco Company, which almost completely controlled the manufacture of ciga-rettes in the United States and also held a prominent position in other tobacco markets. Under the Sherman Antitrust Act, the Justice Department forced American Tobacco to divide into four smaller companies. These firms – R. J. Reynolds, Liggett and Myers, P. Lorillard, and American Tobacco Company – still represent the bulk of the industry even though two-thirds of a century has passed since the division occurred.

Antitrust legislation is also used to prevent *mergers,* the process by which two corporations can be combined into one. The rationale behind antitrust legis-lation is that many small firms are preferable to one large one; that is, small firms will compete with each other and in doing so will drive prices down to levels that reflect costs.

The Efficiency Implications of Monopoly Regulation

How effective are alternative control measures in achieving allocative efficiency? When should monopolies be regulated? When should they be broken up? Let us check on the price regulation practiced by public utility rate commissions. The public utility commission does not apply the Sherman Antitrust Act to break up electric light and power companies into smaller units. What would happen if there were ten competing electric power companies in the same town? Once Mexico City had two telephone companies, each with its own network, com-peting for service. What was the implication of this type of competition?

The answer is that for industries that are natural monopolies, a single firm provides *greater efficiency.* Ten electric companies mean ten sets of power lines criss-crossing over the rooftops, wasting resources, and needlessly duplicating facilities. This inefficiency is reflected in the cost curves of the firms. Public utili-ties are industries with decreasing unit costs when output increases. There are economies of large-scale production. Figure 15.7 is drawn to represent a firm with economies of scale in production. Assume that $Q_2 = 2Q_1$. Consider the so-

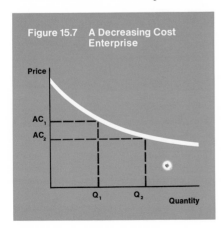

Figure 15.7   A Decreasing Cost
Enterprise

cial alternatives of having one firm produce Q_2 or two firms each produce Q_1. Costs are plainly lower with one firm than with two. To determine this fact, one need only note that unit costs are higher when each firm can produce only Q_1. From the cost side it would be inefficient to break up such a monopoly into many smaller firms, since smaller firms have higher per-unit costs. Yet if one firm is left alone and free to maximize its profits, society will end up paying not the marginal cost but some higher price. So something must be done to make certain that society gets the *benefit* of the lower costs of production that result from large-scale operations without having to give a monopolist large levels of profit. This is where rate regulation enters the picture.

What price will provide society with allocative efficiency from a decreasing cost monopoly such as the one described above? We know that it should be a price that is equal to marginal cost. But since average cost is everywhere declining (in the relevant range of demand), marginal cost is less than average cost. This creates problems. When price equals marginal costs, it must be less than average cost. A price less than average cost means that the firm loses a little on every sale. This problem shows up clearly when we draw the rest of the curves as in Figure 15.8.

How should we deal with this type of industry? If we could force the firm to charge P^*, we could make $MC = P$ (price) and get an efficient allocation of resources. But we cannot force a private firm to charge that price, since it involves a loss (equal to the shaded area). Price is less than average cost; therefore the firm would be losing a bit on every sale. How about a public utility commission solution? The commission simply acts to eliminate monopoly profits. It requires the firm to set the price at P' ($P = AC$). No monopoly profits are made. Why are resources inefficiently allocated even though monopoly profits have been eliminated? Remember that marginal cost represents social cost. But at Q', marginal cost is below price. Hence social cost is less than the price consumers are willing to pay even after the rate commission has set its rules. Consumers are required to pay price P' even though the additional resources required to expand power

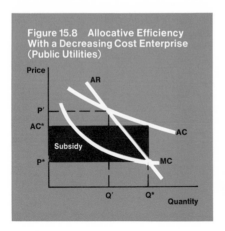

Figure 15.8   Allocative Efficiency With a Decreasing Cost Enterprise (Public Utilities)

production are much less and are equal to MC rather than AC. Just because no profits exist at Q' does not mean that resources are efficiently allocated when output is restricted to this level. Consumers restrict their consumption of the commodity because they face price P'. But society's cost is only MC. It is possible to produce at cost MC goods whose value is P'. If this is not done, happiness is wasted. Resources are efficiently allocated only when price equals marginal cost, and this means producing at point Q^* for price P^* even though it would mean a loss for the firm. A way must be found around this dilemma.

How should societies deal with enterprises that have decreasing costs, such as certain utilities, bridges, lighthouses, roads, canals, etc.? It could make them into state enterprises and run them at a loss, setting price equal to marginal cost. Many countries have publicly owned utilities, railroads, and mail service, as well as roads, bridges, and lighthouses. We now see why running them at a loss may mean greater allocative efficiency than requiring them to make a profit. The fact that many government enterprises run at a loss does not mean they are inefficient. It may mean that they are charging a price equal to marginal cost and are losing money in order that resources be allocated efficiently.

There are two ways to incur losses. One is to be inefficient and not control costs properly. The other is to lower price below the efficient cost level in order to expand sales and take advantage of the economies of large-scale production. If $P = MC$ in a decreasing cost industry, the latter kind of loss will exist. It is a socially efficient loss.

Alternatively, the government could subsidize private firms and then require them to sell at a price below average cost (equal to marginal cost). This would prevent their need to cover costs from standing in the way of consumer sovereignty and allocative efficiency. A subsidy is simply a negative tax that is turned over to the private firms. The public is, in effect, rewarding the firms that do it a favor by charging a price equal to marginal cost.

Thus the elimination of monopoly profits does not guarantee an efficient allocation of resources. It increases output beyond what the monopolist would produce in the absence of legislation, but it will not, in the case of decreasing cost industries, increase output to the level at which price equals marginal cost.

Most taxes, we will see later, also lead to inefficiencies. Thus decreasing cost industries are a major reason why most allocations of resources in the market economies of the world are inefficient. We have to choose between inefficient levels of taxes and inefficient levels of output in decreasing cost industries. There is no *a priori* way to make this choice.

Questions

1. Compare antitrust legislation with price regulation as devices for guaranteeing the existence of efficiency in the allocation of resources.
2. Why do decreasing cost industries pose problems for the efficiency of an allocation of resources?
3. Why does pure competition result in the efficient level of output for an industry?

Concepts Discussed

monopoly
economic profits
accounting profits
pure competition

price regulation
antitrust
merger

APPENDIX: MONOPOLY AND THE PRODUCTION POSSIBILITY FRONTIER

The inefficiency caused by monopolies can be shown with reference to the production frontier. By using the frontier, the effect of the monopolist's action on relative prices and the production of all commodities can be seen. First, we discuss the conditions under which the slope of the production frontier is equal to the ratio of marginal costs in the two industries. Then we use this result to portray the monopoly solution.

We assume that only two industries exist: (1) a perfectly competitive steak industry and (2) a monopolized movie industry. First, let us consider the case in which there are no externalities of production, that is, the case in which producers must pay all their own production costs. In this case, the social cost of a steak—the slope of the PPF—will equal the ratio of the marginal costs of steak to movies. This can be shown as follows.

The social cost of a steak, C_S, is the number of movies that must be sacrificed to produce one more steak. The cost to the producers of producing one more steak is its marginal cost, MC_S. The marginal cost results from the payments that must be made to the extra factors hired and from changes in factor prices that may result when steak production is increased and movie production decreased. As we are concerned with very small changes in production, we assume that there are no changes in factor prices. The marginal cost of producing movies, MC_M, similarly is assumed to be the cost of the extra factors that must be hired to produce one more unit of movies.

To increase steak production by one unit, we must hire more factors and these factors must be hired away from the movie industry if we assume full employment in factor markets. It takes MC_M factors to produce one more movie, $2MC_M$ factors to produce two more movies, and $C_S MC_M$ factors to produce C_S more movies. Now if we increase steak production by one unit, MC_S factors must be hired away from the movie industry. And since by definition the number of movies these factors can produce equals the social cost of a steak, C_S, the value of the factors must be $C_S MC_M$. That is, the value of the factors hired by the steak industry equals the value surrendered by the movie industry and, by definition, those surrendered produce the amount of movies that equals the social cost of steak. Thus

$$MC_S = C_S MC_M$$

or

$$C_S = \frac{MC_S}{MC_M}$$

In words, the social cost of steak equals the ratio of the marginal costs of steak and movies. The slope of the PPF equals MC_S/MC_M if there are no externalities.

When there are external costs of production, a different story emerges. Assume that the production of steaks results in a great deal of noise — mooing and so on — which forces movie producers to install soundproofing to keep the noise out of movies' sound tracks. The more cattle, the more mooing and the greater the cost of soundproofing. When steak production is increased by a unit, the steak producers again hire factors equal in value to MC_S, and these are again equal to those given up by the movie industry. But now the movie industry must take additional factors that had been used to produce movies and use them to produce soundproofing. Thus movie output falls by more than the amount it would fall from simply releasing the factors it does. That is, movie output falls (1) because factors are released and (2) because steak production is increased. Both of these declines in production are a part of the social cost of steak; both are represented by the slope of the PPF. But the definition of the marginal cost of movies is the value of the factors needed to increase output by one unit. This definition does not include the costs that will be experienced if the factors come from the steak industry as opposed to some third industry. Thus the slope of the PPF equals the ratio of marginal costs if there are no external costs of production. Mooing is really a cost of steak production, yet steak producers do not pay this cost, and if they set price equal to marginal cost, their customers will not pay it either. Marginal cost is a good measure of social cost only when there are no external costs of production.

Allocative Efficiency and Pure Competition

Knowing that social cost and marginal cost can be the same, consider the implications for allocative efficiency when *both* the steak and the movie industry are purely competitive. Long-run equilibrium is achieved in both industries when price equals marginal cost. Since we know that the production decisions in each industry will result in a price that equals marginal cost, the ratio of the price of steak to the price of movies will equal the ratio of the marginal cost of steak to the marginal cost of movies (in the long run). Furthermore, we know that firms, in striving for the lowest possible cost at every level of output, will achieve internal allocative efficiency. In fact, in a competitive industry, any firm that does not lower costs to the minimum level will be driven out of business. Other firms will make profits and attract new entrants, which leads to lower prices until only the most efficient firms are left in the industry. Each firm will be making zero monopoly profits. Inefficient firms will be experiencing losses. This means that the output of steak and movies will be on the PPF and not within it.

Wherever firms in pure competition may end up along the PPF, we know that the price of steak in terms of movies will be exactly equal to the slope of the production possibility frontier. That is because the slope of the PPF, as we have seen, represents the social cost of steak in terms of movies. And the social cost equals the ratio of the marginal costs. Since market price equals marginal cost under pure competition, the social cost equals the ratio of the market prices. Thus the price ratio at any point such as B in Figure 15A.1 will equal the slope of the PPF at B. In Chapter 9 it was shown that only when the price ratio equals social cost can an efficient allocation of resources be achieved. Otherwise the price charged to the consumer will not reflect the opportunity cost of production of that good to society. Pure competition with profit maximization will lead to allocative efficiency where private cost equals social cost as long as there are no external production costs.

Allocative Efficiency and Monopoly

What if one industry is a monopoly? Suppose that the movie industry has only a single firm, whereas the steak industry is purely competitive. Profit maximization, we have seen, will still guarantee that $MR = MC$, but since for a monopolist MR is less than AR (price), MC must be less than the price as well. Therefore the ratio of prices between movies and steak will not equal the slope of the PPF at the point where production takes place. We know from Chapter 9 that this will automatically lead to an inefficient allocation of resources. This is shown in Figure 15A.2.

In Figure 15A.2, it is assumed that movies are produced by a monopolist and steaks by pure competitors. If the ratio of prices charged to consumers equaled the ratio of marginal costs, the price line OP would have to be tangent to DE (the production possibility frontier) at the point of production S. Actually the movie industry, in our example, is a monopolist and is charging a price in excess

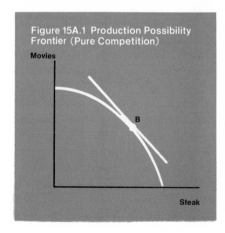

Figure 15A.1 Production Possibility Frontier (Pure Competition)

Movies

Steak

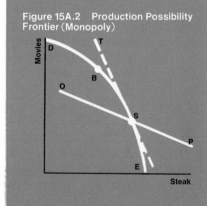

Figure 15A.2   Production Possibility Frontier (Monopoly)

Movies

Steak

of marginal cost. The price therefore exceeds the value of the steaks that society must sacrifice to increase movie production. Consumers must move toward O when they give up steaks for movies, though with prices equal to social costs they might have considered moving toward T. With the high price for movies that the monopolist charges, the individuals cannot afford to move toward T. Individuals select S as the point they prefer to all those on OP. But they might prefer B to all those on OP.

We saw in Chapter 9 why the allocation of resources at point S with the prices implied by price line OP is inefficient. At least one person can be made better off and no one worse off by setting the price equal to the marginal cost of movies for him alone and allowing him to buy more movies. At the new equilibrium, he would be better off and no one else, including the monopolist, would be worse off. If all individuals were permitted to pay the social cost of the commodities they consume, a new equilibrium such as B in Figure 15A.1 would result. The movement to B would make the monopolist worse off as well as all those who own factors better suited to steak than movie production. But once point B is attained, it is no longer possible to improve one person's utility without lowering another's. Point B represents a solution at which resources are allocated efficiently; S does not. A movement from S to B would require increased production of the monopoly good at a lower price. But the movement from S to B redistributes income. As economists, we cannot say which income distribution is preferable. The sovereign voters can choose the one they like best. Therefore we cannot be sure that this movement is a desirable one. We do know that it leads to efficiency and eliminates monopoly profits. Historically, economists have favored such moves.

16 Shades of Gray

Between the extremes of monopoly and pure competition lie most firms in the world today. What happens to efficiency when there are only a *few* sellers in the market, and the decision of one affects the profits of the rest? What happens when a single seller can make his product a little different and change his own conditions of demand single-handedly? Do intermediate market structures permit allocative efficiency? It is to these questions that this chapter is addressed. We shall see that pricing for such firms is no longer a simple question of setting marginal cost equal to marginal revenue because marginal revenue itself can be subject to changes by retaliation of other firms. Pricing then becomes a game of strategy among sellers. The game can be analyzed and its efficiency costs shown, but the outcome cannot be predicted with certainty. The more complex the problem, the more difficult the implications of firm behavior for allocative efficiency. In examining the kind of markets that characterize most modern economies, we see why business for many persons becomes the most exciting game, rivaling even love and politics.

Equilibrium between Two Sellers

The simplest case concerns a market with two sellers producing an identical product. An industry with a small number of sellers is called an *oligopoly*. Suppose that two firms, A and B, are producing mineral water. How will each arrive at an equilibrium price and quantity? This is a much more complicated question than the one facing the monopolist or pure competitor. Why? Because the demand curve of each firm when there are two sellers is unpredictable. The demand curve for firm A depends on what firm B decides to do, and vice versa. Suppose, for instance, that firm A decides to give away mineral water. Then firm B will have no demand curve at all. Suppose, on the other hand, that firm A decides to hoard all its mineral water. Firm B will enjoy the total market demand in this case. The actual situation usually lies somewhere in between. Each firm gets part of the market. Let us see how this works.

Assume for the moment that the boss of firm A is stubbornly independent and acts as though firm B did not exist. He assumes that firm B has fixed its production, though not its price, and therefore he disregards any possible effect his decisions might have on firm B. There is no collusion between the two sellers; each acts independently and without thought about the other. Let us begin with firm B producing Q_B at a price of P_B. The industry demand is DD in Figure 16.1.

This means that firm A begins with demand curve *dd* in Figure 16.2. If it produces nothing, price remains at P_B. If it decides to produce something it can sell it only at a price below P_B. As long as the boss of firm A does not worry about his competitor, he can set $MR = MC$, given demand curve *dd*, and arrive at his maximum profit point. Of course this will change things for firm B, whether or not the boss of firm A thinks about it. Once firm A begins producing, firm B no longer has *DD* for a demand curve. The boss of firm B will probably want to find a new output level as his firm's demand curve has shifted to the left. A new profit-maximizing solution must be found that probably entails lower levels of output. When B changes its production level in response to its new market conditions, A finds that its market conditions change. The situation is such that even though each firm acts independently, each must react to the other's decision.

Solutions to this problem cannot be shown easily in two-dimensional diagrams since we need to discuss the quantities that each firm produces as well as the prices they charge. It is therefore necessary to use algebra to derive the solution. This we do in an appendix. Here we consider a numerical example that illustrates the dilemma faced by these firms.

In Figure 16.3, we have drawn the demand curve for the industry's output, and we have indicated that production takes place under conditions of constant cost, each truckload of mineral water costing $4. To keep the numbers simple, we have drawn the demand curve as a straight line. From Figure 16.3 we can find the average cost and the price for every level of output. This permits us to determine both total cost — average cost times quantity — and total revenue — price times quantity — at each output level. Total profit is the residual — total revenue minus total cost. These figures are presented in Table 16.1.

From this Table the competitive level of output is seen to be eight truckloads of mineral water, because at that quantity profits are zero and marginal cost equals price. The monopolistic level of output, the quantity that will maximize industry profits, is four truckloads or one-half the competitive output.

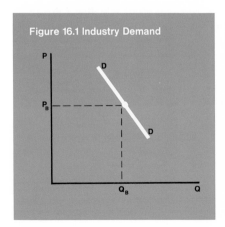

Figure 16.1 Industry Demand

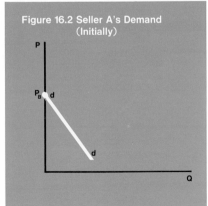

Figure 16.2 Seller A's Demand (Initially)

Table 16.1 Revenue, Cost, and Profit in the Mineral Water Industry				
Quantity Sold	Price	Total Revenue	Total Cost	Profit
0	12	0	0	0
1	11	11	4	7
2	10	20	8	12
3	9	27	12	15
4	8	32	16	16
5	7	35	20	15
6	6	36	24	12
7	5	35	28	7
8	4	32	32	0

A Payout Matrix for One of Two Identical Firms

What will happen to output in an industry with two sellers? This depends upon whether they act independently or in collusion. We can determine the solution that results from each form of behavior by using a device called a *payout matrix,* originally introduced in Chapter 10. Each firm can construct such a matrix once it knows the industry demand. The payout matrix is identical for firms A and B. These matrices are shown in Table 16.2, where we have presented the profits of both A and B as a function of their outputs. Firm A's profit is the first number in each cell; firm B's is the second. Although this table is a bit larger than the payout matrix in Chapter 10, the principle it illustrates is exactly the same. Firm A's profits depend upon the decisions of firm B. This is what is presented in the matrix.

The payout matrix is constructed in the following manner. We start with the outputs of the two firms. These are added together to get the output of the industry. From Table 16.1, we find the level of profit that corresponds to that level of output. Since we know that average cost is constant and that both firms

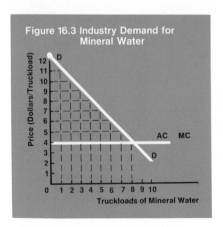

Figure 16.3 Industry Demand for Mineral Water

charge the same price, we know that both firms must earn the same profit per unit. Dividing total profit by the number of units produced gives us profit per unit. The profit of each firm is its level of output times profit per unit. These are the numbers reported in Table 16.2

For example, if firm A produces four truckloads of mineral water and firm B produces two, industry output is six; thus industry profits (from Table 16.1) must be $12. Profit per unit is $2. Since A produced four truckloads, it earned $8 in profit while B with two truckloads of output earned $4. Therefore the entry in Table 16.2 in (vertical) column 4 and (horizontal) row 2 (corresponding to A's and B's outputs) should read (8,4). The other entries are constructed similarly.

Equilibrium without Collusion

We now trace an adjustment to equilibrium under the assumption that the firms act independently, ignoring the possibility that each firm's actions will influence the other's behavior. Let us assume that firm A has been the only firm in the industry; it has been producing four truckloads of mineral water every day, selling it for $8 a truckload, and making a total profit of $16. Firm B decides to enter the market to get a share of the profit. Firm B notes that A is producing four units per time period. If firm B assumes that A will continue to do this, it can find the level of output that maximizes its own profit by looking at column 4 in Table 16.2. Examining the right-hand figures in column 4 — the potential profit for every possible level of output — firm B finds that it will be best off producing two units. Its two added to A's four makes a total of six for the industry. The price will have to fall to $6 a unit to sell six truckloads of water, and at that price B will make $2 per unit for a total of $4.

Once B starts producing, A's monopoly has been disturbed. Its profits have been reduced to $8 a day from the original $16 due to the decline in price from

Table 16.2	Profits for Firms A and B as a Function of Their Outputs*								
A's Output	**0**	**1**	**2**	**3**	**4**	**5**	**6**	**7**	**8**
B's Output									
0	(0,0)	(7,0)	(12,0)	(15,0)	(16,0)	(15,0)	(12,0)	(7,0)	(0,0)
1		(0,7)	(6,6)	(10,5)	(12,4)	(12,3)	(10,2)	(6,1)	(0,0)
2		(0,12)	(5,10)	(8,8)	(9,6)	(8,4)	(5,2)	(0,0)	
3		(0,15)	(4,12)	(6,9)	(6,6)	(4,3)	(0,0)		
4		(0,16)	(3,12)	(4,8)	(3,4)	(0,0)			
5		(0,15)	(2,10)	(2,5)	(0,0)				
6		(0,12)	(1,6)	(0,0)					
7		(0,7)	(0,0)						
8		(0,0)							

*A's profit printed first (profit of A, profit of B).

$8 a truckload to $6. Firm A observes that B is producing two units per time period. It examines row 2 in Table 16.2 and finds that it can increase its profit from $8 to $9 by reducing output to three truckloads per time period. Firm A does this. The price of mineral water climbs to $7 because of the reduced output. Firm B's profit jumps from $4 to $6 a day.

But with firm A producing only three truckloads, firm B finds from column 3 that it has a choice of continuing to produce two units or increasing output to three. Both levels give B the same profit of $6 per day. This is because the higher output will have to be sold at a lower price with a resulting lower profit per unit. Firm B might note, however, that A's profit will fall if B increases output to three units. Whether B does increase output or not will depend on how its management feels toward A. If it wishes evil to A, clearly it will produce three units. If A's management feels the same way about B's, it too will find three units the best level of production, given B's decision to produce three. A *noncooperative equilibrium* can therefore be established with both firms producing three units of output. At this equilibrium, neither firm could make itself better off given the actions of the other.

Cooperative Equilibrium

From Table 16.2, it is evident that both firms could make more profits if they both restricted output to two units. With each firm producing two units, the industry output would be at the level that a monopolist would choose. Total profits would be maximized and with each firm producing half of the maximized total, each would be doing better than if they both acted independently. Is this not the kind of behavior we should expect to see from two firms?

The incentive of higher profit is certainly a force that operates in this direction. Just because an industry has two producers instead of one does not mean that the level of output that maximizes profits for the industry cannot be found. Thus there is a strong reason to expect cooperative behavior. Yet we do not observe explicit cooperation for two reasons. The first is legal. Just as the laws attempt to prevent a monopolist from using his market power to raise prices and restrict output, so they attempt to prevent collusion on the part of more than one seller in the same market. Explicit agreements among sellers are illegal in most countries. This does not mean that collusion is impossible, but only that it is difficult to bring about because it must be done without written agreements.

We call the form of behavior in which firms cooperate without an explicit agreement *tacit collusion*. Just from looking at Table 16.2, we can imagine the form in which tacit collusion could take place. The two firms attain a noncooperative solution with each of them producing three units per time period. Profits are $6 each. One of the firms then produces two units for a few time periods. This has no effect on his own profits but it gives his competitor a windfall. It should not take the competitor long to realize that the windfall will not last forever unless he returns the favor. So he, too, cuts his production to two units and now both firms can enjoy profits of $8 per year. In this case the firms have acted in such a way as to help each other without the need of a formal agreement. In some industries there may exist customary behavior or a code of ethics that restricts the manner in which firms can compete. It may be unethical to enter another's territory or to hire away his researchers. Such ethics can develop whenever the producers recognize their common interest.

Does tacit collusion produce a stable equilibrium? Look at the matrix. Each seller could act independently and increase his profit at the other's expense. There is no explicit agreement to prevent any seller from raising output to three units and profit from $8 to $9 at the other's expense. A 12 percent increase in profits must be tempting. The only thing holding the firm back is the threat of retaliation from its competitor, who might also decide to increase output to three units, cutting both of their profits back to $6 and leaving them both worse off than they would be with tacit collusion.

The first restriction on collusion, then, is legal; the second one is economic. Breaking the implicit agreement can be profitable. With two firms, tacit collusion might work fairly well. One firm can be reasonably sure that the other will react if it tries to disturb the equilibrium. But the larger the number of sellers, the more difficult it becomes to maintain the tacit collusion. What, for example, is to prevent the members of a 1,000 firm industry from realizing that there is a payout matrix for each firm and that they can tacitly arrive at a monopoly level of output in which monopoly profits will be divided up 1,000 ways? Collusion under such circumstances would require a high degree of administration and control. If one seller began cutting his output in half (the others staying put) in an attempt to signal the others how they should behave, he would find to his dismay that his profits had fallen by half and his sacrifice would hardly be appreciated by any of the other firms, since their prices and profits would remain almost the same as before. Total industry output would be reduced through his independent action by only .05 percent. This would have a negligible effect on their profits. This means that the likelihood of attaining a tacit collusion diminishes as the number of firms rises. And if they ever could achieve a collusive bargain, each firm would receive 1/1000 of the monopoly profits. If any firm broke the collusive agreement and doubled its output, it would double its profits. As this would have only a minor effect on the others, they would be unlikely to retaliate. Thus the difficulty of administering any collusive agreement rises with the number of sellers. Agreements in restraint of trade normally characterize industries with only a few sellers dominating the market. There, each firm has a much larger impact on the others' profits. It is more reasonable to expect retaliation when a firm's behavior has a great effect on profits than when it has a small effect. It is easier to maintain the collusive equilibrium when retaliation is expected than it is otherwise.

Defining an Industry

All of the preceding analysis involved the assumption that we could define an industry. We have effectively assumed that an industry is a market in which the *total demand curve* for the product is unaffected by the behavior of other industries. This means that if a monopolist is really a single seller in the market, his demand curve will be unaffected by the behavior of other firms. An alternative definition might be that an industry is a market for a single homogeneous product. But we know that the common use of the term industry requires us to depart from either of these definitions in practice. For example, having a monopoly in the production of natural rubber will be of small comfort to a firm faced with the wide availability of synthetic rubber that can be used for the same purposes. The demand curve for natural rubber will be affected by the behavior of synthetic rubber producers and may indeed appear to be horizontal to its monopolist. What about defining "industry" functionally, as made up of firms producing a product that has the same use? This would mean that in many respects the production of copper and aluminum, two relatively inexpensive, noncorrosive, highly conductive metals, would be defined as a single industry.

This undeniable ambiguity in the definition of an industry poses a real problem for the theory. That is, the problem posed is not just one of finding words to denote the concept "industry," but of finding a concept that allows us to ignore the behavior of other firms. Such a concept would be very convenient for purposes of analysis but, unfortunately, we can see little justification for it. Only limited success has been attained in the attempt to handle this problem formally. The notable attempts include the concept of *imperfect competition,* designed to handle the case of many sellers who produce slightly different products, and *differential oligopoly,* for the case of a few sellers who produce slightly different products.

Imperfect Competition

The whole class of situations in which monopoly profits can be eroded by competitors' producing similar but not identical products is analyzed by economists under the term *imperfect competition* or *monopolistic competition.* Products may be differentiated by style, performance, durability, or other characteristics, and hence become imperfect substitutes for each other. Since products are no longer identical, even when many sellers exist, each firm still observes a downward-sloping demand curve for its particular item. Each firm is to some extent a monopolist because no other firm produces exactly the same product. Yet each firm finds that as long as it makes a monopoly profit, other firms will enter the market producing *similar* goods. The result is that even though its demand curve remains downward sloping (since there are always some buyers who will pay a premium for the special qualities of this firm's product), the increased competition will (1) shift the demand curve for the firm to the left and (2) increase the demand curve's elasticity. Let us see how this happens.

Figure 16.4 illustrates a firm in imperfect competition. Initially its demand curve (AR_1) may allow some economic profits. (Note that average revenue exceeds average cost for many levels of output.) Over time, more and more firms producing similar, though not identical, products enter into the industry. They attract many customers away from the monopolist. Our firm's demand curve shifts to the left until it ends up at AR_2, just tangent to the average cost curve. At this level of output $MR = MC$, but since $AR = AC$ there are zero profits. (Every other level of output would involve a loss.) Here we have a case of a monopolist whose profits were destroyed by other firms that produced goods that were a close substitute for the monopoly goods. They were able to compete with him even though they did not make an identical product. The name *monopolistic competition* accurately describes such industries.

What are the implications of this new equilibrium for resource allocation? Do zero profits imply allocative efficiency as they did under pure competition? Or does $P > MC$ signal an inefficient production point? Let us recall the results for pure competition in Chapter 15. Price equaled average cost *and* marginal cost. That could happen as long as the demand curve was flat. But the downward slope of the demand curve under monopolistic competition means that price is everywhere above marginal revenue. Therefore price exceeds marginal cost at the point of maximum profits. *Clearly under monopolistic competition price is above marginal cost and resources are not being allocated efficiently.* We can make at least one person better off and none worse off by letting him buy one more unit of output at a price equal to MC. But if we required the firm to set $P = MC$, it would lose money since it experiences decreasing costs. It would have to be subsidized in order to survive. The entry of many new firms has shrunk the demand for this firm's output until its profits are zero. At this point, it experiences decreasing costs.

Efficiency requires that price be equal to marginal cost. But with decreasing costs, such a price would lead to losses. Should we subsidize the countless little firms who enter an industry and produce a slightly different product? Such an undertaking would tax the capacity of government and might be likely to perpetuate many inefficient firms. Is society better or worse off with the large number of firms that exist in imperfect competition, each producing a product only slightly different from the others? The downward slope of the cost curves, indicating economies of scale, suggests that something might be gained in terms of

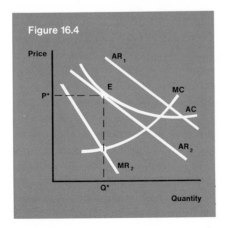

Figure 16.4

lower unit costs by having fewer sellers. On the other hand, the public is served by having slight differences in individual tastes satisfied under such a market. We must balance off the benefits of product variation with the costs of productive efficiency. Let us take the example of small retailers such as gasoline stations and explore the equilibrium they attain to see if variety is worth what it costs.

Gasoline stations differentiate their product not so much in terms of the quality or content of the gasoline as in terms of the station's location. If one gasoline station lowers its price, it gets more sales, but others stay in business because they are more conveniently located for their particular consumers. If large profits exist among gasoline stations, new ones will be built by entrepreneurs who want in on the game. This will cut back on the demand of the existing stations. There will be more substitutes than before among which consumers can choose. Monopoly profits eventually will be driven to zero as more and more stations are added. But each station will still have some consumers who prefer it for location, friendliness of the attendant, cleanliness of restrooms, or other "product differentiation" reasons. At the point where monopoly profits are zero, are there "too many" gasoline stations? This question gets us to the heart of the efficiency implications of monopolistic competition. If gasoline stations have decreasing costs, the fewer stations there are the cheaper the gasoline can be. Assuming we have decided not to subsidize gasoline stations, is it better to have very few stations with very cheap gasoline or very many conveniently located stations with expensive gasoline? The answer all depends on how much the individual who is making this judgement values cheap gasoline relative to the convenience of many service stations. To have fewer stations allows each station to have lower per unit costs and thus lower prices. But fewer stations means less convenience to the buyer. Which does the public prefer?

If customers indeed always preferred cheap gasoline to convenience, their demand curve for gasoline as seen by an individual station would be horizontal. Assuming that all gasoline is a perfect substitute for all other gasoline (something the firms deny), perfect competition would then exist in the filling station industry and resources would be efficiently allocated. Any firm that lowered its price would get all the customers. This would tempt them all to lower price until they reached a level of costs below which they could not go. This is minimum average cost and this is the equilibrium for perfectly competitive industries.

The fact that the demand curve for each station is always slightly sloped indicates that at least *some* consumers prefer to buy gasoline at a specific location or from one particular firm and are willing to pay for that convenience. Suppose that there are four gasoline stations at a main intersection. And suppose people would prefer the price that would exist if only one seller were there. (This price would be much lower than with four stations due to decreasing costs.) How could they signal their preferences to the station owners? They would buy from the cheapest of the four. The other station owners would have to lower price in order to retain their business. A price war would ensue and if there were decreasing costs, three of the stations would be driven out of business. The remaining one could then set its price at a level low enough to permit more profit than he had been making originally. (This is possible because its costs are much lower with high levels of sales than with low levels of sales.) This argument indicates that the public gets what it wants. If it wants cheap gasoline, the demand curve to each station will be horizontal. The firm charging the lowest price will get all of the sales. Firms will be encouraged to lower prices. But since costs are decreasing, losses will ensue to those firms with low levels of sales. They will be driven out of business. The consumer will end by having very few stations with very cheap gasoline.

If, on the other hand, the public wanted conveniently located stations, it would patronize new ones as they opened despite the increase in price. They would end by having very many stations with expensive gasoline. Thus consumers' preferences, as reflected in the slope of the demand curve faced by each station, determine whether the consumers are to receive cheap gasoline or many stations. In fact, if some prefer convenience while others prefer cheap gasoline, we might find a few very large stations that sell cheap gasoline and many small ones located all around the city that have higher prices.

Of course, collusion might prevent a price war even if consumers wished to have cheap gasoline. The losses that the victor of a price war would have to sustain in order to win the war, plus the fact that his chance of surviving is only one out of four, might well cause him to prefer the present four-station arrangement to any alternative scheme. The chance of being the only station on the corner may not appear to be worth the risk of going out of business. Sales competition does not seem very attractive in this case and the four stations might have a gentlemen's agreement to act as one in terms of the price they charge. Because of their size they need not fear prosecution from the federal government. They could easily keep an agreement secret.

Competition among the four firms would then shift to measures other than price cutting. Each would look at additional aspects of its sales function in an effort to make its product superior to that of its competitors and thereby take away some of their demand. Each gasoline station would attempt to make its product different from and better than that of its competitors by offering faster service, free glassware, a fancier building, cleaner restrooms, and so on. These are efforts to shift the firm's demand curve to the right, rather than to move along a given demand curve by lowering price. Is it possible to imagine a "quality war" among products in imperfect competition? Of course, the loser of such a quality war could always save his skin by lowering price.

Differential Oligopoly

We have been analyzing industries in which there are *many* sellers who produce slightly different products. We have seen that under those circumstances, even though price ends up above marginal cost, no monopoly profits are earned. But what about the case of industries in which products are differentiated but there are only a *few firms*? This type of industry is called *differential oligopoly* (it is distinct from "pure oligopoly" in which there are only a few sellers who produce identical products). The situation of a seller in differential oligopoly is not dissimilar to the situation of a seller in monopoly. There are some barriers to entry, such as patents or a large initial capital requirement, that permit monopoly profits to be earned over the long run. In the case of two sellers we saw how this was true for identical products (mineral water). If the products are slightly different, the firm's demand curve will have a different shape from the industry's demand curve (since different consumers will have preferences for the product of one or another seller even when prices are the same). In fact, it will be possible for firms to charge *different prices* in such a market. Take, for example, the automobile industry. Each auto brand name has its own unique demand curve with a shape slightly different from that of its competitors. Each firm can charge a somewhat different price for its cars, since they are not identical.

If one firm lowers the price of its cars, it can steal some but not all of the demand away from its rivals. There are always those willing to pay more for a favorite brand of car. Loyalties die hard, along with prejudices. ("Ask the man who owns one.") And if the cars are really different, this is not an irrational preference. Certain people may prefer gasoline economy to style, others prefer performance and cornering ability, and so on. In such industries we might also see the kind of tacit collusion regarding price that takes place in industries with few sellers of homogeneous products. But we would also expect a great deal of effort to be spent on shifting the preference of consumers from one make of automobilt to another by adding special design and performance features to make their models as distinct as possible from those of competitors. A large share of advertising expenditure goes to divert demand from one seller to another seller within an industry of differentiated oligopoly or imperfect competition. The advertising might be regarded as jockeying by the firm within a given payout matrix, or even as an attempt by the firm to change the demand curves in such a way as to increase the payout within a given cell of its matrix.

The resource allocative implications of differentiated oligopoly are complex. Price certainly exceeds marginal cost. Monopoly profits are frequently earned. To the extent that the firms in the industry wind up producing at a point of decreasing costs, economies of scale are being sacrificed for product differentiation, just as under imperfect competition. Where does this leave the consumer? Monopoly profits clearly leave him worse off. But we have seen that price may be above marginal cost even when there are no monopoly profits, in the case of imperfect competition. The consumer may be willing to pay this higher price for the privilege of product variation. Who knows? Still, the solution is inefficient, but it may be preferred by consumers to an efficient one with less choice. What should our policy be toward these industries? It is another example of the difficulty of evaluating industries when dealing with shades of grey. For government to subsidize all firms with decreasing costs might be technically impossible. It might require more resources to administer the subsidy branch of the government than the effort is worth. (Of course, this does not say that we should not subsidize the natural monopolies like electricity where output is homogeneous and close substitutes do not exist.) Lack of such a subsidy will leave us with an inefficient allocation of resources.

Summary
We see that whether or not collusion takes place, and whether or not product variation exists, an industry between the extremes of monopoly and pure competition is not likely to result in allocative efficiency in the free market. Consumers in some cases may wish to sacrifice efficiency for product variation. But with industries that earn *monopoly profits* through collusion or other restraints on trade, the consumer is clearly disadvantaged, with or without product variation. Since most markets in the world today are in the grey area in between, the implications of these findings are universal. We have to live with certain inefficiencies and it is up to us to choose which ones. Most firms cannot set price equal to marginal cost without losing money. And we are unwilling to subsidize them all as this would require vast levels of taxes, which themselves are likely to lead to inefficient resource allocations. If we restrict entry into such fields through a form of licensing and if we control the pricing of those with licenses, we might result with price equal to marginal cost and a much smaller variety of output. Some would applaud this, others would feel worse off. As with any action that redistributes satisfaction, we cannot determine *a priori* whether or not to undertake it. It all depends on whose satisfaction matters to the voters.

Questions
1. What problems are encountered when attempting to define an industry?
2. Why might there be more than one possible solution to output and profits in a two-firm industry?
3. Why is it difficult to assess whether or not the existence of many small sta tions is superior to a smaller number of larger ones?

Concepts Discussed
oligopoly
noncooperative equilibrium
cooperative equilibrium
tacit collusion

differential product
imperfect competition
monopolistic competition
differential oligopoly

APPENDIX: THE ALGEBRA OF INDUSTRY EQUILIBRIUM

We have seen how a monopoly will produce less output than a competitive industry would when faced with the same demand curve. To see how much less, it is useful to look at an algebraic example. The example we choose is a very simple one, namely, that of a linear demand curve. We will show that if the demand curve is linear, a monopolist will produce exactly half the output that a competitive industry would. Furthermore, we will show that in this case, if there are two firms in the industry, output will be two-thirds the competitive level and if three firms exist, it will be three-fourths that level, and so on.

To keep the example simple, we assume that the industry is one of constant costs. That is, marginal and average costs are constant at all levels of output and therefore equal to each other. Using the symbols Q for output, P for price, C for total cost, and c for marginal cost, we can define the industry by the following two relations. First, the fact that average and marginal costs are constant is expressed in equation 1.

1. $C = cQ$

Second, the linear demand curve is given by equation 2, where a and b are some positive constants.

2. $P = a - bQ$

The symbol a denotes the price at which the quantity demanded falls to zero; b shows how much price must fall if sales are to be expanded by one unit.

Case I: Perfect Competition

If this industry is characterized by perfect competition, we know that at the solution, price will be equal to marginal cost. Accordingly, substituting c for P in equation 2 and solving for Q will give us the level of industry output. The solution is shown in equation 3.

3. $Q = \dfrac{a - c}{b}$

Case II: Monopoly

The monopoly solution differs from that just shown because the monopolist takes account of the fact that his actions affect the price of output. Specifically, profit maximum with monopoly occurs where marginal revenue equals marginal cost. We can show this algebraically by defining profit π as the difference between total revenue PQ and total cost C.

4. $\pi = PQ - C$

Profit is maximized by differentiating equation 4 with respect to Q, using elementary laws of calculus, and setting the derivative equal to zero. First substitute equations 1 and 2 into equation 4 so that the symbols P and C are replaced by expressions containing Q. Then differentiate.

4'. $\pi = aQ - bQ^2 - cQ$

5. $\dfrac{d\pi}{dQ} = a - 2bQ - c = 0$

Solving equation 5 for Q, we get equation 6, which is the level of output when the industry has only one profit-maximizing firm.

6. $Q = \frac{1}{2}\left(\dfrac{a-c}{b}\right)$

Note that the monopoly level of output is exactly one-half the competitive level.

Case III: Duopoly

An industry with two firms is called a *duopoly*. In the body of the chapter, we saw how there need not be a determinate solution to the level of industry output when there are a small number of firms. The reason for this is that one firm's choice of how much to produce depends not only on how much it thinks the other firm will produce, but on how it thinks the other firm will respond to its actions. We said that if the firms cooperate fully, they can produce the monopoly level of output and divide the maximized profits between themselves. We have also discussed the case where no cooperation is assumed and where each firm assumes the other firm's level of output will be unaffected by its own decision. That is the case we examine here.

First, we need an additional equation to show how industry output Q is now the sum of the outputs of firm 1, Q_1, and firm 2, Q_2.

7. $Q = Q_1 + Q_2$

If we substitute equation 7 into equation 2, we get equation 8, which describes the demand curve faced by firm 1.

8. $P = a - bQ_1 - bQ_2$

The equation for firm 1's profit is now equation 9.

9. $\pi_1 = PQ_1 - cQ_1 = aQ_1 - bQ_1^2 - bQ_2Q_1 - cQ_1$

And the maximum profit occurs where the derivative of equation 9 with respect to Q_1 equals zero.

10. $\dfrac{d\pi_1}{dQ_1} = a - 2bQ_1 - bQ_2 - c = 0$

Solving for Q_1

11. $Q_1 = \dfrac{a-c}{2b} - \frac{1}{2}Q_2$

Note that the output of firm 1 would equal the monopoly level of output if firm 2 produced nothing. But for each extra unit of output firm 2 produces, firm 1 decreases its output by one unit. Thus industry output will exceed the monopoly level of output whenever firm 2 produces anything.

To show the industry output explicitly, we must look at firm 2's behavior. Assuming that it acts exactly the way firm 1 acts, its profit-maximizing output level will be given by equation 12.

12. $Q_2 = \dfrac{a-c}{2b} - \tfrac{1}{2}Q_1$

Substituting equation 12 into equation 11 and solving for Q_1, we find that in this case the profit-maximizing level of output of firm 1 is one-third the competitive level.

13. $Q_1 = \tfrac{1}{3}\left(\dfrac{a-c}{b}\right)$

Firm 2 produces exactly the same level of output as firm 1, so industry output, in this case, is two-thirds the competitive level. The reader can try for himself the case of three firms or n firms to see that industry output will always be $n/(n+1)$ times the competitive level of output if firms ignore the effect their output will have on the decisions of the other firms.

It should be remembered that the derivation of precise numbers such as $n/(n+1)$ requires that we have precise demand curves and cost functions. In this case, we took the simplest example—a linear cost function and a linear demand function—and got neat simple results. More complex examples will lead to more complex results.

17 Real Firms

What Really Goes On?

Enough of theory, says the practical businessman. Let us get down to brass tacks. What does economics have to say about my firm? Can these generalizations go further than good horse sense in talking about social welfare and allocative efficiency? After all, are things not far more complex than the simple models of the last few chapters would suggest?

Political extremists at both ends of the spectrum mistrust economic analysis. One group rejects the idea that the market can ever misallocate resources. The other group is slow to believe that the market can ever bring any beneficial effects to mankind. Both groups rest their case on evidence that the assumptions of economic analysis oversimplify conditions in the real world.

Who is right? The first step in checking on what we have said so far is to set the assumptions of our analysis against the practice of real firms. That is what we do in this chapter. We find that some of our earlier simplifying assumptions must be relaxed so that we may deal more realistically with the problems of enterprise. Because of the immense complexity of the production process in the real world, the reader can only be introduced to these issues. It would take a shelf of books just to begin to handle them in detail. When he is confronted with the immense number of ways in which the organization of production affects our lives, the response of the economist is to abstract a few key concepts and analyze them. The shorthand economists use — economic theory — allows us to formulate principles that are general enough to cover many different situations. Unfortunately we must pay a price to attain that generality and the price involves ignoring many of the specific ways in which the organization of production affects us.

We have presented in the past chapters the general issues that economists usually discuss when considering the organization of production. In this chapter we attempt to expand the domain of analysis in a few dimensions by discussing some additional issues. This glimpse into business in practice shows how the tools of analysis may be applied by the reader in countless cases to draw conclusions about the usefulness of economics and its role in evaluating allocative efficiency in the production process. The first problem we handle in checking on the relevance of our theory is one of communication.

Economic Jargon outside the Classroom

The readers of *The Wall Street Journal, Fortune, Forbes,* or *Business Week* will note that the models of the firm presented in the preceding chapters, and the issues they raise, do not correspond to the terminology of the financial press. Is there simply a failure to communicate because different terms are being used to discuss the same thing, or have we misrepresented firm behavior and goals? Where is there any mention of marginal cost and marginal revenue in the business media?

Most of the issues that economists discuss using professional jargon are handled in a more colloquial, if ambiguous, way in the press. Take, for example, *automation*. Automation to the businessman is a complex production process that he can employ to cut costs. To an economist automation is a way of substituting capital (machines) for labor to cut costs. We have seen in Chapter 13 how firms seek to minimize cost at each level of output by deciding on the optimal combination of labor and capital. When an automated process comes along, this changes the conditions for cost minimization. It may then be possible to produce each level of output at a lower cost by using more machinery and less labor.

What about *mergers*? Discussion of the union of great corporations or the absorption of smaller by larger firms fills the financial journals. What are the reasons for mergers? Here again economic analysis provides several possible answers. It can show how a merger can improve or worsen resource allocation, depending upon the reason for it. A merger can permit both merging firms to decrease costs if economies of scale exist. On the other hand, the merger might result in a restriction of competition since the two competitors are now one. The different types of mergers have different implications for allocative efficiency, though they share the goal of profit maximization. The preceding chapters permit us to analyze their respective welfare implications.

New entrants into an industry were discussed earlier as an example of firms wishing to get a piece of the action where monopoly profits exist. Strategies used to prevent entry into markets, another subject of the financial press, were also discussed in terms of the profit-maximizing objectives of the initial producers. We dealt with the *creation of new products* as efforts by entrepreneurs to earn a return in excess of costs by attracting consumers to a different pattern of expenditure. In all these cases the observed behavior of individual business enterprise in its most newsworthy aspects can be subjected to the kind of analysis we have presented. Beneath all of these activities lurk marginal cost and marginal revenue. They are so general that they can serve to explain each issue mentioned above. Yet because profit maximization is so general, it is usually taken for granted and finds little mention in the press, any more than "love" is mentioned in wedding announcements.

References to markets, sales, consumers, revenue, competition, or restraints on trade have implications for *marginal revenue*. Mentions of technology, labor disputes, the rate of interest, or investment plans relate to *marginal cost*. Thus economists and businessmen are really talking about the same things but in different words. At this point we still have left unsaid many important things about firms and their problems. Some of these issues emerge, however, when we examine the assumptions of the models we have presented.

Uncertainty

For example, a set of revenue curves was shown to be an abstraction from a general sales function. We assumed these curves to be known with certainty and to be predictable, when, in fact, they are subject to unpredictable shocks. Even when current demand is known by the firm with certainty for the whole range of its demand curve (which is seldom), no firm can be sure of future demand for its product. This means that production decisions that involve long-term commitments, such as investment in plant and equipment, must be made even when there is no guarantee that the goods produced will be sold. And even when present prices of factors of production are known, there is no guarantee that they will remain fixed over time. So far we have ignored a host of problems about the future, all of which introduce uncertainty into the firm's decision-making process. Some of these problems will be considered during the discussion of capital markets in the next section. Uncertainty makes the cost and revenue curves become fuzzy, thick lines, rather than sharp, clear lines, for most producers. Profit maximization is no easy process when cost and demand conditions are blurred by the possibility of changes beyond the firm's control.

Research and Development

In addition to disturbances outside the firm's control, there is one major dimension of uncertainty in which the firm does play a major role: *future technology*. What products will be produced in the future? What will the new methods of production be? How will this affect cost and revenue? Firms are continually engaging in research and development (R and D) expenditures to create new products that will raise profits. We know that in the long run competitive industries (whether perfectly or imperfectly competitive) make no monopoly profits. But the dark clouds in the future need never darken the present profit situation of an imaginative and creative seller. Monopoly profits exist for the first firm in a new industry. The short run may be long enough for the first firms in a market to make an initial profit, plow it back into R and D, develop new products, and keep ahead of the game. A firm with a good research and development team can stay forever in the short run this way, by coming up with major innovations every two or three years. In effect they are a monopolist in one new product, then another. They just hope that it takes many years for their competitors to catch up.

In the preceding chapters our models were all static, covering only a single point in time. But the world is changing. Instead of letting cost curves remain in one place, the seller can use R and D expenditures to improve production techniques and raise profits in this manner as well as by product development. As cost curves shift down, other firms will follow suit as quickly as they can, but the existence of lags in adjustment to new technology provides profits in the short run for the farsighted firm. We see now that there is far more flexibility for profit maximization within a competitive enterprise than our earlier analysis suggested. Expenditures on R and D can change the conditions of cost and revenue, permitting the seller to equate marginal revenue and marginal cost at entirely new points and increase profits. The additional dimensions of profit maximization introduced by dynamic considerations such as the foregoing, and the problems created by uncertainty from outside the enterprise itself, make the business manager's and entrepreneur's roles fascinating and exciting. But the problem of economic analysis also becomes much more complicated than was true for static firms with perfect certainty.

Decision Making under Uncertainty

It is tautological to say that whatever the nature of these additional problems facing the businessman, profit maximization will occur where $MR = MC$. That statement provides no insight into the actual decision-making process of the firm. In fact, economic theory is still searching for a general theory of the firm that includes the explicit cost of decision making, the possibilities of research and development, and other problems associated with uncertainty. Our current dynamic theories are mere extensions of static models to show how static problems might be solved over time. But we do not know what the production function for new ideas looks like, when it is more efficient to establish a bureaucracy than to make day-to-day decisions, or the precise manner in which the finite lives of stockholders and managers affect corporations of infinite life. We have not yet found a convenient device to simplify these dynamic problems that will predict anything beyond what can be inferred by knowing that firms set marginal revenue equal to marginal cost.

The student of economics, engineering, social psychology, history, and other related disciplines should be challenged to probe further into the problem of decision making under uncertainty. One way to see the difficulties that face the firm in this regard is to look more closely at the tools business managers use to determine whether or not they are making profits and how much the firm is worth. Profits must equal revenues minus costs. This is true by definition for all firms. But the actual determination of revenues and costs is not a simple problem. As a result, firms are never even sure of their current levels of profits! Information is indeed a scarce commodity. In order to bring this to light, we introduce the two basic accounting statements of the firm, the *income statement* and *balance sheet,* which are used to take the pulse of the firm.

BUSINESS ACCOUNTING PROCEDURE

> Like pictures, numbers are perceived and interpreted in different ways. Sometimes a cursory glance is enough, more often it takes time to comprehend them fully and deeply.
>
> DMITRI V. PAVLOV

The Income Statement of a Firm

The income statement is used by the firm to measure profits and losses. It also shows the basis of profit in a given period by listing the sources of revenues and costs. We might view an income statement as the following simple equation:

profits = revenue − costs

In Table 17.1 a typical income statement is presented. Revenues and costs are broken into their major components. Although many alternative accounting procedures exist, the one presented here is representative of those most commonly used.

"Other income" usually includes interest earned on securities owned by the firm or on facilities rented out for a brief period. Material costs represent the cost of goods purchased from other firms. Interest costs are payments on the debt the firm has incurred.

One item that deserves particular attention is depreciation. This represents the wear and tear on plant and equipment during the period covered by the income statement. These costs are included at the time that the firm's assets are actually used up, rather than at the time the assets are initially purchased. Such a convention enhances the reliability of the profit figure for the current year. But it also makes profits depend on just how the firm decides to distribute the wearing out of plant and equipment over time. This is analyzed in more detail later.

Table 17.1   Profit and Loss Statement

Firm A

(For the period Jan. 1, 197X to Dec. 31, 197X)

Revenues (or Income)		
Sale of Goods	1,000	
Other Income	100	
Total Income		1,100
Costs		
Costs of Goods in Process		
Labor	300	
Materials	500	
Interest	100	
Depreciation	100	
Taxes Other Than Income	50	
Total	1,050	
Minus Additions to Inventory	100	
Costs of Goods Sold		950
Earnings before Taxes		150
Taxes		75
Earnings after Taxes (Accounting Profits)		75

The item "additions to inventory" is included as a minus. Why? Remember that the term revenue refers to the value of goods sold. Costs refers to the costs of goods being made. But all the goods sold during a given year need *not* correspond to the goods that were *made* during that year. When a good is produced it is shipped either to a warehouse or directly to a consumer. While it is being stored or shipped, often it is still owned by the firm that made it. Such goods are a part of the *inventory* of the firm. *Inventories are the goods (finished or unfinished) and materials that a firm owns and intends to use or sell but has not used or sold yet.* If a firm buys a huge shipment of some material that it plans to use later in production, costs go way up, but its revenues stay constant. This material will eventually be turned into finished goods. When these goods are sold, revenues will go up though current material costs will not change. We wish to have current profit figures that tell us whether goods *currently* being sold are providing a revenue in excess of *their* cost of production. That is why we take away from costs the share of expenses that goes into producing goods that have not yet been sold. We add to costs the expense of producing goods we sell out of inventory. Both items appear in the entry "additions to inventory."

Depreciation and Uncertainty

Accounting is sometimes considered to be a rather straightforward reporting of the revenues and costs of a firm, but only by those who are unfamiliar with its intricate workings and the many arbitrary judgements that it requires. Actually, accounting procedures for the same firm can be very different, giving a completely different view of the pattern of that enterprise's profits over time. Of the many ways in which accounting techniques can be used creatively to vary the appearance and even the nature of profits, we choose as an example one having to do with alternative treatments of depreciation as applied to the same firm.

A mineral water producer has invested $100 in the plant and equipment needed to produce that energy-vitalizing and morally unimpeachable fluid. For the time being his firm is the only seller, and his planned sales amount to $100 a year for the first three years. His plant was designed to last exactly three years, at which point the engineers tell him that it will collapse in a pile of rust. The "other costs" are minerals and other inputs purchased from suppliers, and they amount to $50 per year for the level of production that yields $100 worth of mineral water. How would the producer estimate his profits for each year? Clearly this depends on how he decides to distribute the cost of plant and equipment ($100) over the three years.

Horatio A. Economicus happens to work for the firm during the summer as an accountant. In this first test, young Horatio is asked by the boss how he plans to go about costing the wearing out, or depreciation, of plant and equipment and what this will mean for the firm's profits. Without a moment's hesitation, Horatio responds by giving three of the many alternatives that face the firm. All of the depreciation can be taken in the first year, half in each of the first two years, or it can be distributed evenly over the three years. Does this make any difference,

Table 17.2   Alternative Income Statement

Mineral Water Firm

(Immediate Depreciation)

Year 1		Year 2		Year 3	
Revenue	$100	Revenue	$100	Revenue	$100
Cost		Cost		Cost	
Plant	100	Plant	0	Plant	0
Other	50	Other	50	Other	50
Total	150	Total	50	Total	50
Earnings before Taxes	−50	Earnings before Taxes	50	Earnings before Taxes	50
Taxes	0	Taxes (with Allowance for Initial Loss)	0	Taxes	25
Earnings after Tax	−50	Earnings after Tax	50	Earnings after Tax	25

asks the boss with a sneer, when sales and costs are the same regardless of how they are written down?

Quickly Horatio pulls out three accounting tables that he worked on the evening before in a discotheque during the breaks. The boss recognizes them to be alternative income statements, each of which depends upon a particular depreciation technique that might be used by the firm. They are reproduced as Tables 17.2, 17.3, and 17.4.

Table 17.3   Alternative Income Statement

Mineral Water Firm

(Steady Depreciation)

Year 1		Year 2		Year 3	
Revenue	$100.00	Revenue	$100.00	Revenue	$100.00
Cost		Cost		Cost	
Depreciation	34.00	Depreciation	33.00	Depreciation	33.00
Other	50.00	Other	50.00	Other	50.00
Total	84.00	Total	83.00	Total	83.00
Earnings	16.00	Earnings	17.00	Earnings	17.00
Taxes	8.00	Taxes	8.50	Taxes	8.50
Earnings after Taxes	8.00	Earnings after Taxes	8.50	Earnings after Taxes	8.50

Using immediate depreciation (Table 17.2) provides misleading figures in the first year, particularly for any outside observer or potential investor who does not know the life of the assets being depreciated. It looks as though the mineral water enterprise is losing money. The public will be discouraged. Over the three years, its net after-tax profits turn out to be $25 (since the loss of the first year is permitted by tax authorities to be offset against the profit of the second year). Because of the negative public image that the firm will get in its initial year of operation by publishing these figures, the boss goes on to look at Horatio's other two tables (Tables 17.3 and 17.4). (He also fears the reaction of the other stockholders to the huge losses that are reported. They may feel that there is a better man for the job of firm manager.)

Table 17.3 depreciates the plant equally over the three years. The even distribution of plant costs gives a balanced view of the firm's profitability to the public. Earnings are identical in each year and no one is misled. This looks like an attractive scheme since the firm ends up with the same profit and taxes as before, but without creating any adverse image in the first year. However, there is also the possibility of using a faster rate of depreciation without having to report losses in any given year. This method is presented in Table 17.4.

At first glance it would appear that whether depreciation is instantaneous, steady, or fast the boss is correct in saying that profits will be the same in the end. Not so, says Horatio, if the firm is on its toes. He points out that for tax purposes many firms depreciate as rapidly as possible. The tax authorities, on the other hand, try to limit the rate of depreciation. Why? Under the even depreciation method shown in Table 17.3 taxes were $8.00, $8.50, and $8.50 for three years, or a total of $25.00. Under fast depreciation, Table 17.4, taxes were $0, $0, and $25.00 for the same three years, or a total of $25.00. Why might the

Table 17.4   Income Statement

Mineral Water Firm

(Fast Depreciation)

Year 1		Year 2		Year 3	
Revenue	$100	Revenue	$100	Revenue	$100
Cost		Cost		Cost	
Depreciation	50	Depreciation	50	Depreciation	0
Other	50	Other	50	Other	50
Total	100	Total	100	Total	50
Earnings	0	Earnings	0	Earnings	50
Taxes	0	Taxes	0	Taxes	25
				Earnings after Taxes	25

firm prefer to use the faster depreciation method shown in Table 17.4 to that shown in Table 17.3 for tax purposes? With even depreciation the firm pays taxes of $8.00 and $8.50 in the first and second year. But with fast depreciation the firm pays no taxes in those years. The money that is kept in reserve for future taxes ($25.00 in the third year) can be invested in some other project to earn *interest*. Thus with fast depreciation the firm gets to invest $8.00 in some other project during the first year and $8.00 plus $8.50 during the second year. The accumulated interest from these deferred tax payments can be added to the firm's income. Let us see how this works.

The bright young accountant works out the details and shows the boss that by taking the tax savings during each of the first two years and investing them in government bonds at 5 percent, it is possible for the firm to make $.618* of additional profits during the three years by paying taxes at the end of the period. By year 3 the firm has earned a total profit of not $25.00 but $25.618, thanks to "other income" earned using the depreciation scheme of Horatio. Thus the choice of accounting methods can affect the level of profits as well as the manner in which they are reported.

The Balance Sheet of a Firm

Let us turn now from the income statement, which indicates the flow of profits and losses during a period of time, to the *balance sheet*, which presents the worth of a firm at a point in time. Table 17.5 presents an example of such a balance sheet for our mineral water firm at the beginning of the three-year period, before it has earned any profits or made any depreciation. Notice that the main headings are assets, liabilities, and net worth. *Assets* are those items owned by the firm. Those items owed to other firms or individuals are *liabilities*. *Net worth* is the difference between the two. It is the share of the owners of the firm in the value of its assets, after taking out everything owed to third persons (liabilities). The balance sheet is simply an equation, just as the income statement is also an equation:

assets − liabilities = net worth

Assets and liabilities are both traditionally broken into two groups: current and noncurrent. Current assets include cash, securities, inventories, and accounts receivable. Accounts receivable are items owed to the firm by others, representing the credit that has been extended by the firm. Current assets represent assets that can be transformed readily into cash at their market value if necessary. Noncurrent assets such as plant and equipment are less immediately

---

The accounting calculations are as follows. At 5 percent interest per year, the firm earns $.40 on its initial tax saving of $8.00 in the first year, pays tax of $.20, and receives a net "other income" of *$.20. Reinvesting the $8.20 in the second year it receives $.41 in interest reported as "other income," or *$.205* after taxes have been paid on the interest. But in addition to this the firm is able to invest the tax savings during the second year ($8.50) for one year and earn $.425, which leaves *$.213* in "other income" after taxes to be added to the earlier amounts. Thus all of the "other income," which is italicized here, can be summed to get *$.618* in additional profits, thanks to the deferred taxes resulting from using accelerated depreciation.

Table 17.5 Balance Sheet at Beginning of Year 1

Mineral Water Firm

Assets		Liabilities	
Current Assets		**Current Liabilities**	
Cash	$50	Accounts Payable	$10
Inventory	0		
Accounts Receivable	0		
Noncurrent Assets		**Noncurrent liabilities**	
Plant and Equipment	100	Bank Loans	50
Total Assets	150	**Total Liabilities**	60
		Net Worth	
		Common Stock	$90
		Earned Surplus	0
		Total Net Worth	90
		Total Liabilities and Net Worth	150

Assets − Liabilities = Net Worth
(150)   (60)   (90)

marketable. Once the firm has purchased them, their principal value results from what they will produce subsequently for the firm (rather than what they would command if disposed of immediately). Noncurrent assets, if sold immediately, might have to be disposed of at a loss. They include, in addition to plant and equipment, real estate, natural resources, and the ownership participation of the enterprise in other firms.

Current liabilities include those liabilities that will have to be paid off shortly. They include short-term borrowings, accounts payable, taxes, or dividends owed, wages owed to employees, and so on. Noncurrent liabilities represent long-term borrowings. These include bonds, mortgages, and other debts not immediately repayable that the firm might have incurred in the process of setting up its facilities and running them. What is the firm's actual share of its assets? Its *equity* or *net worth*. This depends upon how much it has borrowed and owes to third parties. That is why net worth is best regarded as a residual between the total value of assets and the total value of liabilities. That part left over after taking out the firm's obligations to outsiders is its equity.

From the Income Statement to the Balance Sheet
What is the relationship between a firm's income statement and its balance sheet? Each provides a different but altogether important element of information to its managers, potential investors, economists, and tax authorities. The balance

sheet tells how much more a firm owns than it owes. An income statement tells whether or not it is *adding* to its assets faster than to its liabilities. That is because the income statement measures the flow of profits over a period of time (such as one year). Profits that are not paid out in dividends to shareholders are added to the book value of the corporation. They appear on the right-hand side of the balance sheet as part of net worth ("earned surplus"). They appear on the left-hand side as an addition to assets in the form of cash, securities, additional plant and equipment, or whatever else the proceeds were used for.

For example, if management decides that our mineral water producing firm has earned $8 of profit in the first year (following the method in Table 17.3), and if these profits are not paid out in dividends, they appear in the balance sheet at the end of that year. The new balance sheet would increase earned surplus by $8 as well as cash by $8 (if they are held in cash). The left- and right-hand sides of the balance sheet remain in balance, and net worth is larger by the amount of retained profits. In a similar manner the funds that the firm sets aside for depreciation during the first year might appear as cash in the amount of $34 (see Table 17.3), offsetting a reduction of $34 through depreciation in the value of plant and equipment. In this instance total assets would remain the same, though the value of fixed assets would decline and the value of current assets would rise. Notice that the choice of depreciation method has an important effect on the balance sheet from year to year.

Profits that are not paid to shareholders increase the book value of the company. If a firm earns profits during the course of a year its balance sheet at the end of the period will show a greater net worth than at the beginning. If the firm incurs a loss, its net worth will decline during the year. Thus the balance sheet is like a photograph of the firm at any point in time (sometimes "touched up" by the accounting department). Changes in the condition of the enterprise show up at a glance when one looks at several of these "photographs" for different points in time. If one is interested in knowing what accounted for the profits of a given period, it is necessary to go to the *income statement*. Here the details of revenue and costs are presented. The income statement presents the *flow* of profits over a period of time (usually one year). The balance sheet shows the *stock* of profits minus dividends that has been accumulated in the history of the firm. The balance sheet, therefore, needs only one date as it is a picture of the firm at a point in time. The income statement, on the other hand, measures how the firm is changing over a period of time. That is why economists call items in the balance sheet *stock variables* and those in the income statement *flow variables*. Both stocks and flows must be studied to get a complete picture of the enterprise over time.

The Accountant's Dilemma

We have seen that there is no one correct way to handle the bookkeeping of the firm. Among our three alternative methods of depreciation accounting, each has its advantages and disadvantages. Horatio A. Economicus has done his job well by showing that accelerated depreciation will maximize profits by deferring taxes. What will the boss decide to do? Since the government permits it, the boss might well adopt accelerated depreciation for tax purposes. But what about the public? Using the method in Table 17.4 will mislead the observers to think that the firm is unhealthy, since it earns zero profits in the first two years. This not only endangers the jobs of management, but it gets them in trouble with the Securities and Exchange Commission (SEC) as well. The SEC requires that firms publish accounts that portray as accurately as possible the "true" state of the firm. This is to prevent managers from publishing figures that indicate losses in order to drive the price of the firm's stock down. The managers might then buy the stock, publish huge profits, and watch the stock appreciate. Bearing in mind his three major considerations, namely, the SEC, the stockholders, and the profits that result from accelerated depreciation, the boss nervously asks Horatio if there is any way to use accelerated depreciation for tax purposes but to publish different figures for the public. Horatio suggests that the company publish an income statement for the public such as the following, Table 17.6, which will give them a fairer picture of the actual profitability of the enterprise year by year. Depreciation is charged at a steady rate, similar to that in Table 17.3, even though it is presented to the tax authorities at an accelerated rate, as in Table 17.4. The amount that eventually must be spent on taxes is charged as provision for future taxes in the report shown to the public. The concept of *gross earnings* has been created to let the public know what profits would be if the firm did not keep a different set of books for the tax authorities.

Table 17.6 presents a picture of profitability at a constant rate over the three years so as not to mislead the public. This satisfies the SEC. But the use of accelerated depreciation for tax purposes has increased the profitability of the firm by $.618 over this period. We have seen why the boss uses accounting methods for the public different from those he uses for the tax authorities. Many firms keep a third set of books to provide management with information about the profitability of the firm. These presumably take account of factors that are firm secrets and cannot be divulged even to stockholders. Some firms with conservative managements understate their expectations of future profitability in the written text accompanying their annual income statement and balance sheet. Others exaggerate the future prospects. We can assume that their choice of accounting methods is similarly affected by their corporate personalities.

Uncertainty Once Again

The whole discussion of which accounting method is optimal indicates how uncertainty can affect the *current profits* of the firm. Horatio's boss must know the future before he is able to charge the true depreciation in the present. Will his machinery really turn to rust in three years? What if the equipment becomes obsolete before that time? What if tax rates increase? Would it then be better to spread depreciation over a longer period? What if the price level rises? Would it then be better to deduct depreciation as soon as possible? Uncertainty about the future leads to uncertainty about current depreciation, which in turn leads to uncertainty about current profits. This is true no matter how definite our current revenue and other cost figures are. The current profit figures published by firms are really only the *best possible guesses* of their accounting departments, internal auditors, finance managers, and top management. We have seen the wide latitude management has in determining *measured profits*.

This latitude exists not only for depreciation but also for a host of other current expenditures that could legitimately be charged to future output. Consider research and development expenditures. Should we deduct them from current revenue or should we create a fund of future expenses to be added to costs once we sell the goods that were discovered through the research? For tax purposes most firms declare these R and D costs as current expenses. But in reporting them to the public they are often presented as an investment to be depreciated later rather than as a current charge against profits. (Of course they cannot be depreciated later on for tax purposes, since they have been deducted from rev-

Table 17.6   Published Income Statements

Mineral Water Firm

Revenue	$100.00	Revenue	$100.00	Revenue	$100.000
		Other Income	.40	Other Income	.835
		Total	100.40	Total	100.835
Cost		Cost		Cost	
Depreci- ation	34.00	Depreci- ation	33.00	Depreci- ation	33.000
Other	50.00	Other	50.00	Other	50.000
Total	84.00	Total	83.00	Total	83.000
Gross Earnings	16.00	Gross Earnings	17.40	Gross Earnings	17.835
Minus Provision for Future Tax	8.00	Minus Provision for Future Tax	8.50	Minus Deferred Taxes	16.500
				Plus Past Provision for Tax Payments	16.500
Adjusted Gross Earnings	8.00	Adjusted Gross Earnings	8.90	Adjusted Gross Earnings	17.835
Taxes	0.00	Taxes	.20	Taxes Chargeable to Current Earnings	8.917
Net Earnings	8.00	Net Earnings	8.70	Net Earnings	8.918

enue once already.) Which is more accurate, the charge to current costs (for taxes) or to future costs (for published reports)? It depends on whether or not the R and D eventually pays off. If it does, then research and development in creating future income might well be considered as a future cost. If it does not, it might as well have been regarded as a current expense, since it brings no future payoff.

Firms with large and fluctuating research and development costs and large changes in the level of investment have the greatest latitude in deciding how to distribute charges against current earnings. They present a challenge to accountants and the public as well as to their own managements. The more they report as earnings this year (by deferring charges) the less they will have to report in the future. The decision of whether to report earnings in the present or future rests not with Horatio but with the boss. Thus our determination of the profitability of an enterprise requires a careful scrutiny of all the footnotes and comments in its income statement. These comments describe the depreciation practices used and many other factors in which the management exercises its discretion in reporting figures.

We saw at the beginning of this chapter why management is justified in exercising discretion in financial reporting. It is because current earnings are indeed uncertain, as are future costs and sales. The future is blurred, and even the manager of the firm itself does not have spectacles that will clear up the horizon and tell him with certainty what actual profits are.

The Organization of Production Decisions

For five chapters, we have used the term "firm" to denote an institution in which decisions about production are organized. Yet much of what has been said is relevant to different forms of organization as well. All economies in the world today can be called mixed systems in the sense that they contain many different forms of organizations to carry out the production needs of their citizens. There are centrally managed institutions that are owned by a sovereign, there are private competitive firms with private owners, there are publicly regulated monopolies. There are cooperative enterprises, there are nonprofit institutions, and there is the nonmarket production by consumers of goods they use themselves. All economies have all these forms of organization though the relative importance varies from nation to nation. All these institutions share common problems: they must attempt to minimize cost; they must decide whether additional production is worth the cost; they must forecast the uncertain future in order to make current decisions; and they must measure their own activities in order to know where they stand and how well they are succeeding in solving their problems. The problem a firm faces when deciding whether or not to automate is the same as that faced by the post office or by a university considering the introduction of television to classrooms. The fact that one institution is privately owned, another publicly owned, and the third—in the case of private universities—of unclear ownership does not alter the basic problems of production.

If a society owns *X* and wants *Y*, it tries to find a way to transform *X* into *Y*. If different ways exist, it must decide how much *Y* to produce and how best to produce it. These are the decisions we have studied.

Ownership and Control

When an individual buys a share of the common stock of a firm, he has become a part owner. How much control does he exercise over the decisions of the firm? A letter from a stockholder to a corporation president receives about as much attention as a letter from a customer. If the executive gets a great deal of mail supporting one side of a particular issue, it may affect his decision just as it would affect the decision of a Congressman. The point is that when ownership is dispersed, the feeling of control on the part of stockholders vanishes. The relevance of this issue for the alternative forms of organization is the following: The manager of a publicly owned enterprise has as much freedom as the manager of a privately owned one. And the customers have about the same possibilities for getting action on complaints. (Does the post office or the telephone company respond most rapidly to the desires of consumers?)

Economies of scale characterize the production processes currently available and this means that large organizations are necessary if we are to have cheap commodities and therefore high levels of material satisfaction. Large organizations are very much alike regardless of who the titular owners are or in whom the legal powers of decision making are vested. There will be a manager or group of managers at the top who are responsible for large decisions, for formulating the strategy of the enterprise. They will be held responsible for their decisions by legal owners, public or private, who know a great deal less than the managers about how best to run the enterprise. Thus the managers will be largely immune to criticism and will be able to paper over all but the grossest of strategic errors.

Below these managers will be managers who have specific tasks assigned to them by the top management: "Run that factory," "Sell this product," "Develop new products," or "Find tax loopholes." They in turn boss lower managers who must "Hire twenty machinists," "Get ten new customers," "Create a nickel cigar," or "Analyze the proposed tax bill." The number of managerial layers will vary depending on the size of the enterprise, but eventually the orders are given to "Tote that box" and "Lift that bale." The individuals who work for the firm care very little who owns it as that does not appear to affect the manner in which their jobs are defined for them. Questions of legal ownership do not seem to change the day-to-day operation of large organizations.

Although this argument may be a reasonable apology for why we could look at the production decision from the vantage of the firm, it also may be viewed as a criticism of the way we looked at it. We viewed it as a problem of profit maximization, yet now we see decisions being made by paid workers. Why should these workers not attempt to do what is best for themselves instead of what is best for the firm? The answer is that workers *can* be expected to look out for themselves and therefore one of the largest problems facing management is how to structure a system of rewards — salaries, promotions, comfort — that motivates individuals to do what is best for the firm. This problem too is shared by all managers regardless of who their legal bosses are. Successful organizations are the ones that have established systems to detect and reward superior performances on the part of their employees. The models we have discussed assumed that organizations could solve this technical problem and could act in a unified manner toward achieving their stated goals. In the real world, many cannot.

Questions

1. Why do we not know for sure the value of any particular enterprise? Or whether the value of their output exceeds their costs?
2. Who should decide when a plant manager is to receive a raise or a promotion and how might they decide? A professor? A corporate lawyer? The number two man of a corporation? A research assistant? A two star general? A salesman? A janitor? A secretary? A teacher? In a world that needs great amounts of technical expertise, must the experts have power?

Concepts Discussed

income statement   assets
balance sheet   liabilities
depreciation   equity
net worth

18 Central Planning

Why Planning?

Some governments, faced with shades of grey and unappealing income distributions, see red. In order to eliminate the apparent inequity of decentralized market systems, these governments adopt a system of centralized planning for production decisions and public ownership of capital equipment. They feel that this strategy will accomplish the purpose of eliminating the large fortunes that might accrue to certain capitalists in market systems. In addition, they feel that it can guarantee full employment, cut down on the costs of product differentiation — advertising, etc. — and eliminate problems that can arise whenever private interests are,in conflict with public interests.

Does planning accomplish these desires? Can we produce what the public wants without the "invisible hand" to guide us? In this chapter, we look at the technical problems of organizing production decisions centrally. We find that markets and prices must still be used if the planners are to know what to produce, but that under ideal conditions, the planners can attain the same solution that would be attained under pure competition. It would seem that our choice of systems hangs not upon an abstract analysis of a system's properties when ideal conditions prevail, but rather upon a tedious empirical analysis of what the real conditions are and how well or badly off the different systems perform in that environment.

The Ideal Case of Central Planning: Assumptions

In the case of central planning under ideal conditions, consumers are permitted to use the market to allocate their income. Consumer sovereignty is preserved; price tags are placed on every item. Consumers are permitted to buy as much as they want at that price. This assumption corresponds to the way some centrally planned economies today actually allocate commodities to consumers. In addition, we assume that if the item is sold out and excess demand arises, the price is raised. If an item does not sell and inventories build up, the price is lowered. The job of the planning authority is to maximize the value of the output produced. Since prices are used as a measure of value (what other measure could be used?) we know that as soon as the price of one good rises, its importance in total output rises and the planning authority may be induced thereby to increase the output of that good and decrease the production of goods with falling prices.

How does the planner make such decisions? When does he increase production and by how much? Here we intend to look at a very important tool of planning called *linear programming*. It is a device that can guide the planning of production and provide the answers to questions we have just asked. After examining this tool, we look at some of the real problems facing planners today.

Remember the commissar in Chapter 7 who was faced with the problem of maximizing corn production in an agricultural economy? His fortunes have changed and he is now head of the Central Planning Bureau of an economy that produces nothing but steak and automobiles. During his rapid ascent to power he has learned a great deal, in particular, to solve problems using linear programming. This is an essential tool in the kit of any technical manager, including capitalists, and is especially important for a central planner who must manage an entire economy. In this chapter we see how the commissar applies the tool of linear programming to solve his production problem. We use diagrams throughout, even though in practice he is accustomed to employ algebra and work out solutions on a computer, since this is more efficient when there are more than two dimensions to a maximizing problem. Table 18.1 shows us what goods (but not how many) can be produced and the amount of resources at the planner's disposal during the planning period.

The Commissar's Problem
The commissar has been asked to maximize output. What is "output"? It is some mixture of steak and automobiles. How many steaks equal an automobile? We must know this to be able to determine the meaning of output. With consumer sovereignty, the answer depends on the price of steak and automobiles. So the planner's first problem is to assign prices to the two commodities so that he will know their relative values and be able to add them up into a homogeneous total. The planning prices that he picks are

    1 automobile = 2,000 rubles
    1 steak   = 2 rubles

Of course our assumption that he is responsive to consumer demand means that if deficits or surpluses arise at these prices, he will have to alter the planning prices later on. That is, the consumers get to tell him whether he has chosen the correct prices or not. But in the meantime he acts as though the prices are fixed. Having established the planning prices, he is able to define output, *Y,* as a function of the numbers of steaks and cars.

    $Y = 2{,}000(\text{no. autos}) + 2(\text{no. steaks})$

Table 18.1	
Factors in the Economy	**Goods To Be Produced**
1. Labor—2 million manhours	1. Automobiles
2. Land—1 million acres	2. Steak
3. Factories—30 factories	

If he has chosen the correct prices (2,000 and 2), an auto is worth 1,000 times what a steak is worth. Increasing production by one auto should be as good as increasing it by 1,000 steaks. His formula for output reflects this and his problem becomes one of maximizing output.

The Production Relationships for Steak and Automobiles

The next step in approaching the planning problem is to specify the technical relationships between inputs (factors of production and intermediate goods) and output for both steak and automobiles. We need to know the production functions. Here we simplify things by leaving out intermediate goods and simply relate output to the basic factors of production, that is, labor, land, and capital (factories). Recall that under pure competition it was assumed that the producer already knew the technical relationships in his production function. Similarly, we now assume that under ideal central planning the planner also knows these relationships. (There is many a slip between assumptions and actuality in either case.)

Table 18.2 shows the production relationships facing the central planner, as prepared by his staff of engineers. They express the production functions in terms of the resources necessary to produce 1 unit of steak or 1 unit of automobiles. It is assumed in this table that the economy has no increasing or decreasing costs. Average costs are the same whether one or many units are being produced. This is called a "linear" relationship. It is essential for the application of linear programming. In the case of increasing or decreasing costs, far more complex planning devices are necessary that cannot be illustrated here.

Once the commissar has in hand information about the availability of resources (Table 18.1) and resource requirements for the production of each good (Table 18.2), he can go to work. The linear programming problem involves the maximization of a particular output subject to resource and production constraints. This is also what the market does. In the market economy each firm tries to produce as much as it can with a given set of resources (this is the cost-minimization problem). Consumers would like to get to the point on the production frontier that has the highest value. The result under ideal market conditions is to reach that point where the slope of the production possibility frontier equals the ratio of prices of the products. Central planning under consumer sovereignty has exactly the same goal.

Table 18.2	Resource Requirements	
Inputs	**Output**	
	1 automobile	**1 steak**
Labor (Manhours)	500	1
Land (Acres)	0	1
Factories	1/100	0

Production and Resource Constraints

Production and resource constraints are expressed in the form of inequalities. Take land, for example. There are one million acres of land available (Table 18.1). Each steak requires one acre of land. This means that if all the land were used to produce steak, total production could not exceed one million steaks. But it might not even reach this level. Why? Because we see from Table 18.2 that steak requires labor as well as land in its production. If the consumers desire a great number of automobiles, there will be very little labor left over for steak production—perhaps not enough to utilize all the land. But the amount of land *constrains* steak production to be *no more* than one million per year. Mathematically the *land constraint* can be written as follows:

no. steaks ≦ 1 million

(This means steak production can be less than or equal to one million steaks, because of the limitation of land available.)

The *factory constraint* in this example applies only to the production of automobiles because factories are not needed to produce steaks. With 30 factories and the resource requirement of 1 factory for every 100 cars (Table 18.2), we know that the number of factories constrains auto production to be less than or equal to 3,000 cars during the planning period.

no. automobiles ≦ 3,000

The *labor constraint* is somewhat more complex. Labor can be used in both automobile and steak production. Thus its constraint must be expressed in the form of two variables. Each steak produced needs 1 manhour whereas each auto needs 500. The total amount of labor used for auto production (500 times the number of autos produced) plus the total needed for steak production (1 times the number of steaks produced) must not exceed the 2 million manhours available. Thus the labor constraint is

500 × no. autos + 1 × no. steaks ≦ 2 million (manhours)

Since labor is used in the production of autos and steaks this constraint shows us that the more labor assigned to auto production, the less will remain for steak production (assuming full employment). Now that the three inequalities have been determined, the commissar is ready to solve his problem. Let us reproduce these inequalities below for convenient reference.

1. steaks ≦ 1 million
2. autos ≦ 3,000
3. 500 × autos + steaks ≦ 2 million

Solving the Commissar's Problem Graphically

Although the commissar might prefer algebra, we can solve his problem graphically. Since there are only two unknowns (steaks and autos), one diagram can include all the constraints. Inequalities 1, 2, and 3 combine the production processes and resource constraints. A graph shows clearly how each constraint limits the possible zone of production from the impossible.

The *land constraint* is shown in Figure 18.1. It separates the possible production points (clear area) from the impossible production points (shaded area). Since no land is needed for auto production, any amount of autos could be produced if land were the only constraint in the economy (factories and labor being in unlimited supply). Figure 18.1 is a graphic way of saying that the amount of land limits steak production to one million units but places no limit on auto production.

The *factory constraint* is superimposed on the land constraint in Figure 18.2. It limits the production of autos to 3,000 units regardless of the other resources available. The result is a box (the clear space within the shaded boundaries) that indicates the total possible production given the two constraints. Land limits steak production and factories limit auto production. The boundary of this area of production possibilities is the familiar production possibility frontier (PPF). An economy with only two constraints (land and factories) could produce any combination of autos and steaks along this square frontier. The greater the number of constraints we add, the more likely that the production possibility frontier will assume the more familiar curved shape.

The *labor constraint* is added in Figure 18.3. It is determined by inequality 3, which says that if only steaks are produced and labor is the only limiting factor, society can produce 2 million steaks (point *A*). If only autos are produced under the same limitations, production is 4,000 units (point *B*). The line connecting *A* and *B* shows all the other possible combinations of steak and auto production given the limited amount of labor. For example, when 2,000 autos are produced, only 1 million steaks can be supplied as well (point *C*).

The resource and production constraints have permitted us to draw a production possibility frontier that shows the space within which the commissar is free to move. Any of the output combinations on that frontier are available to him. He must pick the combination that is worth most to the consumers. He will do

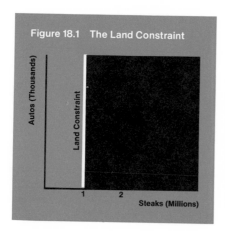

Figure 18.1 The Land Constraint

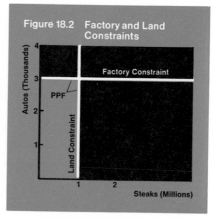

Figure 18.2 Factory and Land Constraints

this, we recall, by maximizing the value of output (Y) where output is expressed in equation 4.

4. $Y = 2,000(\text{no. of autos}) + 2(\text{no. of steaks})$

Remember that the coefficients in equation 4 are prices and that prices represent relative value to the consumers. In this case, consumers feel that automobiles are worth 1,000 times as much as a steak. Therefore 1 automobile increases Y by as much as 1,000 steaks do. The problem of the commissar is to pick from the possible points in Figure 18.3 the one that gives the highest value to Y and therefore pleases consumers most. For example, at point C where 2,000 cars are produced and are worth 2,000 rubles each, auto production is worth 4 million rubles. One million steaks are also produced at a value of 2 rubles each, so steak production is worth 2 million rubles. Total output is worth 6 million rubles.

Is point C the maximum level of output available? The answer to this can be found by drawing a number of possible curves along which the value of output is constant. This is done in Figure 18.4.

Each diagonal line in Figure 18.4 represents a different total value of production. For example, the line for 8 million rubles represents all the possible combinations of steak and autos that will be worth 8 million rubles, *given the planner's prices* that were assumed at the beginning of the chapter. Once we know the planner's prices from equation 4 we can draw these lines. Output worth 2 million rubles may be represented by any point along the first line, by 1,000 autos, by 1 million steaks, or by 500 autos and ½ million steaks. From Figure 18.4, the solution is obvious. As long as the prices are those in equation 4 the commissar should end up producing at point D and maximizing the value of output. Clearly 7 million rubles is the highest possible value of output under present conditions. He should call for the production of 3,000 autos and ½ million steaks. If he chose to produce at C, his value of production, as we have seen, would be only worth 6 million rubles, and he might be dismissed from his post and sent to administer a hydroelectric power station in Uzbekistan.

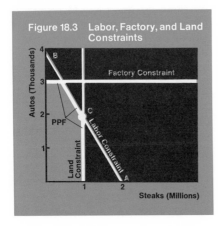

Figure 18.3 Labor, Factory, and Land Constraints

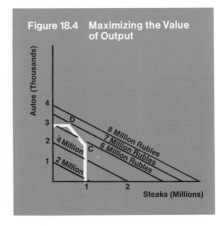

Figure 18.4 Maximizing the Value of Output

Computerization of the Problem

The graphical solution we obtained in this chapter indicates the nature of the algebraic solution that can be achieved much more swiftly by computer. As all of the functions are straight lines, we see that the solution will always contain a corner point somewhere on the production frontier regardless of the prices we choose. Try different prices and see if it is not always a corner that maximizes output. The computer can be programmed to proceed by trial and error to examine various corner points until it has found the maximum. The method by which it proceeds from point to point to find a maximum is called an *algorithm*. In this case, the algorithm is a set of instructions to the computer that tells it the order in which to examine the corners. For example, one algorithm might tell the computer to start at any corner (such as *C*), move to the adjacent corner with the highest value, and continue until it is impossible to increase output any further by moving to an adjacent corner. These instructions applied to our problem would cause a move from *C* to *D* and no additional moves. Since our graphical example has only two products, and there are therefore only two ways to move from any corner (rather than many dimensions and many possible moves), such an algorithm will get us to the maximum with lightning speed. It would never involve a move away from the maximum point *D*. If, by chance, we started at *D* we would remain there. If we started anywhere else, the algorithm would make sure that we moved toward *D*.

Selecting a Specific Production Process

Now that we have shown how linear programming might be applied to achieve an overall planning solution for the commissar, let us look at its usefulness in selecting one from among various alternative production processes for a *given product*. In the example above we assumed that there was only one way to produce steaks. Assume now that a new production process for steak is devised but that everything else in the problem remains as before. Suppose that engineers have developed a way to make steak using ½ unit of labor and 2 units of land per steak. There are now two processes for producing steak that may be labeled "steak no. 1" and "steak no. 2." (see Table 18.3)

The problem is now to maximize

$$Y = 2,000(\text{autos}) + 2(\text{steak no. 1}) + 2(\text{steak no. 2})$$

Note that steak no. 1 and steak no. 2 are identical in quality. Therefore, they get

Table 18.3		
	Steak No. 1	**Steak No. 2**
Labor	1	½
Land	1	2
Factories	0	0

the same coefficient in the output equation. But to the computer, they are different commodities. When the computer selects steak no. 1 over steak no. 2, he will be doing so because steak no. 1 uses fewer scarce resources, that is, requires that we give up fewer automobiles. The three resource/production constraints are now the following:

1′. 500 (no. of autos) + (no. of steak no. 1) + ½(no. of steak no. 2) ≤ 2 million
2′. (no. of steak no. 1) + 2 (no. of steak no. 2) ≤ 1 million
3′. (no. of autos) ≤ 3,000

A graphical solution to this problem would require three dimensions, since there are now three unknowns (steak no. 1, steak no. 2, and autos). But we have set the problem up so that the solution for automobiles remains unchanged at 3,000 to simplify matters. This means that we can *consider the choice of the production process for steak as a separate linear programming problem.* (Such an approach is called a "partial solution" to a planning problem, since it assumes that the output of all other goods is unaffected by the calculation. In this particular case, the assumption is not violated because we have stacked the deck to make sure it holds.)

For this solution we need only to graph the outputs of steak no. 1 and steak no. 2, assuming an output of 3,000 autos. This is done in Figure 18.5. Recall the number of manhours that were available for steak production from the solution of our earlier problem. Point *D* in Figure 18.4 left ½ million manhours and the total amount of land (1 million acres) available for producing steaks after 3,000 cars had been produced. In Figure 18.5 we draw in these resource constraints.

Each of the lines *LM* and *NO* shows a particular resource constraint. Line *LM* shows the *land constraint* when 1 million acres are available. We know that this allows us to produce 1 million units of steak by the process called steak no. 1 or ½ million steaks by steak no. 2 or any combination along *LM*. Similarly, Line *NO* shows the *labor constraint* for each production technique when there are ½ million manhours available. It is clear from the diagram that the maximum steak production occurs at the corner *E* where 666,666 steaks are produced, half

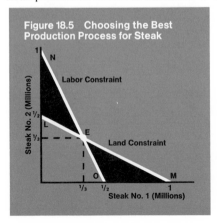

Figure 18.5   Choosing the Best Production Process for Steak

by each process, rather than 500,000 as before using only one process. The existence of the new process delights the commissar and his superiors in the government. It means that all the land now can be fully utilized. (In our earlier solution the production of ½ million steaks by steak no. 1 meant that one-half the land was standing idle, since there was no labor left to work it.) The engineers have devised a new technique, steak no. 2, which uses more land for every unit of labor—hence the added output and efficiency. Total output increases by 166,666 steaks or 333,333 rubles.

Adjusting Planners' Prices for Consumer Equilibrium

We see that the linear programming technique can be used by production planners to *select the proper production method* as well as *to produce the right products*. This corresponds to *cost minimization* as well as *profit maximization* in a market solution. In our simple example, there were only two possible ways to produce steaks and one way to make cars. We could add any number of processes and any number of goods. Linear programming will let us select those goods and those methods that maximize output (or any function we tell it to maximize).

Before looking into the problems of central planning, let us finish the analysis begun earlier. We noted at the beginning of the chapter that planners would set prices of products and let consumers buy what they wished. If it happened that they miscalculated on the prices and ended up with surpluses of some products and deficits of others, they would have to *change prices*. Of course once planners' prices were changed, the optimal output might change as well. For instance, we saw when solving the problem graphically that the commissar relied upon value-of-production lines in Figure 18.4 to determine the best output point. But these lines had slopes representing the relative prices of steak and autos and values determined by their actual prices in rubles. If the planners were forced to change the prices, these lines would have different slopes and values. The maximum might well occur at some other corner if steeper constant value lines were used.

Look at Figure 18.6. The production possibility frontier for steak and autos is now almost a curved line, since many more production processes and resource constraints have been introduced for the sake of realism. (Recall from the chapter (7) on corn production the number of alternative processes confronting the commissar in that simple example.) The final adjustment of prices produces line *AC* touching the production possibility frontier at point *B*. This is where planners end up after adjusting planning prices to clear product markets and after changing output to correspond to the new set of prices.

If point *B* represents the quantities of steak and automobiles that the consumers buy when they face the prices represented by the slope of *AC*, then no other point along *AC* is preferred. This means that *B* is the best possible production point. Using linear programming, *B* will be attained if the prices from *AC* are put into the expression to be maximized.

The Allocative Efficiency Implications of Ideal Planning

In achieving position *B* above, central planning arrived at the same solution as did the market economy under perfect competition. Consumer sovereignty was assumed to prevail in the planning model as it was under pure competition. Of course, there is no guarantee that central planners will respond to consumer sovereignty and set their planners' prices so that all markets will be cleared following the free wishes of consumers. In most planned economies, the adjustment to changes in demand are so slow that long queues form as consumers attempt to purchase many products that are in short supply, while surpluses of others pile up in warehouses. This introduces a number of difficulties for planners. Shades of grey exist everywhere. We now note some of the difficulties planners face.

Shades of Grey in Planning

The commissar is, in practice, confronted with a host of problems that make his life far more hectic than our ideal example might suggest. The first difficulty is one of *computing capacity*. A sophisticated economy has literally thousands of products, each of which can be produced by countless production processes. This means that the number of equations and unknowns in a real-world planning problem are in the millions. Current computers are not large enough to handle such problems. Because of this, the planner must either find a way to break the big problem into small ones that can be solved separately, or he must abandon some detail and plan in a very aggregative fashion, assuming that all fruit is identical and that there is but one way to produce housing.

Furthermore, the *information* necessary to derive the production equations and to determine the exact resource constraints is not centrally available. We saw in an earlier chapter that individual corn farmers knew a great deal about their own particular production functions through experience and training. But this information was not shared by the commissar or his staff at the outset. It had to be acquired from scratch, requiring an enormous effort and involving much trial and error. If planners attempt to duplicate the decision-making processes of thousands of private producers, it requires learning all the facts that

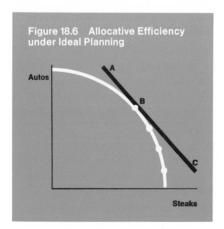

Figure 18.6 Allocative Efficiency under Ideal Planning

those producers have been using to make their decisions. It is not surprising that in practice a number of countries that once attempted to use central planning— with decisions delegated from the top down—are now shifting to greater and greater delegation of responsibility to individual, and better informed, producers. Even large firms in capitalist economies find it profitable to decentralize decision making. For many decisions, it is apparently more efficient to allow the man on the scene to have decision-making power because he has a vast amount of information at his fingertips. If the decisions are to be made on a higher level, the man on the scene must convey all of this information to the decision maker. He must write in a few pages information that took him years to acquire. This is very difficult. The firm is often better off letting the low-level manager make the decision rather than relying on his ability to transmit information. If this is true for firms, imagine how the problem is compounded by centralizing all of the economy's decisions. We should note here that firms also use linear programming to minimize costs. Governments do not have a monopoly on the use of planning tools. US firms, with linear programming and the world's largest computers at their fingertips, choose to decentralize decisions because they find it more efficient.

Information and communication tend to break down as decision-making units become larger and larger. That is one reason why cost curves begin to turn up and sooner or later become U-shaped for most firms in any economy. Any firm may grow too large to be managed efficiently. If this is true for individual enterprises, it is even more true for whole economies. This means that the commissar who tries to manage the entire economy as a single decision-making unit can see his most valiant efforts fail through breakdowns in the communications process. Since the fields of information theory and decision-making costs are still in their infancy, it is not possible for us to determine the allocative efficiency implications of sheer size in the decision-making unit. It is generally believed that the costs of transferring information increase more than proportionally with the size of the firm. Beyond this, little can be said.

What about public goods and externalities? We allowed planners the use of the market to let consumers determine the value of the products, but this leads to inefficiency if public goods exist. If planners do not let consumers determine value, then surpluses pile up and excess demand causes the lines to grow longer and the public to become more and more dissatisfied with the planning bureau. But as for public goods, such as clean air over Moscow, the consumer has no more incentive to pay for them in a planned economy than he does in a market economy. The planner must therefore guess at the value of clean air and place this in the function to be maximized. Production processes that create dirty air would have charges added to their costs to represent their external diseconomies to the public. But these charges are just like taxes that the private economy might assess. Planning gives us no easy way to estimate the value of public goods to consumers. In both planning and private systems, the government must guess at the value of public goods.

What about monopoly? It is here that planning gets to show its colors. The programming model maximizes the value of output, not profit. Even if production processes are such that it is cheaper to have a few large factories rather than many small ones, planners are not plagued by problems of monopolists and inefficiency when they choose the few large plants over the many small ones. Problems of oligopolists fighting for profit and market power, of too many small inefficient gasoline stations, and of product differentiation that results from advertising alone are not met by the planners. They have problems enough, but these are not among them.

Where does this leave the student of economic principles? At the present time the pitfalls of planning seem to be as great as the pitfalls of the market economy. In either case there are methods of avoiding the pitfalls through public policy: in the first case through improvements of information, communications, and computing capacity and computer technology; in the second case through preservation of pure competition, the composition of taxes and subsidies, and the regulation of monopolies. Under both planning and market regimes, public goods and externalities, as well as decreasing cost industries, require special attention. Otherwise neither system will provide allocative efficiency. Perhaps the main implication of this and the preceding sections is that one cannot assume that in the real world, which is colored grey rather than black or white, allocative efficiency will be attained automatically such that consumers may relax their guard and assume that they remain sovereign. Consumer sovereignty is not a free good.

Questions

1. Recompute the maximum level of output from Figure 18.4 under the assumption that steaks are worth 4 rubles each. 6 rubles each.
2. What are the advantages and disadvantages of centralized planning as a device for allocating resources? Should centrally planned economies be free of pollution?
3. If the planners use the price system, how will the resulting income distribution differ from that which we would observe in a market economy?

Concepts Discussed

linear programming   central planning

VI Markets for Productive Resources

An investment in knowledge
always pays the best interest.

BENJAMIN FRANKLIN

In the second section of this book, we presented an analysis of a labor market within a discussion of a simple economy. At that time, we were not ready to entertain the complexities that must be confronted if markets for other factors are to be considered as well. In this section, we repair that deficiency.

First we discuss capital markets. We show how interest rates are determined in the market for capital and how this market, like all others, can be viewed as one in which men's desires for satisfaction are confronted by limited possibilities for satisfying those desires. We accomplish this by looking at the demand and supply of future goods.

Then a closer look is given to labor markets. We discuss the concept of human capital and note the economic similarities between human resources and other resources. Here we note how skill differences, location, and countless other phenomena that make men unique affect wage rates, and how it takes time for an increase in demand in one labor market to spill over into others. The roles of unions, minimum wage laws, and automation are among the issues explored.

Then we discuss natural resources. To what extent will their limited nature affect the quality of our lives in the future? We attempt to separate real from superficial reasons for fearing their limited nature. Since economics is designed to discuss the efficient use of limited resources, it gives us particularly useful insights into this problem. Certain fears of shortages are shown to result because the potential role of prices in allocating resources had never been considered.

19 Capital

Perhaps no theoretical question studied by economists has raised so much emotional and moral interest as the question of capital. The words "profits" and "interest" have evil connotations in the folklore of most nations; the owners of capital have been painted as oppressors from the earliest days. And in modern times, it is difficult to think of the political implications of the concept of capital without thinking of a group of ideas that can loosely be called Marxism.

To the student who has viewed capital as a key determinant of the relations among men, its modern treatment at the hands of neoclassical economists will be quite disappointing. Capital, it seems, can be studied as a special case of the theory of production and profit maximization. The efficiency of free markets for capital rests on the same criteria as does the efficiency of any other market. This is because, to a neoclassical economist, the market for capital can be viewed as a market for future goods. There is a supply and a demand for future goods and a price that clears the market. We will show how that price is related to interest rates, how the decisions of savers and investors affect those rates, and how certain technical mathematical problems arise in this market that are absent from the markets we have already studied. We reserve an appendix for Marx.

Much of the analysis we present owes its parentage to Irving Fisher and his 1930 classic, *The Theory of Interest*. There Fisher treated capital as a special case of the already developed theory of markets. The technical difficulty of capital theory more than any other reason may explain why it took economists so long to construct a view of capital that was consistent with the rest of their apparatus. Another reason, of course, might be the folklore and the way *a priori* beliefs about how the world "ticks" cloud men's ability to think clearly.

Capital: The Man-Made Factor of Production

The first ape to seize a stick and knock down a banana was pioneering the principle of capital. He took time out to get the stick. He was rewarded for the delay by getting more bananas than he could have gotten by just shaking the tree. Capital (the stick) is a commodity that is obtained through the postponement of present consumption in order to increase future consumption. Like the ape's innovation, the invention of tools marked a turning point in history. Man-made factors of production, when combined with labor and natural resources, have permitted men to take income from the present and increase resources in the future. The resulting increase in productivity has allowed *Homo sapiens* to come out of the trees and into the marketplace.

IRVING FISHER (1867–1947)   Possibly the first of the great modern American economists, Irving Fisher is associated with numerous major advances in economics and statistics, including some important work in index numbers, which he presented in the course of a highly prolific writing career yielding at least 28 books. Almost all of his professional life was spent as a professor at Yale University, although he traveled widely and championed a number of causes not related to the teaching of economics, for example, health foods and temperance.

Although Fisher in his doctoral dissertation (Yale, 1892) made some original contributions to the theory of consumer choice, and although much microeconomic apparatus similar to his now forms part of the body of modern economic analysis, our interest in Fisher stems from his work on the theory of interest. Early in his career Fisher turned his attention to the distribution between stocks and flows as economic magnitudes and to relations between capital (a stock) and interest (a flow). He developed these ideas in such later works as *Rate of Interest* (1907) and *Theory of Interest* (1930). By the use of the ratio of the value of future income streams discounted to the present and then divided by the current cost of an asset, Fisher was able to show that conceptually there is no difference between interest as a flow return on capital, rent as a flow return on land, or any other flow return. The concept of interest as the measure for discounting the future thus was shown to be of universal application. Fisher based the need for payment of interest on impatience (time preference), foregone opportunities for investment that the lender of capital suffered because he chose to lend rather than to invest himself (productivity), and risk and uncertainty. The second (productivity) was clearly an opportunity cost notion and contributed

Real Assets Versus Financial Assets

Capital to the economist is a real physical asset that is endowed with *real productivity* and costs *real resources* to produce. It should be distinguished from financial assets such as currency, stocks, and bonds that may be lumped under the term "capital" in everyday speech. Since, in this section, we wish to compare resource allocation in capital markets with that in other commodity markets, it is essential that the economist's definition of capital as a *physical commodity* rather than as a financial asset be retained.

Physical capital represents consumption foregone. Goods produced in the past could have been consumed then but were not. Hence the price of capital must reflect the rate at which present and future consumption can be traded. Savers pay now and get goods later. Borrowers can get goods now and pay later. Just as there is a market in which swords can be turned into plowshares, so there is a market in which present consumption can be turned into future consumption. *The price in this market represents the terms at which present goods exchange for future goods. It equals the interest rate plus one.*

Suppose, for example, that someone wished to engage in future consumption from a dollar of current income. He may put that dollar into a savings account where it will earn interest. He will receive back $1 + i$ dollars in the future, where i is the rate of interest. Assuming that the prices of commodities are

to the integration of interest theory with the main stream of price theory as a set of laws dealing with costs and choices. It also was quite consistent with Fisher's own earlier work on indifference curves and on the equilibrium condition that the marginal utilities divided by prices would all have to be equal.

His notions of interest were related to his intellectual forebears, the Austrians, notably Böhm-Bawerk, and to Keynes. To the Austrians' productivity notions Fisher added the need for redressing the impatience of the lender, that is, his rate of time preference or intensity of desire for present gratification over future satisfactions. For Keynes the notion of the future productivity of capital and its attendant income stream was essential to his explanation of the inducement to invest. Fisher's system, though logically very tight, was attacked as presenting no specification as to how interest rates were actually set in the money or other markets, and it evinced little historical sense as to how the right to interest as a return had been established.

Fisher's work with the rate of interest and with income flows naturally led to a consideration of the role of money in the system. He asserted a rigid quantity theory accompanied by his equation $MV + M'V' = PT$, and in so doing made a useful analysis of the role of money-type assets (for example, checking deposits). Unfortunately he seemed to go off on the wrong track about the velocity of circulation of money, and although he attempted to present a general integration of all aspects of production, income generation, and money flow, he failed to concede enough importance to the turning points in economic cycles. These, as Keynes was to show and to analyze so well, are the stuff of which unemployment, social unrest, and the need for government stabilization policy are made.

---

constant (the problem of inflation will be handled below), he will be able to buy i percent more goods than if he had not saved. He sacrificed one dollar's worth of present consumption and received $1 + i$ dollars to spend on future consumption. So one unit of present consumption can be transformed in the market to $1 + i$ units of future consumption. We have already defined prices as the ratios in which two commodities trade. Therefore $1 + i$ must be the price of present goods in terms of future goods. Or $1/(1+i)$ must be the price of future goods in terms of present goods. So the *interest rate* tells us the terms on which present and future goods can be traded in the market.

Note that future goods are cheaper than present goods if i is positive. One unit of present goods has the same value as $1 + i$ units of future goods. Since the rational consumer knows that he can sacrifice one unit of present goods for $1 + i$ units of future goods, we can assume that he adjusts his consumption until

$$\frac{MU_{present}}{1} = \frac{MU_{future}}{1/1 + i} \text{ or } MU_{present} = (1 + i)MU_{future}$$

As future goods are cheaper than present goods, he consumes them until their marginal utility is less (by the interest rate) than that of present goods. Of course, he cannot consume future goods in the present. The way we determine his consumption of future goods is through observation of the quantity of resources he saves. Due to the existence of positive interest rates, future consumption should be pursued until it yields less utility per unit than does present consumption. With future goods worth less than present goods, consumers can be said to *discount* their value. The percentage by which the marginal utility of a unit of present goods must exceed that of a unit of future goods can be called the *discount rate*. Thus consumer equilibrium requires that the interest rate equal the discount rate.

How about consuming in the present from income to be earned in the future? Is that possible? It is, and it is called *borrowing*. When borrowing, one receives dollars to spend on present goods in return for a promise to pay future dollars. Of course, every dollar one receives in the present must be repaid by more than one dollar in the future. Thus future consumption can be traded for present consumption, and vice versa. Such trading forms a market in which the price of future goods (one plus the interest rate) is determined.

The interest rate fluctuates, like the price of any other commodity, as the supply of present or future dollars changes. If more people try to borrow than lend, then the interest rate should be positive. If more people want to lend than borrow, one might expect the lenders to have to pay the borrowers to take the money; the interest rate would be negative. In fact, there are usually more savers than borrowers, yet the interest rates are positive rather than negative. Why?

The answer is capital. Any person wishing to save (to trade present for future goods) need not find a borrower in order to accomplish his objective. Instead, he can purchase a real asset with his dollar and sell it in the future for purchasing power then. If he is a shrewd saver, he can choose to buy an asset with a high rate of return, one that is worth more dollars in the future than it is in the present. For example, he can build a house and rent it. In this way he can transfer present money into a whole stream of income in the future. Thus saving and borrowing need not be equal. Part of saving (net saving) can be used to buy real capital goods. It is net saving that interests us now.

Capital and Future Goods

We have just treated the consumer's decision to save as we have treated any other decision of a consumer to buy a particular commodity. Similarly, we can treat the decision of the producer to transform physically present into future goods just as we have treated his decision to transform some present goods into others. The decision to turn present coal into present steel is not very different from the decision to turn currently produced bulldozers into future highways.

To show how similar the two decisions are, in Figure 19.1 we illustrate by a conventional production possibilities frontier the choice that must be made concerning the production of present and future goods. Remember that the slope of the frontier equals the rate at which present goods can be transformed physically into future goods. This minus one is the *rate of return* on capital. In equilibrium, of course, this physical rate must equal the interest rate, or the rate at which present and future goods trade in the market. Thus in equilibrium the slope of the frontier in Figure 19.1 equals in absolute value one plus the interest rate.

The frontier bows outward just as do the frontiers drawn previously to illustrate production possibilities between different kinds of present goods. It does so for the same reason: Future goods use resources in different proportions from those used to produce present goods. Where the slope of the frontier exceeds one, the interest rate is positive. In this range, the society can trade one unit of present goods for more than one unit of future goods. Below, we construct a simple example showing how this is possible.

Consumer purchases of future goods from present income we have called *saving*. The consumers are giving up present goods in order to receive future goods. Producers, on the other hand, *invest* in currently produced plant and equipment in order to produce future goods. Economists call *investment* the amount of real goods an economy puts aside for future use. It is convenient to view consumers as saving—trading present goods for future goods—and firms as investing—trading future goods for present goods. That is, consumers are demanding future goods, firms supplying them. And since in equilibrium the quantity demanded must equal the quantity supplied, so saving must equal investment.

We return to a discussion of the market for future goods in a moment. Meanwhile, it is useful to understand how capital can be physically productive, or how one can give up one unit of present goods and get back more than one unit of future goods.

An Illustration of Capital Productivity: The Case of Robinson Crusoe's Fishing Pole

A simple illustration shows how capital may be productive. Robinson Crusoe lives on his island. By swimming out into the sea, he is able to catch one fish per day. If he had a fishing pole he could catch double this amount and improve his diet. But it takes an entire day to build a pole. To produce this capital good

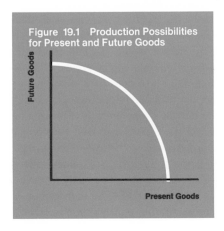

Figure 19.1 Production Possibilities for Present and Future Goods

Future Goods

Present Goods

means the sacrifice of a day's consumption of fish. With the pole in his possession, however, he can consume two fish tomorrow and on each additional day until the pole wears out. That is one fish more per day than if he does not build the pole. How productive is the pole? If it wears out after one day of use it is neither productive nor unproductive. That is, instead of having one fish each of two days, he has no fish one day, two fish the next. Crusoe just gets back the fish he sacrificed in order to build the pole. If it takes more than one day to wear out, the pole is productive. If it decays before the end of the first day, it is unproductive — the initial sacrifice of one fish is never recouped.

Nature does not guarantee that technology will be productive. But historically, most capital has been productive, rewarding current savings with increased future consumption. As long as the pole lasts one day or more, Crusoe is at least breaking even. He gives up one fish today and tomorrow gets back one more than he would have had without the pole. That is a one-for-one trade. If the pole lasts two days, he has made a profit. Nature has been bountiful in providing a way in which one present fish can be converted into more than one future fish. In the real world, nature is bountiful in this way. There exist many ways to turn present goods into greater numbers of future goods.

Mathematical Problems

If the problem of capital were as simple mathematically as the presentation we have just made, it is doubtful that it would have taken economists so long to understand it. And it is doubtful that social theories of great emotional appeal would have been constructed around misleading views of it. The mathematical difficulty arises from the fact that although there is only one present time period, there are an infinite number of future time periods. Thus if we buy a car instead of traveling to Europe, we have given up present travel for future transportation. But the transportation we are to receive will extend over many future periods. Though the problem of deciding to buy a car is similar whether there are many future periods or just one, there are ways to look at capital that obscure this similarity. And unfortunately, that is the way economists looked at it for a long time.

To get an idea of the mathematical problems involved, we only need think of the difference between buying a new car and renting a car for a day. If we looked at a consumer's daily budget constraint, we would see him consuming food, other goods and services, and using many durable capital goods. If a consumer has $40 per day to spend on consumption, how does he handle the purchase of a $3,000 automobile? The $40 per day will allow him to buy and use a car if we give him enough days and if the car lasts long enough. But from his $40, the consumer really pays for the use of his car for one day. Economists might have a reasonable theory about how a consumer allocates $40 per day and still be uncertain how to include his consumption of durable goods such as autos. This is because these durables require an analysis that simultaneously takes into account spending over many days. The decision to purchase an auto cannot be analyzed without considering future income and future consumption needs. On the other hand, the decision to rent a car for a day can be incorporated easily into the decision concerning the allocation of the $40. The mathematical difficulties arise when one attempts to convert the decision concerning the purchase of an auto into one concerning the rental of an auto, a decision that cannot be handled automatically in the conventional framework. To show how this conversion is made, we first have to discuss the difference between the variables *car* and *car-day*.

Stocks and Flows
Certain variables are defined with respect to a unit of time: a salary of $10,000 per year, an output of 20 cars per day. Other variables are defined independently of time: a savings account of $1,000, an inventory of 50 vacuum cleaners. Variables defined with respect to time are called *flow* variables or *flows*; those defined independently of time are called *stock* variables or *stocks*. To be able to combine these two different kinds of variables in a single analysis requires us to incorporate time in a very particular manner. To see how time might affect the relationship between variables of these different kinds, consider the following examples.

A forest is a *stock* of trees. But the rate at which new trees spring up is a *flow*. So is the rate at which old trees die or are cut. Thus a forest may hold a stock of 20 million board feet of standing timber and yield a flow of output of 1 million board feet *per year*. The forest is a stock, the output of wood a flow.

To see how stocks and flows can be combined in a simple economic model, consider the following example of a capital *stock*, a *flow* of new investment (additions to the capital stock), and a *flow* of depreciation (wearing out of the stock). In Figure 19.2, we have portrayed this relationship between these variables by making an analogy to a tub of water. The level of water in the tub represents the capital stock, the flow from the tap is investment, and the leakage from the tank depreciation. Water flows out through a given-size hole in the bottom of the tub. So the depreciation rate is assumed to be *constant* in this example.

Note that we cannot compare the amount of water entering the vessel with

Figure 19.2

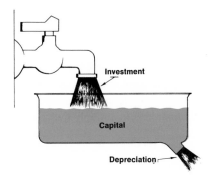

the amount in the tub unless a *time period is specified* (such as one year). At an instant in time no water enters the tub. The longer the period, the more water flows in. What happens to the level of water (stock of capital) over time? If the rate at which water flows in exceeds the rate at which it flows out, the vessel eventually will fill up and overflow. If the rate at which the water flows in is less than the outflow, the tank eventually will empty. Only if the inflow equals the outflow will the water level achieve equilibrium somewhere between the bottom and the top.

The relationship between the rates of inflow and outflow and the water level in a tub is strictly technological. But capital theory adds the element of human behavior. Hence we add to our tub analogy a man who turns the tap, regulating the flow of water (investment). By adjusting the flow he is able to control the level of water in the tank. If the water is above the desired level, he closes the tap and the level falls. With a man in the picture, equilibrium can occur at whatever level he prefers. Once that level is reached, he sets the flow of investment equal to the depreciation outflow. The investor who desires a given capital stock is like the man who wishes to bathe in a leaking tub. He first fills the tub to the desired level by opening the tap wide (he saves a great deal every month). Then he closes the tap to the point where inflow and outflow are equal (he saves just enough to keep his wealth constant). Economists use elaborate mathematics to study actual investment behavior, but the intuitive problem of relating stocks and flows to achieve equilibrium is no more complex than our problem of the leaky tub.* Let us now use this knowledge of stocks and flows to examine the market for capital.

Factor Markets

Like labor and land, capital is a productive factor. This means that producers demand its *services*. It is clear that producers hire labor and rent land. In the same way, firms will hire capital if it is cheaper to increase output using additional services of capital rather than labor or land. In previous chapters we saw how the amount of capital used by a firm will be determined by its attempts to minimize costs and maximize profits. Let us restate the decision rule that determines whether a given factor should be hired or fired.

> If hiring one more unit of a factor contributes more to revenue than to cost, hire it. If it contributes less to revenue than to cost, fire it.

This simple rule serves for capital, labor, or land. The only extension it requires over the rule for labor developed in the one good economy in Chapters 6 and 7 is that *cost* and *revenue* are now expressed in money terms rather than in corn. All that is needed to make the transformation is to multiply the contribu-

---

*Engineering students will recognize in the leaky-tub problem the simplest of differential equations. Economists often use differential equations and the calculus of variations to handle dynamic problems where stocks and flows both are to be determined.

tion that one additional unit of labor (or capital) makes to corn output by the *price* of corn. Thus

$$\begin{pmatrix} \text{a factor's marginal} \\ \text{contribution of} \\ \text{revenue} \end{pmatrix} = \begin{pmatrix} \text{marginal contribution} \\ \text{to revenue of 1 extra} \\ \text{unit of output} \end{pmatrix} \times \begin{pmatrix} \text{total addition to} \\ \text{output made by 1} \\ \text{extra unit of factor} \end{pmatrix}$$

$$MRP_{labor} = MR \cdot MP_{labor}$$
$$MRP_{capital} = MR \cdot MP_{capital}$$
$$MRP_{land} = MR\_MP_{land}$$

The labels in the equation above are shorthand. The first term (MRP) represents the "marginal revenue product" of a factor. The other terms have been encountered before. MR represents "marginal revenue" and MP is short for "marginal product" of a factor. For example, it is MRP_L that is compared with the price of labor, P_L, to determine whether an additional unit of labor adds more to revenue than to costs. The decision rule in terms of this shorthand tells us the following:

If $MRP_L > P_L$, hire more labor; if $MRP_L < P_L$, hire less labor. When $MRP_L = P_L$, then the correct amount of labor has been hired given the quantities of other factors used.

The decision rule can be extended to all factors including capital. We see below how it works to provide equilibrium in the market for capital services.

The Market for Capital Services
In accordance with the decision rule above, once the marginal revenue product of capital services is made to equal its price, the market for capital services reaches equilibrium. Firms compare the cost of hiring more labor with the cost of *hiring* more buildings or machines. Thus the relevant price of capital to the firm in the framework of Chapter 13 is not the price of the building but the price of using or *renting* the building. To analyze the capital market, we must find a means of converting the cost of a physical asset (stock of capital) into the cost of the services of that asset. We must find a way of expressing rental rates on houses (the price of the capital services) as a function of the price of houses (the price of a capital good). Obviously, when the price of houses changes, rents as well must change. But how do we convert the price of houses into rents? This can be done by using the interest rate. The interest rate represents the opportunity cost of foregoing consumption during the present period in favor of future consumption. If a capital good initially costs $100 and lasts forever, the *annual* cost of using that capital good is the interest rate times $100. The easiest way to see this is to assume that the firm borrowed the $100 to buy the machine. Every year it pays interest on the loan. That is the only cost of using the machine because we have assumed, for simplicity, that the machine never wears out.† Thus

†Note that the opportunity cost of capital to the firm is the same whether it uses its own funds or borrows them in the free market if lending and borrowing interest rates are equal.

$$\begin{pmatrix} \text{total cost of} \\ \text{a machine} \end{pmatrix} \times \begin{pmatrix} \text{annual interest} \\ \text{rate} \end{pmatrix} = \begin{pmatrix} \text{cost of a} \\ \text{machine-year} \end{pmatrix}$$

The cost of a machine-year determined here becomes the price of the services of capital that is relevant for firms. It is the rental rate on capital. It can be inserted into the inequality that relates the marginal revenue product to price in order to determine whether it is worthwhile to invest (increase the stock of capital) a given amount. Will the marginal revenue product of an additional unit of investment exceed its cost per machine-year? That is the question firms ask themselves when trying to decide whether to rent more machines or hire more labor. At least that is the question we must view them as asking if we are to use the framework of Part V to decide how much capital the firm will demand.

Note that interest rates are measured in terms of numbers per unit of time, usually percent per year. When multiplying an interest rate—say, 5 percent per year—by a number representing the cost of a machine—say, $1,000—we get a number measured in terms of dollars per year—$50/year. Thus interest rates can be used to convert stock variables into flow variables.

If one reads the economic classics, he will find only hazy distinctions between stocks and flows. There exist analyses in which households add their savings (a stock) to their income (a flow) to get a measure of total purchasing power. Technically, such additions cannot be performed unless one takes into account the important role of time in making these variables different. The classicists had trouble with such analyses and therefore with theories of interest and capital. Today, all economists who do research in this field have a grasp of the distinction and are acquainted with differential equations, the mathematics one must use to combine stocks and flows explicitly.

The concept of capital seems simple enough when presented in Crusoe's world. Capital is the device that allows Crusoe physically to transform present fish into future fish. Questions such as exploitation cannot arise in Crusoe's world. If they do, they have nothing to do with social injustice since Crusoe himself is the whole society.

In more complex worlds men are not self-sufficient. Firms do the producing. Thus firms have a supply curve for fish and households a demand curve. Similarly, there is a supply and demand for future fish. If households demand future fish from their present income, they need not invest personally in fishing poles. All they need do is save. Firms, on the other hand, can supply future fish by buying boats, poles, and nets today. The households loan money to the highest bidders, expecting to buy future fish when the loans are repaid. The firms borrow the money from the households and invest in the equipment that allows them to produce those future goods for which they forecast high demand. If the firms forecast the households' desires exactly, the rates of return on all the investments they make will be the same. If the firms make errors in their forecasts or if the households change their minds, some assets will yield more than others.

Saving, Investment, and the Market for Future Goods

Figure 19.3 illustrates the simplest possible view of capital and interest. There exist demand and supply curves for goods at some future date. These are like any other demand and supply curves. To transform the behavior illustrated by Figure 19.3 into saving and investment behavior we need to take into account two things: (1) There are many future time periods like the one illustrated in Figure 19.3. Thus individuals must own or expect to own assets sufficient to allow them to buy goods in all those periods, and firms must own or expect to own enough productive capital to allow them to sell in all those periods. (2) Saving from current income is just a small part of the assets an individual owns. Thus saving is designed to *change* his asset level to one that allows him to consume what he wishes in the future. He may save very little if he already has a large quantity of wealth because he is already able to consume many future goods. Similarly, firms owning an abundance of plant and equipment need not buy more in order to produce in the future.

Making these two adjustments in Figure 19.3, we can create a market where savers and investors meet, a market like that shown in Figure 19.4. Although the two adjustments are simple enough conceptually, advanced mathematics is necessary to make them explicit.

Note that the amount of investment (the quantity of future goods supplied) is assumed to increase when the interest rate falls (the price of future goods rises). That is equivalent to assuming that the supply curve for future goods is upward sloping. On the other hand, we do not know immediately whether saving functions slope upward or not. An intuitive understanding of why we do not can be gained by thinking of the elasticity of households' demand for future goods. If demand is elastic, households will spend more present dollars on future goods when their price falls. That is, they will save more present dollars when interest rates rise. But if demand is inelastic, the reverse will be true—the amount of saving will decline when interest rates rise. Thus the vertical saving

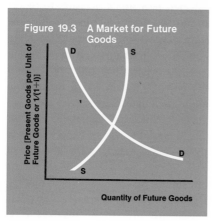

Figure 19.3 A Market for Future Goods

Price [Present Goods per Unit of Future Goods or 1/(1+I)]

Quantity of Future Goods

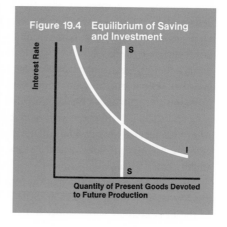

Figure 19.4 Equilibrium of Saving and Investment

Interest Rate

Quantity of Present Goods Devoted to Future Production

function in Figure 19.4 is equivalent to the assumption that the elasticity of demand for future goods is unitary.

Remember that a competitive supply curve is a locus of points at which the price of a commodity equals its cost, whereas a demand curve is a locus at which price equals value. Since the saving and investment functions of Figure 19.4 are really supply and demand curves, we can say that the investment function is a locus of points at which the interest rate equals the rate of return on capital (derived from the PPF and therefore a measure of social cost), whereas the saving function is a locus of points at which the interest rate equals the discount rate (derived from the relative value to savers of present and future goods). Allowing interest rates to clear the market guarantees us that at equilibrium, the social cost of future goods must equal their value.

Uncertainty

The market for investment is plagued by uncertainty. The investment demand schedule moves about in a fashion difficult to predict, since its position and shape are determined by sellers' expectations of future productivity and sales. Remember that the act of investment is an act that transforms present into future goods. Obviously, the terms on which those future goods can be sold affect the demand for investment. And no one knows those terms until the future arrives. Robinson Crusoe was assumed to know with certainty (1) the life of his fishing pole, and (2) its marginal revenue product over all future periods. But we know that in practice sellers who purchase capital goods with lives longer than one period are forced to guess about the future productivity and sales from the production of those goods. The more optimistic the expectation, the further to the right the investment demand curve shifts in a given period. The worse the forecast, the further to the left the demand curve shifts. Even when resources in an economy remain fixed, expectations can change, altering the quantity of investment desired at each interest rate.

We saw in Chapter 17 how this is reflected in a firm's decision to report depreciation. Here we see how uncertainty plagues firms' decisions to turn the "tap" of investment and increase or decrease the level of the capital stock. In later parts of the book we illustrate how an entire economy can move *inside* the production possibility frontier for a time, as a result of adverse expectations and their effect on the capital market. This gives us a preview of the kind of problems that can cause business cycles, booms, and depressions.

The theory of interest and capital is further refined in Chapters 33 and 34, where we discuss money and financial assets. There, the role of expectations in creating boom and panic will be shown to be compounded by the creation of sophisticated financial machinery.

Thus we see that in the market for future goods, just as in any other market, it is the desires of individuals and the constraints of nature that determine price. In the next chapter we see how individuals may also invest in themselves to increase their future consumption and cause the economy to grow. In this respect everyone, fat or thin, is a capitalist, as long as he is willing to postpone consumption and invest in his future.

Questions

1. Assume that individuals' major motive for saving is to provide for their own consumption needs when they retire. What should happen to saving if a social security fund is established that guarantees individuals a retirement income? Is your answer affected by whether the administrators of the fund invest their tax receipts for the participants or pay them out immediately to different participants?
2. How should apartment rents vary with changes in construction costs? In interest rates? In the durability of the buildings?
3. How are interest rates linked to the price of future goods?

Concepts Discussed

capital	saving
interest rate	investment
discount rate	stocks and flows
rate of return on capital	marginal revenue product

APPENDIX: MARX ON CAPITAL

The Labor Theory of Value

Given the theory of capital presented in Chapter 19, what can we say about Marx's theory of capital? Marx had his own explanation as to why interest is earned, namely, that labor is not paid its marginal product. By paying labor very low wages, the capitalists could keep a great deal of revenue for themselves.

But the theory of capital we have presented assumes that labor *is* paid its marginal product. If interest payments are not taken from labor, where do they come from? asks Marx. Surely all capital today was produced by labor, natural resources, and old capital; and the old capital was produced by even older capital, labor, and natural resources. In the beginning there was no capital. Man has produced it. Does this not mean, therefore, that paying man his marginal product would leave nothing to capital itself? Capital is not an "original" factor and therefore should receive no payment in excess of its production cost. So goes the Marxian argument. Not only that, but even the value of natural resources is the cost of digging them from the ground (except for rent, which we analyze in Chapter 22). So, except for a few rents, all output is due to labor inputs. Therefore current labor should be paid the whole product. The fact that interest — that is, a payment in excess of the production cost of capital — is paid is due to the exploitation of labor. Labor must be receiving less than its marginal product.

This argument was not thought to be revolutionary at all in Marx's time. All economists of the era including Ricardo and Mill subscribed to the labor theory

KARL MARX (1818-1883)   Capitalism is doomed! There is nothing anyone can do about it! This is the message of Karl Marx, a great economist who fashioned his tools not as an end in themselves, but rather as explainers of historical processes and justifiers of particular political actions. As Joseph Schumpeter said, Marx's economics formed but a part of his philosophy of history and comprised a segment of a general analytical and evangelical package that included theories of history and sociology and that was supercharged with a prophetic vision. Marx, unlike Smith, Malthus, and Ricardo, wrote at a time when the Industrial Revolution seemed to be producing not only great increases in income but also great amounts of misery. To the crowding of the slums was added the affliction of unemployment and the instability of the business cycle. Conditioned by many years as a German radical journalist and political agitator, Marx felt that these phenomena demanded logical explanation, fueling his hope with the belief that they were destined to pass. His beliefs and his many years of careful scholarship yielded *Das Kapital* (*Capital*, 3 vols., 1864-1890), an analysis of the capitalist system and its outcomes. These were supplemented by a volley of books, pamphlets, and tracts, among which one of the most important was the *Communist Manifesto* (1848).

From student days Marx had imbibed of Hegel's philosophy and its dialectical method: Thesis evokes antithesis, which blends with thesis to form synthesis, which evokes another antithesis, and so on. According to Marx's dialectical materialism, the "mode of production," that is, the nature of technology, was the major force of change and the generator of the sequence of theses and antitheses throughout history. All political, cultural, and religious arrangements were merely superstructure on top of economic reality and all were modified by changes in the mode of production despite their appearing to be independent forces. In Marx's view, European capitalism was the work of the bourgeoisie who had emerged triumphant over their predecessors, the feudal aristocracy, as the discoverers and carriers of the capitalist organization of production and economic activity. However, despite their most impressive achievement, the creation of modern industrialism, the capitalists, like the aristocrats, were destined to be superseded by the proletariat, the propertyless wage earners who

---

of value. What was revolutionary was the prediction Marx made, based on this theory, of how capitalist economies would eventually destroy themselves. The labor theory of value itself, however, was believed by most economists until the development of marginal utility in the 1890s.

The labor theory of value is essentially a theory of cost. Ricardo attempted to resolve Adam Smith's diamond-water paradox by explaining that diamonds took a great deal of labor to produce whereas water took very little. This, we have argued, would lead to a very high supply curve for diamonds and a very low one for water. But we have also noted that supply curves may slope upward. That is, cost may depend on the level of output. Therefore a complete explanation of value must explain the level of output as well.

In the modern theory, this is done by introducing a demand curve that has its roots in marginal utility theory. Thus in the modern theory, both cost—

were the true men of the industrial future.

In *Das Kapital* especially, Marx set out to dissect capitalism's workings and to show that its decline was inevitable and not amenable to any therapeutic action; no reforms could save the system. Necessarily, those who had this insight to the workings of history could occupy appropriate positions and, with the proper tools, aid in capitalism's downfall and in the guidance of mankind to the new system, which, however, would be beyond the dialectical process. Marx's analysis was definitely classical in that he followed Ricardo in the labor theory of value although he rejected Malthus's population theories. To Marx, the fact that workers' wages were kept at a subsistence level by the competition of the "industrial reserve army" (made up of displaced entrepreneurs, obsolete workers, and dispossessed peasants) meant that capitalists could realize a surplus from the difference between wages and the value of what the workers produced. Exploitation of the workers could not continue, however, since the competition of more capital and the increased capital intensity of the production process would lead to reduced margins of surplus and falling rates of profits, hence less accumulation, hence less investment, hence less employment. The system would be subject to increasingly severe crises and would ultimately collapse. Disciplined by the routines of industry, the workers would be well organized to take over the system and would expropriate the expropriators in the name of the people. "Workers of the world, unite!" was his rousing call at the end of the *Communist Manifesto*.

Marx left little guidance for the transitions to socialism and communism, or for the operation of a postcapitalist society, much to the later embarrassment of the Soviets and many of his intellectual followers. He did, however, leave a potent political legacy and turned the attention of economists to such crucial social and economic issues as the income distribution, the possibility of underconsumption and underspending generally, and to the questions of vested interest and entrenched economic power. To many Western economists he has always provided a goad to find better ways to make the capitalist system work and to demonstrate a responsibility for the human as well as the theoretical side of economics.

---

working through the supply curve—and utility—working through the demand curve—determine the value of a commodity. The value of a commodity depends not only on how many men it takes to produce it, but also on how well it satisfies men's material wants.

Thus the labor theory of value should be thought of as a labor theory of cost. But even as a theory of cost, it has problems. This is because a unit of present consumption has a greater *social cost* than a unit of future consumption. And that in turn implies that present labor is worth more than future labor. Once that is granted, the existence of productive capital has been admitted.

The Modern Explanation of Interest

If an individual chooses to consume one more unit in the present (save one unit less), his total future consumption will fall by $1 + i$ units, where i is the interest rate he could have earned by saving. If, on the other hand, he chooses to save one more unit, his future consumption will be higher by $1 + i$ units. And since capital is productive, his decision to save will permit society to have more production in the next period. If, in fact, the market rate of return on capital is i, no one else is made worse off by the extra interest we are paying this saver. For every unit he saves now, the society can give him back $1 + i$ future units *without hurting anyone else*. Why? *Because of the fortunate fact that capital is productive.* If Robinson Crusoe sacrifices a fish today in order to build a canoe, he gets back an extra fish tomorrow and the next day and the next, and so on. He receives interest all by himself. Yet no exploitation is involved in a one-person economy. Interest is therefore a reflection of the fact that the sum of present and future outputs will be larger if we save some present goods than if we do not. This excess can be given to the savers without lowering anyone else's consumption.

It is ironic that the Communist countries today appear to have great faith in the productivity of capital. Khrushchev's boast that the Soviet Union would overtake the United States in production by 1970 was based upon a faith in the productivity of capital. The Soviets have chosen to devote their resources to investment industries at the expense of current consumption. If the sacrifice of one unit of current consumption would give back only one future unit, it is doubtful that the Soviets would continue their heavy rate of investment. They are investing for the simple reason that output becomes higher when capital is accumulated. The productivity of capital is a technological—not a behavioral—phenomenon.

Not only did Marx write before the modern theory of value had been created, but he also wrote before the theory of capital and monopoly had been established. The theories of capital and interest, of course, is a special case of value theory. Once economists had realized that both supply and demand were necessary to explain value, they had only to apply this analysis to the trade of present for future goods to get a theory of capital and interest. It should be noted to Marx's credit that his work provided a great stimulus for future research and that he probably accelerated the development of the subsequent theories a great deal.

To be generous to Marx in the light of the more recent theoretical developments, we would have to describe his work as a premarginalist attempt at monopoly theory. Marx had an intuitive feeling for the existence of exploitation of workers who were being paid less than their marginal products. In modern economics, we believe that monopolies can make large profits. One side effect of the monopoly solution is that all productive factors (capital as well as labor) are paid less than their marginal products in order to benefit those who earn monopoly profits. Thus if one feels that exploitation of labor exists, he should rail at monopoly, not at capital. If such monopoly exploitation were severe, we could expect the savers of the world to unite with the workers of the world and throw off their common chains. Even in the instances where monopoly and capital are difficult to separate (for example, where the owners of capital are taking home monopoly profits in addition to interest), we should be careful to keep our *analysis* of the problem precise by remembering that it is monopoly and not capital that is exploitative. Then our use of political action to cure the evil will be directed at the source of the problem and will be more likely to be effective than if misdirected.

The theory of value presented in this book (termed the "neoclassical theory of value" because it is a modern extension of the classical doctrines of economists such as Smith, Malthus, Ricardo, and Mill) is a marginal utility theory, not a labor theory. "A good has value in proportion to its contribution to men's happiness" is the implication of marginal utility theory. "A good has value if men make it" is the implication of Marx's labor theory. Technically, an old-fashioned Marxist must believe that the employment of men to create sand castles or to dig holes and fill them in creates as much value as any other occupation of their time (including leisure), and that national output would have the same value if everyone spent his time digging holes. Marx's value theory therefore has been of little help to the Soviets in their own planning problems. It cannot tell them which goods to produce or how to find which goods are worth the most since anything a man might produce has the same value as anything else he might produce.

The labor theory of value is a part of the folklore, however. Students feel that if they complete their assignments, they deserve a good grade. If they actually work hard while writing a paper, they believe that the paper should get a good grade. *But it is output that counts, not input.* The folklore runs the other way, however. Farmers know that the value of their labor and capital would earn a great deal more in industry than in agriculture; therefore they feel that they deserve subsidies. One who follows a labor theory of value might conclude that farm prices "should be" raised to give farmers a *fair* income. An economist would conclude that if this is the case, the farmer should devote his resources to industry, not agriculture, and thereby produce commodities that contribute more to men's happiness than does *extra* food. Of course, if the farmer really enjoys farming he should count that enjoyment as a part of his income. We would all like to be paid a great deal to work at what we like to do most. But a rational market system rewards us only to the extent that we contribute to other men's happiness. *To each according to his contribution to the general welfare* is the rule in a perfectly competitive economy.

20 Labor Markets

The Value of Labor

When the pyramids were new, it was common for human beings to be bought and sold in the marketplace. Like beasts of burden men were fed, watered, and driven to labor by their owners. People were equated with real assets. Along with levers, hoists, mules, and elephants, they represented present and future productive power. They were depreciated as their productive time ran out. The ownership of human beings represented ownership of a stock of "human capital," valued for the flow of services that it could provide over time. This ownership was transferable from one slave owner to another just as ownership of machines is exchanged today. The value of a human being to a slave owner depended upon the slave's productivity. Additional slaves were acquired as long as their marginal revenue product exceeded their price. If their marginal revenue product (per unit of time) fell below their price (per unit of time), they were disposed of. The slave market presumed to place a worth on human beings in terms of their capital value.

Today the value that society places on human beings far exceeds that placed on them by the slave owners of ancient times. Involuntary servitude is condemned and has been declared illegal in most countries. The worker himself is now in a position to decide how he will allocate his time between work and leisure. Does this make the concept of "human capital" obsolete? Actually economists are increasingly rather than decreasingly recognizing the usefulness of this concept. It reflects the understanding that not only does a worker represent the embodiment of a future stream of productivity but he is also capable of *investing in himself* (through education and experience) to *increase* that stream of productivity over time. The worker in deciding what his time is worth is in effect placing a value on himself as a capital good.

We might conceive of twentieth-century pyramids being built by the attraction of workers through the labor market rather than through coercion, since the value that the worker places on his time is not infinitely high. For example, if modern pyramid builders were willing to offer wages to those now in command of labor services (the workers themselves), they would not have to offer an infinitely high price to attract many into the effort of moving great blocks of stone. Why? Because workers will accept a wage at which they can buy goods whose value is greater than or equal to the value of the time they spend working. Still, the cost of labor services is likely to be higher in the market than under slavery because an individual places a much higher value on alternative uses of his time than does the typical slave owner on the alternative uses of a slave's time.

The Value of Life

Is it immoral to calculate the value of a human life? We know that such calculations are being made continually. People make decisions daily that require them to place values on their lives, implicitly if not explicitly, in various acts of production and consumption. While smoking, driving, or flying we are risking our lives. Yet, even though we know this, we are happy to take the risk. Why? Because material consumption provides satisfaction even when it represents a threat to survival. A smoker knows that there is some probability of an earlier death from lung cancer caused by smoking, but to him the satisfaction he receives from smoking is worth the risk of a shorter life. Part of the value of a marginal unit of life is reflected in the price he is willing to pay for a cigarette. With the act of buying a cigarette, an individual is in effect saying, "There are some material things for which I would trade a part of my life." In driving a car downtown, a man says, "I will risk my life for transportation." If no material consumption were worth the risk of life and limb, we would stay home all day long. As President Kennedy said, "To be perfectly safe, we must stay in bed — and even then we can't be sure."

A life devoted to the avoidance of danger has few rewards. Therefore we maximize utility by trading away safety for other satisfactions. The equilibrium we attain implies that there is a price on life itself. We are willing to trade life for a finite amount of material goods. Thus the material value of life can be inferred from these trades.

The trade of life for goods is not so obvious when it is expressed in terms of probabilities — when my use of worn tires instead of new ones increases my chance of dying this year by three parts out of a hundred thousand parts. But my decision to use worn tires despite my knowledge of the greater likelihood of death can be used to get an estimate of the value of life. Consider 100,000 people who have chosen to use worn tires. They are gathered in a stadium and told that they must either contribute one hundred dollars each (the cost of a new set of tires) or three of them will be chosen at random to be shot on the spot. If they are consistent, they will choose the shooting. Their probability of dying is the same in the shooting as it is through using worn tires. They have already demonstrated their preference of one hundred dollars to the elimination of a 3/100,000 of a chance for death. Collectively, they prefer ten million dollars to three lives.

Decisions about the value of others' lives must be made every day by public authorities who decide how much to spend to make airports and highways safe, how much to devote to cancer research, and whether to engage in military ventures. Without a value for life, the results of such decisions will be consistent with staying in bed all day — with avoiding danger at all costs. We do not comment on the morality of the decisions made. We merely note that they are eco-

nomic decisions; that is, they involve weighing alternatives and choosing between different bundles that contain different quantities of lives and goods. That
people place a material value on life can be deduced from their behavior. What
that value should be is not a question for economists, however. Some social
evangelists may look to the example of the ants and value production for its own
sake; others will look to Epicurus and value the pursuit of pleasure. Who is right
we cannot say. What life should be worth is a question for philosophers to
ponder. What it *is* worth can be seen from the marketplace.

Humans as Capital

Individuals value their own lives in a manner that can be compared to the way
they value goods. The value they place on life can be thought of as its consumption value—a value that is derived from life's ability to yield satisfaction. Another measure of interest is the value of a man's or woman's future productive
power. How much is it worth today to be able to earn wages in the future? The
value of one's future earnings is called one's *human capital*. Ever since slavery
was declared illegal, there has been no market for stocks of human capital. The
flow of productive services yielded by that capital, however, is sold just as any
other commodity is. To show the similarity between human and physical capital,
we need only look at how the decision to invest in human capital is made.

Education: Investment in Human Capital

Robinson Crusoe has to worry about the relative values of present and future
consumption when he decides whether or not to make a fishing pole. Consider
now the possibility of studying the habits of fish for one day and then being able
to catch two fish a day even without a pole. Studying for one day gives Crusoe
knowledge about the behavior of fish that allows him to double his catch each
day. If we look at the stream of fish consumption available to Crusoe as a result
of this study, we find that it is identical to that available to him from building a
pole. Crusoe has sacrificed fish for one day in order to receive an extra fish for
all future days. Whether he decides to study about fish depends on the value of
future fish relative to present ones. That is exactly the consideration he has to
make when deciding about the pole. To Crusoe, the fishing pole is worth the
same as the knowledge about fish. He is indifferent between sacrificing a fish in
order to build a pole and sacrificing a fish in order to learn how to fish better
without a pole. Both the pole and the knowledge are devices that allow Crusoe
to convert present fish into future fish. The difference is that the pole is physical
capital that can be sold whereas the knowledge is human capital that cannot be
sold.

Implications of the Analysis

If labor is indeed a form of capital, and if expenditures on education, health, and
welfare serve to increase the stock of human capital, then equilibrium in the
labor market must be subject to the same type of analysis as equilibrium in the

capital market. It includes considerations of (1) the supply of savings and demand for *investment* (*flows*) *in human capital*, and (2) supply and demand for the *stock of human capital*. A market for human capital as a stock does not exist anymore, at least between individuals, now that slavery has been abolished. But every time an individual decides whether or not to invest in himself, or society decides whether or not to invest in education, a decision is being made to increase or decrease the total stock of human capital. Like any other capital market decision, the result affects the level of total resources in the economy and future production possibilities.

This means that if persons wish to exchange present for future consumption they can purchase financial assets, physical assets, or human capital (by investing in themselves). The rate of return on these alternative uses of savings must be the same in equilibrium, once a discount is taken for differing degrees of risk. In fact, economists have discovered that the rate of return on investments in human capital is not notably different from the rate of return on physical capital; both are approximately equal to the interest rate (the return on financial assets). This is to be expected if the market is working properly and if individuals are looking for the lowest possible price of future goods (the best possible rate of return on their savings).

The rate of return on education is calculated just as is the return on any other investment. The cost of the investment is noted — the tuition, books, etc., and most important, the income that students forego by attending college rather than working. Then the returns are calculated; computations are made concerning the effect of education on earning power. This is done by applying statistical techniques to a large sample of people in order to find how much more income is earned by those with education than by those without. The extra income earned minus the cost of education is the total return to the investment. To convert this into a rate of return per unit of time requires that we take into account the timing of education and the extra income. Rates of return on education are competitive with those on other investments.

This does not mean that the marginal revenue product of investments in human capital is the total return to society from education. Such calculations ignore the nonmarketable value of education to an individual, the consumption value of education to him as well as education as a public good. Crusoe might delight simply in knowing the principles of fishing and being able to swim better, independent of any greater catch. As incomes go up, the marginal utility of fish falls relative to the marginal utility of simply knowing how to catch fish. Experienced anglers in high-income countries often throw the fish back after catching them, because they regard the production side of the activity as satisfying in itself (the work of catching the fish becomes itself an element of consumption). They study to improve their technique as fishermen whether or not it means a greater consumption *per se*. The principle is important. Some economic philosophies stress the consumption of the act of production itself, rather than the consumption of material goods. Considerations such as these do no violence to our analysis. They simply mean adding another factor to the marginal revenue product of education (the psychological marginal product of consumption of education) before setting it equal to the cost of educational services in determining whether the human capital market is efficiently allocating resources. Many disciplines, including those usually labeled liberal arts, are studied because they make us aware of ourselves and the world around us. Such awareness, aside from increasing our ability to communicate, often adds little to our ability to produce. But it increases our satisfaction enormously.

Uncertainty

Slavery having been abolished, labor markets no longer allow sale of human assets themselves, but only the *services of those assets*. The demand for labor services is similar in concept to the demand for capital services. It is as if buildings no longer could be sold but still could be rented. The demand for these services depends on their expected marginal revenue product. Similarly, the supply of labor services by the workers reflects considerations of the alternative uses of time; workers who use this time to study might increase future marginal revenue products. What should the rental market for labor services look like? Would capital theory predict a high or a low rate of return on human capital? Later, when we study asset markets more fully in Chapter 34, we will see what characteristics allow different assets to have different rates of return. For now, we can anticipate some of the results of that chapter by saying that savers like assets with high rates of return. But they also like assets that are not risky. In fact, they will only own risky assets if they yield a higher rate of return than do nonrisky assets. What makes an asset risky? An inability to predict the value of its future services. If we can predict its returns easily, it is not risky. But more of that later. Human capital is a risky asset. The readers of this book are not sure of their future wages. In fact, they may be very uncertain of them. They may, therefore, demand a very high rate of return on human capital before investing in it.

Another interesting characteristic of human capital is the *heterogeneity of labor* itself. No man is the same as any other. No worker will do a job the same as another will. Unlike machines, the human being is too complex a mechanism to be very predictable. It is this quality that helps make life exciting and the labor market more challenging to buyers and sellers than perhaps any other market. Each worker has different qualifications and preferences for a given job. Heterogeneous assets take a longer time to sell because buyer and seller must be carefully matched. When buying a dump truck, a manager must choose among twenty or thirty kinds whose characteristics are known with great certainty. But when hiring the driver, the manager must choose among hundreds of different men who have different qualities, some of which are unknown.

Stickiness of Wages

The most important implication of human capital as a heterogeneous asset is that the price of labor is sticky; that is, wages respond very slowly to changes in supply and demand. This occurs for reasons we will explore in Chapter 29. For now, all we need to know is that markets will not always clear if prices do not respond rapidly to changes in supply and demand. One result of this for labor markets is unemployment. The quantity of labor supplied can exceed that demanded at the going wage. The difference is unemployment. The reason prices change so slowly in labor markets is that there are literally millions of wage rates because there are millions of different kinds of labor. No one knows for sure what any particular wage rate should be, so the rates tend to stay constant or move at a constant rate until large amounts of evidence accumulate to indicate that that rate is wrong. If there were only one national wage rate and one kind of labor, the market could be cleared daily and there would not have to be any unemployment.

Reasons for Differences in the Quality of Labor

What major characteristics distinguish one laborer from another and therefore make the labor market heterogeneous? In addition to education and training differences, there are differences in natural skills (talents). Some men are born smart or strong, quick or graceful. The value of their labor as productive services depends upon the value that society places on these services. For example, an artist who is considered a genius by one person and a fraud by another has his talent subjected to the tastes of both. What will happen to the marginal revenue product of his artistic labor if the person favoring his talent is a wealthy promoter of the arts and the one despising his work is penniless? What will happen to his marginal revenue product if the tastes of these two observers are reversed? The intrinsic quality of his painting is a subject for seminars in aesthetics. But market value is arbitrated by the consuming public. This is also true for exotic dancers, flagpole sitters, or any other seller of labor services.

Location is also an important factor in determining the value of human capital. In the United States labor is cheap in Appalachia, while 250 miles north in central Ohio and Pennsylvania, the same quality labor receives twice the wage. Why do unemployed workers in Appalachia not move? Possibly they are not aware of opportunities in the North. More likely, they prefer to live where they were born and are willing to offset the difference in wages by the greater utility that "being home" affords. Labor moves from country to country because wages for the same skill are widely different around the world. But national preferences combine with both natural and legal barriers to mobility, preventing migration (including the "brain drain") from equalizing international wage rates.

In addition to the skills and other labor characteristics required for a certain job, the wage must also reflect the *desirability* of that form of employment. Dangerous, noisy, hot, dirty, or third-shift jobs must pay more to attract the same quality of labor than safe, quiet, comfortable, clean, first-shift jobs. Jobs in the tropics or in the Arctic must pay more (for the same American or European workers) than jobs in more temperate climates, unless other considerations such as moral values or missionary zeal offset the geographical features of the employment.

Just as there can exist simultaneously a glut of workers in Appalachia and a shortage in Ohio, there can exist a shortage of computer programmers and an excess of agricultural labor. Since the skills required for these two jobs differ, it is unlikely that much migration from one class to the other will take place. Different men and different jobs can be only partially substituted for each other. All the action in the labor market — quitting, hiring, firing, newly entering, retiring — occurs at the borders of each market and is determined to a large extent by the degree of substitutability of men and jobs. The substitutability of one man for another or one job for another ties all the markets together. That this substitution is only partial leaves all markets a bit isolated from each other.

To get a feel for the way the markets affect each other, consider the distribution of unemployment during a recession among the different categories of skills that exist. Generally, it is the poorly educated, poorly trained, unhealthy who are out of work. When unemployment rates are 6 percent, we do not observe 6 percent of the professors, the nuclear physicists, or the business executives out of work. They retain their old jobs or easily find new ones if dismissed. But promotions are delayed so that men fall behind in their expected career progress. The new jobs that can be obtained are not as impressive as they would be in normal times. Thus for those men with a great deal of skill, the effect of a recession is to keep them at a lower status than they would otherwise attain.

But what happens to the man who would normally fill this lesser job? He, too, must move down the job ladder and fill a position normally filled by even lesser trained men. If we follow this process to the bottom of the ladder, with everyone moving down a step, we can see that someone must step off and become unemployed. Thus one effect of a recession is to increase the level of skills possessed by men at all job levels. Machinists become operatives, operatives become janitors, and janitors become unemployed.

A casual observer of the structure of the unemployment might conclude that even an upturn in business could not cure it, because an upturn in business would create demand for skills at all levels. The unemployed, however, seem to be the least skilled of all men in the whole labor force. But that is precisely the structure of unemployment we expect if men, during recessions, are adaptable enough and willing enough to take jobs requiring slightly less than the skills they possess. This pattern of unemployment yields us some insight into the degree of substitutability of different men for different jobs.

Labor Unions

What is the role of labor unions in determining wage rates and other labor market variables? A *union* is a group of laborers who act jointly as a seller's monopoly when selling their labor services. Economic research suggests that in the case of the United States, unions tend to affect the distribution of income between unionized and nonunionized labor, although the share of interest, rent, and monopoly profits remains about the same as before. Unions, according to such studies, have little effect on the distribution of income between labor and capital. Still, a union might raise the wage rates of its own members. How could it do so?

It is important to remember that a union is a monopoly. Just as the creation of a monopoly out of an otherwise competitive industry can increase the income of sellers of physical commodities, so it can for sellers of labor. The union can restrict the number of men allowed to perform a particular skill—say, carpentry—and thereby raise wages above the level they would attain if entry into the profession were free. The effect is the same as that of any other monopoly. All consumers pay higher prices for carpenters or for goods that required carpentry in their production. The allocation of resources becomes inefficient as the wage of carpenters exceeds that necessary to encourage more men to take up the craft.

The more inelastic the demand for their skill, the more successful will be the craft unions at raising wages. This can be seen from Figure 20.1, where the restricted supply of carpenters raises the wage rate from W_c to W_u.

It is not clear what unions maximize. If they attempted to maximize the wage rate, they would find it optimal for there to be only one carpenter. If they maximize total carpenter income, they may find it optimal to have the competitive amount of carpenters. Some have suggested that unions maximize the income and power of the union leaders. Since we do not know their motives, we cannot determine where in Figure 20.1 the vertical portion of the supply curve should be placed. We have drawn it merely to indicate the potential for raising wages, not to demonstrate any understanding of optimal union behavior.

Professional organizations, which are similar in many ways to labor unions, also act against the interest of all consumers by restraining entry into their professions. They do this by limiting enrollment and scholarships in accredited schools and by controlling the state professional examinations. It is possible for both labor unions and professional organizations to raise the price of their product (labor services) above its marginal cost, just as any monopoly is able to do in the product market.

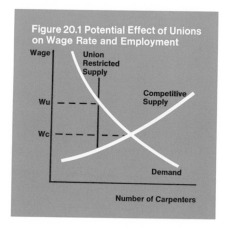

Figure 20.1 Potential Effect of Unions on Wage Rate and Employment

The growth of labor unions in the United States has involved a long and bloody history and is filled with bitter memories of worker-management strife and the misery resulting from periodic economic depressions. In 1935 the Federal Government passed the Wagner Act, which established the National Labor Relations Board. The Board for the first time provided active support for the formation of labor unions. Workers in any industry engaged in interstate commerce were enabled to elect freely representatives to bargain collectively with their employers for higher wages, shorter hours, and better working conditions. The Supreme Court, in supporting this and subsequent legislation as constitutional, recognized the right of workers to act collectively against employers who might be making noncompetitive decisions in the labor market.

One result of the Wagner Act was to allow the creation of large industrial unions, unions whose members were bound together not by a common skill but by a common employer. The steelworkers and autoworkers are major examples of this type of union. It is impossible to tell the effect of these unions on resource allocation. The auto industry, for example, is dominated by a few large firms and it is naive to think of it as having a competitive demand for labor. Just as monopolists have no supply curve for goods—they merely pick the point on the consumer's demand curve that maximizes profit—so they have no demand curve for factors. They choose the point on the competitive factor supply curve that maximizes profit. To confront these large auto firms with a monopolist who sells labor—the autoworkers' union—need not make a bad situation worse; it may actually improve the allocation of resources. There is no way to tell whether resources are more or less efficiently allocated because these two giants, the autoworkers' union and the automobile industry, sit down together to determine wage rates between them.

Minimum Wages

Many countries have passed legislation that establishes the minimum wage workers must be paid. What effect does this have on employment? Labor is not homogeneous. There are workers with marginal products of all levels. Some of

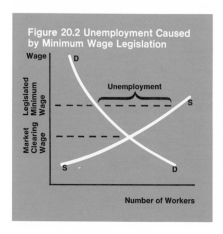

Figure 20.2 Unemployment Caused by Minimum Wage Legislation

the less fortunate have very low marginal products. A high enough minimum wage (since it does not require that a person be hired, but only that he be paid the minimum wage *if* hired) will cause such persons to be unemployed.

This can be seen in Figure 20.2, where we have drawn the supply and demand for labor of a very, very simple skill. Those who would work at such jobs have few alternatives and must either work for very low pay or not work at all.

Figure 20.2 shows how unemployment must result if minimum wage legislation is to be effective—if it is to raise wages above their competitive level. The purpose of the law is to guarantee people with few skills at least a minimum level of income, when in fact it achieves this only for those who keep their jobs when the wage floor rises. The rest of the workers are disemployed and lose all their income. Later on we examine some alternative schemes for guaranteeing a minimal income, such as the negative income tax.

Conclusion

The labor market is marked by complexity and uncertainty. Wages, as a result, tend to be sticky, and allocative efficiency is impeded to the extent that sticky wages produce wider swings in unemployment and a failure of prices to adjust quickly to changing conditions of demand. This is due to the vastly different kinds of labor that exist and problems that arise in linking different labor markets together.

Skills can be acquired. Through education each worker can increase his future income (and consumption), provided he is able to save (or borrow) to this end. This means that no one need look forward to the same wage level throughout his life as long as he is capable of learning a new skill or improving on his present education, and as long as this training corresponds to the future demands of society. A further benefit both of education and work itself is the utility one derives from feeling productive. Workers of the future, as their material consumption rises, may gain increasing satisfaction from the act of production itself and the creative demands it places on the individual. No amount of income redistribution can give such feelings to all men. They arise only from contributing as much to the world as one takes out of it. The ultimate challenge in creating a truly egalitarian system is to create one in which every man actually is useful, productive, and important.

Questions

1. What is the opportunity cost to you of a year at college? What is the cost to the society?
2. Why are the least skilled more apt to be unemployed than the highly skilled?
3. What makes the value of life different from the value of human capital? How could we measure either concept?

Concepts Discussed

human capital   minimum wage
unions

21 Natural Resources

Natural Resources and History

Until recent years the limits on our consumption and material well-being were set by the availability of natural resources. "Nature's bounty," in the form of arable land, minerals, water, and climate, set barriers to economic progress for any civilization, in the absence of conquest and expropriation of other territories. In the nineteenth and twentieth centuries, capital accumulation and technological progress have become the most important determinants of increases in per capita income. But in earlier times, mineral and other resource discoveries played that role. It is not surprising that before the Industrial and Agricultural Revolutions, rulers bent on increasing their national wealth looked across the frontier at the natural resource endowments of their neighbors. *Lebensraum*, the living space allegedly required for continuing imperial expansion, was used to justify calls to arms against neighboring states as recently as the past few decades in both Europe and Asia. Even today the possibilities for increasing national income and wealth through peaceful avenues of saving and investment, rather than through the predatory seizure of the assets of others, have yet to be recognized fully in all quarters of the globe.

History's tales of adventure are filled with the accounts of territorial aggrandizement, tribute, plunder, and searches for mineral treasures in distant lands. The relative strength of monarchs used to be measured by the amount of gold and other precious minerals they could amass in a lifetime, usually through conquest, plus the amount of land under their control and the taxes it afforded. The broader definition of wealth introduced by Adam Smith into the common parlance included much more than natural resource assets. It constituted the entire resource endowment of a nation, including all forms of physical and human capital.

In 1800 natural resources were of great importance in determining a nation's potential income and wealth; the advances in science and technology since then have concentrated on transforming existing amounts of matter to release greater amounts of energy and output. A surprising amount of success has been achieved to date, so that in the latter part of the twentieth century we live in a time when the physical limitations of matter are relatively unimportant compared with the virtually limitless possibilities for production from physical and human capital. At such a time, it may be hoped that saving and investment in one's own economy will replace the compulsion to plunder the assets of others. Similarly, it may be hoped that saving and investment in one's own personal productivity will allow all men to rise to a level of affluence without doing so at the expense of their neighbors.

Even though less important than the constraints of physical and human capital, the boundaries that nature has placed on her own resource endowments continue to figure prominently in the limitations of production possibilities of all economies. We have seen in earlier chapters how, for example, in agriculture, the limited supply of land results in decreasing marginal productivity of investment in agriculture. These limitations can be overcome by finding more land or by making technical improvements that shift up the marginal productivity curves on given amounts of land. The latter expedient will prove increasingly important in the future as the world's land area fills up with human habitations.

The scarcity of natural resources causes them to command a price in the market. Thus they constitute an important element in the exchange of goods and services in any economy as one of the three basic factors of production (capital, labor, and land). This chapter is directed to the problem of how prices are determined in markets for natural resources. Are natural resources allocated to their best possible use in perfect markets?

The Special Character of Natural Resources

Natural resources are similar to any other asset in that they provide a stream of income over time. The value (in present prices) of the future earnings of natural resources constitutes their present worth in the marketplace. A parcel of land will sell at a price equaling the sum of future rents that it is expected to provide after these rents have been transformed into current values by multiplying them by their present prices. In Chapter 19, we showed how future goods were apt to be worth less than present goods; thus the prices future rents are multiplied by must be less than one. A natural resource asset is the same as any other asset from the point of view of its value in the marketplace. Savers will exchange it for capital goods (or securities) in terms that depend on its efficiency in transforming present wealth into future wealth (or present consumption into future consumption). What makes natural resources different from other assets? Certainly not their value. Rather, it is the fact that they are "natural" rather than man-made. Physical and human capital can be increased in supply through saving and investment. Suppose, for example, that the return to investment in human capital rose in the marketplace. Individuals might be expected to save and invest more in themselves. The stock of human capital would increase over time, reflecting this higher rate of return. In other words, human (and physical) capital is responsive to price. But natural resources, by definition, cannot respond to price. Their supply is inelastic (they have a vertical supply curve). Of course, we know that land can be created from swamps and by filling and draining harbors. Minerals can be discovered through exploration and development. In such a sense the supply curve of natural resources is not perfectly inelastic; there is some potential response to price. We will get around this problem by calling man-made natural resources capital. Man-made land is capital. Then, by definition, natural resources cannot be produced. *It is the fact that natural resources cannot be produced that distinguishes them from other factors of production.*

Renewable Resources

There are two basic kinds of natural resources of interest to economists, those that maintain their productivity over time (renewable resources) and those that are used up in the process of production (nonrenewable or "wasting" resources). The former might be compared with capital goods that have perpetual lives while the latter can be thought of as capital that is subject to depreciation. The valuation of a natural resource is the same as that of any other capital good. Each is an asset that can provide revenue in future periods of time. Once the expected future earnings of a natural resource have been transformed into current prices (using a rate of discount equal to the market rate of interest, as we saw in the chapter on capital goods), the sum of discounted future earnings represents its present value.

Potential savers and investors may compare the present value of a natural resource with that of any alternative asset (such as a capital good or a financial asset). Suppose that an individual wishes to postpone consumption by purchasing an asset that will increase his possibility of future consumption. He will buy the asset (natural resource, capital good, or any other asset) that most efficiently does the job of transforming present income into future income. That is, he will buy the asset that has the highest rate of return. As asset holders care very little whether an asset is natural or man-made, natural resources have a value equal to their discounted future earning power just as capital has, even though they cost nothing to produce. And we can discuss the efficiency of markets for natural resources in the same manner that we discuss efficiency in any other market.

Rent and the Single Tax

One social evangelist of the United States in the 1880s proposed that all government revenue might best be derived from a land tax. Henry George wrote a best seller, *Progress and Poverty*, outlining his theory that the rent from land represented to unproductive members of society a windfall that could be taxed away without affecting the nature or extent of land use. Obviously, labor sellers should receive their full wages because they make very real sacrifices in time and effort. And savers must be rewarded for postponing consumption, a real sacrifice. But land owners sacrifice nothing. Why should they be rewarded?

Henry George's theories had world-wide repercussions and even today are influential in land-tax legislation. He argued that a tax on land rent would not affect the output of land because it is in effect a tax on unearned income. As there is no sacrifice involved, people will continue to offer the same amount of land as before the tax. They have no alternative. Was he correct? To answer this question, we examine the economic definition of rent more precisely.

Economic rent is that part of total factor payments over and above what the factor could earn if employed in the next most profitable way. It can be thought of as the amount beyond that necessary to induce the owner of the factor to offer its services in production. In the case of land, how much payment is necessary to bring a parcel of land into production? We are not considering here the payment to other factors such as labor and capital that might be used on the land but simply the amount necessary to keep the land from lying idle. A vertical supply curve for land suggests that no matter how low the payment, any finite price will cause that amount of land to be brought into production. Hence if the marginal revenue product of a unit of land is greater than zero, the land will be brought into production. Although a rather extreme assumption, as we shall see, this is a useful point of departure for theory. Figure 21.1 shows the amount of rent that a parcel of land of 100 acres (OQ) might obtain if the demand (MRP_{land}) were *dd*. Note that at any lower price the same amount of land is offered. Therefore, the total payment to the land is rent.

Total rent amounts to the area of the box *AEQO* (shaded area) in Figure 21.1. Since the supply of land *QS* is price inelastic, the same amount of land would be offered in the market each year regardless of the price it commands for its services. Hence the total payment for land during the period when demand is *dd* ($10 per acre times 100 acres, or $1,000) represents *rent* by the economic definition. It is now possible to show the allocative effect of a single tax on land, such as Henry George proposed, *if the conditions of supply are as shown.* In Figure 21.2, we impose a 10 percent tax on the payment to land. What this means is that the demand curve *as the land owner views it* now shifts down by 10 percent and becomes the dotted line *d'd'*. Notice that of the $10 per acre being paid by the users of the land's services (rent), $1 now goes to the government for each acre. *Yet the quantity of land in use has not declined* even though the land owner receives only $9 per acre under the new single-tax system. This is precisely Henry George's point. Some of the rent is being taxed away without affecting land use.

The total payment for the service of land is still $1,000. The government

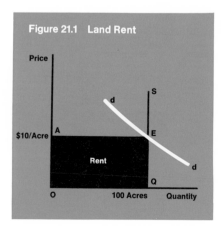

Figure 21.1   Land Rent

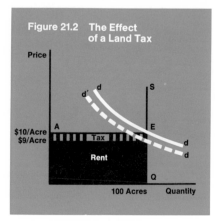

Figure 21.2   The Effect of a Land Tax

receives 10 percent of this amount and land owners 90 percent. Output from the land remains as before (nothing has happened to the marginal revenue product of land to society), though the marginal revenue product received by the land owner has fallen by 10 percent. Since we have assumed implicitly (by drawing a vertical supply curve QS) that there is no alternative use for the land if taken out of production, its use in production is unaffected by the tax. Those who might derive aesthetic value from looking at the uncultivated undergrowth or who simply enjoy hunting might decide to keep the land idle if the price of its services falls too far. If this were to happen, the supply curve would not be vertical—at a low enough price it would have a positive slope, reflecting the fact that alternative uses of the land represent an opportunity cost to its use in the market. *Only when the supply of land is completely inelastic can we agree with Henry George that a single tax on land would have no effect on overall production.*

Is the supply of land completely inelastic? We have mentioned that land can be created by draining swamps or filling in bays. Existing land can be improved in quality by the application of fertilizers, or it can be run down through mineral depletion or erosion. High rents encourage good maintenance of existing land and a high rate of improvement. In fact, the equilibrium market rental rate (when the supply of land is price elastic) would bring about the creation of new land at a rate consistent with the marginal utility of land to consumers. In such cases, a tax on payment for land use tends to distort the creation and maintenance of land and can lead to withdrawal of land from the market to be used for hunting or other forms of private consumption. Let us see what the total supply of land might look like once we have recognized that its use entails certain costs. In order to compare land of different intrinsic qualities on the same diagram, we must add to the gift of nature those costs per acre (for fertilizers, irrigation, and other improvements) that will bring all land up to a similar level of productivity. This we have done in Figure 21.3.

The supply curve for land, SS, rises as the land area increases, since the in-

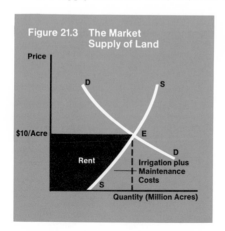

Figure 21.3   The Market Supply of Land

clusion of less and less intrinsically productive land means that more and more costs are necessary to raise its productivity to competitive levels. Hence the land that is most productive by nature (at the far left in the figure) will be used first.

If demand were small enough (if *DD* were far to the left), only this most productive land would be used. But as demand shifts to the right, more and more marginal land will be added to production by improving its productivity through expenditures on draining, irrigation, fertilizer, and so on. Hence *SS* slopes upward and to the right. In our figure, the market equilibrium is at a price of $10 per acre with 300 million acres in production. Note that for the last acre drawn into production, the payment per acre is exactly equal to the cost of improvement of the land and no rent is earned. But for the more productive land, rents are earned since the price of $10 per acre exceeds the cost of putting the land into production. Hence the entire shaded area in the figure represents economic rent to land.

The figure illustrates the difficulty of putting Henry George's tax proposal into practice. How are tax authorities to determine which share of the return to land represents the land's rent (shaded area) and which is compensation for the expenditure on improvements in the land (area below *SS*)? Clearly, if the tax is in excess of the rental share, or if it falls equally on all land regardless of its intrinsic productivity, then resources will not be allocated efficiently. Less land will be used in production than before. What happens in Figure 21.3 if we shift the market demand downward by 10 percent to reflect a proportional tax on land? Clearly in this case the quantity of land used will decline, since the supplied quantity of land varies with price (*SS* is upward sloping rather than vertical). Henry George was unable to solve this problem.

Extension of the Principle of Economic Rent
The definition of economic rent as that part of total factor payments over and above the amount necessary to induce the factor's owner to offer its services in production can be extended to factors other than land. What about the natural abilities of man? We are not all created equal in terms of our potential strength, agility, intelligence, or creativity. Individuals are able to earn income because of natural abilities that exceed those of their fellow-men even in addition to the differential productivity they can achieve through investment in human capital. For example, some of the beauty of a film star is a gift of nature. Greta Garbo, Raquel Welch, Brigitte Bardot, Julie Christie, and Lassie are all able to earn an income that includes a share of economic rent. No amount of investment can create another Greta Garbo, though some fine breeding might result in another Lassie. If one-half of all Elizabeth Taylor's film income were taxed, it is unlikely that she would make fewer films. (She would emigrate.) If we taxed away one-half the labor income of Joe Namath, Melvin Belli, Hugh Hefner, or Lou Alcindor, it is unlikely that they would offer fewer labor services. This shows us that a

good deal of labor income can be thought of as a rent paid to a resource that is fixed in supply.

A return to fixed resources also characterizes part of the income of doctors, lawyers, scientists, and educators. A chemist who enjoys his work so much that he would do it for $10,000 per year may actually be paid $20,000 per year. Half of his salary is rent. Why does his employer not pay him only $10,000 per year? Because some other employer will offer him $20,000 and lure him away. And why is $20,000 the going price for chemists? Because they are able to produce output worth $20,000 per year. Therefore each employer is willing to pay this amount, and if he does not, he loses his chemists. Note that if the price falls, there will be fewer chemists. Some chemists, not as inspired by their profession as the individual above, might have become engineers or biologists or physicians if the price of chemists had fallen to $19,000 per year. Figure 21.4 shows the supply and demand curves for chemists. If the wage fell to $10,000 per year, there would be only one chemist. Even he would not have been a chemist at a lower wage. The higher the wage, the more chemists there are.

As we have drawn the curves, the equilibrium price is $20,000 per year. For all chemists but one, some rent is being received as part of their salary. For example, the 100,000th chemist would remain a chemist even if the wage were only $13,000 per year. He receives $7,000 in economic rent. Now that economic rent has been defined as a return in excess of that necessary to obtain the services of a factor, *it is clear that if there were some way to tax economic rent we could do so without adversely affecting resource allocation.* This follows from its definition. Those who would support such a tax must show that only the economic rent will be taxed.

Nonrenewable Resources

Natural resources that are used up in the process of production are capital assets that can be used only once. They depreciate immediately when used and the major question facing the owners is when to use them. It is possible that we may

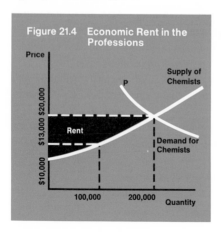

Figure 21.4   Economic Rent in the Professions

run out of certain of these resources. To what extent should this problem concern us? Consider the following imaginary newspaper article:

NICKEL SHORTAGE PREDICTED

Doctor John Smith, noted mineralogist, warns that the world will exhaust its known reserves of nickel in ten years if use continues at the present rate.

What should our reaction be to that article? Should we ask Congress to pass laws forbidding the use of nickel in all but essential commodities? Or should we ignore the article and let the market continue to allocate resources? If we did the latter, how would the market preserve the supply of a scarce natural resource if preservation were needed?

Let us look at the problem in terms of the owner of the wasting resources (for example, a firm or a governmental agency). The owner will attempt to sell them in such a way as to maximize profits. If the shortage of nickel is indeed to be a severe one, the owners will recognize this and ration the nickel among its competing uses by raising the price. The seller recognizes that the value of his nickel will increase if he restricts its supply now; he also realizes he will still be making profits more than ten years from now by such action. By attempting to maximize the present value of all future profits, he takes into account the fact that nickel will be scarce and therefore expensive in the future. If cutting down on sales today adds more to discounted future profits than it subtracts from present profits, he will cut down on sales. If it does not add more to future profits (expressed in present values) than it takes away from present profits, he will not sell less now, nor should he, because nickel is already being most efficiently allocated among its competing uses. If future profits are not very high, the society will not place a great value on nickel in the future. We might as well use it now while it is worth something.

Even if the owner of the wasting resources foolishly disregards his own best interests by trying to sell all the nickel today, it only takes one smart speculator (individual or government stockpiling agency) to buy it from him and ration it out to maximize the present value of all future profits. The speculator will be rewarded for economizing in the use of society's scarce resources. In fact, the speculator who places the highest value on the nickel reserves is probably the one who owns them already.

If the market is indeed allocating resources properly, why are we going to run out of nickel in ten years? First of all, one should not believe everything he reads. We are unlikely to run out of nickel if the market is allocating resources properly. The present price of nickel and the rate at which it is being drawn from the ground reflect the following considerations on the part of buyers and sellers:

1. The likelihood of new ore discoveries.
2. The likelihood of the creation of a chemical synthetic or other metal alloy that can perform the same chores nickel does (the possibility of discovering a close substitute).

3. The knowledge of how much a future price increase would affect future demand by forcing users to substitute other metals for nickel.
4. The likelihood that new production techniques will be created that do not need nickel if its price should be increased.

All these reasons and more indicate that there may exist substitutes for nickel or for any wasting natural resource and that these substitutes will be used when and if the price rises. *These factors have already been taken into account in determining the current market price of nickel.* If the current production rate would in fact exhaust the reserves in ten years, this is a reflection of the fact that good substitutes exist. The demand curve is therefore elastic—there is little profit to be made in raising the price of nickel. Future prices for nickel will be no higher than present prices.

The fact that other resources are said to have an expected life of 100 years simply may reflect the fact that poor substitutes exist. Therefore the owners have restricted current supply to increase present and future profits. Those assets that have low levels of reserves are either cheap to discover or have good substitutes.

Exploration and Discovery

The story of natural resources is one of discovery. When your grandfathers were in school, there was a scare about the adequacy of the amount of coal remaining in the ground to satisfy future energy needs. When your fathers were in school, the scare was about petroleum. In this generation, the scare is apt to be about uranium or whatever future primary sources of energy may be. But the known reserves of coal, petroleum, and uranium have all increased rather than decreased over time. Coal reserves are now adequate for hundreds of years, petroleum for about 100 years. Both these estimates used to be lower. At this writing, the known reserves of uranium will last for 12 years at the current rate of utilization, but use is growing at a phenomenal rate because uranium has become cheaper than coal at some locations as a source for electrical energy production. Will we run out of uranium? The best bet is that massive ore strikes will be made during the next decade, and/or that a new energy substitute will be discovered, so that 12 years from now the world will have uranium reserves adequate for 25 more years of use. If the ore strikes are not made, the price of uranium will rise and we can go back to coal and petroleum.

With current technology we have just begun to scratch the earth's surface, laying bare only the greatest concentrations of ore. Many regions of the globe have not yet had even preliminary geological surveys. With better technology, deposits of lower concentrations of ore can be worked. The chemical flotation technique introduced in the copper industry in the late nineteenth and twentieth centuries made it profitable to work low-yield porphyry ores for the first time, not because the price of copper had risen but because the new methods of processing lowered the cost of removing a given quantity of copper from poorer quality ore. Certainly, if the price of copper does increase, we can expect poorer and poorer ores to be used. As a last resort, the oceans contain in one form or another almost all chemicals. It is a matter of *cost*, not *availability or technology*, that prevents us from mining the oceans today. It is cheaper to take copper from the ground than from the ocean. But it is cost that determines which chemicals are to be used in any production process. Markets are designed to allocate resources efficiently in exactly these cases where cost is the primary factor of consideration.

Unless space travel develops at a pace far beyond its current rate, one eventual resource limitation will be *Lebensraum*, or square footage per person on the surface of the earth. Population cannot continue to soar without people eventually running out of room. We will examine the growth of population later. For now it is sufficient to state that any compound rate of growth of population will eventually get us to and beyond the point where there is standing room only. Population size can be thought of as a public good. We all wish to live in an uncrowded world. We therefore hope that our neighbors have very few children so that we are not overcrowded. But when we determine the size of our own families, overcrowding is a minor consideration. "What effect can one more body have on crowding anyway?" we might ask. Just as the motorist who wants clean air does not voluntarily buy a smog control device, a family who purports to despise the population explosion may not voluntarily restrict its own size. The tiny bit cleaner the air or the tiny bit less crowded the planet as a result of an individual's actions is too small an effect to induce him to behave the way he wishes everyone else would. And just as the motorist would find it hard to collect from others for installing a smog control device, a family practicing birth control receives no reward except the knowledge that they are good citizens. If only one family limits its size, it receives some economic benefits but has little independent influence on general overcrowding. But if most families limit their size, society at large is spared the spectre of standing room only. For this reason, some governments and social leaders recognize the usefulness of subsidizing birth control information and devices. Those who oppose birth control are in effect passing on to others in society the external diseconomies of overcrowding whether or not they are the direct recipients of this doctrine. This is a sticky political issue because of the religious problem. Some people, by belief, feel this is no problem at all, while others are very concerned.

In any case, the possibility of overcrowding exists because the bounty of nature is limited. It is likely that long before we reach the point of standing room only, some unknown function of social equilibrium will slow the growth of population. It is to be hoped that this function will depend not upon the four horsemen of the Apocalypse, as in the past, but upon the intelligence, foresight, and creativity of man. At the beginning of the nineteenth century, the first hypothesis of social equilibrium was proposed by Thomas Robert Malthus, a British political economist and member of the clergy. He saw that population growth must eventually be limited by the available food supply and predicted that eventually we would all be on subsistence diets, living in abject poverty.

The fact that this seemed imminent to Malthus over 150 years ago should provide some relief to us in this day and age when there are so many prophets of doom. Yet we should not forget that empires have fallen as well as risen; there is no assurance that men will always overcome the material obstacles placed before them soon enough to forestall the dangers of famine, pestilence, fire, and the sword.

Questions

1. How might a country adjust to a water "shortage"? To declining petroleum reserves? To a scarcity of timber? To a desire for wild territories? Can the market be used to satisfy these needs?

2. To what extent would Henry George's single tax probably distort a resource allocation?

3. The earnings of many people with very high incomes are largely rent. Would a progressive income tax be likely to distort their occupational choice? Their decision as to how hard to work?

Concepts Discussed

rent

the single tax

VII   The Public Sector

Any economist who wants the government
to act whenever the market falls short
of perfection is like a judge in a
singing contest who awards the prize
to the second singer merely on the basis
of having heard the first.

GEORGE STIGLER

In the next two chapters we discuss the public sector. We show how centralized policy can affect the allocation of resources in a market economy. Economists call the study of this problem *public finance*.

Chapter 22 is devoted to efficiency. We collect all the previously established results concerning market failure, and we discuss the policies that might be taken to offset the resulting inefficiency. We note how taxes and other activities of the public sector may themselves be a source of inefficiency. All of this is done within the framework of a model of general equilibrium. Then we get a glimpse of the concept of political efficiency by looking at models of voting. The chapter serves as a good review of the principles of efficiency because we must discuss them all in order to be able to prescribe policies for correcting market failure.

Chapter 23 is concerned not with efficiency but with equity. We note the concept of equity and how its meaning can vary from group to group. Then we discuss income distributions and the ways in which government policy can affect them. Many of these ways are those shown in Chapter 22 to lead to inefficient allocations of resources. We are left with a political dilemma. How much inefficiency would we tolerate in order to obtain an equitable distribution of goods?

22 General Equilibrium, Efficiency, and the Public Sector

We can now collect from all the previous chapters the results concerning the efficiency of the market and look for policies to prescribe when markets fail to allocate resources efficiently. We do this in the context of a model of general equilibrium—a model of simultaneous equilibrium in all markets.

The Meaning of General Equilibrium

Anyone who has stood on the shore and looked at the sea can imagine the concept of general equilibrium. The sea is never at rest. Forces continually disturb its repose. Oceans move within oceans, and rivers within these seas. Mountains rise, valleys are dredged, and larger creatures devour the smaller in an interacting process of survival. Yet despite this continual movement, the boundaries are circumscribed by the physical limitations of nature. Extremes of heat and cold, phases of the moon, positions of the planets, and, more recently, the activities of men all play a role in determining these boundaries. Because they exist, the sea is continually moving within a "general equilibrium."

The economic marketplace is similar to the sea, in that it is restless yet bounded—by the conditions of supply and demand. In Part III we saw in an extremely simple economy how individual efforts to maximize utility can lead to a unique market equilibrium in the marketplace. Only one commodity was produced, corn, in exchange for leisure time. Only two factors were employed to produce it, labor and land. The process of exchange led to an equilibrium in which the price and quantity of corn were determined, income was distributed, and all markets were cleared. This was a *general equilibrium* in the economic marketplace. In reality, there are close to an infinite number of goods and factors that could be produced and exchanged in a great number of markets.

When only one of these goods or factors is analyzed separately, the study is called *partial equilibrium analysis*. In partial equilibrium analysis, it is assumed for convenience that other things remain unchanged, so that only the single commodity or market experiences an alteration in the conditions of supply or demand. This *ceteris paribus* approach is taken in a number of the preceding chapters. It is a useful approach when we wish to generate results that are rele-

LÉON WALRAS (1834–1910)   Names and concepts are often linked. Such is the case with Léon Walras, the originator of modern general equilibrium analysis, which is often called Walrasian equilibrium. Son of the economist Auguste Walras, Léon was trained as an engineer, then labored long as a journalist, petty official, and bank officer before attaining, in 1870, a university position as an economist, and then not in his native France but at the University of Lausanne in Switzerland. Throughout his varied career, however, Walras focused sharply on major theoretical issues in economics as well as on problems of social reform and change, notably the question of land reform.

Coming out of a French tradition and incorporating concepts from his father (scarcity), Cournot (mathematical formulations), and the physiocrats (general equilibrium), Walras fashioned a brilliant set of analyses of both theoretical issues and practical problems embodied in three major works, *Éléments d'économie pure* (1874–1877), *Études d'économie sociale* (1896), and *Études d'économie politique appliquée* (1898). In the *Éléments* is found most of his system of general equilibrium analysis; here Walras tied together all of the production and exchange relationships found in an exchange type of economy. Beginning with the notion of marginal utility (*rareté*), he defined the equilibrium condition of the consumer, subject to limited income, as that state in which he equates his gains in satisfaction per unit of money among all purchases. No alteration of his purchasing pattern will gain him any more utility or satisfaction, barring a change in his tastes. Proceeding from the equilibrium of an individual consumer, Walras showed that all demands for all commodities can be systematically identified. By an analogous process he developed the equilibrium of the producer, tying purchases of inputs to their costs, to their usefulness in production, and to the returns that they will generate. All demands for all inputs are then collected as for consumer goods. Walras emphasized the similarity of the conditions in input and output markets by noting that sellers of factors (that is, land, labor, capital) must make choices at the margin as to the allocations of their factor services among various alternative uses, choices that are also made subject to constraints. Using the technical relations between inputs and outputs as his connecting vehicle, Walras then developed a set of simultaneous equations that provided a model for the interrelated operations of an exchange economy. To

vant for one market only. Then supply and demand — a partial equilibrium model — can be used as a convenient abstraction to portray the impact of a particular action on the price and quantity of a single market. But if we are concerned with broader questions, it is necessary to use a model that allows us to handle many markets simultaneously.

The study of the interaction of many markets is termed *general equilibrium analysis*. It deals with the effect of initial changes in the conditions of supply and demand on the price and quantity of all goods and services traded in one or more markets. Customarily such analysis begins with the assumption that all markets clear and that the economy is at rest. Then a disturbance is introduced (a change in conditions of supply or demand for, say, wheat) and the process of adjustment to a new equilibrium is analyzed. General equilibrium analysis is identified in the

make certain that the solutions were determinate he introduced the concept of the *numeraire*, or unit of account, in which all prices and costs were stated. Since the price of this unit was equal to one, the number of unknowns equaled the number of equations. Obviously this counter was a stand-in for money in a conventional exchange system although as used by Walras in this way it had no relation to money as a medium of exchange.

In outlining his equilibrium system he literally showed that everything depends on everything else, including all consumption and production outcomes. The mutually consistent equilibria in the system were to be achieved in a dynamic sense by the process known as *tatonnement*, under which prices would be called out and consumers and entrepreneurs would bid and buy according to their requirements and means. Under this system he was able to show that the incomes earned by factor owners (that is, laborers, capitalists, landlords) re-entered the system as the demand for products and that under a regime of pure competition the entrepreneurs would receive nothing like true profit, having to content themselves with returns on their management and labor and on their own capital.

The final set of relations that Walras defined for his equilibrium system was concerned with the demand for money, which he later integrated into the whole structure of interrelated production and exchange relations. The demand for money thus assumed the same nature as the demand for other commodities, subject to calculations as to costs and satisfactions. This integration of money provided the capstone of the general equilibrium system.

Walras's work underlies much of the modern theorizing about the simultaneous movements of an exchange economy. It has also proved of value in the development of input–output analyses by which allocation of commodities among various uses is identified, and it has put various types of planning systems (both market and nonmarket) on a more solid intellectual foundation. However, it failed in dealing with some of the problems raised by Walras himself. It was restricted to full employment, to a system of pure competition, and to constant returns to scale, and thus it was inappropriate to the issues of massive technical change, economies of scale, industrial concentration, and instability so prevalent in the modern economy.

---

popular mind with the Frenchman Léon Walras, who in the latter part of the nineteenth century gave mathematical expression to the simultaneous interaction of all markets in the economy, effectively linking the processes of production, exchange, and financial transactions. He formalized the generally accepted proposition among economists that "everything depends upon everything else." Walras made this formalization possible through ingenious selective simplification, reducing markets to their elementary components, and subjecting them to a set of limiting assumptions, including pure competition, perfect knowledge on the part of all participants, an auction method of effecting transactions, and no increasing returns to scale.

But what about the interaction of many markets in the real world? Can the sea of trade be described as a "general equilibrium"? And if so, is that equilibrium stable? Is it efficient? These are questions that continue to occupy economic researchers. In this chapter we look briefly at some of these issues. First we review the question of efficiency as it applies to equilibrium in the whole economy, or general equilibrium. Then we show how taxes can be used to attain efficiency where it would not otherwise exist. We also demonstrate how most of the common taxes that are levied violate the conditions of allocative efficiency. Finally, we discuss problems of political efficiency, of using the voting mechanism instead of the market to allocate resources. The chapter is intended to convey the problems of efficiency that arise in the real world because of the public sector's existence as well as to show its role in alleviating inefficiency in the private sector. This chapter can serve as a good review of all the efficiency problems we have so far encountered.

Historical Stability of Markets

Just as individual markets have short- and long-run conditions of supply and demand, and therefore short- and long-run equilibria, so the economy as a whole possesses both short- and long-run equilibria. Yet in practice markets are always in the process of clearing, some in excess supply and others in excess demand, prices are adjusting continually, and the whole economy is perpetually moving toward some theoretical equilibrium. Is the process of movement toward that general equilibrium stable? Some social philosophers believe that economic systems harbor within themselves forces that will produce trends, such as increased inequality in income distribution, leading to increased social tensions and political explosions that in turn will have disrupting effects on the market mechanism itself. Others feel that the economy itself has internally destabilizing characteristics, such that one need not introduce any other social or political elements to justify the prediction of revolution in the marketplace. We have seen in earlier chapters how destabilizing expectations may produce cumulative movements away from equilibrium in single markets. In the remainder of this book we examine conditions under which the economy may experience business cycles leading to sustained unemployment (excess capacity) or inflation (excess demand).

Yet one of the most noteworthy characteristics of economic history is the relative stability of so many key economic relations over long periods of time. Despite the disturbing influences of the four horsemen of the Apocalypse, and despite the upsetting nature of trade cycles, relative prices have demonstrated an amazing degree of stability for generations. The distribution of income among wages, profits, and rent has not fluctuated widely even over 100-year intervals. and under widely differing technologies. The real rate of return on capital is reflective of highly stable individual preferences between present and future consumption over the long run. As a result, explanations of economic behavior dating back to Adam Smith still retain validity, population explosions, massive migrations from old to new lands, technological revolutions, and corresponding revolutions in tastes notwithstanding. These factors indicate that markets are generally stable, that basic needs and resources remain relatively constant, and that the economy may well be viewed as being close to some general equilibrium, even though this hypothetical state may never in fact be reached any more than the sea will someday come to rest. Thus we feel justified in employing an analytical framework constructed around the concept of a general equilibrium. In this framework economic events are best understood in terms of the way in which markets individually and collectively approximate the conditions for general equilibrium. And general equilibrium itself may be examined in terms of its approximation of the conditions for allocative efficiency.

Efficiency of Equilibrium in the Marketplace

Many requirements must be satisfied if the allocation of resources is to be economically efficient. We summarize those requirements here before analyzing the effect of taxes on them. Let us first examine efficiency when there are no externalities—when one man's purchase of a commodity affects another's utility in no way except by changing the prices he faces. Then we bring in externalities and public goods.

(1) EFFICIENCY WITH NO EXTERNALITIES. Without externalities, our rule for the efficient allocation of resources is simple (recall Chapter 9). For any person, the ratio of marginal utilities to marginal costs must be equal for all commodities. That is, $MU_x/MC_x = MU_y/MC_y$ where x and y represent different commodities. This rule must be satisfied for each individual. Since we cannot compare utility among people, the ratios may be different for different people. If we rewrite the ratio to read $MU_x/MU_y = MC_x/MC_y$, then the ratios must be equal for all since MC_x/MC_y is a variable common to all in equilibrium. In this latter form, the equation says that the relative value of a commodity must equal its social cost.

We have seen that in market economies this result is obtained by having price equal marginal cost (in perfect competition) and by allowing consumers their free choice of commodities, given the prices they face. The definition of marginal cost given above says that it is the cheapest way to increase the output of a commodity by one unit. Efficiency in the combination of productive resources is necessary if the resulting cost is not to be an arbitrary figure. Three basic allocative rules, therefore, are implicit in the definitions of the variables and in the statement that marginal utility divided by marginal cost is equal for all commodities. These are the following:

1. Consumers are able to maximize utility by setting $MU_x/P_x = MU_y/P_y$ for all commodities.
2. Producers set price equal to marginal cost for all commodities.
3. Producers minimize costs by combining factors efficiently.

(2) EFFICIENCY WITH EXTERNALITIES. When one person's increased consumption of a commodity affects another's utility, the above rules must be altered. This is because the above rules allow only the utility of the buyer to matter. If the purchase of a commodity by individual A increases B's utility, for

example, as in the decision to landscape one's property, efficiency is only attained when B compensates A for the utility he receives from a more attractive neighborhood. Such a "payment" may be made in practice by B's agreeing to landscape his own property as well. This helps to explain why some neighborhoods are generally well maintained and others are generally run down. If B does compensate A, A will take account of the "payments" and consume more of the commodity than otherwise. He may even put in a swimming pool without a fence around it. Or if the externality is negative, such as the creation of noise from A's stereo or smoke from his incinerator, A should have to pay B for the inconvenience he causes. In this way the price of the commodity to A will be increased, so that it equals not only its production cost in terms of physical resources but also its cost to others in terms of annoyance.

TAXES AND EFFICIENCY

How do taxes affect efficiency in a market economy? They can move us toward or away from efficient allocations. Certain taxes are specifically designed to improve the allocative mechanism. Others, however, are designed to yield revenue. The latter form of tax frequently violates one of the rules of allocative efficiency. We look first at these revenue-producing taxes to examine why they are inefficient. Then we look at taxes that are efficient, and finally, at taxes whose purpose is the correction of inefficiencies that would otherwise exist.

The Income Tax

The income tax is used to raise revenue and to redistribute income. Problems of redistribution are examined in Chapter 23; here we are interested only in efficiency. As the tax appears to affect no particular commodity, one might think that it violates no efficiency considerations. But it does.

   Income taxes affect the choice between work and leisure. As one does not receive all the fruits of his labor once an income tax is imposed, one makes sure that the value of the commodities that can be bought by the last dollar earned *after* tax is equal to the value of a dollar's worth of leisure. That is, when the last hour spent working yields goods whose value equals the last hour spent on leisure, the consumer is in equilibrium.

   The effect of this can be seen through the basic equation of efficiency just presented. A consumer will be in equilibrium when the value of leisure relative to goods equals their relative cost—the ratio of prices. To the consumer, of course, the cost of a unit of leisure is his after-tax wage. Thus we have

$$\frac{MU_{leisure}}{MU_{goods}} = \frac{\text{after-tax wage (\$/hour)}}{\text{price of goods (\$/good)}}$$

   Note that the units in which relative prices are measured here are goods per hour, or what economists call the real wage rate. The social cost of leisure is the marginal product of labor. With a perfectly competitive market, this will be equal to the before-tax real wage rate. Thus the social cost of leisure will be the before-tax wage whereas the private cost will be the after-tax wage. In equilibrium, the *value* of a unit of leisure to an individual would be the after-tax wage rate. Yet it is possible for the individual to trade that unit of leisure through some production process for an amount of goods equal to the before-tax wage – the marginal product of labor. Such a trade would affect no one else yet it would make this individual better off because he would be receiving goods that are worth more to him than the leisure he sacrificed. Since an income tax prevents this trade from being made, the resource allocation with an income tax must be inefficient.

For administrative simplicity, certain income is exempt from taxation. Traditionally, this includes the rent on houses occupied by owners, the income of housewives, and all do-it-yourself activities. Trade-offs between income of this sort and taxable income clearly are affected by the income tax. Individuals will pursue do-it-yourself activities until the marginal product of their labor is less than it is in the free market.

Another impact of the income tax is on the market for future goods. If the imposed income tax taxes interest earned on saving (as is usual), it serves to bias the choice toward consumption. Consumption of future goods is taxed in a manner that the consumption of present goods is not. That is, the after-tax return is lower than the social return to saving. Thus, although the consumption of leisure may not be taxed at all, the consumption of future goods may be taxed twice. If we allowed an individual to increase his saving without having to pay tax on the increased interest, he would choose to do so. He would be better off, and no one else would be worse off.

Sales Tax

The sales tax has efficiency implications that are almost identical to those of the income tax, although it has different implications for distribution. The sales tax does not tax leisure, rent of owner-occupied houses, housewife services, or do-it-yourself activities. All commodities that escape taxation under the income tax also escape under the sales tax. But the sales tax does not bias the choice between present and future goods since it taxes only consumption. If one saves, one avoids taxation until the return from the saving is spent; but then the tax must be paid. With the income tax, one pays twice – once on the earned income and once again on the interest of the income that is saved. Except for this difference, the sales and income taxes have identical efficiency implications.

Sales taxes are generally collected at the time of the sale and therefore are very difficult to avoid. A variation of the sales tax, called an expenditure tax, is collected by requiring taxpayers to file a form similar to the income tax. One lists income and saving and then pays a tax on the difference. The disadvantage of this form of collection is that it makes it easier to cheat. An advantage is that it allows the sales tax to be used for income redistribution. That is, the sales tax can be made progressive so that the rich pay a higher percentage than the poor, a situation impossible when taxes are collected at the time of sale.

The Property Tax

Most communities tax real estate — land and buildings — while some tax autos and even furniture or other real property. Financial holdings are exempt from most of these property taxes; such taxes clearly bias one in favor of financial wealth and against real property. Of course, it was pointed out above that income from real wealth is often exempt from the income tax. Thus a property tax on real wealth and an income tax on income from financial wealth could average out to the same level of taxation on all forms of wealth. They will not be the same for all individuals, of course. Those with high incomes pay the income tax at higher rates than those with low incomes, but both pay the property tax at the same rate. Thus if both a property tax and an income tax exist with the income tax exempting income from real property, we would find the tax system pushing the rich toward real assets while pushing the poor toward financial assets. This is because the different rates at which the rich and poor pay tax on income from financial assets make this tax the cheapest one to the poor but the most expensive one to the rich.

Excise Taxes

Excises are sales imposed on some commodities and not on others. Clearly they bias choice in favor of the nontaxed commodities. All the taxes above can be considered as special cases of an excise tax. The income tax, for example, is equivalent to an excise tax on all goods except leisure and those goods produced within the household, while future goods have a higher excise rate than present goods. Thus one can use our argument concerning the inefficiency of the income tax as an example of the inefficiencies that derive from excise taxes.

EFFICIENT TAXES

Can efficient taxes exist? Can we collect revenue without affecting the allocation of resources? There are a few taxes that do not distort resource allocation, although the discovery of some of them required some real stretching of imaginations.

Lump-Sum Tax

A tax that does not depend on any economic magnitudes is called a lump-sum tax. It is determined by noneconomic criteria. One example is the head tax, which requires every individual to pay an equal amount of money to the government. There is no way to avoid such a tax by changing one's economic decisions. Therefore, such a tax cannot create an inefficiency. Lump sums can be apportioned randomly among the population or can be apportioned once and for all on the basis of some *historic* economic phenomena. That is, we could require larger taxes from *today's wealthy* but with a clear statement that wealth will never be used as a criterion again. Without that statement, we would affect adversely the decision to accumulate wealth, thereby biasing the choice between present and future goods.

Tax on a Factor in Fixed Supply

Henry George's single tax, which we discussed in Chapter 21, is efficient if the supply of land is fixed. The single tax taxes rent on land. Taxing by the acre does not affect the decision to use land although no one would wish to own the marginal land on which rents were less than the tax. Taxing a percentage of rents will not affect the owner's allocation decisions *unless* he prefers the land to be used one way rather than another. That is, since he has no choice but to offer his land on the market to the highest bidder, a tax on the rent he receives will not affect how the land is used. Of course, to the extent that fertilization and land maintenance are necessary to maintain land values, the tax on rents exerts a bias on the owner, causing him to prefer to neglect the land and to invest in enterprises that are not taxed.

Tax on the Price of a Factor

Since misallocation occurs through affecting an individual's decisions about the quantity of a factor to sell, a tax that depends solely on the price of the factor would have no effect on the allocation of resources if we were sure that at least some of the factor would be offered for sale anyway. If a man received the same pleasure from all jobs, we could tax him on the basis of his existing wage rate and there would be no allocative inefficiency. In this case, we say that if a person can earn $5 per hour, he must pay $1,000 per year in taxes. It will still be in his interest to make his wage as high as possible because he gets to keep more income from the high-wage jobs than from the low ones. This is true under our current income tax as well. But unlike the income tax, the wage-rate tax does not bias the work-leisure choice. If he chooses to work an extra hour, he gets to keep the whole $5. His tax bill is unaffected by his economic decisions. The wage-rate tax is like a head tax that is assessed according to one's ability to earn.

Of course, some jobs are more enjoyable than others, so this tax would have some allocation effects. That is, the tax would make the low-wage jobs relatively more attractive than they had been. The inefficiency arises because there is no tax on the pleasure derived from the job although pleasure derived from goods is taxed, albeit in a lump-sum fashion.

Thus most taxes cause distortions in the allocation of resources and make the allocation inefficient. Once the taxes are imposed, decisions are made differently and it then becomes possible to improve one man's welfare without hurting another's. The kinds of taxes that do not affect economic decisions are very *regressive*. A regressive tax takes a larger percentage of the income from the poor than it does from the rich. A head tax, for example, would tax all people equally, regardless of their ability to pay. The poor would be paying a large fraction of their income, the rich a very small fraction. *Ability to pay* is one of the criteria used to determine the appropriate tax structure. Since the best measures of one's ability to pay are income and wealth, these are the common variables used to determine one's tax bill. Once these variables are taxed, however, decisions are affected and inefficiency results. Apparently, one must choose between efficiency and ability to pay. Most nations sacrifice efficiency in order to distribute tax burdens equitably. Equity, however, is the subject of Chapter 23.

TAXES THAT RESTORE EFFICIENCY

Throughout the chapters above, we have referred to taxes and subsidies that might be used to make allocation efficient. We now review them.

Subsidy to Decreasing Cost Industries

Where there are economies of large-scale production, charging the efficient price ($P = MC$) leads to a loss since marginal cost is less than average cost whenever average cost is decreasing. Thus the firm would lose a little on every sale. Examples of such cases are bridges, railroads, postal systems, hydroelectric power, water from dams and irrigation systems. If the government subsidizes these industries they can charge the efficient price without going out of business. As subsidies are negative taxes, we can think of this as a tax that encourages efficiency.

Taxes for Externalities

If the consumption of a good has an external effect on another's utility, it is possible to tax that commodity so that the buyer will be forced to consider the other's utility when making his spending decisions. For example, alcohol is thought to have negative external effects. Users bother other people by making noise (particularly late at night), by being personally abusive, by causing auto accidents, and in some cases by costing the state money if alcoholism results and the user becomes a ward. If we did not tax alcohol, the user would have to pay only the cost of production. But there exists a cost of use in terms of the lessening of others' utility as well as a cost of production. Efficiency requires that the user pay both costs. Thus in the case of alcoholic consumption, an excise tax can encourage efficiency by making the user consider the effects his drinking has on others. He will not consider these effects consciously, but will do so implicitly when deciding whether the cost of alcohol plus tax is worth the money required. Of course, much of the original motivation underlying taxes on alcoholic beverages was the desire to be one's brother's keeper.

Political Efficiency

In the chapter on public goods, the chapters on industrial organization, and those on central planning, we have implied that ideal governmental behavior can often improve the allocation of resources by positive action in cases when the market misfires. We have seen how governmental behavior in the form of taxation may also misfire, producing inefficiency. Here we examine briefly the possibilities for ideal behavior on the part of government if we interpret that ideal as being the satisfaction of the wishes of the masses. How efficient is the voting process at expressing the desires of the people? In answer to that question, we present a puzzle and some discussion that indicates that the political system itself can fail just as easily as the market. Often we must estimate whether the government is more or less efficient than the market before we encourage it to intervene in a particular area.

The Voter's Paradox

The problems of political choice are so complex that they merit a special branch of the social sciences. Political science exists to study the working of the political marketplace. Only a few words can be said about these problems here, but it is useful to know how difficult it is for an electorate to express its will.

The political marketplace can also be inefficient. It is possible that the existing political solution is not the one that is desired by the sovereign body. A Yes-No vote once every two to six years cannot begin to describe how the electorate feels on literally hundreds of issues, both qualitative and quantitative, that bear upon questions of resource allocation and economic welfare. As an example of pitfalls in the political marketplace, we present an illustration of what is called the *voter's paradox*.

Assume that there are three voters, 1, 2, and 3, in society. An issue exists with three possible choices, A, B, or C; and the voters must select from among A, B, and C.

Voter 1 prefers A to B and B to C. (Rationality requires that he prefer A to C.)
Voter 2 prefers B to C and C to A.
Voter 3 prefers C to A and A to B.

If the voters were presented with a choice of all three possibilities in an election, a tie would result, a single vote being cast for each outcome. Some other scheme must be devised to break the tie. Suppose that voter 1 proposes the following scheme: "Let us first choose between B and C. Then we take the winner and choose between it and A. May the best proposal win." The other voters reject this scheme. Why?

What will happen if it is followed? Choosing between B and C initially gives *two* votes to B (voters 1 and 2) and only *one* vote to C (voter 3). Then choosing between the winner in the first round, B, and A gives *two* votes to A (voters 1 and 3) and only *one* vote to B (voter 2). As a result, A wins. Society appears to prefer A to B, and then B to C. A must be the socially optimal proposal. *But does the society prefer A to C?* Let us have another ballot on this question. Choosing between A and C, A gets only one vote while C gets two.

We hypothesized a society composed of rational individuals, each of whom had well-defined preferences and voted on them properly. Thus no irrationality is involved in this voter's paradox. What happened is the result of a lack of *transitivity (If A is preferred to B, and B to C, then transitivity requires that A be preferred to C); transitivity does not exist for a sum all of whose components are transitive*. This means that intransitivity is possible for a society with a rational electorate. Voting on issues in sequence need not yield the optimal action as a result; rather, the order in which the voting is conducted may affect the result obtained. Small wonder that political meetings involve fights over the order of items in the agenda.

The problem above is insoluble. Had we made the problem quantitative so that one outcome would give more dollar satisfaction than another, making decisions sequentially might still have resulted in less than optimal results. The point made by this short example is that political systems no less than economic systems must satisfy rigid requirements if utility is not to be wasted. In this book we have pointed to economic market inefficiencies as problems the government must handle, when, in fact, there is no guarantee that the government has a way of discovering the will of the people in an unambiguous fashion. Indeed, the very definition of "the will of the people" encounters the same problem of interpersonal comparison that is met in defining social utility. For people are not unanimous in their opinions. Ultimately, policy must be made, but almost any policy will have enemies. It is difficult enough for a government to determine who likes what, let alone to determine which of these "likers" is to be favored politically.

Social science helps us to attain the kind of society we wish. When men disagree in their wishes, however, there is nothing social science can do. We know of no way to compare utility among people, no way to determine whose wishes are to be granted. Ultimately, some political battles occur to determine what actions are to be taken. We merely point out that it is difficult to devise rules within which such a battle can occur that guarantee an accurate expression of the will of the body politic. Political machinery can be inefficient and some judgement about the importance of that inefficiency must be made when deciding to circumvent the market. Inefficient markets may be the best of a bad lot.

Questions
1. Why does an income tax lead to an inefficient allocation of resources? A sales tax? A property tax?
2. When does a tax that depends on the price of a factor not affect resource allocation?
3. Show how one person could be made better off without making anyone else worse off if that person is paying prices for commodities that differ from their social costs.

Concepts Discussed
general equilibrium   regressive tax
partial equilibrium   ability to pay
efficiency   voter's paradox
lump-sum tax

23 Equity and the Public Sector

In much of this book, we have been concerned only with economic efficiency. Now it is time to turn to *equity*, or justice, and consider its meaning in relation to the division of total output. What is an equitable distribution of income? Can the public sector provide it? What are the costs of providing it?

Social Attitudes and Equity

Attitudes toward equity differ within societies and among different societies. Our opinion of what is a fair way to divide the spoils is different from the opinions held in the past as well as those held elsewhere today. For example, at the time of the founding of the United States, many of its leading citizens placed the preservation of existing property rights, and the right of income from that property, alongside the rights of life and liberty to be guaranteed by the Constitution. While such an extreme defense of the moral rectitude of the status quo was never written into the Constitution, it has remained a cardinal principle for many. Indeed, that document required an amendment before it became legally permissible for the federal government to tax a citizen's income. And the right of *eminent domain*, by which the government may expropriate an individual's property for the public interest (to build a road, a dam, or for urban renewal), carries with it the obligation of just compensation.

Thus in the United States, the idea of equity that has been written into the law by the sovereign political body has guaranteed individuals that their property will not be taken from them without compensation. It has been deemed fair and equitable that individuals be able to hold their property securely and be guaranteed the income from it. Although such ideas do not represent the vanguard of radical political thought today, at one time they were thought to be just that.

In eighteenth-century Spain and its colonies the ultimate property and income rights were vested by divine law in the Crown. The king, as sovereign, was trustee of the realm, administering his trust on behalf of the entire community. At will he could take or bestow land, buildings, and the right to engage in trade or production. In a number of countries today, a similar principle holds in practice, although there is rarely an appeal to divine sanction. The state represents the ultimate repository of property and income rights, which it may administer with or without acceptance of the principle of just compensation. It is not surprising under the circumstances that disputes over questions of economic equity arise among nations today, just as they did on the American frontier among persons educated under entirely different systems of law and social ethics.

The question of equity revolves around moral principles. These principles are subjective—they cannot be proven right or wrong—and while they can be expected to differ among individuals, there is no way to establish once and for all what an equitable distribution of income really is. That is why the question is hotly debated within every society. Some believe that "to the victor belong the spoils." Others argue that income should be passed "from each according to his ability to each according to his need." While few would accept either extreme, the question of equity remains open, because equity, or justice, is what people think it is. Although it may be possible for an electorate to agree on abstract principles of economic justice and to write these principles into law, there is no *a priori* way to claim that any one principle *should* be used. Decisions concerning the desirability of a principle depend on the values of the society. And those values have undergone great historical changes.

To get an idea of why it is difficult to define equity, let us examine the difficulties encountered in trying to define equal opportunity, a principle thought by many to be a necessary part of any equitable system. Consider the following situation. A race is to be run to determine who gets the goods produced by a particular society. Everyone is to have an "equal opportunity" to obtain the goods. But how can we define equal opportunity? We list below varying interpretations of the term, each of which has some parallel in the politics of the real world.

1. The race is held at an unannounced time and place. Everyone has an equal opportunity to show up randomly, since no one is told the time and place.
2. Notice of the race is posted in one place one week ahead of time. Everyone has an equal opportunity to pass the notice, read it, and act accordingly.
3. Everyone is notified by mail two months in advance of the time and place for the race. Equal opportunity is guaranteed since everyone will be allowed to run.
4. Equal opportunity requires that everyone be allowed to train for the race. Therefore it must be announced two months ahead of time, use of training facilities must be guaranteed with free access to food, coaching, rest, and all the other elements that go into good running.
5. Equal opportunity requires an equal opportunity to win, not just to run. Allowances must be made for sickness, injury, age, background, and just plain physical weakness. Then equal work will yield equal results.
6. Equal opportunity requires that we account for psychological barriers to racing that make some run harder than others out of compulsion, not out of physical (or moral) superiority. Being born aggressive is no better than being born submissive.
7. Equal opportunity means simply that everyone gets an equal share regardless of how he runs.

The idea should be clear by now that equity is difficult to define. What is an equal opportunity of attaining success? What is fair and just? Each person may be able to select one of the above seven ideas of equal opportunity as representing equity, but he must admit that the decision was arbitrary. In the light of some intuitive feeling about fair play, one of the statements is preferable to the others. But different people have different feelings about what fair play is. Thus we will not all select the same number as our idea of constituting fair play.

Once we have decided that opportunities should be equal, we still have to decide the income distribution. All that was decided above was who is to be first, not how much he is to get. One alternative is winner take all. Another is that the first three finishers divide the pot in proportions 3:2:1, while a third possibility is to have the first seven finishers divide 10:6:5:4:3:2:1. The rules of the race do not determine the distribution of the spoils.

Below we examine how the public sector affects the income distribution in market economies. For background, we first review how income is distributed in a market economy. Then we look at the actual distribution in the United States, and finally we discuss the most commonly used tools of income redistribution.

Income Distribution by the Market

In Part III, we presented a simple example of how market forces can bring an economy to a general equilibrium in which all markets clear, wages and rents are determined (along with interest in a more complex economy), and income is distributed among the factors of production. This is the income distribution that the market itself brings about, in the absence of any private or public intervention in the competitive process of production and exchange. Following Part III, we discussed many economic forces in greater detail. To place these details in their proper perspective, we have constructed a chart, Figure 23.1, that illustrates the role of each force in determining the income distribution.

Each of the arrows in Figure 23.1 represents a behavioral or technological relationship that we examined in the preceding chapters. They can be viewed as

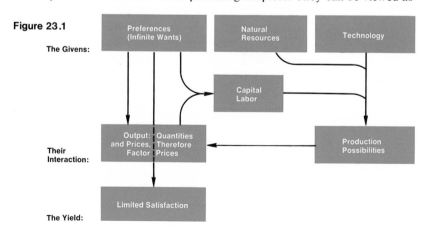

Figure 23.1

The Givens:
Preferences (Infinite Wants)   Natural Resources   Technology

Capital Labor

Their Interaction:
Output: Quantities and Prices, Therefore Factor Prices   Production Possibilities

The Yield:
Limited Satisfaction

equations that must be solved simultaneously. In a system of simultaneous equations, the solution value for each variable depends on the solutions for the other variables.

The following set of conditions are given:

Tastes
Natural resources
Capital
Labor
Technology

All of these conditions except the availability of natural resources are subject to change by human decisions. Even the known quantity of natural resources can, as we have seen, be increased by discovery. But at any point in time it is convenient to regard these factors as given. Together they determine the level and distribution of output among alternative goods and services.

The distribution of output determines the distribution of factor income. And the distribution of factor income, subject to the tastes of consumers, determines in turn the distribution of output. All are simultaneously determined. The end product or yield is not goods produced, or income received, but a distribution of utility among the individuals in the society derived from the process of production and consumption. This utility is always less than it might be if the resources of the economy were more bountiful, if technology were more productive, or if society were less desirous of material satisfaction as opposed to the other possibilities offered by life.

The most obvious interaction among these forces has been pointed out. The income distribution clearly affects the composition of output. Luxury goods will be produced in great quantities if the income distribution is very unequal. The composition of output can then be changed by income redistribution. This is true even if the redistribution takes place among people with similar incomes. If one person enjoys books and another enjoys autos, a redistribution of income from one to the other will change the composition of output.

But the composition of output in turn determines the income distribution. Producing more autos and fewer books means higher wages for steelworkers, glass workers, rubber workers, and lower wages for editors and lumberjacks. So the composition of output and the income distribution are *simultaneously determined*. A model of general equilibrium has a solution in which the value of any variable depends on *all* the structural relations in the system. That is what we attempt to show in Figure 23.1.

We have also drawn a more complete chart, Figure 23.2, to emphasize how all the relationships affect the final solution. This chart is designed to show how each decision affects all other decisions and how the result of all the economic activity is a distribution of limited satisfaction (or welfare). This more complete chart allows us to examine the effect of a change in any of the givens on the result; in other words, to see the allocation of the limited satisfaction. For example, a change in tastes in favor of automobiles and against books may well lead to the following results: The price of autos rises, that of books falls; the prices of steel, rubber, glass, and other commodities used in automobile production rise. The prices of paper, ink, leather, and other items used in book production fall. The incomes of land owners, foresters, and paper makers fall. The net result of the change in tastes toward automobiles and away from books is that a lot of people are made better off and a lot of people worse off. Those who are made best off are those who make autos but like to consume books (the relative price of which falls). Those made worst off are those who make books but like autos.

What about changes in technology? Suppose that new techniques, such as photo offset, greatly increase the productivity of factors employed in the production of books, while automobile technology remains unchanged. The change in technology shifts out the PPC, more in the direction of books than that of autos. A new solution will be found that can yield more of both goods or more of one, less of the other, depending on taste. If tastes are such that the demand for any good is proportional to income, it is likely that the price of books will fall relative to the price of autos, and that output of both books and automobiles will increase with that of books increasing most. The change in techniques can influence the book producers' demand for factors of production in different ways. It is possible that the new technology will make capital more productive relative to labor; or the reverse may be true. The different kinds of changes will have different implications for the distribution of income between labor and capital. As the big picture shows, all markets are interconnected just as the tides of the sea are part of one interrelated flow of ocean currents. No disturbance anywhere in the economy is likely to occur without repercussions elsewhere. A change in one market leads to changes in other markets. The end result is a reallocation not only of output but also of satisfaction. Income distribution is subject to the winds of trade.

Figure 23.2   The Big Picture of the Economy (More Detail)

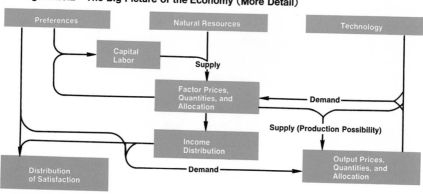

Income Distribution

Once equilibrium has been achieved, it is appropriate to ask, *Who gets the income?*

This question has two important dimensions. The first concerns the share of national income going to the different factors of production. This is termed the *functional distribution of income.* It is concerned with the distribution of national income among capital, labor, and natural resources. The second dimension has to do with the way in which national income is divided among individuals and households in the economy. This is termed the *personal distribution of income.*

Economists interested in the process of resource allocation, technological change, and economic growth are most concerned with the functional distribution of income. Economists interested in social welfare are concerned with the personal distribution of income. The bridge between the two has to do with the distribution of ownership of assets and the relative productivity of those assets. If all the assets are owned by a few individuals or households, then even if the distribution of income among physical capital, human capital, and natural resources is approximately equal, the distribution of personal income can be very unequal.

But if all individuals owned capital, natural resources, and human capital in equal quantities, they would all receive the same income. Then the functional distribution of income would be of academic interest only and would have no social importance.

It might be useful to look at some actual numbers to see how these two ways of looking at the distribution of income differ. In Table 23.1, we have listed the distribution of income by functional share in the United States for the years 1929 and 1969.

Table 23.1   Functional Distribution of Income in the United States

Factor	Income (Billions of Dollars) 1929	Income (Billions of Dollars) 1969	Share (Percent of Total) 1929	Share (Percent of Total) 1969
Wages and Salaries	50.4	509.8 ⎤	58.9	73.1
Fringe Benefits	0.7	54.4 ⎦		
Income of Self-Employed	9.0	50.2	10.4	6.5
Farm Income	6.2	16.1	7.1	2.1
Rental Income	5.4	21.6	6.2	2.8
Corporate Profits before Tax	10.5	88.7	12.2	11.5
Net Interest	4.5	30.6	5.2	4.0
Total	86.8	771.5	100.0	100.0

Source: US Department of Commerce

From Table 23.1, we can see that labor not only gets the lion's share of output but that this share has grown since 1929. It is important to remember that farm income and income of the self-employed are partly payments to labor and partly payments to capital. Thus total payments to labor in 1969 were more than the 73 percent indicated in Table 23.1.

But the functional division of income tells us little about inequality. To see how income is actually distributed among people, we must be concerned with their total money incomes, not the sources of that income. Table 23.2 shows the distribution of total money income to families in 1947 and 1969.

Redistributing Income

The figures in Table 23.2 do not result solely from the working of the market economy. Some redistribution of income as well is represented in those figures. How is the redistribution accomplished?

The most typical method of redistributing income is through government taxation and expenditure. There are three basic redistributive devices that are generally used. These are (1) outright redistribution of money from the rich to the general population; (2) cash payments to those thought to be needy according to specific characteristics such as age, infirmity, number of dependents, and employment status; (3) payments in the form of specific commodities (or subsidized commodity prices) to the general population or the poor. Table 23.2 includes the latter two forms of payments received by the poor, but it does not take account of income taken from everyone, but particularly the rich, in the form of income tax payments. Let us look at these three devices in some detail.

INCOME TAXES. The major device for redistributing money from the rich to

Table 23.2   US Families by Total Money Income, 1947 and 1969

Total Money Income	1969 Thousands of Families	Percent	1947 Thousands of Families	Percent
Under $2,000	2,404	4.7	10,203	27.4
$2,000 to $3,999	5,075	9.9	15,528	41.7
$4,000 to $5,999	5,785	10.3	7,187	19.3
$6,000 to $7,999	7,007	13.7 ⎱	3,322	8.9
$8,000 to $9,999	7,389	14.4 ⎰		
$10,000 to $14,999	13,682	26.7 ⎱		
$15,000 to $24,999	8,005	15.6 ⎰	1,008	2.7
Over $25,000	1,889	3.6 ⎰		
Total	51,237	100.0	37,237	100.0

Source: US Department of Commerce/Bureau of the Census, Series P-60, No. 70

the population at large is the income tax. Most countries have adopted progressive income taxes. A *progressive tax* is one that taxes a larger percentage of the income of the rich than of the poor. Progressive income taxes generally leave some small amount of income free from taxation. Higher levels of income are taxed at higher rates and the rates increase as income increases. Figure 23.3 shows how the US income tax works for a married family with two children. Income before tax is measured on the horizontal axis, income after tax on the vertical axis. The difference between the two lines (shaded area) represents tax payments as a function of pretax income (assuming a standard deduction). It is clear that the size of the tax payment is an increasing fraction of income.

Some social scientists have noted that the greatest increase in tax rates occurs at the point where taxes are first paid. There the tax rate changes from 0 to 14 percent of additional income. These scientists have suggested that one simple way to redistribute income from the rich to the poor is to continue the tax function at this point so that people with very low income receive payments from the tax system. This solution is represented in Figure 23.4, the shaded area denoting *negative tax* payments to those with low incomes.

INHERITANCE TAXES. Even after income is taxed progressively, many countries, including the United States, tax inheritance as well. This can be rationalized by noting that vast fortunes can be built through loopholes in the income tax law and that the inheritance tax guarantees that a good piece of all large fortunes gets paid to the state. The inheritance tax is probably justified on grounds of equity, however. Even though income is taxed progressively, it is possible, through savings, to build large fortunes. Our inheritance laws are designed to prevent these fortunes from being parlayed into monumental fortunes that create a moneyed class. The law effectively tells the wealthy, "Money is for consumption, not for the creation of dynasties."

The Distributive Effect of Expenditures

Taxes by themselves do not tell the whole story of how the government affects the distribution of income. Expenditures affect that distribution as well. In a

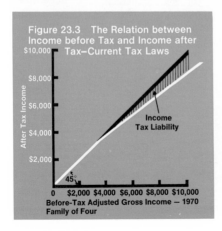

Figure 23.3   The Relation between Income before Tax and Income after Tax—Current Tax Laws

Income Tax Liability

Before-Tax Adjusted Gross Income — 1970 Family of Four

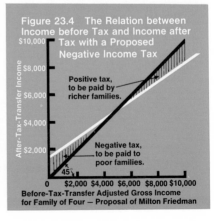

Figure 23.4   The Relation between Income before Tax and Income after Tax with a Proposed Negative Income Tax

Positive tax, to be paid by richer families.

Negative tax, to be paid to poor families.

Before-Tax-Transfer Adjusted Gross Income for Family of Four — Proposal of Milton Friedman

number of countries the middle class pays a disproportionately high share of income taxes. Taken at face value, this would suggest that the effect of government policy was to make the middle groups worse off relative to the others. But if we look at the other side of the coin, government expenditures in such countries also heavily favor the middle class. The poor are taxed little and receive few benefits, the middle class is taxed more and receives more benefits, while the upper class is taxed little but receives few benefits. Thus what appears to be a partially progressive (from lower to middle income) and partially regressive (from middle to upper income) fiscal distribution system is in fact virtually a *proportional* system. The net benefits and taxes balance out among the income groups.

TRANSFER PAYMENTS. It is more difficult to determine the distributive effect of many kinds of government expenditures than of taxes, though some direct expenditures to specific individuals are easily identifiable. These are called transfer payments, many of which are designed quite clearly to favor lower income groups. For example, a whole class of payments to the poor exists, payments that depend upon particular qualifications of the recipient. Apparently the electorate feels that some poor are more needy than others and restricts eligibility for cash payments to those who satisfy certain well-defined criteria. Among these criteria are age (with both very young and very old favored), disability, sex, previous work experience, and location of residence. Poor people who do not have the appropriate qualifications receive no payments from the government. This form of redistribution differs from the negative income tax noted above in that the negative tax would pay money to all the poor, not just to those deemed worthy of support according to criteria in addition to poverty. Since it costs money to determine who satisfies the appropriate requirements, it has been claimed that the negative tax will be cheaper to administer. In some areas, for example, one of the current forms of welfare, aid to dependent children, requires that payments be made only to families without fathers. In these areas, inspectors are employed to visit recipients at unannounced times to see if fathers in fact are present. Aside from how one feels about the propriety of such visits, such inspectors cost money.

Another difference between the negative tax and many of the present welfare schemes concerns the economic incentive to work. Under the negative income tax, the more one earns the more he can keep. Many current programs attempt to minimize welfare payments by subtracting all outside earnings from the size of the welfare check. Thus every $1 earned by a welfare recipient leads to a welfare check that is $1 smaller. There is no incentive for the recipient to work harder because there is a 100 percent tax on all his additional earnings. Encouraging people to work through a negative income tax program may actually lower the benefits paid out, even though these benefits will go to people who are substantially better off than are those who receive today's payments. Research is currently being conducted to determine the potential effects of a negative tax proposal on work effort.

PUBLIC GOODS. A third set of redistributive devices includes those goods the government buys and provides below cost to the public. These are the bulk of government expenditures. Some of these, such as education, parks, and police protection, are provided to the whole population, whereas others, such as Medicare, food stamp programs, health clinics, and rent supplements, are provided only to certain poor or otherwise needy people.

Why should we give the poor particular commodities rather than money to spend as they choose? After all, we demonstrated in Chapter 8 that a consumer is better off if he has the freedom to choose how to spend his income. That argument suggests that if we gave money to the poor, they could choose to buy the commodities we now give them or they could choose other commodities if those other commodities made them happier. Why do we restrict the possibilities for happiness by giving particular commodities rather than generalized purchasing power?

Many rationalia can be offered. First, the sovereign body may feel paternalistic toward the poor. They may feel that the poor are incapable of making decisions properly and if given income instead of goods, they would not buy enough food, housing, and medical care. Second, they may feel that their responsibility toward the poor does not demand that they make the poor happy, but only that they provide them with food, shelter, and other essentials. That is, the majority of the electorate may feel unhappy if the poor have good television but poor food, even if the poor are happier that way. The electorate may feel that for their own satisfaction it is only necessary to house and feed the poor and that it is immaterial that the poor prefer other commodities to food and shelter.

Another group of laws attempts to prevent the poor from entering into undignified contracts. These laws include legislation concerning minimum wage rates and maximum interest rates. Such laws are constructed with either a lack of knowledge about supply and demand or from a belief that monopoly profits can be eliminated in this fashion.

Equity and Efficiency
Equity considerations lead us to tamper with the market mechanism. There is no way to tax the rich without taxing income or wealth. Either way, the prices faced by individuals are changed by the tax laws and inefficiency results. People make decisions differently with tax laws present than they do in the absence of such laws. In Chapter 22 we outlined the nature of the inefficiency that results from this kind of tax policy. It appears, then, that there can be a fundamental conflict between efficiency and equity. The electorate must choose between these two goals because it may be impossible to attain them both simultaneously. The choice goes beyond the conventional limits of economic analysis. Economists can present the nature of the choice in practical terms — the costs of redistribution in terms of total output lost — but it is the voter who must choose.

The choice involves comparing income levels with income distributions. Do we prefer a world in which X has 100 apples and Y ten apples to one in which they both have 50?

Many socioeconomic problems require such a comparison. Unions may be able to raise the wage rate of their members by exerting monopoly power over employers. This leads, we have seen, to an "inefficient" allocation of resources and a waste of potential utility. But there is no question that it makes *some people* better off (the union members). An economist is in no position to say whether the increase in wage rates brought about by the union will increase or decrease social welfare. Welfare is redistributed in such a way that someone's utility increases as someone else's decreases. There is no objective way to compare these utilities. But it may be possible to point out the allocative implications of the change in wage rates. Since political decisions depend in part on such calculations, a branch of economics called *welfare economics* exists to explain the effect of such decisions on income distribution, output, employment, and growth.

Income Distribution and the Political Marketplace
We have seen how the economic marketplace automatically allocates resources and distributes income and we have noted the efficiency requirements for that allocation. Those who are dissatisfied with the result may turn to the political marketplace for redress of grievances. The citizenry may decide that it wishes to reallocate income. The voters are forced to make a subjective decision concerning the amount of income they wish each person to have. Usually, the vote determines the rules within which individuals are free to maximize their utility rather than a specific allocation of goods. Welfare economics exists to remind us that such decisions must be made. But it does not give us any criteria to use in making these decisions. How much should we take from Peter to pay Paul? Who knows? The sovereign body decides such matters in a way that depends on its moral values. The sovereign body must attempt to maximize social welfare by making comparisons of utility between people. It should be pointed out that even in the case where there is no redistribution, this implies that the sovereign body prefers the existing distribution to all others since it always has the power to change it. Of course, there is no guarantee that the political marketplace reflects the people's desires any more than does the economic marketplace. Dictators, oligarchies, and even popular majorities may impose their views of equity on the rest, distorting the process of production and income distribution to their own advantage.

Recall the concept of the social compact introduced in Chapter 1. Individuals were shown to sacrifice certain freedoms if the mutual sacrifice of all served to increase the welfare of each. Persons might choose, for example, to buy social insurance (social security). Under an insurance scheme in which benefits are proportional to need, those with relatively low incomes tend to draw a larger share of the benefits than they bear in costs. Although our previous analysis tells us that allocative inefficiency is likely to result from such a program, the citizens may decide that they prefer a world with the greater income security of such insurance than a world without it. Does this make sense? If the citizenry is happier with the "inefficient" result after the social insurance scheme is put into operation than they are with the "efficient" results before it, then *the voters must feel that those with increased utility gained more than the others lost through decreased utility.* Thus the total utility of society has been thought to increase after the redistribution of income resulting from social insurance. The loss due to inefficiency may not be as great as the gain due to reallocation.

Economists, therefore, have no more qualifications than students to decide what is equitable for society, let alone how we should trade equity for efficiency. There is some cost in terms of goods foregone that makes us balk at moving toward a more equitable distribution of income, regardless of how we define equity. Where does this leave us? Standards of justice are subjective. Equity is what people think it is. Only 100 years ago, most of the advantaged persons in even the wealthiest countries would have argued that the poor were poor because they were lazy, promiscuous, unintelligent, or drunkards. To give them more than token charity would be to "pour money down the drain." Charity itself was felt to be at best good for the soul but not for the economy. Today attitudes have changed. Poverty is being viewed increasingly as a vicious circle in which people may be poor because of their environment rather than vice versa. Meanwhile economic progress has increased average incomes, enhancing the ability and willingness of the advantaged members of society to pay for improved conditions for the poor. Moreover, such contributions no longer reflect simply charity but also the recognition by many of the complex interdependent nature of society. Others' poverty may affect one's own living standard in many ways. Equity is taking on broader connotations over time, influencing demands by society on the body politic for redistributive measures. But given that different people have different morals, there continue to be disputes about what equity really is. Imperfect political processes must somehow hammer out customs for each society that permit practical decisions to be made about income distribution.

Questions

1. The average income of every man, woman, and child in the United States today is about $3,500. How much lower would you be willing to make that figure in order to bring about what you consider to be an equitable distribution of income? Is it possible that the means necessary to give you your desires would lower output by more than the amount you wish to sacrifice?

2. Outline the conventional means of redistributing income by public action. Note their relative advantages.

3. Note the differences between the functional and the size distribution of income and their social implications.

Concepts Discussed

equity	progressive tax
eminent domain	negative income tax
functional distribution of income	welfare economics
size distribution of income	

VIII International Trade

People of the same trade seldom meet
together, even for merriment and diversion,
but the conversation ends in a conspiracy
against the public, or in some contrivance
to raise prices.

ADAM SMITH

Trade is what economics is all about. Trade between members of different nations, *international trade,* is just a special case of the trading activities we have already discussed. In the next three chapters we analyze various aspects of international trade and apply the previously discussed criteria of efficiency to the situations that result from several kinds of trading behavior.

In Chapter 24, we present the pure theory of trade. We discuss the benefits to both parties that can be derived from trade and point out why no nation has to fear that another will be able to undersell it in the production of all commodities. We note how different resources will make different nations relatively more efficient at producing some commodities than others and why each nation should be content to allow foreigners to produce those commodities at which they have a relative efficiency advantage. We point out how the total goods available for consumption in all countries can be increased if free trade is permitted, but that the distribution of these goods may be such that some people are worse off with free trade than without it.

Because of the effects of national trade policies on income distributions, such policies are subjects for political controversy. In Chapter 25, we explore how restrictive trading policies can alter income distributions both within and between nations, and we conjecture about the political implications of these economic realities.

Most of this book contains analyses of frictionless worlds, the simplest models available to describe the results we wish to present. Sometimes, however, discussions of friction are useful. Cases occur in which the predictions of the frictionless model would be seriously misleading or in which a study of the friction reveals something important that we otherwise would not understand. Thus in Chapter 29, considerable time is spent discussing costs of information. Uncertainty about the future plays a large role in Chapters 17 and 35.

Chapter 26 is concerned with transportation costs. First, the analysis of international trade contained in Chapters 24 and 25 is modified with the addition of these costs. Then we describe how they are important in explaining the location of industry and population. We note how the location of these activities within an urban core might be determined and present a capsule of the economic history of a growing city. Some insights into the economics of ghettos, suburbia, high-rise apartments, and school segregation are offered. From the vantage of Chapters 24 and 25, transportation costs can be viewed merely as friction—a nuisance that makes the analysis more difficult but explains nothing more about the pure theory of trade and trading policy. Yet when studied by themselves, as in Chapter 26, transportation costs are seen to be important determinants of why the world looks the way it does.

24 The Open Economy: the Theory of Trade between Separated Markets

When Marco Polo brought samples of the silks and spices of the Orient to the fairs of Europe he was behaving like any other merchant in search of profit. Yet the activity of traders such as he brought about revolutions in welfare that affect us even today. The word "exotic" originally referred to foreign commodities. Its current meaning gives us a good idea of the value that men have placed historically on consuming intriguing and different commodities from abroad. With exchange between countries now commonplace, stores around the world are stocked with radios and cameras from Japan, textiles and toys from Hong Kong, woolens, records, and whiskey from England, hams from Poland, caviar from Russia, coffee from Brazil, spices from the Orient, food and appliances from the United States, and, in most places, cigars from Cuba. These goods must give more pleasure to buyers than do domestic substitutes. This suggests that there would be a great loss in utility to any country forced to do without them. If it were also forced to do without foreign raw materials, many domestically fabricated goods would be much more expensive. Apparently copper from Chile, iron ore from Canada, bauxite from Guyana, tin from Bolivia, and gold from South Africa are much cheaper than they would be from any other country. Use of these foreign materials for domestic production lowers the price of the final commodities in which they are incorporated. Therefore we can say that there appear to be significant gains from trade.

Some claim, however, that there are losses from trade as well. Because foreign wages are lower than those in the United States, some goods can be produced more cheaply abroad. And the purchase of these cheaper foreign goods by Americans denies jobs and incomes to America's own laborers and to American employers who pay "fair" wage rates. It is claimed that the US steel industry cannot survive in the face of foreign competition; that more and more foreign automobiles, textiles, agricultural products, and petroleum will soon be imported, to the detriment of domestic industry. Should this be allowed to happen?

American objections to goods produced abroad are echoed in other countries. Even the most efficient nations in Europe cannot compete with the United States in the production of goods that require vast amounts of capital, highly educated labor, or complex systematic organization of production. Thus domestic industries in all countries fear foreign competition, even as these countries' consumers enjoy foreign products. How can we compare these losses to the gains from trade? Are we better off with greater or lesser freedom in the movement of goods and productive factors across national borders? Will local firms be able to respond to the challenge of foreign competition and lower costs, or must they go out of business? Will more jobs be created in industries that sell goods abroad than are lost by industries forced to shut down because of foreign competition? To whom do the gains and losses from trade accumulate? These are some of the questions that will be touched upon in this chapter. In subsequent chapters, we examine questions about nationalism and trade policy, balance of payments deficits, and the role of gold and the dollar in international exchange. Trade is clearly an area of great interest to the world's politicians. Their decisions as to the openness of our lives to foreign commodities affect every citizen. It is therefore important that we understand how and why these decisions are made.

The Uses of Diversity

The advantages of free trade in a single marketplace have been shown in previous chapters. Here we discuss trade between markets that are physically separated. The most important characteristic of separation is that the markets do not share the same factors of production. Each region has its own natural resources, its own labor, and its own capital. Later we show how labor and capital can migrate in response to price differentials among regions. But the present discussion of gains and losses from trade refers only to trade between different geographical regions, each having fixed factor supplies. These regions can be *within* a single country or can be separated by a national boundary. Here we are not interested in where political lines are drawn between regions, but only in how the separation of markets for factors affects resource allocation. The role of national boundaries in trade is discussed in Chapter 25.

Trade and exchange are what economics is all about. When is it profitable to use up resources in producing commodities? When should one sacrifice guns to buy butter? Early in the book, we showed how the answers to such questions revolve around relative costs and values. If a commodity is worth more than it costs, we should buy it. The profitability of such a transaction does not depend on whether one of the participants is a foreigner or not. It depends upon whether the two parties would assign different relative values to the two commodities in the absence of trade.

Viewed in this way, international trade becomes merely another example of trade between individuals, some of whom happen to be foreign. If A thinks an apple is worth two oranges and B feels an orange is worth two apples, A should trade an orange to B in return for an apple. Both parties will be made better off by this. Adding the fact that A and B reside in different countries does not change that conclusion. Whenever two people assign different relative values to commodities, there are gains to be had from trading. In equilibrium—when no further trading is profitable—all parties must assign the same relative values to commodities. The theory of international trade, we will see, is merely a special case of the theory of exchange. It is useful to examine that special case in order to understand the implications of exchange when a national trading policy is pursued.

Trade and Efficiency

Trade theory is developed within the context of a perfectly competitive economy. Only with perfect competition do prices represent social costs. We know that at a perfectly competitive equilibrium, production for a particular country will take place at some point on the production possibility frontier (PPF) and that the slope of the frontier at that point will equal the relative prices faced by the consumer. The PPF can be viewed as a statement of the terms on which it is possible to trade, one good for another, with nature.

Indeed, the entire production process can be viewed as a trade with nature. We are able to trade land, labor, and capital for textiles. The production process receives the input of factors and returns an output of commodities. The production frontier for textiles and computers, for example, tells how it is possible to trade textiles for computers with nature—by withdrawing certain factors from one production process and reallocating them to another. The rate at which such a trade takes place we have called the social cost of the commodity.

The possibility of international trade allows an economy an alternative way of trading computers for textiles. In trade theory, economies compare the two ways of acquiring textiles—by trading with nature or by trading with other nations—and choose the cheaper way. Of course, the trade with nature involves domestic production of textiles whereas the trade with another country does not. But in trade theory the location of production is important only through its effect on relative cost. That is, we should find out whether the international cost is cheaper than the domestic social cost. If so, we will be better off to sell computers abroad and buy textiles than to shrink the domestic computer industry and expand that for textiles. Such purchases from abroad are called *imports*; sales abroad of domestic production are called *exports*. Once we have determined that textiles are cheaper abroad than at home, we know that if we trade, we will have more computers left over than if we reallocate production, though in both cases we get the same amount of textiles. This illustrates that gains from trade can exist.

If all countries or regions are already producing at efficient points on their production possibility curves, one might wonder how it is possible for there to be gains from trade *for all*. If one region is enabled to consume more than the limits of its production possibility frontier (PPF), is not some other region forced inside its own PPF? The answer is no, *if* at the outset the social costs of various

DAVID RICARDO (1772-1823)   Credit for the first really theoretical exposition of economics in English should probably be given to David Ricardo. Though he was not an academic like Smith and Malthus, his long and productive career as a man of affairs (starting at age 14 in his father's stockbrokerage firm) gave him many insights about the basic structure and functioning of England's eighteenth- and nineteenth-century economic system. He wrote pamphlets and speeches at a prodigious rate (notably some on paper currency and on Bank of England policy) but made his major theoretical expression in his *Principles of Political Economy and Taxation* (1817).

Like Malthus, Ricardo was trying to identify some of the economic forces at work in the Industrial Revolution in England. Reasoning, as had Smith, that the capacity of a nation to grow is determined by the amount of available productive capital and holding that the best policies were those facilitating capital accumulation, Ricardo set about an analysis of the determinants of capital formation. To him, accumulation derived from profits. In order to isolate the prospects for profits he had to show how society's product was divided up among the various types of income receivers: laborers (wages), landlords (rent), and capitalists (profits). To do this he had to devise a theory of value much as Smith had had to devise one. Presuming that commodities had to have use before they could have value, Ricardo argued that value was determined by the amount of labor effort contributed to generating a unit of a commodity, including that imbedded in the capital goods that aided in production. Clearly there were problems; for example, differing qualities of labor, art objects, and gems, a standard of value, and various forms of capital goods. Nonetheless, his theory of value lasted for many years and formed much of the foundation for the work of Marx and others. Working from his labor theory, accepting Malthus's theories of population, and reasoning in the light of the law of diminishing returns (which he was among the first to enunciate clearly), Ricardo alleged that the long-run prospects for capitalist development in England and indeed in most growing countries were dim. Wages and rents would take an increasingly larger share of the total product, leaving smaller amounts for saving and investing. The whole system was thus doomed to stagnation at best. Adding to this long-range gloom were his later pronouncements about the possibility of the displacement of labor by machines, a condition that could result in the progressive unemployment of much of the laboring class. This idea was seized on by Marx as a starting point for some of his own analysis.

For Ricardo the escape hatches from his pessimistic system lay in technical

---

commodities differ among various regions. If social costs do initially differ, it is possible for the two regions to trade at some price between their own independent prices and both be better off.

For example, if the domestic cost of 1,000 tons of textiles is three computers in the United States and one computer in Hong Kong, it is possible for the United States to trade two computers to Hong Kong for 1,000 tons of textiles. The United States has attained an amount of textiles for two computers that would cost three computers if domestically produced. And Hong Kong has received two computers for an amount of textiles that could be converted into

change and foreign trade, and it was in connection with the latter that he developed his theories of mutual advantage that undergirded so much free trade theory in the nineteenth and twentieth centuries. Adam Smith, in his attack on the mercantilists and in his pursuit of the advantages of a widened market, had argued that mutual benefits were to be gained from international specialization and division of labor. His argument had presumed that each country or people had some specialty or specialties in which they were more efficient than all other people or nations, for example, bananas from Honduras and computers from the U. S. They enjoyed an *absolute* advantage over anyone else and could benefit themselves and others by specialization and trade. Ricardo asserted the rather startling idea that trade could and would bring gains even if some countries were more efficient than others in the production of *everything*. He reasoned that not all of the advantages would be of the same magnitude and that the more efficient country could benefit itself and everyone else if it concentrated on those commodities in which its productive advantages were the greatest.

Ricardo's theory of comparative costs (or advantage) worked as follows. Suppose that in England it takes the labor of 100 men to produce a quantity of cloth and the labor of 120 men to produce a quantity of wine that will exchange for that cloth. If Portugal, however, finds that she can produce the same amount of wine with 80 men and the cloth with 90 men, it would be to the advantage of both England and Portugal to trade. England would get wine (costing her 120 men at home) through the efforts of 100 men producing cloth, whereas Portugal would get cloth (costing 90 men at home) for the labor of 80 men whose wine output would be traded. Ricardo held that each consumer's country would have more product and that capitalists could employ their capital more efficiently. However, although this theory provides a powerful intellectual justification for international trade based on comparative costs, it says nothing about the actual prices at which that trade will occur. This task was left for John Stuart Mill and later trade theorists.

Ricardo in a real sense embodied the whole English classical school although he did not write its great synthetic work. (That was John Stuart Mill's contribution.) Ricardo's style of abstract analysis set the standard and form for much of Anglo-Saxon economics in the nineteenth and twentieth centuries and still provides a model for many deductive expositions in the discipline. Lean, clinical, and highly refined analysis ("high theory") is still regarded as the highest type of effort in the field, an opinion largely due to the influences of David Ricardo's *Principles*.

---

only one computer at home. *Thus where social costs differ, trade may allow both countries to consume amounts of goods that lie outside their production frontiers. Both can profit from trade.*

The power of this idea and the effect it has had on the world's standard of living is hard to overstate. David Ricardo, an English economist, was the first to provide a rigorous proof that trade could benefit both countries. Despite the insights of earlier writers, the popular view prior to Ricardo had been that the world economic pie was predetermined and that the bigger the slice earned by one country, the less available to all others. National policies were designed to try to guarantee that all profits stayed at home. Ricardo showed how the effect of these policies was to inhibit trade and to lower well-being. The fact is that the pie analogy is not accurate; trade can profit both parties. Russians, with much cheap caviar and few fine cigars, are happy to be able to trade with Cubans, who have many fine cigars but no caviar. Both countries can be better off from trade and both can consume goods in amounts that it would be impossible for them to produce. It is small wonder that economists have long been staunch advocates of the free movement of commodities across international borders. It may be good politics to point out the advantages of trade accruing to the other guy, but it is bad economics. Trade benefits both parties.

The Graphics of the Gains from Trade

It is quite simple to show the gains from trade graphically. Assume a country has attained an efficient equilibrium on its own production possibility frontier, say, at point *B* in Figure 24.1. Remember that the slope of the PPF at *B* denotes the social cost of textiles in terms of computers, that is, the number of computers that must be sacrificed to get another unit of textiles. Assume that the international price of textiles in terms of computers is different and that reasonable amounts can be traded without affecting that price. If production is to stay at point *B*, the possibilities for trade must be indicated by moving from *B* along some line whose slope is the international cost of textiles. *LBF* is such a line in Figure 24.2. Any point on *LBF* is attainable by trade. *LBF* might be called a *consumption possibility curve*. This means that if country *A* continues producing at point *B*, its consumption possibilities might extend well beyond its own production possibility frontier. *LBF* represents a new consumption possibility curve along which, we will assume, society is best off at point *F*, a point beyond the PPF. Under these circumstances, country A will be willing to export *GF* in computers in exchange for the importation of *BG* in textiles.

The consumption at point *F* will provide a better life than did the old level at point *B* without requiring any change in the structure of production. But this is

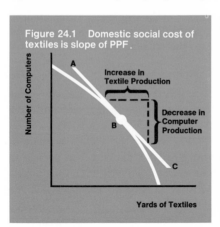

Figure 24.1   Domestic social cost of textiles is slope of PPF.

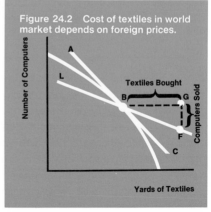

Figure 24.2   Cost of textiles in world market depends on foreign prices.

not the end of the process induced by the new possibilities of interregional or international trade. Readers will recall that at point B the private cost of production (indicated by the tangent to the production possibility curve AC) is *not* equal to the social cost of the commodities (indicated by the slope of LF). Note that because trade abroad is cheaper than trade with nature, the social cost has now become the foreign price. This is consistent with our practice of always defining social cost as the cost using the most efficient production process. In this case, foreign trade is a more efficient way of producing textiles than increasing domestic production. Because of the difference between social and private prices, the economy is not in equilibrium in Figure 24.2 even though it is better off at point F than at point B.

We have seen that the initial effect on the United States, for example, of a lower world price for textiles relative to computers is an increase in the consumption of textiles through the exportation of computers. Nevertheless, at the new social cost of textiles in terms of computers (GF/BG) the US producers are no longer in equilibrium at point B. Producers choose point B from all the attainable production points only when the slope of ABC represents the price of textiles. If LBF is the price of textiles, they will be tempted to shift resources away from the production of the now cheaper textiles toward the now relatively more expensive computers if the new international price ratio prevails in the domestic market.

Hence there will be a movement of production upwards along the production possibility frontier until that point at which private costs become equal to social costs once again. Computer production will be increased, textile production curtailed. Provided that the world international price ratio for the two commcdities is not altered by the entry of country A into international trade, the slope of the consumption possibility curve LF will not change. Under these circumstances producers will eventually wind up at point R (Figure 24.3) where their private cost of production (represented by the slope of the tangent to the PPF at that point) is precisely equal to the slope of the consumption possibility

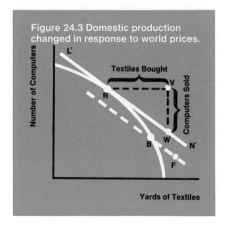

Figure 24.3 Domestic production changed in response to world prices.

curve $L'N'$ in Figure 24.3. The new consumer equilibrium will be that point on $L'N'$ that yields the greatest utility to those who have income to spend. We may suppose that this point is represented by W. Then the United States will export VW in computers in exchange for RV in textiles. Consumption has improved in two stages, first by moving from B to F in Figure 24.2, and then from F to W in Figure 24.3.*

Note the gains from trade. Point W has more computers and more textiles than point B. By switching production from B to R and trading to point W, consumption of both commodities can increase. Clearly, with more of both commodities, the country as a whole is better off; total consumption is higher regardless of how textiles and computers are valued.

It may be surprising to find that *both* countries can end up consuming more of *both* commodities. Both A and B can get more textiles *and* more computers. To see this graphically, look at Figure 24.4. Countries A and B produce and consume at points B and B' respectively in the absence of trade. Since the social cost of textiles at B is different from B', we know that trade would be profitable. If A and B trade the amounts indicated in Figure 24.4, it is possible for them to consume at points W and W' respectively, and these points are obviously superior to B and B' for both countries. Both countries get more of both goods. The geometry makes that quite clear.

What economic principles underlie that geometry? Note that the PPFs were drawn differently for the two countries. Country A's PPF is quite steep throughout, whereas country B's is relatively flat. This is because A has resources that are relatively well suited to producing computers while B is endowed with resources that are relatively well suited to textile production. The relative advantage a country may have in producing particular commodities is called its *comparative advantage*.

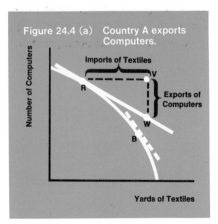

Figure 24.4 (a)   Country A exports Computers.

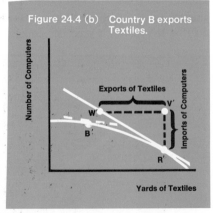

Figure 24.4 (b)   Country B exports Textiles.

*Those who read the appendix to Chapter 8 will recall that if there were only one consumer in country A, or if all consumers were identical, then points, B, F, and W represent points on successively higher consumer indifference curves, indicating successively higher levels of consumer utility. Clearly point W would be preferred to point B only if it provided a higher level of social welfare.

The Principle of Comparative Advantage

Comparative advantage is expressed in terms of the relative cost of producing tradeable goods. The principle says quite simply that no nation need fear that it has nothing to export since it is the *relative* cost of commodities that determines their tradeability. If computers are cheaper in terms of textiles for one country, then textiles must be cheaper in terms of computers for some other country. A country simply cannot be at a *relative* disadvantage in the production of all commodities. The definition of the word relative guarantees that. If one country takes twice as many computers to build a ton of textiles as another, then the other must take only half as many textiles to build the computers. If the ratios of costs of two commodities differ in two countries, one good must be relatively more expensive, the other relatively cheaper. As it is relative cost that corresponds to social cost, it is relative cost that is relevant for trade theory.

In our illustration above, we could think of the United States as having a comparative advantage in the production of computers vis-à-vis the rest of the world. Notice that nothing was said or had to be said in the example regarding the *absolute* cost of production of computers in terms of manhours, machine-hours, and the like. It was only necessary to demonstrate that in terms of textiles, computers could be produced more cheaply. The demonstration of this point by Ricardo proved the existence of the doctrine of comparative advantage. Countries trade and consume goods, not factors, so it is the price of goods in terms of each other that matters for trade, not the price of goods in terms of factors. Some areas of the world may be extremely inefficient producers in the sense that they use more manhours, etc., in the production of *all* commodities than do the most productive countries; nevertheless they can gain from international trade just as the productive countries can.

The theory of trade is useful in that it applies to the separate regions of a single nation as well as to commerce between nations. The previous analysis can be used to determine why, for example, the state of Montana should export raw copper to the state of Connecticut in exchange for copper wire, brass plumbing fixtures, and pipe from the Connecticut Valley. It also explains why agricultural products from the Ukraine are exchanged for manufactures from the Russian Republic. The advantages of individual specialization as championed in Adam Smith's doctrine of "division of labor" may be extended to regional and national specialization as well. This theory of regional specialization begun by Ricardo reached a high point in the twentieth century through the contribution of Swedish economists Eli Heckscher and Bertil Ohlin. Their argument is that various regions of the world are unequally endowed with natural resources, labor, and capital. They point out that factors of production may even be said to include climate, rainfall, and quality of the soil, in which some regions are relatively better equipped than others. For example, the arid regions of California and North Africa are well suited for the production of date palms, whereas the tropics excel in fruits, nuts, and sugar cane. Other regions are better suited to a completely different set of products, such as coal and iron ore producing regions of the northern Midwest of the United States and the Ruhr Valley. Since regional differences in resource endowments have partly accounted for the pattern of world settlement, it is not surprising that regional and national patterns of production tend to reflect these differences.

Comparative and Absolute Advantage

Think of the many different kinds of agricultural land that exist. Some is fertile — rich in minerals and rainfall, level and with no rocks — while other land is infertile — arid, parched, hilly, and rocky. The fertile land is better than the infertile land at the production of both corn and beef, as shown in Table 24.1, when an equal amount of complementary factors (labor and capital) is used on both plots of land. It is in fact ten times better at beef production and twenty times better at corn production. If these were two countries, one might feel initially that the country with fertile land need not import beef or corn as it can produce both more efficiently than can the other country. The country with infertile land should be able to export nothing because it is bad at producing everything. But this is obviously bad reasoning. Domestic output clearly will be higher in the infertile country if the land is used to produce something. How should it be used?

Consider the following. There are 10 acres of bad land in one country, 1 acre of good in another. Initially, both plots produce both corn and beef and no trade exists. The acre of good land produces 50 bushels of corn and 250 pounds of beef. The 10 acres of bad land produce 25 bushels of corn and 250 pounds of beef. Trade is thought by both countries to be impossible because of the inefficiency of one and the efficiency of the other.

But we have seen how trade is profitable whenever social costs differ. In this case, a speculator could observe the different social costs and make a bundle buying in one country and selling in the other. Enter Hiram Garsh. Who would guess that by dint of fast buying and selling of commodities he will make enough to buy a Cadillac and a Florida condominium? How does he do it? First, he observes that the fertile region is exchanging 5 pounds of beef for 1 bushel of corn (its social cost). He then notes from the *Farm Journal* that in the infertile region, 10 pounds of beef trade for 1 bushel of corn (the social cost of corn in the infertile country). It does not take Hiram a year of economics to tell that he has a chance to make a buck by trading beef and corn between the two markets. Since there are potential gains from trade whenever social costs differ, he sets out to secure these gains for himself.

Table 24.1 Output per Acre		
	Corn	**Beef**
Fertile Land	100 bushels	500 pounds
Infertile Land	5 bushels	50 pounds

Hiram first approaches the beef producers in the infertile country, promising for every 10 pounds of beef purchased 1 bushel of corn in exchange. That is the going price of beef in the infertile country. He takes the beef, drives it down the trail to the fertile country, and sells every 10 pounds for *2* bushels of corn net of weight loss from the drive (having nobly resisted the temptation to water the livestock heavily before weighing it at the time of sale). He then brings the corn back to the infertile country, repays the beef producers their *1* bushel per 10 pounds, and ends up with profits of nearly a bushel of corn for every 10 pounds of beef sold. Hiram has reaped the gains from trade. He continues to do this until beef starts to get as scarce in the infertile country as corn in the fertile country. Beef prices eventually rise in the infertile country and fall in the fertile country while corn prices rise in the fertile country and fall in the infertile country. The success story of Hiram Garsh is not lost on the crafty farmers in both regions. They observe the change in prices and adjust next year's planting accordingly. The fertile country produces more corn in response to higher corn prices and the infertile country produces more beef. By this time Hiram has turned the trading over to his son and retired with his wife, Cadillac, horse, and dog to his Florida sea-view apartment.

Thus we see that even an absolute efficiency advantage held by one area in the production of everything is not an obstacle to trade. *Relative* or *comparative* production costs matter. Though one country might be absolutely more efficient at the production of all commodities, it cannot be *relatively* more efficient at all. As long as *relative* costs differ, a country must have a comparative advantage in the production of at least one commodity.

Trade will have to be profitable if relative costs differ. Speculators will be able to make fortunes if they are allowed to buy and sell at different prices in the two markets. The story of Hiram Garsh illustrates a trading behavior called *arbitrage*. Arbitrage involves buying in cheap markets and selling simultaneously in expensive ones. This activity guarantees that commodities will get to the places where they are worth the most. It also guarantees that prices will be equal everywhere since the arbitrage increases demand where prices are low and supply where they are high.

History yields many examples of behavior like Garsh's, and many resulting fortunes. For example, when Perry opened Japan for trade with the outside world, the ratio of the price of gold to the price of silver was three inside Japan while it was sixteen in the rest of the world. A shrewd Japanese speculator took boatloads of gold to China and brought back boatloads of silver. This activity quickly changed the prices of gold and silver within Japan to correspond to those elsewhere. In the process, however, the speculator made such a fortune that he established a banking firm that is still one of Japan's largest.

Who Gets the Gains from Trade?
When the social costs of commodities differ in two areas, there are gains to be had from trade. These gains can be shared by the two countries or captured by

arbitragers. Since the different social costs will be reflected in different relative values in the two places, the movement of commodities from where they are worth less to where they are worth more can increase satisfaction. Who gets the extra satisfaction?

Consider again the case of Hiram Garsh. After his commodity transactions had changed relative prices, some farmers ceased producing the crop that had become inexpensive in their region and switched over to producing the good that had become expensive. This is what we hoped would happen if all the gains from trade were to be exploited. Farmers in the infertile country switched over entirely to beef production, producing 500 pounds per year, while farmers in the fertile country, specializing in corn, were able to produce 100 bushels. Before trade, total output in the two countries was 500 pounds of beef and 75 bushels of corn; with trade it is 500 pounds of beef and 100 bushels of corn. The reallocation of production due to the change in prices brought about by trade has allowed each country to specialize in the production of that commodity at which it has a comparative advantage. This specialization is responsible for the increase in total production of 25 bushels of corn. Though the infertile land is worse than the fertile land for producing all commodities, it is relatively worse at producing corn and therefore *relatively* better at producing beef.

Since the different products use factors in different proportions, the switch in production from one commodity to another changes factor prices. Increasing cattle production and decreasing corn production in the infertile country results in higher prices for cowboys, jeeps, branding irons, and Stetsons, whereas prices of tractors, plows, and farm laborers must fall. Of course, the reverse must happen in the fertile country where sales of the *Farm Journal* are booming and country music echoes from the plains. The changes in factor prices are responsible for the eventual attainment of equilibrium because they change the relative costs of the products in the two countries until they are equal.

We have noted that there are 25 extra bushels of corn now in existence. Who gets them? Hiram could capture them only so long as the relative prices remained different in the two areas. If trade is pursued until these prices are equal, there will be no profit for arbitragers. Who gets the gain depends upon what happens to factor prices. Land owners in the two regions may get part of the gains. Cowboys in the infertile country, tractor makers and laborers in the fertile country may all be better off. But what about the cowboys in the fertile country? Are they not worse off? Has the demand for their services not fallen?

The answer depends on how many cowboys can shift their occupations to become farm laborers. If the switch is easy, we may find that the increased demand for farm laborers raises wages sufficiently to tempt many cowboys to sell their boots and switch jobs. If cowboys become scarce as a result of this, their wage may rise. On the other hand, no cowboys may switch jobs. In this case, the decline in the demand for their services will lead to a lower wage for them. Thus the 25 bushels of extra corn need not be distributed equally around the two countries. The change in factor prices may make some people worse off even though more is being consumed in the aggregate.

Can we then be positive that free trade will increase satisfaction? No. If some people are made better off and others worse off, we would have to be able to compare the utilities of these people to arrive at a conclusion that is valid in the aggregate. We cannot do that. But because the trade increases total output, we know that prohibiting trade is inefficient. We know that with trade prohibited, there remain opportunities for making some people better off without making anyone else worse off. The problem with initiating trade is that resources may be reallocated in such a way that some people *are* made worse off. Although there are more goods for all, some may have less than before. And that explains the existence of opposition to free trade.

US steelworkers will be out of work if the United States imports steel rather than produces it. Textile firms may go bankrupt if textiles are imported. Clearly the steelworkers and the owners of the textile firms would prefer to have no imports. The rest of the citizens may prefer imports, however, because then they will have cheaper steel and textiles and therefore a higher standard of living. Also, if the United States increases computer production for export, computer prices may rise as the factors used for their production become more scarce. Domestic buyers of computers may become worse off because of this price increase.

Thus an analysis of the gains from trade is not a straightforward matter. We can show that more goods are available with trade than without, but we cannot tell for sure that this is an improvement in total welfare because we do not know who is getting these goods and how to compare their satisfaction with the dissatisfaction of those who may be made worse off because of trade. We can conclude' that trade policy will become a ticklish political issue as those who stand to gain do combat with those who stand to lose from any change in trade policy.

The Sources of Comparative Advantage

Comparative advantage is an elusive characteristic since it depends upon a number of interrelated factors, including the conditions of supply and demand in every trading region. Country A had a comparative advantage in computers only because its factor endowments and final demand tended to bring about a higher relative price for textiles before trade than did those of country B. However, it is quite possible to conceive of a circumstance under which the comparative advantage of country A could revert to country B without altering the production possibilities curves one iota. All that would be necessary is a very strong consumption bias in favor of computers in country A and textiles in country B. Under these circumstances country A would begin at a point far to the left on its production possibility curve, at a relatively high price of computers in terms of textiles. Country B, on the other hand, would be producing and consuming before trade at a point far down on its production possibility curve and at a relatively low price for computers in terms of textiles. Under these circumstances, the process of exchange would be reversed and sharp traders would begin by purchasing computers in country A and exchanging them for textiles in country B at a sizable profit until once again relative prices equalized. This illustrates how both production and consumption interact to bring about comparative advantage so that there is no *a priori* means of determining what a country's trade position will be simply by looking at its production possibility frontier.

Another way of looking at the problem is to observe the behavior of trade in country A when it is faced with three alternative international price ratios for computers and textiles. Looking at Figure 24.5, let us suppose that country A begins by producing and consuming at point *B* in the absence of international trade according to the consumption possibility curve *ABC*. If by chance the international price ratio is the same as the slope of *ABC*, there will be no reason for country A to enter into trade since nothing will be gained on the part of buyers or sellers by doing so. However, if the international price ratio is represented by the slope of *QRS*, so that computers are relatively more expensive abroad, then it is likely that country A will enter into trade and begin exporting computers and importing textiles until it reaches a production equilibrium at *R* and consumption equilibrium at a point such as *W*.

If, on the other hand, the international price ratio shows foreign textiles to be relatively more costly than computers, the reverse pattern of trade will take place. Country A will begin exporting textiles and importing computers until it achieves an equilibrium where the international price line *VTU* is just tangent to the production possibility curve at *T* and the new consumption point stabilizes at some point such as *X*. *In this diagram we see that the comparative advantage of country A depends on world prices as well as on the domestic conditions of supply and demand.* This is an important point. It is possible that if textiles become sufficiently expensive relative to computers in the world market, country A may become a complete specialist in textile production, producing at point *E* and importing all of its computers. Similarly, if computers become sufficiently

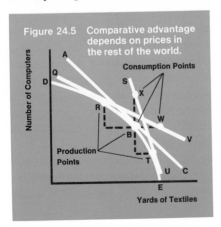

Figure 24.5 Comparative advantage depends on prices in the rest of the world.

expensive in the world market, it is conceivable that country A will become a complete specialist in computer production at point D on its production possibility frontier, importing all of its textile needs.

While such "corner solutions" do not alter the theory of comparative advantage, they occur in practice quite frequently among developing countries. Natural resource endowments often make such regions especially suited to the production of one or two major exports. With relatively high prices for capital and skilled labor, it is cheapest to import all manufactured goods. Under these circumstances complete specialization renders such countries relatively more vulnerable to the fluctuations in world prices. It is more difficult for them to react to such price changes by shifting their pattern of production away from coffee, cocoa, or copper into textiles or computers. Such countries, while experiencing *gains* from trade, may also be plagued by the *strains* caused by fluctuations in the price of their principal exports. Clearly, the greater the diversity of its production, the less vulnerable such an economy will be to the vicissitudes of world tastes and technology.

Achieving Equality in Relative Prices without Trade

There are methods of equalizing relative prices among regions or countries without exchanging commodities through trade. One of the most customary practices, which has already been mentioned above and which forms the basis of the following chapter, deals with barriers to trade imposed by commercial policy that artificially raise the price of imports and lower the price of exports. For example, in the case of country A in Figure 24.5 one method of avoid competition from textile imports would be to increase their price through a tariff in the exact amount of the initial price differential. Alternatively, it would be possible to place an export duty on computers of a like amount, either measure having the effect of shifting the international price observed by domestic producers to a slope exactly equal to that of line ABC. This is an artificial method of bringing about international price equality at the level of the consumer.

Another way, mentioned above, is through the movement of factors. In Chapter 26 on location and transportation we explore these movements further and see how they can bring about equalities in factor prices across regions. A third method would be for both production possibilities and tastes to converge between the two trading regions so that production possibility curves and consumer preferences would become similar in all regions. This could happen if new technological advances in production and transportation free a region from dependence on its own natural resources and if increased communications allow people to explore and acquire the tastes of others. If this occurs, then each region might again become self-sufficient with relative prices equalizing since all regions would tend to have identical production possibility and consumption possibility curves and identical consumer preferences. However, as long as production possibilities differ, no amount of convergence of tastes would eliminate the gains from trade. Similarly, as long as tastes remain different among regions, no amount of convergence of production possibilities could eliminate those gains.

In addition to these considerations, it is important to keep in mind the fact that transport costs constitute one of the great obstacles to interregional and international trade. With the advance of transport and communications technology, the lower cost of exchanging goods and services may tend to increase rather than decrease the gains from trade, despite the fact that tastes and technologies around the world seem to be following an amazingly similar evolution. So it is that despite the influence of the media in the United States that tend to fuse the market into a homogeneous consuming monolith, and despite the spread of manufacturing throughout the world in similar production units, international trade represents a greater share of national output than ever before.

Interregional and international trade are here to stay, constituting some of the most interesting economic forces in the world today. They are interesting not only because the exchange of goods and services gives each of us a stake in the welfare of all nations, but also because along with the trade of commodities there goes an exchange of concepts, systems of values, culture, and art. Such transactions enrich the lives of each participant in the marketplace of ideas just as trade in goods and services expands his material well-being. The international convergence of tastes that appears to be taking place hopefully represents a new culture comprised of the best of the old. If not, many new problems are in store for both social evangelists and social scientists.

Questions

1.   Can we show that trade allows an increase in the consumption of goods if relative prices differ across countries? Can we show that free trade unambiguously makes a country better off? What if the losers from trade received sufficient compensation from the gainers to be no worse off than before?

2.   How do arbitragers make money? Is anyone made worse off by their actions?

3.   If Japan has lower wage rates than the United States, will not the day arrive when there is nothing the United States can sell to Japan? If the Japanese are more efficient at producing everything than anyone else, is it possible for others to export to them?

4.   What are the sources of comparative advantage? Why do some countries export figs whereas others export computers?

Concepts Discussed

imports   comparative advantage
exports   arbitrage
gains from trade

25 The Open Economy: Trade Policy

Nationalism and the Pattern of Trade

Although the economist may see the world as an interlocking set of markets, to the political scientist it is a picture puzzle of nation states. To the historian it is not a fixed but a changing map on which boundary lines are in continual flux. But whatever its aspect on the map, one's own native land tends to evoke an emotional reaction that is often heralded in the mind by the roll of drums. This reaction, which we term *regionalism* within countries and *nationalism* between countries, provides the basis for more than just military or political rivalry. It is also used to justify interventions in the market mechanism that can have important implications for the pattern of resource allocation and social welfare.

This chapter takes us from trade theory to trade practice through a discussion of the importance of national frontiers in the process of exchange. We look at the implications of using national currencies for international transactions and how the rate at which one currency exchanges for another is determined. Then we examine the policy of fixed exchange rates and the economic consequences of commercial policy including the application of tariffs and quotas. In the process the reader is shown how in certain cases trade policies can work to the advantage of a single country and to the detriment of the rest of the world, provided that there is no retaliation from its trading partners.

The existence of nation states gives rise to national boundaries. Transactions between regions become conspicuous at the point where borders cut across the flow of trade. Even if world trade were conducted on a barter basis, the existence of frontiers would raise questions of national policy that economists must answer. Should goods and services be allowed to pass the frontier freely without regard to their place of origin or destination? The question is a real one, since the flow of commerce may be blocked easily by "robber barons" along waterways, turnpikes, or mountain trails, or by national governments at points of entry on a patrolled frontier. It is both physically easiest and politically least objectionable to tax the commerce of foreigners. Hence those who come from abroad to ply their wares have always tended to bear a disproportionately heavy share of the cost of government. Even today revenues on trade comprise a major source of tax receipts in developing countries.

Competition among nations has taken many forms. Initially it was believed that one nation could gain at the expense of others only through foreign war. Economic means such as the hiring of mercenaries were relied upon to increase one nation's military strength over that of another. In this respect the wealth of one nation was used to purchase troops that, by defeating other states, could increase the territory and therefore the wealth of the aggressor. Since payment had to be made using some form of money, gold and silver being the most common, it was believed that the power of a nation could be measured by the quantity of precious metals it owned. Precious metals were equivalent to an ability to wage war. On the basis of this belief, the object of national trade policies was to increase the amount of precious metals held at home. This policy is called *mercantilism*.

By the late Renaissance, the advent of new industrial and agricultural technology made it possible for emerging nation states to think in terms of other forms of aggrandizement. Countries such as France and England began to think in terms of investment in the internal production of goods and services as an alternative to the forcible acquisition of property from other states. Other countries such as Spain and Portugal continued to regard trade as a means of obtaining precious metals and thereby wealth and power.

At this time England was beginning to listen to pamphleteers such as Sir Thomas Mun, who wrote his famous treatise *England's Treasure by Forraign Trade* in 1664. In this work he pointed out that a country wishing to maximize its wealth should increase its domestic supply of resources by engaging in the exchange of goods that it holds in abundance for those that are scarce locally. He showed that this could be done through expanding "forraign trade." Since trade required seed capital, Mun advised the Crown to encourage even exports of gold, if that were what was necessary to purchase scarce goods from far countries. He pointed out correctly that it was not gold but the volume of goods and services a country could command that represented its true treasure. Having an abundance of goods to sell represents an ability to acquire gold and therefore to wage war. One need not acquire gold itself, but merely the capacity to earn gold. We have seen from Chapter 24 that it took several centuries to formalize these arguments in terms of trade theory. And although today's patterns of trade are much changed from those of mercantilist times, countless commercial barriers still remain.

To evaluate trade policy in terms of social welfare, it is essential to know the social preferences of a nation state. How does a country assess its true wealth? Is it in terms of national security through military might, the level or distribution of its income, its rate of economic growth, the level or rate of growth of its technology, the nation's conquest over earthly or extraterrestrial elements, or the relative position in any of these areas that one country maintains over its major competitors? If goals of national policy are expressed in *relative* terms, so that one nation gains only at the expense of another, economic growth that permits the expansion of absolute income per capita may prove unable to alleviate international tension. Under such circumstances the existence of wars, whether hot or cold, whether in terms of trade or weapons, is guaranteed.

Trade between Nations

If all governments were content to permit the free flow of goods and services, if perfect competition prevails, and if each country's factors of production remained within its borders, the free trade solution discussed in Chapter 24 would result, with its associated implications for efficiency and welfare. Each nation would be expected to exchange those commodities in which it had a comparative advantage for those in which it had a comparative disadvantage until relative prices equalized among all countries of the world (net of transport costs). Once this solution was obtained, no change could benefit any participant in the market except at the expense of someone else. If, however, one country thought it possible to gain at the expense of another, it could justify tampering with the process of free trade. It is precisely this type of consideration that underlies almost any application of commercial policy in the world today.

International Supply and Demand Curves

To demonstrate the effect of commercial policy on resource allocations, it is convenient to create a new tool—the *excess demand curve*. An excess demand curve measures the difference between demand and supply at each price. Therefore it can be constructed quite simply from an ordinary supply and demand curve as shown in Figure 25.1.

The excess demand curve shows zero as the excess quantity of wheat demanded at the price at which the quantities supplied and demanded are equal. At that price, demand minus supply is zero. At higher prices, demand minus supply is negative, whereas at lower prices, demand minus supply is positive.

The excess demand curve shows how much wheat this country would demand from abroad at each possible price in the international market. At interna-

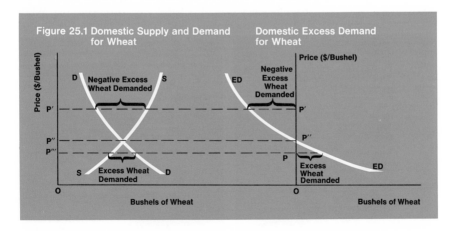

Figure 25.1 Domestic Supply and Demand for Wheat   Domestic Excess Demand for Wheat

tional price P'', for example, no wheat is demanded or supplied abroad since that is the price at which the quantity of domestic production equals the quantity of domestic demand. At lower prices, domestic demand exceeds production. Therefore, if price P''' reigned in the international market and this country traded freely, it would import the quantity labeled "excess wheat demanded." On the other hand, if a much higher international price prevailed, say P', domestic production would be much larger, the quantity demanded much smaller, and the country may choose to export wheat. Thus whether a country is to be an importer or an exporter of wheat depends quite simply on whether the international price is less than or greater than the domestic price.

Defining an excess supply curve as the quantity supplied minus the quantity demanded at each price, we can see that it is the negative of the excess demand curve. That is, a positive quantity of excess demand is a negative quantity of excess supply, and vice versa. Thus an excess supply curve could be constructed as the mirror image of an excess demand curve. This is done in Figure 25.2.

If we now consider this country's excess demand curve for wheat and the rest of the world's excess supply curve (created by adding horizontally all other countries' excess supply curves), we can determine an international price for wheat and decide whether this country is to be an importer or an exporter. This is done in Figure 25.3.

On the basis of the figure, free trade will have the domestic country import the quantity of wheat indicated from the rest of the world. This is because in the absence of trade, the domestic price (P'') would have been higher than the foreign price (P''''). Once trade occurs, domestic and foreign prices must become equal. This occurs at price P''' in Figure 25.3.

The efficiency implications of free trade can be described using supply and demand curves if we remember that a demand curve is a locus of points at which value equals price and that a supply curve is a locus of points at which cost equals price. We know that efficiency cannot occur if value exceeds cost. When

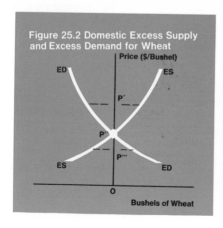

Figure 25.2 Domestic Excess Supply and Excess Demand for Wheat

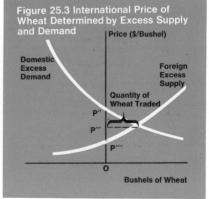

Figure 25.3 International Price of Wheat Determined by Excess Supply and Demand

something is worth more than it costs, one should give up the objects of lesser value in order to increase utility. With no trade, a unit of wheat is worth more to domestic consumers than the goods they would have to sacrifice to buy it. Efficiency requires that they make the trade.

Commercial Policy: Tariffs

A *tariff* is a tax imposed on imported commodities. For example, the United States taxes automobiles that are produced abroad but sold within the United States. This increases the price to the purchaser but not to the seller. Tariffs distort the allocation of resources in two ways. (1) By changing the prices individuals face, tariffs do not present individuals with the true social cost of a foreign good. Individuals will therefore buy fewer foreign goods than they would if they could pay the price that foreigners receive. As a result consumers forego utility. (2) The higher domestic price for certain goods leads to more domestic production of those goods than would exist if producers faced the international prices. As a result resources are misallocated and efficiency is lost both at home and abroad.

The effect of a tariff on resource allocation can be shown graphically by using excess supply and demand curves. With a tariff on imported wheat, consumers must pay a higher price for each unit. Now they not only pay enough to induce producers to sell, but they must pay an excise to the government as well. This is shown in Figure 25.4 where a tariff of 50 percent of the price of wheat has been added to the supply curve. The supply curve shows us the price producers must receive, and the supply curve plus tax shows us the price consumers must pay. Thus equilibrium in Figure 25.4 occurs with imports of Q_1 instead of Q_2. The shaded rectangle denotes the government's receipts from tariff payments.

Consumers pay price P_1 with the tariff, a higher price than they would pay without the tariff, P_2. Producers, on the other hand, receive price P_3, a lower price than they would receive without the tariff. With P_1 denoting the value of

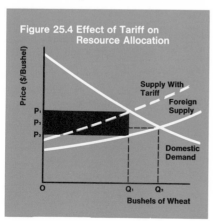

Figure 25.4 Effect of Tariff on Resource Allocation

wheat to domestic consumers and P_3 the cost of producing wheat abroad, it is clear that Q_1 represents an inefficient allocation of resources. At Q_1, the value of wheat exceeds its cost. Consumers would be happy to buy one more unit at a price less than P_1. Producers would be happy to produce one more unit at a price greater than P_3. No one would be made worse off by allowing the producers and consumers to get together and conduct an additional transaction. The tariff effectively prevents the transaction, however, and therefore is responsible for the inefficient allocation of resources.

If tariffs waste satisfaction, why are they used so commonly throughout the world? There are many answers.

First, as shown in Chapter 22, almost all taxes lead to inefficient allocations of resources. Thus if tariffs are used to raise tax money, the choice is not between efficiency and inefficiency but rather the kind of inefficiency that is to be tolerated.

Second, we showed in Chapter 24 how the gains from trade need not be shared by all. Internal politics may allow the potential losers to prevent trade from occurring via tariffs. In our example here, it is likely that domestic wheat producers will not enjoy the foreign competition. They will use their political power to keep the cheap foreign wheat from entering the country. Their arguments may take the form of appeals to patriotism, requests for sympathy, or may merely play on the fears of the rest of the voters that theirs may be the next industry to fall to the inexorably lower costs of foreign producers.

A third reason tariffs may be used is in an attempt to capture a larger share of the gains from trade for the home country. Even though the total gains will be smaller because of the tariff, it is possible that the country invoking the tariff will be better off with it than without it. To see this we have to note the effect of a tariff on both cost and value of goods received from abroad. We use the concept of consumer's surplus (see Chapter 8) to get an accurate measure of the value of the imports.

In Figure 25.5, the area $P_2 \times Q_2$ denotes the total resources that must be

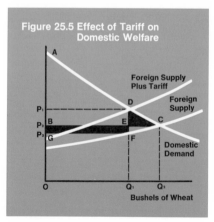

Figure 25.5 Effect of Tariff on Domestic Welfare

spent to obtain Q_2 units of wheat when no tariff is imposed. This is the free trade solution. The large triangle, ABC, measures the consumer's surplus derived from the Q_2 units of wheat and can be thought of as the gains from trade accruing to the importing country.

When a tariff is imposed, imports fall to Q_1. This results in a loss of consumer's surplus of CDE, the small shaded triangle in Figure 25.5. But the decrease in imports lowers the supply price of wheat so that now fewer resources must be spent for each bushel. Foreigners now receive a payment equal to $P_3 \times Q_1$ for the Q_1 bushels of wheat. The rectangle $BEFG$ denotes resources that are saved by the home country due to the lower price of wheat.

Thus the tariff has two effects on domestic welfare. First, it lowers satisfaction because of the loss of consumer's surplus; wheat is worth more than it costs. But second, it lowers the price of wheat and allows the domestic country to keep resources that would otherwise be shipped abroad to pay for the wheat. Whether the domestic country loses or gains depends upon whether triangle CDE is larger or smaller than rectangle $BEFG$. In the case where the triangle is smaller, the domestic country will gain by the imposition of a tariff.

The relative size of the gains and losses depends on the elasticities of the supply and demand curves. In Figure 25.6, we draw two extreme cases: (1) a case where the supply curve is horizontal so that the tariff cannot change the world price, and (2) a case where the supply curve is almost vertical so that the tariff has a great effect on the supplier's price. In case 1 we have made the demand curve inelastic so that there are large losses in consumer's surplus whereas in case 2 we have made the demand curve perfectly flat so that there are no losses in consumer's surplus. Obviously, a tariff would make the country in case 1 worse off and the country in case 2 better off. There is no way to know whether a tariff would benefit or hurt a country without knowing something about the elasticities of supply and demand.

Although a tariff may, in certain circumstances, increase welfare in the home country, it always decreases it abroad. To see this, we need only note the

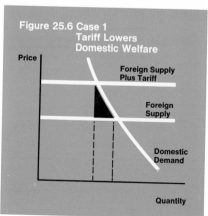

Figure 25.6 Case 1
Tariff Lowers
Domestic Welfare

Price

Foreign Supply
Plus Tariff

Foreign
Supply

Domestic
Demand

Quantity

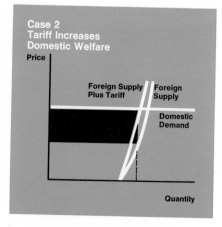

Case 2
Tariff Increases
Domestic Welfare

Price

Foreign Supply
Plus Tariff

Foreign
Supply

Domestic
Demand

Quantity

two ways in which tariffs affect home-country welfare. First, a tariff causes a loss of consumer's surplus. This is a pure waste. The commodity is worth more than it costs and the consumer's surplus measures a part of that difference. But secondly, a tariff transfers resources from the exporting country to the importing country. The rectangle we described above measured resources saved by the home country that *otherwise would be sent abroad*. Thus the rectangles do not represent a net gain in satisfaction for both countries together but merely a transfer from one to the other. The triangle, on the other hand, constitutes what economists call a "dead-weight" loss since the loss cannot be recouped anywhere else in the system.

If two trading partners both thought of themselves as being in a position where tariffs could increase domestic welfare, they might both institute tariffs. A war over trading policy could result in which each country attempted to improve its position at the expense of the other. Such a trading policy is called a "beggar-my-neighbor" policy. With each round of tariff increases, welfare is transferred from one country to another and then back again. But with each round, total welfare declines since consumer's surplus is sacrificed that is never recouped. The only certain effect of the attempts of each nation to increase its slice of the pie is that the pie shrinks.

In recognition of a common interest among nations to keep tariffs low and therefore reap the maximum gains from trade, international conferences are called periodically where attempts are made to reach agreement concerning the appropriate level of tariffs. With different countries exporting different commodities, the bargaining at such conferences takes the form of "You lower the tariff on chickens by 20 percent and I'll cut the tariff on automobiles by 10 percent." It is difficult to reach agreement at these conferences since what is being determined is the size of the slices of the pie. Many arguments are given as to why a certain protected domestic industry is a special case and should be exempt from any movement toward across-the-board tariff reductions. A common argument of this form is the "infant industry" argument in which it is claimed that a certain domestic industry is not yet on its feet. It needs protection in the short run al-

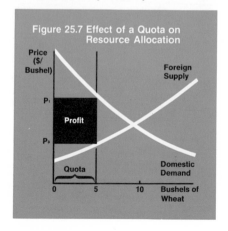

Figure 25.7 Effect of a Quota on Resource Allocation

though it is expected to be a vigorous competitor in the long run. Such expectations do not always materialize.

There are other tools of commercial policy besides tariffs. Their effects are roughly the same, however, since they tend to waste some of the satisfaction that would be available from the free market. A *quota*, for example, is a restriction on the quantity of a particular product that can be imported. A quota might say that 5 million bushels of wheat can be imported and no more. Licenses will be issued until the quota is exhausted and then further imports are prohibited.

Looking at Figure 25.7, we see a problem associated with quotas, namely, that there are profits to be made by those who obtain the licenses. They are able to buy in the world market at price P_3 and sell in the domestic market at price P_1. With tariffs, this difference is collected by the government, but with quotas it disappears into the hands of whoever has been able to obtain a license. What an invitation for corruption!

In Chapter 38, we will describe the monetary aspects of international trade and discuss financial forms of trade policy. Their effects are the same. One nation may attempt to benefit at the expense of others by restricting the free flows of goods and services. These attempts redistribute income not only among nations but also among individuals within nations. Because of this, they are hot political issues. Small lobby groups who would profit a great deal from a tariff can often barrage the government effectively with propaganda for their cause. Consumers, who generally are the losers from tariffs because of the higher prices they must pay, are so dispersed that they tend to be an ineffective lobby. The consumers lose so little from each single tariff that it is not worth their while to complain when increases are proposed. If the price of candles goes up by 10 percent, consumers will not be much worse off. Candlemakers, on the other hand, may stand to make or lose a fortune depending on whether the tariff is imposed or not.

Since those who lobby for tariffs are really asking for an inefficient allocation of resources, economists think of them as the "bad guys." Given the nature of the political process, the bad guys often win.

Questions

1. How can the international price affect the decisions of a country to export or import commodities?
2. How do tariffs affect the welfare of importers and exporters and how do these effects depend on the elasticities of supply and demand?
3. How do the effects of a quota differ from those of a tariff?

Concepts Discussed

mercantilism	beggar-my-neighbor
excess demand curve	infant industry
tariff	quota
dead-weight loss	

26 Transportation, Location, and Urban Development

Why do big cities have tall buildings? Why are steel furnaces located near coal fields, bakeries in cities? What determines the character of suburbia: Which suburbs will contain the really rich as opposed to the not so rich, which will contain factories, research centers, or offices? The answers to these questions depend importantly on the economics of transportation. It is the purpose of this chapter to provide insight into those questions through a consideration of transport costs. First, we show how the analysis of the previous two chapters must be modified if transport costs are substantial. Then we discuss the economic factors that affect the location of industries and population. Finally, we present a model of urban development as an example of the interplay of transport costs with other natural and social forces.

Transport Costs

In the previous two chapters, we claimed that there exist potential profits whenever the social cost of a commodity is different in two locations. We illustrated this by the example of a shrewd speculator reaping those profits when he established trade between two regions. We then showed how specialization in production could increase welfare in both areas. The argument was conducted using only a knowledge of the relative costs of commodities in the two regions, with the assumption that transport costs were unimportant.

To show how the existence of transport costs affects that conclusion, it is useful to use a simple two-commodity example as we did before. This time we choose steel and computers. Let the cost of a computer be 1,000 tons of steel in the United States and 2,000 tons in Japan. With no transport costs, it would clearly benefit the United States to specialize in computers, Japan in steel. This is illustrated in the following table. It is possible, however, to imagine transport costs so large that there would be no gains from trade. Let us express the social cost of transport in terms of steel and find a level of costs that just eliminates the gains from trade. Assume, for example, that it costs two-thirds of a ton of steel to ship a ton of steel from Japan to the United States, whereas it costs 200 tons of steel to ship a computer from the United States to Japan. These transport costs are just high enough to eliminate the gains from trade as can be seen from Table 26.2.

The argument is conducted using steel to denote costs because we have not yet discussed money. However, it may be simpler to understand when money prices are considered. Thus let steel cost $100 per ton in the United States, computers $100,000 each. In Japan steel costs 20,000 yen per ton and computers 40,000,000 yen each. Knowing that each yen is worth $.003 (ten yen equal three cents in value), we can convert the Japanese costs into dollars. Steel in Japan is worth $60 per ton, computers $120,000. Trade is obviously not profitable since it costs $20,000 to ship a computer to Japan and $40 to ship a ton of steel from Japan to the United States.

Transport costs, therefore, are one reason why prices can differ around the globe. If there is free trade, the difference in the prices should be no greater than the transport costs. That is, with steel in the United States costing $100 a ton and transport from Japan to the United States $40 a ton, steel prices in Japan should be at least $60 a ton. If steel in Japan is cheaper than $60 a ton, trade will be profitable despite the costs of transportation. Transport costs place limits on the amount by which prices can differ around the globe. Timber and coal, for example, are cheaper in the United States than in Europe, haircuts and houses are more expensive. Yet the costs of transportation are large enough to prevent these differences in price from permitting profits to be made by shipping commodities from one market to the other. Thus the existence of transportation costs adds a footnote to the theory of trade presented in Chapters 24 and 25. In the next section, we will see that transportation costs explain many other things as well.

The Location of Industry

Transport costs help to explain the location of industries. Certain bulky natural resources that are used up in the production process do not have to be trans-

---

Table 26.1 Gains from Trade — No Transport Costs

Social Cost of a Computer

United States	1,000 Tons of Steel
Japan	2,000 Tons of Steel

1. The United States can build one more computer if it produces 1,000 tons less steel.

2. The extra computer can be traded to the Japanese for 2,000 tons of steel, the cost of a computer in Japan.

3. The Japanese can produce one less computer, 2,000 tons more steel; thus Japanese consumption can be unaffected by the trade.

4. The United States receives 2,000 tons of steel in return for its sacrifice of 1,000 tons. Net gain: 1,000 tons of steel.

ported very far if production takes place at their source. This explains the location of iron and steel mills near the source of coal. Transport costs are lowest with the mills near the coal. Similarly, aluminum plants are located near sources of hydroelectricity, food processing plants near farms, and consulting firms near universities. If it is more expensive to transport the raw materials than the finished product, industry should locate near the raw materials.

But in industries where it is more expensive to transport the finished product than the raw materials, the plants should be located near the consumers, wherever they may be. Examples of these industries include automobile assembly, bakeries, and service industries such as plumbing, retailing, or dentistry. It is more expensive to transport autos than auto parts and raw materials. Thus auto assembly plants should be near population centers, not near raw materials. Since baked goods must be sold rapidly, air freight would have to be used if the bakeries were set up in the wheat fields of the Midwest. Air freight is much more expensive per pound than transportation by rail, the method used to get the wheat to the flour mills and bakeries. Thus bakeries are located near the consumers, not the wheat producers. Likewise service industries must perform their

---

Table 26.2   Gains from Trade with Transport Costs

Social Cost of a Computer:

United States	1,000 Tons of Steel
Japan	2,000 Tons of Steel

Social Cost of Transportation:

Steel, Japan to United States	2/3 ton of steel per ton of steel
Computer, United States to Japan	200 tons of steel per computer

1. The United States can build one more computer if it builds 1,000 tons less steel.

2. The extra computer can be transported to Japan at a cost of 200 tons of steel. Cost of a delivered computer is thus 1,200 tons of steel.

3. The delivered computer can be traded to the Japanese for 2,000 tons of steel.

4. 1,200 of those tons of steel can be transported back to the United States if the other 800 tons are sacrificed to transport them.

5. Thus the United States receives 1,200 tons of steel in return for its sacrifice of 1,200 tons of steel. There are no gains from trade if transport costs are this high.

operations near consumers. It is very expensive to have consumers fly to their dentists or vice versa. Therefore the second way transport costs affect the location of industry is by making it cheapest to have some industries exist where their consumers are.

A third impact of transportation on location derives from the fact that water transport is the cheapest way to move bulky commodities long distances. But water is not found everywhere. If it is necessary to move commodities partly by land and partly by water, there must exist terminals where the transfer of goods from one mode of transport to another can occur. These terminals will be where it is physically easiest, and therefore cheapest, to make the transfer, usually where water is deep and calm at the shoreline. It will be most convenient to locate offices of transport firms' managements at such terminals where equipment and labor can be observed most easily. Industries that sell services to transport industries will find it convenient to locate next to the transport managers. Thus at ports we expect to find not only busy terminals but also insurance, banking, and other financial services. And once the ports exist, we might expect to find that many industries locate there to take advantage of the cheap water transportation and to eliminate the handling costs that result when goods are transferred from rail to water.

In the United States, these reasons have determined the location of most of the large cities. Boston, New York, Philadelphia, Baltimore, and Miami are on the East Coast, New Orleans and Houston on the Gulf Coast. Seattle, San Francisco, Los Angeles, and San Diego are on the West Coast, and Milwaukee, Chicago, Detroit, Cleveland, and Buffalo on the "north coast," the coast connected to the Atlantic by the Erie Canal and the St. Lawrence Seaway. Other cities on the Mississippi-Missouri-Ohio river network include Minneapolis-St. Paul, Kansas City, St. Louis, Cincinnati, and Pittsburgh. In fact, the only very large cities not on major waterways are Denver, Dallas-Ft. Worth, and Atlanta, all essentially products of the twentieth century in which transport costs have become less and less important in determining location. Why? As economies become technologically more sophisticated, products contain smaller amounts of raw materials and greater amounts of engineering know-how and precision equipment. The result is a product whose value is large per pound. Industries that produce these sophisticated products are relatively less dependent on transportation for determining their location since transport costs will be a small part of the final value of the product. Even if the *value* of raw materials stays constant, the *weights* of those materials used can decline if there is a shift from cheap simple materials such as iron to expensive sophisticated materials such as molybdenum and titanium. If transport costs become very low, what will determine the location of industry? Population will.

The Location of People

Historically, people have moved to where jobs are — generally at ports and sites of mineral deposits. With low transport costs, however, people can live where they wish and the jobs can follow the people. If enough men like sun, mountains, and oceans to the extent that they will accept wages $500 lower per year in California than in the Midwest, it may be profitable to ship raw materials from the Midwest to California, have them processed, and then ship the final product back to midwestern consumers. For modern sophisticated industries, transport costs for the materials and products one man works with and produces in a year may be less than $500. Thus the extra shipping costs may be less than the saving due to lower wages. A modern example of this is a firm that ships computer cards to Hong Kong to be punched and shipped back. The low Hong Kong wages make this profitable despite the costs of air freight. Thus when there exist industries using sophisticated technologies that have low transport costs, men can live where they wish and the jobs can follow them.

The twentieth century in the United States has seen both kinds of movements of men: (1) from the country to the city, where the jobs are, and (2) from the eastern and central areas to the South and West, where there is natural beauty and agreeable climate. More and more the location of plants is being determined by the location of men.

All the movement will not be to the sun and mountains, however. Many men do not like to undergo the financial and emotional costs of moving and severing roots. Thus old cities will continue to offer trained labor forces as an inducement to firms to locate plants there and these old cities will continue to grow long after the original reason for their existence has disappeared. That is, they may grow despite a disagreeable climate and high transportation costs.

Boston, for example, developed in the seventeenth and eighteenth centuries as a port due to the quality of its harbor and its proximity to timber, a resource useful in shipbuilding and in scarce supply in Europe. Port services such as insurance and finance developed as well. In the nineteenth century, Boston's relative importance as a port declined because of its inconvenient access to western markets. It was kept alive by its financial industry, which directed the investment of old capital into new industries, primarily rails and the manufacturing that developed along nearby New England rivers. When electric power became economical in the early twentieth century, Boston stagnated as its textile industry moved to the South to be near cheap labor and cotton.

But the second half of this century saw a remarkable resurgence in Boston, this time largely due to the fact that many highly educated people preferred to live there and that educated men are precisely what is needed by new industries. Electronics and scientific research are the new industries of Boston just as they are in areas of southern California. Proximity of old friends and cultural resources makes Boston attractive to educated people. Southern California's climate is also attractive. These two areas have no natural resources that their industries need; they are poorly located if transport costs are important. But research is an industry that needs no natural resources and has no transport costs. It can follow men to new locations or stay with them at old ones. Since old friends and cultural resources are things that can exist wherever great quantities of men congregate and put down roots, cities that owe their origin to transport costs might continue to exist long after the original effects have disappeared.

Cities and Agglomeration Economies

We mentioned cultural reasons for preferring one location to another as a place to live. The primary determinant of the quality and quantity of cultural offerings associated with a particular city is the number of people who live there. This is an example of what is called *agglomeration economies* by urban economists. It is another form of economies of scale. It tells us that wherever people choose to live, they will wish to live close enough to each other to be able to support symphonies, restaurants, and athletic teams. Big cities not only have more of the same activities than small ones do, but they have some activities that small cities cannot support because there just are not enough people.

Of course, tastes differ among men. Some will prefer one climate, others another. The relative value of open space as opposed to cultural activities will vary from man to man so that some will be happiest in small towns, others only in metropolitan areas. Different cities will have different personalities as well, and their different attractions may draw different men.

Location of Urban Population

One thing that transportation costs and differences in taste can help to explain is the location of people within a metropolitan area. Metropolitan areas tend to have cores or centers wherein many of the cultural activities and sources of employment exist. People are spread around this core in rings, each successive ring having a lower population density than the one closer in, with the outermost ring virtually blending into the countryside. This general pattern is caused by the costs involved in getting from one place to another and the diverse tastes of men.

If, for example, we built a city with the opera at one end of the fringe, the football stadium at another, and places of mass employment at other edges of the metropolitan area, transport costs would be very large. Massive highways or mass transit lines would have to connect each of these outer points with each of the residential areas. Since there are economies of scale in transportation, such a duplication of facilities would be very wasteful. People would choose to live in that residential area nearest their job in order to minimize transport costs. But this might place them very far from the activities they enjoy most. On the other hand, a city with all activities centralized needs only highways from this one center to each of the residential areas.

If all of the activities and many of the sources of employment were located in the center, one would expect people to prefer to live in the center in order to minimize transportation costs and have easy access to these facilities. But there is only so much room in the center. Not everyone can live there. With supply fixed and demand very high, it is not surprising that real estate values are very high near the city's core. They are so high that the people who live there must economize on space in every way they can. Thus in the center of cities, we expect to see buildings full of small apartments. It is uneconomical to live in the city's center the way one lives in the suburbs — with trees and lawns, etc. At the edges of the city space is much cheaper, thus much more space can be used per family.

This model of city real estate prices depends only on transportation costs. We assume that if a man could choose between the identical structures and environment close in or far out, he would choose to live close in because he would be nearer to work and recreation. Because of this, real estate prices will be higher close in and we will find that the man will not have the choice of identical structures because the real estate values are important determinants of the mode of living available. Lawns are prohibitively expensive in Manhattan precisely because that is where everyone would choose to live if it were possible to have a lawn there.

Given a city that conforms to this model, each man is faced with a choice of where to live. Living in close will make it easy to get to work, concerts, theatres, restaurants, and sporting events. Transportation costs will be low. Living far out will make transportation costs very high, but space will be cheap. Large houses will be possible with lawns, quiet streets, trees, and gardens. Those who live far out will find transportation so expensive that they will forego many activities that they would otherwise buy. Thus the choice of living far out or close in boils down to one's preferences for open space as opposed to the activities of the central city. Each mile further out one might move involves cheaper space but higher transport costs to the central city. The ideal spot to live is determined by moving outward from the center of the city until one finds that area where the additional value of cheaper space is less than the additional transport cost. Surely no one would live 200 miles from work simply because of the lower real estate prices that far away. The reduction in real estate prices is not worth the increase in transport costs that must be sacrificed to live on that real estate. On the other hand, once one is five minutes from work, further savings in transport costs are unlikely to be worth the higher prices one would have to pay for the real estate closer in. Somewhere between the two extremes, a man can find a place with the proper tradeoff between transport costs and real estate prices.

Different individuals will find it optimal to live at different distances from the center. This is because tastes will differ for open space as opposed to the events in the center. For those who partake of the center culture, the relevant transportation costs are higher at any given distance from the center than for those who do not partake because more trips must be made. For those who visit the city often, the optimal distance from the center at which to live is clearly less than for those who make fewer trips. Similarly, those who like open spaces and want to buy some for themselves will have larger than average space costs and will find it profitable to live where space is cheap.

As important as taste in determining location is income. This is because the most important element of transportation cost is not gasoline or subway tolls but time. If a man must pay $1 for transportation to get to work and the trip takes one-half hour, the true cost of the trip is $1 plus the wage the man could have earned in that half hour. If the man's time is worth $10 per hour, the total cost of the trip is $6. Since time costs vary with wage rates, different men will experience different costs for the same trip. The trip just mentioned will cost $11 to a twenty-dollar-an-hour man and $51 to a hundred-dollar-an-hour executive. Those with high wage rates will have a greater incentive to economize on the time they spend traveling. Therefore, they will find it economical to live in close in order to keep transport costs low, whereas those with low wage rates will live further out, the lesser value of their time making transportation less costly. Space costs the same for all men, but transportation is more expensive for the rich than for the poor. Thus the rich, other things equal, can be expected to live closer to the center than the poor. The tradeoff between transport costs and space faced by the rich is different from that faced by the poor in such a way as to exert more pressure on them to live in close.

Let us summarize the predictions of our simple transportation cost model of urban location before we add some real-world considerations that qualify the results. In the simple model just described, we have group activities and sources of employment located in the center of the city. Demand for real estate will be very high there as men attempt to live near their jobs and sources of stimulation. The high real estate prices will lead to tall buildings and small apartments in an attempt to economize on the use of land. Further out from the center, land will be cheaper and used more lavishly. Individuals will decide where to live by offsetting the high costs of space close in against the high costs of transportation further out. Those who are rich and those who travel to the center often will have higher transport costs than the others and will wish to live further in. Other things equal, we would expect to see the very rich living in close and to encounter suburbs of lower and lower income levels as we move out from the core.

Urban Problems and the Location of Population

Although this general prediction is useful to remember when considering metropolitan areas, there seem to be many important real-world exceptions. We now consider three qualifications to the model just presented in order to gain a more sophisticated view of urban development.

(1) HOUSING TECHNOLOGY. Perhaps if we built a city overnight, we could build it as the model above predicts it would be built. In fact, however, cities grow slowly with the center expanding to the edges. More and more of the surrounding farmland becomes residential while real estate values rise everywhere as people are pushed further and further from the core. The model above predicts that the quality of housing will slowly improve at every point as the near-rich and the not-so-rich are gradually forced to move further and further out in their attempt to escape escalating rents. New commercial buildings are placed in the center, moving the very rich out a few blocks. Housing becomes denser at every point to economize on land costs, and each point receives an influx of wealthy people moving out from the core while its less wealthy residents move

further out in search of cheaper rent. Thus the average wealth of the residents living at any point increases with the growth of the city.

The technology of houses, however, is such that they last a long time. As they grow older, they tend to deteriorate in relative quality because of both depreciation and their inadaptability to new improvements and inventions. Housing technology is such that we would expect houses to be lived in first by the very rich, then the almost rich, and so on until finally when they are old, decrepit, and outmoded, the houses are lived in by the very poor. Thus the technology of housing tells us that each particular dwelling should be occupied by poorer and poorer people each decade. This is in direct contrast to the model of urban location that tells us each parcel of real estate should be occupied by richer and richer people as it stands relatively closer to the urban core. Which of these two factors will dominate depends on how rapidly the houses deteriorate. If they depreciate rapidly, they can be torn down and replaced by new buildings with little loss. If they last, however, it may be efficient to leave them standing for a while and build high income housing further out that can be connected to the core by rapid transportation. That is, it may be efficient to have the poor live in close and the rich far out even though this increases transportation costs. Housing costs may be lowered sufficiently to offset higher transport costs. Thus in some cities we can see tall buildings directly adjacent to decaying neighborhoods. The technology of houses is such that rich and poor will be distributed more evenly than the simple transportation model predicts. Houses will be allowed to grow old before they are torn down.

Rarely, however, do we find rich and poor sprinkled within the same neighborhood. Rather we see neighborhoods of rich and neighborhoods of poor sprinkled throughout the metropolitan area. Why?

(2) Neighborhood Effects. The reason we rarely see the rich living next to the poor is due to neighborhood effects or externalities. Neighborhoods with a majority of poor people are not desirable places to live. The two most important reasons for this are crime and poor schools. Crime is apparently related to income. One of the luxury goods we can afford as income increases is to obey the legal code of the society. For the rich, the fruits of crime have a lower marginal utility than for the poor, and the penalties for being caught threaten a greater loss of future income when income is already high. Moral—or legal—behavior is therefore cheaper for the rich than for the poor. Since many crimes tend to be committed in the criminal's neighborhood, we can expect to find more crime in neighborhoods where poor people live; these neighborhoods therefore become less desirable places to live.

The quality of schools depends on the quality of the students. One learns more in a school where others are well prepared and willing to obey than in a school where others pose problems of discipline and slow down class progress because of a lack of understanding. Poor families tend to be uneducated and undisciplined. These are some of the causes of their poverty. The children, therefore, have had few of the advantages of wealthier children and pose greater problems in the school system. To live with the poor means that one's children will receive a poor education.

Schools and crime are just two of the reasons why the rich and the poor rarely live in the same neighborhood. Because of reasons like these, the rich move away from the poor. Prices of real estate rise where the rich go, making it possible for the rich to segregate themselves by using a barrier of real estate prices to keep all of their positive neighborhood effects to themselves. Zoning laws that stipulate minimum lot sizes increase the effectiveness of the barrier. This of course makes it all the more difficult for the poor children to grow up being anything but poor because they are never exposed to the patterns of behavior of the nonpoor.

(3) AGGLOMERATION DISECONOMIES. The location model described above assumed that all jobs were in the central city. In fact, as cities grow very large and turn into vast metropolitan areas, it is no longer necessary for all employment opportunities to be located at the core. Factories and other employers of low-skilled labor can locate anywhere because transportation costs are less important to their workers than they are to those with more valuable time. Thus, the larger cities become, the more we expect certain employment sources to locate at the periphery where real estate is cheap. Although presumably employers must pay their employees' transportation costs in wage differentials, these costs are not so large as to warrant the firms' location in the city's center.

When a city is big enough for only one factory, it might be expected to locate in the center. But as cities expand, one finds factories ringing the outskirts, locating where the low-wage labor and cheaper land are found. A laborer then would have not only the choice of living at a particular distance from the city center, but also the choice of living at a point in the ring near his job, assuming that the zoning laws do not preclude the existence of low-cost housing at that point. As cities grow, more and more different kinds of activities find it profitable to locate out near their labor until finally, in the largest of cities, all that is left in the downtown area is financing—banking, insurance, brokerage—activities that use very little space, pay relatively high salaries, and benefit from being located near each other for the face-to-face communication necessary to conduct business.

To get an accurate idea of the determinants of the location of activities in a particular city, we would have to keep in mind all of the above plus the peculiar geography of the city (rivers, lakes, and mountains) as well as the transportation decisions made by the city management (location of subways, highways, and airports).

A Profile of Metropolitan Development

A capsule of the history of a hypothetical metropolitan area's growth might be the following. Some natural resource drew industry to the city. A swell in population followed, people moving as close to their jobs as they could afford. As the city grew, all downtown houses (the houses of the rich) were bought for expansion of the commercial core. The rich moved a bit further out, forcing the poor out further yet. In some places, however, the poor had gathered in large enough clusters to make these neighborhoods undesirable. The rich skipped these locations and moved much further out. When increasing rents forced the middle class to move further out, they did not move into poor neighborhoods because of both the neighborhood effects and the quality of housing. It was cheaper for them to undergo the large transportation costs of living in the suburbs than to renovate poor housing in areas where the poor lived. As the city grew further, clusters of polite suburbs developed and exerted an attraction for industries that used primarily middle-class labor (research and development, for example). The location of such a firm in a suburb lowered transportation cost a great deal. All of its workers chose to live near it, of course, rather than in the other polite suburbs on the opposite side of the metropolitan area.

Thus our final solution is a batch of clusters. Clusters of the rich who enjoy cultural offerings and who work in the center continue to live in the center; the rich who like space live on estates in the distant suburbs (some maintaining residences in both places); clusters of middle class live on the main transportation lines to the city or near newly erected sources of middle-class employment; clusters of laborers live in the city near their jobs in neighborhoods that are old and declining; other groups of workers live in small new houses on the fringe near new factories; clusters of the very poor are jammed together in older decayed urban neighborhoods that have become too large to be reclaimed; and other clusters of poor live near sources of unskilled employment at the fringe.

The cost of moving men and equipment from place to place explains a great deal of the present pattern of urban growth. Businesses and residences locate so as to minimize, among other things, the cost of transportation. And transportation routes are designed to permit upper income groups to "leap" the slums. One of the results of this pattern of growth is to eliminate communication between rich and poor and to make it difficult for poor children to imagine what it is like to be well off. The tendency for the rich to cluster together and retain for themselves the beneficial effects they might otherwise yield the poor is a tendency that urban planners must take into account when considering how best to tamper with the location of activities in metropolitan areas. The benefits of cheaper private costs of transportation must be weighed against the social cost of denying the poor access to the mainstream of the society's culture. How we feel about a divided society should be an important consideration in forming a transportation policy, because transportation exerts a powerful influence on the location of men and economic activity.

Questions

1. What economic factors helped determine the location of Pittsburgh? New York? Chicago? Liverpool?
2. How might a metropolitan transportation policy affect the rate at which suburbs devour farmland? How would it affect real estate prices in the center? At the fringe? Why might owners of suburban real estate be tempted to exert pressure on the planners of metropolitan transportation?

3.   Consider the future effect of a current policy of building structures of "mixed" quality in new neighborhoods, structures that wear out at different rates. Could this alleviate future neighborhood effects? What might happen to the price of the better built structures in such a neighborhood as opposed to what would happen in a homogeneous neighborhood?

Concepts Discussed

transport costs   agglomeration economies
location of industry   neighborhood effects
location of population

IX Theory of Economic Growth

The death of one man means
bread and butter for another.

SWEDISH SAYING

Economic growth can solve many problems. If the whole economic pie grows rapidly, fights over its division are apt to be less severe. When all parties recognize their common stake in economic growth, their disagreement over the appropriate distribution of income may result in battles of lesser intensity that use fewer economic resources.

But how is growth possible if we have limited natural resources? Are we doomed to poverty in the long run if the population keeps exploding? How can we foster increases in output per man? What is the role of technology, saving, and a population policy? These are the questions discussed in Chapters 27 and 28.

27 Economic Growth: Technology and Population

Inhabitants of the Western world have grown accustomed to a steady improvement in economic well-being. Parents expect their children to have a better standard of living than they themselves were able to enjoy. On average, these expectations are realized. Credit for these improving conditions must go to the incredible technological development that has characterized the last 200 years in the West. New products have been invented so that the poor of today are in some respects better off than the kings of history; they have television, movies, and better medical care than could be bought just a century ago.

Not only have we new products, but we have discovered new ways to produce old products so that now there is an abundance of food, clothing, and shelter. These commodities were in such short supply historically that mere existence was a precarious occupation, requiring all the effort of most of the people. Mass production is but one of many devices that have been used to increase the amount of commodities men receive for their labor. Better transportation has linked the world into a single huge market so that goods are no longer scarce at one point of the globe and abundant at another. Better transportation, division of labor, and the growth of technology have created living standards in the West never seen before.

Steady economic growth of any magnitude, let alone that observed recently, has been a rare historical occurrence. In the past, the growth of an empire was accompanied by a temporary improvement in living standards, but the sources of the improvement indicate why the change was temporary. First, empires created peace and stability (law and order), thereby protecting the locals from marauding tribes and avaricious neighbors. This meant not only that crops were no longer burned but also that fewer resources needed to be devoted to defense against one's neighbors. The saving of these resources, we have noted, is one of the strongest motives men have for signing a social compact. A second reason for improvements in living standards was that the trade of goods increased greatly when huge areas were unified under a single government. Not only could the goods be protected from theft in transit, but the taxes on internal trade were often much less oppressive than those imposed on foreign goods. Trade, we have seen, can greatly increase well-being by redistributing goods to where they are worth the most.

But these reasons do not allow for improvement in living standards every generation. Once the barbarians cease burning one's crops, they have simply ceased burning one's crops. While cessation of this act may allow for a doubling of production in one generation, it cannot double it again for the next generation. The next generation will have to find some new device if it is also to increase production. Historically, the new devices were rarely found. Thus the creation of an empire led to a once and for all improvement in living standards, not to a state of permanently increasing production. Basic production techniques were not affected by politics. The politics affected how much of the potential production could actually be produced and eventually consumed, but it did not affect the potential for production. Once the potential was realized, further gains were not possible.

The idea of perpetual change in production techniques is a new one. It differentiates modern Western culture from its predecessors and from many other current cultures. The changes in technique that occur allow potential production to grow steadily. Steady growth brings with it many social problems, some of which we discuss later. But it also brings with it better living standards.

Parson Malthus

Any major treatise on economics written in the 1700s or 1800s devoted a great deal of attention to population. The most famous treatment of the population question was that of Parson Malthus. Malthus was concerned with the amount of population that could be sustained in the long run by the earth's fixed resources. The key to Malthus's analysis was the law of diminishing returns. Adding more and more population to a fixed resource base leads to declining living standards due to diminishing returns. Population brings with it, of course, more labor, which is an input into the production process. But the addition of more and more labor to a fixed amount of land results in diminishing returns to labor. Double the population and output will not double; it increases, but by less than 100 percent. Eventually, reasoned Malthus, enough labor could be added to the fixed land to reduce living standards to a subsistence level, to a level that would keep everyone on the brink of starvation. Attempts to increase population beyond this point would be thwarted by the lack of enough resources to keep the new people alive.

Malthus, of course, was unaware of the possibility of continuing technical progress. The effect of this ignorance was to make his forecasts woefully inaccurate. Changes in production techniques have allowed us to squeeze more and more output from each input to an extent never imagined by Malthus or anyone else alive in his time. The recent huge increase in population has been accompanied by rising, not declining, living standards. Technological progress has been such a powerful force that it has more than offset the effect of diminishing returns on living standards. That Malthus, the expert of his day, could have been so wrong about the number of people that can be maintained by a fixed level of resources should be a source of comfort to us today, surrounded as we are by gloomy predictions of ecological disaster as a result of the population explosion.

Population Growth

A key hypothesis in Malthus's theory was that population *would* expand to its natural limit. Diminishing returns tells us that with a given technology a natural limit exists, but it does not tell us that population must grow until that limit is attained. Malthus believed that man is similar to other species and would expand in numbers to the limits of his food supply. No other species practice birth control. The level of animal populations is determined by enemies and the available food supply. There is a long-run equilibrium level for each of the species determined in the huge simultaneous ecological system; this equilibrium could be called the balance of nature. Wild animals are always at the brink of starvation. If there is food to spare, they breed until all food is used intensively. Malthus interpreted human behavior in that light.

In Malthus's time the general level of education was low; birth control technology was poor. It was difficult to imagine a conscious limitation on population growth in order to keep living standards high. History yielded countless examples of population growth whenever food supplies had increased. Empires that allowed food production to grow found population growing as well. Malthus saw no example of a population that limited its own growth in order to maintain a high living standard.

Is the Malthus forecast likely to be correct? There are three possibilities that must be considered in attempting to answer that question, two of which allow Malthus to be wrong. First, it is possible that men will limit population growth. This might happen through either a centralized policy or voluntary limitation on the part of families. Between the world wars, population stayed constant in much of Europe without any policies to encourage birth control. Perhaps the horror of war convinced enough families that the world was not a pleasant enough place to wish on children. Perhaps the tragedy of the Great Depression made them fear the economic future of their offspring and they therefore attempted to prevent endless division of the family wealth. Today many young urban families feel they cannot afford children because of the high price of housing, which will increase further if population continues to expand. Thus history does yield examples of conscious birth limitations by humans in response to deteriorating social and economic conditions.

The second possibility for Malthus to be wrong lies in a perpetual continuation of the behavior of the last century. Technology may proceed at such a rate that we can continue to have high living standards despite population growth. One can imagine a very advanced technology—that of today's science fiction—in which planets are colonized and resources are combined into many wondrous products. With that technology, population growth is no threat to men's future.

The third possibility is that Malthus is right. Perhaps men do expand their

THOMAS ROBERT MALTHUS (1766-1834)   Author of the Malthusian theory of population, and (in Keynes's phrase) "first of the Cambridge economists," Parson Malthus came in for vitriolic attack both during his life and after. His father knew Hume and Rousseau and sent him to Cambridge; thus Malthus was early acquainted with many intellectual currents of his day, including the works of Rousseau, Condorcet, and Jeremy Bentham, whose pleasure-pain calculus set the goals of much of Malthus's work. This knowledge provided part of the framework within which Malthus tried to find economic laws or theories whose observance would maximize human welfare, a search similar to that of Adam Smith.

His labors yielded a number of works, of which the most important were the *Essay on Population* (1798 and six editions) and the *Principles of Political Economy* (1820). In the *Essay*, Malthus set forth what has since become known as the Malthusian Doctrine or theory of population; according to this theory the human population always tends to outrun the means of subsistence. He asserted that all men need food, and that all men have an urge to marry (mate). Since population size is a function of food supply, since population will always grow as long as there is food, and since population, which grows at a geometric rate, will ultimately tend to grow faster than food supply, which grows at an arithmetic rate (implicitly because of the law of diminishing returns), mankind will always be up against the margin of subsistence and will have its numbers checked by natural restraints. Usually the checks will apply only after population has grown too large, and men therefore will be subject to the disciplines of vice and misery, that is, famine, pestilence, and war. In such a world, labor's wages could not remain above subsistence levels because population would rapidly grow if they did and drive them back down. Unless men embraced continence and other "preventive checks," the long-run prospects for humankind were bleak indeed, a conclusion that led Thomas Carlyle later to dub economics "the dismal science" and that gave to political economy a generally gloomy outlook in marked contrast to the rosy visions of Adam Smith. In later editions Malthus actually modified his early pessimism somewhat by a stronger advocacy of "moral restraint," a stance that subverted his earlier, more deterministic assertions.

Actually this type of preventive control apparently lies behind the demographic experience of much of the Western world during the Industrial Revolution, since birth rates and rates of natural increase have been more modest than the expansion of incomes would have led a Malthusian to expect. During Malthus's life and for much of the nineteenth century, his population ideas were both

numbers whenever they have food to spare. The Industrial Revolution greatly increased men's ability to produce commodities, and the population growth of the last century may have been a result of that. Although the food supply and the resource base are still more than adequate, that is only because men have lacked enough time to adjust their numbers to their new starvation level. What is that level?

Today there are respectable scientists who claim that the earth can support only one-half billion people in the long run, roughly one-sixth of the current population. Others think of 10 or 20 billion as possible. Ultimately, the potential for

derided and used as justifications for attacks on reform and public health legislation; they may have been implicated in the draconian changes in England's Poor Laws in 1834. It is only somewhat belatedly, as a result of the overwhelming population pressures in the Third World, that the Malthusian spectre has again risen, this time in a much more devastating form than even Malthus himself imagined.

Malthus did not confine himself to the long-run population question, however; he also looked to the shorter run in his *Principles*. Noting that not all productive resources were everywhere in use as his *Essay* had suggested, he reasoned that the demand for goods, and hence for the labor that produced those goods, was determined by the capacity and willingness to spend. Obviously, inadequate demand for labor came about because of inadequate demand for the things produced by labor. Workers generally had inadequate purchasing power because of subsistence-level wages and, since capitalists saved and accumulated (often independently of profits) and did not spend all their incomes, the only groups outside the productive process whose spending could pump total demand were the landlords and the government. Because the aristocrats' incomes came from land rents and were independent of their productive efforts, they and their dependent servants could be counted on to consume society's excess output and keep the nation's labor force at work. Although Malthus's assertion of a tendency to underconsumption and resulting depression and unemployment has a notably modern ring, as does his advocacy of a remedy through public works, one of his other policy prescriptions, that is, to stimulate aristocratic consumption, does not. He was, however, attacked by his friend David Ricardo and others, who argued the Say's Law proposition that production creates its own demand and that there could be no "general gluts" as Malthus argued. Moreover, many economists regarded Malthus's bias in favor of the aristocracy as dangerous because it tended to emphasize unproductive consumption at the expense of productive accumulation and investment.

Malthus's analyses suffered from the same weaknesses as those of the other English classicists: they were too limited. He failed to consider the interrelatedness of economic growth and failed to see that men could change habits and customs of family formation. He did contribute useful long-run analyses of untrammeled population change as well as very useful underconsumption theories of a shorter term level of economic activity. Had both of these contributions been incorporated in nineteenth-century analysis, Western capitalism and a good deal of the Third World would have been spared much subsequent misery.

---

numbers will be determined by technology, but the actual numbers will be determined by men. We are now a laboratory in which Malthus's hypothesis is being tested. He may be right or wrong. For some, the suspense itself is killing.

The Optimum Population

The discussion of population has illustrated an important issue to be remembered when considering the possibilities for economic growth. That is, the existence of more men leads to the production of more output, but because of diminishing returns the increase in population leads to lower levels of per capita output. This shows the importance of distinguishing between the growth of total output and the growth of output per capita. Both total output and output per capita are important measures of the wealth of a country.

If we are concerned with the economic well-being of each citizen, it is *per capita* growth of income that must be considered as material progress, assuming, of course, that there is no change in the relative distribution of income. From this view, the growth in the number of people may lead to fewer resources being available for each person and would therefore be of negative value. On the other hand, we may be concerned with total output when comparing the relative strength of two countries. Population also contributes to military might, not only through the provision of "cannon fodder," but also through its effect on total output. Even though the addition of more population makes each person poorer, it leads to a greater production of goods that can be used for any purpose, public or private.

Thus there are reasons we might prefer to reduce the number of people. How far should it be reduced? Surely one is too small a number to aim for. Even if we thought that the ideal population figure would be the one that maximized per capita income, we would still want a reasonable number of people around. This is because diminishing returns may not occur for a small amount of people on a large amount of land. Division of labor and specialization of skills may allow two to produce more than twice what one produces. Possibilities for such specialization exhaust themselves, however, as the number of people increases, so that 4 billion people cannot produce twice as much as 2 billion do. We have expressed both forces graphically in Figure 27.1. As population increases to P', specialization of skills allows output to increase more than proportionally. When population increases beyond P', diminishing returns causes output to increase less than proportionally. Thus output per man, a measure of the living standard, is at its maximum for a population of size P'.

It is important to note that specialization of tasks is only one reason living standards can increase with population. Doubling the population may double the

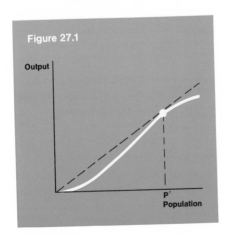

Figure 27.1

Output

P'
Population

number of artists and therefore the number of great paintings that all can enjoy. If we double the number of television channels, for example, everyone can have greater variety in his life. Thus the sheer diversity of the experiences that constitute life depends in part on the number of people around. So one answer to the question of the optimum population would be that level that maximizes per capita satisfaction.

Other issues must be considered when deciding on a level of population. Children yield a great deal of pleasure to their parents. Therefore a decision to shrink the population by birth control would require great sacrifices from the shrinking generations. Taking into account these sacrifices will soften any policy of population control. There are also ethical questions concerning the sheer number of souls that could be prevented from existing due to the material desires of those existing now. Thus the question of an optimum population is not an easy one.

So far, mankind has had the luxury of allowing each family to determine its own size. This need not be efficient. A family may desire four children for itself, yet wish that the total population remain constant. One of these two desires must be sacrificed. If satisfaction is to be maximized, we would want the greater desire to be satisfied. Yet with free choice about the size of one's own family and no control over the size of the total population, individuals will satisfy the desire within their control. Thus everyone may have four children and prefer a world in which everyone had two.

The payoff matrix shown in Table 27.1 illustrates the choices facing me (whether to have two or four children), the choices facing others, and the total populations that will result in the United States under each of the four possible outcomes. The numbers in parentheses indicate my ranking of the four possible events. Clearly, with no constraints on my actions, I prefer four children to two regardless of what others prefer. But if others feel the same way, we will all have four children and wind up at the third-best alternative. If, on the other hand, we band together and agree to have only two children each, we can attain everyone's second-best alternative. The possibility I prefer most is not available to everyone, because when everyone attempts to attain it (by having four children), we are reduced to the third-best alternative. This indicates the external effects of

Table 27.1   Total Population of United States in 1990

Others Have	2 Children	4 Children
I Have		
2 Children	200,000,000 (2)	200,000,002 (1)
4 Children	300,000,000 (4)	300,000,002 (3)

decisions concerning family size. When externalities exist, some form of intervention in the market is justified. What kind of intervention might work best here?

Tastes are not identical; some will prefer the alternative labeled three to that labeled two. Thus a simple law prohibiting births is not necessarily optimal. Some kind of payment scheme may have to be devised to compensate people for not having children. If the compensation level reflects accurately the loss of satisfaction caused to others by the existence of one more body, then an individual faced with the choice of accepting the compensation or having a child considers the social cost of his actions. That is, if one more child reduces others' welfare by $1,000, then I should have the choice of collecting the $1,000 or having the child. Others will be indifferent to my actions and I will be free to pick the alternative that makes me happier. Distributing the burden differently, we might make me pay a tax of $1,000 whenever a child of mine is born. Both schemes are efficient, but they have different distributive implications.

A mathematical fact of interest when considering population growth rates is the timing of births. If parents are forty years old when their children are born, the population growth rate will be much smaller than if they are twenty years old. A doubling of population every generation obviously implies a doubling every forty years in the first case but every twenty years in the second case. Thus an additional policy that could be followed for growing populations is to offer compensation if births are postponed as well as if they are prevented. Stretching out the generations leads to smaller equilibrium population levels even when the growth rate is zero.

The question of population is a hard one that must be faced in the future. Alternatives are (1) a conscious policy of birth control with large financial incentives, (2) the Malthusian solution of starvation and abject poverty, or (3) an equilibrium determined by some as yet not understood process of social equilibrium. Policy 1 with the appropriate financial incentives is economically efficient.

Technology

Technology we said was responsible for a good deal of the growth in per capita output that we have witnessed recently. Even with a zero population growth rate, economic growth—an improvement of well-being—can continue with technological progress that allows us to squeeze more and more output from the world's fixed quantities of inputs.

Some ecologists have recently claimed that all economic growth places strains on our resources. This is not correct. Certain kinds of technical progress allow us to gain satisfaction without requiring greater resource inputs, while others, admittedly, are of the kind feared by the ecologists. Some inventions, it is true, merely augment the productive power of labor; they allow one man to be as productive as two used to be. This means that one man can dig twice as much iron ore from the ground, make twice as many automobiles, use twice as much fuel. Such inventions, called labor augmenting, place an additional strain on the natural resource base. Other inventions can be called resource augmenting. These allow us to build the same buildings with half as much steel (by redesigning girders), to get more energy out of a pound of coal (by making more efficient dynamos), or to make more efficient use of a given amount of energy (by inventing the wheel). They may be merely a way to harness natural forces already in existence. Hydroelectric power is such an invention. Thus economic progress need not be accompanied by destruction of the environment. As resources become relatively more and more scarce (expensive), there will be more and more incentive to develop resource-augmenting technology in order to lower costs. Historically, natural resources have been worth little more than the cost of digging them from the ground. The largest element of cost has been that of labor. Thus the largest effort has been directed toward finding labor-augmenting inventions. When prices change, or are forecasted to change, the direction of research effort will be likely to change as well.

Automation

An issue that has been revived every generation since technological progress began is that of automation. If we keep creating machines to do men's work, will there ultimately be no work for men to do? In its most recent manifestation, the process of replacing men by machines has been called automation because it has involved the installation of complex automatic machinery.

Whenever technical progress has led to the replacement of men by machines, there have been widespread rumblings of discontent accompanied by intellectual arguments to show how men are made poorer in the process. Yet when we look at history, the share of labor in total national output has remained relatively constant; if there has been a change, it has been one in the opposite direction of that forecast by seers of doom. Payments to labor were 70 percent of total output at the turn of the century and they are 80 percent now. It is hard to see how the replacement of men by machines has made men poorer. The real value of per capita payments to labor has doubled, not fallen, during this century. Thus the data yield no evidence of machines impoverishing workers.

Although the term automation is modern, the concept is at least as old as the Industrial Revolution. Weavers rioted and broke the first power looms out of fear for their jobs. The reason automation and its predecessors have been able to instill such fear in observers results from the heterogeneous skills that are possessed by men. It is true that technological progress makes some skills obsolete. Blacksmiths, harness makers, and saddle makers all had problems adjusting to the automobile. If we looked only at transportation when forecasting the demand for blacksmiths, we might fear that machines would completely eliminate man- and horsepower as objects of economic value.

If we observe the economy as a whole, however, it is clear that progress is possible only by such inventions. Only by increasing the output that can be produced by a manhour can the standard of living increase. The replacement of horses and harness makers by autos allows for the same amount of transportation with much less input—or for much more transportation for the same amount of input.

Looking at history, we can see that only by the elimination of the need to perform certain tasks have we gained the manpower needed to staff the new industries responsible for improvements in living standards. Progress creates new products and therefore new needs for employment. The men to perform these tasks are found by eliminating old jobs. Recently, the character of the progress has been such that the dullest of jobs have been eliminated and the most interesting have been created. This was not true of the early Industrial Revolution when complex production processes were broken down into simple tasks. Some fear that the elimination of dull jobs will lead to a kind of structural unemployment with unskilled men forever out of work. The fears are not yet realized. In fact, the labor force has been upgraded through education at a rate sufficient to provide the newly needed skills. This is exactly what we would expect given a simple understanding of the laws of supply and demand. Increasing demand for skilled workers would lead to higher wage rates in these occupations, thereby encouraging unskilled workers to acquire these skills. As the demand for skills changes with technology, the quantities of the various skills supplied can be expected to change as well. Historically, the supply and demand for skills have changed in such a manner as to keep relative wage rates fairly stable. There has been no marked deterioration of the income of unskilled labor relative to that of skilled labor. The claimed evil effects of automation just cannot be found in the aggregate data. This does not imply that such effects are impossible but only that they cannot yet be observed. Statements about aggregates are small comfort to those whose jobs are destroyed by the invention. They may very well be made worse off even while the total quantity of goods is being expanded.

Long-Run Social Equilibrium

The two forces just discussed, the growth of population and the improvement of technology, pose great problems of social adjustment. A new invention like the automobile completely disrupts old patterns of life and drastically alters the relations between people. Suburban living, a product of automobiles, is different from the life style of cities. The new environment faced by children differs from that faced by their parents; each generation must overcome new problems in order to declare peace with its society. Old solutions to problems become inadequate when the magnitude of the problem changes; new problems arise that demand alteration of social patterns if they are to be solved. The result is a society that is forced to change its complexion every generation. The result can be chaos.

The modern Western world is the first civilization to be faced with the problem of continuing adjustment to new demands and opportunities. Old civilizations appear to have been more stable from our vantage point although admittedly they may not have appeared that way to their inhabitants. Now we must rethink all our basic institutions and assumptions every generation. It is not clear that our social relations are durable enough to take such a strain. It is not clear what the character of a society will have to be if it is to be able to absorb this change gracefully. One can imagine a society built around dynamic assumptions — where change is a fact of life. Such a society would have a few enduring principles that would be embodied in ever-altering relationships. The institutions could be changed frequently but the principles would be stated broadly enough to accommodate a host of institutions. It is difficult to imagine how such institutions could be established or how a society could easily differentiate the permanent from the transitory principles. But that is the challenge a society must face if it is to reap the potential benefits of technological progress.

It is clear that technology and population growth change the nature of society. It is not clear that the present society is able to endure these changes while maintaining its principles intact. Economic growth brings with it great problems as well as the great opportunity of wealth for all.

Questions

1. How could a society determine an optimum population? What alternative policies could be followed in an attempt to attain it?
2. Why must technological progress eliminate jobs if it is to make men better off?
3. To what extent should economic growth be an objective of government policy? Is it per capita growth or total growth that matters?

Concepts Discussed

optimum population
labor-augmenting technological progress
resource-augmenting technological progress
automation

28 Capital and Economic Growth

The Malthusian interaction of technological progress and population growth is obviously the most important determinant of long-run economic well-being. Unfortunately, as we pointed out in previous chapters, economists know too little about the determinants of either of these forces to be able to forecast the likely nature of the long-run solution. Technological progress results from men's creative genius and we have little insight into the nature of the creative process. The desire for progeny is basic to all living beings yet we do not understand how less basic cultural, social, or economic desires can temper its effects. Accordingly, these variables are discussed only in very hazy ways by economists. Models to be used for formulating a policy toward economic growth must concentrate on those variables over which control can be exerted. Therefore the most common variable emphasized in such models is capital.

It is well known that capital is a factor of production, that more capital can be created from current output, and that, other things equal, the more capital in a society, the higher its level of production. These facts have dominated the models of economic growth constructed by economists. The rest of this chapter contains a brief introduction to the analysis of economic growth from the viewpoint of capital accumulation. First, we look at the effect of capital accumulation on the production frontier and the problems associated with the notion of the *economic growth rate*. Then we analyze alternative means of transferring present purchasing power to the future. Finally, we look at the effect of the saving decision in a simplified world with no constraint on natural resources.

Present versus Future Consumption

The ability to transform present goods into future goods can be illustrated by the now familiar production possibility frontier (PPF). By decreasing present consumption, we may devote more resources to the production of capital goods that can in turn be used to produce goods for future consumption. Thus through the sacrifice of present consumption, future consumption can be increased. To an individual, this is the choice of how much current income to consume and how much to put into saving accounts that can be used for future consumption. To the society, the reflection of this choice is seen as the decision to produce buildings and bulldozers, which will produce future goods, as opposed to haircuts and food, which are immediately consumed. In Figure 28.1, the sacrifice of current consumption, a movement from D to C, leads to an increase in future consumption, a movement from E to F.

Before extending this simple analysis to the long run, it is useful to get a better understanding of the nature of the tradeoff between present and future as well as to see some problems that are hidden by simplifying the problem of capital to one of a choice between time periods rather than one between particular commodities.

Capital

Capital, we claimed in Chapter 19, was a produced factor of production — present goods that have been set aside to augment future production. It is important to remember that capital is more than just plant and equipment, that there are more ways to convert present consumption into future consumption than by accumulating physical capital. Capital can be embodied in humans as well. Going to college involves a sacrifice of current income, yet it is expected to increase one's future income. Education, training, and prevention of disease are investments in human capital; they involve the expenditure of current resources and are expected to augment future income. Similarly, natural resources can be conserved or consumed. Coal can be left in the ground or dug up and burned. Water can be fouled in the present or left pure for the future. Current resources can be devoted to research that will change the technology of the future. Thus there are many ways to trade present output for future output; machines, equipment, and inventories comprise just one way, albeit a very important one.

Each generation faces the choice of how much resources to leave the generation that follows it. It is possible to deplete the environment, spend nothing on education, and build no new roads, buildings, and machines. Or it is possible to consume as a monk and devote all income to the production of education, physical capital, and the preservation of natural resources. The usual choice is somewhere in between these two extremes. We treat our children about as well as our parents treated us given the resources at their disposal.

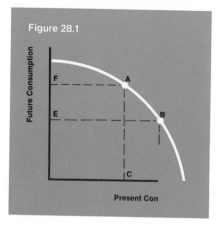

Figure 28.1

The first half of this book has been concerned with efficiency, getting to that point on the PPF that is of maximum value for a particular distribution of income. By using a production possibility frontier (PPF), we gave a two-dimensional illustration of an *n*-dimensional problem — *n*-dimensional because there are many possible goods. The question of growth is one of increasing the PPF for future goods. In Figure 28.1 we have seen a PPF drawn between present and future goods. There will be many kinds of future goods, however, and if we drew a PPF for any two of them — say, transportation and housing — the very height of the PPF would be affected by our decision to save.

Figure 28.2 shows two production frontiers for housing and transportation. Think of PPF_1 as representing the possibilities available in 1970 whereas PPF_2 represents those in 1980. The outward shift is due to the growth of the factors and to technological change. Since one of the factors that grows is capital and the quantity of capital created results from an economic decision, we see that the height of future PPFs depends on how much saving we do today. It is possible, for example, to invoke policies that push the future PPF out at the expense of current consumption. Whether or not such policies should be invoked depends on the relative values and costs of present as opposed to future goods.

The Economic Growth Rate

In the last two decades, economists have rediscovered the wonders of compound interest. The *economic growth rate* — the percentage rate at which total annual output grows — has become a policy goal in its own right. For the United States, the growth rate has been historically about 3½ percent per year, recently about 4½ percent per year. Growth rates vary around the world from negligible amounts to the 10 percent per year maintained by Japan for the last two decades.

How important is a growth rate? The mathematics of *compound interest* is such that small changes in growth rates, if maintained, can result in huge differences in output in a few generations. This is because the small difference is mul-

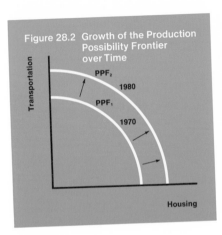

Figure 28.2 Growth of the Production Possibility Frontier over Time

Transportation

PPF_2

1980

PPF_1

1970

Housing

Table 28.1   Output at Various Annual Growth Rates (in Millions of Dollars)

Year	1 Percent	3 Percent	5 Percent
1970	1,000,000	1,000,000	1,000,000
1971	1,010,000	1,030,000	1,050,000
1972	1,020,100	1,060,900	1,102,500
1973	1,030,301	1,092,727	1,157,625
1974	1,040,604	1,125,509	1,215,506
1975	1,051,010	1,159,274	1,276,281
. . .			
1980	1,104,622	1,343,916	1,628,893

tiplied and remultiplied many times over. In Table 28.1 we have three possible time paths for an economy whose output is initially measured at one trillion dollars, roughly the value of US output. In Table 28.1 we see what would happen to output if it grew by 1, 3, or 5 percent per year for an entire decade. By 1980, output will be 50 percent larger if it grows by 5 percent per year than if it grows by 1 percent per year. The difference is $500 billion, roughly $2,000 for every man, woman, and child alive in 1980—not an inconsiderable amount.

These results are even more striking when longer periods are considered. In Table 28.2, using Brazil as an example, we show the results of a century of growth at various different rates:

The results speak for themselves. The power of compound interest would permit the Brazilian economy virtually to triple its output after 100 years if the growth rate is 1 percent per year. If the rate of growth could be increased and sustained at 2 percent, however, output would have increased sevenfold. Look

Table 28.2   A Century of Growth at Different Annual Rates (Output at Beginning of Period = 1 Billion Cruzeiros)

Growth Rate per Annum (%)	Output after 100 Years
0	1.0 billion cruzeiros
1	2.7 billion cruzeiros
2	7.2 billion cruzeiros
3	19.2 billion cruzeiros
4	50.5 billion cruzeiros
5	131.5 billion cruzeiros
6	339.3 billion cruzeiros
7	867.7 billion cruzeiros
8	2,199.8 billion cruzeiros

at the results of a 5 percent growth rate sustained over a period of 100 years. Output would be 131 billion cruzeiros at the end of the period even though it was only 1 billion at the start.

An historical example to illustrate compound interest is the case of the United States and Britain between 1871 and 1968. In 1871 British output was worth $10.4 billion, US output $21.6 billion. Since then, British output has grown at the rate of 2.20 percent per year, while US output has grown at the rate of 3.87 percent per year. Thus in 1968 the United States had an output equal to $860.6 billion, while that of Britain was $86.9 billion. Had Britain grown at the US rate, British output in 1968 would have been $413.6 billion. Clearly the growth rate matters. Current policy toward growth can have a dramatic effect on future well-being.

Problems in Measuring Growth

Hidden behind the single number for a growth rate is the manner in which the various components of total output change. The growth rate is a weighted average of the growth rates of all sectors of the economy. When total output increases by 5 percent, the value of autos produced may have increased by 6 percent while that of housing increased by only 3 percent. The way autos and houses are added together affects the computed growth rate. There is no way of adding them together that gives us an unambiguous measure of how much total output has increased. This is because the composition of output may change over the period. The problem this poses can best be illustrated by a diagram.

In Figure 28.3, we have drawn three points representing different amounts of housing and transportation. It is possible to say that point *B* is 50 percent larger than point *A*. It contains 50 percent more of all commodities than does *A*. But what about point *C*? How much larger than *A* is it? In the absence of a unique set of weights to use in adding up housing and transportation, we cannot tell. We do not even know if *C* is larger or smaller than *B* since it contains more housing but less transportation than does *B*.

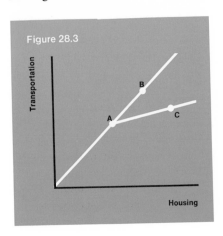

Figure 28.3

The traditional way of comparing points like B and C is to multiply the appropriate quantities by their prices to get a measure of value. If there were a unique set of prices, we could do this. But if prices change over time and if B and C are outputs from different time periods, it is not clear whether we should use the prices that prevailed when B was produced or those appropriate to C. The different prices will give us different answers about the relative magnitudes of B and C.

This problem is called the *index number problem* and it is just one of many problems encountered by economists when they attempt to make comparisons of aggregates. There is no way to solve the problem, no way to get an unambiguous measure of the rate of growth. Still, the rate of growth is a useful fiction to maintain and we will act in the remainder of the chapter as if we are comparing points like A and B, comparisons for which the index number problem does not arise. We do this because we believe that aggregates like the growth rate are not misleading. Also, if necessary, it is possible to specify different indices that give the extreme values to the growth rate, that is, indices that can tell us that the growth of output was between, say, 4 and 5 percent last year.

Capital and Growth

We have seen that in the long run, the rate of growth of output for a mature economy is determined by the growth of technology, labor, and natural resources. In the short run, however, the rate of growth output can be affected by capital accumulation, by building more factories, roads, and warehouses. This short run may be of particular importance to underdeveloped countries as we shall see in Chapters 39 and 40. The short-run growth, we have seen, involves a sacrifice of current consumption due to the savings that must be done in order to build the factories.

For policy purposes, it is useful to know what the long-run effect on consumption of a change in saving behavior would be. But as we saw in Chapter 27, economists are not sure of what the long-run level of population growth will be. Because of our lack of knowledge, we have ignored the long-run Malthusian problems and concentrated on analyses of some intermediate length of time during which population can be expected to grow.

The simplest of such analyses explores the nature of the solution for per capita consumption in a world in which population grows at a constant rate. Because of its simplicity it is the model we will use here to examine a few questions concerning longer run equilibria.

We might wish to know, for example, what would happen to the rate of return on capital if a constant fraction of output is saved every time period. Because of diminishing returns, we know that if the quantity of capital increases relative to that of other factors, its marginal product must fall. We can ask of the simplest model of growth whether falling marginal products—and therefore falling profit rates—must result when a constant fraction of output is added to the capital stock every time period. Or in other words, if saving rates are constant, can an equilibrium be attained at which capital grows at the same rate as the other factors and therefore its marginal product remains constant?

A Model of Economic Growth

The simple model we use ignores the existence of limited natural resources, technological progress, depreciation of capital, and unemployment. More complex models that take account of these variables, however, reach roughly the same conclusions we will get with the simpler model. In this simple world, we can think of only capital and labor as productive factors. A constant marginal product of capital then will exist whenever the percentage growth rates of capital and labor are equal, because then, the expansion of the capital stock through savings will not result in diminishing returns to capital.

The growth rate of capital will be the amount of new saving (a constant fraction of output) divided by the existing stock of capital. If we call the fraction of output saved *the saving rate* then the requirement that growth rates be equal becomes

$$\text{growth rate of labor} = \frac{\text{saving rate} \cdot \text{output}}{\text{capital stock}}$$

or, using obvious symbols

$$g_L = \frac{s \cdot O}{C}$$

Dividing both sides of the equation by s, we can express the requirement of equal growth rates as

$$\frac{g_L}{s} = \frac{O}{C}.$$

Note that the right-hand side of this equation is merely the ratio of output to the capital stock whereas the left-hand side is the growth rate of labor, assumed to be constant, divided by the chosen saving rate. Since the left-hand side consists of constants, we see that the requirement for equal rates of growth of capital and labor can be satisfied with the proper ratio of output to capital. That is, for every saving rate, there exists a different ratio of capital to output that will yield a long-run equilibrium in which capital grows at the same rate as labor and therefore at which the marginal products of the factors can be constant. Positive saving rates need not lead to diminishing profit rates, contrary to the forecasts of Marx, Keynes, and others, if the labor force is growing.

With labor and capital growing by the same percent each time period, output will grow by that percent if the production processes exhibit constant returns to scale. Such a long-run equilibrium has been called a *balanced growth* equilibrium since all important variables—capital, labor, output, consumption, saving—grow at the same percentage rates. Obviously, all ratios of these variables to each other must be constant.

To gain an intuitive understanding of how it is possible to avoid the effect of diminishing returns on profit rates, we need only note that this model assumes that the labor force continues to grow. As long as there is new labor every time period, it is possible to create some new machines (capital) every time period without changing the ratio of machines to men. Long-run equilibria involve levels of output and capital at which the number of new machines is exactly the amount that can be used by the new laborers without changing the ratio of machines to labor.

The growth of output and consumption over time can be shown graphically. In Figure 28.4, we exhibit the paths of these variables over time, assuming that a balanced growth equilibrium has been obtained.* Different paths will exist for different saving rates. Higher saving rates bring about higher levels of capital, of course, and therefore will be associated with higher paths for output.

Changing Saving Rates

If higher saving rates bring about more output, one might ask why we do not espouse policies designed to make saving rates very high. But such policies need not make people happier; there are two reasons for this, both of which result from the fact that it is consumption that makes people happy, not output. (1) Increasing the saving rate will lead to a decline in consumption in the very short run. It takes a while before enough machines can be built to get the economy to the new balanced growth path with a constant higher level of output per capita. (2) Consumption need not be higher in the long run even though output is. With a larger fraction of output being saved, it is possible for consumption to fall permanently when saving rates are increased. At a saving rate of 100 percent, for example, consumption will be zero even though a very large capital stock will result, bringing about very high levels of output.

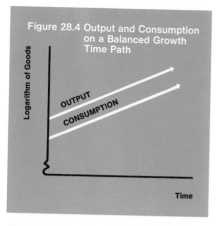

Figure 28.4 Output and Consumption on a Balanced Growth Time Path

*It is convenient to graph the logarithm of such time paths because when a variable increases at a constant geometric rate, its logarithm increases at a constant arithmetic rate. Thus the time paths drawn in Figure 28.4 are straight lines.

If an economy attained a balanced growth path and then the saving rate were increased, in the short run the rate of growth of capital would become higher than that of labor. And remember that due to constant returns to scale, the rate of growth of output can equal that of capital only if labor grows at the same rate as capital. Thus in this case, the growth rate of capital would exceed that of output. Or in other words, the ratio of output to capital would fall so long as the growth rate of capital exceeded that of labor.

From the basic equation of growth,

$$\frac{g_L}{s} = \frac{O}{C}$$

we can see that the higher the saving rate becomes, the smaller must be the ratio of output to capital at the new equilibrium. That the new equilibrium will be attained can be seen quite simply from the fact that an increase in the saving rate makes capital grow faster than output. Thus the right-hand side of the equation must shrink whenever the left-hand side does.

The time paths of output and consumption are affected by the change in saving rates, as can be seen from Figure 28.5. At time t, the saving rate is suddenly increased to be held at a new constant level. This can be seen by the decline in consumption in period t. After t, however, the higher saving rate means that more capital is being produced and therefore output becomes higher than it would be otherwise. Consumption is now a new constant fraction of output; thus its path must look like that of output except when saving rates change. Note that as time passes, the growth rate of output (the slope of its time path) tends to revert to its original level. This is due to the fact that a new equilibrium is being approached at which the growth rates of capital and labor are equal. Since the growth rate of labor has not been changed, it is the old rate of growth at which the equality must occur. Output, of course, must be growing at this rate too.

To see why increases in saving rates need not be desirable, we only have to compare the time path of consumption in Figure 28.4 to that in Figure 28.5. One

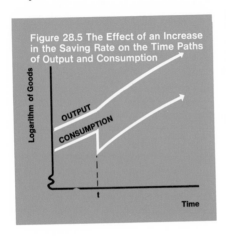

Figure 28.5 The Effect of an Increase in the Saving Rate on the Time Paths of Output and Consumption

path results from a constant saving rate, the other from a change in the rate. Figure 28.6 makes this comparison for us. Note that when the saving rate is increased, some consumption is sacrificed initially although the higher capital stock yields more consumption in the distant future. Whether or not saving rates should be increased depends on whether we feel that the shaded area is worth more or less than the slashed area.

The second reason increases in saving rates need not increase satisfaction is that consumption must be very low when saving rates are large because most of the output is devoted to producing machines, not consumer goods. In Figure 28.7, we illustrate this by showing the effect of a change in the saving rate on the time paths of output and consumption. For purposes of comparison, the alternative time path of consumption – when the saving rate is held constant – has been drawn to illustrate that the new consumption path need never surpass the old path even though output is obviously higher.

This simple model has obvious limitations, yet it has given us some insight into the problem of intertemporal resource allocation. The desirability of a perpetually higher rate of economic growth can be shown by a simple examination of tables of compound interest. But this model shows how capital accumulation need not lead to perpetually higher growth rates. By accumulating more and more roads, machines, and buildings, we can grow faster in the short run than if we do not accumulate them. But diminishing returns to capital forecloses the establishment of a perpetually higher growth rate by this route. Eventually, the economy must grow at a rate dictated by its natural limits: the increase in population, natural resources, and technology. And in the very long run, the natural limits are dictated by the technology and natural resources themselves with even population being forced to adjust.

Capital allows us to trade present consumption for future consumption. Whether or not such a trade is desirable depends on the relative value of those goods. Without knowing the relative value of present and future goods, we cannot say whether or not it is desirable to pursue a policy of increasing the

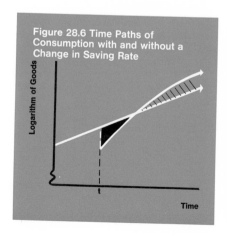

Figure 28.6 Time Paths of Consumption with and without a Change in Saving Rate

Logarithm of Goods

t

Time

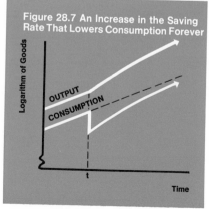

Figure 28.7 An Increase in the Saving Rate That Lowers Consumption Forever

Logarithm of Goods

OUTPUT

CONSUMPTION

t

Time

growth rate in the short run when such an increase comes at the expense of current consumption.

Questions

1.   Private saving and investment decisions are designed to allocate resources between present and future in a way that maximizes individual utility. Can you think of any evidence of market failure that makes the private market solution inefficient? Should there be a national policy toward growth?

2.   Why do higher saving rates, and therefore higher capital stocks, not always lead to higher levels of consumption?

3.   Why is an aggregate growth rate a number to be handled with caution? Is it an exact measure of the growth of output?

Concepts Discussed

economic growth rate   the saving rate
compound interest   balanced growth equilibrium
index number problem

X Unemployment: Theory and Policy

The ideas of economists and political
philosophers, both when they are right
and when they are wrong, are more powerful
than is commonly understood . . . Practical
men, who believe themselves to be quite
exempt from any intellectual influences,
are usually the slave of some defunct economist.

JOHN MAYNARD KEYNES

The depression of the 1930s was an economic disaster of such impressive dimensions that it ranks as one of the greatest social ruptures in modern history. Fact: Money incomes fell on average by one-third. Fact: Some people's income fell by 100 percent. Fact: Unemployment was the state of life for 20 percent of the labor force for almost a decade.

Adjustment to these facts required a complete rethinking of social relationships. Basic assumptions on which people created constructive, rewarding lives were destroyed. Individuals were forced to relive the agony of adolescence and its search for terms on which peace could be declared with one's environment and for premises on which one could erect an identity and life style. Needless to say, the scars from such a wound fade slowly.

These scars are evident in many ways. The thinking of people who lived through the depression is different from that of those who did not. Parents value security and material comfort more than do their children who have never seen these standards threatened. Economics teachers structure whole courses around the problem of unemployment as if it were the most pressing of all social problems.

Another residual of the depression is the body of institutions created in the 1930s that still exist today. These institutions exist not as scars or relics from the past but as evidence of the new social relationships that emerged from the cataclysm. The new institutions, such as unemployment insurance, social security, and bank regulation, were created to blunt the impact of future economic tidal waves. Their existence today is testimony to a bitter lesson of history.

In the next four chapters, we are concerned primarily with a third reminder of the 1930s, namely, the intellectual effects of the depression on economic thought. Stimulated by the vast social problem around them, the economists of the era focused their thinking on solutions to this problem. The result was a body of thought associated with the name of John Maynard Keynes that analyzes ways in which men can control their economic environment. In these chapters, we discuss the reasons economists feel that major depressions need never recur and what to do if one threatens.

The ability to prevent unemployment is the newest major accomplishment of applied economics. The profession is still in the process of digesting this accomplishment and of polishing the tools it requires for complete effectiveness. As such, this body of analysis occupies a large place in all texts of economics. It is the body of thought about which economists have most recently had reason to be proud of their profession. The success of the profession at developing and applying this analysis has resulted in the production of many billions of dollars' worth of output that would not have existed otherwise. The success has also averted much of the potential human tragedy caused by holocausts such as that of the 1930s. The analysis shines brightly even to those of us who were not around during the depression and did not experience its costs.

29 Unemployment and Wage Adjustments

Can involuntary unemployment exist? If there is a free market for labor which we could represent with supply and demand curves, will not a price eventually be reached at which the quantity supplied will equal that demanded? All our previous analysis about the way markets work indicates that involuntary unemployment can exist only as a temporary short-run phenomenon. In this chapter, we take a closer look at the labor force to see what special characteristics it has that allow unemployment to exist—characteristics that, we will find, make the "short run" very long. We will argue that peculiar forces exist in the labor market that make the adjustment of prices very slow, so slow that short-run disequilibrium can exist for many years. This disequilibrium is apparent as an excess of quantity supplied over that demanded; that is, unemployed laborers who would like to work at the going wage.

When observing the labor market, we find the following relationships between unemployment and wage rates. Any hypothesis about labor market behavior must be consistent with these observations. (1) Unemployment rates are never zero; (2) wages increase even when prices stay constant; and (3) wages increase more rapidly when unemployment is low than when it is high. We now explore a modern hypothesis about labor market behavior that is consistent with these observations.

Labor Is Heterogeneous

The previous chapters on supply and demand were concerned with the nature of equilibrium in a market for a homogeneous commodity such as steak or corn. Each bushel of corn is more or less like every other bushel of corn. Therefore one price clears the market. But labor is not homogeneous. A computer programmer, a plumber, a history teacher, and a fireman have very different skills. They sell their labor at different prices in different markets. Men differ by the talents and temperament they are born with as well as by the skills and education they have acquired since birth. Accordingly, the portrayal of the national labor market by a single supply and demand curve is a gross oversimplification—one that may lead us to erroneous prediction if we are not careful.

Figure 29.1 is such a diagram. Clearly, the equilibrium wage is w^*. If the present wage is w', unemployment will exist because supply exceeds demand at that price. What Figure 29.1 does not show us is the speed at which wages will fall from w' to w^* and that the indicated wage rates are really averages of many different rates in many different jobs. For some purposes, abstractions such as Figure 29.1 are useful. But to understand the behavior of labor markets, we must study the speed of adjustment and the implications of the heterogeneous character of labor. After such a study, Figure 29.1 will be more meaningful and useful.

Markets for heterogeneous commodities differ from those for homogeneous commodities in the following two characteristics: (1) Many different prices for the commodities can exist simultaneously; (2) information costs are very expensive.

Enough has been said about the differences among laborers that lead to the existence of different wage rates for different skills. To see the importance of information costs for heterogeneous commodities, consider the manner in which one would explore the market for selling a house as opposed to a bloc of General Motors common stock. To sell the stock, one calls one's broker and finds the going price. That is all there is to it.

There is no going price for houses however. If one calls a realtor, he will demand to inspect the house before suggesting a price that should be charged. Even then there is no guarantee that a sale will be possible at the suggested price. It may be necessary to wait six months or more before the sale can be consummated. Prospective buyers will all demand an inspection for themselves before making any decision. Clearly, it is costly in terms of time and effort to inform the market of the exact nature of the house you have chosen to sell.

Why the difference in the manner of sale? Heterogeneity. All houses are not alike, all shares of General Motors common are. Once one knows the price of General Motors common, no more information is necessary. There is nothing else to tell the broker because he knows exactly what General Motors common is. In the case of the house, however, neither the realtor nor the prospective buyers have any idea what is for sale until they examine it for themselves.

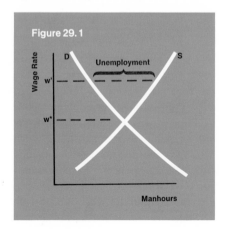

Figure 29.1

What does this imply about labor markets? Labor is heterogeneous. Before signing a job contract, the management will demand a lot of information from the employee — his past employment record, health, reliability, skills, and talents. The employee will demand to know the wage, location, working conditions, and possibilities for promotion before accepting any job offer. The inspection of the market takes a great deal of time.

Frictional Unemployment

Consider a man who makes $5 per hour. He has just been fired and is looking for work. He is offered a job at $3 per hour. He turns it down. Is that rational? It probably is. He turns it down because he has the feeling that his skill is worth $5 per hour. His neighbor, with a similar skill, continues to earn $5 per hour. The few ads in the paper for his skill offer $5 per hour. He so far has not responded to them early enough to pick up a job. His best guess, however, is that he will soon find a $5-per-hour job. Should we count such a man as being unemployed when he has refused work? In fact, our statistics do count him as unemployed. Such unemployment we call *frictional unemployment.*

Frictional unemployment occurs because of the diversity of the labor market. It takes time to transfer from one job to another, to fit round pegs into round holes. If we lowered frictional unemployment by forcing people to accept the first job offer that came along, we would seriously misallocate resources by having plumbers become janitors and so on. This reasoning tells us that *there exists an efficient amount of frictional unemployment.*

The efficiency can be seen simply by observing why the man declined the $3-per-hour job. He declined because he thought a $5-per-hour job would come along soon. He was willing to absorb the current losses of being unemployed in order to reap the future gains of having an extra $2 per hour every hour. Thus his expected income is higher from being unemployed currently; that is, he expects eventually to produce more goods and services by waiting for a $5-per-hour job than by accepting a $3-per-hour job now. Thus waiting is efficient. It should be noted that the waiting is efficient for the society as a whole as well. Total output will be higher in the future if we properly allocate men to jobs today than if we do not. Frictional unemployment can be viewed as an investment. Current income is being sacrificed in order that future income can be higher. The investment takes the form of men searching for jobs and the return arises if the search results in a better matching of skills and needs. Although we may wish to invoke policies that will reduce the level of frictional unemployment, just as we would like to lower the cost of any investment, such policies must be designed with the understanding that there is an efficient amount of frictional unemployment. The present value of the future output lost by eliminating all frictional unemployment will exceed the present output gained from such a policy.

The existence of frictional factors explains why unemployment will exist even in long-run equilibrium. Even in the long run, men will be changing jobs, new skills will be needed, men will retire, and young laborers will enter the labor force. Thus we can never expect to observe unemployment rates of zero. The first of our three observations about the labor market has been explained. Unemployment never goes to zero.

The Importance of Expectations
In our outline of how the labor market worked, an important role was given to the forecasts made by the employers and the unemployed. They would forecast the prospects that they expected to encounter and use these forecasts to determine whether to accept an offer or not. Economists call these forecasts *expectations*. Expectations are our beliefs about what the future will be like. We cannot be certain about the future, but we have some ideas and feelings about it and we must act on those ideas and feelings. It is because of expectations that a man can decline a $3-per-hour job. Presumably $3 is better than nothing. But a man can prefer nothing to $3 per hour in the present if he thinks his choice will result in a future job at $5-per-hour rather than $3-per-hour. Because these expectations play such a large role in the adjustment process, it is important to understand how they are formed and how much time and evidence are needed to change them.

Our man above expected to receive $5 per hour partly because he used to receive it, partly because his neighbor receives it, and partly because the ads he observes in the paper offer it. Similarly, the employers placing the ads are offering $5 per hour because that is what they have been paying recently, what they are paying now to current employees, and what they observe other firms to be paying. These forecasts are correct if the equilibrium wage is in fact $5 per hour. But what if the forecasts are wrong? What if technology changes and demand shifts so that a new equilibrium exists? How can the labor market adjust to that new equilibrium? Assume, for example, that our man above has been fired because of some innovation that reduces the demand for his skill. The market for his skill will clear only if the wage falls to $4.50. Let us now examine what must happen before the market can adjust to the new equilibrium.

At first, no one realizes that $4.50 will be the new wage. How can they? They realize that the firing was due to the innovation, but they do not know what effect the innovation will have on long-run equilibrium. The man looking for work does not find any for quite a while. Perhaps it takes him four weeks to find work instead of the usual two. Eventually, he is the first in line for one of the jobs advertised in the paper and receives a job. The other unemployed with his skill similarly take longer to find work.

This increases the amount of frictional unemployment. If the same people become unemployed as before but now spend twice as long finding a job, there will be twice as many people unemployed. If, for example, everyone is unemployed for four weeks out of the year instead of two weeks, the average annual unemployment rate will be about 8 percent instead of 4 percent.

Thus in the short run, unemployment increases because of the decline in demand for this particular skill. But this is only a short-run adjustment. Eventually the employers realize that they can raise their standards and still get men for the job. Or they can offer $4.92 per hour and get someone, presumably one who has looked for four weeks already and is beginning to change his mind about his prospects. This realization comes to them from the fact that their ads get immediate responses from more people than they can hire. Thus employers offer $4.92.

Now the unemployed's expectations must change. Part of what determined his expected wage was what he read in the paper. Now he reads $4.92 and, realizing that this is still in the ballpark of $5.00, he adjusts himself to expecting it. But even at $4.92, there are more applicants than jobs and there is a pressure for lower and lower wages. The speed at which the wages fall depends on the speed with which the new information about the state of the market is assimilated by the buyers and sellers. As there are information costs in learning about the market as a whole, no one really knows the true equilibrium. Slowly, they perceive the state of the market from their own experiences. The rate of accumulation of knowledge determines the speed at which prices can change. Because knowledge is accumulated slowly and expectations change slowly, we can expect wages to adjust very slowly and that, in the short run at least, most of the burden of adjustment will fall on the unemployed. That is, those who change jobs will find that the interim is much longer than they had expected. The market wage exceeds the long-run equilibrium wage and the quantity supplied exceeds the quantity demanded. The difference can be called *demand unemployment.*

Though it is difficult to predict the speed at which the long-run equilibrium is approached, it is not difficult to describe the basic facts of the adjustment process. These are that when the demand for labor falls, the immediate result is unemployment. Eventually, wage rates will fall and a new full-employment equilibrium can be established. Thus the long-run adjustment occurs in wage rates, but the short-run adjustment occurs in the quantity of employment.

The Adjustment Process

Such a dynamic market is hard to diagram because the adjustment occurs very slowly. No simple supply curve can illustrate this dynamic adjustment because each supply curve is drawn to an assumed fixed set of expectations. As expectations are continually changing, we would need a whole set of supply curves (one for each set of expectations) to describe completely what is happening. Such a diagram would be so complicated as to confuse the issue rather than to simplify it. The purpose of diagrams, after all, is to illustrate and simplify issues, not to confuse them.

Accordingly, we have drawn a simple diagram, Figure 29.2, that indicates the behavior we have just described but does not exactly duplicate it. Our technique has been to draw the demand for labor as fixed and to include two supply curves, one denoting long-run supply responses, one denoting short-run. The difference between the long and short run is that in the long run, expectations have adjusted to reality whereas in the short run they have not. The short-run supply curve must be specified with respect to some unit of time. It can be thought of as representing the supply response after one month's learning has occurred. For shorter learning periods, the curve should be flatter. Indeed, for an instantaneous curve, we could think of a perfectly flat curve at the existing wage rate. Thus the shorter the short run, the flatter the curve.

Now the demand curve shifts, as described, from D_1 to D_2 (Figure 29.3). In one month the equilibrium shifts from A to B. That is, wage rates fall from $5.00 to $4.92 per hour. Employment falls from OF to OE. One could think of the difference (EG) as unemployment in addition to the optimal frictional unemployment. Workers expect to be unemployed between jobs for two weeks in order to find the best possible deal. But because they had the wrong idea about the state of the labor market, they found that on average they were unemployed for four weeks. This extra two weeks' unemployment occurred because of erroneous expectations. Because the unemployment was caused by a change in demand, it is sometimes called demand unemployment to distinguish it from frictional unemployment. *Demand unemployment is that unemployment due to changes in the conditions of the labor market that have not yet been learned by the participants.*

To continue with the adjustment story of Figure 29.3, we see that a long-run equilibrium occurs at C. At C, wages have fallen below their level at B so that employers use more of this skill than they previously found profitable. With the lower wage, some laborers seek other work. These are represented by GF. In the long run, there is nothing but frictional unemployment again — unemployment that cannot be incorporated easily into our diagram.

Thus a typical adjustment pattern in a market for heterogeneous commodities is for the initial adjustment take place in the quantity sold while the eventual price adjustment occurs slowly. Disequilibrium can exist for long periods of time because of the costs of information that must be incurred before an equilibrium can be reached. Initially, in our example above, there is a sharp increase in the amount of unemployment due to the decrease in demand. Eventually prices adjust and the market clears again. Since it takes a long time for the quantity sup-

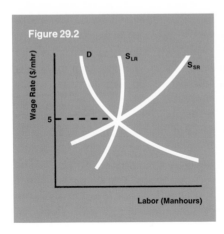

Figure 29.2

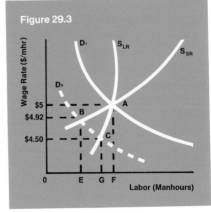

Figure 29.3

plied to become equal to that demanded, unemployment can be observed for a long time.

Examining the pattern of wage-rate changes and unemployment predicted by this model, we find that when wage rates are falling, unemployment rates should be larger than normal. When wage rates are rising, unemployment rates should be smaller than normal. This predicted pattern is close to the one actually observed, as can be seen from Figure 29.4. It is the pattern we summarized above as one of the three facts that would have to be explained by any hypothesis of labor market behavior.

The only one of our three facts left unexplained is that wages tend to increase even when prices are constant. To explain this, we need an additional observation.

Changes in Productivity

Technological progress enables us to derive more and more output from the same quantity of inputs. Changes in technology are inventions that allow products to be produced more cheaply. The invention may replace a man by a machine, make machines cheaper, or it may simply involve a new manner of organizing these productive inputs.

By the very nature of technological change, the demand for certain inputs must be lowered in certain industries. A celebrated example of this goes by the name "automation" (see Chapter 27), which simply means the replacement of men by automatic machinery. Certain jobs are eliminated through automation; the adjustment to this change by the affected workers is a painful and difficult process.

But on the whole, technical progress is a blessing, not a curse. It allows us to produce the same level of output with less inputs. Or alternatively, it allows us to produce more output with the same level of inputs. In the United States in the post-World War II years, investment and technical progress have occurred at a pace that increased the output available from a unit of labor by about 3 percent

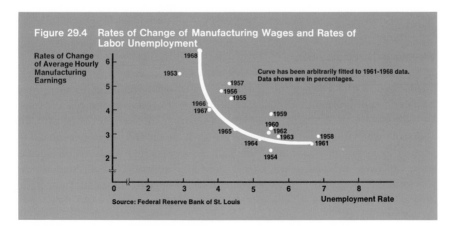

Figure 29.4 Rates of Change of Manufacturing Wages and Rates of Labor Unemployment

Source: Federal Reserve Bank of St. Louis

per year. That is, if our labor force had remained constant in size, total output could have grown by 3 percent per year. Since our labor force grew by 1½ percent per year, total national output grew on average by 4½ percent. Although technical progress may have dramatically increased unemployment rates for particular occupations at particular times, average unemployment rates have not increased. Thus, on average, investment and technical progress have increased output per unit of labor by 3 percent with no perceptible change in unemployment rates.

The change in average labor productivity has made labor a more valuable input. As a result, wages have increased by about 3 percent per year as well. With total sales per man having gone up by 3 percent per year and labor costs also having gone up by 3 percent per year, the difference — profits per man — must have gone up by 3 percent per year as well. Wages, rent, profits — all the components of income — can increase by 4½ percent if the total increases by 4½ percent. For labor, the 4½ percent increase in earnings results from wage increases of 3 percent and an increase in the labor force of 1½ percent.

Thus the fact that wages increase even when prices remain constant can be explained by the fact that, on average, technical progress has increased labor productivity and made it a more valuable productive input. In the United States, wage rates could have increased by 3 percent per year if prices had remained constant. If all prices increase by 2 percent per year, money wage rates can increase by 5 percent per year.

Combining the history of productivity and wage increases with the previous theory about the formation of expectations, we might expect labor market participants to anticipate further technical progress in the future. Thus laborers might expect wage increases of 3 percent if other prices remain constant. If other prices are expected to increase by 5 percent, laborers might expect an 8 percent wage increase. Thus, on average, we would expect wage reductions only if prices were to fall by more than 3 percent per year. Since we rarely observe price declines of this magnitude, we rarely observe wage decreases. Wage rates increase even when unemployment rates are high though they do so by less than they would if unemployment rates were lower.

Structural Unemployment

It is possible for a man to have skills whose value is close to zero. A completely uneducated, untrained man brought up in a rural agricultural environment may be able to contribute little of value to an industrial economy. The market wage for such labor may be less than that needed for survival. It may even be zero. Of course, those of this group who do find work will find it at a wage high enough to support them as employers find it difficult to pay less than such minimums. So some will work for subsistence wages, other may never find work. Such unemployment can be called *structural unemployment* because it results from basic differences between the structure of skills needed by producers and those possessed by laborers.

In wealthy nations, there may still remain small pockets of poverty where children receive no training at all and may therefore be unemployable when they become adults. The situation is much more severe in poorer nations, however. In poor countries, there exist millions of untrained, unemployed people who have left their small agricultural plots to head for the citites. Once there, they vastly outnumber the jobs available for unskilled labor. Life-long unemployment can be a fact of life for a preindustrial man in an industrial world. Such unemployment constitutes one of the major economic and political problems of poor nations.

Social Unemployment

In addition to the unemployment that arises from gaps between the skills of labor and those demanded by the production process, there remains what might be termed *social*, or *psychological*, *unemployment*. This is labor that is unemployed because of its race, sex, religion, political persuasion, or age, rather than for reasons of technical skill. Here the labor market fails to function smoothly owing to noneconomic factors of a social or psychological nature. The result, along with the personal hardships arising from unemployment and discrimination, can be a considerable reduction in economic efficiency.

Policies To Eliminate Unemployment

The structural unemployment just mentioned can be eliminated only by training the labor or by expanding the industrial economy in a manner that increases the need for unskilled labor. Training programs may be organized in an attempt to give these workers skills. Managing these programs is very difficult because the labor market operates in a decentralized manner. No central authority knows whether an additional 100 men of skill Z could be readily employed. Thus a large risk is taken when a training program is begun. In addition, it is very difficult and costly to create a skilled worker from an illiterate farmer who has no mechanical experience. The results from past retraining programs have been mixed. Some men return to the ranks of the unemployed even after they have been trained. Social unemployment cannot be entirely eliminated although laws against discrimination can alleviate the problem. The cure for this kind of unemployment requires a change in men's values; no one is sure about how to accomplish such a change.

A different policy is needed to eliminate frictional unemployment. Some amount of frictional unemployment is efficient. An amount less than the efficient amount is associated with placing round pegs in square holes; that is, getting $5-per-hour labor to perform $4-per-hour jobs. But improvement in the information available to the unemployed may speed up the process of switching jobs, thereby lowering the efficient level of frictional unemployment.

We are left with demand unemployment. Many of the following chapters will be devoted to an analysis of policies designed to eliminate demand unemployment. Demand unemployment results from erroneous expectations. People expected the world to be one way but it was really another. If we ignore demand unemployment, expectations will slowly adjust to reality and the unemployment will be eliminated. An alternative way to eliminate the unemployment is to adjust the reality so that the expectations become valid. If workers expect the labor market to clear at a wage of $5.00 per hour but $4.50 per hour is in fact the equilibrium, unemployment will occur unless something is done to drive the equilibrium wage up to $5.00 per hour.

Our knowledge about policies that change the reality was to a large extent stimulated by the contribution of John Maynard Keynes in the 1930s. Keynes showed (1) that errors in forecasts could lead to unemployment, and (2) that the old ways of eliminating unemployment would not work in all situations. He proposed new policy actions that would work in these cases. He showed how government policy could increase the demand for labor by increasing the demand for goods. This action could change the equilibrium wage to equal its forecasted level, thereby eliminating the unemployment that was due to forecasting errors.

Much of the rest of the book examines government policy to see how and why it works—how it can affect the demand for goods and thereby eliminate unemployment.

Questions

1. In Chapter 4 the long-run supply curves were drawn flatter than the short-run curves. Why? Yet in this chapter, we have drawn the long-run curve steeper than the short-run curve. Why? Are your answers consistent?
2. Why is it efficient to have at least some unemployment?
3. Describe the reasons that wage rates increase even when prices are constant, that they increase faster when unemployment rates are low than when they are high, and that unemployment rates are rarely ever zero.

Concepts Discussed

heterogeneous commodities
frictional unemployment
costs of information

expectations
demand unemployment
structural unemployment

30 Measuring National Income

To understand the ways in which policy can affect employment, it is necessary to understand how national income is measured. *National income* is the total of the incomes received by all citizens of a country over a specified period of time, usually one year. It is a measure of the economic well-being of a nation. Other things equal, the higher national income is, the more goods and services the citizens can afford to buy. National income is closely related to national output, the total value of all goods and services produced by the citizens of a country over the same period of time.

Clearly, the production of goods and services requires the use of productive factors: land, labor, and capital. Thus, other things equal, an increase in total production (national output) will be accompanied by an increase in employment. Therefore, to show how policy affects the level of employment, we only need show how it affects the level of production. This chapter is concerned with the measurement of total production and income, concepts that must be measured if we are to know what policy to use to change employment.

Value Added

To measure total production, we must add up the output of all the nation's firms and individuals. One simple and wrong way to do this would be to add together all the sales of all the firms and individuals. This is wrong because it leads us to count certain production twice. For example, if we count the final value of the automobiles sold by General Motors as part of their sales and also count the value of the glass sold to General Motors by Pittsburgh Plate Glass as part of the sales of Pittsburgh Plate Glass, we will have counted the glass twice. The glass was only produced once; an accurate measure of total production will count it only once.

Therefore, the sales of a firm are a misleading measure of the amount it contributes to total production because sales include the value of the production of other firms as well. To avoid double counting, it is necessary to use only the *value added* by each firm. Value added equals the value of goods produced minus purchases from other firms. Thus the value added by General Motors in the production of an automobile is the value of the auto minus the value of the glass, steel, tires, and so on. The glass, steel, and tires will be counted in national output as the production of Pittsburgh Plate Glass, US Steel, and Goodyear. Since value added is a measure of the contribution of a single firm to total production, the sum of the values added by all economic units must be equal to total production.

Final Sales

Another way to avoid double counting is to ignore the sales from one firm to another when adding up total sales. That is, we could add up the sales to consumers, to government, and to foreigners only. Such sales are called *final sales*. In this way, the sale of the auto by General Motors – a final sale – gets counted but the sale of the glass to General Motors – an intermediate sale – does not.

Final sales is a measure of the rate at which goods are being claimed by their ultimate users. Thus it is a measure of the rate at which satisfaction is being yielded by the national economy. Presumably satisfaction is the purpose for which the whole economic machine is organized. But production and sales are not the same thing. If we wish to focus on the determinants of the level of employment, it is production that interests us for it is production that requires labor input.

Production can differ from final sales in two ways. (1) Inventories can change. Inventories are goods that have been produced but not yet used or sold. They exist on the shelves of stores, in warehouses, trucks, trains, and planes, as well as on the assembly line. (2) Production can differ from final sales through the production of producer goods such as plant and equipment. Economists define new purchases of these goods as *investment* expenditures. Although an individual can invest by buying securities, an economy can invest only by building physical capital. Chapter 19 discusses investment and capital. Producer goods differ from intermediate goods in that they are intended to be used and worn out in the production process while intermediate goods are expected to be transformed into other goods. The iron used by a blacksmith is an intermediate good; his hammer is a producer good. Examples can be dreamed up in which the distinction becomes fuzzy, of course, and some arbitrary classification of the borderline cases is necessary. We wish to maintain the distinction here, however, because it becomes useful below when we discuss changes in the level of production. Accordingly, let us define *total net sales*, hereafter called *sales*, to include final sales plus sales of producer goods to producers. Thus sales differ from production only by the changes in inventory. Production must be sold *or* added to inventories. A basic accounting relationship thus becomes

production = sales + change in inventories

This relationship could be thought of as a definition since it results from the separate definitions of sales and production. Whatever is produced and not sold must be added to inventories.

Some Jargon

Gross national product is the term used by economists to denote the total production of all the economic units of a nation. It is equal to sales plus change in inventories. Its initials, *GNP*, though not a household word, are frequently used by the press as well as by economists as an abbreviation for gross national product. It is the statistic most frequently reported in the newspaper as a measure of the material satisfaction being yielded by the economy.

National income, the sum of everyone's income, is closely related to GNP. National income is the sum of the wages and salaries, profits, interest, rents, and royalties that constitute the incomes of individuals. The relationship between national income and GNP can be exposed most clearly by examining an *income statement* for a single firm. This exercise will lead to a discussion of the relationship between saving and investment, a concept that must be understood if one is to understand how employment is determined.

A firm's income statement is merely an elaboration of the definition of profits. Chapter 17 discusses the income statement of firms in greater detail and, in particular, discusses the problem of depreciation charges, a problem we will only mention here.

production - costs = profits

Now production must also equal sales plus change in inventories. And costs include purchases of goods and materials, wages and salaries, interest, rent, taxes, and the wear and tear on plant and equipment. This last item, called depreciation, results because producer goods last for many years.* This simple elaboration of the firm's income statement is printed in Table 30.1, which is arranged vertically, the conventional manner in which income statements are presented. The income statement really just defines profit. Although income statements are generally computed every three months or so, they must hold at every instant of time because they really just define how profits are to be computed as the difference between production and costs.

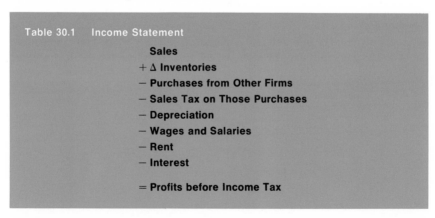

Table 30.1   Income Statement

    Sales
  + Δ Inventories
  − Purchases from Other Firms
  − Sales Tax on Those Purchases
  − Depreciation
  − Wages and Salaries
  − Rent
  − Interest

  = Profits before Income Tax

---

*If the blacksmith needs a new hammer every five years, he might count one-fifth of a hammer as part of his annual cost if he is to obtain an accurate measure of the profitability of his business. We could say that the hammer wears out by one-fifth every year and so its value falls. The decline in value of the hammer is one of the costs of being a blacksmith.

If we rearrange Table 30.1 by putting the bottom six terms on one side of the equation (changing the signs of those terms shifted), we get Table 30.2. Table 30.2 still defines profits, only now we have added equal terms to both sides of the definition.

From our discussion above, it should be clear that the top three terms in Table 30.2 represent value added by the firm; they represent total production minus purchases from other firms. On the other hand, the bottom four terms represent income received by someone from this firm. Table 30.2 therefore can be rewritten as the following equation:

value added = depreciation + sales tax + net income received

Remember that this still is derived from the definition of profits as being equal to the value of production minus costs.

We have defined GNP as the sum of the values added for all firms and productive entities in the economy. We have defined national income as the total income received by all members of the society. Therefore, adding up this equation for all firms and economic units in the economy gives a new aggregate equation:

GNP = depreciation + sales tax + national income

This equation was derived from the profit statements of firms. The fact that profits equal production minus costs can be transformed to say that GNP equals national income, depreciation, and sales tax. An additional definition that will not concern us here is that of net national product (NNP). NNP equals GNP minus depreciation. NNP is a measure of the value of production that is derived from this period's inputs. It subtracts from the total production a number that represents the wearing out of machinery and plant.

Components of GNP

We could break GNP into different components in many ways. For example, we could divide it by industry, by state, or by any arbitrary classification such as

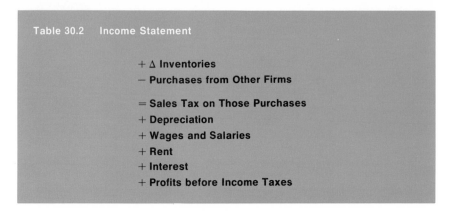

Table 30.2   Income Statement

+ Δ Inventories
− Purchases from Other Firms

= Sales Tax on Those Purchases
+ Depreciation
+ Wages and Salaries
+ Rent
+ Interest
+ Profits before Income Taxes

color. One useful way to break it down is by the final use of product. In particular, we would find it interesting to know whether the product was consumed or was invested for future production. To classify GNP in this way, we must look at final sales rather than at value added.

To convert value added into final sales, one need only cancel intermediate sales and purchases such as the aforementioned sale of glass by Pittsburgh Plate Glass to General Motors. Then our measure of GNP will consist of entries such as the value of autos sold (and added to inventories) rather than entries describing the value of the glass produced by Pittsburgh Plate Glass and the value of assembling autos contributed by General Motors. Such cancellation must eliminate all intermediate sales from one domestic firm to another. The only purchases that do not cancel are those from foreign firms. For example, if General Motors buys radios from a Japanese firm, it would be wrong to count the whole value of the auto as US production without subtracting the value of those goods purchased abroad.

After such cancellations, GNP can be rewritten as follows:

$$GNP = \text{net sales} + \Delta \text{ inventories} - \text{imports}$$

We are now ready to break down sales into components denoting its end use. Some sales are used for consumption, some, called investment, are used for future production. Some go to foreigners (exports) and some are bought by governments for public consumption or investment. Thus Table 30.3 shows one of the many ways in which GNP can be broken down.

Purchasing Power and National Income

Every sale results in an exactly equal increase in purchasing power. The money flows into the cash register from the sale and out again to people in the form of payments for wages and salaries, etc. The money that remains is profit—income to the owner of the business. Depreciation and sales taxes also represent purchasing power even though we do not define them as income. Some of the payments made from the cash register wind up in the coffers of the government, others go to those whose plant and equipment were used (and worn) during the

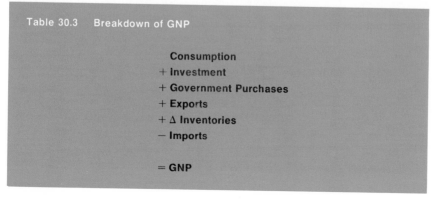

Table 30.3   Breakdown of GNP

  Consumption
+ Investment
+ Government Purchases
+ Exports
+ Δ Inventories
− Imports

= GNP

production of the commodity. These payments are not defined as income, yet they are purchasing power and can be used to buy the goods that GNP represents. Every sale counted in GNP results in equal flows of goods and money. Clearly the sum of the payments received equals the value of the goods sold.

We now wish to divide the purchasing power into the groups that control its disposal, namely, households, business, and government. To do this, an important category of transactions that has been ignored so far now must be considered, namely, transfer payments. *Transfer payments* represent purchasing power that is transferred from one group to another but does not represent a purchase of a good or commodity. An example is dividends. Firms pay dividends to their owners. This transfers purchasing power from business to households without the households' selling anything to business. Other examples are taxes—transfers from households and business to government—and social security payments, unemployment compensation, welfare payments, and so on—transfers from government to households. After taking account of all these transfers, GNP appears as in Table 30.4.

Saving and Investment

We have been looking at GNP in two different ways. One way is derived from adding up the sales figures of different firms. These figures can be classified in many ways according to the characteristics of the products produced. Another way to look at GNP is to look at purchasing power and income. These figures we have classified by the groups receiving the purchasing power. Both ways must give the same total.

If we now wished to break GNP into two components, one to represent goods consumed today and the other to represent goods produced today but to be used in the future, we would also find two ways to do it. One would be to look at the goods sold and classify them as consumption or investment goods,

Table 30.4			
Purchasing Power	=	**Income Received**	+ **Transfers**
Purchasing Power of Households	=	Wages + Salaries + Interest + Rent	− **Income Tax** + **Dividends** + **Government Transfers**
+		+	+
Purchasing Power of Business	=	Profits + Depreciation	− **Dividends** − **Profits Tax**
+		+	+
Purchasing Power of Government	=	Sales Tax	+ **Income Tax** + **Profits Tax** − **Transfers**
GNP	=	**GNP**	+ **0**

the other would be to look at the disposition of purchasing power to see if it is saved or spent on goods for consumption. If our classification of consumption goods is consistent, we will find that those goods classified as consumption goods for the first way of measuring GNP will be equal in value to the spending from purchasing power on consumption goods. They should, in fact, represent the same goods. Goods sold for purposes of consumption should be equal in value to the amount of purchasing power spent on consumption. And since we have two equal measures of GNP and two equal measures of consumption, what is left over must be the same in both cases. And with a few additions and subtractions to what is left over, we can show that the value of new investment equals the amount of income saved. To show how this accounting works out, we need a few further definitions.

If we sell more goods to foreigners than we buy from them, they owe us money. As proof of this, we acquire an IOU from them or some other security. This increase in their indebtedness to us can be considered an investment by us abroad. By this process, we acquire ownership of foreign assets. Just as the purchase of securities is considered to be an investment by an individual, the purchase of foreign securities by domestic citizens is an act of national investment. Thus exports minus imports can be called *foreign investment.*

Government saving can be defined as government tax receipts minus government spending. *Business saving* is retained earnings—profits not paid out in taxes or dividends—and depreciation. If we define household purchasing power as *disposable income* (wages and salaries, interest, rents, and royalties and dividends), *household saving* becomes disposable income minus consumption expenditures. Note that in all these definitions, the terms "saving" and "investment" have referred to flows of income over a time period. They are measured with a time dimension, for example, $80 billion per year. The terms *savings* and *investments* (with an "s" added) will not be used here. They refer to entirely different concepts—stocks of assets acquired at any time in the past. We refer to them here only for purposes of clarifying the notion of saving and investment. Saving and investment do not refer to savings accounts or portfolios of securities. They refer to the rate at which individuals are putting aside income and the rate at which the economy is acquiring productive assets.

If we now write down GNP in the two ways listed above, subtract terms from both sides, and substitute our new definitions, we find that saving equals investment.

Subtracting depreciation from both sides would leave net investment equal to net saving. (Depreciation appears as part of gross business saving and gross investment in Table 30.5.)

That saving equals investment should not be a surprise when we see that the two concepts represent different ways of viewing the same thing. Sales generate purchasing power equal to their own value. Sales must be of consumption or investment goods. Purchasing power must be consumed or saved. Therefore, saving equals investment. Saving is the rate at which income is being put aside to be used in the future; investment is the physical representation of saving in the specific goods that are to be used for future production of consumption goods.

The Role of Inventories

Despite the accounting proofs just presented, it still may be difficult to understand *why* saving must equal investment. Do purchases of plant and equipment increase if one decides to save his income rather than spend it? Does someone increase his saving when AT&T announces plans to invest $5 billion next year? The answers to such questions are not obvious until we study more about the behavior of people and the interaction of the whole economic system.

For now, let us respond to those questions by noting the role of inventories in the saving-investment identity. Changes in inventories are counted above as investment. This is because investment goods are those goods produced now to be used in the future; such a definition presumably includes changes in inventories. But inventories differ from other forms of investment (plant and equipment) in that their owners have only indirect control over their level. This is because sales can increase or decrease in an unexpected fashion, making inventories above or below their intended levels. A sudden increase in the demand for autos, for example, results in an unintended reduction in dealers' inventories of autos. The reverse would result from a sudden decrease in demand.

If one should suddenly decide to decrease the rate at which he is saving and increase his consumption spending, there need not be an immediate matching

Table 30.5

Concept	Symbol			Symbol	Concept
Consumption	C			DI	Disposable Income
Investment	$+ I$			$+ S_B$	Business Saving
Government Purchases	$+ G$	$= GNP =$		$+ T$	Taxes − Government Transfers
Exports	$+ X$				
Imports	$- M$				
Δ Inventories	$+ \Delta$ Inv.				

Subtracting C and G from both sides leaves gross saving and investment.

Table 30.6

Investment (Domestic)	I			$DI - C$	Household Saving
Foreign Investment	$+ X - M$	$=$		$+ S_B$	Business Saving
Δ Inventories	$+ \Delta$ Inv.			$+ T - G$	Government Saving

decision by someone else to decrease his investment. Instead, the former's increased purchases could bring about declines in inventories. Thus in the short run, inventory investment would decrease by the amount of his decreased saving or increased consumption spending. Similarly, had a firm decided to invest more – say, by buying an additional truck – inventories of trucks could have declined by the same amount so that total investment remained constant. Equipment investment could increase while inventory investment decreases. Thus saving and investment are equal at every instant by definition and the trick in the definition is that changes in inventories are considered to be an investment. Thus intended investment and intended saving can differ. But, by definition, measured saving and investment cannot.

But inventories play their role only as a buffer stock in the short run. Ultimately, the owners of the inventories assert their control and attempt to restore them to some desired level. We can see only the first step of how this is accomplished here. The next steps await the next chapter.

The store owner ultimately realizes that his inventories are declining. His natural response is to order more. This runs down inventories at the factory and eventually the factory manager must respond, perhaps by increasing production. In the auto example, we might have total inventories of new unsold autos at the factory, on trucks, in storage lots, and in showrooms of 1,000,000 autos. Production and sales might be 200,000 cars per week so that inventories remain constant. If sales now jump to 250,000 per week, inventories will fall by 50,000 per week unless something happens to production. After ten weeks, inventories will be down to 500,000 – half their usual level – unless some action is taken. The producers may decide to increase production to 250,000 per week – the level of sales – or to increase prices to discourage the additional sales. Their decision is likely to depend on whether they have idle plant capacity and an idle labor force. If so, it is easy to increase production. If not, it is very costly to do so, and they are likely to raise prices. Whatever they ultimately decide, it is clear that changes in inventories allow an adjustment of investment in the short run to guarantee that saving equal investment. But in the long run, something more fundamental must happen. In our auto example, the price of autos or the level of production could be changed in an attempt to restore equilibrium. At the new equilibrium, inventories are constant again, and saving equals noninventory investment. But this means that, at the new equilibrium, intended saving and/or investment must be different from what it was at the old equilibrium.

From this analysis, we can conclude that when firms and individuals desire different levels of investment and saving, the economy is not in a long-run equilibrium. The acts of satisfying the conflicting desires will lead to changes in inventories that will lead to changes in prices or output until a long-run equilibrium is attained at which the intended levels of saving and investment are equal.

In any market, the quantity of goods demanded equals that supplied at the equilibrium price. For other prices the equality need not hold. For the economy as a whole, the intended amount of saving equals the intended amount of investment at the equilibrium levels of output and prices. For other levels of output and prices, the intended quantities can be different from each other; that difference is represented by an unintended inventory change that guarantees the equality of defined saving and defined investment. This is because inventory changes, whether intended or not, are defined to be a part of investment.

Questions

1.   If I take money from my mattress and buy a new car, have I destroyed the equality of saving and investment?

2.   Market prices are used when measuring gross national product. Why does this allow GNP to be a measure of the *value* of goods and services produced?

3.   If we import and export the same amount of goods, GNP as defined above will equal $C + I + G$ only. But the exports and imports are goods of value and should be counted somewhere. Are they?

Concepts Discussed

value added

final sales

GNP

national income

NNP

transfer payments

saving

investment

disposable income

savings

investments

31 Induced Spending: a Simple Model

At a long-run equilibrium, desired saving must equal desired investment. To understand that equilibrium, we must understand the determinants of saving and investment. Chapter 19 outlined the role of interest rates in equating the quantities of desired saving and investment within a model of full employment. Here we are building up to an analysis of a model of unemployment and we will focus on the role of a different variable, namely total sales, in attaining equilibrium. We look first at the manner in which saving decisions are made to see how changes in income affect them. Then we review the link between sales and income established in the previous chapter, and finally we create a simplified model of long-run equilibrium between saving and investment that incorporates saving behavior of the kind to be presented.

The Saving Decision

One popular theory of the saving decision is called the life-cycle hypothesis. In its simplest form, the life-cycle hypothesis merely notes that we should expect consumers to attempt to maintain a stable level of consumption. The reason we should expect this is derived from diminishing relative value. There is no psychological reason to believe that people prefer present to future consumption. Thus a simple assumption is that consumption in all years will yield equivalent amounts of utility. If the principle of diminishing relative value holds for consumption of goods in different time periods as well as for the consumption of different goods, then the 15,000th dollar spent on consumption this year will yield less utility than the 5,000th dollar spent on consumption next year. The value of present consumption relative to future consumption is lower with that allocation than if $10,000 were spent on consumption in each year. Thus if an individual has income of $15,000 one year and he expects to earn only $5,000 the next year, one should expect him to spend less than his income the first year and more than his income the second year. This is because the consumption sacrificed by reducing spending below $15,000 in the first year is worth a great deal less than the consumption gained by increasing spending above $5,000 in the second year. The principle of diminishing relative value tells us that if he has no particular preference for consuming in one year or the other, he will be happier spending only $10,000 the first year and $10,000 the second year. Even spending $10,001 the first year and $9,999 the second year should be an inferior allocation of resources because the 10,001st dollar of consumption gives less satisfaction than does the 10,000th.

Generalizing from this simple observation of the implications of diminishing relative value, the life-cycle saving hypothesis tells us that consumers will attempt to maintain fairly stable levels of consumption over their entire lives. If income fluctuates widely, consumers will save much in years of extraordinarily high income and dissave or borrow in years of very low income. Income may be received at a variable rate but consumption is done at a constant rate. Changing the level of saving allows income to exceed or fall short of consumption.

One of the largest variations in income that must be smoothed by saving is retirement. After age 65, wage income goes to zero yet consumption must continue. The life-cycle hypothesis predicts that individuals will save during their working years in order to be able to dissave when they retire. We observe a great deal of saving for retirement being accomplished through financial mechanisms designed specifically for that purpose. Contractual saving in the form of social security taxes, pension fund contributions, or annuities attached to life insurance policies are common ways to provide for retirement. Many people save for retirement in other ways besides these contractual forms of saving. Even the paying off of a mortgage on a house represents saving for retirement. If one owns a house, he can live rent free when he is retired.

The life-cycle saving hypothesis does not explain behavior exactly, of course. There are always complicating factors that prevent any simple hypothesis such as this one from predicting behavior perfectly. It is interesting, however, to explore what its precise predictions are since behavior will more or less approximate these predictions if the hypothesis is more or less true. What, for example, does the hypothesis predict that an individual will do if his income increases by $1? How much will he be induced to increase consumption spending because of the increase in his income?

(1) If he already anticipated the increase in his income, he will not be induced to increase his spending at all. A man with $5,000 income in one year who expects $15,000 the next year may borrow in order to augment consumption during the first year. When the increase in income occurs, he uses it to pay off the loan and continues to consume at the same rate. A perfectly forecast increase in income may not induce any increased consumption the moment it occurs. The level of consumption already reflects the fact that income was expected to increase.

(2) If the increase in income was unanticipated and is not expected to occur again, it is likely that small amounts will be consumed in the present while most of the income is saved. If forgotten Aunt Harriet dies and leaves in her will $25,000 to her nephew whose income is $10,000 per year, he realizes that it would be foolish to consume this year as much as those who earn $35,000 per year consume. Because next year he would have to cut his spending back to the $10,000 per year level since the extra $25,000 will be all gone. The life-cycle hypothesis tells us that if the nephew is 50 years old and expects to live another

25 years, he will spend $1,000 extra this year and $1,000 extra for each of his remaining years. And if we take account of the interest that could be earned on this money, we find that he could spend closer to $2,000 per year for each of the next 25 years. Thus unexpected income that is nore expected to recur induces him to consume some more immediately but not a great deal more.*

(3) If the increase in income is unanticipated but is expected to last for a long period of time, a great deal of it will be consumed. If one is suddenly offered a job with a different firm at a salary that is $5,000 per year higher, he can consume a large portion of that $5,000 as he will get $5,000 extra in all the future years he works. He can increase consumption this year and maintain it forever at a higher rate because his income will be higher forever. The exact prediction of the life-cycle hypothesis is that he will increase consumption to a level that he can maintain forever. Thus if retirement is 30 years away and he expects to be retired for 10 years, he could increase consumption by $3,750 this year and all future years (ignoring interest receipts) in response to the increase in his current income.

There are complicating factors that prevent the life-cycle hypothesis from predicting exactly. Before we explore those factors, we should state the lessons learned from the exact predictions of the examples above. These lessons are that consumption spending will increase more in response to increases in income that are unanticipated and that are expected to continue than it will to increases that are forecast and temporary. These effects will hold generally even though the predictions are inexact. The role of saving is to allow consumption to fluctuate less than income. If one knows about future fluctuations in income, he can plan for them now and consumption need not vary when they occur. If unanticipated changes in income occur, consumption plans will have to be adjusted. Adjustments will be larger the more permanent the change in income is expected to be.

This model can be applied to very short periods of time as well as to longer ones. If pay checks are received once a month, one does not spend all his income on payday by living in grand style and then attempt to scrape by on nothing for the rest of the month. Instead, one lives in the same building, uses the same durable goods, eats the same food throughout the month. Consumption is smoothed out because the extra pleasure received from the one-day bash is worth less than the pleasure sacrificed by being forced to grovel in poverty for the rest of the month. The life-cycle saving hypothesis extends the reasoning behind this monthly behavior to longer periods of time. Income that is received once and is not expected to be received again is spread out over a long period for consumption purposes, just as the monthly pay check is.

Among the many complications that make the predictions of the life-cycle hypothesis differ from those just presented are the following. (1) With technolog-

---

*Note that the purchase of an automobile that will last five years cannot all be counted as consumption in the year of purchase. It represents present and future consumption. Thus *spending* may increase greatly in response to unanticipated increases in income, but *consumption* will increase by less than spending if many durable goods are bought.

ical progress, we can expect wage rates to increase on average. Most people, therefore, expect their future income to be higher than their current income. If the life-cycle hypothesis is correct, we would predict that young people would attempt to borrow a great deal to increase current consumption above income. But forecasts of future income are not exact. When one is not sure of future income or even of future consumption needs, it is wise to have a cushion of savings to absorb any unexpected impacts that arise. Therefore consumption may be held a bit lower in the early years than the naive theory would predict because one wishes to insure a minimum level of consumption for the future should an unforeseen disaster occur. As wage increases materialize, consumption can increase with them because the uncertainty has been eliminated and the worst has been prepared for.

(2) Despite this, many young people borrow a great deal. And many would like to borrow more than they are able to. They are not able to borrow because banks are aware of the uncertainty of their future income and fear their ability to repay. Thus when income increases to this group, even temporary income is spent to a greater degree than it would be if it were possible for them to borrow all they wished.

(3) The very rich leave large estates. Perhaps their consumption is unaffected by changes in income, all such changes having an effect on the size of the estate they leave.

(4) Interest rates allow positive returns to saving. That is, the sacrifice of a dollar's worth of consumption today allows for the consumption of more than one dollar's worth in the future. This may encourage less consumption in the early years and more in the late years as the interest earned on saving allows one to consume more goods in total if consumption is done late rather than early.

(5) Some economists maintain that consumption standards are in part determined by the consumption of others. At its worst this can be translated as "keeping up with the Joneses." At its best, this theory states the fact that the realization of possible pleasures to be derived from increased consumption requires one to be aware of the existence of the consumption goods. One way this observation is accomplished is by observing others. Other ways are through advertising and sales efforts. Rich people own summer houses. If one did not know that and then became rich, the possibility of owning a summer house might never dawn on him. If our consumption depends on standards derived from observing others consume, we might expect the poor to consume a larger fraction of income than the rich if they both observe the same standards. In the end, of course, it is impossible to consume more than one's income. Keeping up with the Joneses in future years requires that one keep up with their bank account today.

If we now attempt to bring together these observations on the consumption decision and ask how much of any increase in aggregate household income will be respent, we must realize that there will be varying responses from various households. On average, some of it will be respent, some of it saved. We know that the answer depends on whether the increase in income is expected to persist or whether it is viewed as temporary, whether it was forecast or not, and even on the age of the income recipient. Our best estimates are that in the short run, about two-thirds of any increase in consumer income is respent. This number, however, includes much spending that economists classify as investment or saving rather than as consumption. This spending includes all spending for durable goods such as autos and appliances that are to yield future satisfaction as well as present satisfaction. The theory just described referred to the actual consumption of goods and services, not to the purchase of goods. It is satisfaction that must be spread out, not spending. The purchase of durable goods represents present spending but yields a whole stream of future consumption. Our theory above said that consumption from once-in-a-lifetime income might be spread over the rest of one's life. But one way to do this is to buy a house. The purchase of the house represents present spending, but the house yields consumption services on into the future. Our estimate that two-thirds of income is respent must therefore imply that much less than two-thirds of the changes in current income is added to current consumption.

Sales and Income

We have just seen why consumption spending increases in response to changes in income. In Chapter 30 we showed how increases in sales led to increases in incomes of the same amount if the managers of the inventories could regulate them at a desired level. Here we will assume that the inventory managers are able to do this; that is, that we are considering a time period that is long enough so that inventory managers can respond to any of the unanticipated changes that might beset them. In such a world, sales are equal in value to production. And production, we saw, creates an amount of purchasing power equal to itself. For now we will ignore depreciation, sales taxes, and all other forms of purchasing power that are different from income. Their inclusion clouds the analysis but does not contribute to it in any substantive way. Thus we will assume them away.

With these two assumptions, the value of income is equal to that of sales. We now use a very simple model to describe how changes in the level of sales can bring about equality between intended saving and intended investment. In this simple model, we ignore the changes in other variables that also can occur to bring about this equality. Later we note how their existence qualifies the predictions we derive here.

A Simple Model of Equilibrium

If intended saving is to equal intended investment at an equilibrium, must someone change his investment decision when someone else changes his saving decision? Not necessarily. To show why not, we assume that desired investment remains constant as we trace the path to equilibrium of a simple economy.

Assume that initially an equilibrium exists with intended saving equal to intended investment. Someone now decides to spend $1,000 that he had previously intended to save. To attain a new equilibrium either (1) intended investment must decrease by $1,000; (2) saving by some other party must increase by $1,000; or (3), some combination of (1) and (2) must occur. Here is what happens.

The $1,000 deduction from saving is seen as an increase in sales of $1,000. Producers immediately increase production by $1,000 to guarantee that inventories remain constant. Thus the receipts from the increase in sales pass directly into the hands of those who sold the extra labor, etc., to produce the extra $1,000 worth of goods. Thus income rises by $1,000.

Those who receive the income must either save it or consume it. Above we pointed out that it is not unreasonable to expect them to consume two-thirds of any increase in income and therefore to save one-third of it. That is what we will assume here for all changes in income. Thus the $1,000 increase in income brings about an increase in consumption spending of two-thirds of a thousand.

But this increase in sales will also result in an increase in income. And this increase in income will lead to a further increase in consumption sales, implying further increases in income leading to still further increases in consumption, and so on. An endless progression of induced spending results from the initial increase in consumption spending of $1,000. It would be wrong, however, to assume that because the progression is endless, the total increase in sales is not finite. Each round of induced sales is smaller by one-third than the previous round. The total increase in sales, therefore, is the sum of a declining series and, as we show below, the series has a finite sum as long as each round of spending is smaller than the previous round by a constant percentage.

The table shows how the initial increase in spending leads to an increase in consumption spending of $667, which leads eventually to a further increase in consumption spending of $444, leading to still further increases of $297, $198, $132, and $88. The respending never dies, but it does fade away. Elementary algebraic manipulations allow us to add up infinite series such as the one below. In the right-hand column of Table 31.1 is a series consisting of the fraction two-thirds raised to all of the integers. The sum of this series is two.* When we add to this induced spending the initial increase in autonomous spending of $1,000., we find a total of $3,000 of spending that results from the initial increase in consumption of $1,000. The footnote shows why.

---

*An infinite series of the form $1 + a + a^2 + a^3 + \ldots$ can be multiplied by 1 written in the form $\left(\dfrac{1}{1-a} - \dfrac{a}{1-a}\right)$ to yield another infinite series of exactly the same value. Writing the terms down in order shows the second series to be $\dfrac{1}{1-a} - \dfrac{a}{1-a} + \dfrac{a}{1-a} - \dfrac{a^2}{1-a} + \dfrac{a^2}{1-a} - \dfrac{a^3}{1-a} + \dfrac{a^3}{1-a} - \dfrac{a^4}{1-a} + \ldots$. From this series, we can cancel all terms but the first and last, that is, all terms but $\dfrac{1}{1-a} - \dfrac{a^\infty}{1-a}$. If a is less than one, a^∞ is zero. Thus if a is less than one, the sum of $1 + a + a^2 + a^3 + \ldots$ is $\dfrac{1}{1-a}$. In the example above, we added up $a + a^2 + a^3 + \ldots$, which must be equal to $\dfrac{1}{1-a} - 1$ or $\dfrac{a}{1-a}$. For $a = \dfrac{2}{3}$, the sum $\dfrac{a}{1-a}$ equals 2.

Thus total sales increase by three times the amount of the initial increase in sales when two-thirds of all increases in income are respent. The percentage of an increase in income that is respent on consumption goods is called the *marginal propensity to consume*. Thus the footnote tells us that in this model, the *expenditure multiplier* equals one divided by one minus the marginal propensity to consume. The expenditure multiplier tells us by how much an initial increase in sales is multiplied because of the induced spending it causes.

$$\text{expenditure multiplier} = \frac{1}{1 - MPC}$$

In our example, the expenditure multiplier is three since the marginal propensity to consume is two-thirds. If consumers respend three-fourths of all increases in income, the multiplier will be larger—four. The more consumers respend, the larger the multiplier. In fact, if they respend everything, the formula tells us that any increase in sales will cause induced sales of an infinite amount! Respending goes on and on, never diminishing in size.

Now we can return to the problem we posed earlier. Someone has reduced his saving by $1,000. How does intended saving remain equal to intended investment? The $1,000 increase in his consumption increases incomes by $1,000 and the chain of induced consumption expenditure that results increases them by an additional $2,000. Thus incomes have increased by $3,000. Two-thirds of the increase is spent on consumption and *one-third is saved*. Thus we see that saving is restored to its initial level and remains equal to intended investment. Reviewing the adjustment to equilibrium, we have the following: (1) Saving was reduced and consumption increased by $1,000; (2) the extra consumption expenditures increased incomes by $1,000; (3) the recipients of incomes saved $333 and spent $667 for consumption goods; (4) this caused incomes to increase

Table 31.1   Changes in Sales in Response to an Increase in Consumption of $1,000

Sales Δ Sales	Production = Δ Production	Income = Δ Income (= 2/3 Δ Income)	Consumption Δ Consumption
$1,000	$1,000	$1,000	$667 = 2/3 of 1,000
667	667	667	445 = $(2/3)^2$ of 1,000
445	445	445	297 = $(2/3)^3$ of 1,000
297	297	297	198 = $(2/3)^4$ of 1,000
198	198	198	132 = $(2/3)^5$ of 1,000
132	132	132	88 = $(2/3)^6$ of 1,000
...	...	...	...

by an additional $667, causing additional respending and saving; (5) ultimately, respending totaling $2,000 occurs, making the total increase in incomes $3,000. Of that increase, $2,000 is spent for consumption and $1,000 is saved. Equilibrium is attained only after the $1,000 decrease in saving is replaced by other saving. Only then does intended saving equal intended investment; thus only then can inventories remain constant and only then can production be equal to sales.

This simple model can be stated algebraically or graphically and such presentations might clarify the reader's understanding of the process by which equilibrium is attained. Since we will be using this model in the next chapter to describe how government policy can influence employment, it is important that the student master it and learn how to manipulate it.

If models are cartoons of reality, this model should be thought of as a cartoon of a cartoon, since the actual models used by policy makers are much more complicated. Here we have ignored taxes, imports, depreciation, business saving, induced investment, and changes in interest rates and prices. Any model actually used for making policy must take account of these factors. But we are interested in principles, and the principle of a macroeconomic equilibrium can be illustrated most easily using a simple model.

The Algebra of the Simple Model

The choice of algebra or graphics for purposes of exposition is one of convenience; both yield the right answers, though the algebraic answer is usually more precise. For purposes of illustration, however, economists generally choose the one that seems easiest to them or their audience. The reader can make a choice on the same grounds, since comprehension of the workings of either the algebraic or graphical exposition involves comprehension of the ideas contained in the model.

The simple model can be represented by just three relationships. The basic behavioral relationship of the model is the *consumption function*. Given our simplifying assumptions, we can state that consumption spending depends on income. When income (Y) increases, consumption (C) increases as well, according to the theory just developed, and the increase in consumption is less than the increase in income. Remember that the percentage of increases in income that are respent is called the marginal propensity to consume. Algebraically,

1. $C = aY + b$

where a, the marginal propensity to consume, is a constant between zero and one and b reflects consumption spending that does not depend on income.

The second behavioral relationship allows us to ignore the role of inventories as a buffer between sales and production. We assume that producers set production exactly equal to sales. This behavior will result in inventories remaining at a constant level. Since we know that production equals income when there are no taxes or depreciation, we can express the behavior of producers as setting income (Y) exactly equal to sales (Q). Thus

2. $Q = Y$

The third relationship tells us that total sales (Q) is the sum of sales to consumers (C) plus sales of investment goods (I) plus sales to the government (G).

3. $Q = C + I + G$

To keep the model simple, we have assumed that the level of investment (I) is determined independently of the other variables in the system. Thus, in our model, the symbol I can be thought of as a constant, not as a variable.

The algebraic solution of these three equations is straightforward. Substituting equation 2 into 1, equation 1 into 3, and rearranging terms, we find the solution for total sales.

4. $Q = \dfrac{1}{1-a}(I + G + b)$

Equation 4 describes how output is affected by the level of investment as well as by government spending. An increase in investment of $1,000 will lead to an increase in output (and income) of $3,000 when $a = \frac{2}{3}$. Of this $3,000, $2,000 will be spent on consumption goods and $1,000 will be saved. Note that whatever the marginal propensity to consume, saving will increase by an amount exactly equal to the increase in investment. If, for example, the MPC is one-half, income will increase by $2,000 when investment goes up by $1,000. But half the increase is saved so saving increases by $1,000. If the MPC is four-fifths, income will go up by $5,000, but with only one-fifth of it being saved, saving again increases by exactly $1,000.

The Graphical Solution
We can perform the same exercise graphically. Figure 31.1 is a diagram on which income is measured horizontally and sales are measured vertically. In

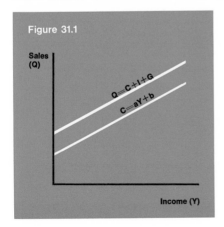

Figure 31.1

Sales (Q)

$Q=C+I+G$

$C=aY+b$

Income (Y)

Figure 31.1, we have graphed the consumption function of equation 1. There is some consumption (*b*) that exists when income equals zero. After that, consumption sales rise by a constant percentage of the increases in income. In Figure 31.1, *a* is taken to be 66⅔ percent.

The definition of total sales, equation 3, tells us that sales of investment goods and sales to the government must be added to consumer sales. This has been graphed in Figure 31.1 as well as in Figure 31.2. This relation tells us that as income increases, sales increase but by a lesser amount. Each dollar increase in income causes two-thirds of a dollar of increased sales.

The fact that sales must equal income (see equation 2) is graphed in Figure 31.2 as a 45° line from the origin. The intersection of these two curves shows us the equilibrium levels of sales and income, Q^* and Y^*.

It is essential to grasp the ideas that determine the equilibrium. The two relationships graphed in Figure 31.2 represent two independent sets of behavior, each of which determines a relationship between income and sales. One relationship says that sales increase when income increases due to the existence of induced spending. The other relationship says that production (which equals income) is determined by producers who watch the level of their inventories carefully and attempt to make production, and therefore income, exactly equal to sales. Given these two forms of behavior, there is only one level of income at which an equilibrium can exist — one level at which sales equal income and at which that level of income induces people to buy that level of sales.

To understand how such an equilibrium is reached, it is useful to consider what would happen at any other level of income. At income levels below Y^*, sales exceed income. But if sales exceed income, they exceed production. Producers therefore would observe declining inventories and they would increase production. Restating this analysis succinctly, we find that if production is less than Y^*, producers increase it. Similarly, if production were to exceed Y^*, producers would lower output because sales would be less than production. Thus any level of income but Y^* could be observed only momentarily because pro-

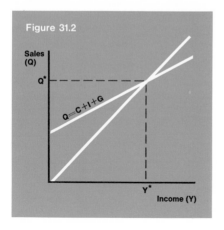

Figure 31.2

Sales (Q)

Q^*

$Q = C + I + G$

Y^*

Income (Y)

ducers would be changing it. This argument indicates not only why Y^* is the equilibrium, but that it is a *stable* equilibrium. Should the level of production ever deviate from Y^* due to some random event, there are forces that operate to restore it to that level.

This model is a useful way to expose the idea that intended saving must equal intended investment at equilibrium. It also shows us how any deviations in saving or investing behavior get multiplied and lead to larger changes in output and employment. Because of this latter property, we will use this model in the next chapter to describe the basic problem of policy. We do this despite the fact that there are many important real-world complications absent from this model. In the succeeding chapters we will attempt to incorporate the most important of these qualifications and show how they modify the results we obtain here. For now, it is useful to note a few of them just so that we keep our feet on the ground and so that we do not attempt to use the model as a standard against which to judge real-world government policy.

Complications

Even if we hold interest rates and prices constant, complications arise for three reasons: (1) because all increases in spending do not increase income; (2) because all increases in income do not reach consumers; and (3) because investment spending also depends on the level of sales. These complications do not change the nature of the policy result we have just derived, but they do change the size of the multiplier. We now look at the major reasons for these complications.

(1) Spending need not increase income if some of the spending is for products made abroad. Remember that imports are subtracted from final sales to get a measure of production. If part of any increased spending by consumers is spent abroad, then the multiplier will be smaller because this spending does not result in increased income and employment at home. Although this complication is relatively minor for the United States where most products are made at home, it is a major qualification for small countries that import half their consumption goods.

(2) Increases in produotion do not lead to increases in consumer income of an equal amount for two reasons. The first is taxes. Only a part of the increased wages and salaries are left in take-home pay after the tax authorities get their share. Thus for every increase in total income, household income increases by a smaller amount because of the fact that taxes are a fraction of income. Thus the decision about how much to respend refers to a smaller bundle than the amount by which output has increased.

The second reason consumers do not receive all of the increases in output is due to corporate profits. Profits usually increase more than proportionally when output increases. Dividend payments are not increased proportionally, however. Firms show a great reluctance to lower dividends; thus when profits increase, dividends are not increased proportionally if the increase in profits is thought to be cyclical. Due to this, the large cyclical changes in profits lead to large changes in corporate saving rather than to changes in dividend payments. Of course, consumers own firms. They could observe the higher corporate saving and be willing to spend more. But by doing so, they are betting that their knowledge of which changes in profit are permanent and which are cyclical is more complete than that of management.

(3) As business improves, firms find a need for greater amounts of plant and equipment. Increases in production therefore lead to greater investment spending on the part of firms. While we have concentrated only on induced consumer spending, we must note that a dollar's worth of induced spending by firms is just as important as a dollar's worth by consumers. Sales expand, leading to further increases in income and therefore to further spending on plant and equipment. In fact, the induced spending by firms plays an important role in many theories of the business cycle, one of which we explore in an appendix to this chapter.

These qualifications are not the only ones that affect the impact of government spending on output, but they are among the most important. Note that the induced investment spending increases the size of the multiplier whereas the other qualifications reduce it. Were we to specify these additional factors as algebraic relationships, the formula for the expenditure multiplier would become more complex, containing parameters in addition to the marginal propensity to consume.

Complications To Be Studied Later
We mentioned earlier that changes in interest rates and prices could further complicate the predictions made using the simple multipliers. These complications are important enough to warrant further study in later chapters when we present analysis concerning the role of money. For now, we must be content with the simple statement that these further complications tend to decrease the size of the multipliers. The net effect of these additional complications is to leave us with an expenditure multiplier that varies with monetary conditions but can be thought of as being in the range of two.

Questions
1.   We gave an example above in which a decrease in saving of $1,000 caused a chain of events that resulted in the restoration of that saving. How did it happen?
2.   What factors determine how much of an additional dollar of income will be respent by a consumer?
3.   Outline the role of the managers of inventories in the process of adjusting to a macroeconomic equilibrium.

Concepts Discussed
life-cycle saving hypothesis   expenditure multiplier
marginal propensity to consume   consumption function

APPENDIX: A THEORY OF BUSINESS CYCLES

One theory of business cycles is derived from the existence of induced investment spending. The marginal propensity to spend can be thought of as the marginal propensity to consume plus the marginal propensity to invest. It tells us how much consumption and investment spending is induced by $1 of autonomous spending. If the marginal propensity to invest exceeds one, instability is possible. Each dollar of spending induces more than $1 of additional spending and each of these induces still further spending. The possibility for instability is evident from the fact that an autonomous increase in spending of $1 could lead to ever-increasing amounts of induced spending.

A business cycle can be constructed from such instability once we find a way to limit the extremes of the expansions and contractions. But before constructing such limits, it is useful to explore more carefully the nature of induced investment spending in order to understand why the marginal propensity to invest can be large enough to create instability.

The marginal propensity to invest is often called the *accelerator*. The accelerator tells us how much firms increase investment spending in response to changes in their sales. One of the responses of producers to increases in sales is to increase production. If, however, plant and equipment are already fully utilized, the only way to increase production is to buy new plant and equipment. Since the cost of plant and equipment may be very large relative to annual output, it may be necessary for a firm to purchase $3 million worth of these capital goods if production is to expand by $1 million. Thus a $1 million increase in sales might lead to $3 million of induced investment spending. And this $3 million might lead to further induced spending on the part of the firms producing the plant and equipment. Thus the accelerator itself may exceed one and may lead to large unstable variations in the level of production.

Production cannot increase without limit, however. Full employment of labor and plant is soon reached and further increases in output must await the creation of further capital goods. Thus the existence of a finite quantity of resources places a ceiling on the level of production. Production may expand in an unstable fashion due to the accelerator, but soon it hits the ceiling and can expand no more. At the ceiling, producers' desires for further plant and equipment are satisfied slowly. There are no additional inducements to invest since production remains relatively stable and producers are acquiring the capital goods consistent with that high level of production.

Slowly the plant and equipment is built and soon producers are satisfied with the new higher level of capital goods they own. But satisfaction means that they now need only invest for replacement purposes. No expansion of capacity is needed; only the replacement of old worn out goods is needed. Thus investment, purchases of new plant and equipment, declines. This decline in spending causes some producers to lower production levels. With lower production, they cancel plans for some of the replacement investment they were intending to make in order to allow their plant and equipment to shrink to a level consistent with the new level of production. Thus investment spending declines in a destabilizing accelerating fashion, causing production to fall rapidly.

Just as a ceiling exists, so a floor exists. The floor is reached when gross investment reaches zero. No further declines are possible. Slowly plant and equipment wear out and the value of the capital goods used in production falls. But all the plant and equipment cannot wear out. Some is needed even for the lower level of production. Ultimately some equipment must be replaced; gross investment increases. This increase leads to further induced increases and the cycle begins anew.

The cycle we have described is one in which the equilibrium level of production is unstable but there exist natural bounds to this instability. These bounds can be called floors and ceilings. In such a model, production moves from floor to ceiling and back again.

Many factors exist in the real world to soften the impact of such destabilizing behavior on the part of investors. First, investors may respond slowly to increases in sales. Sales fluctuate randomly and it is not easy to determine when they are increasing steadily enough to warrant the purchase of new plant and equipment. Thus firms often respond with a lag to changes in sales. Second, there are many industries and they do not all experience the same sales behavior. Newly invented products generally experience sales increases even when sales for the whole economy fall. Thus all industries do not order new plants at the same time. Third, there exists a capital goods industry that produces plant and equipment. As orders increase rapidly, one of their responses is to delay delivery time. Thus when spending increases rapidly, the plant and equipment industry often does not increase production; it merely promises delivery 12 months, 18 months, or even two years in the future. Similarly, if orders decline, this industry has the option of reducing the delivery lag or even of building inventories rather than restricting production. And fourth, financial mechanisms blunt the cycle. Firms often borrow in order to gain cash with which to pay the producers of plant and equipment. If all firms attempt to borrow at once, lenders raise interest rates substantially. The increased cost of borrowing may discourage some firms from investing and they may choose different responses to the increase in sales — raising prices, for example.

Thus the simple floor-ceiling model is a cartoon of a business cycle. It describes why movements of production may increase in a self-reinforcing fashion yet ultimately reverse themselves. The accelerator alone gives one an exaggerated notion of the speed at which the level of sales changes and of the sharp division between expansion, ceiling, contraction, and floor. Nevertheless, the cartoon illustrates behavior that is sufficient to yield cycles and is therefore worthy of study even if the exact predictions of the model are too severe.

32 Aggregate Policy

In Chapter 29, we saw that labor markets take a long time to attain a long-run equilibrium and that this is partly due to the massive amounts of information that must be processed by each market participant. The decentralized manner in which these markets operate leaves no one certain as to what the long-run solution looks like or what the optimal action to pursue consists of. In the process of groping toward an equilibrium, demand unemployment—involuntary unemployment—may exist for quite some time.

In this chapter, we explore the possibilities for centralized policy to control the level of employment. Keynes outlined ways in which the government could affect the level of employment by affecting the level of sales. Here, we introduce the choices available to the government when it observes involuntary unemployment. The first of these choices involves the decision to use policy or to let unemployment take care of itself. An economist analyzes such a choice by comparing the costs of the policy to the costs that arise from having no policy. Since the government is merely the political arm of the society, the relevant costs to be compared are those to the society as a whole, not just those that appear on the government budget. Our strategy is to determine the costs of inaction, compare them to the costs of the potential policy, and choose the action that is cheaper.

Next we look at the issue of the effectiveness of policy. Does it work? Why? What are the problems associated with using it properly? We list the major avenues of policy available to the government and note how the choice should be made from the alternatives available. Finally, we return to the simple model of the last chapter and examine some policies in that framework.

The Cost of Unemployment

First, let us assume that there exists a policy that could eliminate the unemployment. We examine this assumption later in the chapter. If, in fact, there is such a policy, all of the costs of unemployment must be assigned to the choice of inaction. That is, the fact that less output is being produced than it is possible to produce is one of the costs of leaving the unemployment in existence. How large is that cost?

A certain amount of unemployment is necessary if the labor market is to perform properly. We can never be sure of what this amount is, but many observers feel it is about 4 percent of the labor force in the United States. Therefore, for convenience, let us label all unemployment in excess of 4 percent as demand or involuntary unemployment. Looking at the postwar history, we see that demand unemployment has varied between −1.3 percent and 4.0 percent of the labor force. With a labor force of approximately 100 million people, each percentage point represents one million people. With national income about $900 billion per year, 1 percent of output is about $9 billion. This crude guess would tell us that an unemployment rate of 7 percent—with demand unemployment at 3 percent of the labor force—implies that national income is $27 billion lower than it might be.

There are reasons that such crude guesses are thought to understate by large amounts the goods foregone due to the existence of unemployment. First of all, when unemployment rates become large, they are thought to understate the level of unemployment. This is because the labor force shrinks during *recessions*, the word applied to small temporary increases in the level of demand unemployment. The reason it shrinks is because many people choose to do other things than look for work if they feel that the search will be fruitless. Some people retire earlier than they had planned. Others stay in school longer than they had expected. Middle-class housewives who tend to let work seek them rather than vice versa do not enter the labor force because no work seeks them. And some, often in the ghettoes, give up looking for work because they have been discouraged so often. Thus when unemployment rates increase by a single percentage point, the labor force generally declines by about two-thirds of a percent. For every three people counted as being unemployed, two others have quit the labor force because work is too hard to find.

A second reason why unemployment rates understate the amount of output lost through recessions is that some firms do not lay off employees when sales fall. They cut the work week instead. In recessions, many workers are counted as being employed when they are working less than five days a week. A final reason to suspect the quantitative usefulness of unemployment rates is the fact that often only the production division of a firm is laid off during a recession. The white collar workers retain their jobs, partly because they are hard to rehire and partly because their work is necessary for future output although not a direct input into present output. The research department, for example, is working on next year's products. They are fired only if next year is expected to be as bad as this year. With the production division out, total output falls by a greater percentage than the decline in the labor force would indicate.

Adding up these three effects, we find that an increase in the unemployment rate of one percentage point corresponds to a loss of output in excess of 2 percent of GNP. Thus we must double our initial crude guess of the costs of unemployment. An unemployment rate of 7 percent—3 percent of it involuntary—means that output is 6 percent lower than it might otherwise be. That means that $54 billion of a potential $900 billion would be wasted annually because of difficulties encountered in clearing the labor market. This is a loss of $270 for every man, woman, and child in the country—almost $1,000 per family. Clearly, the costs are very high. And clearly, the returns to effective economic policy are great. If economists can espouse policies that prevent the periodic loss of $54 billion, the profession can afford to be proud. The example, incidentally, is not far-fetched, for unemployment rates have exceeded 7 percent even in the post-war era. In the year 1958, unemployment averaged 6.8 percent of the labor force. In the Great Depression, unemployment rates averaged 20 percent. To-day, such a rate would cost us $360 billion every year, or $6,000 per family per year.

The costs just described were averaged over the entire population for pur-poses of illustration. In fact, the costs would not be borne equally. Each change in the unemployment rate of one point does not signify a change in the income of everyone of 1 percent. Some people are fired, others continue to work full time. The distribution of the costs over the people is not random. We have just noted that production workers tend to get fired more often than nonproduction workers. It so happens that production workers tend to be less well off than nonproduction workers and are less able to bear the costs of unemployment.

During recessions, such inequities are accentuated. The poorest, least skilled workers become unemployed and bear the brunt of the costs of recession. The reason this occurs becomes clear after an examination of the way the labor force works. During periods of high unemployment, it is possible for manage-ment to raise the standards they demand for their new employees without dimin-ishing the number of workers hired. As the unemployed slowly learn the realities of the job market, they lower their sights and accept lower pay as well as less enjoyable jobs. The result is that the quality of the labor force improves at every level of employment. It is as if each man took one step down on the job ladder. But the man at the bottom has nowhere to go but off the ladder. As he looks for work, he finds that he is competing with workers much better qualified than he is for jobs no better than the one he left. Management, looking for the best man they can find for each job, hires skilled men for unskilled jobs. The unskilled go jobless. (This phenomenon is further described in Chapter 20, which is devoted to labor markets.) This unequal distribution of costs leads to human tragedy as certain unemployed find no work day after day. Simple desires for useful lives are destroyed. These extra costs of recession take the form of alienation and may lead to additional costs in the form of social disruption.

The Costs of Policy

If the costs of doing nothing are so large, can there be anyone who advocates just that? If so, either he must not believe that it is possible to eliminate unem-ployment by government policy, or he must attribute very large costs to such a policy. First let us look at the costs and then at the question of effectiveness.

Some see a political cost in pursuing any conscious policy designed to elimi-nate unemployment. Because these costs are political, not economic, we will do little with them other than acknowledge their existence. These costs are (1) that a powerful central government is a threat to individual liberty, and (2) that guaranteeing full employment will cause the public to lose some independence by making it unnecessary for them to look out for themselves.

Not only does the independence have intrinsic political value, but it is argued that workers will become less productive when no longer threatened by unemployment. The threat of unemployment is to a man what the threat of going out of business is to a firm, and in the absence of such threats a more easy-going but less productive attitude may be adopted. One can imagine political beliefs in which these costs exceed the costs of unemployment. Such beliefs appear to be held by a small minority of citizens, however, as both political parties claim to pursue conscious policies designed to make full employment a continuous reality.

The claim that policy is ineffective deserves more serious attention. There are economists who claim that their research indicates that policy actions do not work fast enough to be effective in eliminating unemployment. They claim that policy is so slow that actions designed to eliminate unemployment will not take hold until the unemployment is well on the way toward curing itself. The reasons for this delay are as follows:

1. There is a lag in collecting data. The figures for what happened in June become available in the middle of July, sometimes later. It would be diffi- cult to design a policy for June that depends on observing what is happen- in June.

2. There is a lag in detecting problems from the data. There are random variations in the data we receive. Occasionally, the unemployment rate changes by three-tenths of a percent in one month, only to reverse itself the following month. When one observes a change in unemployment, when can he be sure that it is real and not random? How many months of continually rising unemployment rates are necessary before one detects the need for policy action?

3. There is a delay in implementing policy. The worst of these delays is Congress. We will learn that changes in tax rates and government spend- ing are important tools in the fight against unemployment. Congress con- trols these tools. When the administration requests a tax cut, Congress must decide who gets that cut, the poor, the rich, or the special interest groups. In 1961, the Kennedy administration requested a tax cut as part of its anti-unemployment policy. In 1964, the tax cut was granted. Lags of this length can destroy policy effectiveness.

4. There is a lag in the impact of the policy in its effect on unemployment. Before discussing the specifics of this last lag, we must know what policy is, what tools are available to the government and the way these tools work. We look at these tools after a discussion of the methodological problems encountered in trying to estimate the lag.

The economics profession is currently divided in its beliefs about the speed of the response of employment to policy actions. The largest group claims that the lag is no longer than six months or so whereas their opponents feel that it may be as long as eighteen months. In the postwar period, recessions have followed each other every three to five years. If policy is eighteen months late in its impact, it is likely that unemployment will be on the way toward curing itself before the impact is felt. A conscious use of policy when the lags are very long may find us stepping on the gas right when the economy itself is accelerating and braking when it is slowing down anyway. We might accentuate the cycle rather than dampen it.

The reason the profession is divided on this issue is that the measurement of lags is a very difficult operation. *Econometrics* is the name given to the science of forecasting and measuring economic magnitudes. It is an interesting, difficult study in which there exist large social rewards for important breakthroughs. The first Nobel Prizes in economics, awarded in 1969, went to Jan Tinbergen and Ragnar Firsch for the important roles they played in the birth of econometrics in the 1930s. Although the science is moving ahead rapidly, it appears to be still in its infancy relative to the magnitude of the problems it confronts.

Econometrics

Econometrics is the name used to denote the body of mathematical statistics used by economists to test hypotheses and measure economic relations. Those economists who specialize in the use of econometrics are called *econometricians*. The purpose of econometrics is to prescribe the rules under which we can infer truth from data—to tell us how confident we can be in our beliefs about the way the world is. Although great progress has been made in this field recently, there are still many questions that we cannot answer as precisely as we might wish. A brief look at how the econometrician operates will give us some insight into the limitations of the field.

The econometrician, like the economic theorist, builds models for the phenomena he wishes to explain. He first borrows from the theorist hypotheses about how the economic variables involved are related to one another. These are usually expressed in the form of *qualitative* information (for example, that aggregate consumption C should be positively related to aggregate income Y) and generally include a statement of the *direction of causation* between variables.

For example, in the simple model of Chapter 31 the lines of causation between C and Y run as follows: $Y \rightarrow C$, because of the consumption function, but also $C \rightarrow Y$ since $Y = C + I$ in that model, where I stands for aggregate investment.

The econometrician wishes in some sense to *measure* the relationships in the model. That is to say, not only will he want to confirm the hypothesis that the marginal propensity to consume (MPC) is positive, but he will want an *estimate* of its size and a means by which the precision of that estimate can be evaluated. The usefulness of the measures he derives is due to the desire of government to affect the levels of aggregates like C and Y, and the need of business to have good forecasts of them for planning purposes.

Obtaining an estimate of the MPC that is of good "quality" depends on several things. First, no matter how sophisticated the model we construct may be, it cannot *impute* more quality to our estimate than is available from the basic data we use to produce it. If our national accounts are imprecise, for instance, it will be impossible to obtain a precise measure of the MPC.

Another problem concerns the manner in which the hypothesis is expressed. Besides incorporating the available qualitative and causal information given him by the theorist, the econometrician must specify precise mathematical functions for the relationships of interest in forming his model. For the example at hand, he might assume that C is proportional to Y. Then the relations $C = \beta Y$ and $Y = C + I$ form the model, and the problem is to measure β. This step in the process — the choice of a particular mathematical form for the model — is most important. The mathematical form of the model must be treated as a *datum*; it cannot be scrutinized by objective means with today's techniques.

Given the model's form, we can proceed to evaluate the theorist's hypothesis, that is, to estimate the MPC and, when needed, to forecast C from a knowledge of Y with established statistical methods. These methods, which are quite complex, also allow us to express, in probability terms, our "confidence" in the estimate (or forecast); that is, they allow us to evaluate its "quality" within the context of the given model. But different models are likely to yield different estimates of the same concept based on the same data, and often we will be hard-pressed to choose between them on the basis of these same statistical methods. Some subjective means must be used at this point to determine which model and therefore which estimate is better. A common device is simply to use both models for a while to see which one forecasts better. Although this procedure has intuitive appeal, and although it seems that any good predictive model must survive this test, it is still an arbitrary decision. We have no scientific way of comparing estimates derived from different models, of knowing how much better one estimate is than another, or which estimate is best for use for policy purposes.

Since we must assume that the data have been generated by a particular model, accurate forecasting requires that economic behavior be stable. If people suddenly change their minds about how much of their income to save, our forecasts of consumption will be wrong. We will forecast, instead, how much they would have consumed if they had continued to exhibit their past pattern of behavior. To get around this problem, we would need a more profound model to explain how consumers change their minds.

To summarize, given high quality data and a mathematical model with all its implicit and explicit assumptions, statistical methods exist to estimate the values of behavioral concepts, to evaluate the quality of these estimates, to test hypotheses about parameters, or to forecast one set of variables from another. The matter of which model to use for forecasting purposes rests on an evaluation of its results, but it is very difficult to compare the quality of these results *across* alternative models. The task of constructing and estimating models that may be used with confidence to answer questions concerning the magnitude of responses of one economic variable to changes in another is indeed a difficult one. This is particularly true when estimating dynamic relations—the amount of time it takes for an increase in one variable to affect another. Thus the use of econometrics is both an art and a science. The econometrician must be schooled in the methods of advanced mathematical statistics, but he also must have a good feeling for the manner in which to use those methods. The lack of either good judgement or a mastery of statistical tools will make one's estimates or forecasts very inaccurate. Econometrics is difficult in many ways.

Given the difficult technical problems, there exist many different estimates of the length of the lags necessary for policies to be effective. We are slowly sorting out the evidence that indicates why some estimates should be discarded in favor of others. In the meantime, some policy advice must be given. Since economists, like other people, are political animals, should it surprise us that those who fear a large role for a central government claim that the lags are too long for policy to be effective anyway? And those who like to use the government to achieve social goals claim that the lags are short enough to make conscious policy desirable. Despite our claims about the progress of economics and econometrics, the tools we have developed so far have been used only to confirm what we suspected existed there all along. So far, our findings have confirmed our beliefs. And the differences in the findings have corresponded to the differences in our beliefs.

The Tools of Policy

The three major ways in which the government can expand the level of unemployment are studied in further detail in this and succeeding chapters. All three are ways to affect unemployment by affecting the level of sales. Here we merely present them in order to conclude our discussion of policy choice—in this case, the question of how to choose among the alternative tools available.

1. The government simply can buy goods. It need not always buy tanks and guns but may buy schools, housing, hospitals, and roads as well. The production of these goods requires additional employment. This can be called *expenditure policy*.

2. The government can give the people money with which they may buy goods. Generally this is done by lowering tax rates. With lower tax rates, people have more money left over to use as they see fit. Generally, people spend a share of this money. This policy is called *tax policy*. Together with expenditure policy it makes up a branch of policy called *fiscal policy*, the term that refers to actions that work through changes in the federal budget. Of course, there exist channels other than taxes through which the government can transfer purchasing power to the public. Social security payments, welfare, and unemployment compensation represent a few of the important ways. These latter channels represent specific groups of people who now receive payments from the government. The payments all can be analyzed as a part of tax policy, however. In theory, the government

could choose to pay any group according to any characteristic it wished. Of course, the nature of political equilibrium is such that the resulting recipients of government's largesse are not chosen randomly.

3. The government can induce people to spend by lending them money. They do this by depositing money in banks; banks have to lower interest rates in order to relend it. With lower interest rates, we saw in Chapter 19 that the price of present goods is lower in terms of the future goods that will have to be sacrificed to repay loans. Individuals may find it worthwhile to save less because the return has fallen. Furthermore, firms may find it profitable to borrow more and invest in real capital. The production of such capital leads to more employment, of course. With more money in the banks, credit is easier to obtain. This form of policy is called *monetary policy*.

Ignoring the question of effectiveness, how might the government choose which of these policies to pursue at a given instant to eliminate observed unemployment? All of the policies lead to increased sales and employment, but they differ from each other in the kinds of goods that are sold initially. Thus preference for one policy or another depends on which goods the government feels would yield its citizens the most satisfaction. The choice comes down to choosing between publicly and privately consumed goods as well as between present and future goods.

For example, if government spending is pursued, we will get more roads, schools, clean water, or whatever governments usually buy. If a tax cut is enacted, we will have more to spend on anything we wish—food, clothing, shelter, or other goods and services. If interest rates are lowered, much of the increased spending will come from firms for plant and equipment or from consumers for durable goods. This will expand future productive capacity and therefore expand future consumption possibilities. Thus our choice of policies revolves around our preferences for one bundle of goods as opposed to another.

The different policies also imply different income distributions. Low interest rates make borrowers better off, lenders worse off. Private consumption is done by different people from those who consume publicly. Although there may exist changes in tax laws that could be used to guarantee that the public-private choice not affect the income distribution, these changes are difficult to design and are not generally made. We should also re-emphasize the fact that policies leading to high rates of unemployment are particularly tough on the poor.

A Final Word on Effectiveness

The decision to increase government spending requires political agreement about which goods are to be bought. Once such agreement is reached, there are technological lags that prevent spending from increasing immediately. For example, if the decision is made to build more highways, plans must be drawn up telling where the highways are to be built and to what specifications. As this takes a great deal of time and involves very little immediate expenditure, some economists have argued that it is most efficient to have the blueprints already drawn up so that spending on direct construction can begin immediately once a decision is made to eliminate unemployment. Even then, the impact will be delayed. First, land and equipment must be purchased before the construction workers can be hired. Then the actual process of building may take two or three years and last far beyond the need for anti-unemployment measures. One might advocate a start-stop policy in which construction takes place only when unemployment rates are high. But start-up costs are large and the cost of the road will be much greater if it is built in many short periods of work rather than in one continuous burst. Besides, there is a cost in an idle road that is almost completed just as there is in an idle man.

If taxes are cut, money can be channeled to consumers immediately. Whether or not they increase spending immediately is one of the open intellectual questions mentioned above. It is possible that they adjust slowly to larger paychecks and use the raise to pay bills in the short run. It is possible that they spend a large part of the extra funds immediately. More research is needed to determine which response is more likely.

If money is channeled into banks to encourage them to lend, there may be a delay in the bankers' willingness to lower interest rates, a delay in borrowers' observation of the increased ease of borrowing, and a delay in their responses to these lower rates. We are not sure of the length of these delays and therefore of the speed at which monetary policy achieves its impact.

No one believes the lags to be longer than two years. Therefore no one believes that prolonged unemployment at rates of 15 to 25 percent, such as characterized the entire 1930s, is excusable any longer. The lags simply are not that long. A decade of excessive unemployment need never recur. A year or two of unemployment slightly in excess of 4 percent is a possibility. It is recessions of such magnitude over which our cures have uncertain effects. Larger declines in output must eventually be reversed if a proper policy is followed.

The next section outlines the use of fiscal policy in terms of the simple model developed in the previous chapter.

Fiscal Policy in a Simple Model

One of the insights gained in Chapter 29 concerned the likelihood of observing wages and prices to be rigid in the short run. The uncertainties and costs of information that plague the labor market lead to behavior in which wages move slowly in response to changes in market conditions. Producers will find it very difficult to lower prices when wage rates are fixed since wages represent a large part of their costs. Accordingly, prices too are rigid, at least in a downward direction. Thus when we observe demand unemployment, we are likely to observe a world in which prices are fixed in the short run and in which all changes in market conditions result in changes in production—and presumably employment—rather than in prices. The simple model presented in Chapter 31 is one in which output levels rather than prices change in response to changes in the demand for goods. Therefore the model may be useful in studying policy to combat unemployment, although it will be a less useful way to describe worlds where there is no unemployment.

THE POLICY PROBLEM. Within the framework of the simple model, the problem of unemployment can be represented in Figure 32.1. Here, we see an equilibrium level of output that is below the full employment level. The difference has been called the *gap*. How might we eliminate the gap by expenditure policy?

EXPENDITURE POLICY. In this model, the answer to that question is quite straightforward, as can be seen in Figure 32.2. Since the level of sales depends on sales to the government as well as to everyone else, all the government need do is increase its expenditures by the amount labeled ΔG in Figure 32.2, if it wishes sales to increase by the amount ΔQ. Remember that total sales increase by more than just the sales to the government because of the expenditure multiplier. The multiple by which ΔQ exceeds ΔG is that multiplier.

We can give a numerical example of that policy once we write down the algebraic solution derived in Chapter 31. We will not rewrite the model since we have changed no equations or symbols. The solution to output, exhibited in equation 1, can be seen to depend on the level of government purchases (G), autonomous investment (I), and autonomous consumption expenditures (b), as well as on the marginal propensity to consume (a).

1. $$Q = \frac{G + I + b}{1 - a}$$

If we let $I = \$100$ billion, $G = \$200$ billion, $b = \$33\frac{1}{3}$ billion, and $a = \frac{2}{3}$, the solution for sales is $1,000 billion. If, however, there is idle capacity and unemployment, and the government calculates that sales of $1,030 billion per year are possible, what change in government purchases will close the gap? With a multiplier of three and a gap of $30 billion, a change in spending of $10 billion will

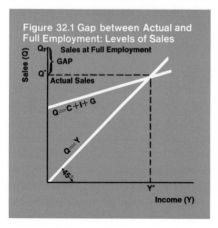

Figure 32.1 Gap between Actual and Full Employment: Levels of Sales

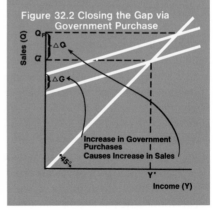

Figure 32.2 Closing the Gap via Government Purchase

bring the economy back to full employment. To check that, change G to $210 and substitute it with the other numbers into equation 1.

TAX POLICY. This model can be expanded to include tax policy. We do this by noting that taxes make private income different from production. Taxes, which can be thought of as the government's income, plus private income (Y) must be equal to the value of production. This constitutes another equation for the model ($Q = Y + T$) and those who wish to solve it again algebraically may do so. We do it graphically.

In Figure 32.3, we have included taxes by noting that sales no longer equal the value of private income, and therefore there is no longer a 45° line emanating from the origin. Now sales equal taxes plus income, and therefore the line must be higher by the amount of the taxes. A constant level of taxes raises the line a constant amount and therefore it retains its old slope.

Taxes can be used to influence the level of sales. Tax reductions appear to individuals to be increases in their incomes and should be treated just as any other increases are. Large parts of them will be consumed if they are thought to be permanent and if they are unforeseen. In Figure 32.4, we assume that individuals treat the tax cut just as they would an average increase in their incomes; they consume two-thirds of it. A tax cut of the size drawn in Figure 32.4 (ΔT) can lead to an increase in sales of ΔQ and therefore constitutes an alternative way of eliminating unemployment.

In our highly simplified model, that is all there is to the creation of policy recommendations. Find out the size of the gap and the appropriate multipliers and then compute the necessary tax or expenditure changes. In the real world, the recommendations are more difficult for many reasons, a few of which follow.

1. Because we are not sure that investment will remain constant, we must forecast its level carefully.
2. Similarly, the levels of exports and autonomous consumption must be forecast.

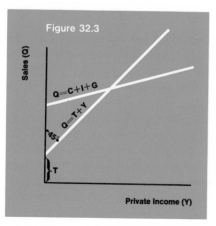

Figure 32.3

$Q = C + I + G$

$Q = T + Y$

45°

T

Sales (Q)

Private Income (Y)

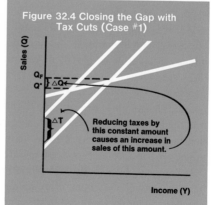

Figure 32.4 Closing the Gap with Tax Cuts (Case #1)

Q_F

Q^* ΔQ

ΔT

Reducing taxes by this constant amount causes an increase in sales of this amount.

Sales (Q)

Income (Y)

3. The more sophisticated consumption function discussed in the last chapter does not imply the existence of a constant marginal propensity to consume. Thus we are not certain of the size of the multipliers.
4. The introduction of changes in interest rates and prices complicates the behavior greatly.

Thus the exercise we just performed would be a very inaccurate and imprecise way to devise policy. But it indicates how policy can be devised in a more complex world.

We have claimed that one difference between expenditure policy and tax policy is in the kind of goods that get produced. Another difference as far as policy is concerned is in the magnitude of the effects. A tax reduction of $1 has a smaller impact on employment than an expenditure increase of $1. The reason is quite straightforward. When government increases spending by $1, the total increase in sales equals that dollar plus the spending that is induced by the increase in people's income of $1. With tax policy, we increase income by $1 and thus get induced spending, but there is no initial increase in spending to increase sales. Thus the difference between spending policy and tax policy is the amount of the initial autonomous spending. Both policies initially increase incomes by $1. Expenditure policy does this through purchasing goods, however, whereas tax policy does it through transfer payments. Thus expenditure policy is more potent per dollar by the amount of the initial purchase.

The difference in potency per dollar warns us that an examination of the government budgetary deficit alone will not tell us the total impact of the federal budget on the economy. For example, if the budget is initially balanced, it is possible to create a deficit, say, $10 billion, in an attempt to decrease unemployment. If the deficit is caused by expenditure policy, more unemployment will be eliminated than if the deficit is caused by tax policy. This does not mean that expenditure policy is always to be preferred to tax policy. The choice between them must be made by choosing among the different goods that get produced from the different policies. Since tax policy is weaker per dollar than expenditure policy, we need only invoke more dollars of tax policy than expenditure policy to get the same effect.

If it is understood that the same budget deficit can correspond to different effects on employment, it should not be surprising to find that it is possible to affect the level of employment without affecting the budget deficit. Such exercises are called *balanced budget exercises,* and they leave the size of the deficit unaffected.

If, for example, we increase both taxes and expenditures by $10 billion, we find the following effect on sales. The increase of expenditures results in $10 billion in sales immediately. It also increases income by $10 billion and therefore might cause additional induced spending. But the tax increase of $10 billion reduces income by exactly that amount so that no induced spending can be expected. The tax and expenditure policies exactly cancel each other in their effect on after-tax income and induced spending. But the government expenditure has still increased sales by the amount of the initial purchase. Thus sales and employment can be increased without increasing the budgetary deficit.

The balanced budget exercise can be shown graphically by shifting both relationships upward or downward by the same amount since taxes and expenditures are in the intercepts of the two functions. If both functions are shifted upwards by exactly the same amount, the intersection point must also shift upwards by exactly that amount. This tells us that total sales increase by the amount of the increase in expenditure but that after-tax income remains constant.

The tax of primary importance to the federal government, of course, is the income tax. This is not a tax of a given number of dollars; rather it is expressed as a percentage of one's income. Changes in tax policy are accomplished by changing the rates at which income is taxed, not by changing the actual dollar amount of taxes. That is, taxes are reduced by cutting tax *rates*—say, from 20 percent of income to 19 percent—rather than by changing specific dollar amounts. This leads to a peculiar result, namely, that the change in tax rates is not proportional to the change in tax receipts. Why? One might think that a reduction in tax rates from 20 percent to 19 percent of income would lead to a 5 percent decline in tax receipts. But this is not true because of the existence of induced spending. When tax rates are reduced, after-tax income increases and consumers spend more. This increased spending leads to increases in income and therefore to additional tax receipts. Thus a reduction in tax *rates* has two effects on tax *receipts*. (1) Tax receipts decline because a smaller percentage of income is taxed; (2) tax receipts increase because income increases and taxes are a percentage of income. In most cases, the first effect outweighs the second, but there is a peculiar case discussed in an appendix to this chapter where a decrease in tax rates actually can lead to an increase in tax receipts. Needless to say, when it is possible to stimulate the economy with large changes in tax rates that have little impact on tax receipts, political opposition to tax cuts is reduced.

Graphically, income taxes can be handled by noting that with them, private

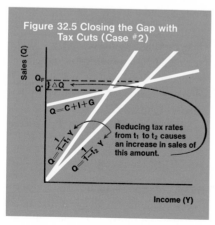

Figure 32.5 Closing the Gap with Tax Cuts (Case #2)

JOHN MAYNARD KEYNES (1883–1946) Savior of capitalism (at least to some), advisor to governments, darling of the intellectuals, and millionaire, John Maynard Keynes was one of those larger-than-life geniuses who left the world irretrievably changed. As the son of a famous economist, John Neville Keynes, and a pupil of Alfred Marshall at Cambridge, Keynes early set out on the track to making a career in economics in the business world, academia, and in government.

His first major work, *Indian Currency and Finance* (1913), reflected his experiences in the India Office of the British Civil Service. In it and in his later *Economic Consequences of the Peace* (1919), Keynes asserted the necessity for appropriate governmental economic policies, including good monetary management. The latter book brought not only fame but also much criticism, as a result of his attacks on what he believed to be the punitive and dangerous economic penalties exacted from Germany and Austria-Hungary after World War I. Keynes reasoned that Germany (and even less the shrunken husk of the Austrian Empire) could not manage to pay the exactions of the Allies and that the resultant economic chaos in central Europe would inevitably lead to another war. The hyperinflation of 1923 in Germany and Austria's inability to sustain huge Vienna on a tiny economic base were seemingly to prove Keynes right, as was the central European collapse of 1928, a disaster that moreover was in part caused by the United States' bad money management. Keynes also authored *A Tract on Monetary Reform* (1923) and a multivolume *Treatise on Money* (1928), in both of which were to be found some of his more important formulations on correct money management and on the theories of spending, saving, and investing.

Keynes's greatest work was, however, *The General Theory of Employment, Interest, and Money* (1936). This monument, like those of Adam Smith and Karl Marx, was general, often vague (some have said deliberately so), synthetic, and somewhat discursive, yet it was supported by systematic logic and by a framework on which a huge body of future analysis was to be built. It is fair to say that with the *General Theory* Keynes not only founded a new school of economics but also set the whole discipline of economics on its head, reorienting it in two important ways: a return to more concrete questions of policy, that is, away from theory and towards political economy, and a greater concern with the

---

income increases by less than a dollar when production increases by a dollar. For a tax rate of t percent of income, taxes equal tQ and after-tax income (Y) equals $(1 - t)Q$. Thus the relationship between sales and income that used to be represented by a 45° line is now represented by a steeper line whose slope is $1/(1 - t)$. In Figure 32.5, we show how a decrease in tax *rates* can be used to close the gap. The tax line is *rotated* when tax *rates* are changed, whereas it is *lowered* when fixed dollar taxes are lowered.

The Impact of Keynes

These models, we repeat, are simplified versions of those actually used to formulate policy. We have presented them not only to point out the way the policy maker solves problems, but also to help in gaining an understanding of the roles

overall volume of employment and production in the system, that is, with macro-economics rather than with Marshallian microeconomics.

The external stimulus to the writing of the *General Theory* was the massive unemployment and depression that hit Britain in the early 1920s and the United States in 1929. Traditional economic theory acknowledged depressions but held them to be transitory adjustment mechanisms for weeding out the weak and assuring the efficient functioning of a competitive system. Most analysts saw the persistence of the depression as stemming from imperfections in the price mechanism, particularly downward inflexibility of wages and prices. Keynes's task was to show that even with flexibility and in a perfectly operating competitive economy, depressions could occur. For Keynes, the traditional workings of a free enterprise, capitalist system held little hope for the automatic curing of such fluctuations, largely on the grounds of price and wage rigidity and on mutually inconsistent behavior by consumers, investors, financial institutions, the central banks, and governments.

Fortunately the Keynesian system was not all hopeless since the monetary and fiscal authorities could influence the economy through manipulating interest rates, money supplies, taxing, and spending. This reliance on government also marked a shift from traditional economics, because it made conscious therapeutic policy a key aspect of the functioning of the economy and because it reinserted the economist in the policy arena. Necessarily these tasks required good data, and Keynes's theorizing led not only to a revolution in theory but also to more sophisticated means of gathering economic information and to the whole panoply of official reporting that is so much a part of the modern governmental scene in the developed world.

Necessarily Keynes's work also evoked howls from the Marxists as well as from the orthodox economists, who either damned him for finding a way out of capitalism's demise (which Marxists confidently expected with the Great Depression) or cursed him as a charlatan who failed to wrestle with the real problems of capitalist instability. Thus far the apparent success of the developed nations in staying at or near full employment would seem to vindicate Keynes, although persistent inflationary pressures suggest that his basic analysis may have to be significantly modified to deal with the problems of an "overheated," fully employed, industrially advanced economy.

---

of taxes and government expenditures in determining the equilibrium level of sales. All models are abstractions from reality and these are no exception. They are useful in describing the real world only if the assumptions they require are more or less satisfied or if these assumptions concern elements of the system that have no important effect on the solution. Prior to the 1930s, the assumption used by economists was that prices were perfectly flexible. In Chapter 29, we showed how this assumption, if realized, would always lead to full employment. In this and the preceding chapter, we made the opposite assumption, namely, that prices as well as interest rates are completely inflexible. The implications of the case where wages and prices as well as interest rates are inflexible were first explored by Keynes in the 1930s. Accordingly, the analysis we have just traced might be called Keynesian. Once we admit the possibility of inflexible wages and prices, involuntary unemployment becomes a theoretically admissible possibility and fiscal policy becomes a useful tool to fight it. The work of Keynes had such a profound effect on economists that models that assumed prices and interest rates inflexible came to dominate professional thinking during the 1950s. The graphic model we presented, called the *Keynesian cross,* is what a large body of the profession thought of when they considered which employment policy to espouse.

But prices and wages do seem to be flexible in the long run and interest rates have been very active in the past decade. Accordingly, there has been a shift of interest away from the simple fiscal model to more complex models that allow for a study of inflation and of the impact of monetary policy. The results predicted by the simple fiscal model hold qualitatively in the more complex models but all of the multipliers are smaller. Tax cuts lead to increased spending even in the larger models but not to as much as they would if prices and interest rates were constant.

Keynes's book *The General Theory of Employment, Interest, and Money* also contained analyses of cases where interest rates and prices were flexible. But the shocking part of the book was the part that showed how there could exist situations in which the simple fiscal model, the Keynesian cross, was a good characterization of the real world. Accordingly the label "Keynesian" became attached to models that ignored the importance of money. Keynes himself was a monetary theorist and his book had many chapters devoted to money, just as the title suggests. It is unfortunate, therefore, that the recent surge of interest in models in which money plays a large role is thought to be associated with a decline in Keynes's influence. In reality, it is just a return to a more balanced view of the world after an overreaction to the special case described by Keynes of what happens when prices and interest rates are sticky.

It took many years before Keynes's point was generally accepted. He published in 1937. Yet the tax cut of 1964 was hailed as the first explicit use of Keynesian policy on the part of the US government. It is interesting to look back at the fiscal policy that was followed during the Great Depression to see the degree to which Keynesian principles were invoked then. Today, some still claim that massive federal spending was attempted in the 1930s and that it was not effective in eliminating unemployment. They conclude that Keynesian principles are wrong. These people may even understand intuitively that the goods the government buys must be made by men, yet they refuse to admit that a conscious use of expenditure policy can have any effect on employment.

To illustrate this point, we reproduce here an actual discussion on fiscal policy that took place between a famous senator and an undergraduate student of economics. Then we look at the actual history.

Student:	How do you know that government spending can't eliminate unemployment?
Senator:	Because we tried it in the thirties and it didn't work.
Student:	What did work? How did we cure the depression?

Senator: World War II ended it.
Student: How can a war cure depression?
Senator: Because of all the equipment and materiel that had to be made. We had to hire men to make them.
Student: Then why don't we build tanks and guns today and dump them in the ocean. That should eliminate our present unemployment, according to your theory.
Senator: That would be wasteful.
Student: Then why not build schools or houses? War expenditures aren't the only kind that can employ men.
Professor   (interrupting): I believe that's enough questions for today for Senator X who has been kind enough to give us a bit of his valuable time.

A Bit of History

The senator is correct in his statements that the war eliminated the depression and that the increased spending in the 1930s still left vast numbers unemployed. But he drew the wrong conclusion from these statements. An alternative conclusion might be that the spending in the 1930s was not large enough to cure the unemployment. To examine this possibility, we have presented in a table at the end of this chapter the size of government expenditures, the size of the deficit, and the percentage of the labor force that was unemployed. We will describe the history of these numbers. First we wish to remind the student of a lesson just learned, however, which is that the size of the deficit as well as the size of the budget affect the level of employment. Therefore in the table we present both the size of the deficit and the size of government expenditure to give an indication of the expansionary force of fiscal policy, even though we note only the level of spending in the text.

The unemployment rate was 3.2 percent in 1929. It rose annually to 8.7, 15.9, 23.6, and, finally, to 24.9 percent by 1933. It fell slowly until 1937 (14.3 percent) and bounced back in 1938 (19.0 percent). Then with the expected onslaught of war and its actual occurrence, unemployment dropped steadily so that it was 17.2 percent in 1939, 14.6 percent in 1940, 9.9 percent in 1941, 4.7 percent in 1942, 1.9 percent in 1943, and 1.2 percent in 1944. The war ended in 1945 and unemployment started to creep upward again, although it has remained relatively low throughout the whole postwar period.

What about the level of government expenditure corresponding to these years? To test the senator's hypothesis that "we tried that in the thirties," let us look at the levels of spending of all governments, state and local as well as federal. In 1929, government spending was $22.0 billion measured in constant 1958 dollars. In 1933, it was $23.3 billion and it increased annually to $26.6, $27.0, $31.8, $30.8, $33.9, $35.2, and, finally, to $36.4 billion in 1940. The senator is right that we did try. This is about a 50 percent increase in government spending. But it is only $13 billion, not a very large amount. Observe what spending could become in response to wartime needs. In 1941 it became $56.3

billion, a $20 billion increase. That was just a warm-up, however. In 1942, government spending reached $117.1 billion, followed by $164.4 billion in 1943, and a whopping $181.7 billion in 1944! No wonder the war ended the depression. In 4 years, government spending was increased by $145 billion on an annual basis. It had been increased only $13 billion on an annual basis over the whole 11-year period between 1929 and 1940. Did we really try it in the 1930s? Spending was increased (on an annual basis) by 10 times as much in 4 years of war as it was in 11 years of depression. If we consider the levels of war expenditure, the depression expenditures do not look very large.

One of the theories that had been circulating prior to Keynes was that of "pump-priming." It is this theory that was really tried in the depression. According to the pump-priming theory, all one had to do was insert enough autonomous expenditure to get the ball rolling. By this theory, a great deal of induced spending would then result. Money would pass from hand to hand, leading to large increases in employment. No one guessed in the early 1930s that the expenditure multiplier was about 2, not 100, and that the government would have to increase spending by one-half the amount it ultimately wished production to increase.

But now we know and therefore we should have no more depressions; that is, now we know until some new problem occurs. Economists are very good at

Table 32.1

	Unemploy-ment Rate	Government Expenditures (1958 Prices) (Billions of Dollars)	Government Surpluses and Deficits (Taxes Minus Spending) (Current Prices)
1929	3.2	22.0	1.0
1930	8.7	24.3	−.3
1931	15.9	25.4	−2.9
1932	23.6	24.2	−1.8
1933	24.9	23.3	−1.4
1934	21.7	26.6	−2.4
1935	20.1	27.0	−2.0
1936	16.9	31.8	−3.1
1937	14.3	30.8	.3
1938	19.0	33.9	−1.8
1939	17.2	35.2	−2.2
1940	14.6	36.4	−.7
1941	9.9	56.3	−3.8
1942	4.7	117.1	−31.4
1943	1.9	164.4	−44.1
1944	1.2	181.7	−51.8
1945	1.9	156.4	−39.5

solving yesterday's problems. Since solved problems rarely recur, the new economic crises of the future will occur because of something we do not yet understand. We do understand about demand unemployment, however, and we should be able to prevent depressions like the one of the 1930s, a depression that was due to an inadequate demand for goods. Our next catastrophe will result from something we have not yet thought to study.

Questions
1. On what basis should the government choose between the alternative policies it could pursue to eliminate unemployment?
2. What is at issue in the dispute over the effectiveness of policy actions in attaining desirable goals?
3. Which policy would you espouse to eliminate unemployment if you felt that more private consumption were needed in the present?

Concepts Discussed
recession	fiscal policy
econometrics	monetary policy
expenditure policy	balanced budget exercise
tax policy	Keynesian economics

APPENDIX I: THE CAUSES OF THE GREAT DEPRESSION

There are conflicting explanations of the actual causes of the depression. Many events occurred simultaneously and it is difficult to sort out which were the causes and which were the effects. Here we list a few of the candidates.

(1) Long Cycle Theory
One theory is that large new inventions occur occasionally and when they do, they require a complete rebuilding of the country's capital stock. The auto was such an invention. The boom of the 1920s saw the whole countryside rebuilt as suburbs became economical due to the existence of autos. Roads and houses, to say nothing of autos themselves, required vast investments. But once built, there was nothing to replace them as a source of autonomous spending. All that was needed to keep auto consumption rising after 1929 was sales for replacement plus small levels of additional sales. Before, however, huge percentage increases occurred every year in a once-and-for-all building spree while everyone bought his first car. Not only that, but because much speculative building occurred, there were huge quantities of unsold houses to be worked off once the bubble was broken.

This explanation is an example of the *accelerator* developed in the appendix to Chapter 31. The accelerator tells us that when people wish to increase consumption of durable goods by a small amount, huge expenditures must be made.

For example, an increase in consumption of housing by 5 percent would require more than a doubling of new construction of housing because new construction is generally only 2 to 3 percent of the existing stock. For a nation to acquire a stock of 30 million autos in a few decades requires high rates of production. But to keep the stock constant at 30 million requires much less production, and so auto sales can decline by a great deal even though auto consumption is higher than before. Similar problems are experienced for road-building, housing, and so on. Since these industries are very large, a simultaneous collapse in their sales leads to massive reductions in induced spending, and a huge decrease in employment can result.

A modern example of the accelerator boom and bust is the story of bowling equipment in the late 1950s and early 1960s. For a while, it looked as if everyone would go bowling. The manufacturers of automatic pinsetters had sales increasing at very rapid rates. Then, suddenly, everyone was bowling. And the pinsetters were not wearing out. Sales fell to zero. To add to the difficulty, a few snobs stopped bowling and a few alleys started returning equipment. The equipment makers would have had negative sales had their accountants been sportive enough to label them as such. Losses were huge. (Brunswick common stock plummeted from 75 to 7 as a result.) If the bowling equipment industry had been a large one, a major economic readjustment would have been necessary. An economy-wide accelerator is one possible explanation of the Great Depression.

(2) Stock Market Crash

A second hypothesis about the cause of the depression concerns the stock market. The stock market crash wiped out much saving. Life-cycle savers found that they had not provided for retirement after all and therefore had to decrease consumption in an attempt to replace the lost wealth. But the increased saving resulted in decreases in sales and then in production via the familiar inventory route. Consumption would not return to normal until the stock market would, and the stock market would not until consumption would.

This, too, is interesting, although there is evidence that there was a slowdown in effect before the market crashed.

(3) International Monetary Problems

For a complete understanding of this hypothesis we must wait until we learn about international money in Chapter 38. Basically, this hypothesis says that world-wide depression ensued because of a complete disruption of world trade due to attempts to correct balance of payments deficits by limiting imports. And since everyone's imports are someone else's exports, sales fell. Major readjustments to the disappearance of trade had to take place. Aggravating the situation was the fact that certain key nations (the United States and the United Kingdom) abandoned the gold standard at various times, creating a great deal of uncertainty as to the value of their currencies. Financial panics ensued, which resulted in bank failures, further market crashes, and general economic chaos and disruption.

This hypothesis is interesting, but the data show that the international panics occurred after the domestic depressions were underway. Thus this hypothesis must be interpreted as an explanation about why the depression was so long and so severe rather than as an explanation of why it began.

(4) Bad Monetary Policy

The next chapters introduce us to the concept of monetary policy. Here we can only intimate the nature of the criticism that some economists levy at the financial authorities for the way they acted during the depression. Briefly, the authorities did not lend banks the vast sums of money they needed to meet the massive deposit withdrawals that occurred during various bank panics. The banks, realizing they could no longer rely on the authorities to bail them out, became much more conservative and would not make the loans that were necessary to finance a recovery.

The fact is that the quantity of loans did fall by a great deal between 1929 and 1933. It is not clear, however, whether this was in response to bankers' unwillingness to lend or to firms' unwillingness to borrow. Furthermore, since the first link in the chain of this explanation concerns the response of banks to panic, it is not an explanation of how the depression began or why panics started. Rather it is a reason for the depression to become worse and last longer than it otherwise would. Some other explanation is needed for the panic.

There are other hypotheses as well, but we cannot examine them all here.

Common to all of these explanations is one of the basic foundations of Keynesian theory. This is that what people expect of the future dominates their current behavior and that these expectations are fickle. If everyone expects the stock market to crash, it will crash. If everyone expects a recession, they will cease spending on plant and equipment and cause a recession. Keynes argued that psychological parameters such as the propensity to consume and the expected profitability of investment determine the demand for goods. Clearly, one of the most important roles for government policy is to guarantee that sensible expectations exist. This will occur if the government convinces everyone of its power to determine future events and of its willingness to do so. Otherwise, the cycles of expectations will cause real problems. President Roosevelt's famous statement, "We have nothing to fear but fear itself," can be interpreted in this light. If a fear of depression causes people and firms to stop spending, a depression may result because of the decline in sales. Fear is its own justification.

APPENDIX II: TAX RATES AND TAX RECEIPTS

We promised to discuss a perverse case in which tax receipts fall when tax rates are increased, and vice versa. We will show this algebraically using the equations and symbols already discussed and described in the body of Chapter 31. The model consists of a consumption function, equation 1, a definition of total sales, equation 2, and a relation between after-tax income and sales, equation 3.

1. $$C = aY + b$$

2. $$Q = C + I + G$$

3. $$Y = (1 - t)Q$$

Solving for Q, we get equation 4.

4. $$Q = \frac{I + G + b}{1 - a(1 - t)}$$

Total tax receipts (tQ) are represented in equation 5.

5. $$tQ = \frac{t(b + I + G)}{1 - a(1 - t)}$$

To show how tax receipts vary with changes in the tax rate (t) requires us to take the derivative of equation 5 with respect to t, using well-known rules of calculus.

6. $$\frac{dtQ}{dt} = Q + t\frac{dQ}{dt} = Q + \frac{-atQ}{1 - a(1 - t)}$$

There are two terms in equation 6 of opposite sign. If the negative term is larger in absolute value, then tax receipts fall when tax rates are increased. This is because the decline in income caused by the higher tax rates is so large that it offsets the fact that a larger quantity of income is now taxed. To find the exact conditions for this, we require that equation 6 be negative.

7. $$\frac{dtQ}{dt} = Q - \frac{atQ}{1 - a + at} < 0 => 1 - a + at - at < 0 => 1 - a < 0$$

Thus if $a > 1$, the perverse result holds. Note that a is the marginal propensity to consume, generally thought to be less than one. Thus the perverse case is unlikely, albeit possible. If output increases by enough, people will not only have more money to spend but they may pay more taxes as well.

In the early 1960s, the Kennedy administration attempted to convince the Congress that a large change in tax rates would have little effect on tax receipts. Their argument rested not only on the analysis we have just presented, but also on an expectation that the economy would naturally grow over time and yield larger and larger revenues anyway. If next year's output will be 5 percent larger than this year's output, next year's tax receipts will be higher as well, even if rates stay constant. Thus we can lower rates a bit without experiencing a decrease in receipts.

XI Money

The most effective way to destroy a society
is to destroy its money.

NIKOLAI LENIN

No sophisticated economy could operate long without money. Yet we have been able to devote thirty-two chapters to the study of important issues of economics without finding it necessary to consider money. In the next three chapters we attempt to make up for that neglect.

Chapter 33 argues that money exists in order to make it easier to trade—to buy and sell—and it presents a brief history of money from the viewpoint of convenience of making transactions. So far, with few exceptions, we have ignored the possibility of transaction costs. With no such costs, there was no need to consider money. We left it out of our discussion in much the same spirit as a physicist would leave out friction in describing how a pulley works. As long as the pulley is well oiled, the predictions made by the physicist's frictionless model will be reasonably accurate. Similarly, in economics, as long as the monetary and financial systems function smoothly, we can ignore them for many purposes.

But lubrication is important to pulleys and monetary systems are important to economies. Should the pulley ever become rusty from lack of oil, the frictionless model will cease to predict accurately the experiences one would have with it. Similarly, when financial panic ensues or monetary systems threaten collapse, the nonmonetary model of an economy will not yield reliable insights into resulting behavior. The next three chapters are designed to acquaint us with the risks and benefits of financial systems.

Chapter 33 concentrates on money—what it is, what it was, and what it probably will be in the future. The role of banks and checking accounts is developed as well. Chapter 34 discusses other financial assets and devotes particular attention to the question of risk—what it is and how financial markets allow us to avoid it. Here we see the gains to be derived from an efficient financial mechanism and the risks that are implicit in these gains. Chapter 35 discusses how a centralized authority can protect the economy from many of these risks. It explores the problems that monetary authorities face and the tools they use to reach their goals. This chapter also discusses how the monetary authorities can affect the demand for goods. Such actions are called *monetary policy* and are complementary to the fiscal actions that were discussed in Chapter 32. We wait until Chapters 36-38 for a synthesis of these two forms of policy.

33 Money

Money must be classified with the wheel as one of the greatest inventions in history. Like the wheel, money is a very simple idea that has vastly magnified the productive efforts of men. Just as the wheel facilitates motion, money facilitates the act of exchange, and it is exchange, after all, that allows the separation of production and consumption decisions, this separation being responsible for the level of living standards we enjoy today. Because of the possibility of exchange, we need not be self-sufficient Robinson Crusoes, each engaged in his private battle against the elements. We need not grow our own food and make our own clothes, but instead we can devote our labor to a single task and use the rewards from that performance to buy those goods we desire. The gain from exchange of all kinds is the glue that holds society together, that makes it worthwhile for us to become involved with other people to such a degree that our very livelihood depends on the acts and decisions of strangers. It is exchange that economics is all about. And exchange—and with it, social development—would be very difficult without money.

Exchange without money would require us to trade our productive services directly for the commodities we wish to consume. Needless to say, it would be very difficult for a nuclear physicist to find a dairy farmer who needs nuclear physics whenever the physicist wants milk. Money separates the act of exchange into two separate transactions. The sale of labor is to the highest bidder. Then the money that results from that transaction is traded for other commodities. It is much easier to conduct the two separate transactions than to accomplish the single direct exchange. Imagine the costs of transactions in the absence of money—the costs of finding others with exactly reciprocal desires. We would spend all our lives transacting instead of producing. Thus money exists to lower transaction costs. The reason we have money in our pockets now is to lower the cost of transactions, to facilitate exchange.

We will now look at a history of the development of money and note the relation between money and the costs of transacting. We will see that each step in the development of money occurred because it lowered transaction costs. As transaction costs are still with us, we can be sure that there will be future developments in the technology of money. These developments, by making transactions even more convenient than they are today, will reduce one of the primary sources of friction in a market economy—transaction costs.

Fables about the Development of Money

Money is an asset that is used as a medium of exchange. The first assets used as money were physical commodities. We have no record of what the commodities were or where they were used since the use of money predates the keeping of historical records. We can surmise, however, that in the beginning there was *barter*. With barter, goods were traded directly for other goods that were expected to satisfy human wants. Some bright trader then discovered that two transactions were sometimes easier than one. This event may have occurred this way: Coming home from a hunt in which he had been particularly fortunate in killing two boars, a hunter puzzled over the disposal of the second boar. Finding a friend who owned a desired bow but who wished no meat, and another friend who wished some meat but would trade only unwanted knives, the hunter had the bright idea of asking the bow owner if he would trade his bow for knives. The affirmative reply enabled the hunter to execute man's first three-way trade, in which knives served as money.

As societies became more organized and complex, the patterns of trade became more stable, and it was found that certain commodities were more efficient than others for use in making transactions. These commodities were used regularly. The reason some commodities might be preferred to others as money is directly related to the costs of transacting. A commodity is likely to be good money if it is

(1) *divisible*, so that it can be used in transactions of any size;
(2) *portable,* so that there are low transportation costs associated with delivery;
(3) *homogeneous*, so that time is not wasted in evaluating the quality of the money whenever it shifts hands;
(4) *durable*, so that it can be stored and need not be reused immediately; and
(5) *predictable in value,* so that the person accepting the money undergoes no greater risk of capital loss than if he owned any other asset.

Gold

Guided by these criteria, societies around the world independently selected gold as the commodity that made the best money. The reasons are obvious. Due to its scarcity in nature, gold is very difficult to produce; but due to its beauty, it is highly desired as an ornament. Therefore the price of gold will be very high and can be expected to remain high relative to other commodities of similar weight. Its high value per ounce makes it as portable as any common commodity can be. Even today at a price of $35 per ounce, six and one-half pounds of gold will pay for an average new American car. Smaller amounts can certainly be carried for smaller transactions.

Gold is durable and can be stored easily. Its durability means that the supply of gold in existence will be affected very little by variations in current production. With a stable supply, price can be expected to remain stable as well and therefore there will be little risk of capital loss associated with the use of gold.

Gold is a basic element and in its refined state is homogeneous. In the form of dust, it is easily divisible and can be used for transactions of any size. Thus gold scores pretty well as money, leading to very low transaction costs. Of all the commodities that were available to early societies, gold apparently made the best money and had the lowest possible transaction costs associated with its use. Alternative commodities such as wheat, horses, and guns, all of which have been used as money at one time or another, make inferior monies because transaction costs are higher with them than with gold.

But still gold is a commodity and all commodities have some disadvantages when compared to other possible monies. The further development of the history of money illustrates this fact.

Gold Coin

An obvious disadvantage of gold as money is the need to weigh it at each transaction and to attest to its purity. Some party in the transaction must have a scale and both parties have to examine the dust or nuggets carefully to determine their value. The next step in money's history circumvented these problems. In all highly developed societies, government mints were established to produce *coins*. Originally, the role of the mints was to weigh the gold and authenticate its purity. The mint would then stamp its seal of approval on the metal and it could circulate in its stamped form, users assured of its properties. The stamped commodity is a coin. If one had faith in the king or the government, one could accept the coin as being worth what the mint said it was worth.

Of course kings and governments are not saints and their seal of approval alone need not give value to coins. If, however, the government would accept the coin as payment for taxes or would allow any holder to come to the mint and trade the coin for the amount of gold it purported to be, the gold coin could be accepted as gold because the government agreed to accept it as gold. If one ever got stuck with a doubtful coin, he could turn it in for real gold. The importance of this point should not be lost because it forms the basis for the next step in the history of money, one of the most important steps ever taken. This point is that the gold coin had value not because it was gold, but because it was coin. It had value because the sovereign said it had value and that he would stand behind it as if it were the real thing. Thus the confidence with which one could accept the money depended on one's confidence in the government. If one expected the government to be around next year and to honor its promises, one could accept the coin for what it claimed to be regardless of how much gold appeared to be in it.

Base Coinage

The next obvious step was to circulate coinage that was made from base metal but that the government would accept as if it were gold. The coin would still offer the holder the right to transform it into gold at the mint when he wished. To see why this was a step forward in the history of money, let us see how it might have been invented.

Running a mint is often unprofitable. It is particularly unprofitable if one puts an ounce of gold into every coin that claims to have an ounce in it and then finds these coins returned years later, worn almost to the point of being unrecognizable. After seeing that three of these thin "ounces" had to be melted down to create one new ounce, the keeper of the mint spent a great deal of time puzzling over ways to curtail the losses of his operation. He was forced by law to surrender an ounce of gold to those who turned in the worn-thin coins. Fine gold dust was being spread over the countryside as coins jingled together in the pockets of traders. This loss was eventually registered at the mint and continually forced the mint keeper to buy newly mined gold just to keep the amount of coinage constant.

The losses of the mint were vast. Natural losses from wear and tear would have been bad enough. But these losses were augmented by those of artificial wear and tear. One of the profitable occupations of the day was to shake a batch of new coins vigorously in a sack. Just as in modern testing labs, the effect of a few years wear could be artificially duplicated in minutes. The profit in this activity was the layer of gold dust that remained at the bottom of the sack after the worn-thin new coins were removed. The less artful members of the profession contented themselves with clipping little pieces from the edge of a coin so that it eventually took on a scalloped appearance. Clearly the mint business was not an attractive calling to aggressive young entrepreneurs.

If, however, the gold was kept safely locked up while copper coins circulated, the losses could be cut drastically. On each copper coin could be stamped a value in terms of gold or even a promise by the mint to pay that amount of gold if the owner of the coin so requested. Note that it is now the promise that is being used for money rather than the gold itself. With the losses of gold curtailed, there was less need to go to the expense of mining more gold in order to have a currency. Thus transaction costs could be lower with base coins than with gold coins.

Paper Money

Once the decision had been made to lock the gold in vaults and to circulate claims to the gold rather than the gold itself, it was not a difficult step to move to paper money. After all, both base coins and paper money had little or no intrinsic value. Their value lay in the promise of the mint to redeem them for gold, not in their use as a commodity. With intrinsic value unimportant, the distinction between coins and paper currency became one of convenience only. Paper is more convenient for some transactions, coin for others. But both clearly have the advantage, as far as the mint is concerned, of being cheap to replace. Worn bills can be turned into new ones at a very low cost. Coins can be made from the cheapest metals even if they do not have a satisfying "ring" when struck. Thus the mint entered a new era when it decided to lock up the gold. And the shakers and clippers were not the last to have their jobs destroyed by technology.

Fiat Money

Clearly base coins and paper money were a step forward in the battle of men against the elements. Now they had to spend less time scratching gold from the ground in order to transact their business. The social loss involved in the spread of gold dust across the country had been stopped. Furthermore, because any number could be printed or stamped on the new money, it was physically more convenient than the gold coin had been. The mint keeper's decision was applauded.

But more progress was yet to come. Although it was true that the gold in the vaults was safe and that no new gold had to be mined to keep the quantity of the currency constant, it was also true that new gold had to be mined whenever the coinage was to be expanded. The new gold was deposited in the vaults and locked up forever to protect the value of the coinage. Some thought this wasteful. The social science fiction writers of the era were writing tales about how the gold could be stolen and nothing would happen to the currency. Evil rumors circulated about the mint keeper's new-found affluence. Eventually, the government had the courage to announce that in the future it was going to cease the practice of "backing" its currency with gold. That is, it would no longer allow currency and coin to be presented for payment in gold. It recognized that with the level of tax rates prevailing at that time, the guarantee that the currency would be accepted as being as good as gold for tax purposes was all that was needed to guarantee its value. Furthermore, because the government had almost unlimited taxing power, it could always eliminate the "bad" money by taxing it all in. The government immodestly finished the announcement with the statement that it recognized that the value of gold had been maintained in recent years by the fact that gold could be converted into currency, not vice versa. It announced a plan to sell all its gold at the previous price; that is, a coin with "one ounce of gold" stamped on it would buy one ounce of gold at this sale. It invited all fearful holders of its currency to turn it in because the government preferred the currency to the gold.

Only a few cranks accepted the offer. The currency did not collapse, the government did not fall, the factories did not shut down. The social science fiction writers had been right. The gold locked in the vaults had been a drag on the economy, forcing the people to pay for vaults and guards and gold miners when they could accomplish all their transactions without that paraphernalia. Thus the selling of the gold marked a further development in the history of money—a further decrease in the costs of transacting. It became clear that the real backing of the money was confidence in the government. As long as the government would take it for tax purposes, one could be sure that others would accept it as well. And as long as others would take it, one might as well take it oneself.

This last observation gives us a general principle about money that is valid for all ages. One is content to accept and hold money only if he feels others are willing to do the same. Generally, we attribute reason to others and feel that they will be content to hold money only if it has some intrinsic value or if it is guaranteed to buy certain commodities or services. The government money we have just been examining is called *fiat money*. It is money because the government says it is. The fact that it can be used for tax purposes gives it value. Convertibility into taxes is almost as good as convertibility into gold as a guarantee of value.

Generally, governments strengthen their fiats by declaring their money *legal tender*. That means that the money must be accepted by all citizens of the country in payment for debts. The government has used its sovereign power to declare that its fiat money is as good as gold and that no one can demand payment in gold instead of fiat money. Fiat money that has been declared legal tender is one of the brilliant inventions of all time. It frees men from the costs of scratching commodities out of the ground in order to conduct transactions. With a stable popular government, one has no risk in accepting fiat money.

That last statement indicates that fiat money does have risks associated with it, however. The money is as good as gold because a particular government says it is. If the government falls, the next one may not observe the same promise. Or if the government prints a great deal of the money, foreigners may begin to demand payment in gold because they fear that the price of the money will fall. They are not covered by the legal tender proclamation of the local government.

Another risk exists when the government ceases to sell gold for the currency. There is nothing to guarantee the price of the currency in terms of any other commodity. If large amounts of it are printed, its price may fall as any supply-demand analysis will tell us. This decline in the price of money—or increase in the price of all commodities relative to money—is called *inflation*. If the public starts to fear that too much money is being printed and that inflation is about to occur, they will attempt to get rid of the currency. They can do this by buying commodities, real estate, foreign securities, and the like. Transaction costs can become much larger if the fear of the value of money necessitates additional transactions. Thus fiat money requires the confidence of the public that its value will remain relatively stable if it is to be an improvement over money that is convertible into gold. Predictability of value was one of the attributes that made gold such good money. Similarly, if fiat money is to be good, its value must be predictable. Confidence is all that guarantees the acceptability of fiat money. That confidence can be destroyed, and with it the advantages of fiat money, by an indiscriminate use of the printing press. When such an inflationary situation results, no one wishes to hold the money. Although it is still used for payments, people exchange it for goods as quickly as possible after they receive it. A great deal of additional transactions, and therefore costs, result from such inflation. Such inflations are a step backward in the history of transaction costs and payments mechanisms.

When two different forms of money exist side by side, it is logical to expect people to attempt to get rid of the one that they suspect may decline in price. Thus they will hold on to the "good" money and use the "bad" money for all their transactions, passing it on like a hot potato. This phenomenon is called *Gresham's Law*. Put simply, it states that "Bad money drives out good money." Historically, when coin and gold circulated together and the coin was becoming more suspect because the government was losing power, coin was used for all transactions and gold was squirreled away. Similarly, today, if one suspected that the rate at which currency could be transferred into gold was about to fall, he might attempt to spend the currency and buy gold, commodities, or other currencies whose value was more predictable. Thus the principle that bad money drives out good is valid for all eras.

Bank Money

Parallel to the development of the technology of currency there occurred a development of a completely different form of money—checks. It would be incorrect to think of checks as the only form of bank money. Private banks in many parts of the world were and are able to issue currency to depositors and borrowers. And in most countries today it is the central bank, a quasi-public institution, that still issues the currency and monitors the nation's financial affairs. Thus currency has as much right to be called bank money as checks do. But now we are interested in checks and the advantages they have over currency for some transactions. It should be noted that checking accounts are used for making payments and therefore they constitute money.

Currency can be stolen. Checking accounts cannot. For this reason firms and individuals prefer to use checks for all large transactions. With checks it is possible to use the mail for payments, a great increase in convenience and a great decrease in the cost of conducting a large transaction. Thus checks clearly have certain advantages over currency. Of course, for numerous small transactions checks are tedious. Thus most people carry small amounts of currency with them for the minor transactions that must be conducted daily. The risk of loss or theft exists, of course, but for small amounts it is preferable to take that risk than to have to write out a check for every cup of coffee. We can expect currency to be used for transactions when it is the cheaper form of money and checks to be used when they are cheaper.

Before seeing how checks work, let us note that one way of viewing money is as a device for keeping score. People are allowed to buy commodities equal in value to the ones they sell. But if the purchase and sale are separated by time and place, some device must be used to guarantee that one's purchases do not exceed one's sales. Money is that device; it is a way of keeping score. Currency can be thought of as a decentralized score-keeping device. The mint has no idea who has accumulated the largest amount of currency. The currency passes from hand to hand in private transactions. And this is the reason theft is possible.

An alternative device would be a centralized scoreboard with a paid scorekeeper. That is how checking accounts work. Each individual has a score on the scoreboard. When he makes a transaction, he notifies the scorekeeper to deduct an amount from his score and add it to someone else's. The bank can be viewed as a scorekeeper and a check is really just a letter to one's bank that instructs it to change the score — to pay money to someone else. Checks happen to be small, convenient in size, and constructed from special durable paper, but they are stationery nonetheless. In fact, one has the option of using any other form of stationery to inform the bank of changes in the score. Stories often hit the newspapers of checks that have been written on shingles or bricks. Most often such "checks" result from bets that have been lost. The loser then mails a C.O.D. brick check to the winner who pays more in postage than the brick is worth. The banks will accept these checks although often they add a service charge to compensate them for the inconvenience in handling.

Because the money is really the score that is registered on the scoreboard, losing checks (stationery) is not the same as losing money. Similarly, the cartoon wife who writes out checks whose value exceeds the money in the account and feels rich because she still has checks left has missed the point that the checks are just stationery. Checking accounts represent a centralized scorekeeping device. One can lose such money only through forgery or through a collapse of the scoreboard.

Because the scorekeeping is centralized, there are costs associated with checking money that do not exist for currency. Someone must change the scores and that someone must be paid. Therefore, technological progress in bank money consists of lowering the costs of keeping score. A discussion of the progress that has been made in lowering the costs of scorekeeping is really a history of banking.

The Development of Bank Money

Originally, banks were storehouses for gold. People feared theft so they kept their gold and currency with whoever owned a vault, usually the local jeweler or goldsmith. The goldsmith would charge for this service. He issued a receipt to the depositors and kept their valuables in a little sack. Today safety deposit boxes in banks serve the same function. Safety deposit boxes are merely little drawers in a big wall safe in which one can keep one's valuables. One must pay the bank for the service.

Because gold and currency were homogeneous, it did not matter to the depositers whether they received back the same gold they deposited. As it was cheaper for the goldsmith to throw the gold in one big pile, he charged lower rates to those who would accept receipts for any gold or currency rather than for a particular item. At this point, the value of one's account was what was written in the goldsmith's ledger. He no longer knew which pieces of gold or currency represented which accounts.

If an individual wished to use his deposited gold for a transaction, he had to go to the goldsmith, turn in his receipt, take physical possession of the gold, transport it to the seller, and trade it for the desired commodity. The seller then had to carry the gold back to his own vault. Not only does this process risk theft, but it forces the buyer to trek to the bank, perhaps at a very inconvenient time.

The next step in the history of bank money reduced this inconvenience. It was the agreement on the part of the goldsmiths to pay out the gold not only to the depositer, but to any person the depositer designated. Thus the depositer might write a letter to the goldsmith saying, "Please allow Smith to withdraw a pound of my gold." Once the goldsmiths have agreed to allow their depositers this convenience, they can be called *banks,* and the letters they agree to accept can be called *checks.* Smith, of course, might wish to make sure that such a letter actually gets written and mailed. The easiest way to guarantee that is to give the letter to Smith and to let him mail it or carry it to the bank when he wishes. At the time of the transaction, it is the letter, or check, that is traded for the commodity. The check is now money.

Had there been only one bank in the world, the introduction of checking privileges might have eliminated all necessity of moving gold physically. If a record of everyone's account had been kept in the same ledger, it would have been very easy to receive a letter from a client, subtract an amount from his account, and add it to someone else's. One could have ignored the vault in the back room. But because there were many goldsmiths, physical movement of coin and currency was still necessary. If one signed one's deposited gold over to someone who used a different goldsmith, the money had to be shifted between the two vaults. This was very expensive.

Thus the next development in banking was the creation of *central banks* to unify the whole banking system. Each little bank made a deposit in the large central bank. Now a check written to someone who used another bank could be deposited in that other bank. That bank in turn could mail the check to the central bank and increase its own deposit there. The central bank deducted the check from the account of the original bank and turned the check over to it. That bank in turn docked the account of the person writing the check. According to the scoreboard analogy, a central bank became a central scoreboard on which the total scores of the individual boards were registered. With central banks, most of the physical transfer of gold and currency was eliminated. Thus the costs of checking transactions were reduced to the costs of scorekeeping — writing down numbers in books.

With the advent of electronic data processing, a further reduction in the costs of checking took place. The impact of this technological progress is still being felt today as new methods of payment evolve. Now the score is kept on magnetic tapes inside computers. This means that the great embezzlers of our generation will be computer programmers, just as they were bookkeepers in past eras.

Future Money

Electronic data processing has lowered bank costs a great deal over maintaining rows of clerks writing numbers on pads. Each customer has a statement prepared for him showing his deposits, withdrawals, and current balance. The amount of record keeping that will be done by banks in the future is likely to increase as it is very inexpensive to program the computer to keep track of many details.

Checks bear magnetic marks that allow them to be read by machines. In the future we can imagine individuals stamping numbers on their checks to signify the amounts paid. The machines will be able to read the numbers and can then do all of the clerical work. No record keeping will have to be done by hand by the bank's clerks. Other innovations that reduce transaction costs or the costs of record keeping can be imagined.

In Switzerland today, one can arrange to have the bank make payments for utilities, charge accounts, and other similar regular transactions. When one's statement is received, automatic deductions have been made for the phone bill and so on. The telephone company receives from each bank one large check representing the sum of the payments of all the bank's customers. It is likely that the company keeps accounts in all banks so that it can be credited automatically with the payments. Thus, instead of mailing bills to individuals, the phone company mails them to the banks, who pay them immediately. This system eliminates the costs of handling checks by individuals, companies, and banks, as well as saving postage. It is one more step forward in the history of lowering the costs of transactions and checking accounts. Soon we can expect similar systems to be used around the world.

Another device of the Swiss system that is gaining acceptance in the United States is the automatic overdraft. This simply means that negative balances are allowed on checking accounts. A loan is automatically extended when the amount of checks to be paid exceeds the deposit balance. Deposits of new money automatically pay off the loan. Coupling this with the automatic payment of bills, we see that consumer credit can be extended directly through the banks rather than through individual firms.

A similar development in the United States is the use of bank credit cards. With these cards, one can charge many items at different stores and receive a loan from a single bank to pay for them. One check to the bank pays all the bills. Thus the costs of transactions are lower than if many bills were received. It is a simple step from the separate credit card and checking account to a system wherein one's credit card and checking account have the same number and the bill (or a part of it) is paid automatically.

Banks envision a day in the future when credit cards will replace checks and even currency. Stamping a credit card on to a sales receipt is just as good a way to inform the bank (or the bank's computer) that a payment should be made as is a personalized check. They are both stationery, after all. With costs falling for computer services, we can envision a day when the payments will be made instantaneously. When a customer hands a waitress his credit card, he can observe her stamp it on the form, fill out the appropriate numbers, and so on. Today the credit slip gets thrown into the cash register. Tomorrow the slip will be fed into a computer console and the customer's checking account will be docked for the champagne before it is even digested. Vending machines can be designed to dispense products when a credit card is inserted in a slot and then withdrawn. The payment will appear on the next accounting statement from the bank. Gasoline pumps may dispense gas when credit cards are inserted; pay phones, subways, buses, and toll booths can all respond to the plastic card with a record of the transactions automatically appearing on the next bank statement. Since the cost of transferring funds from one account to another will be very low, some envision daily paychecks, utility bills, tax payments, and so on. Much smaller accounts can be held, on average, for these many small payments than must be held today for the large monthly checks we write.

This future payments mechanism has been described as a moneyless society. But it is not without money. Money will be comprised of marks on computer tapes as it is today. A great convenience of the system may be that we carry less currency than we do today or that we need lower average balances to finance the same transactions. The very sophistication of the money may allow us to get along with very little of it. But there will still be money. After all, money is the means of payment.

Questions

1.   Why might the following commodities make good or bad monies? Ice, diamonds, IOUs, elephants, wheat.
2.   Why might gold be preferred to more sophisticated monies in times of political turbulence?
3.   How would you be made worse off if all the gold in Fort Knox evaporated? Do you know anyone else who would be hurt?
4.   Why do international transactions pose particular problems in terms of the choice of money to be used? How might a central bank for central banks work?

Concepts Discussed

money	inflation
barter	bank money
coin	Gresham's Law
fiat money	checks
legal tender	

34 Other Assets

Modern assets used as money, such as checking accounts, currency, and credit cards, are not physical commodities; rather, they are financial assets. In this chapter we study financial assets and financial institutions in general to see why they exist and how they affect the decisions of savers, borrowers, and investors. This will make clear the role of banks in the monetary system. We will see how asset prices are determined and how sharp changes in the demand for assets can cause stock market crashes, bank failures, and financial collapse. These are interesting not only for their intrinsic drama but for the effects they have on economic variables that help determine our material well-being.

Markets and Buffers

Supply and demand rarely mesh exactly at every point in time. In principle, a perfect auction market could take place once a day to satisfy the accumulated demanders and suppliers. In such a market, there would be an exact equality of supply and demand just as we discussed earlier in the book. It is more convenient, however, to forego the benefits of this exact equality and allow people to buy and sell whenever they wish. Thus many markets operate continually with transactions being made whenever it suits the whim of the buyer or seller. In such markets, the sudden appearance of a buyer does not automatically call forth the appearance of a seller. Thus to operate efficiently, these markets need some way to allow the temporary excess demand of this instant to offset the temporary excess supply an hour from now. We can call the various mechanisms that exist *buffers*.

One obvious buffer is inventories. Factory output occurs at a pace dictated by the costs of the production process. Consumer demand occurs at a pace determined by household convenience. The two do not occur at the same rate. If an inventory exists, however, we can allow the minor variations in supply and demand to affect the size of the inventory rather than the price of the output. Thus between the producer and the consumer lies a network of distribution industries whose role is to move commodities from places where it is convenient to produce them to places where it is convenient to consume them and to manage the level of inventories in this pipeline. The convenience this inventory yields to buyers and sellers is worth the cost of maintaining it.

Some goods cannot be inventoried because they are services that must be used when produced. Examples are haircuts, concerts, restaurants, and the like. The buffering device used here consists of lines or queues. If ten people walk into a barbershop at once, some will have to wait. They have the opportunity of bidding up the price of haircuts to determine who goes first, but they cannot all buy simultaneously.

Money is a buffering device, as we saw in Chapter 33. It allows the purchase of goods and services at times other than when one sells one's labor. It smooths out the differences between an individual's supply to others of goods and services and his demand from them for different goods and services.

When the buffers are inventories, the costs of managing and maintaining these inventories must be absorbed. Retailers generally make their income from managing and maintaining inventories. The cost represents a difference between the demand price and the supply price that is paid in order to have convenience in transactions. Thus the role of overseeing the market, of guaranteeing some long-run average equilibrium between supply and demand, turns into an industry. This is true in financial markets as well. The industries are called *financial intermediaries*. Examples are banks, insurance companies, savings and loan institutions, and stockbrokers. These institutions guarantee an equality between the quantity of borrowing and lending and between the amount of saving and investment. Apparently the cheapest and most convenient way to run the lending market is not to line up borrowers and lenders once a day to bargain about the interest cost on loans. The existence of banks tells us that the cheapest way to operate this market is to allow borrowers and lenders to go when they wish to the bank to conduct their transactions. The bank as middleman will eventually raise interest rates if borrowers exceed lenders for a long period of time. The bank's activities cost money, of course, just as those of all retailers do. Therefore we observe an interest rate on borrowing different from that on lending. The saving rate could be thought of as the wholesale interest rate while the borrowing rate is the retail interest rate.

Thus financial institutions merely oversee the transactions of their markets. The reason for the existence of any of these institutions is the convenience they provide or the savings they can create by lowering transaction costs. Such institutions are the cheapest way we have yet devised of operating certain markets. Therefore, in our analysis below, we separate our reasons why financial assets exist in various forms from our reasons why certain institutions exist to create those assets. It is possible to have vegetables without grocery stores. People can always buy directly from farmers. Similarly, it is possible to have loans without having banks. Always our reason for the existence of financial institutions will be that it is most convenient to conduct a particular market through an intermediary. The reason for the existence of the market is a separate story.

The Role of Wealth
Wealth is accumulated because people wish to have the power to buy future goods. When an individual decides to save some of his present income, he is deciding to spend in the future rather than in the present. In Chapter 19, we showed how the interest rate could be expressed in terms of the price of future

goods. High interest rates mean that future goods are cheap, that one unit of present goods can be traded for a larger number of future goods due to the interest earned on saving. As the interest rate falls, fewer future goods can be obtained for any amount of present goods one has saved. With the interest rate thereby denoting the price of future goods, it is clear why changes in its level induce changes in the rate of saving—the amount of present goods being put aside to augment future purchasing power.

There is no single interest rate, however. Individuals are confronted with a variety of rates at which present income can be transformed to future income, each associated with an asset having unique characteristics. These characteristics make certain assets preferable to others for some purposes but not for others. Among these characteristics are those we discuss below, namely, riskiness and the ease, convenience, and cost of managing and selling the asset. Each saver attempts to transform present into future purchasing power in as efficient a manner as possible. He does this by buying those assets with the highest yield after taking into account the value of risk and the other characteristics.

In order to understand the impact of financial intermediaries and why various financial assets exist, we study the saver's dilemma as he attempts to convert present into future goods. First we assume that no financial machinery exists. Slowly, we relax this assumption by allowing first one market and then another to exist, showing how the saver's utility is increased by each innovation. We point out which intermediaries oversee the various markets we develop.

Goods That Yield Future Consumption
Of the many goods and services we wish to consume in the future, there are only a few that individuals buy directly in the present. Among these are wines and the services from durable goods. I can buy future housing by owning a house, future transportation by owning a car, and future entertainment by owning books and a television. Similarly, furniture, art, china, land, jewelry, appliances, and a host of other commodities represent future services as well as present ones. Accumulating wealth in this form is one way of guaranteeing future consumption. These goods, except for the land, can be called *capital goods*. They represent output that has been set aside rather than consumed immediately. In Chapter 19, we noted how nature has made it possible for one unit of current output to be transformed into more than one unit of future output. That is what makes capital profitable.

Capital
But all goods cannot be accumulated. Food will spoil; modish clothes, hit records, and many other stylish commodities cannot be bought now for future consumption unless one is to be content with old-fashioned goods. New books will be written, new art painted, new consumption goods invented. There is no convenient way to buy these ahead of time. The new firms that will exist to sell services in the future cannot sell us contracts for them now. For this reason,

generalized future purchasing power that can be used to buy the future commodities is desired. But purchasing power does not exist in nature.

To get future purchasing power, an individual must buy something now and resell it in the future. In the absence of financial markets, that something can only be land, a commodity, or a capital good that can be used to create future goods. Because of this restriction, three basic problems confront the potential saver when he is denied access to financial markets.

(1) Because future prices are unknown, he must make careful forecasts before deciding which commodities or capital goods to buy. Not only do these forecasts take time to create, but they cannot be expected to be realized with certainty. Thus even when acting on the basis of careful forecasts, the saver is not guaranteed any specific level of future consumption. This is in contrast to the situation when he buys a house, for example, and is virtually guaranteed housing services in the future.

(2) His forecasts may show him that productive capital goods have the highest expected rates of return (though not certain). But because many production processes are very complex, ownership of physical capital places great strains on the saver's management capacity. It takes time and money to see that his capital is utilized efficiently.

(3) Many capital goods are not infinitely divisible. If big bulldozers have higher expected rates of return than small ones, then the saver will wish big ones. Thus there may be minimum amounts of saving that are necessary if one is to receive the highest possible rate of return.

We will see how financial markets have been formed to handle these three problems: uncertainty, management of capital goods, and indivisibilities.

Equity

The problem of divisibility is handled by dividing the ownership legally although not physically. Therefore the aforementioned bulldozer that costs, say, $30,000, may be divided into 1,000 legal pieces, each of which is initially worth $30. The legal pieces of ownership may be represented by pieces of paper called *securities* on which is printed the equivalent of "The owner of this paper owns 1/1000 of bulldozer #24689165." Thus securities make it possible to invest very small sums in bulldozers. As the bulldozer is used, the owners of the securities receive payments that they can convert into goods or other assets. These pieces of paper can be thought of as the common stock or *equity* of the bulldozer corporation. The corporation can be viewed as an intermediary whose purpose is to allow people to own small pieces of large capital goods for various intervals of time. The size of a physical capital good need not affect the size of the financial investment individuals can make if it is legally possible to divide ownership.

The many owners of the corporation must appoint someone to see that the bulldozer is used efficiently, that it is properly maintained and does not lie idle. The job of overseeing the bulldozer is done by a manager. For a fee, he handles all of the paperwork associated with keeping the bulldozer running. Thus corporations exist so that owners can have their capital conveniently managed. Because of corporations and the securities they issue, one can buy into pieces of capital at any time and sell at any time that is convenient. If the costs of information and communication were low enough, one could accomplish the management of the capital without a corporation. Professional managers might work for fees as lawyers or accountants do. Similarly, with low bargaining costs, one could sell pieces of a unit of capital without forming a corporation. But apparently the corporation with full-time employees is a convenient form in which to accomplish these transactions.

The buying and selling of shares of equity is organized in most countries on stock exchanges. Brokers exist around the country to take orders and transmit them to the central market. At the market, there exists a specialist who matches the buy and sell orders. He maintains an inventory of securities that acts as a buffer to smooth out the differences between demand and supply. Generally, these inventories are very small relative to the demand and supply so that prices of equities change daily.

The existence of corporations and stock markets may solve the problems of management and instability noted above. But they do not get around the fact that future prices are unpredictable. And it so happens that the prices of corporate securities are less predictable than most other prices. Why? The price of a piece of equity in a specific activity depends on the expected future profits. When one buys a share of stock, he is buying the right to future profit. It is clear that as the estimate of those profits changes, the price of the security will change. Future profits depend on the future supply and demand for the product being sold. Future supply and demand, in turn, depend on whether new substitutes will be invented or new processes designed to make existing equipment obsolete and whether new firms enter the industry to expand supply, as well as on the supply and demand for all the commodities the firm must buy in order to produce output. Future profits will be the difference between future revenues and future costs. In fact, profits are the most volatile form of income in the whole economy. When unemployment rates change by 3 or 4 percentage points, profits can fluctuate by 50 percent. And the profits of an individual firm fluctuate more violently than do total national profits wherein a lot of individual fluctuations cancel out. Thus forecasting future profits is very difficult. Similarly, forecasting future equity prices is almost impossible. Thus the ownership of equity is a very risky way to transfer present purchasing power to the future.

The problem is compounded by the fact that the price of equity can fluctuate independently of the fluctuations in actual future profits. This is because of the uncertainty about these profits. The price of equity depends on the present price being paid for expected future profit. That price can change not only if the actual future profits change but also if their expected value changes (our forecast of them), or if the price of future profits changes as individuals reallocate their consumption toward or away from the present. Thus, as one who follows the stock market can tell you, stock prices move up and down not only in response to news stories about the forecasts of future sales and costs, but also for many apparently unexplainable reasons as well. The simple fact is that stock prices go down when people try to sell stocks. They may suddenly decide to sell for a whole variety of reasons that are independent of their forecasts of future sales. Given the violent swings in stock prices that we observe, many speculators claim that there is little to be learned from examining the facts about future profits for a given stock and a great deal to be learned by looking at the psychology of the market.

Keynes likened the stock market to a beauty contest. In London in his time, newspapers would conduct beauty contests by printing one hundred pictures of girls and asking readers to select the ten prettiest. The girls with the most votes won and the readers who had selected the ten winners won prizes for being astute judges of beauty. A contestant could approach this problem in a naive way by trying to determine the prettiest girls and writing their names on the ballot. But then if we look into the problem a bit more deeply, it is evident that one is not trying to pick the prettiest girls but to forecast the winners of the contest. And the girls who win will be the ones whom most of the other people select. Thus one must guess which girls others will find to be pretty even if they are different from one's own choice. Of course, the truly subtle man realizes that others are approaching the game in this way too and are not going to submit as their selection the girls they find to be prettiest, but the ones they think others will find prettiest. And soon there are an infinite number of dimensions to the game. One guesses the girls that others think that others think that others think that others think, etc., are the prettiest. And that is Keynes's view of the stock market. If one wants large purchasing power in the future, he wants to buy today those stocks that are going to go up regardless of the reason. He wants to buy the stock that others will want in the future. Forecasting profits is hard enough, but predicting man's whims is virtually impossible. Needless to say, speculation is not a simple game. How then can one transfer wealth to the future without taking on these risks?

Before answering that question, let us point out why risk is disliked. Stocks can go up or down. You might think that as long as there is an equal chance of their going up or down, one should not care. We can guess at their return on average (their expected return) and it is the average of the future possibilities that should matter. This reasoning ignores the basic psychological law described in Chapter 2 — diminishing marginal utility. Because of diminishing marginal utility, students do not bet $100 on the flip of a coin. The reason is that the utility to be gained by winning $100 is not great enough to offset the utility to be lost by losing $100. The extra $100, if won, would allow one to consume enjoyable commodities, but less enjoyable than the commodities one would have to sacrifice if he lost $100. The pain of losing $100 exceeds the joy of winning $100, so such bets do not take place.

Similarly, in the stock market, the possibility of winning $100 is more than offset in value by the possibility of losing $100. This means that risk is to be avoided if possible, but not at all costs. Think of considering two investments: one would yield $1,000 for sure, while the other would yield perhaps $500 or perhaps $1,500 with equal probabilities. One has to pay $900 today for either investment and the payoff will occur next year. If risk is undesirable, most people will pick the sure thing. After all, the risky investment is just like the sure one but with a $500 flip of a coin tacked on. If people do not like to flip coins for $500, they will not like the risky investment. But what if the risky investment had possible returns of $550 and $1,550; that is, what if when the coin were flipped one paid $450 if he lost, but he got $550 if he won. Or what about $600 and $1,600 and $700 and $1,700? There comes a time when the high return on the risky asset makes it preferable to the sure thing.

This tells us one of the general principles of asset markets: *People demand higher rates of return on risky assets than on sure things*. We can expect people to be unwilling to buy risky assets if their rate of return is the same as that of unrisky assets, but we can also expect that there will be some difference in the the returns that makes an investor indifferent between two assets. For larger differences he will buy the risky asset, for smaller differences the sure thing.

A while back, we asked if one could transfer purchasing power to the future without taking on risk. Now we have seen that investors must be compensated in the form of higher returns for the risk they take on. The market will reflect this general desire to avoid risk by placing lower returns on the less risky assets. Thus one can transfer purchasing power with less risk if he is willing to accept a lower rate of return.

But we have pointed out that all capital is risky. Some investors may wish to take on even less risk than exists in the least risky of capital assets. How can their desires be satisfied? Financial intermediaries allow them to do this in two ways by creating assets that do not exist in nature. Before looking at the particular assets available to those who dislike risk, let us examine how it is possible for financial markets to affect the risks a particular investor must shoulder.

Risk and Insurance

One way of lowering the risk to asset holders is through *diversification*. That is, two $50 flips of a coin are less risky than one $100 flip. With two $50 flips, one-fourth of the time $100 is lost, one-fourth of the time $100 is won, and one-half of the time one breaks even. Thus if there exist two risky capital goods to be bought by two investors, they can lower their risk by buying half of each good. Buying half of two $100 flips is less risky than buying all of one $100 flip. Of course, for diversification to lower risk, the possible future outcomes from the two assets must be independent. One does not lower risk very much by buying one-half of each of two different bulldozers. Risk is lowered by buying half a bulldozer and half a restaurant.

Financial markets and intermediaries allow individuals to diversify in many ways. First, one can buy securities of many different corporations. That is, an individual can conduct his own diversification. Second, single corporations buy many different kinds of capital and sell many different products so that their equities already represent diversification. Third, mutual funds and pension funds buy many different kinds of equities. Buying a piece of a mutual fund is like buying a piece of many corporations simultaneously. Thus no one need bear the high risks that result from owning a single piece of capital. He can buy instead small percentages of many different capital goods.

But what of the physical capital investors actually do buy? We noted earlier that people own houses, wine, antiques, and art. How do they avoid the risks associated with these assets? (The risks here result not so much from an inability to forecast price and the desires of others as they do from an inability to forecast fire, theft, and vandalism.) One way to diversify would be to have 30 people each buy 1/30th of thirty different houses. Then if one house burns down, no one undergoes the huge loss associated with losing an entire house.

An alternative way to organize the same diversification is through insurance. People can agree always to recompense the fire victims. Anyone wanting a guarantee of repayment in case his house burns can buy such a guarantee by agreeing to pay for a fraction of all the other houses that burn during the year. If on average one house out of 500 burns down every year, one's expected payment would be 1/500th of the value of his house. Individuals can accomplish these transactions themselves, but instead insurance companies have developed to sell this form of protection. Presumably this is because such companies save individuals' bargaining costs. An insurance policy is an asset that pays a great deal of money if a specific event occurs. By coupling this asset with another (like a house) that is worth a great deal if the event does not occur, one has a sure thing. It is like buying both the "heads" and the "tails" sides of the same flip of a coin. Heads the house burns down and one owns $30,000 in cash, tails it does not and one owns a $30,000 house.

Thus diversification lowers risk. Because of this, we observe financial assets and securities whose purpose is to pool many independent risks. The transaction costs involved in buying the many securities needed to diversify means that on average, the return on diversified wealth will be lower than on undiversified wealth. These transaction costs are large enough that insurance companies charge 1/400th of the value of a house as a premium if the house has 1/500th of a possibility of burning. The buildings occupied by mutual funds and insurance companies, the equipment they use, and the salaries of their workers are testimony to the costs of diversification. These costs make the rates of return lower on less risky assets than on the risky assets that are used to create them.

Selling Risk

One way in which financial markets allow individuals to avoid risk is diversification. Another way is by selling risk, by bribing others to shoulder more of it. Diversification lowers risk to all and is an obvious way to increase everyone's utility. It will be done whenever the returns exceed the transaction costs. If tastes differ, however, so that some people are more willing to take on risk than others, financial markets allow these people to get together and trade risk for return almost as if these attributes of assets were different commodities.

Consider the following example. A share of an investment has an equal chance of yielding either $500 or $1,500. Two investors each own one share, but one wishes to avoid risk more than the other. For example, one investor would prefer an investment that yields a certain $900 to the one he now owns while the other investor prefers an investment that has an equal chance of yielding $100 or $2,100 to his current one. That is, one prefers the certain $900 to the current risky investment that brings in $1,000 on average while the other investor would be willing to take on an even riskier asset if its average return were $1,100.

These two investors can get together and each acquire the asset he prefers. Consider that their total income from the two shares will be either $1,000 or $3,000. Currently, they are dividing these two possibilities equally. But split the $1,000 into pieces of $900 and $100, and the $3,000 into pieces of $900 and $2,100, and both investors can be made happier. The first investor gets his sure $900 while the other gets his equal chance of $100 and $2,100. One investor has accepted a lower rate of return in order to avoid risk. The other has agreed to take on extra risk because of the higher rate of return he receives. It is as if one investor had paid the other to take on risk.

This form of transaction is made convenient by the corporations who issue two forms of securities. Many corporations buy capital with money raised from selling bonds as well as stock. Legally, all payments must be made to the bond-holders before the stockholders receive anything. Thus the bonds of the same corporation are much less risky than the stocks. If things turn out very badly for a particular corporation, its stockholders may get nothing while its bondholders are paid off. If things go well, the bondholders receive their safe reward but the stockholders get rich. Thus if a corporation issues both bonds and stocks it al-lows individuals to trade risk conveniently for return. The bondholders, by ac-cepting a lower rate of return, have compensated the stockholders for shoul-dering all the risks.

Of course, if someone wishes to take on exactly the risk and return inherent in the capital that the corporation owns, he must buy both stocks and bonds. By buying some of both, he is able to re-create the returns to the capital owned by the firm because the sum of these returns must be the sum of the returns to the bond- and stockholders.

Other Financial Markets and Institutions

Of course, the bonds of a corporation are not completely risk-free instruments. If things turn out very badly for a particular company, it may go bankrupt and default on its bonds as well as on its stock. Even less risky than a bond is a loan to a firm. Not only does the law say that the loan must be paid before the bond, but most loans are for very short duration while bonds are generally much longer. It is more difficult to predict default in the distant future than in the present.

A hierarchy of claims exists to the earnings on the corporation's capital. This hierarchy distributes the risk and return in different proportions to the different claims. The least risky claims receive the lowest rates of return, of course. These are generally loans.

But even the least risky claim is not risk free. Any venture can go under. Therefore one who was very averse to risk might even wish to diversify among these almost riskless claims and lend small amounts to many different firms in different industries. This is one of the functions of banks. They have diversified their holdings of the least risky claims to firms' income across many firms. Thus a bank's portfolio (a portfolio is a collection of assets) is less risky than most single securities are.

But there is a slight degree of risk even in a collection of loans. The holders of the collection may wish to sell even this risk to others. The bank accomplishes this unequal distribution of risk and return by having stockholders as well as depositors. That is, the bank too has common stockholders who absorb the greater part of the risk. If the bank's loan portfolio turns sour, these stockholders lose everything before the depositors lose a penny. The depositors lend money to banks in the same way that bondholders lend to corporations. It is as if the depositors and the stockholders got together to distribute the risk and return as we described above. Thus a bank deposit represents claims to a diversified group of the least risky claims to physical capital; and the deposit represents the least risky of the claims on that diversified group. As safe as it is possible to get? No. Even a bank deposit is not risk free.

Banks have defaulted on deposits in the past. To avoid this possibility one might even wish to diversify his holdings across banks. Or one might buy deposit insurance. As the latter alternative has lower transaction costs, it is used more widely today. In the United States most banks insure the first $15,000 of an account with the *Federal Deposit Insurance Corporation*, a quasi-public institution. Thus an account at an insured bank represents a claim to capital from which risk has been squeezed many times.

Intermediation: The Broad View

A broad view of capital and financial markets gives us the following insights. The society owns bulldozers, restaurants, factories, and inventories. Of course, individuals own all this wealth but in its natural form it is so inconvenient that they have divided up its properties in many legal forms that could never exist in nature. The role of financial intermediaries is to perform the division efficiently, to minimize the bargaining time, supervision time, and calculations required of individuals to hold wealth in convenient forms. Thus savings accounts, checking accounts, insurance, mutual funds, bonds, and stocks are apparently much more convenient to hold than bulldozers, skyscrapers, and computers. If we look at savings accounts and the like, it is very difficult to observe the financial characteristics of bulldozers in them, but they are there. The sum of everyone's stocks, bonds, insurance, bank accounts, and so on must have all of the characteristics of the sum of all the physical capital.

A checking account represents a legal claim on a bank or, more correctly, on a bank's assets. Therefore it is the bank's assets that guarantee this claim, or that "back" it. If one wishes to withdraw his money from the bank, the bank must dispose of an asset. Of course the assets the bank owns are loans to firms, legal claims to the firms' assets. And the firms' assets are physical capital. Thus indirectly one's ownership of a bank account is ownership of physical capital. Most of the risk has been removed as has all the headache of management. But nonetheless ownership of bank deposits corresponds to ownership of physical capital by someone. If we look at the whole economy, it is as if all the real assets had been poured into a mixer and turned into equity, savings accounts, and insurance.

Expectations and Financial Assets

The picture we have just painted is one of docile equilibrium. Shrewd financial magnates have found ingenious ways of tailoring the characteristics of assets to suit people's desires. We can all have the convenience of checking accounts without depriving the society of physical capital. By dividing and reshuffling the characteristics of bulldozers and lathes, we have become able to use them as money. Rather than waste the time necessary to scratch gold from the ground in order to have money, we use purified bulldozers. Ingenious financial devices have allowed us to get around commodities' physical inconvenience to use a part of them as money, namely, that part represented in checking accounts. Since bulldozers are productive capital and earn interest, total output is higher when checking accounts are used for money than it is when gold is used. This financial structure appears to be the picture of sanity.

But some risks are heightened by financial sophistication. Remember our description of the determination of equity prices: Equity prices fluctuate much more violently than the prices of physical capital in response to changes in expectations. This potential for violent fluctuation exists throughout a financial structure. One of the primary goals of financial policy makers is to prevent such fluctuations and to maintain stability in asset markets.

The reason financial structures exaggerate fluctuations in asset prices can be understood by observing all the gains of intermediation we have just discussed. People are much happier holding the financial rather than the physical assets during normal times for all of the reasons we have described, particularly risk avoidance and convenience. But when some shock changes their expectations about future prices and makes them doubt the value of the assets they hold, they do not know what to do except to "get out while the gettin's good." And "gettin' out" means giving up all of the advantages of financial sophistication, giving up a great deal of the utility one expected to derive from one's wealth. The shock not only changes expectations of the value of real wealth; by inducing people to flee from financial instruments into safer real assets that they understand better, the shock reduces the value of wealth a great deal more.

To understand this point better, let us examine the possible repercussions of a change in expectations with and without financial superstructure. Assume first that there are no financial assets or markets. Provision for future consumption is accomplished by purchasing real goods only. Now a change in forecasts of future prices suddenly occurs so that on average the capital goods now owned are expected to yield a return of minus 2 percent rather than 15 percent profit. That is, they turn out to have been bad investments rather than good ones. This, of course, is a cataclysmic change in expectations. But in the case where only real goods are held by individuals, the change means that now $1.00 worth of present goods can be turned into $.98 worth of future goods rather than $1.15 worth. There is a decline of about 15 percent in the value of future goods that wealth holders will now be able to buy with their savings. It is a tragic event, but one can readily adjust to it. Because everyone owns and manages his own capital, he is forced to know a great deal about future prices. He knows enough not to sell his capital if its price falls by more than 15 percent. With its forecasted value down by 15 percent, it is a bargain at prices more than 15 percent lower. Thus an adjustment to the new forecast occurs and the world moves on.

Consider the same change in average expectations in a world with a sophisticated financial apparatus. Now profits are expected to be negative on average with some firms having much greater losses than others. Because individuals have found it convenient to let others do the management and decision making, they do not know which firms will be the ones with the large losses. But they know what the conservative thing to do is. *Get out of equities!* The stock market collapses as people rush for the exits. The value of many bonds is genuinely threatened but no one knows which ones are likely to go under: Again, rush to the exits. Some firms may be so threatened that they will have to default on their loans. That means some banks may go under. Thus even bank deposits are threatened. To the lifeboats!

The resulting panic on the part of the public undoes all the advantages of the sophisticated structure as people attempt to get back to the security of a world without finance, a world where a man owns real goods and is guaranteed a minimum level of consumption in the future. Suddenly, no one knows which assets to buy. How best can the future be guaranteed? As people attempt to turn savings accounts into canned goods, furniture, art—something they understand— violent changes in relative price take place. Common commodities become very expensive. All financial assets decline in value relative to these commodities. Thus the market value of wealth in terms of these simple commodities falls violently. The withdrawal of deposits forces banks to sell loans and securities to get cash. But no one will buy the loans. They must call them in. That means they call up their borrowers and say, "Hey, get down here and pay off this loan, man! I need cash!" But the borrower owns bulldozers, not cash. "Then sell the things," the urbane banker replies. A bulldozer auction is held but few buyers appear. The tiny amount of cash obtained from the auction cannot pay off the loan. The borrower must default and go bankrupt. That is, he pays back what he can and the rest is a loss to the bank. The company's bondholders get nothing. Thus the stockholders get nothing. With firms paying off only part of their loans, the bank's losses are so great it goes under. Its stockholders lose everything, its depositors lose something.

Thus the financial panic wipes out all the financial intermediaries—corporations, banks, and brokers. After the panic, a violent readjustment in prices has taken place. The world looks the same, but its financial structure has collapsed. Men want to work, but firms have been destroyed. No one hires. Idle factories have been sold to help pay off bad loans. The banks acquired the factories and then when the banks went under, the depositers who had not yet withdrawn got them. It will take the courts years to sort out the bankruptcies and defaults to find out who owns what. Certainly someone owns those factories and whoever he is, he would probably like to see them running. But the violent reshuffling and redivision of financial claims occurred in such a whirl and panic that no one knows what is going on.

The cataclysm just described is more violent than most. It is merely an illustration of what can happen. One of the roles of monetary authorities and government agencies is to see that such events do not happen. Central bankers, we will see in the next chapter, have been given the role of spoil sports. The awesome responsibility they shoulder leads them to see evil in all financial innovations. "The bigger they are, the harder they fall" is the central banker's belief about financial superstructures. Couple this with the fact that an irrational fear of panic on the part of the public can touch off real panic and we see that the authorities will have an easier job in a simple world where panics are less dangerous, therefore less feared, therefore less likely than in a complex world. Sophisticated readers of the financial press find great amusement in the battle that goes on between the regulatory authorities and the financial intermediaries. The intermediaries are attempting to make more profit by inventing new and more efficient ways to bring together borrower and lender, saver and investor. Done properly, this increases the utility of wealth as well as the sophistication of the financial superstructure. But the authorities view each innovation as one more story being built on the house of cards. Their ulcers act up, their dreams become nightmares, their martinis get stronger. They attempt to prop up the house of cards with new laws, new threats, and promises of action when needed. They may prevent certain forms of financial activity, claiming them to be too risky. It is a dramatic and important battle to watch.

Smaller cataclysms and different kinds of cataclysms can result. We assumed a specific form of shock—a massive change in the forecast of profits. Only a fear of revolution or natural disaster would be likely to cause a shock of this magnitude. But other shocks are possible, some of them caused by the monetary authorities themselves. What happens, for example, if the monetary authorities print too much fiat money and oversupply the market to a degree that the price of money starts to fall at a rapid rate? Suddenly all those assets that we have described as safe, insured checking accounts, etc., are threatened with loss due to inflation. The reaction and adjustment to the shock of inflation cause a complete reshuffling of financial claims by investors and in severe cases can pull down all the institutions that deal with money. Cataclysms are not identical.

In Chapter 35, we show how the central bank can control the supply of money and the cost of credit in order to affect the prices and quantities of real goods. We will see how the authorities can bail out the banks when they are threatened to prevent them from going under, how they prevent certain dangerous financial practices, and how they encourage banks to act responsibly. We will also see how their actions have impact even on institutions not directly regulated.

Questions

1.   Distinguish between the two different ways in which financial markets allow individuals to avoid risk. Give examples of both kinds of risk avoidance.
2.   Why do risky assets generally have higher rates of return than nonrisky ones?
3.   What are the advantages and disadvantages of a sophisticated financial superstructure?

Concepts Discussed

buffers	diversification
financial intermediaries	risk
equity	insurance
securities	

35 Overseeing Financial Affairs

We have just seen how a financial superstructure can destroy itself, how panic is possible. It is the job of the monetary authorities to see that this does not happen. This chapter is devoted to a study of the monetary authorities and how they carry out their policy: the conflicting objectives they face; what actions they take to secure their goals; and why these actions work or are supposed to work. We will see why the manipulation of just one asset, currency, has repercussions in all financial markets, how the banking system magnifies these manipulations, and why no intermediary or individual is immune to their effects.

Objectives of the Monetary Authorities

STABILITY. The last few pages of the previous chapter are testimony to the reason why stability is a policy goal of all financial authorities. If things can be kept from changing too rapidly, a speculative panic is less likely to develop.

EFFICIENCY. On the other hand, we want to enjoy as much as possible of the fruits of efficiency that are obtained by allowing borrowers and lenders to make all the transactions they want to. That is, we would like to permit any transaction that makes both parties feel better off. Efficiency requires untrammeled financial markets. The goals of stability and efficiency are clearly in conflict.

Underlying the possibility of panic is a domino theory of financial markets that shows how the actions of individuals can have external effects. Individuals, out to save their own skins, consider the possibility of their own financial collapse when they decide how much debt to take on—or if they do not, they should. But they do not consider how their own collapse can affect others. Considering just that is the job of the monetary authorities. And when individuals enter into new kinds of bargains with each other, the monetary authorities must develop new strategies for action in case panic develops.

Monetary authorities are tempted, therefore, to retard the introduction of new efficient forms of financial contracts until all of their associated implications and potential dangers are understood. In an era when computers are causing revolutions in the technology of intermediation, there are bound to develop many new and interesting forms of contracts for individuals to buy. Thus in an era that is likely to see vast gains in efficiency in financial markets, the regulators have a particularly difficult time. Old regulations that were once merely nuisances become stinging barriers to competition. It suddenly becomes profitable to exploit old loopholes. The neat divisions of the market that once existed are now

458

blurred as it becomes profitable for all institutions to compete with all others in all markets. The beleaguered regulator is tempted to forego all efficiency when he surveys such a scene. Just as he is finished shoring up one column in the edifice, he hears creaking elsewhere and observes massive new towers and wings being constructed with no apparent support. Martinis and tranquilizers become his bread and butter.

CONTROL OF UNEMPLOYMENT. The authorities not only have the power to strengthen the structure against ill winds, but they can set up countervailing winds to blow in any direction they desire, causing changes in the willingness of borrowers to lend and vice versa. This power gives them some control over the level of demand for goods and services and therefore over the level of employment. We will see below how the power works and how it is exercised.

CONTROL OF INFLATION. Chapter 29 makes the point that as unemployment falls, we can expect prices to rise. Financial authorities particularly fear inflation because of the rapid redistribution of wealth that it causes and the actions that individuals will take to prevent that redistribution. Not only might the redistribution lead to default of certain assets, but the attempts of individuals to protect themselves from the inflation can bring down the whole financial superstructure. Inflation and unemployment, both evils, appear to be short-run alternatives. The monetary authorities have to choose between these alternatives when setting policy.

Tools of Monetary Control

We now turn to a description of the tools the authorities use to pursue their goals and the reasons why the tools work. First we look at those designed to prevent panic. Stability is enhanced if the authorities can prevent the collapse and bankruptcy of any of the "dominoes" in the system. In practice, monetary authorities concentrate most of their attention on banks and attempt to prevent them from becoming overextended. There are regulations for all intermediaries, however. Because the list of tools of monetary control varies from country to country, US examples are used. But the discussion of their effectiveness is general enough to indicate the potential effectiveness of all forms of regulation.

DEPOSIT INSURANCE. In the United States, the Federal Deposit Insurance Corporation (FDIC) insures bank deposits up to $15,000. The individual banks pay insurance fees to FDIC, which invests the proceeds in a fund to be used to pay back the depositors should a bank collapse. If banks collapse simultaneously and exhaust the funds of FDIC, the federal government has the responsibility of honoring the FDIC's commitments by printing additional currency to be given to the depositors. A similar institution, the Savings and Loan Deposit Insurance Corporation (SLDIC), insures savings and loan institutions. Thus small depositors are virtually guaranteed that they will receive back their currency even if the banks collapse. This means that there is little reason to withdraw funds from a bank whose solvency is feared. We saw how a fear of collapse could actually bring about such a collapse if depositiors withdrew all their money. The incentive for such speculative collapses does not exist if the depositer is guaranteed that his funds will exist even if the bank goes under.

CASH RESERVES. Banks in most countries are required to hold certain amounts of cash in reserve to be able to meet sudden deposit withdrawals. Generally, these amounts are specified as some percentage of the deposits the bank has received. In the United States, these percentages are about 15 percent of all demand deposits (checking accounts) and 5 percent of all saving deposits. The central bank—the Federal Reserve System—has the power to change these percentages and should lower them a great deal to allow the banks to pay out the cash when it feels that a speculative wave of withdrawals is imminent. The regulation guarantees that the banks will not endanger the quality of the superstructure by making too many loans.

LENDER OF LAST RESORT. Central banks often guarantee to support individual banks by agreeing to lend them money in the event that massive withdrawals materialize. During a panic, a bank finds it difficult to turn its assets into cash. Securities markets are collapsing and the banks cannot get much money by selling their assets. Indeed, their attempts to do so would drive the market down even further. The central bank, as lender of last resort, will help out the local banks by lending them money with securities as *collateral*. That is, the local bank must deposit securities with the central bank if it is to receive a loan. The central bank will own the securities if the local bank defaults on its loan. This ability to convert securities rapidly into cash regardless of the prevailing price of securities is a guarantee to the local banks of cash when they need it. Not surprisingly, the local banks will think of securities as being as safe as cash once they have this guarantee.

INTEREST RATE RESTRICTIONS. The interest rates that banks pay on deposits must be below a legislated ceiling. Currently, banks are allowed to pay nothing on checking accounts and about 5 percent—the exact amount depending on the form of the savings account—on savings accounts. The banks' reaction to this is to attempt to pay interest to depositors in a form other than money whenever the free market rate would exceed the legislated ceiling. On checking accounts, the depositors receive a great many free accounting services. The existence of branches, long hours, many tellers, and even beautiful buildings all increase the convenience of using a bank and are a nonmonetary form of interest payment.

The reason for the restrictions on interest payments is a belief that competition among banks would force them all to pay the same interest rates on deposits. Inefficient banks would go bankrupt because these payments would increase their costs a great deal. Bankruptcies are one of the things authorities wish to prevent. One aspect of a bank's struggle to stay alive would be an attempt to increase its income by buying riskier and riskier assets. This would endanger the financial superstructure. In most industries, inefficient firms can be driven out. But in banking, they can stay in business by buying many risky loans with high interest premiums. In a world with no bank regulation, individuals would have to determine which bank to choose by examining the quality of its portfolio. Even today, when deposit insurance makes this unnecessary, banks publish statements of their financial position in order to assure depositors of the safety of the deposits. They brag about how old they are to show how many past panics they have survived. Whether or not it is wise to shelter the inefficient banks behind a wall of regulations is an open question. There are obvious losses in efficiency. But there can be gains if the regulations cause the public to have more confidence in banks and if the confidence prevents panics that would otherwise occur.

PORTFOLIO RESTRICTIONS. Banks are not allowed to own common stock. This means that banks can no longer enter into what is called investment banking or underwriting. Investment bankers are securities wholesalers. They buy directly from the issuing firm and distribute the securities to brokers and large institutional investors. Banks were allowed to perform this function until the 1930s. When the new law was passed preventing this activity, certain banks, such as the house of Morgan, divided their operations into two parts, an investment banking part (Morgan, Stanley Trust) and a commercial banking part (Morgan Guaranty). The purpose of the law is to prevent a stock market crash from destroying the banking structure.

Insurance firms, savings and loan institutions, and banks all have restrictions on the nature of the securities they can own. This not only makes them less likely to go bankrupt, but it also acts as a truth-in-labeling law that guarantees the customer what he is getting when he buys an insurance policy without forcing him to examine the company's assets.

BROKERS' LOANS. Many individuals borrow money in order to hold common stock, corporate bonds, or other securities. Banks and brokers are restricted as to how much they can lend with securities as collateral. These restrictions are called margin requirements. The intent of the restrictions is to prevent a bad decline in securities prices from becoming worse as those who paid for securities with borrowed money sell them while they are still worth something in order to be able to pay back the loan.

Discretionary Intervention

The regulations we have listed are not complete but they give an idea of the way the financial structure has been and can be strengthened by laws. Laws are only one way in which financial collapse can be fought. Discretionary policy is another. If, for example, individuals have a sudden urge to sell bonds and the market starts to collapse, the authorities can support it by buying bonds. They can only do this as long as they have unlimited quantities of money. But if the money is fiat money that is printed by the very same authorities, they can always print more.

Clearly, discretionary intervention can affect securities prices. And because the price of securities is intimately tied to the cost of buying goods in the future with present money, monetary policy can affect the allocative decisions individuals make between present and future. Because panic and collapse are rare events in well-managed economies, the majority of the day-to-day decisions of monetary authorities concern the attainment of the goals of low unemployment, price stability, and economic growth. These goals are pursued by inducing individuals and firms to buy more or less present goods, less or more future goods. The chain of pursuit is as follows.

INFLUENCING THE DEMAND FOR GOODS. Future goods are more expensive with low interest rates than they are with high ones. More dollars must be set aside to buy a given future object when interest rates are low than when they are high because the high interest rates will turn each present dollar into a greater number of future dollars than the low rates will. When future goods are more expensive, individuals have less desire to buy them, but firms have a greater desire to produce them. Individuals buy lesser quantities of future goods (save less) by buying more present goods; firms produce more future goods by buying more capital equipment (they invest more). *Thus a decline in interest rates can lead to an increase in the demand for goods,* because it causes individuals to consume more and firms to invest more.

That is the *first link* in a chain of events designed to show how monetary policy works. *If* the monetary authorities can *affect* interest rates, they can influence the demand for present goods. The next link shows how they can affect interest rates if they can influence the willingness of bankers to lend.

Banks, remember, are only an intermediary in the lending market. Their function is to allow borrowers and lenders to come together easily and efficiently. As an intermediary, the bank quotes prices, or interest rates, at which it is willing to lend and borrow. The difference between the rates is kept by the bank to pay for the costs of operation and as its profit. These costs include buildings, computers, tellers, and executives, as well as the fact that no interest is received on the idle cash that the bank must hold for safety and convenience.

If there is a sharp increase in the demand for present goods, a bank will experience an increased demand for loans. It cannot satisfy the increased loan demand without lending out its needed cash reserves. The bank's response to this is to raise interest rates in an attempt to discourage borrowing and to encourage individuals to increase their deposits. The bank's role as an intermediary forces it to transmit the change in demand and supply into a change in price. In this case, the demand for borrowing has increased; therefore the bank must raise the price. If the bank receives a sudden inflow of funds or a decreased demand for borrowing, it can lower interest rates in an attempt to lend out the extra money and to discourage additional deposits.

Thus the second link in the chain of monetary policy is the bankers. *Bankers raise or lower interest rates in response to outflows or inflows of funds.* The third link is simply the action of the monetary authorities themselves. If they can cause the deposits of banks to be increased, banks will lower interest rates and the lower interest rates will induce people and firms to borrow and spend more and to save and lend less. How can the central bank increase bank deposits? There are many ways.

The most simple way would be to deposit their own funds in the banks. In most countries, it is the central bank that prints currency so it is never at a loss for funds. They can print up some currency, open accounts with the banks, and deposit it. The local banks will be flooded with cash. They will try to lend some of it because they have more than they need to operate the bank safely. The interest they can earn on a loan more than compensates them for the safety of the cash if they had been in equilibrium before the deposit was made. Of course, as they lend more, the safety represented in a dollar of cash increases. So only a part of the new deposits are lent out. (Below, we will see how the total amount of new lending for the system can exceed the amount that the central bank deposits.)

An alternative way to increase deposits is to increase the cash in the hands of firms and people and let them deposit it. One way to do this is to send them money in the mail, of course, or drop it from airplanes. Such a method is the equivalent of a tax cut, however, and has implications of fiscal policy about it that are best kept separate while we learn how monetary policy works. Monetary policy gets money into the hands of people not by giving it to them, but by buying something from them. When we give it to them, they are wealthier. When we buy something from them, they are not. And the conventional thing that is bought from them is government bonds.

OPEN-MARKET OPERATIONS. The purchase of government bonds by the central bank is called an *open-market operation*. This is simply because the bank buys the bonds in the open market just as you or I would buy them if we wished to. The bank works through the same dealers that all big transactors use. This way, they buy the bonds from those most willing to sell, from those who will sell at the lowest price. The seller of the bonds deposits the check in his account and his bank finds itself with increased cash that it can lend. One advantage of open-market operations over simple deposits is that the central bank cannot be accused of favoring one bank over another. The central bank does not know who is selling and does not know which bank will receive the deposits.

The monetary authorities can influence the demand for goods by buying and selling government securities in the open market. We have just outlined the reasons such actions are effective. We summarize them here. The firms and individuals who sell the bonds generally deposit the money they receive in a bank. The bank notes the increase in the quantity of funds available to be loaned and it lowers the interest rate charged to borrowers and paid to depositors. Firms and individuals note the lower interest rates and decide to buy more present goods and fewer future goods.

RESERVE REQUIREMENTS. Another way to give banks more cash is to ease up on reserve requirements. Remember we said that banks could be required to hold reserves in the form of cash that are equal to certain percentages of its deposits. If the reserve requirement is ineffective, that is, if the banks hold a great deal more cash than the reserve requirement demands, lowering the reserve requirement may have no effect on the bank's lending behavior. If a certain bank, for example, is forced to hold $50 million in cash but chooses to hold $100 million, believing that that is the amount that maximizes profits, then a change in the bank's required cash holding from $50 million to $40 million may encourage no additional lending at all. If, on the other hand, the bank would like to hold only $50 million in cash but is required to hold $100 million, then a change in required holdings to $90 million might have an immediate effect on bank behavior.

It is possible that banks do not view required cash holdings as cash at all. Remember that one of the main reasons banks want cash is to be able to meet sudden deposit withdrawals. If, however, required cash reserves must remain intact, then the bank will have to hold additional cash if it is to be able to meet the withdrawals. Cash has value to a bank because it is immediately available. If it cannot be touched, it does not serve this function. In this view, a reduction in *required* cash holdings increases *available* cash even though *total* cash stays constant. The increase in *available* cash may make the bank feel more secure and it may be more willing to lend than before.

Changing reserve requirements will be an effective way to influence the lending behavior of banks in two cases: (1) where the requirements force the banks to hold more cash than they would otherwise choose to hold; and (2) when the banks do not view the required reserves as cash that is available to meet deposit outflows. Control over the reserve requirement can be, therefore, an alternative to open-market operations as a tool of monetary policy.

DIRECT LENDING. In many countries, although not in the United States, the central bank is also a private commercial bank that can lend directly to the public. And since the central bank is a significant part of the banking system, its decision to expand or contract its own willingness to lend is sufficient to affect borrowing and thereby the demand for goods. The increased willingness to lend on the part of the central bank leads to lower interest rates. Where central banks do not make loans to the public, as in the United States, they must use other methods, described above, to expand borrowing.

Even in the United States, however, the central bank will lend to the local banks. When the central bank of the United States, the Federal Reserve System, was formed in 1913, the provision of lending to local banks was intended as a safety valve to prevent bank collapses. Despite the intention of the legislation, local banks frequently avail themselves of the privilege even when collapse is unthinkable. When interest rates are high and banks are short of cash, they tend to borrow continually from the Federal Reserve. The interest rate they pay on these borrowings is called the *discount rate*, or the *rediscount rate*, to note the fact that the loans turned over as collateral can be called discounts. This is because the securities represent more future dollars than present; it is as if the future dollars were bought at discount. When a bank makes a loan to a firm whereby the firm agrees to repay $100 next year, the bank may give the firm only $92 this year. The difference between the $92 and $100 is interest, of course, but we could view the bank as buying the future $100 at an 8 percent discount. If the bank in turn wishes to borrow from the Federal Reserve, it must turn over loans and securities as collateral and it too must pay interest; thus the future dollars that are to be paid by the firm are *rediscounted* at the central bank. When the central bank changes the discount rate, the member banks' cost and therefore willingness to borrow are affected.

Monetary policy therefore consists of having the monetary authorities intervene in some financial market to affect the cost of borrowing. They may increase the supply of lending directly by lowering their own interest rates. They may buy bonds in the open market and thereby decrease the amount of bonds and increase the amount of cash people hold. They may deposit money directly in banks to increase the supply of funds in the lending market. They may relax the requirements on cash holdings on the part of banks to leave more funds available for investment. These interventions work through the securities and lending markets to raise or lower interest rates and thereby to affect the demand for present goods.

INDUCED LENDING EFFECTS. Once the central bank has injected currency into the system, the currency can be lent and relent and the number of loans may increase many times. The currency can be deposited in banks, lent from the bank, deposited in some other bank, lent again, and so on, and therefore the single currency injection can lead to a much larger increase in the amount of checking money being used. As a first step in an analysis of the effect of induced lending on checking money, we need to show that banks can indeed create money.

Banks and Money Creation

If checking accounts are a part of the money supply, then banks create money. There was a time when bankers claimed that they did not create money at all, that they merely lent out a part of the money that was deposited with them. It was not evident to them that this was money creation. But a cursory look at a bank's balance sheet reveals the true story.

In Table 35.1, we present the balance sheet of a typical bank. Note that cash makes up only 15 percent of its assets whereas checking accounts are 50 percent of its liabilities. (A checking account is a liability to the bank because it represents the fact that the bank owes the depositor money.) If Table 35.1 represents a typical bank, as it claims to, then we know that banks create money. This bank has only $15 million in cash that has been deposited with it whereas there are $50 million in checking deposits. If the checking deposits exceed the cash, the banks must have created money.

Of course, the argument of the simple banker was that he relent some of the cash. And that is exactly how the money was created. Suppose someone deposits $1 with a banker. The banker relends $.85. These two transactions increase the volume of checking accounts by $1 and decrease the currency outstanding by only $.15. Thus the money supply has been increased by $.85. When the bank lends money, the borrower increases his holdings of money. No one else's holdings are decreased. Thus when banks lend money (or buy securities), the money supply increases by the amount of the loan (or purchase).

What gives banks this magical power? Why can one person not lend another money and thereby increase the money supply? In principle he can. Remember that a bank exists only as an intermediary. It conducts the transactions in a particular market only because it is more convenient for people to use the bank than to do it without the bank. The loans and checking accounts of a bank really represent loans from the depositors to the borrowers. Thus except for transactions costs, the depositors and borrowers could get together and reach the same solution outside the banks as they do within the banks. Thus in principle, one person's loan to another can create money. If, for example, the IOU person A gives person B in return for the cash can be used to make payments to others, then it too is money and their transaction increases the money supply.

In practice, the ordinary individual's IOUs are not well enough known to allow them to be used for making payments. Others might not accept them. But the bank's IOUs (checking accounts) are well enough known to be used as money, and therefore an expansion of these constitutes an expansion of the money supply. But note that the bank's IOUs are really a composite assortment of loans. That is, the bank buys batches of loans from individuals and firms and distributes their characteristics across its checking accounts. Thus checking accounts could be labeled as inspected, diversified, managed IOUs of firms and individuals. Apparently that kind of IOU can be used for money whereas the ordinary loan of an unknown cannot be.

Thus the power of banks to create money involves no magic. It is merely the power to create an almost riskless asset through diversification and through shifting most of the risk of the portfolio from the depositors to the stockholders. But even though the banks are able to create this asset, they still are not free to do so unless the borrowers and depositors choose to use the bank. The bank's power to create money derives merely from its ability to lower the costs of transforming loans into deposits. The actual transformation requires willing borrowers and depositors, however. So to a degree the simple banker was right

Table 35.1	Balance Sheet of Typical Banks (Millions of Dollars)		
Assets		**Liabilities**	
Cash	15	Checking Accounts	50
Loans	60	Savings Accounts	40
Securities	20	**Net Worth**	
Building	5	Capital	10

when he protested that he was at the whim of the market, that he could lend only as much as people wished to borrow.

And to a degree, he was wrong because it is possible for him to induce additional borrowing merely by lowering the interest charges on loans. Remember that behind the whole financial superstructure lie millions of firms and individuals patiently allocating between present and future. If an interest rate changes, this behavior changes. If, for example, the cost of borrowing falls, more people will buy automobiles and houses on credit, more firms will borrow in order to build plant and equipment. If the borrowing rate falls, the quantity of loans demanded will increase. Buyers and sellers are always affected by each other's behavior. That does not mean, however, that they have no control over events.

But the banker attains an equilibrium when he has lent all he wishes to lend at the going rate. Given the amount of cash he has, he does not feel that the rate of return on loans is high enough to induce him to take on further risk. Remember that he may be subject to massive withdrawals at any moment and he must have cash on hand to meet them. The more loans he buys, the less cash he has. Thus although more loans mean more profits because of the interest he will earn, they also mean more risk. Thus the banker voluntarily restricts the amount of loans he makes in order to protect his stockholders from bankruptcy. If he should ever change his mind about how much cash is needed for emergency, he can autonomously change the money supply. Should he suddenly feel he has more cash than he needs, for example, he can lower interest rates, thereby increasing his lending. And it is the act of lending, we have seen, that creates money. Thus once he is in equilibrium, the banker's actions are at the whim of the market. It is the banker's job, however, to determine what that equilibrium is.

Multiple-Deposit Creation

The same dollar can be relent many times. If person A lends person B a dollar and he lends it to person C, who lends it to person D, etc., that one dollar has passed through many hands and created many loans. One could say that the net effect is that person A has lent D a dollar. But if the IOUs they all gave each other can be used as money, then there has been a great increase in the amount of money available. Bank's IOUs are money. Therefore if one person lends his bank a dollar and it lends a dollar to another person who pays it to someone who lends it to his bank, and his bank lends it to a fourth party who lends it to his bank, we will find that deposits have increased a great deal. The relending process can go on and on and on, creating money all the while. One dollar deposited in a bank could theoretically be relent a million times.

But the process does not usually go on forever for two reasons.

(1) *Required reserves.* When deposits increase at a bank, its required reserves increase because they are a certain percentage of the deposits. Thus it cannot relend all of the cash it receives. If I deposit $1 in my bank, it can only relend $.85 since the other $.15 must be held in the form of cash as a reserve.

(2) *Risk.* If a bank relent every penny it received, it would be in no position to meet withdrawals. This would be very risky. Banks need some cash to be able to run their business. And the more deposits they have, the more cash they need. Thus banks would probably increase their holdings of cash in response to an increase in deposits even if there were no required reserves.

These two reasons show why banks lend out only a fraction of the money deposited with them. A deposit of one dollar of currency will probably not lead to a million dollars worth of new loans. How many loans will result? To answer this, we need some simplifying assumptions. Assume that all the money banks lend out eventually is redeposited in some bank. Thus each loan creates a checking deposit but does not decrease the bank's cash. Either the people to whom the borrower writes checks deposit them in their accounts, or the borrower leaves the borrowed money in his own account. If we also assume that all banks relend the same percentage—say, 80 percent—of all the money that is deposited with them, then the mathematics of the relending are such that four dollars of loans are created for every dollar deposited in the bank. It works out as follows.

We have assumed that $.80 of every $1 deposited is relent. Thus for a deposit of $1 we have $.80 worth of new money and new loans created initially. But this new money is deposited in some bank. Thus some banks (maybe other banks) have received $.80 worth of new deposits. They relend 80 percent of this, or $.64. This $.64 gets deposited in another bank; 80 percent of it gets relent again. Each time the money is redeposited, less of it is relent. The final amount by which deposits increase is $1 + $.80 + $(.8)^2 + $(.8)^3 + $(.8)^4 + etc. The sum of this infinite series is $\dfrac{\$1}{1-.8} = \$4$, as is shown in Chapter 33. This number has been called the *deposit creation multiplier.* Mathematically, it is identical to the spending multipliers of Chapter 33. There the amount of induced spending generated by a dollar's worth of autonomous spending depended on how much of each additional dollar of income was respent. Here the amount of induced lending depends on how much of the initial deposits are relent.

The impact of monetary policy is therefore magnified by bank behavior. If the central bank increases bank deposits in an attempt to induce lending, the banks will further increase those deposits by the act of lending. The power of the banks to create money allows them to multiply the effect of any central bank operation.

Other Intermediaries

The central bank's action has powerful repercussions. By changing the quantity of currency, the bank can induce individuals and local banks to change some spending decisions and buy more or fewer present goods. All intermediaries will feel the effects of this. Remember that intermediaries exist only to conduct the transactions individuals wish to make. When the environment changes and individuals wish to change their decisions, all intermediaries will feel the effects.

A savings and loan institution, for example, will feel the effects of "tight" money through the following chain. The central bank wishes to induce individuals and firms to buy fewer present goods. To accomplish this, it sells bonds in the open market. Individuals pay for the bonds by check and banks experience an outflow of funds. This outflow leaves the banks in a risky position. To regain some funds, they raise interest rates on deposits to encourage more inflows and on loans to discourage borrowing. Individuals with accounts in a savings and loan institution now observe higher interest rates in banks and withdraw some savings and loan shares and deposit the funds in banks. Borrowers observe lower mortgage rates in the savings and loan institutions and they cease borrowing at banks. Therefore, as a result of the higher interest rates in banks, the savings and loan institutions observe an increased demand for borrowing and a decreased supply of funds. They, too, are forced to raise rates.

Thus policy affects all institutions even if these institutions are not directly under the control of the central bank.

Policy and Speculation

Destabilizing speculation is much more likely to occur with financial assets than with real assets and it is one of the primary reasons we need monetary and financial authorities. It is possible for everyone to get together and bid the price of any asset to zero or infinity in the manner we outlined as far back as Chapter 5. But real assets have an element of safety in them that is absent in financial assets. If everyone agrees that an individual's holdings of francs that were worth $30,000 yesterday are worth zero today, he is wiped out. He has lost $30,000 and he has no reason to expect ever to receive it back. If, on the other hand, the price of his $30,000 house is bid to zero, he is sad because he has lost a great deal of financial flexibility. But he is not wiped out. His house continues to exist and he can live rent free for the rest of his life. He still can receive as much utility over his lifetime as he had expected to before the price changed.

This basic difference between real and financial assets — that real assets can yield satisfaction whereas financial assets can be traded only for satisfaction-yielding objects — makes one much more fearful of a decline in the price of his financial assets than a decline in the price of his real assets. If one believes that people will need housing in the future, he can feel fairly confident that he will be able to sell his house at a reasonable price. He can feel no such confidence, on the other hand, in the future value of the dollar — in the rate at which a dollar will be able to be traded for goods in the future.

Since the prices of financial assets are less closely tied to utility than are those of real assets, speculation can be expected to be more prevalent. One of the major roles of the financial authorities is to put a damper on such speculation by promising to act in a manner that will guarantee the future value of financial assets. And since the monetary authorities are a part of the government, they represent the people's collective desires. By setting up monetary authorities, the people as a group are saying, "We fear that our own greedy speculative behavior would destroy the financial system in the absence of an agreement among us as to the future real value of financial assets." Through the monetary authorities, individuals attempt to guarantee to each other that there is no need to speculate on financial assets. Financial stability is desired by all even though each individual may, in order to protect his own net worth, act in such a way as to create instability. Recognizing this, individuals band together and create monetary authorities that protect their net worths and eliminate the need for certain forms of speculative behavior designed to do just that.

Questions
1. Why do central bankers fear increases in the rate of inflation?
2. Consider the tools used by the central bank to prevent panic and financial collapse. What transactions does each one prevent and how does this prevention affect the stability and efficiency of the financial system?
3. Can banks create money? Can they do it if no additional borrowers come forth when they lower interest rates?

Concepts Discussed

monetary policy	reserve requirements
collateral	discount rate
open-market operations	multiple-deposit creation

XII The Policy Dilemma

If you don't know where you're goin',
you're gonna wind up somewhere else.

YOGI BERRA

Formulating macroeconomic policy is a tough game. The game can be broken into three distinct parts, all of which are important problems to the policy maker but only one of which occupies much space in this text.

The first problem is one of theory. How do we expect men to act? Given their actions, what are the predicted impacts of various policy actions on quantities that matter, such as the unemployment rate. It is these questions that have concerned us most here. We have postulated ways for men to act that seem reasonable to us. We feel that men will attempt to watch out for their own interests; that this will lead them to consume a part of any unexpected increases in income; that they will change their ideas of what constitutes an acceptable wage rate very slowly; that they will borrow and spend more when interest rates are low than when they are high.

We spent time defending each of these hypotheses about human action. Then we described how certain actions of policy makers would work when men behaved in the hypothesized manner. We showed the effects of tax cuts, open market bond purchases, and increases in spending.

It is inappropriate to spend a great deal of time in an introductory text explaining the tests that have been performed to accept or reject these hypotheses. But, as with any scientific principle, these hypotheses may be wrong. There may be some much more useful way to organize our thinking about men's behavior, a way that predicts their actions more accurately than is possible using the hypotheses we have described. And it is possible that these other hypotheses would predict a completely different effect of, say, tax cuts on the level of employment. Policy makers, therefore, must be concerned with the differences of opinion among economists as to what makes the world go round. We have found it difficult enough to explore one view of how policy works. Although it happens to be the view accepted by most economists, there is not a unanimous acceptance of it, and one of the doubts that must gnaw at the policy maker is whether or not his view of men's behavior is the correct one.

The problem we just described is qualitative. There is also a quantitative problem. If we believe that men do increase spending when income rises, accurate policy making requires that we know by how much. Since we can understand how policy works without understanding how to measure the relevant economic magnitudes, we have spent very little time on this problem. It takes a great deal of the time of the policy maker, however. He is ever refining his guess as to how much of a reaction to expect from his potential actions.

The third problem is also one of measurement, but it involves the policy maker's judgement to a much greater extent than do the other two problems. This problem is the one of actual economic pulse-taking. How much unemployment do we have? How much of it is caused by special circumstances, how much of it is not? For example, if there is a rail strike, many men in manufacturing will eventually be laid off because of the inability of their firms to acquire raw materials. The policy maker must guess how much of the current unemployment will be eliminated automatically when the strike ends and how much will remain. He must know the effect of the current drought on wheat prices, the impact of a new technology on the supply of housing, whether or not a proposed increase in social security benefits has been anticipated, and whether people are optimistic or pessimistic about the future course of the economy. What can we say about this problem here except that it is a tough one?

If we look at the three problems together, we understand why the policy-making game is so hard. The policy maker finds out that last month's unemployment was larger than he had predicted. Was this due to a misconception about how people view changes in their dividend checks? To a bad estimate of the response of inventory managers to changes in sales? Or to the fact that consumers simply find the latest automobile models ugly and are content to wait another year before buying? A misunderstanding at any level leads to error.

The next three chapters attempt to give a more sophisticated view of the problems of policy makers. We continue to emphasize theory and analysis, but we occasionally mention the other problems to show how they confound our attempts to find out how the world really operates.

Chapter 36 brings together the two previously presented simple models of monetary and fiscal policy. It shows how they interact, when one is apt to be more effective than the other, and how to choose between them. Chapter 37 introduces the issue of inflation to the policy discussion, whereas Chapter 38 completes the policy picture by introducing the foreign sector and balance of payments problems.

36 Monetary Policy and Fiscal Policy

We now have two simple models of policy, one in which government spending and tax rate changes affect the demand for goods by increasing consumer incomes, and one in which increases in the quantity of money by the central bank lead to reductions in market interest rates, thereby causing increased investment spending. Now it is time to examine the two kinds of policy simultaneously to see how they work together.

Our procedure is the following: First we examine the different paths through which monetary policy can work. We note the disagreements among economists about these paths. We explore a special case in which monetary policy is ineffective in changing the level of employment. We show why the simple fiscal model of Chapter 32 is appropriate in that case. Then we look at a case with the opposite policy implications, a case in which fiscal policy is impotent but monetary policy is effective. Using these two as polar cases, we examine the middle ground, the case where both are effective. Throughout the discussion we treat prices as given; we assume that all increases in the demand for goods are matched by production increases, not price changes. The next chapter removes this limitation and is devoted to a study of price change — inflation.

Alternative Views of Monetary Policy

The way in which monetary actions influence spending decisions can be described in two ways. One of these ways is outlined in Chapter 35: The increase in the money supply causes banks to wish to lend more; this lowers interest rates and thus stimulates borrowing and spending. An alternative view focuses attention on the demand for money by individuals. It explains the impact of monetary actions by noting the adjustments individuals make to money holdings in excess of the equilibrium quantity. We will describe this view shortly.

There is no analytical inconsistency between the two views. Rather, the disagreement is empirical. The holders of the differing views do not believe that one view is right, the other wrong; they believe that one view is more appropriate than the other or is less likely to be misleading. The difference of opinion is over the strength of the different ways through which policy can be effective, not over the theoretical question of whether or not policies work at all. The most convenient way to describe the difference between the two views is through a look at the demand for money.

The Demand for Money

Money is the means of payment. Thus the need for money holdings arises from the desire to make transactions. The amount of money held by individuals varies over time because money inflows and outflows are not perfectly synchronized. Indeed, the fact that payments and receipts do not coincide is the very reason for the existence of money. Despite the fluctuations in the money holdings of a single individual, we can think of the aggregate quantity of money in existence as a relatively stable magnitude, because the payments by one individual are the receipts of another. If we wish to focus on the quantity of money held by one individual, however, we must speak of his average money holdings. If he deposits $1,000 into his account at the beginning of every month and spends it at a constant rate throughout the month, his average money holdings are $500. What factors influence those holdings?

One obvious influence is the amount of transactions the person wishes to conduct. If the paycheck he deposits every month is $1,500 instead of $1,000, his average holdings are likely to be higher. Since the level of transactions will correspond closely to income, economists often think of income as a key determinant of money holdings.

A second obvious influence is the availability of good substitutes for money. If a person can pay for his month's commodities with a credit card, he will not need to keep cash balances in his checking account for transaction purposes. Instead, when he deposits his paycheck, he can immediately write a check for the amount of his credit card balance and cancel his indebtedness. If credit cards could be used for all transactions, there would be no need to have any money in one's checking account except for the one instant each month in which the payment is actually recorded. Average holdings of checking balances could conceivably be zero. This is the "moneyless" society we discussed at the end of Chapter 33.

A third important influence is the cost of holding money. Currency and checking balances do not bear interest, but other assets do. The opportunity cost of holding money is, therefore, the size of the interest payments foregone. If interest rates are 5 percent per year, a person sacrifices $50 a year for every $1,000 of average money holdings he possesses. The higher the interest rate, the higher this cost and the less willing he will be to hold money. At high enough interest rates, he will find it worth his while to cut his money holdings by depositing and withdrawing cash monthly from an interest-bearing savings account. Every month, when he receives his $1,000 paycheck, he can deposit $500 in his checking account and $500 in his savings account. Half-way through the month, when his checking account balance is close to zero, he can switch $500 from his savings account to his checking account. At the end of the year, if interest has been credited to his savings account daily, he will receive an interest payment that depends on the level of the interest rate. Since his savings account will be on average $250 higher as a result of these transactions, the interest he receives will be $12.50 if the interest rate is 5 percent per year, $25.00 if it is 10 percent.

Clearly, the higher the interest rate, the more he will be tempted to enter into such shenanigans.

Does $12.50 seem worth the bother? That depends on how much bother it is. If it were possible to give one's bank an initial instruction to conduct these transactions automatically, it probably would be profitable. If, on the other hand, physical trips to the bank were necessary for each transaction, it would not be profitable. Thus the fourth determinant of the demand for money is the cost of transferring funds into some interest-bearing form. Individuals compare this cost to the interest return when deciding whether or not to engage in frequent asset transactions. The lower that cost, the more likely such transfers will take place and therefore the lower average money holdings will be.

The last determinant of the demand for money that we will look at is the technology of money. This includes not only the physical form of money, but the whole pattern of payments schedules, record keeping, and the manner in which transactions are accomplished. In our framework, it is obvious that money holdings would be larger if individuals were paid every two months instead of every month. They would be larger if minimum balances were required, if it took many days for transactions to be recorded, and if the fee for each transaction were so large that it would be cheaper to make very few large transactions than very many small ones.

Summarizing, we find that the quantity of money demanded depends on the need for making transactions, the cost of holding money, the availability of substitutes for money, the cost of transferring funds into substitutes, and the very organization of the process of collecting payments. If we take these to be the most important determinants and ignore the others, we can view the quantity of money demanded as being determined in the short run by income and the rate of interest — since the other factors are fixed in the short run.

Ignoring banks for the moment, since they are only intermediaries, we note that the supply of money is determined by the monetary authorities. And since these authorities can fix the quantity supplied at any level they wish, it can be viewed as independent of any other economic variables. The quantity demanded depends on interest rates and income; the quantity supplied is fixed by the monetary authorities. In equilibrium, these two quantities must be equal. But since the authorities fix the level of the money supply, it is the quantity demanded that must adjust if the two are ever different. And the quantity demanded will change only if interest rates or income changes.

Alternative Paths to Equilibrium

When the monetary authorities change the supply of money — say, by open market operations — the money market must attain a new equilibrium. There are two separate sets of forces that drive the money market to that equilibrium. Economists disagree over the relative importance of the two forces. The simplest way to distinguish the two sets of forces is by the most likely response of individuals to excess holdings of money. Individuals, we saw, could determine an equilibrium quantity of money holdings. What do they do if they find their checking account above that level, presumably because they have just sold bonds on the open market? Remember that that is the way the extra money got pumped into the economy.

The Quantity Theory

One school of thought holds that individuals will be most likely to spend this money on goods. Or, more correctly, adherents to this view feel that the most useful way of looking at the workings of monetary policy is to think of individuals as spending excess money holdings on goods. The path to equilibrium, in this case, is quite straightforward. The spending causes income to rise; the increased income leads individuals to require more money for transactions; income rises until all the extra money is needed to conduct transactions; at that point, a new equilibrium is attained.

This theory of money adjustment is often called the *quantity theory*. According to this theory, there is a unique quantity of money needed to conduct each level of transactions. Changes in prices or costs—interest rates, for example—are of secondary importance in determining the demand for money. By this theory, the most profound understanding of the workings of monetary policy can be attained by realizing that for each level of the money supply, there is a unique level of income that must exist if there is to be an equilibrium. If any other level of income exists, forces will arise to change it to the equilibrium level. This theory can best be illustrated by Figure 36.1.

In this Figure, the demand for money is illustrated by the ray from the origin, *DD*; this represents the view that an increase in income requires a proportional increase in money holdings. This view is the crux of the quantity theory. If the money supply is fixed at M_1 by the monetary authorities (supply curve S_1S_1), the equilibrium level of income is Y_1. If the authorities then increase the money supply to M_2 (supply curve S_2S_2), income will have to increase to Y_2 if there is to be a new equilibrium. This income level is attained by the actions of consumers

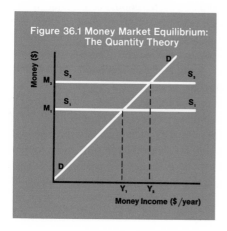

Figure 36.1 Money Market Equilibrium: The Quantity Theory

who spend their excess money holdings, thereby increasing income until the money holdings are no longer excessive.

Note that it is money income that determines the demand for money holdings. This means that if all prices are doubled (including wages) twice as much money will be needed to conduct the same level of real transactions. Thus equilibrium can be attained after an increase in the money supply by either an increase in sales, and therefore real income, or an increase in prices. Whether the adjustment in fact occurs in prices or sales depends on other factors in the economy; for instance, whether full employment exists, prices are sticky, and so on.

Liquidity Preference

A key ingredient of Keynes's theory of aggregate demand (the total demand for goods) is his view of the demand for money. According to Keynes, the demand for money depends importantly on interest rates, and this dependence may be so important as to offset completely the impact of changes in the money supply on income. This view of the demand for money is called *liquidity preference*. To compare Keynes's view to the quantity theory, we again examine the response of individuals to excess money holdings and we assume that these money holdings were acquired by selling bonds on the open market to the monetary authorities.

In the Keynesian view, the way in which money is acquired has an important effect on what individuals do with it. If extra money holdings arise because of wage increases, tax cuts, or additional sales of factor services, people are likely to spend part of their extra holdings because their incomes have increased. They feel richer and are able to buy more present and future goods, and they do so in a proportion related to their marginal propensities to consume. If the extra money holdings arise because people have chosen to sell bonds, they are no richer, and according to Keynes, this will not cause them to increase their consumption. Since they are not richer, any increase in the consumption of present goods requires a decrease in the consumption of future goods. According to the Keynesian theory of consumption, no such reallocation takes place merely because an individual decides to sell his bonds. What then happens to the money?

Before we see what happens to the money, Keynesian theorists require us to answer a prior question. Why did the individual sell the bonds in the first place if he did not prefer money to bonds? We began with everyone in equilibrium. The central bank attempted to increase the money supply by buying bonds. But who would sell bonds if everyone was already in equilibrium? To a Keynesian, the answer to this question explains why individuals do not respend the money. The answer to the question is that the central bank's attempts to buy bonds increase the price of bonds. As the price of bonds increases, individuals become more and more tempted to sell because they fear the price will fall again once the central bank leaves the market. Thus when an individual sells a bond, he does so because he prefers the money to the bond. He sells the bond as a speculation. He fears the price will eventually fall and he wants to sell when the time is ripe. Thus forecasts of future bond prices are a key determinant of the demand for money according to Keynes. Individuals need not respend the extra money pumped into the economy by the monetary authorities.

But if individuals are content to hold the extra money, how does monetary policy influence spending? Is the only effect of open market operations a change in the price of bonds? No. That is just the first step. We must now ask whether a change in bond prices affects spending. Before we can do that, we must understand what a bond is and what a change in its price means.

A bond is a promise to pay future currency, say, dollars. For example, a new bond selling for $1,000 may promise to pay back the $1,000 next year plus $50 in interest, reflecting the current market rate of interest of 5 percent per year. (We have chosen one-year bonds here because their mathematics is simple. With longer bonds, the principle remains the same, however.) The schedule of payments that the bonds promise to meet is fixed. For example, if interest rates go to 6 percent, the bond still will promise to pay back only $1,050 next year even though newly issued bonds must now promise to pay $1,060 if they are to sell for $1,000 today. If new bonds that yield $60 in interest are available, who will buy the old ones that yield only $50 in interest? The answer is no one; that is, no one would pay $1,000 for such a bond. But there must be some price at which one could sell that old bond because it still represents a claim to future dollars. If people will trade $1,000 present dollars for $1,060 next year, how many present dollars will they give up in order to receive $1,050 next year? The answer is $990.57, because individuals giving up $990.57 this year in order to get back $1,050 next year will earn exactly 6 percent on their money. The important result to note here is that bonds are assets that promise to pay a fixed quantity of dollars in the future. If their present price is bid *up*, the rate at which the bonds yield interest *falls*, and, of course, if the price of the bond *falls*, the rate at which it yields interest is *higher*. In our example, a bond that promises to pay $1,050 next year would sell for $1,000 this year if the interest rate were 5 percent per year. If the interest rate rose to 6 percent, the price of that bond would have to fall to $990.57 in order for it to yield 6 percent. Since future dollar payments are fixed, the present price must change when interest rates change. With savings accounts, the reverse is true; the present price is fixed and the number of future dollars paid changes when interest rates change.

Now back to Keynesian monetary policy. The central bank has attempted to increase the money supply by buying bonds. Individuals will not sell their bonds at the original price, but the bank's attempt to buy the bonds drives up their price and therefore *drives down the rate of interest* that bonds yield. The lower rate of interest makes individuals content to hold the additional money. With lower interest rates, there is less incentive to economize on cash holdings, less reason to incur the costs of switching money from checking accounts into other assets. Thus at some lower interest rate, individuals will be content to hold the extra money *even if their incomes do not rise*.

The Keynesian view of money market equilibrium is illustrated in Figure 36.2. In this figure, the demand for money is shown to be a function of the interest rate. At low rates, more money is demanded because bonds are supplied. The supply of money is determined again by the monetary authorities. According to Figure 36.2, an increase in the supply of money from S_1S_1 to S_2S_2 will cause the bond interest rate to fall from i_1 to i_2. At i_2, the price of bonds is high enough that people are willing to sell enough bonds to acquire the newly created money.

How does monetary policy affect spending if individuals are willing to hold the money? The answer lies in its effect on interest rates. With lower interest rates, firms and individuals may decide to spend more on present goods. Firms will find it more profitable to borrow at the low interest rate and invest; individuals will find it less profitable to save. Thus the Keynesian view of monetary policy is that it affects the demand for goods by changing the price of present goods relative to future goods.

Comparing Theories

Which of these views is the most accurate? We cannot answer that question analytically. The demand for money depends on both income and interest rates. The distinction between the two theories lies in their view of the quantitative importance of interest rates in affecting the demand for money. Is there or is there not some price for bonds that makes people prefer money to bonds? One group says that regardless of the price of bonds, their interest yield will make individuals prefer them to idle balances. The other group says that if there is no price at which individuals prefer money to bonds, the money simply cannot be pumped into the economy through the bond market.

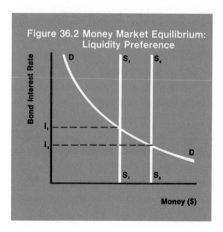

Figure 36.2 Money Market Equilibrium: Liquidity Preference

We will spend no more time comparing theories but will assume that there is a little truth to both views. We now combine our monetary policy model with the fiscal policy model developed in Chapter 32. As an introduction to this combination, we look at the special cases in which the two kinds of policies are ineffective.

Impotent Monetary Policy

The shocking theoretical point made by Keynes is that, in certain cases, monetary policy is impotent. In just those cases, the simple fiscal model of Chapter 32 is a useful way to characterize the economy.

Monetary policy does not work in Keynes's world in either of two cases:

(1) People are indifferent between bonds and money at the prevailing price of bonds. In this case open market purchases do not drive up the price of bonds or lower the interest rate. This case is illustrated by Figure 36.3. Here the increase in the supply of money from S_1S_1 to S_2S_2 does not lower the interest rate. At a low enough interest rate, the risks of holding bonds are equal in value to the meager interest the bonds yield. Individuals will be indifferent between the risky bond with interest rate i_o and the less risky money with no interest yield. Increases in the supply of money are held willingly by individuals without a change in interest rates. With no change in interest rates, no induced spending occurs, and the increase in the money supply has no effect on output.

(2) Monetary policy will be impotent if spending is not sensitive to interest rates. The interest rate is related to the relative price of present goods in terms of future goods. But if the demand for present goods is completely price-inelastic, a decrease in their price will result in no additional purchases. Consumers and investors need not respond to interest rate changes by changing their spending decisions. In this case, monetary policy will not change the demand for goods.

It is important to note that in both these cases, monetary policy still would

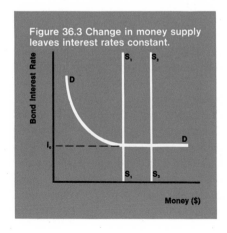

Figure 36.3 Change in money supply leaves interest rates constant.

be effective from the viewpoint of the quantity theory. It is here that the Keynesians and quantity theorists have their greatest disagreements. The Keynesians claim that monetary policy was impotent during the Great Depression, that purchases of bonds by the central bank would not have lowered interest rates further because they were already as low as they could go. Open market operations would merely have resulted in banks holding more funds than could be lent out even at very low interest rates. The quantity theorists claim that further bank lending would have taken place if expansionary monetary actions had been tried. Both groups see the same data but they interpret them differently. History, too, is a tough game.

Impotent Fiscal Policy

How might fiscal policy be impotent? Do not government purchases of goods have to increase sales? The answer is no. Government purchases have to increase sales to the government, but if money is very scarce, there can be offsetting declines in sales to others. Briefly, here is how.

The government must sell bonds to get the money to pay for its increased expenditures. But if money is really tight, no one — not individuals, banks, or firms — will have any extra cash with which to buy bonds. Everyone wili need the money he now has to conduct his transactions. If the government is to sell its bonds, it must bump someone else out of the credit market. Loans to the government replace loans to the private sector and the decrease in loans to the private sector causes a reduction in private spending. The government's attempt to borrow may cause interest rates merely to rise until private borrowers voluntarily leave the market. The increased cost of borrowing causes them to change their plans and they do not make the expenditures they otherwise would have.

In this case, monetary policy would be very effective in changing expenditures, but fiscal policy would be impotent. This case may be a reasonable characterization of an economy when money is very tight and interest rates are very high. The late 1920s and 1960s are candidates for being economies of this kind.

Potent Monetary and Fiscal Policy

The normal case is one in which both kinds of policy are effective. The two polar cases we have just examined should help us understand the interaction between the two policies in the general case.

Increases in government spending that are financed by borrowed funds will, in general, place upward pressure on interest rates. Some private borrowing will be curtailed because of the higher rates and private spending will be lower than otherwise. In the normal case, the decrease in private spending will not be as large as the expansion in public spending. This is because the higher interest rates cause people, firms, and banks to hold less money and to be more willing to lend. Thus government borrowing causes interest rates to rise, but this causes the total supply of lending to increase. The government borrowing, therefore, is only partly done through replacing private borrowing; it is also partly done through new lending that had not existed previously. Fiscal policy usually has some potency, therefore, even though it does not work as effectively as the model of Chapter 32 indicates.

Monetary policy, in the normal case, is not as potent as a naive prediction from the quantity theory indicates. If the monetary authorities attempt to expand the money supply by 10 percent, income will generally expand by less than 10 percent. This is because the increase in the money supply will lead to lower interest rates and with lower interest rates, individuals, firms, and banks will hold more idle funds than before; they will have larger cash balances on average for each transaction they must conduct.

Thus in the usual case, both policies are effective at changing sales, but their strength can vary from near impotence to almost the complete power indicated by the naive models.

Comparing Monetary and Fiscal Policy

A major difference between monetary and fiscal policy lies in their effect on interest rates. Expansionary monetary policy, a policy that is designed to increase income, generally leads to lower interest rates. Indeed, according to one view of money, this is necessary if expansionary monetary policy is to be effective. Expansionary fiscal policy, on the other hand, leads to higher interest rates. As income expands, people need larger money balances and they become less willing to lend. This causes interest rates to rise. Thus expansionary fiscal policy increases interest rates; expansionary monetary policy decreases them.

The importance of this distinction is that the two policies result in a different pattern of production. With expansionary monetary policy, the extra production will be more likely to take the form of plant and equipment, durable goods, or, in general, commodities that will yield production in the future. This is because the decline in interest rates makes future goods more expensive. Expansionary fiscal policy, on the other hand, results in higher interest rates and thereby causes a substitution of the reverse kind. Less investment will occur along with fewer purchases of durables, but there will be more purchases of present consumption goods that become relatively cheaper. Thus our choice of whether to use monetary or fiscal policy depends on whether we prefer to see current consumption or future consumption stimulated.

In conclusion, we should point out that the effects of both monetary and fiscal policy have been discussed in a world of constant prices. Thus our analysis is relevant for the short run in which changes in demand lead to changes in employment. In the long run, as we saw in Chapter 29, the changes in demand lead to changes in wage rates. In the next chapter, we attempt to synthesize the monetary and fiscal analysis into a world in which prices change. Government spending, we will see, may lead just as easily to inflation as it does to increases in employment.

Questions

1.   Under what conditions will open market operations be ineffective in changing the level of employment? How about government expenditures financed by government bonds? Why does government expenditure financed by printing money always work?

2.   Describe the different "routes" by which economists believe monetary actions affect employment. What separates the "quantity theorists" from the "Keynesians"?

3.   Why do expansionary monetary actions and expansionary fiscal actions change interest rates in different directions?

Concepts Discussed

the quantity theory
liquidity preference

37 Inflation

Inflation appears to be one of the facts of life in the late twentieth century. What is inflation? Why does it exist? What are its costs? What can be done about it? These are some of the questions that concern us in this chapter.

The *rate of inflation* is the average percentage rate of increase of all money prices. Usually the rate is expressed in annual terms. Prices, we know, are the ratios at which commodities trade. Money prices tell us the number of units of money that must be sacrificed for a particular commodity. Thus if the money price of an apple changes from 5 cents per apple to 6 cents per apple, it has increased by 20 percent. If on average all money prices had the same percentage increase and if the higher prices existed a year after the lower ones, we could say that the rate of inflation between the two dates was 20 percent per year. Turning the ratios upside down, we see that the average price of money in terms of goods has fallen (though by 17 percent). Thus inflation is a decline in the value of money relative to commodities. When a father tells his son that the value of the dollar is only 39 cents, he means that the price of money has fallen by 61 percent since the days when men were men.

Problems with Dynamics

In most of this book, we have been concerned with *static* analysis; that is, the determination of an equilibrium at a single point of time without explicit consideration of the effect of the passage of time. Recently, we have encountered problems in which present behavior depends on future forecasts, but for simplicity we have tried to present this behavior from a static point of view. Our approach has been to worry about the present behavior only and not about a sequence of behavior. We have not examined many *dynamic* models in which it was necessary to trace out a whole time path of solutions for particular variables.

The exceptions to this procedure have been the discussion of economic growth in Chapters 27 and 28 and the description of wage-rate determination in Chapter 29. In Chapters 27 and 28, we presented a dynamic model that explicitly incorporated the passage of time. In Chapter 29, we discussed the differences between short- and long-run solutions and described the qualitative nature of the adjustment, although we did not choose to talk explicitly about the speed of adjustment. The reason for this avoidance of explicit dynamic models is quite simple. They are very difficult to understand. They require the use of differential equations and other more difficult mathematics, skills that most students have not acquired. Thus the cost of incorporating such models in terms of student hours, faculty hours, and class time is high. Still, we know that if the value of a commodity exceeds its cost, we should buy it. And there is the rub. The more complex the problems we are trying to solve become, the less likely advanced mathematics is to yield satisfactory results. Mathematical models of quite simple dynamic economic behavior have no known solutions. Other models yield solutions that have no intuitive appeal; they do not further our understanding of the problem in any fundamental way. Still others yield conclusions that are very specific to the way the problem was formulated so that we get thousands of unimportant results rather than one or two simple important ones. Thus in first-year courses in economics, the value of explicit dynamics is not thought to be high enough to warrant its costs.

But now we must study inflation, which is clearly a dynamic problem. Unfortunately, inflation is complex enough so that the many explicitly dynamic models of it that economists have studied have yielded many specific results. There is no one simple dynamic model of inflation that we feel yields enough results to warrant careful mathematical study. Accordingly, this chapter will be devoid of explicit mathematics. At times this may make our reasoning seem imprecise—as if we are waving our hands about the conclusion rather than proving it. There are two reasons for this impression: (1) Words are not as precise as symbols and require a great deal of elaboration to convey any precise conclusion; and (2) since the actual conclusions derived from different models are different, there is no unique set of simple results to present. We will describe simple inflationary processes that we feel best characterize the real world and best represent the current viewpoints of economists. But how inflation works, what its effects are, and what should be done about it are questions about which economists do not agree. Slight differences in views of the world apparently result in major differences of opinion about the inflationary process. The lack of generality in the results derived from dynamic models is mirrored in a lack of agreement among economists as to what to do.

Money and Inflation

Inflation can be viewed as a decline in the price of money. Why should there be a greater stir over a decline in the price of money than over declines in other prices? Inflation is considered to be a newsworthy evil. Other price declines pass by largely unnoticed. There are several reasons why changes in the value of money capture a great deal of interest. Two of them are of particular importance.

The first of these, which we hinted at in Chapter 35, concerns fiat money only. Fiat money has no intrinsic value and virtually no costs of production. Its value derives from its usefulness as money and from the fact that the government guarantees to accept it for tax payments. But there is no natural floor to its value. Gold, on the other hand, can always be hammered into rings, teeth, and plate that would have value because of their beauty and usefulness. New gold cannot be produced except at great cost. Thus holders of gold have a natural limit on the risk they have shouldered. With dollar bills or any paper currency, there is no natural limit to the risk. The value of the dollars could go to zero under the right circumstances. This possibility makes everyone more alert to changes in the value of fiat money, and with good reason. Historically, paper currencies occasionally have gone to zero in value. In Germany in 1923, money prices increased by almost 100 billion percent. A savings account that would buy 300 large new houses on January 1 would not buy a cigarette by December 31. Such price changes are not observed for commodities other than money. Thus inflation is more likely on theoretical grounds because of the lack of a natural price for money, and it is likely on historical grounds as well. This by itself makes it a newsworthy phenomenon.

The second important reason that inflation causes such a stir is that many contracts are written in monetary terms. Because money is the means of payment — the most convenient commodity to trade — it is the commodity that gets written into contracts that involve future payment. The mortgage on one's house is a promise to pay future dollars. One's contract to teach is a promise by his employer to pay future dollars. One's savings account is a promise by his bank to pay him a certain number of dollars whenever he wishes. When the price of money changes — that is, its value in terms of goods changes — all these contracts change in value. If money depreciates in value, one will feel richer because his future mortgage payments will require less sacrifice of goods than he thought they would, poorer because his savings account will yield him less future satisfaction than he though it would, and poorer because his salary allows him to afford less consumption than he thought it would. A change in the price of money affects the real value of more assets than does a change in any other price. By the *real value* of money we mean its price in terms of goods. Thus the price of money is one of the most important prices to watch, because a change in it leads to a greater redistribution of wealth than does a change in any other price.

Because of the redistributive aspect of inflation, people are alert to it and attempt to protect themselves from it. How might a borrower and lender take their forecasts of inflation into account when writing a loan contract? Let us assume that person A is to lend person B $1,000 for a year, and they agree that 10 percent is a fair interest rate if next year's dollars buy the same quantity of goods as this year's dollars. That is, they agree that a real interest rate of 10 percent is fair. But they forecast a rate of inflation of 5 percent for the coming year. A dollar will probably buy 5 percent fewer goods next year than it does this year. Thus each dollar person B pays back will be worth 5 percent less than each dollar person A lends him. Person A can protect himself from the inflation by demanding that B pay back 5 percent more than $1,100. That is, if B pays A $1,155 next year, A will have earned 10 percent in real terms on his money. Person A will be able to buy 10 percent more goods than he could today with the $1,000 he lends to B.

Thus if individuals protect themselves in their monetary contracts from anticipated inflation, the monetary interest rates will increase to reflect the depreciation in the value of money. In the example above, person A is charging person B a 15.5 percent monetary rate of interest even though the real rate of interest is 10 percent. With a rate of inflation of 5 percent per year that is expected to continue, all monetary interest rates can be expected to be 5 percent higher than they would be otherwise. Thus the "high" interest rates of the late 1960s do not appear quite so high once we subtract from them the inflationary premium.

The ability of asset holders to protect themselves from anticipated inflation in new contracts should not be confused with the redistribution of wealth that takes place due to unanticipated changes in the value of old contracts. In the examples cited above, an increase in the anticipated rate of inflation does make a person feel richer because his mortgage becomes worth less. But how about his savings account? With a market-determined interest rate on savings accounts, he should be compensated for any newly anticipated inflation by an increase in the rate at which interest is credited to his account. Savings accounts have a guaranteed present value and a future value that depends on the market rates of interest between now and the future. Changes in those rates change the future value of the accounts. Mortgages, on the other hand, have a guaranteed future money value. Changes in interest rates, therefore, change the present value of the mortgages. The reader should not get the impression from this paragraph that the use of savings accounts is a good way to protect his wealth from inflation. This is because there is a legal ceiling on the rates that can be paid. Once this ceiling is reached, further increases in the anticipated rate of inflation cannot be reflected in increases in the interest rate on these accounts. Actual inflation at a rate different from what was anticipated will, of course, continue to redistribute wealth.

Unanticipated inflation traditionally has not been written into contracts specified in terms of money, although there is no theoretical reason why it could not be. Returning to the example above, person A could request that person B pay him an interest rate equal to 10 percent plus whatever rate of inflation actually occurs. Then they both would be protected from surprises. One can only hypothesize that such contracts will become prevalent in the future since they seem to have obvious advantages over the kinds of contracts now available.

Wage and Price Flexibility
Before discussing policy with flexible prices, we must extend Chapter 29's argument about wage dynamics to include prices. In Chapter 29, we examined the labor market and pointed out the difference between the short-run and long-run response of wage rates and employment to changes in demand. If the demand for labor expands, there is an immediate increase in employment without significant changes in wage rates. After a while, the tightness of the labor market leads to increases in wages that alleviate the tightness through their depressing effect on the quantity of labor demanded. Thus ultimately wages increase and employment is unchanged – the opposite of the initial effect. This argument can be ex-

tended to prices as well as wages. To do this we must study the demand for labor and the supply of goods.

The demand for labor and the supply of goods can be studied simultaneously as one behavioral decision by firms if we bear in mind that it takes men to produce goods. That is, once we note that there is a production function that tells firms how many men they must hire to produce each level of goods, it becomes clear that the two decisions are not independent.

How does a firm react when it observes its inventories of produced goods decreasing, presumably from increases in sales? When sales increase, a firm can (1) raise prices until sales return to their old level; (2) increase production by hiring more labor; or (3) do some combination of (1) and (2). Which policy is followed? It depends on many factors. The firm attempts to maximize its profits but is faced by competitors who do likewise. If we assume that competition prevails, we know from Chapter 15 that the price a firm charges for its output will equal the cost of increasing production by one unit, its marginal cost. Thus the amount that prices must increase when output is expanded equals the amount that costs increase. Costs increase because (1) labor costs increase and (2) it is difficult to expand production indefinitely without expanding the amount of productive equipment. We are told by (2) that costs increase less when plant and equipment lie idle than when they are already fully utilized. We are told by (1) that prices will act dynamically the way marginal labor costs do.

If a firm observes sales increasing, it attempts to increase production. If there is much idle plant and equipment and if a great deal of unemployed labor is available, the firm's competitors will be willing to expand employment without significant price increases. The firm will be forced to do the same. If, on the other hand, it and its competitors had no idle plant and equipment, it would be able to raise prices and profits in the short run while placing orders for more productive equipment. Our answer, therefore, partly depends on the amount of idle plant and equipment available. But it also depends on the amount of unemployment in labor markets. If there is little unemployment, labor will be hard to find. Remembering our analysis of labor markets, we know that in the short run the firm may expand employment, but that it would find it necessary to raise wages to keep this labor employed in the long run. Thus in the short run the firm can expand production without experiencing increases in the cost of the labor it hires. In the long run, of course, wage rates will increase. Therefore in the short run the firm can expand output without raising prices, but in the long run its cost per unit will increase and it will decide to raise prices as well.

Thus the dynamics of the labor market are transmitted directly to the goods market. Just as employment increases first and then wages rise in response to a change in the demand for labor, so production increases first and then prices rise in response to a change in the demand for goods. This simple dynamic argument explains the postwar United States behavior of prices and output reasonably well. At the beginning of expansions (1950, 1955, 1960-1963) employment could increase sharply without large price changes. Eventually (1951-1952, 1956-1957, 1965-1970) prices increased quite rapidly without corresponding increases in output. In fact, prices generally continued to increase even when unemployment had begun to rise and the economy was heading into slight recessions. The reasons for such patterns are explained in Chapter 29.

Price Elasticity of Aggregate Demand

When the quantity of goods demanded increases beyond the full employment level of output, prices will begin to rise. Does the increase in prices bring about an equilibrium? In other words, does the aggregate quantity of goods demanded decline when prices increase? It should be remembered that we are discussing now the total demand for all goods by all people. It is therefore not obvious that when prices increase, less will be demanded. Some of the demanders, after all, are those receiving the higher prices and wages. With increased incomes, they may demand more goods to offset the decrease in demand by those who must pay higher prices and whose incomes are unchanged. We cannot predict the aggregate effect on consumption of a change in the distribution of a given quantity of consumer income. All we can look at here is what happens to total income when wages and prices change.

One of the important concepts explained in Chapter 30 is how aggregate purchasing power must be equal to the level of sales. If the sales receipts of firms double because of changes in the price or quantity of sales, the sum of the purchasing power must double. If wages, interest payments, and all factor costs do not double, profits will more than double to make up for it. The cash that goes into the register when a sale is made must end up in someone's pocket. Therefore, if we ignore depreciation, business saving, tax laws, and other real-world complications, we can say that income will increase by the same percentage as sales. Thus when prices double, consumers' incomes on average will double, enabling them to maintain the same level of purchases as before.

Is then the aggregate demand for goods inelastic with respect to price? Is there no price increase that will cause the quantity of goods demanded to decline? The answer to this question comes from the money market. As prices increase, more and more money is needed to conduct transactions. This is because the demand for money depends on the monetary value of income. But if the central bank does not increase the supply of money, something must give. An inflation that has doubled prices has caused $2 to be used for transactions that used to take $1. This decline in the real value of the money supply has the same effect on the demand for goods as if there had been no inflation but the central bank had contracted the amount of money outstanding. Each dollar after inflation is only half as good as it was before. Thus the inflation effectively cuts the real value of the money supply in half.

The increased tightness in money markets causes interest rates to rise. This is because all firms and individuals need more money to pay the inflated prices that exist. With no more money available, they attempt to borrow. This drives up interest rates and leads to reductions in spending. Thus the quantity of goods demanded declines when prices increase because an increase in prices has the same effect on demand as does a contractionary monetary policy. There are other reasons why changes in prices affect the demand for goods but they need not be discussed here.

We have now completed a very aggregative model of an economy by studying the interdependence of the markets for goods, labor, and money. We should know how changes in variables in any of these markets influence variables in the other markets. In particular, we should be aware of how changes in forces in any of these markets affect the equilibrium price for goods. Some of these forces are policy variables controlled by the government. To review how policy works in this world, let us pose a hypothetical problem.

Policy and Prices

Assume that an economy is in a position of long-run equilibrium in all markets. Intended saving and investment are equal, inventories are at their desired levels; workers' and employers' expectations about future wage rates and labor market prospects are being fulfilled; and the supply of money is exactly the quantity needed for transactions at the going level of interest rates. Then an unexpected increase in investment demand occurs due to an innovation. In the absence of policy, the following path of activity occurs.

The producers of investment goods attempt to increase production by hiring more workers. In the short run, they get these workers from the pool of frictional unemployment. The workers respend their incomes, causing the initial effect of the spending to be multiplied. After a while, labor becomes harder to find and workers find that jobs are very easy to find. Wages creep up faster than they would have otherwise. With marginal costs up, producers raise prices. The higher wages and prices lead to increases in the demand for money, but with the supply of money fixed, interest rates rise. Prices increase until the money market gets tight enough so that interest rates increase to the level that induces consumers and investors to decrease spending by an amount equal to the original increase in investment spending. Equilibrium is restored. It may take a few years for all of these things to happen, and the speed at which it occurs may vary from instance to instance. But it is not a bad view to hold of the way the economy as a whole responds to a large increase in the demand for goods in the absence of a countercyclical policy.

Note that a price increase is necessary for equilibrium to be restored. That increase we have defined as inflation. If the policy makers had wished to prevent the price rise, they would have had to reduce the demand for goods by an amount equal to the increase in autonomous investment demand. They could have done this, we know, by increasing taxes, cutting government expenditures, or decreasing the supply of money. In the short run, this policy would have made output lower than in the absence of policy, while in the long run prices would have been lower.

This is really a static view of policy. It is concerned with how policy actions affect the equilibrium level of prices. The dynamics we describe is a description of the process of adjustment to that equilibrium. Inflation occurs when prices change from one equilibrium level to a higher one. But we can incorporate the possibility of a continuous dynamic inflation within this static view of the economy. Our static model tells us the equilibrium level of prices that will ultimately be obtained for every set of values for the autonomous variables. To picture a continuous inflation within this framework, we must think of the autonomous variables as changing continuously. The labor force, capital stocks, level of government expenditures, and supply of money are continually changing. Thus the long-run solution changes before it is ever obtained. For a continuous inflation that is never damped, these variables must change continuously. In particular, when discussing long-run inflations, we must be concerned with the behavior of the money supply.

Money and Permanent Inflation

An equilibrium exists to the level of prices in our static model because the size of the money supply is fixed. The fixed quantity of money prevents prices from rising forever because there just is not enough money to finance the higher volume of transactions that higher prices entail. It is not too surprising that this should be the case when we remember how the general price level is related to the price of money. The general price level is a weighted average of all the prices that have units of money in the numerator. The price of money in terms of goods must be its inverse. With the general price level so closely related to the price of money, we would expect the quantity of money supplied to have an important influence on it.

Permanent long-run inflations are only possible when the money supply is expanding. And sudden dramatic changes in the price level by hundreds of percentage points must be accompanied by large changes in the supply of money. But inflations of this magnitude must not be confused with smaller inflations that last a shorter period of time. The smaller inflations can be caused by a change in any of several variables besides the money supply in a manner that was just described.

The Costs of Inflation

We should now have a reasonable idea of what inflation is, how it might be caused, and how it might be controlled. Now we ask, why control it? What are its costs?

One of the costs, we have seen, is that it redistributes income in a manner not intended by the policy makers. So does theft. Although the total quantity of goods remains fixed, random redistributions presumably are to be avoided if possible.

A second cost of inflation results directly from the attempts of individuals to avoid the redistribution. As forecasts change, attempts are made to dispose of certain assets and acquire others. These attempts lead to large price movements for certain assets, which themselves encourage further speculation. At its worst, the speculation can cause a financial collapse with a massive redistribution of wealth and with very large real costs involved in straightening out the tangle of who owns what. Such collapses historically have led firms to pursue cautious investment policies and the low levels of investment have caused high levels of unemployment.

A third cost of inflation results directly from the cost of making forecasts. Forecasting requires information and information is expensive. The more accurate a forecast must be, the more information is needed and the more expensive the forecasts become. It is difficult to know even the present rate of inflation and very expensive to assimilate the latest information about its expected course.

We saw in Chapter 29 how these costs could lead to a misallocation of resources in the labor market. If individuals have not yet fully adjusted to the going rate of inflation, they will overestimate the real value of the wages they are offered and will be more likely to accept job offers that would not be attractive to them if they knew all about the inflation. This is why unemployment rates fall below their equilibrium levels in the early stages of inflation. People end up taking jobs that yield them less real income than would other available jobs that they would probably have found with a little more search. In the short run, they make more money, of course, because they are employed rather than unemployed. But in the long run, they make less because they are doing $4.00 an hour labor when they are capable of doing $4.50 an hour work. Note that this is a real loss to the whole economy. In the short run output is higher than it would be otherwise because the frictionally unemployed are put to work. But in the long run output is lower than it would be otherwise because men and jobs are mismatched.

This timing of the costs of misallocation indicates that the policy choice where inflation is concerned must take account of preferences for present as opposed to future goods. Increasing the rate of inflation can fool the people. Being fooled means that more output is produced today than otherwise would be, but less output gets produced in the future as a result. If the policy makers feel that the extra present output is worth more than the future output that is sacrificed, they may decide that inflation is socially profitable. Since the labor market participants apparently feel otherwise, a policy maker who adopts inflation should have some reason to believe that the prices faced by the labor market participants are different from the costs faced by society and that these prices cause the workers to undervalue present output. An example of this might be a war waged with goods produced by fooling people to accept the "wrong" jobs and paid for by the way in which labor is badly misallocated at the end of the war. The policy maker chooses the inflation because war is a public good and individual decisions will not take proper account of this.

Unfortunately, this ability of policy makers to fool the people in the short run invites manipulation of the economy from political motivation—pumping it up before elections and paying the price afterward. Where elections are frequent and the citizenry gullible, we might expect to see more inflation than elsewhere.

The costs just mentioned are costs of unanticipated inflation. Are there any costs to an anticipated inflation? Perfectly anticipated inflations do not redistribute income or wealth. For example, what if we all adjusted to expecting a 5 percent per annum inflation and protected ourselves from it in all our contracts? As long as our forecasts were realized, would the world be any different from one in which forecasts of constant prices were realized? Actually, it would not be. Monetary interest rates would all be 5 percent higher than otherwise, and if we could get accustomed to rates at that level and build them into our thinking, the depreciation of future dollars would be anticipated automatically. It is true that there would no longer be a constant measure of value to be used for comparisons over time. Certain calculations would take longer than before, at least until we all memorized the compound interest table for 5 percent. But the cost of these calculations is not too great.

The largest cost associated with a permanent rate of inflation would result from the fact that interest is not paid on currency and in many countries not on checking accounts. This means that holders of money for transactions purposes will see their purchasing power erode by 5 percent per year. The only way to protect themselves from this would be to hold less money, to engage in a greater number of transactions between money and its close substitutes. These transactions are costly. Thus an inflation makes money less convenient. It increases the cost of transacting. Of course, if individuals did not attempt to protect themselves from the interest loss, there would be no cost to the society. Holders of currency would lose wealth, and the taxpayers would gain since the currency is part of their debt. But individuals will attempt to protect themselves, and it is precisely these attempts that constitute the costs of inflation. If it were feasible to pay interest on money, these costs could be avoided. The interest payments would prevent the transactions balances from having their value eroded by the inflation.

The largest costs, therefore, must be assigned to unanticipated price changes and the effect they can have on subsequent forecasts and behavior. Unexpected price changes misallocate resources and invite destabilizing financial speculation. With all these costs to inflation, why is it so prevalent? Are there any advantages to inflation?

Inflation as a Tax

Inflation may be used as a tax. We just noted how even an anticipated inflation transfers resources from the holders of currency to the government that has issued it. This is very much like a tax and can be used instead of other taxes. Consider the following alternatives a country might face. (1) It can balance its budget, hold its money supply constant, and have no inflation; or (2) it can cut taxes by 10 percent and print money to cover the deficit. The money supply grows, leading ultimately to inflation. It is possible to attain a long-run equilibrium with a constant rate of anticipated inflation; in this case the inflation erodes the value of the old money at the same rate at which new money is being printed. Thus the real value of the money supply remains constant. But taxes have been cut. They have been replaced by the losses constantly incurred by the holders of money.

Could inflation, given its costs, ever be preferred to other taxes? That depends on the costs of collecting the other taxes and on their incidence. The money holders may be different people from the other tax payers. Switching from taxes to inflation redistributes the costs of government from the taxpayers to the holders of money. As long as this is what the government wishes and as long as the alternative costs of collecting taxes from the money holders exceed the costs of the inflation, then inflation can be a socially profitable venture. Usually, however, it is only profitable where other taxes are easily evaded or avoided. Inflation may be the only way to tax certain interest groups whose legal staffs protect them from the tax laws but whose business requires them to hold large cash balances.

Inflation and Trade

Inflation is usually listed as one of the evils policy makers wish to avoid. One reason this is so, in addition to the costs listed above, is the effect of inflation on the balance of payments. This is one of the subjects of the next chapter, in which the financial aspects of foreign trade are examined and the problems of policy in an open economy are discussed.

Questions

1. How does inflation redistribute wealth? How can it serve as a tax? How can people protect themselves from the redistribution of an anticipated inflation?
2. Why is the question of inflation as seen by the policy maker tied up with the question of the relative value of present and future goods? Why might policy makers choose inflation in times of war?
3. How does the existence of a given stock of money ultimately determine the price level? Why are runaway inflations impossible without large increases in the quantity of money?

Concepts Discussed

rate of inflation	real interest rate
real value of money	money interest rate

38 International Payments

When Americans buy British automobiles, they wish to pay for them with dollars. When British companies sell automobiles to Americans, they wish to receive pounds sterling as payment. Thus there must be some place where someone with dollars can buy pounds if Americans are to be able to buy British cars. The *international payments mechanism* refers to the organization of markets such as the one in which pounds are converted into dollars. There are many ways in which such a market can be organized. We look at the most common forms in this chapter.

The existence of an international payments mechanism places restrictions on the actions of national policy makers that vary with the form of the payments mechanism. To complete our discussion of policy, it is necessary, therefore, to understand how these mechanisms work and why they pose restrictions. We devote some special attention to the problems of the United States because of its unique position within the current payments system.

International payments mechanisms are monetary systems and they can be analyzed from the same viewpoint used to analyze national monetary systems in Chapter 33. That is, a good monetary system makes payments convenient and inexpensive, and it is resilient to panic and financial collapse. International monetary systems serve the same scorekeeping purposes that domestic systems do; they are designed to prevent any one country from acquiring goods worth more than the goods it sacrifices. Our discussion of these systems will be similar to our discussion of domestic systems in that we will start with the oldest, the gold standard, and proceed to more modern systems, ending with a discussion of the efficiency and convenience of payments systems not yet used by men. While watching the payments system develop, it will be evident that progress on the domestic monetary front in terms of (1) lowering the cost of transactions by changing the monetary system and (2) using conscious monetary policy to offset cyclical excesses usually placed strains on the existing payments mechanism and occasionally necessitated the development of a new one.

The Gold Standard

Gold was originally chosen for international payments for the same reasons it was chosen as domestic money (see Chapter 33). If every nation uses gold for its domestic currency, gold will make an efficient international means of payment. The same costs are associated with its use internationally as domestically, however, and systems that do not share these costs—digging it from the ground, transporting it, guarding it, and so on — will be preferred if they are no worse on other counts.

It is useful to observe how payments equilibrium is maintained in a world using the gold standard. What happens, for example, if one country buys more goods from another than it sells to that country? This situation is defined as a *payments deficit*, the reverse as a *payments surplus*. The deficit country experiences an outflow of gold; that is, it is spending more money abroad than it is earning. This cannot happen forever, of course, because the country ultimately will run out of gold. But far before that point is reached, automatic forces of economic equilibrium correct the imbalance in the payments. The forces act as follows.

Because gold is the national money as well as the international money, a gold outflow represents a decline in the national money supply. As currency falls, the banks find it prudent to restrict lending. But individuals need money to conduct their transactions and they attempt to borrow to get it. Interest rates rise. The higher interest rates discourage consumption and investment spending with the result that output and employment fall in the short run. In the long run, wages and prices fall. But this deflationary cycle does not continue forever. Within it lies the cure of the payments problem.

First, when output falls due to the decline in consumption and investment spending, part of the decline in sales is reflected in lower imports. When people buy fewer goods, they buy fewer foreign goods as well as fewer domestic goods. Thus the short-run decline in output partially corrects the payments problem by causing a decline in purchases from foreigners.

In the long run, wages and prices fall. This makes domestic goods cheaper than they were in terms of gold and more attractive relative to foreign goods whose prices in terms of gold have not fallen. Natives stop buying foreign automobiles, clothes, and watches and instead start buying domestic substitutes. Foreigners start importing more of the now cheap domestic commodities instead of producing them. Thus in the long run, the decline in prices restores equilibrium in the flow of payments. If we observe one country buying more from others than it sells to them, the gold that flows between the countries to pay for the commodities will eventually correct the imbalance.

The process works as well in reverse. The country that is selling more abroad than it is buying will experience an inflow of gold. This is a monetary expansion. Banks will find deposits increasing and will lower the cost of borrowing. Firms and individuals will borrow more and buy more goods. This will increase employment and the price level. Certainly it will increase purchases from abroad.

Thus the gold flow eventually lowers prices in the country that it leaves and raises them in the country that it enters. The price change eliminates the gold flow in the long run. All deficits and surpluses in payments correct themselves. With a gold standard, we can conclude that payments disequilibrium is impossible in the long run.

Gold Exchange Standard

A slight modification of the gold standard is a system called the *gold exchange standard*. In this system, national currencies are used as domestic money rather than gold, but the domestic currencies are all convertible into gold at fixed price ratios. That is, the central banks that issue the coins or paper currencies agree to give gold to anyone who wishes to turn the currency back in. The gold exchange standard functions just as a gold standard except that the gold has been augmented by currencies that are backed by gold, although perhaps backed to some magnitude less than 100 percent. As long as each central bank does not issue new currency to replace the gold and currency that leave the country, the same automatic stabilizing effect that occurred with the gold standard will occur with the gold exchange standard. Payments deficits—purchases from abroad in excess of sales—will result in outflows of gold and currencies. The outflow reduces the domestic money supply, causing a decline in income and eventually prices that restore equilibrium by eliminating the deficit.

The advantage of the gold exchange standard over a pure gold standard is that less gold must be scratched from the ground to operate the system. And gold need not be lost while circulating since only currency is in circulation. For international payments, gold still can be used, or some of the domestic currencies may be used if they are thought to be as good as gold. The more the currencies are used, the more efficient the international payments system becomes. Transaction costs are much lower when dollars are used for payment than when gold is used.

The gold exchange standard is the basis of today's international monetary system. To understand the problems associated with it, we must understand the behavior of the central banks, which have an important role in the operation of the system.

Central Banks and the Gold Exchange Standard

Central banks, we said, guarantee the convertibility of their currency into gold at a fixed ratio. The Federal Reserve System in the United States, for example, at one time guaranteed to give an ounce of gold to anyone who turned in $35. It also offered to buy gold at $35 per ounce from anyone who wanted to sell. Given these guarantees by the central banks, there are various ways in which the conversion of one currency into another might work. Just by looking at these ways we will gain an understanding of the strengths and weaknesses of the gold exchange standard.

Assume that an American wishes to buy a British auto and to pay for it with dollars. The car costs £1,000. The US central bank promises to trade $35 for an ounce of gold; the Bank of England promises to trade £14.6 for each ounce. The conversion might work as follows: The American trades $2,400 into his central bank for 686 ounces of gold. The gold is shipped to the British exporter who is able to trade it to his central bank for £1,000. Many of these transactions are made every day by the banks. When a native buys abroad, the bank sells gold;

when a foreigner buys domestic goods, the bank sells dollars and receives gold. This manner of converting dollars into pounds illustrates the important role of the central banks. It also points out the fact that they must keep a stock of gold on hand as a buffer because the receipts of dollars will rarely cancel exactly the receipts of gold.

The transaction just described is a good picture to keep in mind of how settlements are ultimately reached. But there are other ways to conduct the transactions that are much more convenient and much cheaper. Rather than ship the gold all around at great risk and expense, the central banks might agree to handle each others' currencies. By doing this, gold shipments can be kept to minimal levels. To see the convenience of this system, let us look at the same transaction again.

An American wishes to buy a British car that costs £1,000. He writes a check for $2,400 and mails it to the British firm. The British firm deposits the check in the Bank of England and is given credit for a deposit of £1,000. Note that it is the willingness of the Bank of England to accept the dollars that has provided the great increase in convenience. To complete the transaction, the Bank of England must get its gold from the Federal Reserve, of course. It does this by cashing in the dollars. But with thousands of similar transactions going on daily, by the end of the day the Bank of England has built up a great many dollars and the Federal Reserve a great many pounds sterling. These can be traded, leaving only the excess of one over the other, which must be covered by a gold shipment. Our choice of just one day was arbitrary, of course. The banks could wait weeks, months, or even years before they considered a gold shipment necessary. In the meantime, they would be content to watch their balances of foreign currency grow and contract with the needs for trade. The advantage of conducting the transactions in this manner is not only convenience to the individuals concerned, but since checks are being exchanged rather than gold, much less gold is needed. The domestic currencies are now useful as international currencies as well. Substituting them for gold greatly reduces the system's need for gold and therefore makes it cheaper to operate. When run in this fashion, the gold exchange standard becomes largely an exchange standard. Gold can remain as the unit of account, but its role is one of ultimate reckoning rather than of day-to-day usefulness.

The Cost of Adjusting

The gold exchange standard, as we have seen, has an automatic method for correcting payments imbalances. But in the course of a correction, a country generally must experience a high level of unemployment. In the past few chapters, we have described ways in which policy makers can prevent unemployment. If these policies are used, unemployment will be prevented, but so will the correction. How might a central bank prevent the natural correction from taking place?

The correction occurs because money leaves the banking system. Americans write out dollar checks to British sellers and the dollars get withdrawn from

American banks. This would tighten up money and raise interest rates unless the central bank offset it. The central bank can do this by printing more currency and buying government debt in the open market. Thus domestic money balances can be kept at their original level. This means that interest rates will not rise; thus spending will not fall, employment will not fall, wages and prices will not fall, and thus the payments imbalance will *not* be automatically corrected. How do policy makers get out of the bind? How can they induce foreigners to buy more domestic goods and natives fewer foreign goods, without causing high levels of unemployment in the interim?

Our answer to that dilemma is called *devaluation*. A devaluation reduces the amount of gold that the bank will pay back for each unit of its currency presented for payment. It changes the value of the domestic currency in terms of gold. How does this restore equilibrium?

Equilibrium can be restored once domestic prices fall in terms of gold. But rather than accomplish this by the long painful process through which domestic prices fall in terms of currency, the central bank can do it quickly by changing the price of currency in terms of gold. If a domestic automobile costs a native $3,500 and an ounce of gold costs $35, then a domestic automobile costs 100 ounces of gold to a foreigner. Assume that the price must fall to 70 ounces before foreigners buy enough to balance the payments. This price decrease can be accomplished in two ways: (1) We can let the domestic price of autos fall to $2,000 by deflating the economy and watching all prices slowly fall, or (2) we can devalue the dollar, that is, change the price of an ounce of gold to $50 so that now 70 ounces is worth $3500. Thus a devaluation of the currency lowers domestic prices to foreigners and raises foreign prices to natives. In principle, a devaluation usually can correct the payments imbalance.

Devaluation has costs, however. First of all, it leads to a redistribution of wealth. The imbalance in the payments has caused the foreign central banks to accumulate gold and currency. As long as the foreign price of gold is constant, the bank is indifferent between accumulating gold and accumulating currency. But once the possibility of devaluation arises, the foreign banks may well prefer to hold only gold. This is because the devaluation reduces the value of the currency holdings. A bank holding $700 has holdings worth 20 ounces of gold if the price of gold is $35 per ounce. If the price is raised to $50 per ounce, the dollars are now worth only 14 ounces of gold. Thus devaluation reduces the real value of domestic currency held by foreigners. Because of this possibility, they may feel it necessary to keep their transaction balances in gold rather than in currency. If they do, this will negate a large part of the advantages of the gold exchange system, namely, the saving in real resources that occurs when gold is augmented by fiat currencies. If all international transactions still must be conducted in gold, more gold will be needed than if currencies are used as well. Thus the possibility of devaluation makes central banks wary of the amounts of foreign currency they will acquire. If the devaluations are frequent, the banks may feel it necessary to hold only gold with the result that some of the advantages of using currency for international transactions will be lost.

Key Currencies

Devaluation is not equally likely for all currencies. Some currencies are very stable in value and some countries appear much less likely to encounter deficits in their balance of payments than others. The currencies of these countries can be held with much less risk than others and the central bankers are aware of this. What is likely to happen then is that a few stable currencies tend to be used for international transactions. This allows the system to exploit the advantages of fiat money with the least risk from devaluation.

In our example above, a British automobile was purchased by an American and dollars served as the international currency. They were accumulated eventually by the Bank of England. An Englishman buying an American car could also use dollars if he wished. Rather than write a check in pounds and mail it, he might go to the central bank, convert his pounds into dollars, and mail the check specified in dollars. The American firm then deposits this to its account as it does any other check. What is the difference between this method and the one where the check for pounds is mailed? The difference is that the conversion of pounds into dollars occurs a few days sooner, before the American firm receives the check in the mail and deposits it in its bank, which then sends it on to the Federal Reserve. With the conversion occurring, say, three days earlier, the British purchaser and the American firm have protected themselves from any devaluation of the pound that might occur during that three-day period. Should the pound be devalued before the American firm gets its dollars, the British purchaser would have to write an additional check because it would then take more pounds than before to buy the same American automobile.

It is possible, then, that dollars might be used as the currency in transactions flowing both ways across the Atlantic. If it is felt that dollars are less risky than pounds, everyone will prefer to own dollars for the few days it takes a check to clear. This is merely an example of Gresham's Law: People spend the bad money early in order to hold on to the good money as long as possible. In today's world, dollars are the currency most often used for international transactions. Because of this, all foreign central banks find that they need a supply of dollars on hand to meet the needs of their own citizens who occasionally wish to acquire dollars in order to buy American goods.

But if the central banks will always have dollars on hand, why can these not be used for any international transaction? If an Italian wishes to buy a French car, why should he be forced to choose between lira and francs, currencies with a history of devaluation? Why does he not use dollars to complete the transaction? He does. The Italian goes to his bank, converts lira into dollars, and mails the dollars to the French firm, which converts them into francs. When this happens, dollars pass from the Italian central bank to the French central bank. While they are passing, the owner is free from the risk of devaluation of the lira or the franc. And this is how the world's international business is conducted.

Most international payments are made with dollars. All central banks have a buffer of dollar holdings for transaction purposes and they are frequently called upon to exchange their own currency for dollars and vice versa. The dependence on the dollar is so complete that most banks specify the price of their currency in terms of dollars rather than in terms of gold. The price of one currency in terms of another is called an *exchange rate*. The Bank of England, for example, offers to trade one pound of sterling for $2.40 in either direction. The effect of this guarantee is the same as if it were specified in terms of gold with one exception. It is no longer possible for the United States to devalue its currency relative to the rest of the world. If the United States devalues, the only effect is that the price of gold increases. American goods do not become cheaper to foreigners because the rates at which foreign currencies trade for the dollar are not affected by a United States devaluation.

Currency Markets

It is often convenient to bypass the central banks when trading one currency for another. Markets exist in all the world's financial centers in which currencies can be traded. Thus the British importer seeking to trade pounds for dollars need only call a currency broker in order to find an exporter who wishes to convert his dollars into pounds. These currency markets are so efficient that it is through them that the central banks conduct most of their trades. For example, if there appears to be an excess supply of dollars on the London market—that is, more firms trying to trade dollars for pounds than vice versa—the Bank of England will enter the market and buy up the extra dollars, thereby preventing the price of pounds in terms of dollars from changing. Small limits are allowed for price fluctuations. The price of the pound is allowed to vary between $2.38 and $2.42. The Bank of England permits these fluctuations by guaranteeing to buy an unlimited number of pounds at $2.38 and to sell at $2.42. The Bank is also free to enter the market at any time to move the price anywhere it wishes between the limits.

The world's currency markets are linked by arbitragers. *Arbitrage* is the simultaneous buying and selling of the same commodity in different markets in an attempt to make profits. If the price of pounds is $2.38 in London and $2.39 in Zurich, a smart arbitrager will simultaneously buy in London and sell in Zurich, keeping the $.01 difference. Through the actions of arbitragers, the behavior of the central banks gets transmitted to all the world's currency markets. If the Bank of England guarantees to buy pounds at $2.38 in London, the price cannot fall far below $2.38 anywhere else because arbitragers will buy up the pounds in order to resell them in London.

Speculation

We have noted that central banks are faced with a problem when deficits appear on their balances of payments. The deficits must be paid by the central bank with either gold or its holdings of foreign exchange, which are usually in the form of dollars. If the deficit continues, the bank will run out of reserves. The bank is faced with the choice of (1) deflating its economy (the classical adjustment process) or (2) devaluing its currency. If firms and central banks expect a devaluation, they can protect themselves by selling their holdings of the suspect currency on the open market. For example, many international firms will have two checking accounts, one specified in dollars and one in pounds. If a devaluation of the pound is expected, it makes sense for a firm to sell a large part of its pounds on the open market for dollars and to use its dollar checking account for all transactions.

Thus a fear of devaluation of the pound will cause many pounds to be sold in the world's currency markets. The Bank of England must buy these pounds or else the price of the pound will fall below $2.38. That is, it must buy the pounds or allow a *de facto* devaluation to occur. This kind of speculation has much the same effect as a run on a bank. Holders of pounds are unsure of their value and attempt to trade them for dollars. This forces the Bank of England to use up its remaining reserves all the faster in order to support the price of its currency. Just as fear of a bank's solvency can cause it to go under, so fear of devaluation can bring that devaluation about by hastening the exhaustion of a central bank's foreign exchange reserves.

The dollar is particularly vulnerable to this kind of speculation. This is not because the Federal Reserve has no reserves. To the contrary, the Federal Reserve has more gold and foreign exchange holdings than any other central bank. But because the dollar is used for all sorts of transactions all around the world, there are many dollars available in the world's checking accounts that can be turned in on short notice for other currencies. Not only do the world's central banks hold dollars (almost to the exclusion of other currencies), but all large private banks and firms hold dollar accounts out of convenience because of the many dollar transactions they are called upon to make. Thus if a suspicion that the United States would change the price of gold or would refuse to convert other currencies into dollars should grow, a massive run on the dollar could occur. Although the Federal Reserve's holdings of foreign exchange reserves are vast, they are only about one-fourth as large as the holdings of dollars by foreigners. Thus if all these dollars were presented for payment, the Federal Reserve would have to default.

The payments system is very convenient and cheap to operate since the role of gold has been minimized. Gold has been replaced effectively by dollars for international transactions. This is because dollars are much more convenient and efficient. They do not have to be dug from the ground or guarded while in transit. They can be used in the form of checks that are easy to mail and that cannot be stolen. But to gain the advantages yielded by this more sophisticated form of money, the world has to put up with the risks of a currency collapse. Each holder of dollars look warily at the other holders, knowing that his money is good only as long as the others agree to hold the slightly risky currency.

As collapses of banks only occur when depositors suddenly stampede, the possibility of the international collapse of the dollar depends on the actions of the foreign central banks, the major holders of the IOUs of the United States. Generally, what happens when a reserve currency such as the dollar is threatened is that a loan is extended to the United States by the other central banks to meet the immediate "withdrawals." In the future the loan will have to be repaid, of course. But as long as all of the central banks band together and agree to make loans whenever they are needed, there will be no collapse caused by a run on the bank. If public or private speculation forces dollars to flow rapidly from the United States abroad, loans by central banks can send the dollars back again. Any international movement of gold or currency can be offset exactly by loans of central banks in the reverse direction. Thus the extended position of the United States is only dangerous if the foreign central banks refuse to cooperate.

SDRs

The *International Monetary Fund* is designed to be an international bank that makes the loans needed to offset currency speculations. SDRs, special drawing rights, are overdraft privileges at the IMF. That is, SDRs indicate the amount by which each nation is allowed to have its international checking account go negative before it must ask for additional loans. SDRs are more convenient than specifically granted loans because of their automatic nature. Since they are guaranteed, they can be considered as additional reserves that can be used to finance a balance of payments deficit or to offset a currency speculation. The more reserves a country has, the more able it is to offset such speculations. Speculations are less likely to occur if the speculators feel that the country has the power to stop them. That is, why withdraw your money from the bank if the bank is going to remain solvent? The expansion of SDRs in the future will represent a great step forward in international finance, a step that will free men from clawing the earth's surface for commodities whose only use is to keep score. Magnetic tape can keep score just as well if we but establish institutions that make use of it.

Alternative payments mechanisms can be imagined. One that has gained great favor with economists is a system of freely fluctuating exchange rates. The bankers, as yet, have not been overly interested in such a system.

Fluctuating Rates

If exchange rates are determined in free markets the way the price of a security is, we call the payments mechanism one of *fluctuating exchange rates*. The free market rate may stay constant, of course; the name merely notes the fact that they are free to fluctuate with changes in supply or demand.

The demand and supply of the currencies will depend on the demand and supply for the various commodities and assets between nations. The supply of pounds derives from the demand for foreign assets and commodities by Englishmen. The demand for pounds comes from the demand for English goods and assets by foreigners. The price of pounds in terms of dollars, the exchange rate, will vary to guarantee that the quantity supplied remains equal to that demanded. Given the price of English goods, a high price for pounds will mean that English goods are expensive to foreigners, and a low price will mean they are cheap. Thus variations in the exchange rate make the price of English goods vary to foreigners but not to natives.

Many economists favor such fluctuating rates just as we favor the determination of free prices in any other market. Freely determined prices have aspects of efficiency about them that are discussed in the first half of this book. With free markets people can choose to act as they would in restricted markets, but they also can choose other forms of action. Freely determined prices are preferred by economists for most markets because of the greater possibilities for happiness that they offer.

The disadvantages of such free rates are commonly stated as follows. (1) Destabilizing speculation will be possible if rates are freely determined. With violent swings in price, no one will want to take on the risks inherent in the long-run international relationships that are necessary if trade is to take place. (2) Even if the solution for the exchange rate is generally stable, the possibility of fluctuations leads to uncertainty that will prevent firms of all nations from conducting business abroad.

One might ask if firms do not observe the same uncertainty of future prices when deciding to invest and produce at home; that is, uncertainty depends on the uncertainties of nature that are merely reflected in the exchange rate. One could ask why invisible political boundaries increase uncertainty over real economic magnitudes. The answer apparently has to do with policy. National monetary policies can change levels of employment, output, and interest rates, as well as prices. Uncertainty about the policy of foreign countries and therefore about the price at which a person will be able to convert foreign currency into his own may affect his ability to do business in the foreign country. It may raise transaction costs by requiring the person to insure all contracts by selling them in the international currency markets. Thus the additional uncertainty of fluctuating rates must be an uncertainty about the future policies of the nation-states, policies that will have a great impact on the exchange rate. Such policies, of course, ultimately must affect the exchange rate regardless of the payments system used.

International Securities Movements

One more important concept must be added to this picture of international transactions to make it a useful portrayal of real-world payments mechanisms. That concept is the possibility of ownership of foreign securities and capital goods. Just as financial markets create convenient forms in which to hold domestic wealth, so they make possible additional convenience in the holding of international wealth. The risk of wealth holding can be diversified across the assets of all countries if international financial markets exist.

Because of these benefits from international diversification, an international superstructure of financial assets and intermediaries has been created to allow individuals to satisfy their desires efficiently. We will now examine how this superstructure affects the adjustment mechanisms we have just outlined.

When a country sells more to others than it buys from them, it acquires claims to their goods. These claims are just like those an individual acquires when the value of the goods and services he sells exceeds that of those he buys. Just as an individual can leave these claims in the form in which he received them—that is, he can hold money—so can a country, or the natives of that country. And just as an individual can trade this money for financial assets, so the citizens of a country can trade international money for international assets.

Because of this possibility, gold and currency will flow between two countries not only in response to imbalances in the demand for goods and services but also in response to imbalances in the demand for assets. Payments of money between countries will represent the sum of the excess amount of goods one country has bought from the other and the excess amount of assets. It is possible, we will see, for a country to sell more goods to others than it buys from them and still have a payments deficit. This happens when its citizens buy more assets from other countries than they sell to them and the asset deficit exceeds the goods and services deficit.

The possibility of asset movements yields one more automatic stabilizing device that can correct imbalances in the flow of payments. Above we noted that deficit countries would experience outflows of money that lead to higher interest rates. Investors in all countries would find these higher interest rates attractive and would transfer savings to countries offering them. Similarly, borrowers would be repelled by these rates and would borrow abroad. Thus with assets free to move between nations, the monetary outflow that results from the imbalance in the purchases of commodities would be offset by a monetary inflow that results from investors seeking the highest return possible on their assets. In the extreme case where the assets of all countries are perfect substitutes—that is, they share the same risks and are equally convenient—they would all have to have the same interest rates. A slight deviation in rates would be a signal to investors to shift funds into the high-interest country until the rates equalize again.

Where the assets of different countries are not perfect substitutes, differences among their interest rates will be observed. It will still be true, however, that an increase in the rate on any asset will make it more desirable, signaling investors to buy it. Thus monetary outflows lead to higher interest rates, but higher interest rates lead to monetary inflows as foreign investors buy domestic assets. It is possible, if the assets are perfect substitutes, that the inflow will be large enough to offset exactly the outflow.

Is equilibrium ever restored? Can one country continue forever buying more from the other countries than it sells to them just because of asset transactions? The answer, of course, is no. But with asset transactions, the scoreboard can keep mounting the score higher and higher for one country and lower for the other without forcing a painful readjustment process via unemployment. What happens is that one country keeps accumulating claims on the other's capital stock; it begins owning more and more of the other's machines, although in a conveniently intermediated form. These machines and assets earn interest. So in the long run the income of the country acquiring claims is higher than it would be otherwise because of the extra interest payments. The higher income leads to higher levels of imports and ultimately to equilibrium in the balance of payments.

Thus with asset movements possible, disequilibria in the balance of payments can be adjusted by a very long-run route involving changes in the levels of wealth and income in the two countries. As one country gets wealthier and wealthier, it consumes more and more, including imports. Since people acquire wealth ultimately for consumption purposes, no country will continue to acquire claims against another indefinitely. This process operates when countries' tastes for present as opposed to future goods differ. Essentially, one country lends goods to the other for future repayment.

Policy in Open Economies

Where economies are linked by trade, they all share to a certain extent the same economic experiences. Just as Chicago has high unemployment rates when New York has high unemployment rates, and just as Chicago has high interest rates when New York has high interest rates, so the regions of the world are linked by trade. Unemployment spreads from one area to another because the lack of income in one region causes that region to buy fewer goods from the other regions. Its labor force may migrate to the other regions if immigration is allowed. Similarly, high interest rates in one region attract funds from others. The scarcity of funds that results in the other regions causes the bankers to raise interest rates. Thus trade links regions to a common economic experience. The only buffers are transportation costs and man-made barriers such as tariffs.

If regions are to have more or less the same experience, how can policy be effective? How can monetary and fiscal policy work if different countries are pursuing different goals simultaneously? If the United States wishes to cut down its inflation and raises taxes while Canada wishes to eliminate unemployment and lowers taxes, what will result? The higher United States taxes will lead to fewer purchases by Americans, some of which will be reflected in lower imports from Canada. Thus the anti-inflationary American policy will increase Canadian unemployment. The lower Canadian taxes will lead to increased purchases of goods by Canadians, part of which will be imported from the United States. These imports will contribute to inflation in the United States. If the economies are very closely linked, it will be impossible for the two countries to have independently successful policies without resorting to specific controls. That is, either both countries will have high interest rates or neither will. Attempts to pursue policies aimed at different levels of interest rates or employment will be doomed to failure.

Specifically, we can say that with the gold exchange standard that is being used presently, monetary policy will be much weaker than otherwise. The reason for this is that the tools of monetary policy must be used to guarantee that the rate of exchange remains constant. Remember that the supply and demand for currencies determine their prices both in the world of fluctuating exchange notes and in the world of fixed exchange rates. The difference lies in the fact that with fixed exchange rates, the central banks are committed to enter the market and sell their own currency whenever its price threatens to go up and buy whenever its price would otherwise go down. Thus, at the fixed price, private supply and demand may result in excess supply or demand for the currency and the central banks must mop this up by entering the other side of the market. This agreement by the central banks limits in part their ability to control the level of the money supply.

For example, if a central bank desires to increase the level of employment, it might pump money into domestic banks in order to lower interest rates and induce further borrowing. The lower interest rates, however, induce people to buy foreign securities and sell domestic ones. This results in an accumulation of domestic currency by foreigners, not by domestic banks. The foreigners may present this currency to the central bank for payment in gold. If this happens, the only effect of the monetary expansion will have been a worsening of the balance of payments, reflected in an outflow of gold. The central bank is forced to buy in the international currency market the money it attempted to dump into the domestic economy. If monetary actions are to be successful in this environment, they will have to lead to lower interest rates all around the world. Clearly, a much larger dose of monetary action is required in this case to yield any given results, and this dose must not be offset by foreign central banks.

Fiscal policy is not as hampered. If successful, of course, the increased level of income and prices will lead to increased imports and decreased exports. That is, any expansionary action that is successful will be partially weakened by the effect it has on foreign economies through the balance of payments. Another way of saying this is that all the multipliers—expenditure, tax, and monetary—are smaller in a country whose economy is open to foreign trade than in one whose economy is not. Larger doses of policy are needed in countries that are sensitive to international price movements than are needed in other countries.

Consider how the pursuit of the goals discussed in the last chapter is affected by balance of payments considerations. If, for example, low interest rates are desired to encourage economic growth, the policy maker has to temper his pursuit of them with the realization that low interest rates will lead to an outflow of funds seeking better returns abroad. These funds will be used to buy foreign bonds and bank accounts and will be presented eventually to the central bank for payment in gold. Therefore a country with very low foreign exchange reserves cannot pursue a policy of low interest rates unless it is prepared to prevent a payments deficit by some other means—strict control of capital movements, for example, or even devaluation. Recently the United States invoked a measure called the "interest equalization tax" to enable it to have lower interest rates than those in foreign countries. The tax is a tax on interest earned on foreign assets so that domestic assets with lower interest rates can look equally attractive to investors.

Controls such as the interest equalization tax restrict the free flow of funds between markets and therefore impair efficiency. But without them, independent policies are impossible. Without such specific controls, the limits on the success of policy are determined by policy makers abroad.

All expansionary actions result in increased purchases abroad. If domestic prices increase as a result of the policy, it may even result in lower sales abroad. Expansions, therefore, lead to balance of payments deficits. Occasionally, domestic policy is so strongly affected by this relationship that contractionary actions are invoked even though expansionary moves are desired at home. That is, occasionally, the realities of the balance of payments are such that domestic policies are affected by the need to keep the payments in balance. Thus unemployment is allowed to exist because of its beneficial effect on the balance of payments.

Such disturbances of domestic policy could be called a cost that is associated with the monetary system. With a different system—flexible exchange rates, for example—the payments are always in balance. They take care of themselves because the exchange rate adjusts to guarantee an equilibrium in the supply and demand for currency. Therefore, with flexible rates, domestic policies need not be affected by balance of payments considerations. Of course, with flexible rates, domestic policies affect the exchange rate and therefore the cost of foreign commodities. The price of the currency might therefore be a policy goal.

A system of fixed exchange rates has these costs only if the policy makers are unwilling to change the fixed rate. If a policy action leads to a deficit, the policy makers have the option of changing the exchange rate to right the deficit. Thus we might expect to see economic expansion accompanied by devaluation rather than by balance of payments deficit. Of course, once a particular government became known for pulling such a stunt, it would find its own currency returned rapidly when it began a period of economic expansion. No one would wish to hold a currency that is in jeopardy of being devalued.

Questions

1. Central banks act as "lenders of last resort" to prevent small banks from failing during a financial panic. (See Chapter 35 for details.) How might a lender of last resort be devised for the international monetary system to prevent central banks from failing due to speculation against their currencies?
2. If the Federal Reserve increased the price of gold to $50 an ounce from $35 an ounce, would you be any poorer? How would you be affected if foreign banks increased the price of their currencies in terms of dollars?
3. How important should international considerations be in the determination of domestic policy? How much unemployment would you put up with in order to deflate the economy and defend the integrity of the currency?

Concepts Discussed

international payments mechanism
the gold standard
payments deficit and surplus
gold exchange standard
devaluation

exchange rate
arbitrager
SDR
fluctuating exchange rates

XIII   Economic Development

Every year, if not every day,
we have to wager our salvation
upon some prophecy based
upon some imperfect knowledge.

OLIVER WENDELL HOLMES

Politics, we have seen, complicates economics greatly. Most people will agree that if a policy action exists that can make one person better off without hurting anyone else, it should be carried out. Economics describes the nature of such policy actions. Political disagreement, on the other hand, always centers on the question of dividing the spoils. Economics does not give us any way to determine when it is proper to take from Peter and to give to Paul. Unfortunately, most potential economic policy actions make some people better off and others worse off. Thus the principles of economic efficiency can rarely be invoked in their purest form. The economic policy maker must consider the political implications of his actions.

We conclude this book with an example of the difficulties encountered when trying to apply economics to social problems. The problem we choose is that of economic development. Most of the people of the world are poor. The difficulty in eliminating international poverty poses one of the world's most pressing social problems. And some of the major obstacles to solving the problem are political.

Economic development is a useful problem to consider at the end of a course in economics because its analysis serves as a review of all the concepts of efficiency and equity we have learned. Furthermore, it allows us to apply the principles of trade theory, monetary theory, location theory, and public finance. Because all these factors are simultaneously involved in the problem of development, there are no easy solutions.

How does a country attempt to secure for itself the life of affluence that can be observed in a few Western societies? What are the principles of affluence? How can they be harnessed? Are they consistent with domestic ideas of social justice? What are the raw mechanics of industrialization? Discovering the answers to these questions is the livelihood of the development economist.

39 The Problem of Economic Development

The low level of economic welfare of the majority of the world's population is not a new phenomenon, but the "problem of economic development" is. Although mankind has always been poor, in the last few minutes of the world's history certain individuals and societies have discovered the Aladdin's lamp of economic growth. As these groups improve their economic conditions, those remaining behind are confronted with an increasing gap between their way of life and that of the favored few. Historically, growth has tended to produce inequality among individuals, regions, and nations. At least until 500 years ago, most of the "great civilizations" of the past showed a pattern in which certain social groups benefited at the expense of others. The empires of Akhnaten, Alexander, Augustus, and Athualpa were built from the taxes and toil of subjugated people. It is not surprising that much of mankind still tends to associate the economic prosperity of some with the oppression and plunder of others.

In recent years, however, the picture has begun to change. Technological revolutions in agriculture, industry, commerce, and transport have combined to permit enormous expansions in productivity of the world's resources. Though technological progress is by no means a new phenomenon, the clustering of innovations in a few short centuries, concentrated in a relatively small area of the world (Great Britain, the European continent, North America, and, recently, Japan), has greatly changed the nature of growth. The progress of one group or nation no longer need depend upon the decline of another. Exploitation is no longer a necessary condition for material prosperity. If we may conceive of the world's production possibilities in terms of an international production possibility frontier, there is increasing evidence that the alternatives now open to mankind involve not only movements along this frontier but also an expansion of the frontier itself through savings, investment, and technological progress.

Nevertheless, the growth that has occurred since the Renaissance has not been balanced among regions and social groups. Not all societies have been equally adept at combining natural resources, labor, and capital with the new technological developments. The more successful have left the others far behind, until a situation now exists in which the United States, Western Europe, and the Soviet Union, with less than one-third of the world's population, produce all but one-fifth of the world's economic product. The growth of these presently developed regions has not taken place in isolation. It has involved considerable interaction with the rest of the world, through trade and factor movements. This has brought about the accusation that, regardless of technological progress in the past few centuries, the rich still benefit at the expense of the poor.

Development economics involves an effort to unravel these issues. It examines the pattern of growth as part of the transformation of entire social systems. It attempts to isolate both the proximate and root causes of economic change. And, most importantly for those left behind, it attempts to prescribe policies that will create the conditions for self-sustaining growth in the backward areas of the world. It is quite understandable that the infant study of economic development has yet to arrive at conclusive evidence to support either the complementary or competing theories of economic growth. However, we are much closer to an answer today than we were a few decades ago when the questions were first taken seriously by policy makers. Is it surprising that belief in the exploitation hypothesis is strongest in those areas that remain poor, whereas the rich societies believe they have lifted themselves by their own bootstraps?

The problem of economic development has been studied primarily from a national focus. This is probably a result of the fact that the demand for policies to promote development is derived primarily from nation-states. Governments in power over much of the world see their people in poverty. They see the people in the developed areas living amidst affluence, and they wish to capture the secrets of economic development for themselves.

Poverty, of course, is a relative concept. We can only define a standard of income as "low" if we are aware of the practical possibility of better things. The problem of economic development has therefore become a "problem" only since certain regions have begun to prosper and grow rapidly. Those left behind have become relatively poorer and poorer each year. Thus the demand for development policies has grown with the development of the advanced nations who have demonstrated the possibility of a better way of life. The problem of economic development, then, can be viewed as one of attaining balanced improvement in standards of living—improvement at roughly the same geometric rates—over all the regions of the world and among all social groups. Thus the problem of economic development is that of obtaining social equity through economic growth.

What are the chances for solving such a problem? Are there any natural forces that can be relied on to diffuse the progress from advanced regions to less developed areas in a fashion that is socially equitable?

The "Vent for Surplus"—A Balancing Force

Despite the recent national focus of development policy, the problem of development, when expressed as one of balancing growth rates, or of sharing economic progress, is a problem that exists within national borders as well as between nation-states. Even the United States, which until now has had the world's greatest success in improving living standards, contains important regions and social groups who have not shared equally in the development process. Appalachia is an outstanding example of a stagnant region within a booming economy. The American Indian, the Eskimo, the rural black, and even the urban poor stand out as examples of groups that have missed the gravy train of progress. Thus the problem of balancing growth rates is not a problem that recognizes national boundaries.

One hypothesis of how economic progress is spread from developing industrial centers is called the *vent for surplus*. It is an application of the concepts of trade and location developed in Chapters 24-26. As an urban industrial agglomeration grows, the process of growth changes factor prices. In particular, wages and natural resource prices rise. Those areas that produce the scarce natural resources find a growing market for their goods. And through this process the growth is spread.

The American Midwest looms as an example of successful growth via the vent-for-surplus route. The existence of cheap productive land led pioneers to cross the Appalachian Mountains in an attempt to get rich by shipping food back to the developing regions, namely, Europe and the eastern United States. When iron ore and coal were discovered, the scarcity of these resources made it profitable to establish mining industries that shipped resources from where they were cheap — the mines — to where they were expensive — locations where steel was demanded. In this case, transport costs made it profitable to establish the steel industry in the Midwest near the mines. Thus a heavy industry grew up that, along with agriculture, remains the core on which the economy of the Midwest is built even today.

Oil and cattle in Texas, gold and specialized agriculture in California, copper in Montana, coal in Appalachia, timber in Oregon, and ore reserves in Canada led to the growth of industries that primarily exported natural resources to the developing eastern states and Europe. The growth of these export industries made labor scarce, and the resulting increase in wages attracted immigration from areas that were not sharing equally in the process of growth, namely, New England and the South. As the export industries grew, complementary industries could be established near them; and where many of the conditions for growth were satisfied, the territory could become a growing center, exerting pressure itself for growth on the surrounding regions. Thus today the Midwest, California, Texas, and southeastern Canada are industrialized and growing along with the East in a manner that makes it difficult to determine who is exerting a vent for surplus on whom. These territories are growing in a jointly dependent manner today, although at one time they were primarily raw materials producers.

Not all the territories mentioned above made it, however. Ghost towns dot the West at the sites of depleted mines. Even major ore deposits — copper at Jerome, Arizona, iron ore in the Mesabi range, or coal in Appalachia — did not attract enough other industries to allow these territories to prosper after their ores were depleted or the world's need for them declined. Thus vent for surplus can explain the creation of export industries, but it is not a sufficient reason for economic development to occur. Apparently, many other factors such as climate, convenient transportation, and the like are necessary for a territory to be able to develop a broad industrial base that does not depend on its initial export industry. What these other factors are, or what alternative combinations of these factors work, is still a puzzle. One of the goals of development economics is to unravel precisely that puzzle.

When looking at the world's economy, we can ask, which are the Californias and which the Appalachias of the future? How can we speed up the process of developing the sectors that appear likely to make it? What can be done with the world's Appalachias? When turning from a study of national regions to nation-states, there are a few additional problems to be studied: (1) Migration between nations is restricted; (2) flows of capital are restricted; and (3) flows of goods are restricted. These restrictions complicate the problem.

Within the United States, the answer of economists to the problem of Appalachia has been simple: depopulation. Move the Appalachians to California, because Appalachia appears to be a territory that cannot profitably use as many people per square mile as it holds. Economic incentives appear to be accomplishing this result in a decentralized fashion as many families decide to make such a move every year. But with immigration restrictions, an underdeveloped country that is destined to remain an Appalachia does not have depopulation as an alternative. It needs some other policy—if indeed one exists—to make the best of a bad lot. How much poorer would Appalachia be today if no emigration had been allowed in the last century, if no "foreign aid" in the form of TVA had occurred, and if the area had not existed in a rich country with an apparent policy of subsidizing rural areas via road building, cheap electric power, subsidized air travel, and agricultural price supports? What policies could such an Appalachia espouse to lift itself by its own bootstraps? The problem of development is not an easy one to solve even in a nation teeming with technicians and economic experts. It is all the more difficult where such expertise is lacking.

With emigration virtually foreclosed, the politically ticklish question of birth control as national policy must be raised. Countries whose resources have little value in the world market perhaps can attain high per capita incomes by limiting their population to a scale that the resources can support in a better fashion. Although successful historical examples exist in which emigration played a key role in development—Sweden and Puerto Rico, for example—we have as yet no successful examples of the use of birth control as a primary stimulus to economic development. Even the casual observer of underdeveloped areas can sense the existence of more people than are needed to do the nation's work. Although out-and-out beggary may be widespread in only a few places, the existence of hordes of uneducated, unemployed people in and around the great cities is prevalent. Farmers' plots appear to be too small to make adequate use of their labor. Two men are often hired to perform one job. And rather than shrinking, the population in many of these areas appears to be exploding. The dictum of Malthus appears to be confirmed in many areas of the globe today. Expansions in aggregate income are associated with population increases of such proportions that per capita incomes show little or no change. It appears that some solution to the population problem must be found if development is to be a reality for many areas.

The trade theory of Chapters 24-25, working through the vent-for-surplus framework, tells us that areas with low wage rates should be able to specialize in the production of commodities that use a great deal of labor relative to other factors—labor-intensive commodities. Thus within the United States, we see textile plants in the South, shoe factories in old, depressed mill towns of New England, and the garment industry in New York City, all utilizing the relatively low-wage labor available there.

With a free world market for commodities, we might expect such labor-intensive activities to pass to nations with low wage rates. Though some of this has definitely occurred, the restrictions the advanced nations place on imports have prevented the process from spreading to the extent it would with free markets. The trade policies of the developed nations in many cases prevent the natural economic forces from operating. Thus part of the problem of development is the political one of barriers to free trade.

Trade theory also tells us that capital will flow to areas with low wage rates to take advantage of the cost differential they imply. We should expect to see General Motors assembling autos in Latin America rather than in the United States since Latin American wage rates are lower than US wage rates. And to an extent this expectation is confirmed. But investment abroad is a tricky proposition. The huge foreign investor who exerts a substantial economic force in a small country can always be blamed for the failure of any domestic economic policy. If this route is often used by politicians, and if the populace believes the story, pressure will mount for nationalizing the factories. This policy has been carried out in a few cases and the threat of it is sufficient to keep many potential investors from taking the big step. They continue producing with high-cost US labor because they are not confident that they can maintain ownership of any foreign factory they build. Most foreign investment by US industry occurs in Canada and Europe—countries already developed—partly because threats of expropriation are mimimal there. Thus another dimension of the development problem is political. It must be solved if the vent-for-surplus framework is to work naturally.

Despite the political barriers created by the nation-states that restrict the free flow of goods and services between them, vent-for-surplus economies have begun to appear throughout the underdeveloped world. They form little islands of material prosperity in a sea of subsistence production, exporting to the industrial centers their minerals and agricultural products or their labor-intensive manufactures, and using the proceeds to import capital goods, consumer goods, and to pay for luxuries such as tourism to Tokyo, Paris, New York, and Miami. The question is, Will these islands of development grow sufficiently to swallow up the sea of subsistence production around them? Will they eventually transform the societies in which they are found into "developed countries" in their own right? The historical evidence indicates that success *may* be achieved, al-

JOSEPH A. SCHUMPETER (1883-1950)   No other economist since John Stuart Mill or Karl Marx was as universal and encompassing in his range of interests and knowledge as Joseph Schumpeter. Conservative, as his Austrian Roman Catholic bourgeois origins dictated, he was an exponent of Walras, an adept in modern sociology, an admirer of Marx, and a respecter of the insightful vision that Marx displayed. Trained in the Austrian school of economics around the turn of the century, Schumpeter flavored much of his analysis with the marginal utility ideas of the Vienna school, yet, unlike many of his Austrian colleagues, Schumpeter was mainly interested in the more transcendant questions of what determined the quality of an economy's performance and, more importantly, what determined the course of its development.

Like Marx, Schumpeter sought to identify the basic rules according to which systems developed and to find *the* engine for economic advancement. In so doing he used mathematics, economic theory, sociology, and history. His output over the course of his search was immense, including *Theory of Economic Development* (English edition, 1924), *Business Cycles* (1939), and the encyclopedic *History of Economic Analysis* (1950). His quest for an explanatory variable of development ultimately led to choice of the key role of innovation. Given a closed system operating according to the concept of the circular flow, Schumpeter alleged that there would be no opportunities for growth in the absence of such shocks as those generated by the act of innovation, that is, the activity of applying previously developed engineering and organizational improvements in the techniques of production. Innovating entrepreneurs could attract money capital to finance their improvements because they could compete with existing enterprises inasmuch as they could pay higher interest charges to the bankers, whose function Schumpeter identified as the financing of production and innovation. As development proceeded, other aspiring entrepreneurs would seek to avail themselves of similar opportunities until the resulting competition and a series of bad judgements squeezed out all profit possibilities. The accumulated errors

---

though there is no guarantee that the symbiosis of development automatically will produce an equal rate of development in these outlying regions. The fact that trade routes from Europe have crisscrossed the world for centuries, yet many of the principal trading countries remain woefully underdeveloped, suggests that the latter either initially lacked the necessary and sufficient conditions for growth or lost some of these conditions in the process of resource transfers to the developed centers.

Politics Once More

One more political problem that must be discussed when considering the obstacles to growth in underdeveloped countries is the very problem of political equilibrium. Within each country, there exist groups of people who will be affected differently by economic growth and these groups may be locked in a struggle for control of the government and those mechanisms that affect the distribution of in-

would bring about a process of temporary collapse as the chances for profit disappeared so that only the strong and efficient were left and the way was created for a new generation of innovators and a restart of the processes of growth and development. This innovation and following collapse and sorting process Schumpeter labeled "creative destruction."

Ironically, he believed that though capitalism was outstandingly successful in creating material goods and in pushing forward the process of economic development and change, it was foredoomed. The reason lay not in its shortcomings, as in the Marxist model, but rather in its successes. As capitalism flourished, much of the glamor and excitement of the entrepreneurial challenge would be removed, a removal that would be paralleled by the displacement of small capitalists by large, faceless corporations operated by committees rather than by venturesome businessmen. The result would be a disaffection from capitalism on the part of much of the public, which no longer had any stake in the outcomes. Matching this withdrawal would be that of the intellectuals being in too great numbers for all of them to have meaningful social roles to play and who would, therefore, be all the more motivated to provide leadership for the public's refusal to support capitalist structure and policy. Under this type of assault the system would no longer function as a traditional capitalist system. Although the process of economic development might not be completely aborted, its future was considerably more cloudy. Obviously this projection has faint echoes of Marx, yet it is significantly different in that there is nothing inherent in the economic logic of the system that will make it break down.

It is noteworthy that in all of his analysis Schumpeter venerated the general equilibrium approach of Walras (whom he called the greatest economist), questioned much of the work of the English partial equilibrium analysts such as Marshall, and was particularly harsh with the emphasis on tinkering and on policy formation that he found among English economists such as Ricardo and Keynes.

---

come. There may be powerful groups who are already rich and who will only lose by growth as it drives up the wage rates of servants to a point where, as in most developed countries, personal service becomes a relic of the past. Landowners may resent the creation of a class of rich industrial magnates; small shopkeepers may resent the creation of cheap, efficient supermarkets; and the educated class may resent the loss of income and status they may undergo if education becomes a widespread phenomenon. Although all these groups probably espouse development as a desirable policy for their nation because of national pride or an expectation of a better personal standard of living, they are against many of the specific policies designed to make such growth a reality. If equally powerful groups hold different opinions about the way to grow, political equilibrium may not exist. In such a case it may be impossible to formulate a development strategy since the different groups have different ideas of what kind of society to create. Military coups, rapid changes in governments, and violence in the streets make steady progress toward any clear-cut goal difficult. When the fighting is over the goals, we can see politics as a major obstacle to economic development.

A symptom of the politics is the rampant inflation that is prevalent in many underdeveloped countries. In Chapter 37 we saw how policy makers could fool the people temporarily by increasing the rate of inflation. Where wage earners and industrial owners have no agreement over what an equitable distribution of income is, bargaining can be expected to be particularly bitter. Peace can be bought by allowing each group to set the prices at which it sells its output. Thus labor raises wages, management raises prices, and labor gets its turn again in a never-ending cycle. The government prints enough money so that these price increases do not result in demand unemployment, a result that could topple it. Knowing the government's weakness, labor and industry play their game with impunity.

Inflation, we saw, can play havoc with financial markets. In fact, continuing inflation at unpredictable rates may prevent the development of financial markets and their related mechanisms. This may hinder the generation of saving and its transfer into productive investment. With inflation, frequent devaluation becomes essential. A sad result of such a policy is that a great deal of the scarce brain power that could be used for solving the real problems of economic development may be relegated to solving the financial problems of rampant inflation — problems produced by the politics of the region.

International Redistribution

In whose eyes is economic underdevelopment a problem? Whose problem is it? Most societies attain internal equilibrium in which a substantial amount of resources is transferred from the rich to the poor. How does the arbitrary placement of a national border affect the feelings that produce such equilibria? Should we spend more money on Californian Mexicans than on Mexican Mexicans? Many families span both groups. And many of the arguments raised in favor of or against internal redistribution can also be raised in regard to the question of international redistribution, that is, foreign aid. Redistribution may help to reduce international tension and be thought of, therefore, as a public good that benefits the doner country as well as the recipient. It also may further the development process, as we will see in the next chapter, and thereby expand the international division of labor, ultimately lowering import costs and increasing the exports of the donor country. In the last instance, however, the question of international income transfers probably has to be resolved on the grounds of social equity. And since foreigners do not vote, their desires carry little weight in the policies designed by the rich, developed nations.

Questions

1.   How does the free market diffuse the growth process from developed to underdeveloped areas?
2.   What political factors affect the success of the diffusion process?

3.   Resources play a key role in the problem of development. What aspects of land, labor, and capital are particularly troublesome from the viewpoint of attaining economic growth?

Concepts Discussed
    balanced growth   foreign aid
    vent for surplus

40 Strategies for Economic Development

Social Development

Increasing demands are being placed on social scientists to produce strategies that will both (1) speed up the rate of economic growth in less developed regions and (2) make that growth consistent with the desire for social progress. Developing countries express a variety of alternative desires that they wish the growth process to fulfill, depending upon which individuals or social groups one consults. At one extreme there are those who would be satisfied with the direct transplant of a system of material production, distribution, and consumption from the United States, western Europe, or the Soviet Union to their own shores. At the other extreme are those who express profound dissatisfaction with all foreign materialist systems and would isolate their economies as much as possible from the rest of the world so as to nurture a unique society reflecting purely internal values.

Regardless of which social goals a government pursues, its strategy for economic development must be consistent with those goals. Consistency requires not only the pursuit of one bundle of consumption goods as opposed to another; it also places constraints on the manner in which those goods are to be produced. The very economic institutions used to increase the level of production will have an important impact on the tastes, habits, and life style of the next generation. Economists traditionally assume that individual desires can be taken as given; they view the purpose of the economic apparatus as satisfying those desires. This procedure is useful for discussing marginal changes in economic policy that will not have a profound effect on the character of the social environment. That is, it is a useful way of handling the kinds of policy decisions generally made in advanced economies. But it is a questionable practice when considering development strategies that can alter drastically the basic relations between man and man. It is questionable, for example, when considering how to change a country of rural peasants whose consumption consists primarily of a meager diet into a country of sophisticated urbanites consuming whatever luxuries they wish. The tastes and preferences of the next generation may well be a product of the manner in which production is increased today. The problem of economic development can therefore be viewed as an opportunity for imple-

menting a policy of massive social change without having to tear down the existing institutions that already provide material comfort.

The Existence of Alternatives

The economist is poorly prepared for the role of social architect, a role that must
be played by someone who understands the growth process as well as the culture of the underdeveloped nation. How does one suggest alternative paths of
development? Where does one look to find out what economic institutions would
mesh most easily with the particular strengths and foibles of the native culture?
Is the policy maker to be an artist or a scientist? Such questions remain unan-
swered. They suggest the excitement and challenge to be found in problems of
economic development, or indeed, in attempting to apply economic principles to
any profound social problem, be it poverty, environmental pollution, or urban
decay. But since no one is better prepared than the economist for solving these
problems, he must consider them to be his own.

Economic planners are not social arbiters, even though they are architects
of social systems. As architects, their purpose is to respond to the wishes of the
citizens for whom the plan is to be designed. Presumably, these wishes can be
communicated through their elected representatives. In the case of dictatorships
or oligarchies, the planning problem may appear to be "simplified" to the extent
that a social welfare function of a few is imposed upon the many. Even here,
however, if the preferences of the leaders and the led diverge too widely, the
cost of military and police enforcement of planning strategies may limit their
scope and effectiveness. The planner, as a social scientist, may be better able to
predict these costs than the rulers. He may even be able to predict revolution
and with it the emergence of new goals. Should these potential future goals be
considered when designing the present plan? Does the architect worry about
who will live in the house after the present owners? Does too much arrogance in
an architect make him an arbiter after all?

The economist, searching for alternative candidates for a development strategy, often looks to history. It gives many different examples. Since all countries
that are now "developed" have achieved their present position through a long
and often painful process of trial and error—whether they call themselves "socialist," "capitalist," or "mixed enterprise" systems—there is no single development strategy that has been used with perfect success in any country. Some have
passed through major revolutions and civil wars. Others have experienced costly
panics, business cycles, and sustained unemployment. Still others have been
forced to rely upon massive emigration to relieve population pressures as well as
widespread experimentation with state control measures. Almost all have gone
through major wars and national emergencies in the course of their development.

Of course, social systems never offer ideal conditions for experimentation or
analysis, since so many things are changing at the same time. People move from
place to place, some industries are born and others die, governments rise and
fall, and value systems evolve as well. Still it is possible to look at the historical

pattern of growth of regions and nations that are now highly developed and compare this with the structure of those economies that have lagged behind. Asking development questions of economic history can be extremely helpful to the growth strategist. Some of his most useful propositions have been inferred from comparisons of the structure and rate of change of a given economy at different points of time as well as between economies at a single point.

For example, the vent-for-surplus economies introduced in the preceding chapter can be shown to have structural similarities among many regions and nations over time. The growth of the mining regions of the North American continent and those of Asia, Africa, and Latin America have been subjected to analysis using similar theoretical models, models that have been designed with specific historical cases in mind. These models suggest that the growth diffusion mechanism in such economies is capable of being explained (and even predicted) according to a set of basic underlying principles. This is not to suggest that there has not been a wide variety of development outcomes of these vent-for-surplus economies, in terms of their level and distribution of income, their structure of economic, social, and political institutions, and their underlying goals. Yet these different expansion paths do not invalidate the basic structural similarities of such economies. Rather they reflect differences in initial conditions of supply and demand, ties with third countries, and long-term goals. All these factors help to explain why the actual diffusion of growth in such regions shows marked differences even when their structural properties are much the same.

The historical examples show what has worked before. To know what will work in any particular case requires more detailed knowledge of the cultural characteristics of the region in question and how these characteristics affect the economic behavior of the citizens. To learn this, data must be collected and hypotheses tested. How responsive are the peasant farmers to changes in the prices of the crops they produce? Do they switch from corn to pigs when relative prices change? Do they invest more when interest rates fall? How sensitive is the rural–urban migration to changes in wage rates? Answers to many questions like this must be known before it is possible to choose one of the historical examples as suiting the country's needs. Econometric methods must be used to answer these questions precisely.

Social and political factors often dictate additional constraints on programs for economic development. In some cases, these constraints may be more subtle than purely economic ones, although the obstacles they impose to certain growth strategies are more evident. The reader can probably think of many places where resources are abundant but underutilized, and where growth is inhibited by the structure of the country's social and political institutions. Often a small segment of the population will impose constraints on the rest for its own benefit. We have seen in earlier chapters how this can take place as pressure groups argue for protective tariffs, the prohibition of new labor-saving technology, or the preservation of monopolies and other devices to restrain trade. Those in control may well prefer existing conditions of life to the ones that would arise from sudden rapid change in the economic process.

Whatever the reason, the degrees of freedom open to planners are limited. We may call this area of maneuverability of economic policy makers *policy space*. It has dimensions just as does production space—the PPF. Policy space, the range within which planners may operate, is limited by the following factors:

1. Policy space is limited by economic constraints whenever scarce resources are needed for implementing a particular policy.
2. Policy space is limited by domestic social values. Those in control of society may find particular growth paths, or their consequences, in conflict with values inherited from the past, which in turn depend upon past education in the broadest sense.
3. Policy space may be limited by relations with foreign governments, institutions, or enterprises in the form of trade restrictions or even military action if particular forms of social development are pursued.

In cases where domestic conditions place serious constraints upon policy space, planners may have to pursue growth indirectly through expenditures on social programs including education, skill retraining, health and nutritional support, family planning, community development, training in political participation, as well as changes in the structure of asset ownership including land tenure reform. These may be called expenditures on *social infrastructure*. These expenditures may be viewed as necessary in order to encourage certain groups to participate in the push for progress. Or they may be viewed as goals in themselves, the whole purpose of progress being to attain such conditions.

Although the building of social infrastructure attracts resources away from direct growth-promoting activities, it may serve to forestall social and political disequilibria that would otherwise arise from lack of sympathy with a specific set of policies. Such disequilibria could result eventually in actual disruptions of the economic process through rebellions in the name of reaction or reform, or through revolution, civil war, or foreign intervention, which would retard the rate of development by much more than the short-run cost of social infrastructure expenditures to alleviate these pressures. By ignoring the social and political dimensions of policy space, economists may underdetermine their planning models and fail to predict growth-disrupting aspects of economic change.

Alternatively, policy makers may attempt to alter the dimensions of policy space through ideological "education." Appeals to "manifest destiny" in the United States during its earlier period of expansion, "the Empire" in the cases of England and Japan, and similar calls for patriotism, solidarity, or other social qualities have served as a means of coalescing the population and expanding the dimensions of economic policy space at the time when major political programs needed to be implemented. Many leaders of underdeveloped countries find that an efficient way to fuse the populace into a unified body and get them willing to pursue a particular development path is to raise the spectre of foreign attack. Workers are told that they are defending the country and that the harder they work, the safer their families will be. It may, therefore, be thought by some to be impractical to expect development to take place in an atmosphere of cooperation with other nations. Distrust and verbal pyrotechnics may be useful tools in a strategy of overall development.

An important constraint in the policy space that planners face is the capacity to plan itself. There are many degrees of planning, ranging from modest intervention in the market mechanism to the substitution of entirely new systems of production and distribution for the market mechanism. A comparison of market and planning solutions in terms of their ability to maximize social welfare was provided in Chapter 7. In Chapter 18, we described in a simple framework the solution to a planning problem. We noted that sophisticated machinery for communication and highly trained technicians are an essential aspect of efficient central planning. Yet these are precisely the resources that are scarcest in poor countries. It is the advanced countries that should have a comparative advantage at planning. Yet it is the underdeveloped economies, we will see, that are particularly subject to problems of market failure. Thus a paradox exists: Those economies that may be most in need of effective planning are least capable of achieving this objective.

It should not be surprising to find that underdeveloped countries import planning in the form of development economists and their research. Nor should it be surprising that these countries search for and tend to adopt strategies that combine the best of both worlds; they use the market mechanism to maximize the benefits of individual decision making, and they use economic planning techniques to assure that the price signals and allocation decisions in the market are consistent with economic efficiency and social equity.

The Economics of Development

Although the particular policy space of each nation limits the nature of the development path that can be chosen, there are a few basic economic principles that can be applied in many different cases. Not surprisingly, these principles are the same ones we have discussed in the previous thirty-nine chapters. They concern the efficiency with which the limited resources are used to pursue the stated goals of social progress. In underdeveloped areas, the constraints imposed by limited resources are all the more evident since the resources are no meagre. With severely limited resources and unlimited goals, waste becomes evil, efficiency imperative. How might the principles of efficiency be applied most usefully to the problem of international poverty? What does a policy for national economic development look like?

Export Policy

Most nations are too small for it to make any sense to consider the problem of development independent of the rest of the world. Economies of scale and the gains from trade are too large to be ignored. The only successful example of autarchic development is the Soviet Union, a nation with a huge land mass and many people. Even in the Soviet case, economic considerations alone would have led to the exploitation of many of the opportunities for international trade that political considerations denied. Since most nations are smaller than many of the states of the United States, autarchy is not a viable alternative.

In Chapter 39, we argued that natural forces exist to spread development from one territory to another via trade. A key aspect of any development policy is to exploit these natural forces, to encourage and accelerate them, and to use them to stimulate development in the rest of the economy. An obvious way to do this is through the exploitation of natural resources. Geological surveys are encouraged, agricultural comparative advantages examined to see if new or existing crops might provide products needed by the rest of the world, and climate and location are considered with an eye toward tourism.

But comparative advantage involves more than raw materials. In the chapters on trade and location, we argued that technology is changing in such a way that transportation and raw material costs are insignificant for many new industries; rather, the key ingredient is skilled manpower. One need only look to the example of Japan to see how development is possible even when there exist no important raw materials to fuel growth. Japan imports raw materials and exports manufactured products. One could view Japan as exporting skilled labor because that is what is added to the materials it imports. The decreasing importance of raw materials has been viewed with alarm by some development economists since they are the exports on which many small economies thrive. But when looking at Japan, we realize that this trend can be viewed as an opportunity for development. No territory need think of itself as a doomed Appalachia once its development ceases to be restricted by its natural resource endowment. Japan has shown how a great future awaits any country that can harness the scarce resource of skilled labor. An important aspect of any policy designed to exploit the technology of the twentieth century is education and training of the labor force. This creates a resource around which an export policy can be designed.

Market Failure

Elimination of inefficiencies, we have seen, can create more for all. Making sure that private price is equal to social price is therefore a necessary aspect of an efficient development policy. This problem deserves particular attention in underdeveloped areas for several reasons. First, the small size of the local markets encourages the creation of monopolies even in industries that exhibit economies of scale over only a very small range. But second, and most important, with a social policy that is designed to severely change the face of the nation, the social return to investment in some industries may differ greatly from the private return.

There are cases in which the production of one industry provides positive or negative benefits to other producers or consumers. The case of a polluting factory is a clear example. It has no incentive to reduce its pollution if that will reduce its profits as well, despite the fact that the pollution provides great disutility to the community. Hence the community must consider the pollution as a negative externality and place a penalty on it equal to the disutility it provides. In developing economies, new industries often provide great positive externalities. One example is in the case of activities by the firm that improve the production possibilities of other firms. If, for example, one producer develops a new process that becomes general knowledge, it will benefit not only other firms but also society as a whole. If a company builds a road that can be used by the whole community, it creates benefits that extend well beyond its own internal cost savings. These additional benefits to society are termed *external economies*. Similarly, if a firm trains labor that is free to seek employment anywhere, it provides a return that it cannot completely internalize. Hence on-the-job training programs provide external economies of production. Since certain industries provide benefits to the economy that do not appear in private profits, there are arguments for their subsidization by society as a whole through the public sector. Railroads are a traditional case in point, and the United States government has provided many types of subsidies in the creation of its rail grid.

It has been shown that the market mechanism, however smoothly it functions, must rely upon individual decision making. Therefore it cannot adequately take into consideration those externalities in production or consumption that give rise to the need for public goods and services. Though it is by no means necessary that public goods, whether they be smog control, mass transit systems, education, or regional water development projects, be produced by public enterprise, they will only be adequately supplied if they are demanded collectively.

Economic planners can assist in adjusting the price system to reflect the demand for public as well as private goods. Thus there is a great role to be played by economic planners, not only in the developing world but in countries such as the US and the USSR, as their governments become increasingly responsive to the wishes of the whole community and increasingly aware of the effects of one person's actions on another. This principle has already been recognized by the industrial countries as a basis for the efficient allocation of resources under foreign economic assistance programs. And one of the unexpected and encouraging by-products of such technical assistance programs is its effect on the growth of expertise in development planning techniques that then may be applied within the industrial countries themselves to improve the level of economic efficiency and social welfare.

Some industries stimulate industrialization more than others. They do this by changing the prices other industries face. Development economists have used the term *linkage* to denote the stimulating force an industry can exert on the rest of the economy. For example, the creation of one industry may lower the costs of inputs to another. This is called a *forward linkage*. The development of a copper mining industry may make it profitable to develop a milling, smelting, and refining industry, because of the effect on the price of copper ore. An industry may also raise the prices at which other industries sell their products. The same mining industry can provide an example of this phenomenon—called a *backward linkage*—through its demand for mining equipment, electrical power, and pumps. Production of fertilizer, hoes, and plows will automatically be stimulated by any policy that furthers agricultural development, another example of backward linkage. A *demand linkage* results from the disposal of the purchasing power generated by the industry. Clearly, different goods will be demanded if large amounts of local low-wage labor are employed as opposed to small amounts of expensive, highly trained foreign technicians.

Linkages work both ways. The growth of an industry may lead to a broad industrial expansion if it has large linkages. But its decline must have the reverse effect, namely, eliminating the market for locally produced goods and factor services. If such an industry is built around a depletable mineral resource, the long-range effects of the industry's expansion may be severe unless appropriate steps are taken to eliminate the region's dependence on the mineral before its demise. In these cases, the industry must be used only as a springboard to industrialization. It cannot be used as a permanent foundation for an industrial base.

The search for externalities and linkages is an important part of a development strategy. If firms can be made to consider the social impact of their actions, decentralized decisions will do a large part of the development planning. If, for example, the government can place a value on the social benefit of training employees, it can offer to subsidize such training to that extent. It is still up to the firm to calculate whether training the workers for their particular needs is worth the remainder of the training costs. As long as they calculate correctly, they can be relied upon to make the correct decision from the social standpoint. The government need not worry about which particular skills to give the labor force as long as skills in general have external values; for example, they make other skills easier to acquire, which are passed on to the next generation, or they improve the wage and welfare of the man trained. Firms decide which skills to teach and they make that decision knowing the size of the subsidy they will collect for each man they train.

Saving and Capital Accumulation

Some underdeveloped countries have very low saving rates and very low levels of income. The two factors are related since the very low levels of income make the opportunity cost of each bit of saving that much more expensive. And the low saving rates lead to low levels of capital and thereby to low levels of income. Economists have constructed very simple models of economies in which two equilibria can exist, one with low levels of income and low saving rates, the other with higher income levels and saving rates. Planners sometimes feel that their country is stuck temporarily at the undesirable solution and they view the planning problem as one of constructing a path from one natural self-sustaining equilibrium to another. One way to do this is to raise the saving rate and hold it at its higher level. The analysis of Chapter 28 gives an idea of how this works. Although such a policy is easy to prescribe, it is difficult to practice because of the very scarcity of resources. Where is the extra saving to come from? Do we lower consumption in the short run below its already minimal level? Do we borrow funds from abroad? Do we encourage foreigners to invest within our borders? Political constraints will obviously affect this policy choice.

The economically efficient solution to this problem requires that individual savers and investors be faced with the true social rate of return. In many countries this is not done and the governments find themselves hard pressed to find the savings necessary to implement their plans. They have calculated that dams, irrigation projects, or electric power generating facilities will yield social returns in excess of the private returns they generate. An efficient policy would be to subsidize the profit of these endeavors and let the firms find the savings by paying high interest rates in the capital market. This is not often done.

But even worse is the fact that interest rates are often pegged at levels below those that would clear the market. Legislation designed to prevent "usury" has set arbitrary ceilings on interest rates of 5, 6, or 8 percent per annum. Thus private savers are not faced with the true social rate of return when deciding how much to consume. If the government feels that saving has a social rate of return of 20 percent, it should offer that on saving. Then individuals will decide how fast to approach the new equilibrium. They will decide whether saving is worth it or not even at a rate of 20 percent per year.

Compounding the problem of usury laws is the rate of inflation. We saw in Chapter 37 that the monetary interest rate equals the real rate plus an adjustment for inflation. In some countries, rates of inflation of 20 percent per year are commonly experienced. Thus a rate of interest of 20 percent on money would represent a real rate of return of zero. Yet even in these countries, it may be illegal to charge 20 percent per year as interest. True rates of return on financial assets are negative in such cases. Thus one of the first headaches the development economist faces is the straightening out of national monetary policy. Untangling these puzzles is often quite a job because the problem is compounded by the role of the currency in the international payments mechanism. Appalachia never had to contend with foreign exchange deficits or saving "imbalances" caused by its own financial policies. Because Appalachia was tied to the currency of an economy outside its borders, such problems could never arise, and the efficient decentralized marshaling of local savings could proceed.

With high levels of saving an essential aspect of any movement toward higher living standards, it is a tragedy that financial policies are often pursued that discourage rather than encourage private saving. Instead of being faced with a high guaranteed real return to reward him for helping his country, the potential saver is faced with a low—and sometimes negative—and uncertain return. It should not be surprising that many countries have a problem keeping their savings at home. Their citizens prefer to maintain savings accounts in the United States or Switzerland rather than at home. Thus in response to market interest rates, we have the incredible result that savings are shipped from the poor countries into the United States for investment there. This happens not because real social investment opportunities are greater in the United States, but because its sounder financial policies give a higher private rate of return on financial assets.

If savers faced the true social rates of return, saving flows in the reverse direction could be expected.

Foreign aid is often requested to fill the saving gap, that is, the gap between the level of investment desired by planners and the level of saving forthcoming through taxes and private saving decisions. Foreign aid — international income redistribution — was discussed in Chapter 39. It can be considered not only as a gift, but as part of an international income tax that is to be paid if one is to continue to enjoy the benefits of the international social compact. Antisocial behavior is common among as well as within societies if the social compact does not distribute benefits in a manner that the poor consider to be equitable.

Currently, the amounts spent on foreign aid by the advanced countries is minimal. Historically, it has always been easier to raise funds for defense than for welfare. The United States spends annually more than $20 for every man, woman, and child on the face of the earth simply to defend its borders. Yet it spends less than $1 per person on foreign assistance to alleviate the problem of international inequality. One reason for this discrepancy is the lack of public confidence in aid — the feeling that it will be abused rather than used by both the donor government and the recipient. Often the political and military criteria for foreign assistance greatly outweigh the economic. Aid from European countries has tended to go to ex-colonies, aid from the United States has gravitated toward countries on the periphery of the "cold war" in an attempt to raise bulwarks against real or imagined threats of Communist expansion. Efforts to disentangle purely economic aid from political and military assistance have not been conspicuously successful. The idea of foreign aid as a transfer payment within a world community has not proved to be a very strong force in motivating the rich to give. Historically, transfers within nations from rich to poor have arisen largely as a result of the increase in political power of the poor. With international political power unequally distributed, the preconditions for an international welfare state have yet to be established.

A World Economy

The automatic diffusion of economic growth through the trade mechanism is hampered by trade restrictions. What could Japan do to develop if no one would buy its output? How could it pay for the raw materials needed to build the durable goods that are an important part of the Japanese standard of living? Without the possibility of trade, each nation must develop independently. Some may not have the capacity for this. Thus the tariffs, quotas, and other trade restrictions that result from political bargaining within the advanced countries have a profound impact on the very possibility for development of some poor nations.

Chapter 25 shows how tariffs can redistribute income internationally. When rich nations place tariffs on goods produced in poor nations, the redistributions run from the poor country (and the consumers in the rich country) to the factors of production in the rich country that produce the protected product. The US sugar quota has the effect of making beet sugar growers in California, Colorado, and the Dakotas and cane growers in Louisiana and Hawaii richer. It raises the price of sugar to the US consumers and reduces income in the Philippines and the Caribbean. This forecloses one of the natural paths to development through the free market. The poor nations have a great deal to gain from free trade and we can expect trade policy to be an important demand to be furthered by the foreign policy of these countries in the years to come.

International investment is another aspect of the automatic diffusion process. We noted above the role of such investment in increasing a nation's capital stock and thereby its per capita income, and we noted how the policy of the poor country could encourage such investment by guaranteeing it the social rate of return.

Foreign investment is viewed as a mixed blessing, however. Along with the plant and equipment that industrialize the country comes foreign control over the domestic economy. Those objecting to the untrammeled growth of foreign investment within their frontiers tend to associate control over the economic marketplace with increased control over the society as well. We know that if all markets were perfectly competitive, it would make no difference whether an individual producer were born on that piece of territory or in Timbuktu. But in developing countries where markets are small and producers few, it is far easier to obtain a high degree of control over a particular economic activity and to influence the prices of both inputs and output. Under these circumstances increased foreign investment may mean a loss of local influence over the structure of production and distribution. And since many such regions are governed by an oligarchic rather than democratic political system, it may even be possible for those in command of material resources to exercise considerable influence over the political and social marketplace as well.

International investment, and the multinational corporations that determine its course, searches the world for opportunities to buy cheap and sell dear. In this fashion it serves the function of bridging markets, exploiting the potential gains from trade and specialization and diffusing growth. However in so doing, a single large international corporation may have a greater political influence in a given developing country than the local government. The ability to make or break contracts, to extend or withhold opportunities from a poor and struggling region, places the foreign investor in an enviable position.

The United States and most developed countries have progressively enacted antitrust legislation to restrict malpractices of corporations involved in interstate commerce, while at the same time permitting society to benefit from the efficiency that such competition could provide. By the same token one may look forward to a time in which the international corporation has its activities circumscribed by international antitrust regulations so that individual countries and regions will be protected from unfair business practices while at the same time enjoying the advantages of greater specialization through higher wages, lower prices, and a more rapid rate of growth.

The developing countries as well as international agencies such as the

World Bank, the OAS, and the OECD are seeking to find ways of reducing the risk element in foreign investment and to improve the efficiency of international capital markets. Little has yet been done in the direction of enactment of international antitrust legislation. Such a role properly belongs to an international governmental agency or as a subject for an international treaty.

If we look within the United States at the pattern of corporate ownership, we note that national corporations dominate the economy of California. Californians, on the other hand, own a large piece of all national corporations including those that do not operate within its borders. This pattern causes Californians no concern. They see no reason to want to restrict the actions of non-California firms or to require California citizens to sell the common stock of the national corporations they own in order to invest the money at home. Nor do the citizens of any other state worry about this.

In fact, the discussion in Chapter 34 shows us how this pattern of ownership allows the California citizens to protect themselves from uncertainty. Rather than being restricted to a small number of firms in which to invest, they are able to diversify their holdings across all firms in the nation, thereby reducing risk through the law of large numbers. If we restricted Californians to invest only in California firms and we restricted the activities of non-California firms within California, welfare would decline for two reasons: (1) The uncertainty of return from the investments by Californians would increase; and (2) we would not necessarily have the best firm performing the job within California. Thus there are clear gains that arise from merging the California economy with that of the rest of the nation.

If we now reread the last two paragraphs and insert the words Canada for California, North America for United States, and international for national, the same facts and argument hold. Canadians own common stock in Canadian and US firms. Canadian and US firms invest heavily in Canada and the United States. The gains to be had from diversification make this an efficient pattern of ownership. In fact, as the world's economy grows toward a unified whole, we should expect to see the world's productive assets owned by international corporations that in turn are owned by peoples of all nations. The diversification this permits reduces the risk associated with financial investment.

But countries are of different sizes. And although the Canadian and US economies may be so closely related that for most purposes it is useful to think of them as a single entity, from the point of view of Canadians the entity appears to be the US economy. To Canadians, investments by international firms in Canada seem like US ownership of their assets even though the Canadians in turn own a piece of the very firms that own their assets. If General Motors does 5 percent of its auto business in Canada and 5 percent of its stock is owned by Canadians, should it be considered a foreign firm?

This is one of the sticky questions posed by nationalism that international corporate law has yet to resolve. How much control must the Canadian government exert over US corporations' behavior within Canada before it ceases to feel dominated by the US economy? Should Rhode Island exert the same control? New York City?

When looked at from the vantage of a world economy, Canada is a large country. How should Chile, for example, feel if it were to see all large businesses within its borders run by international corporations while most of its savings were held in the form of financial claims to those companies? Owning one-half of 1 percent of an international giant does not make it into a domestic corporation. Yet this is the pattern of ownership to be expected if international capital movements are to be as free as intranational ones.

Efficiency dictates that we have untrammeled markets. But politics may dictate something else. Small countries may be willing to put up with lower levels of output in order to increase their control over their own economy. Thus there would appear to be large returns to a policy that allowed a nation to control the actions of firms within its borders but that was administered in such a way that the firms still had the incentive to invest heavily in the capital goods so desperately needed in the underdeveloped world. Policies that are both efficient and equitable are in great demand for every social problem. Unfortunately, they do not always exist.

Summary

We have no blueprint for development. In this chapter, we have exposed the issues that must be considered when formulating a development policy. Clearly, the particular policy will depend on the particular constraints and opportunities faced by the economy in question. We have tried to show both the economic nature of these constraints and the broader questions that arise when economic desires confront social and political reality.

Questions

1.   What are the choices that face a government that wishes to increase the rate of capital formation in order to expand future production? That is, what are the alternative sources of capital and what policies must be followed to exploit these sources?
2.   How do politics and social values affect the actions a government can pursue to stimulate industrialization?
3.   What considerations affect the extent to which central planning as opposed to markets should be used to allocate resources in developing economies?

Concepts Discussed

policy space
social infrastructure
linkages

Glossary

Ability to pay. A criterion frequently used to determine who shall bear the cost of government activities. It is usually measured using one's income or wealth and is the rationale for progressive income taxes.

Absolute advantage. The advantage one country or region has over another in the cost of producing a particular commodity in terms of the resources used.

Accelerator. See *marginal propensity to invest*.

Accounting profits. Sales minus costs, where cost does not include the opportunity costs of factors; owned by the firm, usually not the same as economic profit.

Agglomeration diseconomies. Diseconomies of scale (see definition) that occur when a large number of people live close to one another.

Agglomeration economies. Economies of scale (see definition) that occur when a large number of people live close to one another.

Aggregate consumption possibility frontier. The sum of the individual *consumption possibility frontiers* (budget constraints).

Aggregate demand. The total amount of goods and services demanded by the participants of an economy.

Algorithm. A sequence of mathematical operations that constitutes a method of solving a mathematical problem.

Arbitrage. The simultaneous buying and selling of the same commodity in different markets in an attempt to make profits. Its effect is to make the price of a commodity equal in all markets.

Automation. Technological progress that replaces labor by complex automatic machinery whose operations are synchronized electronically.

Average cost. The total cost of output divided by the quantity of output.

Balance sheet. Presents the worth of a firm at a point in time.

Balanced budget exercises. Simultaneous increases and decreases in taxes and government expenditures that leave the size of the budget deficit unaffected.

Balanced economic growth. Growth at roughly the same geometric rates of all commodities produced, and by all geographic regions.

Balanced growth equilibrium. A long-run equilibrium characterized by balanced economic growth.

Barter. The direct exchange of one commodity for another without the use of money.

"Bears." Speculators who feel that prices are going to fall.

"Beggar-my-neighbor" policy. A policy of discouraging imports through tariff increases or other restrictive measures.

Bonds. Financial assets that promise to pay fixed amounts of money at some future date.

Borrowing. The process by which future money is promised in exchange for present money.

Budget constraint. The limitation that income imposes on the individual consumer wishing to purchase goods. It is represented by the boundary of the *consumption possibility frontier*.

Buffers. Mechanisms that allow the temporary excess demand (supply) of one instant to offset the temporary excess supply (demand) of another instant.

"Bulls." Speculators who feel that prices are going to rise.

Business saving. Retained earnings plus depreciation; revenue not paid to households or government.

Capital. Physical goods of economic value produced by man in the past and not consumed then.

Ceteris paribus. An assumption, commonly used in economic analysis, that the values of all variables and parameters other than those being studied are fixed.

Checks. Letters to a bank that authorize it to make payments from a specific account to a designated person.

Coin. A piece of metal whose value as money derives from the symbols stamped on it by a government.

Collateral. Assets that a borrower deposits with a lender with the agreement that the assets become the property of the lender if the borrower defaults.

Comparative advantage. A country or region has a comparative advantage in the production of a particular commodity when its social cost of producing that commodity is lower than the social costs experienced by the other countries or regions for the same commodity.

Compound interest. Interest paid on previously earned interest as well as on the principal sum of an obligation.

Constant returns to scale. If we increase *all* inputs by some multiple, and all output increases by the same multiple, we have constant returns to scale.

Consumer sovereignty. Denotes a system in which consumers decide by their purchasing decisions which goods are to be produced.

Consumption function. The function that describes how consumption expenditures depend on other variables.

Consumption possibility frontier. The budget constraint; the boundary of the combinations of consumption goods that a consumer can afford. It is determined by his income and the prevailing prices.

Cooperative equilibrium. An equilibrium attained by an oligopoly when the firms in the oligopoly decide to maximize their combined profits. The agreement may be explicit or implicit.

Demand curve. Shows the quantity of goods demanded as a function of price. At each point on the demand curve, the consumer is in equilibrium and the value of the commodity equals its price.

Demand deposit. A checking account.

Demand unemployment. Unemployment caused by inadequate aggregate demand; it is unemployment in excess of the efficient or frictional level of unemployment.

Deposit creation multiplier. The number of dollars of induced lending generated by an autonomous increase of one dollar in bank deposits.

Deposit insurance. Insurance that protects the depositor should his bank or savings and loan institution go bankrupt.

Depreciation. The decrease in the value of plant and equipment over a given period of time.

Devaluation. An action by the national government that reduces the value of the domestic currency in terms of gold or foreign currencies.

Diamond-water paradox. A paradox to Adam Smith, who could not explain why diamonds were of high value and water of low value, even though water was a necessity and diamonds a luxury.

Differential oligopoly. An industry consisting of a few sellers producing slightly different products.

Differential marginal productivity. A property of production functions—believed by economists to be quite pervasive—in which the marginal product of a productive factor declines when more of the productive factor is added to fixed quantities of other factors.

Diminishing relative value. A principle that states that the value to an individual of any commodity A in terms of any other commodity B declines if he consumes more of commodity A and sufficiently less of commodity B to leave him no worse or no better off.

Diseconomies of scale. A property of production functions that exists when an equal percentage increase in all inputs causes output to increase by a smaller percentage.

Diversification. The purchase of many different kinds of assets in an attempt to lower the risk of a portfolio.

Double-counting. Counting the same quantity twice when creating a total. Usually double-counting involves the counting of both intermediate sales and final sales when deriving an estimate of total production.

Duopoly. An industry with two firms selling an identical product.

Dynamic models. Models that describe the behavior of variables over time.

Econometrics. The science of measuring and forecasting economic magnitudes.

Economic efficiency. See *Pareto optimality*.

Economic goods. Goods produced from scarce resources.

Economic growth rate. The percentage rate at which total annual output grows.

Economic problem. Unlimited desires confronted by scarce resources.

Economic profit. The excess of revenue over cost when cost includes the opportunity cost of all factors; usually *not* the same as *accounting profits*.

Economic rent. The part of total factor payments over and above the amount necessary to induce the owner of the factor to offer its services in production.

Economics. That branch of the social sciences that studies the creation and distribution of material satisfaction—who gets what.

Economies of scale. A property of production functions that exists when an equal percentage increase in all inputs causes output to increase by an even greater percentage.

Elasticity of a curve. The percentage change in quantity divided by the percentage change in price between two points on a curve.

Eminent domain. The ultimate right of the government to use private property for public purposes. In the United States this right is not absolute, for the government must give the owner a just compensation.

Entrepreneur. An owner-manager of a firm.

Equity. Shares of stocks representing ownership of a corporation; also a term used to describe subjective values of justice regarding the distribution of income.

Excess demand curve. The quantity demanded minus the quantity supplied at each price.

Excess supply curve. The quantity supplied minus the quantity demanded at each price.

Exchange rate. The price of one currency in terms of another.

Expectations. Predictions of the values of future variables; forecasts.

Expenditure multiplier. The amount by which an autonomous increase in sales is multiplied because of the induced spending it generates.

Expenditure policy. The policy that determines a government's purchases of goods and services.

Exports. Domestically produced goods and services that are sold abroad.

Externality. The effect of a transaction on the utility of a person other than the buyer or seller.

Fiat money. A medium of exchange that is accepted as money simply because the government says it is money.

Final sales. The sum of net sales to consumers, to governments, and to foreigners. Final sales exclude sales to producers except sales of durable plant and equipment.

Financial intermediaries. Institutions operating in financial markets that allow buyers and sellers — borrowers and lenders — to meet conveniently.

Fiscal policy. The sum of a government's tax and expenditure policies as exhibited by its budget.

Flow variables. Variables defined as rates per unit of time; for example, $2 per hour.

Foreign aid. International income redistribution.

Foreign investment. Exports minus imports (for a nation); purchase of foreign assets (for a firm).

Free good. A good whose production does not use up scarce resources.

Frictional unemployment. Unemployment that results from the time lag in matching men and jobs efficiently.

Functional distribution of income. The distribution of national income among the different factors of production, such as capital, labor, and natural resources.

General equilibrium analysis. An economic study in which the interaction of all markets is considered.

General equilibrium system. A system (model) that attempts to define all the important market interactions.

Gold exchange standard. An international monetary arrangement in which money consists of fiat national currencies, all of which are convertible into gold at fixed price ratios.

Gold standard. A monetary arrangement in which all national currencies are backed 100 percent by gold, and gold is used for international payments.

Government saving. Tax receipts minus government expenditures.

Gresham's Law. Bad money drives out good money. Gresham's Law refers to the tendency of people to protect themselves from loss by spending money of questionable value and retaining money of certain value.

Gross national product (GNP). Denotes the total production of all the economic units of a nation during a specified time period, usually one year. It is equal to final sales plus changes in inventories. Also see *national income*.

Household saving. Household disposable income minus current household consumption.

Human capital stock. The value of future labor earnings.

Imperfect competition. The case of many sellers producing slightly different products; also called *monopolistic competition*.

Import quota. A protective measure that sets limits on the quantity of a particular product that can be imported.

Imports. Goods and services purchased from abroad.

Income effect. The change in the quantity of a good demanded because a person's purchasing power has changed.

Income statement. Shows the determination of a firm's profit in a given time period by listing the sources of revenues and costs.

Index number problem. An intractable problem that prevents the obtaining of an unambiguous measure of the rate of change of economic aggregates. This problem involves the arbitrary choice of which prices to use when comparing the total value of output bundles whose compositions differ.

Indifference curve. A locus of points of the different combinations of goods that yield the same total level of satisfaction.

Infant industry argument. A common argument in support of import restrictions that claims that certain new domestic industries have not yet reached their ultimate level of technical efficiency and therefore need temporary protection from foreign competition.

Inflation. A decline in the price of money; alternatively, an increase in the average of the money prices of all commodities.

Information costs. The costs (including time) involved in securing information.

Interest rate. The percentage rate at which interest is paid on money; it tells us the terms on which present and future dollars can be traded in the capital market.

Intermediate goods. Goods transformed by production into other goods.

International Monetary Fund (IMF). An international bank that makes loans to countries in order to offset currency speculation.

International payments mechanism. The organization of markets in which the currencies of different countries are exchanged.

Intransitive. Not transitive.

Investment. The amount of real goods an economy puts aside in an attempt to increase the supply of future goods.

Investment expenditures. Purchases of producer goods.

"Invisible hand." A term originally used by Adam Smith to describe the ability of the perfectly competitive market to bring about the greatest good for all, even when every merchant selfishly maximizes his own profits.

Isoquant. A locus of points representing the various combinations of inputs required to produce a given amount of output.

Labor-augmenting technical change. Technical change that has the same effect on output as if the quantity of labor had been increased.

Labor theory of value. A theory of value that asserts that the value of a good is proportional to the amount of labor used in its production.

Law. The study of the resolution of disputes that arise because of ambiguities in the social compact or through violation of the compact.

Legal tender. Money that by government decree must be accepted by all citizens of a nation in payment for debts.

Lender of last resort. The name given to a central bank that agrees to lend money to individual banks whenever they experience massive withdrawals.

Life-cycle hypothesis. A theory of the saving decision that asserts that consumers save in order to be able to maintain a stable level of consumption in the future.

Linear programming. A mathematical technique in which a linear function is maximized subject to linear constraints that appear as inequalities.

Linkage. A term used by development economists to denote the forces an industry can exert on the rest of the economy.

Liquidity preference theory. A theory of the demand for money that asserts that the interest rates on assets similar to money have an important effect on the quantity of money people wish to hold.

Lump-sum tax. A tax that does not depend on any economic magnitude.

Margin requirement. A tool of monetary policy that restricts banks and brokers as to how much they can lend when specific securities are used as collateral.

Marginal cost. The increase in the total cost of production that results from producing one more unit output.

Marginal productivity of a factor. The contribution that one additional unit of a factor makes to physical output while the quantities of all other inputs remain fixed.

Marginal propensity to consume (MPC). The percentage of increases in income that is spent for consumption purposes.

Marginal propensity to invest (MPI). The percentage of increases in sales that is spent on investment goods; also called the *accelerator*.

Marginal propensity to save (MPS). The percentage of increases in income that individuals save.

Marginal revenue. The increase in total revenue that results from the sale of an additional unit of output.

Marginal revenue product. The marginal product of an input multiplied by the marginal revenue of the output.

Marginal utility. The increase in satisfaction one derives from having an additional unit of a commodity is its marginal utility. Also see *value*.

Market. The arena in which buyers and sellers exchange commodities.

Market equilibrium. Occurs when buyers and sellers wich to do no further trading at the prevailing prices.

Market failure. This event occurs when decentralized markets fail to result in an efficient allocation of resources. Market failure often occurs because social cost is not equal to private cost.

Mercantilism. Historically, a national economic policy in which countries measured their power by the amount of precious metals they possessed.

Mixed systems. Economic systems in which resources are allocated partly through decentralized markets and partly in a centralized governmental decision.

Monetary policy. A government policy that attempts to affect the terms on which credit can be obtained in private markets and whose purpose is to regulate the nation's level of sales, employment, and prices.

Money. An asset that is used as a medium of exchange.

Money interest rate. See *interest rate*.

Money price. The number of units of money that must be sacrificed for a particular commodity.

Monopolistic competition. See *imperfect competition*.

Monopoly. An industry with only one firm.

National income. The total of the incomes received by all citizens of a country over a specified period of time, usually one year; it is equal to gross national product (GNP) minus depreciation minus sales taxes and other small items.

Natural monopolies. Decreasing cost industries; industries that experience economies of scale so that the cost per unit is lowest when there is only one firm in the industry.

Neighborhood effect. An externality that is received by those geographically close to the source.

Net national saving. The part of national saving that can be used to buy real capital goods. *Depreciation* cannot be considered as a portion of net saving.

Net worth. Assets minus liabilities.

Noncooperative equilibrium. An equilibrium that results when each of all participants in a market tries to improve his own well being without considering the effect of his actions on the actions of others.

Nonrenewable natural resources. Those natural resources that are used up in the process of production.

Normative economics. A study of economics that incorporates the value judgements of the economist.

Oligopoly. An industry with a small number of producers selling an identical product.

Open-market operations. Operations carried out by the central banking authority in which it buys or sells government bonds in the same market everyone else uses.

Opportunity cost. The value of consumption or production foregone because one decides to consume or produce a particular good.

Packaging wants. An advertising technique in which an advertisement is designed to give the subconscious impression that a product will satisfy basic psychological needs other than the overt needs for which the product has been developed.

Pareto optimality. Characterizes an allocation of resources when it is impossible to reallocate them in such a way as to make at least one person better off and no one else worse off; also known as *economic efficiency*.

Partial equilibrium analysis. A study that focuses on only one market of an economy under the assumption that solutions in the other markets will remain unchanged.

Payments deficit. The excess of the value of a country's imports over its exports.

Payments surplus. The excess of the value of a country's exports over its imports.

Personal distribution of income. The distribution of national income among individuals or households.

Policy space. The range within which economic policy makers may operate.

Political science. The branch of the social sciences that studies how political power is distributed among and exercised by the various bodies of the citizenry.

Positive economics. The study of economics that does not depend on the value judgements of the economist. See *normative economics*.

Price. The ratio in which two commodities trade. For example, three cents per apple.

Private cost. The cost of a specific item to an individual.

Producer goods. Goods intended to be used and worn out through the production of other goods in the future.

Production. The process by which inputs are physically transformed into outputs.

Production function. The list of technologically efficient processes of production for a particular commodity or commodities.

Production possibility frontier (PPF). The boundary of the combinations of goods that can be produced by a whole economy. This boundary is determined by the scarcity of resources and by the available technology.

Productive efficiency. Said to exist when there is no way to increase the production of one commodity without decreasing the production of some other commodity.

Progressive income tax. An income tax that increases as a percentage of income as income itself increases. Also see *regressive taxes*.

Psychology. The branch of the social sciences that studies how individuals mature and adjust to the environment around them.

Public good. A good that yields utility to people in addition to the purchaser. See also *pure public good.*

Public sector. Those industries that are administered by the government.

Publicly provided goods. Goods supplied by the government.

Pump-priming. A term used to describe the policy of a government making a once-and-for-all autonomous expenditure in an attempt to generate a self-sustaining increase in economic activity.

Purchasing power. The value of an economic magnitude in terms of the goods it can buy.

Pure competition. The condition characterizing an industry in which there are many firms producing an identical product, with no barriers to entry and exit, and each firm ignores the effect of its actions on others.

Pure public good. A good consumed in equal quantity by each individual, although the good may be worth different values to different individuals; no one can be excluded from consuming a pure public good.

Quantity theory. A theory of the demand for money that, in simplest terms, asserts that there exists a unique relationship between the quantity of money and money income. The quantity theory asserts that individuals spend excess money holdings, regardless of the interest rate and the manner in which the new money holdings were received.

Rate of inflation. The average percentage rate of increase of all money prices, usually weighted and expressed in annual terms.

Real interest rate. The rate at which one earns future purchasing power on monetary assets; it equals the money interest rate minus the rate of inflation. The real interest rate tells us the rate at which present purchasing power can be traded for future purchasing power in capital markets.

Real value of money. The price of money in terms of goods.

Recessions. Small temporary increases in the level of unemployment.

Reciprocal demand. Said to exist when one man offers what another man desires and vice versa.

Regressive taxes. Taxes that take a larger percentage of the income of the poor than of the rich. Regressive taxes have the opposite effect of *progressive taxes.*

Relative value. The value of one good relative to the value of another good; usually expressed formally as the ratio of the *marginal utilities* of the two goods.

Renewable natural resources. Those natural resources that maintain their productivity over time. An example is hydroelectric power.

Rent. That part of total factor payments over and above the amount necessary to induce the owner of the factor to offer its services in production.

Reserve requirement. A tool of monetary policy that requires a bank to hold cash reserves equal to a certain percentage of its deposits.

Resource-augmenting technical change. Technical change that has the same effect on output as if the quantity of natural resources had been increased.

Sales. Final sales plus sales of producer goods; also called *total net sales*. This term is a convention adopted for this book for the purposes of simplifying discussions about aggregate economic activity.

Saving. The flow of present income that is traded for future purchasing power. See *savings*.

Saving rate. The fraction of income saved; the average propensity to save.

Savings. The stock of accumulated *saving*.

Securities. Documents that represent legal ownership of physical commodities, or legal claims to another's wealth.

Social compact. A framework, originally developed by John Locke, that explains how a society might restrict certain forms of behavior in order to promote the common welfare.

Social cost. That which society must give up in order to produce a good. Social cost equals the slope of the production possibility frontier; also called *social opportunity cost.*

Social infrastructure expenditures. Expenditures for public goods, such as education, highways, health and nutrition, community development, land tenure reform, and so on, which are designed to improve the quality of life of the citizens. The term is most frequently used by development economists.

Social opportunity cost. See *social cost.*

Social sciences. The group of disciplines that study man's behavior.

Sociology. The branch of the social sciences that studies how social groups differ in values, behavior, family structure, and social institutions.

Sovereign. One who holds supreme power in a society.

Special drawing rights (SDR's). The amount by which each nation is allowed to have its international checking account with the International Monetary Fund go negative before the country must ask for additional loans.

Stable market. A market is said to be stable if it *tends* toward an equilibrium whenever it is not already in equilibrium.

Static analysis. The determination of an equilibrium at a single point in time without explicitly considering the effect of the passage of time.

Stock variables. Variables defined independent of a unit of time; for example, 600 machines.

Structural unemployment. Unemployment resulting from basic differences between the structure of skills needed by producers and those possessed by laborers.

Substitution effect. The change in the quantity of a good demanded or supplied resulting from the change in the price of the good after correcting for the change in purchasing power caused by the price change.

Supply curve. The quantity of output supplied as a function of price. The supply curve is a locus of points of equilibrium for sellers; on the supply curve price is equal to cost plus normal profits.

Tariff. A tax imposed on imported commodities.

Tax policy. The policy by which a government determines tax rates. Tax policy has an important affect on the disposable incomes of consumers.

Technical efficiency. Said to exist when there is no way to use less of one input without using more of any other input to produce the same level of output.

Time deposit. A savings account.

Total cost curve. The locus of points indicating the lowest cost at which each possible level of output can be produced.

Total net sales. See *sales*.

Total revenue curve. The locus of points indicating the highest possible level of revenue for each quantity of output sold.

Transfer payment. Purchasing power that is transferred from one group to another but does not represent a purchase of a good or commodity.

Transitivity. A comparison is said to be transitive if whenever $a > b$ and $b > c$, then $a > c$.

Unstable market. A market in which forces of disequilibrium get reinforced so that movements away from equilibrium are not reversed.

Utility. Satisfaction; welfare.

Value. Marginal utility; the value of a commodity is the increase in satisfaction one derives from having or consuming an additional unit of the commodity.

Value-added. Equals the value of the goods a firm produces minus the value of the inputs it purchases from other firms.

Value judgement. A judgement that is based on one's philosophical values and is therefore subjective. One cannot discuss the scientific merits of a value judgement.

Vent for surplus. A hypothesis stating that economic progress spreads from developing industrial centers to less-developed geographic areas by means of the growing demand for goods in the former areas.

Voter's paradox. A hypothetical case that shows that intransitivity of preferences is possible for society as a whole even if each member of the electorate is rational and has transitive preferences.

Wagner Act. Legislation passed by Congress that established the National Labor Relations Board and provided active support for the formation of labor unions.

Welfare economics. That branch of economics that studies the effect of political decisions on income distribution, output, employment, and growth.

Index